P9-DTX-444

2017

Withdrawn/ABCL

Withdrawn/ABCL

The
Beautiful Country
and the
Middle Kingdom

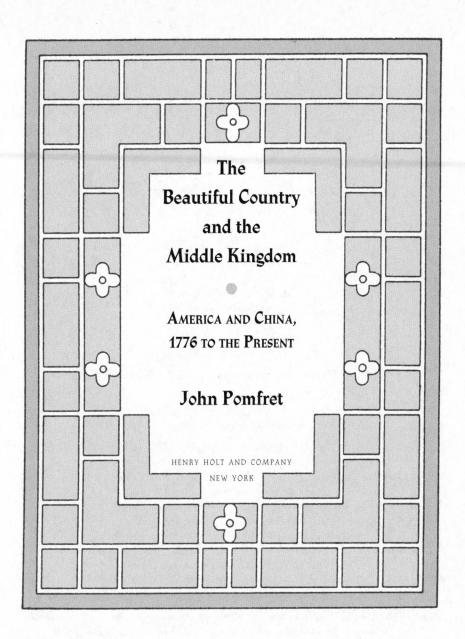

The Beautiful Country and the Middle Kingdom

AMERICA AND CHINA, 1776 TO THE PRESENT

John Pomfret

HENRY HOLT AND COMPANY
NEW YORK

3 9075 05032180 8

Henry Holt and Company
Publishers since 1866
175 Fifth Avenue
New York, New York 10010
www.henryholt.com

Henry Holt ® and 🅗® are registered trademarks of Macmillan Publishing Group, LLC.

Copyright © 2016 by John Pomfret
All rights reserved.
Distributed in Canada by Raincoast Book Distribution Limited

Library of Congress Cataloging-in-Publication Data
Names: Pomfret, John, 1959–
Title: The beautiful country and the Middle Kingdom : America and China, 1776
to the present / John Pomfret.
Description: First edition. | New York : Henry Holt and Company, 2016. |
Includes bibliographical references and index.
Identifiers: LCCN 2016009016 | ISBN 9780805092509 (hardback)
Subjects: LCSH: United States—Foreign relations—China. | China—Foreign relations—
United States. | BISAC: HISTORY / Asia / China.
Classification: LCC E183.8.C5 P58 2016 | DDC 327.73051—dc23
LC record available at https://lccn.loc.gov/2016009016

Our books may be purchased in bulk for promotional, educational, or business use. Please contact
your local bookseller or the Macmillan Corporate and Premium Sales Department at
(800) 221-7945, extension 5442, or by e-mail at MacmillanSpecialMarkets@macmillan.com.

First Edition 2016

Designed by Meryl Sussman Levavi

Maps by Jeffrey L. Ward

Printed in the United States of America

1   3   5   7   9   10   8   6   4   2

To Zhang Mei, who pulled me over the finish line

Contents

Part IV

Part V

Prologue

●

On a barren landmass nine thousand miles from his native Boston, William Dane Phelps stalked his prey. A colony of elephant seals lazed on a narrow beach, safe from the sharks and orcas that fed on them in the open sea. But here came Phelps, a teenager with a spear. Ten people were waiting to eat, and Phelps had been commanded to cook. The only problem: the meat—all nineteen hundred pounds of it—was alive. "I was left alone to get breakfast," Phelps recalled. "I knew nothing of the habits of the elephant, had never seen one killed, and there I was."

Phelps picked what looked to be the most docile of the beasts and leapt into battle. He struck the seal on the nose. The animal reared up on its flippers, bellowing as it towered over the boy. That opened up the monster's midsection. Phelps tried to plunge in his spear, but the animal caught the weapon in its mouth and gave it a jerk, cracking Phelps on the head and knocking him on his back. Phelps righted himself, bashed out the creature's eyes with his club, and, he wrote, "lanced him until he was dead."

It was 1817, and fifteen-year-old Phelps was a six-month sail from home, having just landed on Marion Island, a speck of land one thousand miles from the southernmost tip of Africa. Phelps was one of a crew of twenty-five aboard the *Pickering*, a brig from Boston that was scouring the seas for fur seals. They had struck pay dirt on Marion. While their ship went off in search of more treasure, Phelps and seven others remained on the windswept isle to hunt and skin.

Phelps and his shipmates spent almost two years on Marion, living in a cave and clothing themselves in animal skins as they killed thousands of fur seals and amassed tons of elephant seal oil. But the men's bounty was not destined for the coats, mufflers, and night lamps of the moneyed families of Beacon Hill and Back Bay. When the *Pickering* returned for the hunters, it whisked them off not to New England—but to Canton, China.

In the early nineteenth century, the promise of the China market sent Americans journeying around the world, killing and harvesting in staggering numbers: six million fur seals; the pelts of a quarter million sea otters; tons of sea cucumber and ginseng; forests of sandalwood; millions of silver dollars, all destined for China. Phelps and hundreds of other Americans spun the first threads of an enormous tapestry that they and their Chinese friends, competitors, customers, lovers, and enemies would weave into a story of wild exploits, extreme misjudgments, and unsung impact.

Many Americans believe that their country's ties to China began when Richard Nixon traveled there in 1972, ending the Cold War between the two nations. In fact, the two sides have been interacting with and influencing each other since the founding of the United States. It wasn't just free land that lured American settlers westward. It was also the dream of selling to China. The idea of America also inspired the Chinese, pulling them toward modernity and the outside world. American science, educational theory, and technology flowed into China; Chinese art, food, and philosophy flowed out. Since then, thread by thread, the two peoples and their various governments have crafted the most multifaceted—and today the most important—relationship between any two nations in the world.

Now is the time to retell the story of the United States and China. Today, these two nations face each other—not quite friends, not yet enemies—pursuing parallel quests for power while the world watches. No problem of worldwide concern—from global warming, to terrorism, to the proliferation of nuclear weapons, to the economy—can be solved unless Washington and Beijing find a way to work together.

America's first fortunes were made in the China trade from 1783 until the early 1800s and profits from that commerce bankrolled America's industrial revolution. In the 1830s, the 40-odd Americans living in the tiny trade outpost on the outskirts of Canton boxed far above their weight. Thanks to their labors, the United States became the Middle Kingdom's number two trading partner after the mighty British. Chinese officials then began what would become a tradition: looking at the United States as a bulwark against China's enemies. Over the years, they would propose alliances with the United States to counter the British, the Germans, the Russians (or Soviets), and the Japanese.

The first American Christian missionaries arrived in China in the 1830s. Though they are often held up as an unbecoming example of American cultural imperialism, forcing Jesus on an unwilling people steeped in an older Confucian creed, they were crucial to China's development. Along with Western-educated Chinese, they supplied the tools to break the stranglehold of traditional orthodoxy. They taught the Chinese Western science, critical thinking, sports, industry, and law. They established China's first universities and hospitals. These institutions, though now renamed, are still the best of their kind in China. America's women missionaries crusaded against the barbaric customs of female infanticide and foot-binding, helping to accomplish the greatest human rights advances in modern Chinese history.

As Americans brought Christianity to China, laborers from southern China flocked to California in search of gold. By the 1860s they constituted the largest population of foreign-born people in the American West. Those who didn't pan for gold wound up building the West. They drained the Sacramento River delta, creating one of the richest agricultural belts in history. They laid half of the Transcontinental Railroad connecting the East and West coasts. With their grocery stores, laundries, vegetable patches, and apothecaries stocked with herbal remedies, they provided essential services without which the West could not have been won.

Mainstream Americans turned on the Chinese in the 1870s. Congress made them the first ethnic group to be banned from the United States when it blocked Chinese workers from America in 1882. The Chinese did not stop coming, however, and, using funds collected by Chinese merchants, they hired America's best lawyers to challenge a raft of racist laws and ordinances. Those cases contributed greatly to the advancement of civil rights for all Americans, undergirding, for example, the push in the 1950s to dismantle the "separate-but-equal" educational system for American blacks.

Despite its racism, America remained a land where many Chinese could realize their dreams. The Chinese were hounded across the West not simply because they were different. In their industriousness they rivaled and threatened competing white settlers and they made whites work harder. That ability to thrive in America and make all of America more competitive continues to this day.

While some Americans hated the Chinese, others nurtured a deep concern with China's well-being. Though commercial activity dominated the US approach to Europe, South America, Japan, and elsewhere, the emotional attachment to these places—with the exception of Great Britain—was not nearly so deep as that to China. "Clear your plate; there are children starving in China" was a dinner-table mantra for generations of Americans. So was the "pennies for China" campaign in churches across the heartland.

With the turn of the twentieth century and the dawning of America as a global power, policy makers in Washington took more interest in China and fought to keep the country whole, despite efforts by European nations and Japan to carve it into colonies. American statesmen moved to bind China's best and brightest to the United States, establishing a fund to educate Chinese stateside. The Boxer Indemnity scholarships spawned Nobel Prize winners, scientists, politicians, engineers, and writers and set the scene for a Chinese intellectual renaissance in the 1920s and 1930s.

Those same decades found Americans intrigued by Chinese culture—its food, art, poetry, and mysticism. A Chinese American woman from Los Angeles became the first nonwhite movie star in the United States. American taste buds accepted Chinese food. American tycoons put together the world's greatest collections of Chinese art and endowed museums from Boston to New York, Washington, Kansas City, and San Francisco to house them.

In 1937, the Japanese invasion of China knit China and America closer together than ever. Before the war there had been ten thousand Americans in China; their numbers jumped tenfold in just a few years. But as the war progressed, America came to see its Chinese ally, Generalissimo Chiang Kai-shek, as dictatorial, incompetent and, worst of all, unwilling to fight Japan. As a result, many Americans viewed Chiang's enemies, the Chinese Communist Party, as the true guerrilla David battling a mechanized Japanese Goliath. State Department officials were convinced of the accuracy of this perspective, and steered US policy away from providing aid to Chiang for his showdown with the Communists after the war.

We now know that the reality was more complex. Chiang's armies fought so stalwartly that it was they, not the Communists, who sustained 90 percent of the casualties battling the Japanese. Americans at the time comforted themselves with the notion that the United States had done all it could to help Chiang Kai-shek. But countless promises of aid, weapons, and gold to his government had gone unfulfilled.

Some historians have argued that after the war the United States missed a chance to forge good relations with Chairman Mao Zedong as Communism took hold. But documents from Chinese archives released in recent years show that Mao was not ready for ties with America. Mao used hatred of the US as an ideological pillar of his revolution. Even today, the legacy of Mao's paranoia about America colors China's relations with the United States.

In the 1970s, Western obituaries reporting the demise of American influence in China were premature. Almost from the day China re-opened to the West, American pragmatism, its free market approach, and light-touch regulation have dominated China's economic reforms. American culture has monopolized its movie and TV screens, and Christianity, despite Communist oppression, has experienced a renaissance of unprecedented proportions. American values, education, and even its fresh air are the envy of many Chinese. From Deng Xiaoping on, every Communist leader has sent at least one of his children to the US to study, including the Harvard-educated daughter of the current president, Xi Jinping.

When the two nations rediscovered each other in the 1970s, American sympathetic regard for the Middle Kingdom was rekindled, and Americans again worked to make China strong. Since then, no other country has been more important to China's rise than the United States. Its open markets, open universities, and open society have served as the key foreign drivers of China's return to greatness. Meanwhile, China has renewed its claim on the American imagination and entered every home with the ubiquitous three-word phrase: "Made in China."

For those reading this book in China, the time is also right for a reappraisal of the Middle Kingdom's ties to Meiguo, the Beautiful Country—China's name for the United States. Communist histories have twisted the story of America's two-hundred-year-long association with China. In the early days of the relationship, Chinese are told, the United States schemed to colonize China, acting no better than the imperialist powers of Old Europe or even Japan. They're taught that American charity was a trick. The Chinese version of World War II airbrushes American sacrifices from the tale. China, not the United States, beat Japan, the Chinese learn. As for the Korean War, to this day Chinese textbooks maintain that South Korea, backed by America, started that conflagration, when in truth it was the North Koreans supported by Joseph Stalin and Mao. Over the past five decades, these same textbooks also claim, America has sought to keep China down.

Still, although the Communist Party won't admit it publicly, many

Chinese privately acknowledge America's role in China's ascent and the fact that, more than perhaps any other nation, China has benefited from the Pax Americana—the system of free trade, secure waterways, and globalized financial markets built by the United States and its allies after World War II. It is no coincidence that although China's growth was impressive in the 1980s and 1990s, it became a global trading power only after 2001, when the United States ushered it into the World Trade Organization. As the imprisoned Nobel Peace Prize laureate Liu Xiaobo observed, China "needs challenge, even 'menace' from another civilization; it needs a vast and surging, boundless sea to pound it out of its isolation, its solitude and its narrow-mindedness." America has filled that role.

Year by year, decade by decade, the two nations have bound themselves closer together. America has been China's top trading partner since the 1990s. China surpassed Canada to become America's top partner in 2015. Scientists on both sides of the Pacific cooperate in more fields—fighting cancer, splitting genes, looking for clean energy, investigating atomic particles, discovering new drugs—than their counterparts in any other two countries. Complications between these two great nations abound as the United States and China and Americans and Chinese cooperate and compete across the world.

If there is a pattern to this baffling complexity, it may be best described as a never-ending Buddhist cycle of reincarnation. Both sides experience rapturous enchantment begetting hope, followed by disappointment, repulsion, and disgust, only to return to fascination once again. In the nineteenth and twentieth centuries, American missionaries fantasized that China would become the world's largest Christian nation, while mandarins in Beijing counted on America to shield their country from the depredations of European imperialists and Japan. Neither wish was fulfilled. But new expectations follow inevitable disillusion with every spin of history's wheel.

At present, Americans have entered the disenchantment phase of the cycle, their views clouded by economic and strategic concerns. China, the narrative goes, pilfers American jobs, swipes its secrets, stockpiles its debt, and is now scheming to expel the US Navy from the Western Pacific. In the American imagination, China has traversed the arc from object of benevolence to fount of anxiety. A trip to the Great Wall, the Forbidden City, and the tomb of the First Emperor once topped the bucket list of generations of Americans. Today, US tourist visits to China are flat and public opinion toward the country has soured.

The Chinese feel dispirited, too. Their leaders expected America to make way for China in the Pacific. In the 1970s, senior American officials assured them that the US would pull its troops from South Korea and step aside as China recovered Taiwan, thereby completing China's unification. Many Chinese have also grown tired of Americans telling them what to do. At the same time, other Chinese understand that they are losing the goodwill of many Americans and this has given them pause. While Americans are asking whether they have given China too much, some Chinese are beginning to ask whether they have pushed America too far. These fluctuations, too, are rooted in history. The two nations have feuded fiercely and frequently. Yet, irresistibly and inevitably they are drawn back to one another. The result is two powers locked in an entangling embrace that neither can quit.

William Dane Phelps would graduate from deckhand to captain and make a handsome living killing sea mammals and selling their hides and oil to the Chinese. Generations of Americans and Chinese followed in his wake, weaving together two vastly different cultures. Through all the whipsaw cycles of boom and bust, dashed hopes and exalted dreams, rivers of blood and mountains of trade, the relationship between the United States and China is powered by love and hate, contempt and respect, fear and awe, generosity and greed.

Chinese and Americans arouse deeply conflicted feelings in one another. Yet no other two nations' mutual dependence is as vital to the fate of the world as the one between these two great powers. In search of wiser choices for the future, we look to a story that began three centuries ago, in the founding of a young nation, and the death knell of an old one.

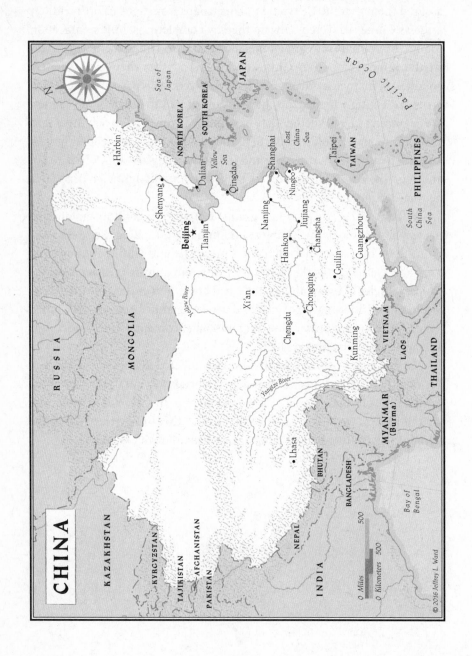

CHINA

KAZAKHSTAN

KYRGYZSTAN
TAJIKISTAN
AFGHANISTAN
PAKISTAN

RUSSIA

MONGOLIA

NEPAL

INDIA

BHUTAN

BANGLADESH

•Harbin

•Shenyang

Beijing ★
•Tianjin

•Dalian

•Qingdao

Yellow
Sea

Yellow River

•Xi'an

•Chengdu

•Lhasa

Chongqing

•Kunming

Yangtze River

Changsha

Guilin•

Hankou

Jiujiang

•Nanjing

•Shanghai

Ningbo

East
China
Sea

•Guangzhou

VIETNAM

LAOS

MYANMAR
(Burma)

THAILAND

Bay of
Bengal

South
China
Sea

PHILIPPINES

TAIWAN

Taipei•

•Taipei

NORTH KOREA

SOUTH KOREA

Sea of
Japan

JAPAN

Pacific Ocean

N

0 Miles   500
0 Kilometers   500

© 2016 Jeffrey L. Ward

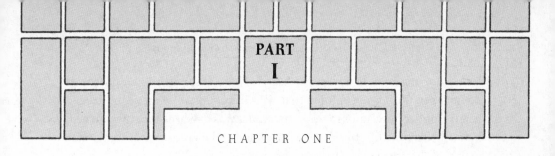

A New Frontier

The year was 1776, and the American colonies were seized with revo-lutionary fervor. But in New Hampshire, a twenty-five-year-old student studying to be a missionary dropped out of Dartmouth College and shipped out with the Royal Navy on Captain James Cook's third and final voyage. Six years later, after Cook was killed in Hawaii, the sailor, John Ledyard, returned to America's shores to proselytize not for God but for trade—with China.

John Ledyard was fired up by a scheme to dispatch Yankee ships around the tip of South America to the Pacific Northwest to collect the pelts of the northwest sea otter for the China market. Coastal Indians would barter a pelt for "only a hatchet or a saw," Ledyard wrote. But the Chinese would pay one hundred Mexican silver dollars for a single fur, a markup that his contemporary Adam Smith could love.

A Connecticut Yankee with a hooked nose, an ample inheritance, and a penchant for trouble, Ledyard was an American visionary in a time of global turmoil. The Spanish and Portuguese empires were crumbling. The Royal Navy ruled the seas. And America's War of Independence had left the United States barely united and deeply in debt.

Britain had shut Yankee merchants out of the lucrative trade with the British West Indies. America's once-thriving shipping industry limped along. Its whaling and cod businesses were in tatters. Its slave trade fared little better. "The town of Boston is really poor," complained the Reverend

John Eliot in a letter to a friend in March 1780. "If some brighter prospects do not open up, it is my opinion that we cannot subsist." Americans needed a new frontier beyond Europe's sway. And it was to China that they turned, planting deep within the Yankee imagination the fancy that China's markets held the answer to American prayers.

In May 1783, Ledyard chased down Robert Morris, the Philadelphia merchant and signer of the Declaration of Independence who had bankrolled the American Revolution. After sharing his China plan with Morris, Ledyard boasted that he would soon be at the helm "of the greatest commercial enterprise that has ever been embarked on in this country." But Morris and his partners dawdled, and the impatient Ledyard left the United States again. Urged on by Thomas Jefferson, he tried to cross Russia's vast expanse to reach America's West Coast. But the Russians stopped him. His next venture led him to Africa, but as he began his journey into the continent in January 1789, he accidentally poisoned himself and died.

Robert Morris stuck with the China idea, however, and on a wintry Sunday, February 22, 1784, the *Empress of China*, a three-masted ship of 360 tons, set sail from New York Harbor bound for the prosperous southern Chinese port of Guangzhou, known to Westerners as Canton. The *Empress* carried a crew of forty-two, a box of beaver skins, twelve casks of spirits, and twenty thousand Mexican silver dollars. But her prize cargo was thirty tons of American ginseng harvested in the Appalachian forests. Philip Freneau, the poet of the American Revolution, celebrated the ship's departure with verse reflecting America's newly won liberation. The *Empress* was heading, he wrote, "where George [the British king] forbade [Americans] to sail before."

At noon on May 11, 1785, the *Empress* returned to New York to a thirteen-gun salute—one for each of the United States. In her hold, she carried more than twenty-five thousand pounds of tea, a load of cloth, and a large selection of porcelain. The venture earned a 30 percent profit of more than $30,000 (nearly $1 million today). The *New York News Dispatch* declared that the journey "presages a future happy period" of trade with China, an example of the high bar that America's fledgling media were already setting for relations with the Middle Kingdom. Morris backed a second voyage, the *Pallas*, which made $50,000, but his luck soon soured. Pouring his earnings into a Pennsylvania land deal that went belly-up, he was tossed into a debtor's prison. Nonetheless, in the next fifteen years, more than two hundred American ships would follow the *Empress* to Guangzhou, a fleet second only to the four hundred vessels of the British.

Tea, which predated coffee as the American beverage of choice, brought American traders to China. The tea that was tossed into Boston Harbor on the night of December 16, 1773, had been shipped out of the southern Chinese city of Xiamen. Within a few years of independence, tea composed nine-tenths of the goods leaving China on American ships. In 1785, American vessels carried less than a million pounds of tea from China; in 1840, they moved nineteen million.

What began as an exchange of American raw materials for Chinese tea soon mushroomed as Asian handicrafts of every variety flooded into the United States. Though today we speak of an American pivot to Asia, American tastes have been pivoting to Asia for more than two hundred years. The American appetite for blue-and-white Chinese bowls, plates, and teacups was so prodigious that New England carracks limped into Boston Harbor with crates suspended over their sides. To a people who only recently had measured wealth by the number of chairs a household owned, Chinese porcelain, known as china, represented status and taste.

China in 1800 was a manufacturing powerhouse, responsible for about one-third of all the goods made in the world. And Americans were beguiled by its products. "Willow pattern" porcelain, inscribed with trees, bridges and pagodas, monks and scholars, "filled us with wonder and delight, Or haunted us in dreams at night," wrote poet Henry Wadsworth Longfellow. Boston's upper crust clothed themselves in Chinese silk. The dining room in George Washington's Mount Vernon boasted a 302-piece dinner and tea set brought to America by the *Empress of China*. Chinese porcelain sparked the founding of an American porcelain industry. Curtains from China inspired the American drapery business.

As there is today, there was fakery on all sides. Chinese artists churned out some two hundred copies of Gilbert Stuart's famed portrait of George Washington. Yankee merchants sold them in Philadelphia until Stuart won a court order in 1802 banning their sale. American woodworkers paired pagodas with Algonquin longhouses on Yankee-made side tables made to look Chinese. In Boston and New York, tea salesmen packaged old Chinese tea in new boxes. The entrepreneurial gumption would only be matched two centuries later when Chinese knockoff artists produced vast quantities of bogus North Face jackets and pirated DVDs.

American fascination with things Chinese went beyond household goods and luxury items. In 1834, two New York businessmen brought a Chinese woman named Afong Moy to the city, where they displayed her in a cage. Dressed in Oriental finery, Moy was part of an exhibition to sell

Chinese knickknacks. The New York press went wild, extolling her bound feet and exotic ways. When she arrived in New York Harbor in October, the advertised price to see her was a quarter. By the time she opened at 8 Park Place a few weeks later, it was up to fifty cents. Moy's success inspired American showman P. T. Barnum to devote a whole museum to the Chinese—as freaks. Among his showpieces was a pair of conjoined twins.

Fused at their rib cages, Chang and Eng Bunker were shipped to the United States in 1829 by Robert Hunter, a British merchant, who believed that he'd struck it rich with a touring exhibition of Chinese mutants. Though they were ethnic Chinese, the pair hailed from Siam, hence the term "Siamese twins." After three years in America, Chang and Eng successfully sued Hunter for breach of contract and set out on their own.

Chang and Eng's case was not the first time Chinese had turned to America's courts for justice. That tradition dates back at least to 1805 when Chinese merchants began filing motions against their deadbeat American counterparts in Philadelphia's courts. Even then Chinese plaintiffs were impressed with what one petitioner called America's "equal protection of the Rich, and of the Poor, and for dealing equal measure to its own Citizen, and to the Alien." Many more cases would follow.

Acting as their own managers, Chang and Eng toured the young nation, appearing in formal wear, performing backflips and somersaults, and hoisting portly spectators on their heads. With their earnings, the twins purchased a one-hundred-acre plantation, with slaves, in Wilkesboro, North Carolina. They married sisters, Sarah and Adelaide Yates, and fathered twenty-one children. They died in 1874 within three hours of one another at the age of sixty-three and were buried together near their plantation.

Although American impresarios promoted Chang and Eng as a gruesome curiosity, their success underlined the opportunities America presented to the Chinese. The pair burrowed deep in the American psyche, resurfacing in a historical novel published in 2000 and again as the characters Terry and Terri Perry in the 2013 animated movie *Monsters University*.

This trade in goods and people reignited America's shipbuilding industry and rekindled its economy. Less than a decade after Reverend Eliot penned Boston's obituary, its shipyards were booming again. In 1789, the *Massachusetts*, at nine hundred tons then the largest ship ever built in the United States, was launched for the China trade. Unfortunately, profit-hungry investors used uncured wood and had the ship built in haste. By the time it limped into Guangzhou Harbor, it was a rotting hulk and had to be sold for scrap.

The fortunes that East Coast merchants amassed in the China trade were vital to the United States' evolution from seafaring nation to factory of the world. The Astors, Greens, Russells, Delanos, Lows, and Forbeses plowed the proceeds earned in China into New England textile mills, Philadelphia banks and insurance companies, New York real estate, and railroads that laid the foundations for American power.

Taxes on the commerce bolstered the fortunes of the US Treasury. "Our trade to the East Indies flourishes," wrote President George Washington to his old comrade-in-arms, the Marquis de Lafayette, on June 3, 1790. "The profits to Individuals are so considerable as to induce more persons to engage in it continually."

The promise of the Chinese market drew Americans to the West Coast, Hawaii, and the South Seas in search of goods to trade with the Celestial Kingdom. From the early 1800s, as the young nation's ambitions expanded, business interests lobbied the federal government to secure deepwater ports on the Pacific Coast to serve as launching pads into Asia.

One hopeful merchant was the New York real estate mogul and German immigrant John Jacob Astor, whose vision for the Oregon Territory as a springboard for American expansion into the Pacific influenced American presidents and secretaries of state. Astor made his fortune trading fur, first with Native Americans in upstate New York and then via ships plying the waters off the Oregon coast. In 1810, he established the Pacific Fur Trading Company and built a settlement, Fort Astoria, on the Columbia River.

The British soon seized Astoria, but other Americans flocked to the coast to collect otter pelts for the Canton trade. A key ally in Astor's struggle to fend off foreign competition was John Quincy Adams, son of President John Adams. First as ambassador to Russia and Great Britain and then as secretary of state and president, Adams blocked Russian and British forays into California and the Pacific Northwest, sweeping the coast clear for America's westward heave toward the Far East. He, too, believed in the promise of trade with the Middle Kingdom.

Even Midwesterners like Senator Thomas Hart Benton caught China fever. In 1819, Benton argued that Missouri's borders should cross the Missouri River Valley to bring the new state just a little closer to China. Contemporary writers imagined an endless wagon trail from Ohio to Oregon lined with densely populated trading posts grown rich on Asian commerce. Despite the fact that trade with China would sputter and slow (in percentage terms it peaked in 1805–8 at about 15 percent of foreign trade), the sobering reality of the present day never dislodged the oversized expectations for tomorrow. As many do today, Americans then believed that their future resided in Asia.

Trade with China also helped cement America's embrace of a rough-and-tumble business model based on individual initiative that became a key to the nation's success. In 1786, Congress rejected a proposal to establish a trading monopoly modeled on Britain's state-run East India Company, which dominated commerce with China. Americans were free traders. "Commercial intercourse," Senator Rufus King wrote then president John Adams, "would be more prosperous if left unfettered in the hands of private adventurers."

In Asia, these "private adventurers" faced off against the mightiest trading empire in the world, the United Kingdom, and from the start the Americans dreamed of replacing the Union Jack with the Stars and Stripes as the dominant standard in the Pacific. To compete, the Americans embraced innovation. Their ships were smaller, averaging 350 tons, but cheaper to build and faster than the lumbering 1,200-ton behemoths of the British East India Company. American ships employed fewer men; 19 hands each compared with the 120 crewmen common on British vessels. Sailors on US ships were paid better and encouraged to move up the ranks from deckhand to captain.

New Englanders, like William Phelps and Amasa Delano, a distant ancestor of Franklin Delano Roosevelt, went to sea as teenagers, at a time when it was not unusual for an American captain to be barely twenty. They sailed with imprecise navigational instruments (calculating latitude had been perfected, but longitude would have to wait for later in the century), lived off maggoty bread, and were often racked by venereal disease. But their lodestar was the prospect of profits in Guangzhou, a shining beacon that persuaded America's best and brightest to choose the sea as a career.

As William Phelps testifies at the start of his memoir: "Born within a cable's length of the sea-beat shore, inhaling with my earliest breath the atmosphere of the Old Ocean, it was not a matter of much wonder that I very early manifested a strong love for the sea, and took to the water as naturally as a duck."

After months onboard, braving storms and scurvy, the Americans would arrive at the coast of China. The first stop was Macao, a spit of land jutting into the South China Sea, eighty miles down the Pearl River from Guangzhou. Though Macao belonged to China, Chinese authorities had allowed the Portuguese to manage it since the mid-sixteenth century as a way of keeping foreigners out of China proper but close enough to trade. There, American sailors found a melting pot of Pacific Islanders, Filipinos, Malays, Africans, Indians, Europeans, merchants, and gamblers, not to mention the Chinese. The climate—Guangdong's winters were mild compared with the bitter cold of the Northeast—delighted the Yankee sailors.

After securing a Chinese boatman, ships would stop at Whampoa, twelve miles from Guangzhou, where traders discharged their cargoes and paid duties. From there, they would head to Guangzhou itself. At various points, the Americans doled out bribes, known as cumshaw, or squeeze, to keep the goods moving.

Traveling up the Pearl River, the sailors confronted a world afloat: coastal junks, sampans, ferry boats, barber boats, and food vendors bobbed along in the muddy waters of the Pearl. "We passed a pagoda of large size, seven stories high," wrote Charles Tyng, who sailed from Boston in 1815 at the age of fourteen. "The houses were curious, similar in appearance as those seen on china plates, and other ware. The country seemed crowded with inhabitants, young and old, all moving about like ants round an ant hill."

To America's founders, China was a source of inspiration. They saw it as a harmonious society with officials chosen on merit, where the arts and philosophy flourished, and the peasantry labored happily on the land. Benjamin Franklin venerated China's prison system and sought information on its census, its silk industry, and how its people heated their homes. George Washington wrote that he had once thought that "the Chinese tho' droll in shape and appearance were yet white." (The American construction of an Asian racial "type" would happen later in the nineteenth century.) The revolutionary pamphleteer Thomas Paine compared Confucius to Jesus Christ. James Madison and Thomas Jefferson admired China's ability to close itself off from the outside world, finding virtue in its isolation.

The Americans who actually went to China, by contrast, were befuddled and awed by the empire. Guangzhou, home to one million people, a quarter of the population of the entire United States in 1800, was the greatest city most of them would ever see. Samuel Shaw, a former artillery officer in the Continental Army who traveled to Guangzhou three times before dying of a fever on a return voyage in 1794, remarked on the "excellence" of the government but pronounced himself glad to be an American. Amasa Delano described China with the wonder of a country hayseed, contending that it "is the first for greatness, riches and grandeur of any country ever known." Still, he too was distressed when he saw what appeared to be the corpses of mixed-blood babies floating down the Pearl River.

Under rules established in the eighteenth century, trade with China was conducted at arm's length. In theory, Westerners could do business only with a special guild of merchants, commonly known as the Thirteen Hongs, which was appointed and taxed heavily by the Qing court. Westerners were confined to a compound of about a dozen buildings, called factories, cut off from the general population in a section of Guangzhou outside the city walls and small enough to be measured in footsteps—270 along the bustling Pearl River and 50 from the riverbank inland. By the mid-1820s, the Americans occupied their own factory on Old China Street.

Westerners in Guangzhou were governed by what were known as the "Eight Regulations," a long list of rules designed to maintain China's political and national security and manage foreign trade. Among these was a ban on Western women, issued in order to prevent families from settling in China. Another outlawed teaching a foreigner Chinese. (To communicate, Chinese and Westerners developed their own language, a mélange of English, Portuguese, Dutch, French, and Cantonese that was called "pidgin," derived from the Cantonese pronunciation of the word "business.") Selling Chinese books to a foreigner was also prohibited, as was spreading Christianity.

The Americans soon learned, however, that though the government was wary of foreigners, the Chinese people were less so. Western women may have been forbidden, but British and American captains occasionally sneaked them in from Macao for a look around. Westerners were theoretically allowed to leave the foreign ghetto only when accompanied by a "linguist," who worked for the government. But as American trader William C. Hunter noted, "We walked when we pleased and remained as long as we pleased while on each occasion a linguist was the last person we ever saw."

Other rules barred foreigners from owning property or conducting business other than trade in Guangzhou. Nonetheless, Americans ran inns and taverns and even, in the case of former slave trader William F. Megee from Rhode Island, hired themselves out as building contractors.

Westerners were prohibited from consorting with Chinese women, but William Hunter kept a Chinese lover. Benjamin Chew Wilcocks, a Philadelphia merchant and famed gourmand who was the US consul in Guangzhou for a decade, fathered a daughter with his Chinese mistress. In 1833, when he was past fifty, Wilcocks's mission to find a wife in Philadelphia was almost derailed when his love child arrived aboard a tea ship in the City of Brotherly Love.

Nathan Dunn, a suspect in the first reported sodomy case in Pennsylvania, managed for eight years to flaunt the Chinese regulation evicting foreigners from Guangzhou after the end of each trading season. It was rumored that he preferred Chinese men. Dunn was also the first American to pursue another passion—Chinese antiquities. On December 22, 1836, he opened a massive exhibition—*Ten Thousand Chinese Things*—in the new Philadelphia Museum, wowing the cream of American society with an Oriental phantasmagoria.

William Hunter's warm feelings for Guangzhou and his Chinese partners were shared by many other American traders who found themselves at sea when they returned to the United States. The banquets, the scenery, the people, the camaraderie with merchants from around the globe, and the unforgettable nature of life in China made America seem dull. Writing of the merchant John P. Cushing, who retired to Boston a multimillionaire in 1830 after twenty-seven years in Guangzhou, a colleague named John Latimer noted that America "was no home to him. His habits had become so fixed, that China was to him a home." Remarked Benjamin Wilcocks on his return to Philadelphia: "I am unhinged, unsettled, idle and of course irritable. . . . Everything here loses in comparison with" China.

One reason the Americans felt loved in China was that in the early days, they were generally well behaved. They had no choice. From the Atlantic seaboard until they reached the Chinese mainland, Americans relied on the kindness of strangers. Their ships could not land at a single port without the approval of Britain or another European power. They traversed the pirate-infested waters of the Indian Ocean courtesy of the French navy. Once in Guangzhou, the American merchants had no military to back up their demands, and no diplomatic representative to negotiate on their behalf. So, unlike the frontiersmen in the American West who fought Indian tribes with an army behind them, America's pioneers in China sought harmony and peace.

When Samuel Shaw first arrived in China in August 1784, it took him days, and the intervention of a French captain, to convince the Chinese that the Americans and the British were not the same. The Chinese initially called the Americans "the New People," Shaw wrote, and the United States the "nation of the flowery flag." But, after trying out at least sixty-one other options, the Chinese settled on a name for the land that these new people came from—Meiguo, or "the beautiful country."

With time, influential scholar-officials in the Manchu court became well disposed toward the Yankee traders. In 1817, the Americans received favorable mention from Ruan Yuan, who governed two southern provinces, Guangdong and Guangxi. He praised Americans as "the most respectful and compliant people" from the Western world. Chinese merchants had a similarly favorable impression of the Americans. In his memoirs, Samuel Shaw recounts a bargaining session with a Chinese merchant who refused to buy Shaw's products at Shaw's stated price. This went on for a week, Shaw wrote, and Shaw negotiated politely throughout. The Chinese merchant was impressed, and contrasted Shaw's civility with the surliness of most British traders. "All China-man very much love your country," the merchant told Shaw in pidgin English when he at last had accepted Shaw's terms. But the merchant also predicted that after a few trips to Canton, the Americans would lose their patience and "make all same Englishman, too."

What pleased the Chinese merchants most about the Americans was that they paid for their tea, porcelains, and cloth with silver. For decades, America's main export to China was silver dollars, mined and minted in Spanish America. From 1807 until 1833, American ships hauled 2,225 tons of silver to China, more than half of all the silver China imported during that time. Just as American consumers injected billions of dollars into China's economy in the late twentieth century, American merchants flooded the Middle Kingdom with silver in the early days of the relationship.

US silver exports to China played a key role in helping the Qing court right its balance of trade and postponed for many years the economic crisis brought on by the trafficking of Indian opium into China. As British drug sales in China skyrocketed, Chinese silver flowed into the coffers of the East India Company and private British trading houses. In 1807, the East India Company took 3.4 million silver dollars out of China—its first sizable export of silver—but Americans brought 6.2 million to China in that same year.

The American trade imbalance with China was tough on the United States and its traders. One Cantonese merchant named Consequa sought President James Madison's assistance in collecting multiple debts. Yankees scoured the globe for products to replace silver. The first boom was in ginseng. Chinese had been consuming the American version of the root since the early 1700s, when a Jesuit priest discovered the plant in use among the Iroquois of North America. In ginseng, Samuel Shaw thought that he had chanced on the charm to unlock China's market. "Useless produce of our mountains and forests," Shaw enthused shortly after the *Empress of China* made landfall, was going to make him rich. But the ginseng boom soon turned to bust. The year before the *Empress of China* landed in China in 1784, ginseng had sold for thirty dollars a pound. But Shaw could only get four dollars. By 1790, a pound of Yankee ginseng fetched barely twenty-five cents. "Because of the Americans, the price has dropped," groused Chrétien-Louis-Joseph de Guignes, the French consul in Canton. Even when the price fell to sixteen cents, the pigheaded Americans just moved more of the stuff. In 1802, they brought 300,000 pounds to China; in 1824, 800,000. (The price of wild American ginseng did finally recover—in the 1990s. Today, it's over a thousand dollars a pound. And most of it still goes to China.)

Sea otter pelts were next. The British had inaugurated the trade in 1784 off the coast of modern-day Oregon. Three years later, the Americans arrived, and over the next decade, the Bostonmen, as the Indians called them, elbowed out the British. American ships took two hundred thousand pelts to China—worth $6 million in the currency of the day. By the mid-1820s, the sea otter had vanished from the Pacific Northwest.

Traders from Connecticut specialized in seals. On Más Afuera, a seven-mile-long rock five hundred miles off the coast of Chile, Americans found three million of the creatures, wrote Amasa Delano in his memoirs. They were soon gone. From the mid-1790s to the 1820s, Americans killed more than six million fur seals. By 1824, the fur seal had disappeared from the waters around South America and from the islands to the south of Africa, where William Phelps had slaughtered them in his teens.

In Hawaii and on Fiji, American traders found sandalwood, used for furniture and incense, and the oleaginous sea cucumber, which the Chinese ate. But in the end, facing a huge trade deficit and hoping to stanch the flow of silver into China, the Americans, like the British, began to run drugs.

The Chinese had been sampling opium since the eighth century. In the early years, it was either eaten or drunk. By the beginning of the Ming dynasty in the fourteenth century, it gained popularity among the well-heeled as an aphrodisiac and an after-dinner relaxant. In the sixteenth century, it became more widespread as it was combined with another import: tobacco. By the late eighteenth and early nineteenth centuries, opium was available in coastal Chinese homes. The American trader

William Hunter observed that among his Chinese friends, "smoking was a habit, as the use of wine was with us, in moderation."

The first American ships to carry opium to China brought it from Turkey in 1804 courtesy of two Philadelphians, Benjamin Wilcocks, the gourmand consul with the love child from Macao, and his brother, James. Chinese smugglers were happy to cut the more potent British product from India with what became known as "turkey." From the end of the War of 1812 to the mid-1830s, Americans bought more Turkish opium than any other nation. One Boston firm alone, Perkins & Company, regularly shipped one-half to three-quarters of Turkey's entire yearly crop of 150,000 pounds to China. By 1818, the Americans were buying opium in India as well, challenging the East India Company's monopoly on the drug traffic there.

The US entry into the opium trade coincided with an enormous increase in opium exports to China. In 1773, British ships moved 75 tons of opium to China. By the 1830s, American and British vessels were carrying more than 350 tons a year. In 1829, total British exports to China accounted for $21 million, about half of it from opium. American exports hit $4 million, of which opium constituted one quarter.

The US opium trade had reverberations at home. Within two decades, the opium traffic reversed America's trade imbalance with China. Silver poured back into the United States, contributing to sharp inflation in the 1830s. One American firm, D.W.C. Olyphant & Company, refused to carry the drug out of religious conviction, but most American merchants saw a good opportunity in moving "turkey" to China.

"I do not pretend to justify the prosecution of the opium trade in a moral and philanthropic point of view," mused Warren Delano, an American opium trader in Guangzhou and the grandfather of Franklin Delano Roosevelt, "but as a merchant I insist that it has been a fair, honorable and legitimate trade." Equivalent, he argued, to importing brandy into the United States.

The vast gap between the Chinese and American cultures made for many clashes. When an American sailor allegedly killed a Chinese woman on September 29, 1821, the small American community in Guangzhou faced its first crisis. Would the Americans conform to the Chinese way of doing things, or would they defy the mandarins?

Francis Terranova was a Sicilian deckhand on the *Emily*, a 284-ton cargo ship from Baltimore. He was buying fruit from Ko Leang-she, a peddler on a sampan, when Ko fell into the sea. The Chinese accused Terranova, who was unimpressed with the quality of Ko's bananas, of throwing an olive jar that hit Ko on the head and knocked her into the water. Others said that Ko had simply slipped into the water and drowned.

Wang Yuanren, the district magistrate, invited US consul Benjamin Wilcocks to view the corpse. There was a gash on the right side of Ko's head, Wilcocks wrote, into which the olive jar "fitted exactly." Terranova, Wilcocks thought, was guilty. The Chinese authorities demanded that the sailor be handed over. In negotiations with Wilcocks, the Chinese agreed to a trial and to a Yankee approach to the proceedings. Witnesses for both the defense and the prosecution would be called.

On October 6, 1821, a flock of Chinese warships surrounded the *Emily*. Led by Magistrate Wang, hundreds of Chinese officials and soldiers crowded onto the deck, dwarfing the American delegation of forty. None of the American witnesses spoke Chinese. When the Chinese interpreters arrived, they approached Wang on their hands and knees, leaving the impression that they would not be translating anything that the magistrate did not wish to hear. Unmoved by testimony from the *Emily*'s sailors backing Terranova's story, Wang cut the hearing short. The Americans accused the Chinese of breaking their pledge to grant Terranova a fair trial. Wang then lost patience and pronounced Terranova guilty. The *Emily*'s captain refused to hand over his deckhand. On October 7, the Chinese suspended trade with the United States.

The prospect of a trade embargo was too much for the Yankees. After sixteen days, the Americans turned Terranova over to the Chinese. Before dawn on October 28, he was taken to the office of the viceroy in Guangzhou and strangled.

The British were shocked, more by American docility than by the execution. The Americans had "barbarously abandoned a man serving under their flag to the sanguinary laws of this Empire without an endeavour to obtain common justice for him," reported the Select Committee of the East India Company. To the British, the case brought home the need to live outside the purview of Chinese law. To the Chinese, it showed that even when China tried to placate foreign mores, the foreign devils would still be unsatisfied.

The matter did not end with Terranova's execution. While the Sicilian was being tried on deck, the *Emily* held a load of opium in its stowage. Tipped off that the captain was smuggling drugs, Chinese authorities confiscated the cargo and sent the ship back to Baltimore empty.

The Terranova case colored American views of China for years. Westerners cited it as proof that they needed extraterritoriality, under which foreigners policed their citizens on Chinese soil, to ensure "universal values" and to protect the rights of the accused.

The potent mix of money, drugs, and cultural differences that swirled around Guangzhou was bound to ignite. Amasa Delano wagered that British gunboats would soon attack China. In Delano's view, the emperor's unwillingness to fully open his country to trade with the West was a strategic mistake. "The English possess great power in Asia both by sea and land," he wrote. "If they attacked, I think it would end in the dissolution of the present government of China." He would eventually be proven right.

For the United States, however, trading with China not only saved but helped shape the new republic. America's discovery of the China market was integral to the rise of the United States. For the Chinese, America also meant opportunity—for their officials, for their showmen, and for one globally minded businessman.

CHAPTER TWO

Founding Fortunes

In the early nineteenth century, the world's richest private business-man was Chinese. Wu Bingjian, a merchant prince from Guangzhou, had amassed a fortune estimated at $26 million in 1834, the equivalent of tens of billions today. He did it without leaving China, but with the help of his American friends.

A cautious, even retiring, man whose Chinese nickname was "the timid young lady," Wu was famed for his uncanny knack for figures and his kindness, especially to the New England merchants, which caused endless grumbling among their British rivals. To the Western merchants in Canton, Wu was known as Howqua or Houqua—the name he did business by.

In the early nineteenth century, Howqua was appointed senior merchant of the Thirteen Hongs of Canton, which were authorized to deal with the "oceanic barbarians" in Guangzhou. At the time, the Hong system, under which a small group of merchants handled thousands of tons of tea and porcelain exports a year and were responsible for one another's debts, was viewed as one of the most efficient trading enterprises in the world. In the United States, this collective guarantee inspired lawmakers in New York to establish the first bank deposit insurance system, a precursor to today's Federal Deposit Insurance Corporation.

Howqua's commercial interests stretched from China to India to London and the United States. His American investments, managed by a trusted Yankee friend, powered the development of railroads, real estate, manufacturing, and insurance. Some 150 years before American capital fueled China's modernization, money from the Middle Kingdom performed the same service in the United States.

What drew Howqua to a series of Boston merchants over the first four decades of the nineteenth century is a story that has gone largely untold in the popular literature about China and the United States. But it is a sterling example of the persistent sense of a shared destiny and mutual self-interest that flowed between Americans and Chinese as they responded to a changing world.

The idea, put forth in histories of the period, that the Chinese did not welcome foreign trade is not true. Although the Qing court adopted a patronizing attitude toward foreigners, and Confucian mandarins sniffed self-importantly at China's merchant class, the dynasty's policies were not anticommerce. China's Qianlong emperor may have told a British mission led by Lord George Macartney in 1793 that "Our Celestial Empire possesses all things in prolific abundance and lacks no product within its border," but his imperial household relied on taxes from China's trade with the West.

The Manchus, a nomadic Asiatic tribe who ran the Qing, even employed trade to save the empire. When Manchu cavalry poured into China from the north in the early seventeenth century, they took Beijing first, establishing the dynasty in 1644 to rule over the Han Chinese. For the next forty years, a struggle for southern China raged between the invaders and the remnants of the Ming court.

In 1684, however, with southern China finally in the Qing's hands, the then emperor, Kangxi, opened the south for trade with the outside world. He promoted commerce to jump-start the economy and win the allegiance of the south. To Kangxi, trade with the West was a glue to keep southern China in his realm.

But the court worried that just as contact with the West could be used to win its subjects' loyalty, it could also shake the empire's foundations. So Kangxi restricted trade to a small group of men—the Thirteen Hongs—in one southern port. Encouraging commerce in Guangzhou made sense as a way to heal the wounds of war. But once Western merchants began to press for access to all of China, the throne saw them as a threat. These conflicting goals—of leveraging the West to strengthen the empire and restricting its impact to guarantee security—defined China's often contradictory responses to the capitalists from across the seas.

* * *

Born in 1769, Howqua specialized in the most profitable sectors of the Canton trade: tea, moneylending, and commodities, which included opium. He turned a profit first as a tea grower and then as a middleman. A portrait of Howqua in middle age shows him swaddled in luxuriant finery, a fur-lined dark blue silk winter coat embroidered with a phoenix. The amber and coral necklaces draped around his neck offered a marked contrast to Howqua's austere, even ascetic, mien.

Howqua adapted quickly to the new trend of replacing silver aboard ships with interest-bearing bonds. When dealing with millions of dollars floating for months on ships around the globe, he found that this scheme could be lucrative. Howqua reached out to merchants in other Asian ports—Calcutta, Manila, and Batavia—and pulled Guangzhou, through which more than $25 million in exports flowed annually, into a global web of trade.

In 1820, Howqua cornered the Asian market in pepper. In the foreign ghetto, he honed his skills as a real estate baron, leasing several of his properties to Western merchants. His 1843 obituary in Britain's *Asiatic Journal* declared him the equal of any European merchant and observed "that to the last he directed his vast and complicated trade, which almost encircled the globe, alone." It called his business sense "astonishing." Howqua did not like the British, the *Journal* acknowledged. "His predilections were American, and justly so, seeing that he was indebted in an early stage of his career to a citizen of that country." That citizen was John Perkins Cushing.

John Perkins Cushing arrived in China in 1804, the first year Howqua did business with the Americans, selling them a boatload of tea. Cushing had been dispatched to China to serve as a clerk for the Boston firm Perkins & Company, founded by his uncle.

Like many Americans in the China trade, Cushing was a teenager, and Howqua took him under his wing. With Howqua's guidance, Cushing matured from a sixteen-year-old with literary pretensions and scant interest in numbers into the shrewdest and most successful of all the American traders in Guangzhou.

What pulled Howqua to the Americans initially was their silver. He did not have to barter his tea for British woolens or manufactured goods. Moreover, as the leading Hong, Howqua was caught between the overbearing British East India Company and corrupt mandarins. The East India Company bought in bulk, so it demanded lower prices. Qing officials squeezed Howqua for bribes. The Americans were a perfect foil, allowing Howqua to sell at a price higher than the British accepted and offering him a place where he could secrete his money beyond the grasp of the Qing court.

New England merchants carried Howqua's tea to London, skirting the East India Company. And Americans took his tea to the United States on their ships, evading the high duties that the US government imposed on goods imported on foreign vessels. The Americans were amazed at the faith that Howqua placed in them. "Unbounded confidence in Americans has never been equaled," wrote Paul S. Forbes, a Guangzhou-based merchant and one of Cushing's cousins, "entrusting to those with whom he had no ties of country, language, or religion between 2 and 3 millions of dollars at one time."

By the age of nineteen, Cushing had taken over the Perkins & Company office in Guangzhou. The eruption of the War of 1812 pushed him closer to Howqua. The Royal Navy chased American merchantmen off the seas, so Cushing had little American trade to conduct. Instead, he ran Howqua's overseas businesses. He moved into drug trafficking, and Perkins & Company soon had a near monopoly on opium from Turkey, supported by loans from its Chinese friend.

Howqua tried to cover his tracks but did not always succeed. In 1821, after opium was discovered aboard his clients' ship, the *Emily*, the emperor ordered that a sapphire button, a sign of Howqua's status as an honorary official, be stripped from Howqua's hat. Still, his Yankee business kept growing.

Together Cushing and Howqua battled their British competitors. They subverted the East India Company's monopoly on British-made cloth and other British products that sold well in China. In one of China's first great intellectual property rip-offs, Americans and Chinese copied the East India Company's packaging trademark and dumped their cheaper cloth on the Guangzhou market. The East India Company complained to the Chinese and pushed the Qing court to crack down. But finally the British government moved to dissolve the monopoly in 1834, in part because it could no longer compete with independent merchants like Cushing, aided by the entrepreneurial Chinese.

When wars of independence shook Latin America in the 1820s, Howqua and Cushing moved in on the trade in silks and tea that Spanish Manila galleons had shipped to South America. In 1825, during a rice famine in Guangzhou, Howqua persuaded Chinese customs authorities to reduce duties on Cushing's ships so long as they carried rice to China. This further spurred American drug trafficking, as Yankee traders buried crates of "turkey" under the grain in their holds.

In 1835, Howqua donated one of his buildings, 3 Hog Lane, to American missionary Peter Parker to open, rent free, the first Western hospital in China. The Hospital of Universal Love heralded the start of American support for China's medical sciences. Howqua availed himself of Parker's care. The great merchant suffered from maddening bouts of itching each winter and chronic loose bowels.

Despite the four months it took for mail to reach opposite ends of the earth, Howqua and his American associates maintained an active correspondence. In 1837, Howqua shipped John P. Cushing fifty-four pounds of mulberry seeds to start a silk industry in the United States. (It failed.) Howqua's friends mailed him soap, a wood-burning stove, a rocking chair, barrels of flour, cookies (favored by Howqua's oldest wife), and a cow that calved during the journey. The beasts were thin but alive upon landing. "With good care and plenty of good food," Howqua replied, "they have both become quite fat and the cow furnishes us with a most liberal quantity of rich milk." The Americans named a clipper ship after the businessman. Madame Tussaud's in London fashioned his likeness out of wax.

Howqua's generosity was the stuff of legend. When Warren Delano prepared to return to the United States in the 1830s, Howqua threw him a banquet that featured two kinds of soup, bird's nest and shark fin, and quail, sturgeon lips, and pigeon eggs. "We were 13 hours getting thro' with it," one American guest recalled. In 1827, Howqua forgave a debt of $72,000 that Benjamin Wilcocks owed him, allowing the Philadelphian to head home with no financial liabilities. Wilcocks had earlier acted as Howqua's principal debt collector in the United States, earning Howqua's lasting gratitude. "You and I are number one olo friend," Howqua told Wilcocks in pidgin, as he ripped up the promissory note.

As Cushing rose in prominence at Perkins & Company, he assigned another young clerk, John Murray Forbes, to Howqua's account. Howqua again treated an American teenager, who had come to Guangzhou from Boston in 1830 at the age of seventeen, much as a son.

While Cushing would live in China for twenty-five years, Forbes stayed only until he turned twenty-three, returning to the United States in 1836 a wealthy young man. Months after he landed back in Boston, the Panic of 1837 rocked the United States, plunging the country into a five-year depression. A year later, Forbes was ready to invest. Using the $100,000 he had saved in China, he established J. M. Forbes & Company, an investment bank. He augmented his seed capital with half a million dollars from his mentor, Howqua.

In his letters, Howqua insisted that Forbes alone manage Howqua's American investments. As he had with Howqua's teas, Forbes held Howqua's money in his own name but kept it separate from his own funds, "although I made it a rule not to buy anything for it which I was not also buying for myself." Forbes invested in land, transportation, manufacturing, and railroads. One of his factories made the first rail ties in the United States. He ran the first passenger trains to Chicago from the East. In came immigrants, out went grain and cattle. Decades before Chinese labor built America's Western railroads, Chinese capital laid the groundwork.

Forbes was not the only American to plant his Chinese proceeds in American soil. After hitting it big in Guangzhou, Abiel Abbot Low returned to New York City, built a fleet of trading ships (christening one of the vessels *Houqua*), and invested in the first transatlantic cable and railroads, too.

Americans in the China trade also became the nation's first great philanthropists. Forbes bankrolled the transcendentalist philosopher Ralph Waldo Emerson. Low supported education for women and funded libraries and hospitals. Low's son Seth built the Low Memorial Library, now the administrative center of Columbia University. The Astor family endowed Harvard; other traders bankrolled Yale, founding its Skull and Bones secret society, and Princeton.

From seventy-five tons a year in the 1770s, the opium trade to China had ballooned to fourteen hundred tons a year by the 1830s. Already, it was sucking millions of dollars of silver from China's treasury into the coffers of British and American trading houses. Its poison coursed through all levels of Chinese society. The Canton trade, which had helped pull the Chinese empire together, was now pulling it apart.

For decades, the Qing court had debated how to deal with opium. A standoff between those who advocated legalizing and taxing the drug and those who favored a crackdown led to the worst possible solution. The trade was banned but tolerated, and a river of profits and payoffs flowed into the pockets of Qing bureaucrats and Chinese smugglers. In 1820, a new emperor, Daoguang, took the throne. Several years later, after his eldest son apparently fell victim to the opium pipe, he vowed to take action.

If the Qing government was conflicted about opium, so, too, were the

Americans, for it wasn't only American business that was interested in China. In the 1830s, American Protestant missionaries started arriving in Guangzhou, bringing with them a negative view of the trade as opposed to the business community's decidedly amoral approach. Trafficking was wrong and had to stop, the missionaries said. The two sides squared off. Which mattered more, profits or principle? Was the goal to make money in China or to foster change? The battle continues to this day.

In 1839, Emperor Daoguang dispatched an official known for his uncompromisingly high moral standards to deal with the scourge. Commissioner Lin Zexu turned his sights away from Chinese drug dealers and addicts and trained them on the Western merchants. He proposed a barter deal, offering to swap tea for opium and a promise to end the traffic. When the Western merchants rejected it, on the afternoon of Monday, March 18, 1839, Lin ringed the foreign ghetto with Qing troops. Hand over all the opium, and legal commerce can resume, he said.

Six days later, Charles Elliot, chief superintendent of British Trade, arrived in the city and assumed responsibility for the drugs. By early May, Elliot had collected 15,400 chests of opium, valued at 6 million silver dollars; a tenth came from the Americans. Elliot handed them all over to Lin Zexu.

The Americans announced that they were willing to forsake the opium trade. American manufactured goods and cloth were gaining traction in China, and the Yankee merchants believed that the dream of the China market was about to come true. "Our staunch friend Howqua says if we don't cut the drug trade 'in toto' he will cut us," wrote Robert Bennet Forbes, a nephew of John M. Forbes who had arrived in China in 1838 as chief representative for Russell & Company.

By May 24, Lin Zexu had lifted his siege of the foreign quarter. The British merchants then pulled out. By June, only fifteen Americans and a handful of men of other nationalities remained in Guangzhou. Unlike the British, the Americans signed a pledge, brought to them by Howqua, to end the opium trade.

Commissioner Lin rewarded the Americans for their good behavior. On June 17, 1838, he invited a group of them, including Charles W. King, a merchant from a firm that had not run opium, and Elijah Bridgman, the first American missionary in China, to witness the destruction of the confiscated drugs.

King and Bridgman were taken to a small island halfway between

Macao and Guangzhou, where they found five hundred workers crumbling cannonball-sized balls of opium into vast pits filled with water, salt, and lime. Once the opium had dissolved, the sludge was sluiced into a tributary of the Pearl River and out into the ocean from which it came. "Have we anywhere on record a finer rebuke administered by Pagan integrity to Christian degeneracy?" Bridgman asked his readers in the *Chinese Repository*, the American-operated paper in the city.

King and Bridgman were ushered into a makeshift bamboo hall where Lin sat on a sofa. Short and stout, with a smooth, full round face and a small black beard, Lin was "vivacious, and exhibited nothing that was 'barbarous or savage,'" Bridgman observed. It was no accident that only Americans had been invited to witness this historic day, Lin told them. They were, he said, "decent and proper" with a "predisposition toward being transformed and cultivated" by Chinese civilization. Despite the patronizing tone, it was the highest compliment he could give.

With his hands clean of opium, King assumed that he was entitled to a special deal and began a long tradition of American commercial behavior in China by seeking privileges during an audience with a Chinese official. King asked Lin to allow his firm to continue to trade during the crisis and to make up for his losses. Lin agreed to the first request but rejected the second.

Lin was more concerned about the British. Why had they pulled out of Guangzhou? he asked. He wanted maps and other intelligence. When Bridgman and King spoke about Britain's naval power and its use of steam to power its ships, Lin "once or twice raised a frown on his brow," Bridgman reported. Unbeknownst to the commissioner, China was on its way to a war with the mightiest power in the West.

Before he withdrew from Guangzhou, British superintendent Charles Elliot visited American merchant Robert Bennet Forbes and demanded that the Americans also depart from China and shut down trade with the empire. "If your house goes, all will go, and we shall soon bring these rascally Chinese to terms," Elliot told Forbes.

Forbes refused, telling the British representative that he would stay put in Guangzhou "as long as I could sell a yard of goods or buy a pound of tea." When Elliot threatened the Americans with arrest, Forbes scoffed. America was a competitor for the favors of the Chinese court—a reality that has not changed much today.

British traders, stuck outside Guangzhou with ships loaded with goods and needing tea for London, were less steadfast than the British superintendent of trade. They couldn't simply dump their cargo and go home empty-handed. So for the next fifteen months, the handful of Americans living in Guangzhou and Macao undertook an astoundingly profitable river trade—sailing British wares to Guangzhou and the payment back to Macao for transfer onto vessels bound for London.

By early 1840, British traders were forking over more to move their goods up and down that ninety-mile stretch of water than it cost to ship the stuff to Europe and back. "While we hold the horns," one British merchant grumbled, the Americans "milk the cow." The river business, Robert Bennet Forbes confided to his friend and partner Samuel Cabot, was the best that Russell & Company had ever enjoyed.

To meet the demands of the trade, FDR's grandfather Warren Delano bought a nine-hundred-ton British-built vessel and renamed it the *Chesapeake*. Then Commissioner Lin asked to buy it, and so the first American military sale to China came to pass. Lin turned the *Chesapeake* into a floating armory, outfitting it with Portuguese cannons and painting two great eyes on its bow to keep the foreign devils at bay.

Charles Elliot would eventually thank Forbes for staying in Guangzhou. When they met later in Macao, he acknowledged that without the cover of the American flag, British merchants would have lost millions. "My dear Forbes," Elliot said, "the Queen owes you many thanks for not taking my advice."

In June 1840, a British expeditionary force under Rear Admiral Sir George Elliot, Charles Elliot's cousin, sailed into the mouth of the Pearl River with a fleet of forty-eight ships ready to punish China for impounding British property even if it was narcotics. The British crushed their Chinese foes. The *Chesapeake* was an early casualty. The Chinese had no one with the skills to sail her; her guns were pointed the wrong way and the casks of gunpowder that had been stored on deck made too tempting a target. British marines boarded her and put her to the torch. When the flames reached the *Chesapeake*'s magazine, the great ship exploded, illuminating the sky for miles around.

As loss piled upon loss, Commissioner Lin Zexu tried to entice the Americans into an alliance against the British. The Chinese offered the Americans a monopoly on the trade through Whampoa, and money for capturing Englishmen, dead or alive. (The Chinese put a $50,000 bounty on Charles Elliot's head.) Ruan Yuan, the governor-general of Guangdong and Guangxi provinces, suggested abolishing all customs duties for American ships as a sweetener. "The American barbarians are sure to be grateful for this Heavenly favor," he predicted, but the Americans did not bite.

In the United States, the public followed the war with a lively interest and generally backed the Chinese. The War of 1812 and the burning of the White House was still fresh in many minds. Americans had supported a movement to turn Canada into a republic and clashes with the British army erupted along the Canadian border. American missionaries in Guangzhou had sounded an emotional appeal on behalf of the Chinese. Their reports on the evils of opium, sent to churches across America, turned many Americans against the war and the trade.

"China has a perfect right to regulate the character of her imports," declared *Hunt's Merchants' Magazine* from New York City. On March 16, 1840, Caleb Cushing, a congressman from Massachusetts, rose to address the House Committee on Foreign Affairs. The British practice of trafficking opium violated, he said, "all law, human and divine." Yankee practicality lurked behind Cushing's condemnation. With China trade in his blood (John Perkins Cushing was a cousin), he understood that Americans could profit from Britain's woes.

But whereas Cushing saw a moral imperative—and an opportunity—in taking a different approach to China than the rapacious tactics of the British, his fellow New Englander, John Quincy Adams, believed that Britain was right to go to war. As the conflict intensified, Adams, who had been secretary of state when the sailor Terranova was executed and was now chairman of the House Committee on Foreign Affairs, argued before the Massachusetts Historical Society that the British were not fighting simply for the right to traffic opium. There were broader principles at stake, such as free trade and the untrammeled intercourse between nations. The British, he said, wanted the Chinese to treat them as equals. "The cause of the war is the kowtow," Adams declared. The war was being fought to battle China's "boasted superiority above every nation on earth."

Adams's view was still in the minority. (The *North American Review*, the leading intellectual publication of the day, declined to publish his speech.) But it foreshadowed a continuing debate on how to deal with China. Should China be allowed to act as if it were a unique civilization that deserved special treatment—or should it be held to Western standards?

In August 1842, China buckled to British military pressure. The court agreed to British terms and signed the Treaty of Nanjing: China ceded Hong Kong to the British crown, opened up five treaty ports for trade, paid an indemnity of 21 million silver dollars, and instituted regular customs duties, abolishing the random taxes and fees that had so bedeviled Western traders.

Writing to John P. Cushing in December 1842, Howqua welcomed the end of the Hong system, which had handcuffed his world-class business acumen, golden though the shackles may have been. "I look forward with pleasure to the time when I will be a free man," he wrote, adding wistfully, "If I were a young man now I should think seriously of embarking for America, to settle down somewhere near you."

His business partner, John M. Forbes, offered one of his ships to take the merchant's treasures and his family to Florida or an island in the Caribbean. "Come to this country," Forbes urged in a letter, "where every man is called upon to pay only his fair share of the expenses of the Government."

Howqua never read the note. On September 4, 1843, thirty days after it was written and three months before it would arrive in Guangzhou, China's seventy-four-year-old tycoon died at the Hospital of Universal Love. According to the notes of Dr. Peter Parker, a bout of diarrhea, brought on by the Manchu demand that Howqua pay another bribe, had "terminated the life of this distinguished merchant."

Defeat in the Opium War finally drove certain leading figures in the Qing court to seek a systematic understanding of the Western world. Before that, Westerners had appeared in Chinese books in weird getups, as devils and monkeys, and always smelling bad. America was thought of as far off, very strange, and of little significance. One Chinese pamphlet placed the United States near Africa. Another called it an "isolated island in the middle of the ocean." Commissioner Lin thought, given the American opium trade, that the United States was somewhere near Turkey.

Now China had to dissect the West, and the Americans emerged smelling sweeter than everyone else. Chinese writers marveled at American democracy and at the idea that the American people, including the president, bowed to law and not to an emperor. American charities fascinated the Chinese. Commissioner Lin was taken with American education. America's prosperity was powered by its schools, which enabled "talents to emerge generation after generation," he wrote in the *Gazetteer of Four*

Continents, one of the tomes on Western powers that were produced during this period. Yankee industry impressed the Chinese. At least 150 years before US pundits would hold up China's economy and its decisive leadership as a model for the United States, the Chinese saw things worthy of imitation in America.

In the 1840s, Emperor Daoguang tasked Xu Jiyu, the governor of Fujian province, just north of Guangdong, with writing a history of the Western barbarians. Published in 1849, Xu's *A Short Account of the Oceans Around Us* lavished praise on America, and especially on its first president, inaugurating a Chinese cult of George Washington that would endure through the era of Mao Zedong.

Xu gathered his information about America from David Abeel, a missionary from New Brunswick, New Jersey. Abeel had been in Xiamen, on Fujian's southern coast, since 1842 and found Xu to be "the most inquisitive Chinese of a high rank I have yet met." He plied Xu with books and maps. Sadly for Abeel, none of Xu's curiosity extended to God. "He was far more anxious to learn the state of kingdoms of this world," Abeel observed, "than the truths of the Kingdom of Heaven."

The story of America's fight for independence was of immediate relevance to a nation struggling to contend with the British crown. So it was natural that Xu devoted the longest section in his book to the United States. Americans, Xu wrote, were "docile, good-natured, mild and honest." No other country came closest to the Confucian ideal that "everything under heaven is for the common good." Americans possessed what China wanted, he wrote: "wealth and power."

Three elements made George Washington's story gripping to a Qing dynasty scholar trying to determine what was wrong with China. First was Washington's selfless dedication to his country, a rebuke to the widespread corruption in the Qing court. Second, Washington had thrashed the British, China's foe. Third, in contrast to China's sclerotic monarchy, where the emperor clung to power until his dying day, Washington's return to civilian life served as a model of the cardinal virtues that Chinese sages had promoted from time immemorial. Just as Washington had mistaken the Chinese for Caucasians, Xu and his fellow scholars saw Washington's virtues as Chinese.

"Of all the famous Westerners of ancient and modern times, can Washington be placed in any position but first?" Xu asked. Those lines would be etched onto a marble plaque and sent by Chinese merchants to Washington, DC, in 1853. There the administration of President Franklin Pierce mounted the plaque inside the five-year-old Washington Monument, where it can still be seen today.

Underlying Xu's *Short Account* was a simple yet profound insight: the old mandarin conviction that China sat at the apex of world civilization no longer held true. China needed to look outside itself for answers to its quest for wealth and power. But most Qing officials were not ready for that perspective and in 1850, when Emperor Daoguang died and was replaced by a more traditionalist leader, Emperor Xianfeng, the court accused Xu Jiyu of "inflating the status of foreign barbarians" and banished him, along with other pro-Western officials, to the edges of the empire.

The signing of the Treaty of Nanjing between Britain and China forced American politicians to pay attention to China. Britain spurred the United States to demand equal treatment. No longer could the United States remain aloof from the interests of American businessmen and missionaries in China.

The first official American political engagement with the Middle Kingdom came with the arrival of the US Navy's East India Squadron at the mouth of the Pearl River in April 1842, just after the Chinese surrender to the British. American commodore Lawrence Kearny told Chinese officials that the United States would expect the same treatment that Britain had won.

The US government also got an inkling of how tortured its China policy would become. On the one hand, in response to merchants' requests, Kearny had been instructed to protect American interests. On the other, in reaction to the missionaries and public opinion back home, he had been directed to halt the American opium trade.

Kearny published a letter warning American drug smugglers that he would not protect them from Chinese prosecution. He seized an American opium ship, the *Ariel*, but soon discovered that no American law justified taking action against narcotics trafficking. He could hold the *Ariel* only because her papers were not in order.

Patrolling China's coast for more than a year, Kearny sought to show the Chinese that the US Navy, unlike the British, had come in peace. On May 9, 1842, he hosted the local commander of the Chinese navy, Admiral Wu Jianxun, aboard his flagship *Constellation*.

Arriving in the afternoon, Admiral Wu was on high alert for treachery. Qing authorities had already ordered Chinese merchants to pay a huge bond, guaranteeing his safe return to shore. When American seamen

conducted an exercise for the admiral's benefit, pretending to repel board-
ers from the *Constellation*'s starboard side, Wu reacted in terror "as almost
a hundred or more men, with swords and pikes and fixed bayonets, rushed
up from the gun-deck," wrote American missionary Elijah Bridgman, who
doubled as Kearny's interpreter. Ultimately, the admiral relaxed, explored
the ship, and lingered onboard until sunset. The next day, he dispatched
two aides to visit the American ship so that they, too, could witness a modern navy. Wu filed a detailed report on the *Constellation* to the emperor,
omitting details of his anxiety attack. "Our ships are slow and clumsy,"
he complained, but the vessels of "the rebel barbarians . . . turn their sails
smartly."

Two days after Christmas 1842, Caleb Cushing, who had fulminated in
Congress against the British a year earlier, warned President John Tyler
in Washington that if the United States did not respond to the Treaty of
Nanjing with its own treaty, the British would seize Japan and Hawaii and,
with them, control of the Pacific. The future of the United States hung
in the balance, Cushing claimed. Three days later, in a special message to
Congress, Tyler asked Congress to dispatch an envoy to China to negotiate an American treaty. Cushing got the job. From the start, Cushing
viewed his mission as key to checking Britain's imperial pretensions and
reinforcing America's interests in Asia.

Cushing was also going to China as a representative of the Western
world. Civilization may have dawned in the East, he remarked during a
speech before his departure at Boston's Faneuil Hall on June 17, 1843, but
now the sun of progress was shining on the West. "We have become the
teachers of our teacher," Cushing said, a line that Americans would hear
tossed back at them 165 years later at the height of America's Great Recession in 2008.

Secretary of State Daniel Webster instructed Cushing to work to
moderate China's "repulsive feelings towards foreigners" and draw a clear
contrast with the British. Tell the Chinese, Webster said, "that the United
States, once a country subject to England, . . . now meets England upon
equal terms." Webster directed Cushing to show the Chinese that unlike
the British, who had grabbed Hong Kong, the United States did not covet
Chinese territory.

Cushing landed in Macao on February 24, 1844, and sent word to the
Chinese that America wanted its own treaty. A few weeks before nego-

tiations started in June, Cushing was handed a convenient pretext for demanding that Americans not be subject to Chinese law. Cushing had brought with him a new flagpole fitted with a weathervane in the shape of an arrow for the US trading post in Guangzhou. The city was in the midst of a drought, and once the flagpole was erected, the Chinese insisted that the arrow, as it gyrated with the wind, was radiating evil spirits.

A mob broke into the foreign ghetto to tear the flagpole down. US consul Paul S. Forbes calmed the crowd by agreeing to remove the weathervane, but elsewhere in the city, another group of Chinese attacked a group of Americans. One of the Americans shot and killed one of the Chinese, Hsu A-man. As in the Terranova case, the Chinese authorities demanded that the Americans hand over their countryman to face justice. Cushing refused and had the man tried by a jury of Yankee merchants. When he was acquitted, Cushing arranged for a payoff to Hsu's family.

In letters to Chinese officials in the run-up to talks, Cushing fixed on what was called the A-man affair to promote the principle of extraterritoriality. He was determined to draw a protective ring around the Americans, allowing them to live in China but not under Chinese law.

Treaty negotiations began on June 16, 1844, in a Buddhist temple just outside the walls of the Portuguese settlement. Cushing's counterpart, Qiying, a garrulous Chinese official, embraced the reserved New Englander upon their meeting. Dressed in a modified major general's uniform designed to impress the Chinese, Cushing offered Qiying books on military tactics and fortifications, delicately suggesting that such information would be of value to China. Qiying, saddled with a superiority complex, declined the gifts. In a few decades, Qiying's successors would be begging America for arms and military advice.

Over the next two weeks, the two men and their staffs hammered out a treaty. In messages to the Manchu court, Qiying sneered at the Americans for their "stupid ignorance" and their inability, compared with the better-trained British translators, to speak Chinese. But Cushing outwitted him. His first demand was for an imperial audience in Beijing. When Qiying rejected it, Cushing suggested that the Chinese agree to his terms for the accord, which expanded significantly on the Treaty of Nanjing. Qiying consented.

The Wangxia Treaty of Peace, Amity, and Commerce between the United States of America and the Chinese Empire set the foundation for American ties with China for more than a century. Fundamental to it were the premises that America required equal access to China's markets and opposed carving China into pieces. Later, these ideas would be called the Open Door.

The US treaty opened the way for Westerners to participate in China's inland trade, giving Americans the right to use Chinese ports to move goods around the country and to send their warships into Chinese waters. Ignorant of economics and the law, Qiying had little idea what he was agreeing to. He focused chiefly on keeping Cushing from traveling to Beijing. The British treaty had stipulated that Westerners involved solely in criminal cases in China would be subject to their country's laws. Cushing, however, convinced Qiying to extend that protection to include civil cases as well. By allowing the treaty to extend the issue of extraterritoriality far beyond what had been detailed in negotiations with the British, the Manchu court created a mechanism that would humiliate China and threaten her sovereignty for a century to come.

Cushing and Qiying concluded the treaty on July 3, 1844, a day before the sixty-sixth birthday of the United States. Cushing set sail for home in August, but not before Qiying gave him another hug and a massive portrait of himself in Manchu garb. It hangs today in the Museum of Fine Arts in Boston.

The American press was fascinated by Cushing's journey to the Far East. In Pune, India, he rode an elephant to a Brahmin temple. On the island of Ceylon, the British governor feted him with a ball. He returned home by way of Mexico, only to stumble on the revolution that led to the Mexican-American War. In January 1845, *Hunt's Merchants' Magazine* declared that the treaty he had negotiated would open "a new era in the commercial world, second only to the discovery of this continent."

Others were bullish, too. Around this time, Asa Whitney, a dry-goods merchant from New Rochelle, New York, returned to the United States from Guangzhou. Twice bankrupted in America, Whitney had struck it rich in China and came home with an idea even more momentous than John Ledyard's sea otter schemes. Whitney became the first great prophet of the transcontinental railroad.

Whitney's principal argument for what he called a "great thoroughfare for all mankind" was the prospect for trade from China. If America could build a railroad connecting its East and West Coasts, Whitney promised audiences across the country, the United States would become the middleman between the Middle Kingdom and the entire world. Chinese commerce appealed to Americans as a way to bind their nation together, profit from Old Europe, and unleash the productive capacities of the United States.

Whitney's plan—to secure federal grants for land from Lake Michigan to the California coast—never got off the ground. By 1852, he had bowed out of public life and retired to his farm, but not before leading a survey mission to validate his route and convincing legislatures in eighteen out of the then thirty states to approve resolutions in favor of the plan.

Asa Whitney brought the idea of a national railroad into the American consciousness and provided the intellectual impetus for the 1862 Pacific Railway Act. Of course, the transcontinental railroad did not reroute global trade, nor did it ensure American hegemony over commerce between Asia and Europe. (The Suez Canal, opened in 1869, ended that pipe dream.) But once again, the inspiration that Americans took from China prompted change in the United States.

Despite China's meandering foreign policy, the connections between China's merchant princes and New England's businessmen persisted. After Howqua's death, John M. Forbes continued to pay regular dividends to Howqua's descendants. From 1858 to 1879, the family received more than sixty thousand silver dollars a year. Business records indicate that the Forbes group made out well, too, turning a profit of close to one million dollars managing Howqua's estate. Forbes's descendants, such as the family of Secretary of State John Forbes Kerry, remember old friends. To this day, a portrait of Howqua hangs at the Forbes estate on Naushon Island just off Cape Cod.

The visionary Yankee merchants who opened relations with China shared an irrepressible faith in the future of the United States and were eager to make their mark on an uncertain world. They found willing partners among the Chinese. The American idea of a "special" relationship with China began in the golden bonds forged between traders such as Howqua and their American peers.

CHAPTER THREE

Blitzconversion

In late March 1847, two Chinese men arrived at the Welting Baptist Chapel in Guangzhou. Wedged between a duck market and a pub, the chapel was the handiwork of Issachar Jacox Roberts, a fire-and-brimstone preacher from backwoods Tennessee. The two men were cousins and an unusual pair. There were fewer than eighty missionaries then, and the rare Chinese who went to see them were usually in search of something other than the light of the Lord, more likely a handout or a job.

But this pair had not come to beg. They wanted to learn the Gospel. When Roberts asked why, one proceeded to tell a wild tale of hallucinations involving an old man with a golden beard and his command to "exterminate the demons." It was just the type of apocalyptic apparition that resonated with Roberts, who had been driven to devote his life to battling Satan by a vision that had come to him as he labored on his farm twelve years before.

Roberts wrote to his friend William C. Buck, a Kentucky newspaper editor, about the two men. Following the hallucinations, one of them had stopped worshiping his ancestors, a practice that Christians considered blasphemous, and had convinced others to follow suit. Their arrival at his chapel, Roberts wrote, presaged "the commencement of the outpouring of the Holy Spirit upon this benighted people." Buck printed Roberts's letter on the front page of the *Baptist Banner and Western Pioneer* in Louisville.

The two men joined Roberts's Bible class. They learned the way a Baptist church operated, memorized hymns, and witnessed a baptism. They informed Roberts that in their village, thirty miles from Guangzhou, many others had "abandoned their idols." They seemed eager to return home to preach, and after two months, the cousin who had recounted the story about his visions asked to be baptized.

Just before Roberts was to immerse the man in the murky waters of the Pearl River, the man asked about employment. Roberts had no patience for what his fellow preachers called job-hunting "rice Christians." He canceled the baptism and, he wrote, "saw him no more."

Not, that is, until 1860, when that man, Hong Xiuquan, stood at the head of the Taiping Rebellion, one of the biggest and bloodiest rebellions the world had ever seen, an uprising that cost the lives of up to forty million Chinese and nearly brought the Qing Dynasty to its knees. In his quest to overthrow the rulers of the world's most ancient civilization, Hong drew on the fevered Christianity of the American frontier and the faith he had learned from a farmer-preacher from Tennessee.

The relationship between Issachar Jacox Roberts and Hong Xiuquan embodies the bizarre but powerful attraction that China and America exerted on one another in the mid-nineteenth century. Their brief encounter illustrates how outsized expectations have bedeviled relations between the two countries and their peoples. Roberts was part of a wave of American missionaries who believed that after its defeat in the Opium War, China was ripe for elevation to the ranks of Christian nations. Hong and others in his movement counted on Roberts to win Western support for their Christian rebellion and to smooth trade and diplomatic relations with the world's great powers. Their story—a proselytizer of American values expecting pro-American changes in China and a Chinese revolutionary counting on American support—would play out again and again, mostly with the same outcome: disenchantment on both sides.

The battle between the Taiping rebels and the Qing empire also touched off a struggle in the United States over how to deal with China. Though an American missionary lit the spark for the rebellion, a Yankee adventurer named Frederick Townsend Ward helped snuff it out. The time of the Taipings shows Americans at cross-purposes in the Middle Kingdom. In American newspapers and church gatherings, Americans argued about what to do and which side to back in China. Some advocated pushing for a transformation of China. Others fought to keep China whole. This remains an ongoing debate.

The rebellion also taught many leading Chinese not only to despise Christianity but to fear it, a lesson that China's ruling Communist Party has inherited. The uprising convinced Qing dynasty officials that the only way to meet the challenges of the modern world was through a Western-inspired program of reforms. To the Qing officials, the Taipings brought home both the danger and the necessity of an accommodation with the West.

Americans had been involved in the mission to convert the Chinese since they first started coming to China. The first Protestant missionary, Robert Morrison, arrived in China in 1807 on a Yankee ship and for months pretended he was an American before acknowledging his British citizenship. China was a reluctant convert. Chinese merchants such as Howqua were delighted to make American dollars and American friends, but most of Howqua's nineteenth-century contemporaries were comfortable with their culture of Confucius, Buddha, and the Tao, and showed little interest in the holy goods the missionaries were hawking. In the first twenty-seven years of their missionary work in China, Protestant missionaries claimed only ten converts. One American preacher called a good year "two baptisms and the marriage of one Christian Chinese couple." In letters, diaries, and books, many of the American believers—Roberts included—displayed an exasperation with, even a hatred of, Chinese culture.

Many missionaries regarded Britain's victory in the Opium War as a sign that God was readying China for the arrival of the Word. "This land of heathenized infidelity has at last been thrown open!!!" proclaimed J. Lewis Shuck, Roberts's Baptist colleague, in a letter to American churchgoers soon after the 1842 signing of the Treaty of Nanjing. "However much we should regret to see war and bloodshed," Roberts added, "we are willing to see anything which has a tendency to accomplish these desirable ends"—the opening of China to Christ.

Roberts had arrived in China in 1837 after mortgaging his Mississippi farm and had started preaching in Macao. While the first group of Western missionaries studied Chinese and hobnobbed with the upper classes, Roberts was drawn to the masses. He preached to a leper colony on the outskirts of town. His first convert was a beggar.

Roberts moved to Hong Kong and then in May 1844 to Guangzhou. For twenty silver dollars a month, he secured four rooms and a kitchen in a building sandwiched between the street and the Pearl River. He was barely a mile from the foreign factories, but he could have been a thousand. To fit in, he donned a floor-length Chinese gown. His neighbors contributed to his wardrobe, donating Chinese socks and shoes. When aspiring mandarins flocked to Guangzhou for the annual civil service examination that year, some of them dropped by Roberts's mission. Roberts had been told that they were implacable foes of his work, but they sat politely through Sunday services.

Roberts was a child of the Second Great Awakening, a revivalist crusade that had swept across the United States in the early nineteenth century. Opting for piety and fervor over education and expertise, the movement sought to fashion a religion suitable for a hardscrabble life on the frontier. The farmer-preacher was the model. To many in the movement, book learning was at odds with God.

The Great Awakening focused on domestic converts—settlers, freed slaves, and Native Americans. Its success, highlighted by massive backwoods tent revivals, swelled the movement's ambitions to bring about not just an American conversion, but a global one. America's view of itself as a nation blessed by God was central to this calling. The American Board of Commissioners for Foreign Missions began sending missionaries abroad in 1812. The Baptists, whose flock would grow from 10,000 before the War of Independence to more than 350,000 by 1845, followed soon thereafter.

The first American missionaries were dispatched to Burma, India, and Ceylon, but China was seen as the biggest prize. The *American Baptist Magazine* called Christianizing China the greatest challenge in the world. "Nowhere has Satan a seat on the earth, to be compared in extent with that he holds in seeming triumph in . . . the so-called 'celestial empire,'" the journal said. "From that seat he must be thrown down."

Convincing Americans to move to China to preach was a hard sell. The tenacity of China's traditional culture, the unpopularity of the Christian message, and the harsh environment were not for the weak of heart. It was not until the 1890s that the number of American missionaries in China surpassed the number in India. Nonetheless, China was always "the lodestar, the goal," in the words of renowned American evangelist Sherwood Eddy, who spent thirty years preaching in Asia. Its market for souls remained as tantalizing to America's missionaries as its nascent demand for goods was to American salesmen. Powered by the twin myths of Chinese need and American appeal, the United States' great spiritual expansion was under way.

China quickly gained a privileged place in American hearts. During the heyday of American missionary activity from the late nineteenth through the early twentieth century, Americans funded a majority of

China's colleges and high schools and scores of Young Men's and Young Women's Christian Association (YMCA and YWCA) centers as well as agricultural extensions, charities, and research institutes. By 1900, as fund-raising campaigns became increasingly professional, one in eight adult Americans—more than five million people—were dropping "pennies for China" into hats passed in church. From the turn of the twentieth century, Americans dominated the missionary enterprise in China, which absorbed one-third of all American evangelists heading overseas. No other country came close to receiving that degree of attention.

Like America's first businessmen in China, its pioneering missionaries hailed from the East Coast. Peter Parker, the fourth American preacher in China, landed in Guangzhou in October 1834. A graduate of both Yale's medical college and its divinity school, he was the first medical missionary to be sent abroad. Parker and the other early Protestants shared some similarities with the Catholic Jesuits who had been coming to China since the sixteenth century. Through good works, they sought to convince the Chinese of the superiority of their faith. Parker opened Guangzhou's first hospital, introduced anesthesia to China, and over his three decades in the country performed more than fifty thousand surgeries—all for free. In his application to the American Board, Parker described dual goals: disseminating "the blessings of science *and* Christianity all over the globe."

The barely literate Roberts, on the other hand, went straight for the Chinese soul. While Parker, in his high collar and starched white shirt, was hard at work at his Hospital of Universal Love, fitting Commissioner Lin Zexu, for instance, with a truss for a hernia, Roberts hit the streets of Guangzhou, peddling pamphlets and inveighing against ghosts. Full-body baptism was his goal for his converts. For China writ large, he imagined a sudden Christian awakening, what his mentor, Karl Gutzlaff, a German Protestant who dealt in opium and God for years along China's coast, called a "blitzconversion."

Peter Parker and Issachar Roberts disagreed about how to change China. Parker and others sent out by the American Board believed that long years of study, an additional specialization, and a healthy respect for the culture were the keys to China's kingdom. They were scholars, not bomb throwers. They wanted, in Parker's words, to "heal" China, to help it become stronger and embrace Western values in the process.

Elijah Bridgman, the first American missionary, translated Western learning into Chinese and founded an English-language newspaper, the *Chinese Repository*. The second missionary, S. Wells Williams, set up printing presses. Both men contended that it was not possible to sweep all of China's past into the dustbin of history and replace it with Christ. God could be discovered in the high moral character of Confucian teachings. China, they believed, had to be Westernized one man and one woman at a time. In the 1950s, Americans repurposed this strategy and called it "peaceful evolution."

Parker and his contemporaries viewed with alarm the arrival of the Baptist strivers who saw little good in Chinese culture and embraced the sword instead of the scalpel. "We are not sorry that new laborers have come to this field of missionary labor," Parker wrote home after the Baptists appeared in 1844. He worried, however, that their bull-in-a-china-shop proselytizing—shouting at people in the street, picketing Chinese temples—would end in violence. Roberts, Parker wrote, was "an indiscreet man, unsuspecting as a child; and unacquainted with human nature and the world."

The Baptists scoffed at their old-school countrymen with their Christ-like patience. The Baptists wanted to cast aside the old China and create a new one, modeled on America. As Roberts's colleague, J. Lewis Shuck, wrote to the Baptist mission in the United States: Parker and company "have no converts, no churches and no extensive militant missionary operations, yet they regard it as interference for Baptist missionaries to come to Canton or Macao. Interfere with what?"

One thing all the missionaries agreed upon, however, was that China was sick. Even as Roberts thundered against Chinese idolatry on the streets of Guangzhou, Parker was at the forefront of recasting the Chinese image in the United States. The Chinese, according to this view, were not a creative, powerful, or mysterious people from a great culture or a nation of carnival freaks, but a diseased mass craving a cure—and an American cure.

For more than two decades, Parker engaged in one of the closest, and strangest, cultural collaborations between an American and a Chinese. From 1836 to 1852, in a studio on Hog Lane, next door to the Hospital of Universal Love, a Chinese painter named Guan Qiaochang, or Lamqua to his Western clients, painted a gruesome series of portraits of 114 of Parker's patients.

Parker had opened the hospital in November 1835 as an eye clinic, modeling himself on Christ, teaching the blind to see. He soon acquired a reputation as a highly skilled surgeon, and ophthalmology gave way to oncology. Parker specialized in removing tumors, many of which had been advancing for years. Nine hundred patients streamed in within the first three months, suffering from massive growths.

Before sending him to China, the American Board of Commissioners for Foreign Missions had ordered Parker to use his medical knowledge only "as handmaids to the gospel." But the Chinese weren't interested in the Gospel. They wanted Parker's "handmaids": American medicine and American science. In 1837, Parker began teaching Chinese doctors Western medicine. By the time he left China in 1857, he had taught scores of students but had logged few if any converts to his name.

Parker asked Lamqua, one of the first Chinese trained in Western portraiture, to paint his patients before they went under the knife. One portrait is of Leang Yen, a thirty-four-year-old woman with one good arm and the other disfigured by a tumor. In the case notes, Parker reported that Leang Yen twice canceled the operation to remove the tumor and her arm along with it. She demanded two hundred silver dollars to let him amputate the tumor. Parker tried to persuade her that he was there to help her, but she did not trust him. Finally, under pressure from her husband, she acquiesced to the surgery.

That interaction highlighted the deep ambivalence that many Chinese felt toward Americans, viewing men of God such as Parker alternately as ghoulish body snatchers or as superheroes. To Parker and Roberts, Leang Yen and her compatriots were either ungrateful wretches or pathetic invalids. How could they not understand that America had come to save them? Parker displayed the portraits on trips to the United States to raise money for his hospital and the Medical Missionary Society of China, which he had founded. The message back home was that China was ailing, and that America had the cure.

Like his preacher Issachar Roberts, Hong Xiuquan was an outsider. He was a Hakka—a subgroup of Han Chinese that had migrated south from north-central China centuries earlier. The natives of Guangdong province called them "guests," implying that they would one day leave.

Hong's introduction to Christianity had come in 1843, after he had failed an examination to become a Chinese official for the fourth time. In a pamphlet written by a Chinese convert, he found an explanation for the feverish visions that had followed an earlier failure on the test. In those visions, Hong had seen a golden-bearded man clothed in black. That must have been God, he thought. There was an elder brother, who had to be Jesus Christ. Together they had slain some demons, who seemed to be Confucius and Buddha. Hong Xiuquan baptized himself a Christian and declared himself the younger brother of Jesus Christ.

Hong's first converts were his cousin, Hong Rengan, and a neighbor. They began proselytizing to friends and family, calling themselves the Society of God Worshippers. By 1847, when Hong traveled to Guangzhou to seek Roberts's guidance, the society counted two thousand followers.

From Roberts, Hong ingested a Christianity that stressed passion and morality. Though his understanding of the catechism was imperfect, Hong learned how to manage a church and deliver a sermon, knowledge that he would later employ in his rebellion. He made the Ten Commandments the bedrock of the Society of God Worshippers. He embraced the Baptist belief that baptism—preferably full-body—was central to the conversion process. Roberts's personal war against Chinese idolatry colored Hong's views on the need to make a clean break with China's cultural traditions.

By 1850, the Society of God Worshippers boasted thirty thousand Han Chinese followers. The Manchu authorities were alarmed. In February 1851, in the Guangxi town of Guiping, the Qing army attacked, but the rebels dealt the Qing forces a crushing defeat. Hong's preaching turned more radical and more anti-Manchu. The Taiping Rebellion had begun.

Roaring north from the mountains of Guangxi, the Taipings sped nine hundred miles to the Yangtze River, gaining converts as they fought. In March 1853, the great city of Nanjing, the first capital of the Ming dynasty, fell to the rebels. That month they proclaimed the founding of a new nation—the Kingdom of Heavenly Peace, or Taiping Tianguo.

Two months later in Guangzhou, Roberts received an envelope bearing the seal of the Heavenly Kingdom. It was from his old student and the newly self-crowned Heavenly King himself, Hong Xiuquan. "Though it is so long since we have met, yet I constantly cherished a remembrance of you," the note began, betraying no rancor over the aborted baptism of years earlier. Hong asked Roberts to join his rebellion, propagate the Gospel, and baptize his followers. "Your ignorant younger brother, Hong Xiuquan, salutes you," it ended.

To have a former pupil in such an exalted position—the rebel king of China!!—presented enormous possibilities for China and for Roberts. "Never were the prospects for usefulness with God's blessing brighter," Roberts enthused to a friend back home. "They almost dazzle! . . . China will be revolutionized, Christianized, & a great multitude saved through these means." Other missionaries shared Roberts's enthusiasm, looking to Hong's followers as the heaven-sent agents of China's "blitzconversion."

Hong's hopes and expectations in reaching out to his old friend were similarly grand. If the American preacher were to become a spokesman for the new Christian China, surely other Westerners would join his cause. There could be trade between the Taipings and their spiritual brothers from the West. If the riches and customs duties of Shanghai on the coast and Hankou up the Yangtze could flow into the treasury of the Kingdom of Heavenly Peace, instead of the imperial household in Beijing, then China would be his.

Among Hong's followers, faith in the United States ran high. His cousin, Hong Rengan, who rejoined the movement in the late 1850s after years in Hong Kong, looked at America as a model for the rebel nation. In a remarkable document, "A New Work for the Aid of Government," identified by historian Stephen Platt as the first platform for reform in China's modern history, Hong Rengan reserved his deepest admiration for the Beautiful Country.

China needed railroads like America's, mines like America's, a legal system like America's, and patent protections like America's, he wrote. China's old way of viewing the world, with its empire as the center of the universe, had to change. Its treatment of foreigners—calling them "barbarians" and expecting them to knock their heads on the ground before Chinese officials—was anachronistic in a modernizing world. Protestant societies, Britain and America, were the world's most successful, Hong concluded. China should become more like them.

Issachar Roberts journeyed from Guangzhou to Shanghai and requested permission from Humphrey Marshall, the US consul, to travel into rebel territory. Responding that this would violate American neutrality in China, Marshall denied the request and threatened Roberts with execution if he attempted the trip.

Marshall had little faith in Roberts's belief that China was ripe for Western salvation. A graduate of the United States Military Academy and a veteran of the Mexican-American War, Marshall was skeptical of the idea that a "blitzconversion" would cleanse China of its heathen culture. Instead, he saw the Taipings as a convenient excuse for Europeans, especially the British and the Russians, to carve up the empire into fiefdoms and close it to American trade. Instead of aid to the Taipings, Marshall advocated providing American military, commercial, and diplomatic support to uphold the Qing state.

Marshall pleaded unsuccessfully with Secretary of State William Marcy for the resources to help the imperial government against the rebels. A weak China was bad for America, Marshall argued. It just made the Middle Kingdom a more tempting target for the empires of the Old World. Marshall appealed to the US Navy squadron in Shanghai to assist the Qing, but its commander had no sympathy for his argument, either. The squadron was led by Commodore Matthew Perry, who was far more interested in wielding his black ships to open Japan than to prop up the Qing. "There is nothing to be hoped for in Japan equal to the advantages now actually enjoyed in China," Marshall wrote Perry in June 1853. Perry set sail anyway, entering Tokyo harbor a month later on July 8, 1853.

Instead of providing troops, Washington sent Marshall a pink slip. Learning of his dismissal in a newspaper article, Marshall left China on January 27, 1854, but his ideas stuck around. Marshall was the first American official to contend that China's weakness was a matter of concern to the United States. In doing so, he added a key corollary to the Cushing-negotiated Treaty of Wangxia. Not only did the United States need equal access to China's markets, but as Marshall argued and generations of Americans would later agree, a strong China was in the interest of the United States.

When Nanjing fell to the Taipings in 1853, the world took notice. The *New York Times* called the rebels America's natural allies. Many Americans saw the conflict in the context of their own history. Here were a people, the Han Chinese, rising up against the Manchus, an alien overlord. Karl Marx, writing in the *New-York Daily Tribune,* framed the rebellion as part of a global uprising against capitalism that had started in Paris in 1848.

W. A. P. Martin, a well-known Presbyterian missionary from Indiana, published an open letter to the US government in the *North-China Herald* declaring that now there were "two Chinas": a Christian China headquartered in Nanjing, overseeing the affluent tea- and silk-producing regions of the Yangtze valley, and the decaying Chinese empire of the north. He called on the United States to recognize "Christian China" and "throw open its portals to unrestricted intercourse." Peter Parker, so recently an opponent of Roberts, had come around as well, writing from Guangzhou that it was time to recognize the Taiping rebels and hasten the fall of the Qing. Critics, however, observed that the rebellion possessed an air of blasphemy. After all, Hong Xiuquan had pronounced himself the younger brother of Jesus Christ and his prime minister had assumed the title of Holy Ghost. No recognition occurred.

Meanwhile, outside Shanghai, an army of half a million Taiping rebels mustered. Panic shook the foreign settlement in the city, which had fast become the most important of China's treaty ports. Wealthy Chinese fled. Those remaining marshaled the city's defenses.

Roberts was getting nowhere in his quest to help spread the word for Hong and his revolution. Refused passage on several ships heading to Nanjing, the Tennessee preacher found himself broke and out of a job. The Southern Baptists had fired him after he ignored a plea from an American colleague who had attempted suicide. His second wife, Virginia Young, whom he had married in 1850, had given birth to a son in 1853 and a daughter a year later. Roberts decided to return to the United States to settle his family and raise funds for the work that awaited him with the Taipings. Helped by his old friend William Buck, editor of the *Baptist Banner and Western Pioneer*, Roberts collected $24,000 from small donors across the South. Energized by a barnstorming speaking tour across the United States, Roberts was again convinced that China stood at the cusp of great changes. Writing from New York Harbor on January 24, 1855, he declared that he was ready to go to Nanjing to guide Hong and his believers "with a vigorous hand . . . in the way of truth as it is in Jesus."

Meanwhile, as Humphrey Marshall had feared, the Manchu authorities, weakened by the Taipings, were bending to British and French pressure for more territorial concessions. Unlike Japan, which would respond to capitalism's challenge with wholesale westernization, China, under the reign of Emperor Xianfeng, who had taken the throne in 1850, had refused to reform. In 1856, the British and French forces attacked China again, beginning what was known as the Arrow War.

The new war found Americans less supportive of China than they had been in the last one. US naval forces joined in several battles, marking the first time that Americans had killed Chinese in combat. Peter Parker, who had since become a US diplomat, argued that America should follow the European lead and seize territory. He advocated annexing the island of Taiwan, located one hundred miles off China's southern coast, as a coal depot for the navy and a base for trade. It was the first time that the island would arise as an issue between the US and China. President James Buchanan's administration ignored the proposal.

In an editorial on August 20, 1858, the *New York Times* praised the British and the French for using their cannons to further force China to open its doors to trade and lambasted Washington for its passivity. It was "humiliating," the paper said, that the United States "allowed others to do the work and reap the honor while we are content enough to pocket the profits."

The British and French assaults on China ended in October 1860 with the sacking of Beijing's Garden of Perfect Brightness, a vast expanse of European-style palaces designed by Jesuit missionaries. Sickened by the news that Europeans had torched his favorite Beijing citadel, Emperor Xianfeng would die within a year.

Defeated, the Chinese signed the Treaty of Tianjin, known with no hint of irony as the "Treaty of Peace, Friendship and Commerce." Ten more treaty ports were opened. Foreigners could travel anywhere. Christians were protected. Opium was legalized. And, most troubling to the Qing court, Britain and the rest of the Western world were allowed to station representatives in Beijing, implying that foreigners were equal in status to the Son of Heaven.

In the American version of the treaty, the Chinese, still believing that the United States was more virtuous than the other powers, added a clause committing both sides to help one another in times of conflict. In return, the American missionary S. Wells Williams, who had joined the US negotiating team in Tianjin, convinced the Chinese to agree to four articles promising to tolerate all religions and to allow Protestant missionaries to buy land anywhere in China, not just in the treaty ports.

For the first time, the United States was advocating not just for Americans in China, but for Chinese Christians as well. This represented an unprecedented escalation of American involvement in China's internal affairs and laid the foundation for the lasting belief that how China dealt with its people was of concern to the United States.

In October 1860, as Western forces were looting Beijing, Issachar Roberts, now fifty-eight and sporting a white beard, finally arrived in Nanjing having hitched a ride on a steamer up the Yangtze River. Roberts had expected to serve as the spiritual adviser to the Heavenly King. Instead, although he had never really mastered Chinese, he was put to work as an interpreter. It took days to arrange a meeting with his old disciple, Hong Xiuquan. The Heavenly King promised to put Roberts in charge of religious affairs. Hong issued a decree proclaiming religious toleration throughout the kingdom and ordering the establishment of eighteen churches in Nanjing alone.

Roberts would spend the next year trying to sway Western policy in favor of the rebellion. He sent letters to newspapers in China, Hong Kong, and the United States. From Hong's cousin, Hong Rengan, he relayed a promise that the Taipings were open to doing business with the West. Facts on the ground proved his point. When Taiping forces took the treaty port of Ningbo just south of Shanghai in December 1861, they asked Westerners to stay. Missionary W. A. P. Martin noted that trade in Ningbo jumped under Taiping rule. But history was not on Roberts's side. With the concessions wrung from the Manchus following the Arrow War, many in the diplomatic community agreed with the British consul, Frederick Bruce, that a weak Qing dynasty was better than a strong Kingdom of Heavenly Peace. Bruce argued that the West should support the Qing.

Western missionaries, dismissive of Hong's claims to being another son of God, distanced themselves from the movement and smeared Roberts. He was a "vexatious" crank, said Tarleton Perry Crawford, a fellow Baptist preacher from Tennessee who visited Nanjing in the spring of 1861. Roberts, he wrote, "lives in a miserable old dirty room, has no power or influence among the Rebels, except in his own vain imagination."

By January 1862, Roberts was the only missionary left in Nanjing. Then, on January 13, even he fled the city on a passing British warship. Crushed because the Taipings had rejected his spiritual guidance, Roberts, once the Taipings' biggest booster, became their fiercest critic. He falsely accused Hong Rengan of killing an aide. He called Hong Xiuquan "a crazy man." Roberts's defection left the movement without a Western patron, severing the flimsy link between Protestant missionaries and a Chinese Christian revolution.

Led by Frederick Bruce and Admiral James "Fighting Jimmy" Hope, commander of British forces in Shanghai, the British entered China's civil war on the side of the Qing. But because they were technically neutral, they needed a cover. That opened the door for another American to bend the arc of Chinese history: Frederick Townsend Ward.

Like many of the Americans before him who had made their mark on China, Frederick Townsend Ward steered clear of the US government. A native of Salem, Massachusetts, Ward did not go to China as a trader, sailor, or diplomat but as a soldier of fortune. Rakishly handsome, with a mane of shoulder-length hair, dark eyes, and a lanky frame, the not quite twenty-nine-year-old arrived in China in 1859 penniless and seeking adventure. He had originally aimed to throw his lot in with the Taipings, but like Roberts, he had trouble making it to Nanjing. So, using a French steamer named *Confucius* as his base, he battled river pirates for Chinese merchants.

Impressed by their hired gun's derring-do, the merchants encouraged

Ward to defend Shanghai's outlying towns against a Taiping invasion. Hong Xiuquan and his generals had decided in May 1860 to attack the city, and word of their plans had crept along the rumor mill into Shanghai.

On Shanghai's docks, Ward recruited a ragtag army of Filipinos, Malays, Brits, Americans, and Europeans, offering them a share of any loot that they could pilfer while protecting the city. Financing for this effort came from a Ningbo banker named Yang Fang. Behind the scenes, Qing authorities lent encouragement while trying not to advertise their reliance on a barbarian American for the city's defense. The authorities knew that ever since the Opium War, Chinese soldiers, even rebels, held Western soldiers and Western firepower in almost mystical regard. What better way to secure Shanghai than with a force of foreign devils?

Ward named his band of mercenaries the Shanghai Foreign Arms Corps. They came equipped with Colt revolvers, Sharp's repeating carbines, and a Babel of languages. From 1860 into the first half of 1861, they fought the Taiping. Despite the high death toll (during one battle Taiping regulars gunned down 40 percent of Ward's force of 250), there was no shortage of recruits. Looting was more lucrative than dock work. For his pains, Ward suffered a shot to the face, leaving his speech permanently slurred. He was also awarded honorary Chinese citizenship, allowing him to escape prosecution for violating American neutrality laws. And he won a Chinese bride—Yang Fang's daughter.

Ward proposed forming a force of American-led Chinese fighters. Qing officials agreed, and Ward became the first foreign officer in the Qing army and the first Westerner to introduce Western military tactics to the Middle Kingdom, unwittingly initiating a long history of American involvement in China's military reforms. In the summer of 1861, Ward established a training camp in Songjiang, northeast of Shanghai near the Taiping lines. At first, the Chinese writers mocked their countrymen under American command, dubbing them "fake foreign devils." But Ward kept training, and by January 1862, he had three thousand troops ready for action.

That winter, Ward led his new army into battle beneath a banner emblazoned with the Chinese character *Hua*, the Chinese approximation of his last name. First a snow-covered town ten miles north of Shanghai, then four other hamlets fell to Ward's forces. Much larger Taiping armies fled before his troops. Ward was wounded again and lost a finger to a musket ball. In one battle near Ward's Songjiang headquarters, the American-led Chinese soldiers beat back an onslaught of twenty thousand Taipings by luring them into an artillery ambush. The Taipings called Ward's men "devil soldiers." In March, the Qing government officially named Ward's contingent the Ever Victorious Army. Ward was allowed to wear a peacock feather in his cap, an exalted honor for a barbarian from the Beautiful Country.

Ward's exploits came to the attention of a brilliant thirty-year-old Chinese officer, Li Hongzhang, beginning Li's half-century association with Americans. The thing that first impressed the Americans about Li Hongzhang was his size. More than six feet tall, he towered over most Chinese and many Westerners. "He has a keen eye, a large head and wide forehead, and speaks with a quick, decisive manner," observed one American journalist. Americans appreciated that Li, unlike many Chinese mandarins, did not fear railroads, mines, or the telegraph and was eager to develop China. He was what the Chinese would call a "self-strengthener," a man who believed that China needed Western technology and even some Western ideas to become rich and strong.

Li had been fighting the Taipings in central China since 1853 with a force of more than one hundred thousand men. In the spring of 1862, the Qing court sent him to defend Shanghai. For Li, who had never before dealt with foreigners, arriving in China's most cosmopolitan city was a shock. Westerners dominated the town and controlled its defenses. British and French troops numbered about three thousand; Ward commanded the same number of Chinese.

Li worried that the British and French would use their military positions in Shanghai to expand their influence. So, as he would do on many occasions in the future, he tried to bolster an American, in this case, Ward, as a counterweight. Ward was happy to oblige, and by June, he was reporting to Li. While Li tried to keep British and French military activity confined to the city limits, he gave Ward freedom to roam, using the Ever Victorious Army as the shock troops of imperial army assaults against the Taiping.

Ward called Li the "devilish governor," and Li was often exasperated by his American lieutenant's incessant demands for payment, but the two generals got along anyway. Ward's men trained Li's army, and Li used Ward's connections on the Shanghai waterfront to acquire guns and ammunition. When another Qing official complained to the court that Ward had refused to shave his head and wear a queue like other mandarins, Li declared that he would not allow "petty faults" to impede their partnership. Li credited Ward with saving Shanghai. "Such loyalty and valor," he told the Qing court, "is extraordinary when compared with these virtues of the best officers in China."

By September, Ward's force had ballooned to more than five thousand men. Li was so impressed with Ward's fighters that he wanted the Ever Victorious Army to attack the Taiping capital at Nanjing. Given Ward's skills as a commander, Li predicted, Nanjing would fall in nine days. But on September 21, 1862, as Ward led his men in an assault on Cixi, ten miles outside the Taiping-occupied treaty port of Ningbo, a bullet pierced his gut. He died the next morning, demanding with his last breath that his family be paid the money Qing authorities owed him. It never was.

Calling the American, Hua, "a great man, a soldier without fear and blameless," the Qing court ordered the construction of altars and a Confucian hall in his memory. The Communists desecrated them after China's revolution in 1949. A British officer, Charles "Chinese" Gordon, took Ward's place, assuming command of the Ever Victorious Army.

As for Issachar Roberts, he returned to his family in the United States in 1866. Five years later, at the age of sixty-nine, he was dead, felled by leprosy contracted in Macao during his early, hopeful days preaching to the heathen Chinese.

Issachar Jacox Roberts represented a major strain of thinking in America's hopes for China: that it could be converted in one miraculous stroke into a nation like the United States. Such hopes did not die with the Tennessee evangelist. Simultaneously, however, Americans with a different vision—of a China that was stable, strong, and open for American trade—were hard at work. One of them was heading to the northern capital, Beijing.

●

CHAPTER FOUR

The Calm Minister

Carried on the shoulders of eight Chinese porters in a sedan chair borrowed from the French government, Anson Burlingame bobbed into Beijing on July 20, 1862. The first American minister assigned to the capital, he arrived, accompanied by his wife, Jane, their two sons, and their six-year-old daughter, with no place to stay and a tiny budget. He also had no guidance from President Abraham Lincoln and Secretary of State William Seward, who had far greater problems on their hands than US relations with China. Nonetheless, Burlingame would become one of the most revered Americans in nineteenth-century China. The Chinese called him Pu Anchen, Calm Minister Pu.

In the mid-nineteenth century, few, if any, of America's tiny corps of diplomats sought positions in China. The relationship was largely in the hands of merchants like John P. Cushing, missionaries like Peter Parker and Issachar Roberts, and adventurers like Frederick Townsend Ward. The pay paled in comparison with postings in Europe. At the time of Burlingame's arrival, the US legation worked out of a rented house in Macao on China's southern coast. The United States, alone among the treaty powers, trained no interpreters. In Shanghai, six men served as consul over a nine-month stretch in 1858. The consulate there occupied a single hotel room and didn't own an American flag.

Although the Treaty of Wangxia had granted the United States, like other Western nations, the right to police its citizens in China, the US would not establish functional jails and courts there until the early 1900s. In the meantime, foreign crooks claimed American citizenship to avoid jail. In Shanghai, a city famed for its foreign brothels, the term "American girl" signified not a perky debutante, but a prostitute. "The United States authority was laughed at and our flag made the cover for all the villains in China," Burlingame complained to his secretary of state.

After a month of bunking at the French legation, Anson Burlingame and his wife found a tiny home near the British, French, and Russian legations that fit his budget of less than $500 a year, one-fifteenth of the salary paid by the British crown. The residence, just south of the Forbidden City, home of the Qing court, was so small that Burlingame could not offer American visitors a bed. The entrance to the courtyard was so narrow that the sedan chairs of Chinese officials could not squeeze through, forcing mandarins to alight in the street and drag their gowns through the mud.

Still, the couple transformed their humble embassy into the social center of the small world of foreigners in the northern capital. As Jane wrote to her father during their first winter, "We are scarcely ever alone. Sometimes there are callers from morning til night."

Like Issachar Roberts, Burlingame was a child of the American frontier and an evangelical of sorts, promoting faith not in God but in the American dream of freedom and equality. He was an avowed abolitionist and the first of dozens of such Americans, most of them members of the Republican Party, who would fight for China with the same zeal with which they had battled slavery.

But where Roberts aggravated even those who agreed with him, Burlingame, with his prodigious side whiskers and expansive forehead, exuded a magnetic combination of Western grit and East Coast panache. He had grown up in Michigan and had accompanied survey parties around the Great Lakes. He had attended Harvard Law School, married into a prominent Boston family, won a seat in Congress in 1855, and helped found the Republican Party. Burlingame catapulted to fame in the spring of 1856 when a Southern congressman, Preston Brooks, challenged him to a duel after Brooks had brutally pummeled Senator Charles Sumner, a passionate opponent of slavery and proponent of Chinese immigration, on the floor of the Senate. Once Brooks learned that Burlingame was a crack shot, however, he backed out.

After Burlingame lost his congressional seat in 1861, the same bumptiousness that had won him praise in the North made him a liability for

the Republicans. Party stalwarts referred to Burlingame and radical abolitionists like him as "noisy jackasses." Lincoln ultimately sent him to Beijing.

If Secretary of State William Seward, the clean-shaven former governor of New York, hadn't spent most of his energy fighting the Civil War,
he would have focused on Asia. Seward believed that America's future lay
in the Pacific. He opposed European plans to carve China into spheres of
influence. He wanted China open for US business and for mission work.
Seward gave Burlingame what Jane Burlingame called "carte blanche" to
fashion a China policy along those lines.

Burlingame agreed that China needed to be modernized, but unlike
many of his more impatient countrymen, he did not hold that "American
progress" could be shoved down unwilling throats. To change the West's
policy toward China, he needed British help. Her Majesty's government
remained the resident power in Asia. In 1861, England's Far Eastern forces
boasted sixty-six warships and eight thousand men. The United States had
neither ships nor sailors: Commodore Perry and his tiny East India Squadron, established in the 1830s, had been called home to fight.

Burlingame directed his substantial charm at British minister Frederick Bruce, who had moved to Beijing from Shanghai, and the two formed
a "mutual admiration society," as Jane Burlingame put it. Bruce would
show up unannounced and deposit himself in an armchair in the Americans' sitting room while Burlingame's daughter, Gertie, climbed into
his lap.

Bruce liked Burlingame's idea of a new approach to China. The Arrow
War had given Britain, France, Russia, and the United States almost everything they wanted—more open ports and more freedom to proselytize
and trade. The challenge now was to nudge the Qing in the direction of
implementation.

Burlingame called the new approach to China the "cooperative policy."
Like the ousted Shanghai consul, Humphrey Marshall, Burlingame argued
that the West should protect Chinese sovereignty. He contended that China
should not only bear the responsibilities of international law but should also
partake of its benefits. "He insists," Bruce wrote sympathetically to the Foreign Office in London, "that this opportunity is unique at the commencement of a new epoch in China's history." In a sense, Burlingame was right.

Emperor Xianfeng's death on August 22, 1861, marked the end of a
decade that featured an aggressive anti-Western foreign policy and the
start of another spasmodic shift toward accommodation with the West.
A five-year-old emperor, Tongzhi, the son of Xianfeng and his favorite

concubine, the five-foot-tall Cixi, assumed the throne. Real power, however, lay with Cixi, known as the Empress Dowager, and a series of senior provincial officials such as Li Hongzhang, who would dominate China until the fall of the Qing.

Western historians have not been kind to Cixi. Following cues from Communist Chinese historians, academicians have generally portrayed her as a scheming autocrat who stymied reforms. But to be fair, she had an impossible job, trying to steer a course between grasping imperialists and competing factions in her court.

In the early 1860s, Cixi's sometime lover, the Manchu prince Gong, who favored compromise with the West, launched a series of economic and educational reforms. He established the Zongli Yamen, China's first government department devoted solely to foreign affairs. Officials who had earlier been exiled for praising the West were summoned back to work.

Among them was Xu Jiyu, the author of the early history of the West who had heaped praise on George Washington. Rehabilitated at age seventy, Xu compared himself, restored to government work, to "an old woman who dreams again of sex." To celebrate Xu's reemployment, Burlingame presented the Zongli Yamen with a copy of Gilbert Stuart's portrait of Xu's hero, George Washington.

Xu was put in charge of the first Chinese government school in the capital to teach Western knowledge, the Tongwen Guan. But like so many Chinese working with foreigners, Xu was hounded by xenophobes and, after a year at the helm, pleaded with the Empress Dowager to allow him to retire. She relented and replaced him with the American missionary W. A. P. Martin, who had so recently backed recognition of the Taipings. Martin would run the Tongwen Guan for the next quarter century.

Chinese hard-liners fought the idea of a Western-style school, especially with a Western dean. "I have never heard of anyone who could use mathematics to raise the nation from a state of decline or to strengthen it in time of weakness," scoffed Woren, a Manchu tutor of the emperor. Besides, he added, if astronomy and mathematics had to be taught, why should it be by barbarians?

Some Westerners also deplored the idea of giving China ideas that it could use in its own defense. When French minister M. Kleczkowski found out that Martin had created a word for "rights" in Chinese and had translated into Chinese a treatise on international law, he shouted: "Who is this man who is going to give the Chinese an insight into our European international law? Kill him—choke him off; he'll make us endless trouble."

Prince Gong realized that to meet the challenge from the West, China needed to follow Japan's tack: open its doors to trade, improve its economy, and build its strength. In a memorial to the emperor in early 1861, Prince Gong laid out a strategy. To counter the West, China needed to show it a friendly face. "Resort to peace and friendship when temporarily obliged to do so," he wrote, but "use war and defense as your actual policy."

According to Gong, China faced three challenges: internal rebellions, of the Taipings and another band in northern China called the Nian; the "near barbarians," Russia and Japan; and finally the "far barbarians," Great Britain and France. Gong proposed dealing with the rebellions first, then with the Russians and the Japanese, and last the Europeans. The Americans got special mention. "The American barbarians are pure-minded and honest in disposition and have always been loyal to China," Gong argued. "The problem is how to control them to make them exploitable by us." That problem would perplex Gong and his intellectual descendants for the next 150 years.

A month into his stay, Burlingame was granted an audience with Prince Gong. With both nations racked by rebellion, Burlingame cannily drew a parallel between China and the United States. He conveyed his sympathies to the Qing court in its fight against the Taipings and expressed support for the empire. China's reformers had found an American friend.

Nevertheless, antiforeign feelings ran deep in both the court and the country. Western missionaries, now permitted to preach and own property in the Chinese heartland, had spread to all corners of the realm. The number of missionaries would jump from one hundred in 1800 to four thousand by the turn of the century, with Americans leading the way. From 1860 on, the fires of a xenophobic, anti-Christian hatred would burn in many Chinese hearts, stoked by those in the upper class and others with bad memories of the Taipings.

To gain traction with the average Chinese, China's traditionalists, men like Woren in the court, needed something dark to say about foreigners that would grip the imagination of China's people. They settled on sex and through pamphlets, popular songs, and posters, they spread tales of Western missionaries and their allegedly aberrant sexual escapades. In 1861, an essay called "A Record of Facts to Ward Off the Cult," written by an anonymous author who identified himself only as "the most heartbroken man in the world," appeared throughout the empire.

The "Record" painted a grim picture of Christian mission activity as a nonstop orgy, including sodomy, pedophilia, and torture. Sunday services, it said, began with a short sermon after which "they copulate together in order to consummate their joy." Converts were said to smear their faces with menstrual blood—which explained the "wild animal" smell of most foreigners. The "Record" was the first major effort by the conservative faction in the Qing court to demonize the West; it would not be the last.

Burlingame was aware of the "Record," but as American officials would do in the future, he paid little heed to anti-Western misinformation and concentrated instead on winning hearts and minds through concrete deeds. He helped the Zongli Yamen wriggle out of a bad deal with the British to build China's navy. He advised Prince Gong on how to wield international law to prevent the Prussians and the Danes from fighting in China's territorial waters during the German-Danish War of 1864.

The records of Qing officialdom are punctuated with glowing accounts of Calm Minister Pu. He was "gentle," "smooth," "respectfully suave," "well-bred," "even tempered," "fair-minded," "noble," and "sincere at heart." Prince Gong had once been fanatically anti-Western. Routine contact with Burlingame mellowed his views. The prince even became comfortable with foreigners and struck Americans as different from the average mandarin. "His voice is low and soft, and his gesticulations more those of an Italian than a Chinaman," wrote one American contemporary.

Burlingame went to bat for China with diplomats from other countries. In what would become an enduring refrain in Chinese-American relations, he insisted that China be held to different standards than other nations. On New Year's Day 1863, Prince Gong gave Burlingame a letter of salutation to President Lincoln from the emperor, who claimed in it that Heaven had commanded him to "govern the world." Burlingame ignored the phraseology, which restated the Chinese belief that the Qing ruler was the master of the globe. This was a marked contrast to the British, who so despised the Chinese sense of superiority that they forced the Chinese to agree to ban the use of the word "barbarian" in their internal documents.

Burlingame believed that the United States was within its rights to demand that the Qing court guarantee the safety of all Americans in China, missionaries and merchants alike. But he did not think that the United States should insist that the Qing give Chinese Christians, for example, similar protection. The Chinese court could treat foreigners one way, he argued, and treat Chinese another.

Unfortunately, approaches like Burlingame's led the Chinese government to believe that it *was* different and that it could bend the rules of international discourse. Bolstering China's ego won Burlingame friends in Beijing, but it would also tempt Chinese officials to capitalize on their theoretical uniqueness to demand special treatment.

In November 1867, a Qing official meeting with Burlingame tossed out an idea. Perhaps the American minister could represent China overseas. The Qing court was worried that Western powers wanted to renegotiate the various treaties of Tianjin and further extend their sway. Prince Gong argued that if China were compelled to make more concessions, an antiforeign backlash would bury all possibility of reform. Only Burlingame could persuade the powers to modify their demands.

In a telegram to Secretary of State Seward on November 21, Burlingame resigned as US minister to China and, "in the interests of my country and civilization," accepted the job as a "Minister Plenipotentiary" on the first major Chinese delegation to the West. When the oldest nation in the world seeks to open relations with the West and requests the youngest nation to be its intermediary, Burlingame wrote, "the mission is not one to be . . . rejected."

Opposition to the mission came from both China and the United States. Woren, the emperor's tutor, argued that including an American barbarian in a Chinese delegation "is tantamount to . . . ignoring the dignity of the empire." Democratic Party–leaning newspapers in America blasted Burlingame, a Republican, for selling his soul to the Chinese.

As the steamer carrying the delegation of thirty approached San Francisco in April 1868, Burlingame fretted that his arrival would be marred by protests. But the crowd at San Francisco's wharf had come to cheer. The circus-like reception was just the beginning of a coast-to-coast party for Calm Minister Pu and his team. Wearied by the stress of Reconstruction and the impeachment of President Andrew Johnson, America was ready for a distraction.

In Boston, the delegation was met by a marching band, sixteen two-horse carriages, and four hundred mounted troops with swords raised. For three hours, the parade snaked through the city. The Stars and Stripes and the Qing dynasty's triangular yellow streamer festooned the path. The next day, more than five thousand Bostonians turned out to greet the Chinese. The poet-doctor Oliver Wendell Holmes wrote verse for the occasion inspired by the vision of a lucrative merger of East and West.

> Open wide, ye gates of gold,
> To the Dragon's Banner-fold!

Builders of the mighty wall
Bid your mountain barriers fall!
So may the girdle of the sun
Bind the East and West in one.

At the welcome banquet at the St. James Hotel on August 21, the idea of this kind of mingling intrigued another American who rose to speak. In 1868, the transcendentalist philosopher Ralph Waldo Emerson was already sixty-five years old. American thinkers like him and Henry David Thoreau had begun to mix an element of Asian philosophy into the rich soil of American spirituality.

Emerson had been inspired by Confucius's insistence that mankind could achieve perfection through self-cultivation and his belief that great men could change the world. The Sage of Concord was so enamored of the Sage of Qufu that he labeled him one of the world's thirteen great thinkers, a member of "the high priesthood of pure reason."

That night at the St. James, Emerson titled his speech "The Union of the Farthest East and the Farthest West." He noted China's early inventions, such as gunpowder and the printing press, and lavished praise on the Chinese as a people. His talk was so compelling that reporters pressed the elderly American philosopher to stay until 1:00 a.m., writing out his remarks.

In Washington, Burlingame's first stop was Seward's home, where the two men, minus the Chinese and in defiance of Qing court orders that no treaties were to be negotiated, began hammering out a revised treaty between the United States and China. The idea that two Americans could rewrite an accord between Washington and Beijing did not strike either as bizarre. Americans had already developed a conviction that they knew China's interests better than the Chinese did. The pair discussed whether President Johnson should meet with the Chinese delegation. The issue was reciprocity. Burlingame had never had an audience with the emperor. Nonetheless, on June 6, 1868, the mission went to the White House and found the typically diffident president in a chatty mood. Johnson compared the arduous early years of the American republic with the Qing empire's current plight. The merriment continued with a state dinner, a military tribute, a private visit to Seward's home, and a reception thrown by General Ulysses S. Grant, the Republican presidential nominee.

In New York City, on June 23, the delegation was treated to a banquet at Delmonico's, at the corner of Fourteenth Street and Fifth Avenue, attended by America's leading capitalists and thinkers. At the close of the dinner, Burlingame rose to speak. Before he had arrived in China, Burlingame declared, the West's view of China had been that "you must take them by the throat." But thanks to his efforts, he said, trade was up, the Chinese had embraced Western education, Christian missions were growing, the number of steamboats had multiplied, and a railroad had been started.

"There is no spot on earth where there has been greater progress made within the past few years than in the Empire of China," he claimed. What should the West and America, in particular, do to encourage more change? "Let her develop herself in her own time and in her own way," he pleaded. If America just followed this course, he promised untold riches. "Let her alone and that silver which has been flowing for hundreds of years into China . . . will come out into the affairs of men." Although he was well aware of the contents of the "Record," Burlingame even claimed that China was prepared to invite Protestant missionaries to "plant the shining cross on every hill and in every valley."

Burlingame's speech, reprinted in newspapers and journals nationwide, touched off a new wave of optimism about China. W. A. P. Martin, who just a few years earlier had urged the United States to recognize the Taiping rebels, now lauded the reforms the Qing had launched. Writing in the *New Englander and Yale Review* magazine in January 1869, he described a "Renaissance in China" during which "the Chinese mind will be brought proportionally nearer to our own." Others depicted China as an America-in-waiting. In the November 1868 edition of *Harper's*, William Speer, another American missionary, described China as one of the freest and most naturally democratic nations in the world. Soon, he predicted, China would resemble, of all places, New England, its pagodas and temples "replaced by the white spires of Christian churches and schools." Businessmen were equally buoyant. American firms, pundits wrote, would soon dominate China's river trade, build its telegraph and railroad lines, and dig its mines.

There were, of course, skeptics. Burlingame's harshest critic was his successor as US minister to China, John Ross Browne, a leading nineteenth-century muckraking reporter, who argued that Burlingame had sold the US public a bill of goods. China was not ready to change, he said in missives to the State Department. He described Burlingame's claims as a "hallucination." The Chinese hated all foreigners, he said, Americans included.

Browne and Burlingame represented two distinct American views of the Chinese. Burlingame was spellbound by China's potential and argued that the only way forward was to nudge it gently—the term of art would later become "manage China's rise"—toward an outcome beneficial to the United States. Browne was obsessed with China's present and contended that the Qing court needed to be forced to abide by international norms. US policy makers have bounced between forbearance and impatience ever since.

Returning to Washington, Burlingame sealed a new treaty with Seward without authorization from the Qing court. The accord, formally titled "Additional Articles to the Treaty Between the United States and the Ta-Tsing Empire of the 18th of June, 1858" but known as the Burlingame Treaty, was revolutionary for the time. It outlawed American ships from transporting Chinese slave labor to South America. It banned discrimination against Chinese workers in America and opened the way for Chinese immigrants to become American citizens. Article 7 promised that Chinese would be welcome at any educational institution under US government control, marking the start of what became the richest intellectual exchange in the modern world.

The Burlingame Treaty was just one of a series of steps that Secretary of State Seward took toward Asia. Even before the Civil War had ended, he had gotten Congress to pass the Pacific Railway Act, building on Asa Whitney's dream of a "great thoroughfare" to China. And at the same time that he was working on the treaty with Burlingame, Seward was meeting secretly with representatives of the Russian czar on "Seward's folly," the $7 million purchase of Alaska. America was becoming a Pacific power.

The Burlingame Treaty was signed in July 1868, the same month that the Fourteenth Amendment, guaranteeing equal protection under the law, was proclaimed a part of the US Constitution. These were hopeful times, with promises of justice for America's blacks at home and a fair deal for China overseas.

The treaty was radical for China, too. For centuries, the Qing court had considered any Chinese who left the realm of the Dragon King to be traitors. China was a continental power and despised those who looked to the sea. Now, two Yankees negotiating in Washington had forced the Qing court to recognize that all Chinese, no matter where, were worthy of protection.

Two Chinese officials accompanied Burlingame on his trip to the US. Zhigang was the senior Manchu official. He praised Burlingame for being "open, understanding, fair" and for working "with such dedication" for

China. But like other members of the Chinese delegation, Zhigang was less interested in diplomacy than in exploring the vast country unfolding before him.

In one of the first official Chinese travelogues describing a visit to the West, Zhigang fixated on American shipbuilding, steel mills, microscopes, and printing presses. His report highlighted the Chinese belief that Western technology was the key to China's regaining its glory. He praised Christian doctrine but noted that in capitalist America "the love of God is less real than the love of profit." He paid homage at Washington's tomb and noted that of all the nations he visited, America was the most sincere about wanting friendship with China.

The mission's translator, Zhang Deyi, would become one of China's most accomplished travel writers. The delegation had arrived in the midst of a messy presidential campaign that pitted Ulysses S. Grant against Horatio Seymour. Zhang Deyi was repelled by the political mudslinging and predicted that it would lead to the nation's unraveling. Yet the system's egalitarian nature, exemplified by President Andrew Johnson's up-from-the-bootstraps résumé, impressed him. He noted that with its civil service examination, China, too, was a meritocracy, another one of the enduring similarities between the Middle Kingdom and the Beautiful Country.

Jealousy, Zhang insisted, was not part of the American psyche. American children were raised not to cry. He detailed meticulously the odd habit of "touching lips," China's first treatise on the Western kiss.

Zhang was leery of American women, auguring a tumultuous relationship between Chinese men and Western femininity. The self-confidence of American females gnawed at him. Women should be confined to the home, he argued; equality between the sexes would spell the end of connubial bliss.

And yet, at an open-air lunch in the Oakland hills, Zhang lost himself. "When the tea was gone, the wine finished, and the dishes in a disarray like a wolf's den, the evening sun shone on the mountains, a fresh wind blew, birds chirped high and low, and the trees rustled in the wind," he wrote. "The ladies left first, trailing long skirts on the ground like the tails of foxes. The fragrant aroma of their whole bodies was enticing, and although their lily feet are a foot long, they still walk with a graceful gait."

Burlingame's mission left the United States in November 1868 on a whirlwind tour of a dozen European countries with a first stop in Britain. After meeting the delegation, the new British foreign minister, Lord Clarendon, announced the end of London's gunboat diplomacy, thanks in part to the Middle Kingdom's magnetic representative from the United States.

Russia was the last stop. The delegation arrived in St. Petersburg in February 1870. On the sixteenth of that month, Burlingame met with Czar Alexander II. Afterward, Burlingame retired to his room with a cold. A week later, he was dead.

The news made it to China by May. Prince Gong and his colleagues at the Zongli Yamen were crushed. "What a pity that Mr. Burlingame was cut off by so untimely a fate, leaving his work unfinished," Prince Gong told William Seward when the former secretary of state visited Beijing later that year.

Among the Chinese elite, the mission's success in winning American and British consent to a less aggressive stance toward China sparked a debate. Xue Fucheng, one of China's first envoys to Europe, heralded the Burlingame Treaty as a clear statement of intention to help China. "America is a strong ally," he declared.

But those arrayed against change saw in the "cooperative policy" an opening to argue that the world was now accepting China on its own terms and that China did not really need to implement its treaties or continue its reforms. The US and British governments' respectful attitude toward the Chinese mission was a sign of weakness, they claimed. Opponents of reform circulated new pamphlets and outlandish rumors, pushing the Chinese people to despise foreigners even more.

In June 1870, a story spread through the northern treaty port of Tianjin that French Catholics were murdering babies in an orphanage, touching off one of the worst antiforeign riots China had ever seen. Chinese attacked the orphanage and raped, mutilated, and murdered ten nuns. Scores more were killed in what came to be known as the Tianjin Massacre. The bloodshed prompted the French to send gunboats to fire on China again. And with that, the cooperative policy was finished.

The tentative steps toward reform taken by Cixi, Prince Gong, and viceroys in the provinces ground to a halt. The only exception was a pet project of Viceroy Li Hongzhang that involved the United States and would begin in 1871. Returning to China with a ream of reports on Western practices, Zhigang found that the tide had shifted once more. "Alas! There is nothing I can do," he wrote.

Anson Burlingame died trying to help China. He believed that America and China were destined to do great things together as they melded the oldest civilization with the youngest republic. To a thunderous ovation at the height of his speech at Delmonico's, he told his fellow Americans: "The imagination kindles at the future which may be, and which will be, if you will be fair and just to China." Burlingame's vision fell victim to his early death and the machinations of those in the Qing court who had their reasons for hating the West and opposing China's reforms. And in pushing the Chinese to despise foreigners ever more deeply, these officials found an unwitting ally—in the United States.

●

CHAPTER FIVE

Men of Iron

The Burlingame Treaty, signed in 1868, pleased Americans because it promised to bring more Chinese workers to the United States. Writing in the *Nation*, editor Edwin L. Godkin predicted that "the coming of the barbarians" would herald nothing short of an economic revolution, liberating Americans from the drudgery of everyday work. Americans dubbed Burlingame's accord "the cheap labor treaty" and anticipated the arrival of Chinese workers, Godkin wrote, with "the thrill of delighted, eager expectation."

Like the poet Oliver Wendell Holmes, former secretary of state William Seward, with Burlingame the treaty's author, imagined a merger between the United States and China. In a speech delivered in Hong Kong and reprinted in the *New York Times* on February 25, 1871, Seward claimed that the more Chinese there were in America, the stronger both countries would become. America needed labor, and China had too many people, Seward said. The interests of the two nations were absolutely aligned.

By the time the treaty was signed, Chinese had been coming to the United States for almost two decades. In 1848, the discovery of gold at Sutter's Mill near the Sacramento River touched off a flood of treasure hunters rushing to California. Southern China was so tightly wound into the web of global trade that the electrifying news of gold's discovery made it to China's coast only days after it hit New York. By February 1, 1849, 54

Chinese had come to the United States. By the end of 1850, 4,000 had arrived. A year later, the number was 25,000.

For thirty years, the Chinese made up the largest population of foreigners in the American West. By the mid-1850s, they represented one-tenth of California's total population, and the state was sprinkled with towns—from Celestial Valley to Shanghai Diggings—bearing their stamp. To these immigrants, California was not the Golden State, it was *gum shan*, the gold mountain. Even today, San Francisco is known in Mandarin Chinese as *jiujinshan*, "the old gold mountain."

Chinese historians have debunked the idea that poverty propelled the Chinese to come to America. The vast majority hailed from six counties around Guangzhou, the richest region in China. They were seeking opportunity—and many found it. Prosperity attained in America was a powerful lure. At sixteen, Lee Chew, a farmer's son from Taishan, ground zero of Chinese emigration, decided that America was in his future after a man returned to his village from the United States and built a "paradise" with gardens, lakes, and a menagerie of animals. He had made his wealth, Lee wrote, "in the country of the American wizards." Lee, like many Chinese at the time, opened a laundry in New York City.

The twelve-week voyage to America was no picnic. Chinese were shipped by the hundreds in the cargo holds of ships, often old "slavers," and kept below deck for the entire voyage in bunks six feet long and three feet wide, with barely twelve inches of headroom. The *Lady Montague* lost 300 of her 450 passengers to disease. When a fire started onboard the *Dolores Ugarte* in 1871, the crew locked the Chinese belowdecks and abandoned ship. More than 500 Chinese perished in that listing pyre.

The first waves of Chinese were mostly men, and for decades, the ratio in US Chinatowns never dropped below ten men to one woman. It was less expensive to sustain a family back in China. Besides, the Chinese had for centuries restricted a woman's freedom to travel. Many of the Chinese women who did come to California were brought over as prostitutes, as were many of the first white female immigrants to the West Coast. With so many men and so few women, the Chinese, when they could, married whites, generally Irish girls, who were equally low on the American totem pole. The first Americans born with Chinese blood were Eurasians.

In the beginning, white America welcomed the Chinese. In 1849, John Geary, the mayor of San Francisco, honored the Chinese in a special ceremony to mark California's admission to statehood. In 1852, California's second governor, John McDougal, endorsed bringing in Chinese to drain the immense swamplands in the Sacramento River delta. Chinese sweat turned five million acres into some of the richest farmland in the world. Sympathetic businessmen praised the Chinese and their work ethic and compared them favorably to white workers. "I tell you they are men of iron," Frederick Bee, a Republican who owned mines, built railroads, and cofounded the Pony Express, told the California State Senate. "I have hung them over the sides of rocks where no white would trust himself. . . . They are hardy, industrious laborers." California's press predicted that the Chinese would one day be on a par with whites. "China boys will yet vote at the same polls, study at the same schools and bow at the same altar as our own countrymen," declared San Francisco's *Daily Alta California* newspaper in May 1851.

At a time of severe labor shortages, Chinese toilers saved the West. By 1870, Chinese made up one-third of the populations of Idaho and Montana, where the key industry was mining. In the 1870s, one-quarter of all miners in the West were Chinese. When white miners abandoned claims, the Chinese would work them, employing a technique called "teaspoon mining," ferreting out the gold dust that earlier, less patient claimants had overlooked.

As laundrymen, cooks, and small-scale merchants, Chinese did the work that white women would have performed if they had been present in large numbers. In the way that Howqua's capital had stoked the development of the East Coast of the United States, Chinese toil and entrepreneurial acumen powered the West.

In 1865, the Central Pacific Railroad sent announcements to every post office in California, offering high-paying jobs to whites to build the transcontinental railroad. Only a few applied. So that year, Charles Crocker, the Central Pacific's construction boss, hired his first fifty Chinese workers. Railroad managers worried that the Chinese, at an average of four feet ten inches and 120 pounds, lacked the strength to do the job. The Chinese proved them wrong. By 1867, "Crocker's pets," as they were called, composed 75 percent of the Central Pacific workforce of twelve thousand men.

The working conditions were horrendous. Winter brought avalanches, spring, landslides, summer, 120-degree heat. Central Pacific records said that 137 Chinese perished building the railroad. But on June 30, 1870, a reporter from a Sacramento newspaper saw a train car filled with Chinese bones. He counted the remains of twelve hundred men inside. The frontier writer Joaquin Miller described teams of Chinese bone collectors who followed the railroad, collecting the remains of dead workers so they could be shipped back to China for burial among their ancestors. They were, Miller wrote, "the caravan of the dead."

On May 10, 1869, on Promontory Summit near Ogden, Utah Territory, the golden spike on the railway connecting California with Council Bluffs, Iowa, was driven home. The uniting of the United States by rail was greeted like a second revolution. Before, it had taken six months to cross the country; now, the trip lasted six days. Not a single Chinese appeared in the ceremonial photographs.

The transcontinental railroad did not turn the United States into the global clearinghouse for Chinese goods. But that did not stop Americans from dreaming about the revolutionary potential of the China market. In 1857, along the eastern slope of Mount Davidson in Nevada, near the California border, Yankee miners discovered the richest vein of silver in American history. The Comstock Lode sparked a silver rush across the West, similar to the Gold Rush a decade earlier.

One of the claim owners was William Ralston, the president of the Bank of California, who was known for his lavish parties and wildcat investment schemes. Ralston had sunk his silver-mining profits in a vast network of businesses across California, from sugar refining to a stagecoach operation. But once the Civil War ended, he had more silver than he knew what to do with. And now that America's foreign trade was picking up again, Ralston thought, what better place to send it than China?

US merchants had relied on the Mexican silver dollar to trade in the Far East. But Ralston hatched a plan with his friend Henry Linderman, a former director of the US Mint, to replace the Mexican peso with a silver coin minted exclusively for the China trade. That would permit Ralston and other mine owners to sell their silver to Uncle Sam. And it would benefit American merchants by allowing them to stop buying Mexican silver dollars at a premium in order to do business with China.

Ralston paid Linderman $5,000 to author the Coinage Act of 1873. The act authorized the minting of the US trade dollar, with Lady Liberty holding out an olive branch on the face and a bald eagle on the back. Over the next four years, America's mints cranked out $36 million in trade coins, absorbing almost half of the production of the Comstock Lode.

Business writers greeted the advent of the trade dollar with the same enthusiasm with which they heralded any business news related to China. In May 1874, the San Francisco *Bulletin* reported that the coins had "gone off like hotcakes." The Philadelphia *North American* projected that the trade dollar would cement America's "leading place in the commerce of the East."

The trade dollar circulated in southern China, but it could not compete with its Mexican counterpart in Shanghai, China's business capital. Chinese made fun of the dollar's look. It was stamped with the motto "In God We Trust," prompting one Chinese trader to quip: "If the coin is good, why you trust God?" America's competitors, such as the Japanese, minted knockoffs.

The larger problem, however, was that by the early 1870s, European nations had stopped minting silver coins. So no matter how many trade dollars the US Mint churned out, it could not stanch the fall in silver's price. Soon the value of the silver in the US trade dollar was worth less than a dollar. And crafty investors showed up at the US Mint offering vast amounts of silver bullion for trade dollars—turning a profit on each coin. Business owners from the West to the Midwest began paying unsuspecting American workers with trade dollars. And with that, what began as a scheme to subsidize silver interests and spur the China trade turned into a nasty political catfight. The Coinage Act of 1873 earned a new name: "The Crime of 1873." By 1876, Congress had stripped the trade dollar of its value. A year earlier, Ralston, his investment schemes in tatters, had turned up dead, floating facedown in San Francisco Bay, a suspected suicide. Today, genuine US trade dollars go for hundreds of dollars apiece. Chinese coin dealers have flooded the market with fakes.

The demobilization of more than one million American soldiers at the end of the Civil War created a huge pool of men looking for work. Hundreds of thousands of veterans from the South and the North headed west. Railroad and port construction boomed as did speculative land deals. But as more capital was caught up in projects with no immediate economic return, the economy slowed. California was hit especially hard. Its young manufacturing sector could not compete with the more efficient factories in the East, which, thanks to the railroad, were less than a week away. For every workingman on the West Coast, there were three without a job.

Once the American economy soured, Americans soured on the Chinese, as they had soured on the Irish several decades earlier. Everyday American racism made the Chinese an easy target. They were so different, with their baggy pants, their shaved heads, and a long braid, or queue, mandated by their emperor, dangling from their heads. Equally important, their unrelenting work ethic unnerved white Americans. A higher percentage of Chinese were employed than white men.

The white response was to stack the deck against the Chinese. State legislatures passed laws to block Chinese entry into America or prevent those already in the United States from working. When those measures failed, there were lynch mobs, arsons, and murders.

Initially, the racial strife was confined to the West. But with the completion of the railroad, businessmen on the East Coast brought in Chinese workers to break strikes in Massachusetts and New Jersey. At a labor rally on June 30, 1870, in New York's Tompkins Square Park, speaker after speaker blamed the Chinese for the woes of the American workingman. That day, John Swinton, a pro-union editorial writer, published a letter in the *New York Tribune* calling "the Chinese-American question" the leading issue of the day. The Chinese, like blacks, Swinton argued, were not intelligent enough to live in a democracy. "It is a question not only for discussion and decision," Swinton said, "but for action."

Action came the next month, when Congress passed a new naturalization act that extended citizenship to Americans of African descent but excluded Asians, who were denied citizenship unless they'd been born in the United States.

Mainstream America was switching sides on the Chinese question. In 1868, James Gordon Bennett, the editor of the *New York Herald*, had welcomed bringing more Chinese into America. But by 1870, he was writing: "Their pagan savageness appears to be impregnable to the mild influences of Christian civilization."

A short poem captured the spirit of the times. In August 1870, the writer Bret Harte was editing the *Overland Monthly* in San Francisco. His deadline was approaching, and there was some extra space in the magazine's September issue, so Harte dashed off a few stanzas that he initially titled "Plain Language from Truthful James." The poem—a mere 372 words—was a rip-roaring success. The doggerel, which would be renamed "The Heathen Chinee," was translated into dozens of languages, set to music, reprinted in virtually every newspaper in the country, sold by the hundreds of thousands in illustrated copies, and turned into a Broadway hit.

"The Heathen Chinee" told the story of a card game between an Irish miner named Bill Nye, a narrator named Truthful James, and a Chinese man, Ah Sin. Nye cheats but loses, then assaults Ah Sin—"He went for that

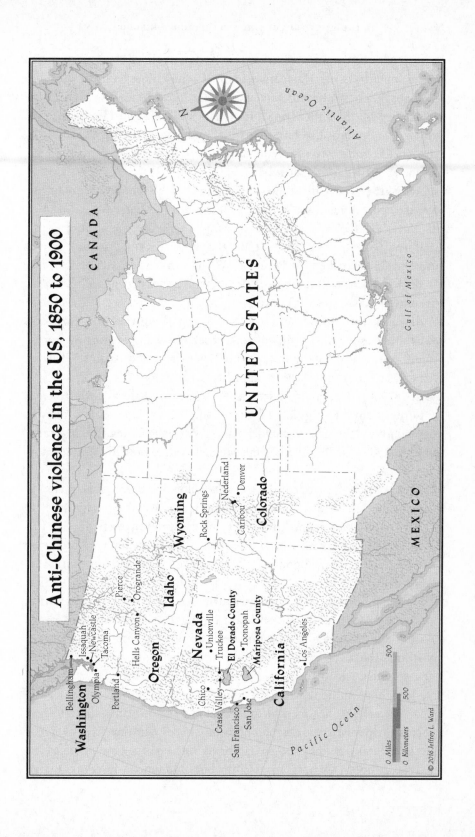

Anti-Chinese violence in the US, 1850 to 1900

CANADA

UNITED STATES

MEXICO

Atlantic Ocean

Gulf of Mexico

Pacific Ocean

Washington
Bellingham
Issaquah
Newcastle
Tacoma
Olympia
Portland

Oregon

Idaho
Pierce
Orogrande
Hells Canyon

Wyoming
Rock Springs

Nevada
Unionville
Truckee
Chico
Grass Valley
San Francisco
San Jose

El Dorado County
Toonopah
Mariposa County

California
Los Angeles

Colorado
Nederland
Denver
Caribou

N

0 Miles   500
0 Kilometers   500

© 2016 Jeffrey L. Ward

heathen Chinee"—only to discover that Ah Sin has been cheating, too. No matter what the game, Harte implied, the Chinese were going to win.

Thousands of Americans "went for that heathen Chinee." In Los Angeles on October 24, 1871, after two Chinese gangs rumbled over the rights to a prostitute, a mob of five hundred white and Hispanic men invaded the city's small Chinatown. Sixteen Chinese were strung up on street lamps. No one was jailed for the crimes.

Across the West, Chinese were rousted out of their homes; Chinatowns were burned; Chinese were lynched. "It is a war of the races here," stated the *Marysville Daily Appeal* about a string of anti-Chinese attacks across California's Central Valley. By 1873, the whole nation had sunk into a severe recession, called the Panic of 1873. Issuing his annual State of the Union address in 1874, Ulysses S. Grant became the first president to call for controls on Chinese immigration.

At about the same time that "The Record," with its allegations of sexual perversity among the missionary set, was taking China by storm, American medical authorities and politicians took aim against Chinese women as a source of infection, impurity, and disease.

In 1875, the Congress passed the Page Act, the federal government's first-ever attempt to regulate immigration. The law labeled as "undesirable" contract laborers, ex-convicts, and Asian prostitutes. The last category resulted in an almost complete ban on Chinese women coming to the United States.

Americans of European stock had a love-hate relationship with Asian beauty. In 1848, a Chinese woman named Ah Toy sailed into San Francisco Bay to become the city's most famous courtesan. At the height of her fame, men would line up for blocks and pay an ounce of gold dust just to "gaze upon her countenance," reported the *Daily Alta California*.

Within a few years, the entrepreneurial Ah Toy had two other prostitutes working for her. By 1852, she was running two Chinatown "boardinghouses." She smuggled at least one shipload of several hundred Chinese prostitutes into San Francisco and was never shy about taking a deadbeat client to court. Ah Toy lived well into her nineties.

Though prominent white customers—judges, politicians, lawyers, police officers, businessmen—skulked into Chinatown in search of illicit charms, in public they championed the crackdown on Asian women. Frank M. Pixley, who served as California's attorney general for a year in the 1860s, imported whores from China but simultaneously led the charge against them. In 1868, the California legislature declared that Chinese bordellos were a public nuisance.

When the California state senate held a hearing to address cheap labor in the spring of 1876, sex grabbed the headlines. Dr. Hugh Toland, a member of the San Francisco Board of Health, testified that the syphilis that Chinese prostitutes carried was more virulent than that of the average American prostitute. Toland claimed that white boys as young as ten had contracted the disease.

"How the Chinese Women Are Infusing a Poison into the Anglo-Saxon Blood" ran the headline in one learned journal. "If the future historian should ever be called upon to write the Conquest of America by the Chinese Government," reported the *Medico-Literary Journal* of San Francisco, "his opening chapter will be an account of the first batch of Chinese courtesans and the stream of deadly disease that followed."

In 1881, the California legislature amended the civil code to prohibit marriage between whites and "Mongolians." Six other Western states followed suit. Though interracial marriages were outlawed for everyone at different times, the prohibition on intermarriage with the Chinese hit that community the hardest because there were so few Chinese women. The percentage of women in the Chinese population dropped from 6.4 percent in 1870 to 4.6 percent in 1880, relegating most Chinese men in America to permanent bachelordom.

In the fall of 1877, anti-Chinese agitators formed the Workingmen's Party. Led by a young firebrand named Denis Kearney, out of County Cork, Ireland, the party would remake politics in California. Kearney was a charismatic orator, capable of diverting anger at robber baron capitalists into rage against the Chinese. At the end of each speech, he would lead the crowd in a chant: "The Chinese must go!"

The Workingmen's Party dominated California's 1879 constitutional convention and inserted two anti-Chinese amendments into the state constitution. The first blocked both public and private corporations from employing Chinese. The second ordered that "no native of China, no idiot, no insane person, or person convicted of any infamous crime shall ever" be allowed to vote.

In 1880, President Rutherford B. Hayes dispatched a team of Americans to China to negotiate limits on Chinese immigration. On November 17, 1880, the two parties signed a revised treaty. The new treaty allowed the United States to suspend the immigration rights for Chinese laborers, although the Americans also agreed that they would never "absolutely prohibit it." The treaty committed the US government to protecting Chinese in the United States, but that promise was not kept. While the American delegation was negotiating in Beijing, three thousand white men surrounded Denver's Chinatown and burned it to the ground. The short-lived era of free immigration from China to the United States was over.

The new treaty didn't placate California's politicians, who used their political muscle in Washington to push for a wholesale ban on Chinese immigration. In May 1882, President Chester A. Arthur, a Republican, signed the Chinese Exclusion Act, which barred skilled and unskilled Chinese laborers from entering the country for ten years. Students, diplomats, and merchants were exempted.

The law marked the first time that the United States specifically denied an ethnic group the right of entry, a crucial shift for a nation founded by immigrants. Tightened progressively over the decades, the exclusion act would not be repealed until the height of World War II, when China allied with the United States against Japan.

The act resulted in an epidemic of mass roundups, expulsions, arson, and murder that spread from California to Colorado, from Washington state to the South. The scattered violence of the 1870s turned into a systematic purge. In Rock Springs, Wyoming, in 1885, twenty-eight Chinese miners were gunned down or burned to death after they refused to join a union. Two years later, the worst massacre of Chinese unfolded in Hells Canyon along the Snake River in Oregon, where a gang of horse rustlers robbed Chinese miners of $50,000 in gold. The mangled bodies of thirty-four men washed up downstream. In California, Chinese residents were hounded out of more than two hundred towns.

The Chinese reacted to American racism and the challenges of living in the United States in a typically American fashion. They fought back, on the streets, in the courts, and at the workplace with boycotts, strikes, protests, essays, knives, guns, and fists. "Poor John Chinaman," as the *Daily Alta California* called him, a weak figure who chose to move on rather than to battle, was nothing but a myth. In Western mining towns, the Chinese armed themselves with bowie knives and revolvers. The Chinese Consolidated Benevolent Association, also known as the Six Companies, run by Chinese merchants and funded by contributions from almost every working Chinese in the country, armed itself with the law, bankrolling more than ten thousand lawsuits challenging the whole legal architecture designed to oppress the Chinese.

The Chinese also battled the exclusion act by sneaking into America.

Almost twenty thousand Chinese were smuggled from Mexico around the turn of the century. Lawmakers called for a "Chinese Wall" on the border to keep the interlopers out. The vast federal bureaucracy designed to limit immigration to America was originally created not in response to Mexicans, but to the Chinese.

Another way around the exclusion law was to create fictitious birth documents. These allowed tens of thousands of "paper sons" to make it to America. The 1906 earthquake and fire in San Francisco was a godsend for this immigrant population, permitting many to claim that their birth records had been lost in the blaze.

The Chinese determination to enter the United States and willingness to fight for their rights underscores two points about their lives in America. First, the Chinese were never as isolated from mainstream society as some historians have alleged. Second, despite withering oppression and violence, many Chinese in the United States achieved the American Dream.

Lue Gim Gong left Taishan at the age of eight in 1868 to work first in San Francisco and then as a strikebreaker in a shoe factory in North Adams, Massachusetts, where he befriended his Sunday school teacher, Fanny Burlingame, who was the sister of US minister Anson Burlingame. Learning of his skill with plants, Fanny hired him as a gardener. When Lue contracted tuberculosis, Fanny sent him to Florida to recover. When she died, she left him $12,500 and two houses in the middle of Florida's citrus region.

Lue took an interest in the fledgling Florida fruit industry. He developed an orange that withstands frost, a new strain of grapefruit, and a sweet apple. Acclaimed in the United States as "The Citrus Wizard," Lue saved the orange business in America after it was nearly destroyed by several years of hard freezes.

Like many Chinese, Lue remained a loyal son. He returned home and brought his inventive spirit with him. He planted orange groves around Taishan. But when he set up a system to pump water uphill to irrigate his trees, local farmers complained that the system interfered with the region's feng shui, and they chopped the grove down. When his parents tried to marry him off to someone he did not know, Lue fled back to the United States, and his name was struck from the family rolls.

To be sure, Lue faced prejudice in America, but as the historian Liping Zhu has written, for the Chinese in America, "the brighter aspects of free soil, free labor, and free gold overshadowed the dark side of exploitation, injustice, and discrimination." Despite its bigotry, America compared favorably to the other options—South America, Australia, or, worse, Southeast Asia, where any single anti-Chinese pogrom left more Chinese dead than all the Chinese killed in America combined. From its early days, America was known in China as a place where the Chinese could succeed.

The Chinese also responded to American bigotry with gumption and smarts. When San Francisco passed the Sidewalk Ordinance, prohibiting Chinese vegetable sellers from using shoulder poles on sidewalks, the hawkers stepped off the pavement into the streets. When the Los Angeles city council, pressed by the Workingman's Party, introduced a special levy of twenty dollars on Chinese vegetable peddlers in 1879, the peddlers called a strike. The City of Angels went without vegetables until a county judge abolished the tax.

Bolstered by the Fourteenth Amendment, which guaranteed equal protection under the law, the Chinese and their white allies challenged laws and ordinances in state and federal courts. California was the main battleground, and Frederick Bee, a prominent Republican and member of the San Francisco bar, led the charge.

With his white whiskers, high-collar coat, and plug hat, Bee did not look the part of a human rights activist. He was first and foremost a businessman. But his belief in the idea that America was a land of opportunity led him to embrace the Chinese cause.

By 1878, Bee was the second-ranking official at the newly opened Chinese consulate in San Francisco. He traveled the West by train, horse, and riverboat to Chico, Denver, Rock Springs, and the Washington Territory, demanding the punishment of vigilantes and mayors alike for attacking the Chinese. On the other side of the continent, John W. Foster, a onetime secretary of state, labored for the Chinese cause in Washington, DC.

Both Foster and Bee were well paid for their troubles. But it took courage to tell the Chinese side of the story. Bee's life was regularly threatened. Still, their combined investigations of anti-Chinese atrocities forced the United States to pay China more than $500,000 in indemnities for the loss of life and property. Fear of their probes also compelled racist American politicians to stop inciting violence against the Chinese.

Testifying before Congress, Bee reminded America's lawmakers that if federal and local authorities continued to ignore the plight of the Chinese in the US, then Chinese would massacre Americans in China in return. In Denver, he proved that the police did nothing to protect the Chinese while a mob set Chinatown ablaze. In Rock Springs, Wyoming, he collected the names of white assailants who had slaughtered Chinese, but when he tried to find the US attorney who was handling the case, he discovered that the man had decamped to Illinois.

Relations between Bee and his supervisors at the Chinese consulate were not always smooth. In February 1887, Congress approved an indemnity of $270,000 to China for the massacre at Rock Springs. The US government paid the indemnity to the Chinese consulate in San Francisco, but less than one-quarter of the funds ever made it into the hands of the victims' families. In a heated argument in late August 1889, Bee accused one of the consuls of skimming money. The consul argued that he had needed to pay senators and congressmen for their votes. It was not the last time that Chinese officials would be slipping funds to US politicians.

Bee died of a heart attack in San Francisco on May 26, 1892. On the day of his funeral, Chinese stood ten deep on the streets of Chinatown as prominent Chinese merchants set off for the First Unitarian Church on Geary Street on the white side of town. Chinese tongs and associations filled the church with wreaths. The Consulate General of the Qing court sent over a gigantic heart made of flowers, with "Our Colonel" emblazoned across the center. White mourners sat on the left side of the aisle; Chinese occupied the right. "Probably never before in America," wrote the *San Francisco Chronicle*, "have representatives of the two races crowded together with one common motive and to express one human sentiment."

In 1884, the Tung Hing Tong, the laundrymen's guild in San Francisco, continued the Chinese practice of hiring the best lawyers in the country when it retained Hall McAllister, a prominent Republican considered one of the greatest litigators in nineteenth-century America, to argue a case before the Supreme Court. McAllister contended that San Francisco's Board of Supervisors had deliberately created a web of permits and business licenses designed to force all Chinese laundries to close while allowing white-owned competitors to stay in business. One of the rules banned wooden structures (traditionally run by the Chinese) and approved brick ones (mainly operated by the French).

Supreme Court Justice Stanley Matthews, writing the unanimous decision in *Yick Wo v. Hopkins*, observed that the laundry ordinances had been administered with "an evil eye and an unequal hand." It was clear, he said, that the enforcement of the law violated the Fourteenth Amendment. The case had vast legal implications. First, it made all people in the United States, not just citizens, equal before the law. Second, it was the first Supreme Court ruling to say that if a law was unfairly enforced, it could be struck down. In the 1950s, the Supreme Court returned to the principles established by *Yick Wo v. Hopkins* to block attempts in the Deep South to limit the rights of blacks and condemn black children to "separate but equal" schools.

In 1892, Congress extended the Chinese Exclusion Act for another decade and added a requirement, called the Geary Act, that all Chinese in America apply for an internal passport—the first in the United States. An organization called the Chinese Equal Rights League convinced tens of thousands of Chinese to defy the Geary Act in one of the nation's first cases of mass civil disobedience. Urged on by the Six Companies, 105,000 of the 110,000 Chinese in America refused to register with the government.

The league's founder was Wong Chin Foo, a magnetic public speaker who had come to the United States in the 1860s as a student. Wong founded the league to fight against discrimination and advocate for voting rights for Chinese citizens of the United States. Wong was different from almost every other Chinese in the United States. He had traveled to America to study, not to work, and he hailed from Shandong province in the north, rather than from Guangdong in the south. Wong harangued both sides of the Chinese-American divide. He locked horns with anti-Chinese agitator Denis Kearney, challenging him to a duel. (Kearney declined.) He lectured his countrymen from southern China that if they wanted to be accepted in the United States, they should throw out their Chinese robes, cut off their queues, stop smoking opium, and start learning English. In 1883, Wong founded the first Chinese-language newspaper in New York City and called it the *Chinese-American*, the first public use of that term. More than seventy years before Martin Luther King Jr. dreamed of an America that judged people by the content of their character and not the color of their skin, Wong declared that only "character and fitness should be the requirement of all who are desirous of becoming citizens of the American Republic." Wong returned to China in 1898 for a family reunion and died there, aged only forty-two.

In 1898, lawyers retained by the six companies took another case to the Supreme Court. Wong Kim Ark had been born in the United States in 1873 to parents who ran a grocery store in San Francisco. In 1895, he went to China and returned to America later that year. At the port of San Francisco, he was denied entry by John H. Wise, an immigration officer who was notorious for banning as many Chinese as he could. (Wise would often send nasty poems to lawyers working for the Chinese, boasting of his exploits.)

Represented by prominent Republican attorneys, Wong sued the United States government, arguing that as a US-born citizen, he had a right to return home. The government countered that the "accident of birth" could never confer the rights of citizenship, since Wong's "education and political affiliations" remained "entirely alien" to the United States. The Supreme Court disagreed. The Wong Kim Ark case answered the question of whether birth in the United States confers citizenship. It does.

In 1904, the exclusion act came up for renewal. China demanded that the United States ease its restrictions on immigration, but Congress extended the act indefinitely, thereby violating the treaty made with the Qing court. The number of Chinese in the United States dropped from a high of more than 110,000 in the late 1880s to some 70,000 in 1910. Partly as a result, "the Chinese-American question" no longer preoccupied American racists and political opportunists the way it once had. The Japanese would soon be caught in the crosshairs, resulting in the 1924 Immigration Act, which extended the Chinese Exclusion Act to include all Asians.

Sentiments toward the Chinese were never simple, however. Even as bigots clamored "The Chinese must go!" other Americans worked to improve education in China and bring Chinese students to the United States.

In 1847, an American missionary arranged for an eighteen-year-old Chinese student named Yung Wing to attend boarding school in Massachusetts. There the young man embraced the work ethic and athleticism of a New England boyhood. He split his own firewood and walked three miles to school and back each day. At the end of four years, Yung Wing won a scholarship to Yale University, paid for by Christian women from Savannah, Georgia.

Yung had grown up fatherless, selling homemade candy and gleaning grains of rice from worked-over paddies. In New Haven, he studied until midnight and took odd jobs to cover room and board. The intellectual hothouse there was heady stuff for this son of southern China. "Old Yale is surrounded with an atmosphere of ambition," he wrote to an American missionary. "I never was subject to such excitement."

Yung became an American in 1852, before the 1870 Naturalization Act banned Asians from becoming naturalized citizens. When he graduated in 1854, he promised to devote himself to a single idea—that "through

Western education China might be regenerated, become enlightened and powerful."

Belief in the capacity of an American education to transform China has endured to the present day. For Yung, the key to China's resurgence lay in the high schools, colleges, and universities of the United States and in educators from America who would soon head to China in droves. For first identifying the transformative effect that Western education would have on China, Qian Ning, a modern Chinese writer, called Yung "China's Columbus."

In November 1854, after seven years in America, Yung returned to China. His English was fluent, but his Chinese was only so-so. He occupied an uneasy place wedged between Westerners and Chinese. In Guangzhou, he was repulsed by the sight of an execution ground, littered with the bodies of men killed without trial. In Hong Kong, the British blocked his efforts to practice law. In Shanghai, he became a local hero when he bloodied an overbearing Scot after he had yanked Yung Wing's queue. Yung eventually found his niche as a tea merchant negotiating the perilous but profitable divide between the Taipings and the Qing.

As one of the few Chinese educated in the United States, Yung caught the eye of senior officials. Viceroy Zeng Guofan, the most powerful and visionary mandarin in the Qing court, tasked Yung with building China's first weapons factory, the Jiangnan Arsenal. Yung did it using machinery from Fitchburg, Massachusetts.

Situated on the outskirts of Shanghai, the Jiangnan Arsenal, founded in 1865, was American down to its nuts and bolts. Half the equipment came from Massachusetts, and the remainder from the American firm Thomas Hunt & Company, the largest machine shop in China at the time. The arsenal soon grew into the biggest weapons plant in Asia and one of the largest in the world. Managed by American and British engineers, by 1867 it was churning out fifteen muskets a day, thousands of pounds of shrapnel, and small howitzers. Eventually it branched out into warships. By 1892, it occupied seventy-three acres and employed almost three thousand people. Its translation department was the largest in China and with its focus on Western technology represented China's first attempt at collecting industrial secrets—by fair means or foul—from the West. When Zeng Guofan visited the factory, he looked at the machines, Yung Wing noted, "with unabated delight." Yung lobbied Zeng to send Chinese boys to the United States to study just as he had.

Yung found himself in the middle of a colossal debate among the self-strengtheners, who wanted to use Western technology to make China strong. Did China require only the machines of the West or did it need something more—Western logic, science, even religion and political philosophy—to become great? Did China require a wholesale transformation of its society so that it could innovate like the West, or could it absorb Western technology without changing China's soul?

In 1871, the year the Burlingame delegation returned to China minus its American chief, Zeng Guofan proposed to the throne the idea of an educational mission to America. The plan would be to send thirty Chinese boys to the United States each year for twenty years, chiefly to pursue military studies at West Point or Annapolis. The United States could be trusted with China's youth, Zeng assured Emperor Tongzhi and his mother, the Empress Dowager Cixi, because Americans were "honest, kind, and have always been respectful and obliging to China." What's more, the right of Chinese to attend American schools had been enshrined in Article 7 of the Burlingame Treaty.

The court approved the plan. Chen Lanpin, a conservative Confucian who spoke no English, was appointed to lead the mission. Yung Wing would be his deputy. The first detachment of Chinese students, ranging in age from ten to sixteen, left Shanghai on August 11, 1872, aboard the *Spirit of Peking*. A month later, the ship arrived in San Francisco, and the boys, wearing maroon robes, with blue silk coats and short round hats, stepped onto American soil. The Chinese Educational Mission—China's first permanent mission abroad—had begun.

Chugging across the Great Plains on the Transcontinental Railroad, the boys came face to face with the American Wild West. Student Li Enfu had never been robbed before. Now, as he peeked out the train's window, he spied "two ruffianly men" with revolvers drawn. Shots were fired. Women screamed. "What we saw," Li wrote, "was enough to make hair stand on end."

Feted in San Francisco, held up on the train, mesmerized by New York, the boys were profoundly affected by their encounter with the United States. They arrived in Connecticut to be kissed by their adoptive mothers, taken to Sunday school, and taught English with tough love. At meals, they were told the names of the dishes once, and were rewarded with seconds only if they could remember them. "By this method," Li Enfu recalled, "our progress was rapid and surprising."

Hartford, Connecticut, shielded the boys from anti-Chinese racism, and many excelled at school. There was Tang Shaoyi, who took the nickname Ajax from the *Iliad*. Yung's nephew, Yung Leang, had a predilection for pranks; he was named By-jinks Johnnie. Cai Tinggan, a chubby, perpetually smiling fellow, became the Fighting Chinee. Breezy Jack, Sitting Bull, Yankee Kwong—their nicknames attested to their assimilation.

Yung Wing and Chen Lanpin bickered over the boys' upbringing. Yung regarded their Americanization with delight; Chen, with horror. When the boys asked Yung whether they could discard their robes and cut off their queues, Yung agreed. Chen did not. They compromised: the boys wore Western clothes but kept the queues. When Chen called the students together to read the emperor's circulars, he demanded that they kowtow. "Hell House" was the boys' name for the mission's building on Collins Street in Hartford where they were forced to study Chinese.

Chen sent agitated reports to Li Hongzhang, the viceroy directly responsible for the mission. Were the boys really taught by women? Li asked. And what's this about a three-month summer break? Chen disapproved when Yung Wing fell in love with an American woman named Mary Kellogg and married her in March 1875. Cross-cultural love set a bad example for the boys. Chen wanted the mission shut.

In 1876, the boys went to Philadelphia for the Centennial Exhibition, the first official world's fair in the United States, which featured thirty-seven nations, including China. Where Western countries and Japan displayed their technology—the telegraph, the phonograph, and the lightbulb were recent inventions—China brought antiques. Statesmen from across the globe congregated in Philadelphia, but the Qing dynasty had only sent a low-ranking customs officer named Li Gui. Meeting the boys, he was struck by how different they were from their counterparts back home. "The outcome of Western education," he declared, "is beyond our estimation."

In 1875, the Tongzhi emperor contracted smallpox and died at the age of nineteen. He would be the last adult emperor to rule China. Breaking the rules of dynastic succession, Cixi installed her three-year-old nephew on the Dragon Throne. He became Emperor Guangxu. Cixi continued to pull the strings of power.

That year, Chen Lanpin was appointed China's first minister to the United States, with Yung Wing as his deputy. Yung split his time between the educational mission and pushing the Qing court to pay more attention to the fate of overseas Chinese. In 1875, he authored a startling report on the brutal mistreatment of Chinese digging fertilizer in the guano pits of Peru. In part because of his efforts, the trade in Chinese slave labor to Latin America was halted. Meanwhile, another conservative Confucian, Wu Zideng, was dispatched to Hartford to run the educational mission.

Communication between Wu Zideng and the boys was so tortured that he wrote a letter to the *Hartford Daily Courant* to get their attention. "If you deliberately neglect the rules of politeness of your native country, on your return home, how can you live in sympathy with your fellow countrymen?" Wu asked. The *Courant* spoofed Wu's notorious refusal to surrender his seat to women on the city's cable cars.

Wu reported to Beijing that some of the boys had secretly joined the Asylum Hill Congregational Church. He charged that they were playing too many sports and neglecting their Chinese. They were becoming "foreign ghosts," he said. Li Hongzhang responded that he would only support the mission on one condition: He wanted the students to attend West Point or Annapolis. But in 1877, the State Department told China that its students would not be allowed into American military academies, thereby violating the terms of the Burlingame Treaty. Anti-Chinese sentiment had spread East, and Washington was no longer in the mood to respect its agreements with the Qing court. The mission limped on for a few more years, until finally, in September 1881, after leading Qing officials complained that the boys had "all plunged themselves into American culture," Cixi shut it down.

Mark Twain, President Grant, and dozens of educators urged the Chinese to reconsider. "We have given to them the same knowledge and culture that we give to our own children and citizens," wrote Yale president Noah Porter to the Zongli Yamen. It was not enough.

Some of the boys decided to stay behind, ditching the trains taking them to San Francisco and absconding to their adopted homes in Hartford. "A bird born in captivity cannot appreciate the sweet odor of the woods," wrote one, "but let it once have free space to exercise its wings, off it flies to where natural instinct leads."

To prevent more defections, Chinese authorities split the mission into three groups and dispatched chaperones to escort the boys home. Once they arrived in Shanghai, they were incarcerated and questioned by police about their loyalty to the empire. Writing to an American friend, Yung Wing's nephew, Yung Leang, confided that he found this welcome "a humiliation I did not expect and did not know how to respond to." How could the students be both Chinese *and* advocates for American science, the police wanted to know. Shanghai's *Shenbao* newspaper called them "half-breeds" and suggested that they be exiled.

After four days in what one described as a "Turkish jail," the boys were freed only to be scattered across China, to mines, to a naval academy, to the customs house. They were thrust into jobs with no promise as the Qing court sought to smother their influence. Yung Wing went to Beijing to plead their case, but no one would see him.

Still, the genie of American "spiritual pollution," the bane of the traditionalists and later of the Communists, was out of the bottle. As the *New York Times* noted presciently in 1881: "China cannot borrow our learning, our science, and our material forms of industry without importing with them the virus of political rebellion." The virus had not died. The same year the Chinese Educational Mission ended, the first Chinese women arrived in the United States to study.

By the late 1880s, Li Hongzhang, who had supported Yung Wing's educational mission, was fed up with the United States. He took the tightening of the exclusion act and the unwillingness of the US government to admit Chinese to West Point and Annapolis as a personal affront. The Americans "make a profession of dealing justly with all the world," he told an Australian journalist. "How have they dealt with China? They refused us citizenship, they suffer our people to be murdered or expelled by armed mobs, they shut us out of their country, except under certain severe restrictions and then when we agree to these they break them off and exclude us altogether."

In the mid-nineteenth century, a growing number of Chinese looked to the United States for education and opportunity, establishing two powerful perceptions of America—as China's teacher and its hope for the future. But conservatives in China reacted in horror at the speed with which their countrymen embraced American values and championed an opposing view of America as a threat to the Chinese way. America, for its part, responded erratically to the Chinese. White workingmen attacked Chinese laborers, giving birth to the idea that their industriousness endangered the United States. American educators, on the other hand, welcomed Chinese students and advocated an alternate view—of China as a deserving disciple of the United States. All of these opposing images continue to do battle today.

CHAPTER SIX

A Good Thrashing

In the 1870s, America turned away from China. The happy hopeful-
ness of the Burlingame era was over. Americans oppressed the Chinese at
home and looked down on them abroad. In April 1879, A. A. Hayes wrote
in the *International Review* that US policy toward China was "a matter of
indifference to the great mass of our people." That year, Harvard College
dropped its sole Chinese course. The *New York Times* noted the "slight
amount of business and diplomatic intercourse we have with China."

Trade, which was $9 million in 1864, fell to just $1 million in 1875. The
great American merchant houses that had led the march to China had
largely gone bankrupt or had pulled out. Russell & Company, the successor
to John P. Cushing's empire in Guangzhou, which had once dominated
China's river traffic, sold its steamships to a firm controlled by Viceroy Li
Hongzhang. Chinese competitors blocked an American plan to manufacture textiles in Shanghai.

American businessmen now thronged to Japan. Since the black ships
of US Navy commodore Matthew Perry's fleet had descended on the Japanese coast in 1853, the Land of the Rising Sun had embraced a political
and economic reform program that soon became the envy of the Chinese.
In 1860, Americans had conducted far more business with China than
with Japan. Twenty years later, Japanese trade with the US overtook Sino-
American trade. While US investment in Japan would grow to hundreds
of millions of dollars, American plans to dig mines, run telegraph and

telephone wires, and open banks in China barely got off the ground. For the Americans, there was just too much money to be made elsewhere to bother doing more than daydreaming about riches in the Manchu kingdom.

Japan's increasing strength pushed up against China's historic sphere of influence, creating tensions that have lasted to the present day. In 1879, Japan annexed an island chain that included Okinawa and stretched hundreds of miles south, to the northern tip of Taiwan. Japan likewise sought to increase its sway over the Korean kingdom. Like the Opium War–era mandarins before them, Chinese officials were intrigued by the idea of using the United States to counter their enemies. "The Chinese like Americans better or rather, perhaps, hate them less than any other foreigner," said former president Ulysses S. Grant, who visited China in 1879. "We are the only power that recognizes their right to control their own domestic affairs." When Grant steamed into Tianjin in May 1879, Viceroy Li Hongzhang requested his help in negotiating with Japan. But there was little that Grant could do.

By the early 1890s, both China and Japan had dispatched armies to the Korean peninsula to back competing factions in the Korean court. Still, the Qing court was so confident that Japan would not dare attack that even as tensions mounted it sent the *Kuang Chia*, the pride of the Chinese navy, to southern China to transport lychees for the Empress Dowager. In the spring of 1894, the Sino-Japanese War began with a Japanese assault. In the ensuing months, little Japan crushed the Chinese army and navy, shocking mandarins and Westerners alike.

In the early morning of December 23, 1894, John W. Foster, China's lobbyist in Washington, was awakened at his Dupont Circle mansion by a telegram from Emperor Guangxu, requesting that he come to Beijing to help China negotiate an end to the war. Working with Frederick Bee, Foster had convinced Congress to pay reparations to China because the US government had failed to protect Chinese workers in America. Now Foster was being asked to champion China's cause on a global stage. He left the United States in late December and arrived in China on a steamship in January 1895. In March, he set off from Tianjin with Li Hongzhang for Japan.

In talks in the port town of Shimonoseki, the Japanese demanded that China agree to all their demands as a condition of a cease-fire. Li Hongzhang wanted the cease-fire first. As Li returned to his residence following a negotiating session on the afternoon of March 24, a would-be assassin shot him in the face. With blood spurting from his cheek, the viceroy calmly requested a handkerchief, walked into his residence, and asked for a surgeon to dig out the bullet.

Li wanted to return to Tianjin, but Foster argued that the incident could be turned to China's advantage. Embarrassed, the Japanese agreed to an unconditional cease-fire. It was, Foster quipped, "the most effective shedding of blood on the Chinese side during the entire war." On April 17, 1895, the two sides signed the Treaty of Shimonoseki.

The final terms were harsh: China lost the island of Taiwan and the Liaodong Peninsula, including Port Arthur, the largest port on the Yellow Sea, known in Chinese as Dalian. The Qing court agreed to allow foreigners to build factories in China, a concession that portended immense economic and social change. Worried that he would be executed for agreeing to such onerous terms, Li convinced Foster to travel to Beijing to explain the treaty to the Manchu court. China needed to end its practice of running away from painful agreements, Foster told the mandarins in Beijing, because otherwise China's recalcitrance would only prompt the foreigners to seize more of China's land. The mandarins peppered Foster with questions. Weng Tonghe, an imperial tutor and one of the most influential government officials of the day, asked Foster, in all seriousness, whether territory had ever changed hands in a European war. "It was the most unique conference I ever attended," Foster wrote.

Foster leaked the treaty's contents to the European powers, reasoning that they could be counted upon to rein in Japan's lust for Chinese turf. As Foster expected, Russia, France, and Germany forced Japan to hand back the Liaodong Peninsula and Port Arthur, a humiliation that the Meiji government would not forget.

Foster was anxious to return to the United States, but the Qing court proposed that he move to Beijing and advise the Grand Council, China's cabinet. Foster declined, invoking Confucius. He had a date, he told Li Hongzhang, with his seven-year-old grandson to go fishing that summer. If he failed to make good on his promise, "I will lose face with him. He will think his grandfather is not a man of truth." That summer, on the St. Lawrence River, Foster landed a muskie that came up to his grandson's shoulder. He sent a photograph of the boy with the fish to Li. The boy's name was John Foster Dulles. Decades later, as secretary of state, he would have a China story all his own.

The American press called the Sino-Japanese War "The Pigtail War," and the Qing empire's trouncing was greeted with glee. In Japan, with its burgeoning economy and powerful military, Americans saw an honorary "white man" in Asia. American pundits called Japan America's "Yankee brother," and crackpot Darwinian theorists speculated that the Japanese would soon evolve into Caucasians.

William Woodville Rockhill, who would one day become the most influential American diplomat in China, saw Japan's victory as a jolting tonic for the Qing court. "A good thrashing will not hurt China in the least," he observed from his perch at the State Department. The *Missionary Review* called Japan's triumph a "highway" that opened China "for the entrance of Christian forces."

China's defeat led to a deepening crisis among its leaders and intellectuals. Yan Fu, who had introduced his country to the ideas of Social Darwinism, used the term "national salvation" to awaken his countrymen to the enormity of their plight. China's elites agreed that China was sick but they bickered over the cure.

A decade before the Sino-Japanese War, a network of a dozen American and British Protestant missionaries had begun experimenting with new tactics to reach the Chinese. The idea of converting China one Chinese at a time promoted by the first wave of American missionaries would require, according to one calculation, half a million years. The fire-and-brimstone method of Issachar Roberts had ended in the Taiping Rebellion. So a cluster of preachers took the controversial step of fostering a new China, instead of evangelizing or blitzconverting the old one.

These men packaged Christianity with Western education, science, capitalism, and political theory, offering the combination as a remedy that would strengthen China. They appealed to China's elite, rather than to the poor and the downtrodden. "Win the leaders of China," claimed American missionary Gilbert Reid, "and China is won." In offering Christianity as a tool to make China great again, these preachers adopted a new technique to sell Western values to China. Out went the argument that Christianity was right and good and in came the claim that it was useful.

Founding newspapers, schools, colleges, and associations as well as advocating reforms, this group of American and British preachers played a critical role in the opening of the Chinese mind, ushering in the most cosmopolitan era in modern Chinese history. With their Chinese partners, they built China's modern educational system, popularized Western medicine, print media, science, and sports, fought foot-binding and female infanticide, organized antipoverty and rural reconstruction efforts, and nurtured generations of Chinese modernizers. Their books and essays roused to action the highest authorities of the land, including the boy-king on the Dragon Throne, Emperor Guangxu.

By the 1880s, every major Chinese city had at least one Protestant church. YMCAs and YWCAs spread across urban China. These institutions were the first places where Chinese men and women mingled as equals. What's more, Protestantism's emphasis on charity, good works, and self-sacrifice appealed to a people longing for a vanguard of men and women willing to devote their lives to saving the nation. This very American type of service, which gave impulse to Prohibition, the suffrage movement, and progressivism in the United States, remained a staple in China through the twentieth century. The techniques that American ministers employed, including street theater and mass mobilization, and the causes they embraced, such as literacy and rural health care, would inspire China's Nationalist Party and the Communists as well. Both would borrow liberally from the Protestant tool kit as they vied for power.

For several decades into the early twentieth century, Chinese Protestants made up more than half of China's college and high school graduates and most of its leading politicians. Protestants or those educated in Protestant schools launched all of China's modern professions: teaching, medicine, law, and industry. American influence inspired many Chinese to embrace individualism, scientific research, nationalism, democracy, women's rights, and a civil society.

In 1859, Young John Allen, the orphaned son of a Southern slave owner, sold the family farm in Georgia and shipped out to China as a Southern Methodist missionary with his wife, Mary, and their daughter, Malvina. No sooner had the family arrived in Shanghai than the American Civil War erupted, leaving Allen with a growing family (within a few years, he and Mary would have six children) and no money as Southern Methodist contributions dried up.

Shanghai in the early 1860s was already home to more than one million Chinese and several thousand foreigners, of which barely one hundred were Americans. In 1863, the Americans folded the small neighborhood they had occupied in the Hongkew section of Shanghai into the much larger British zone to create the International Settlement. Amid the bustle of a growing city, Allen found work teaching English as well as chemistry and physics, introducing his students to the telegraph, the galvanic battery, and other newfangled inventions. Between 1860 and 1867, as Allen averaged a measly one baptism a year, he became convinced that Western knowledge—not religion—was the key to the Chinese soul. He called his work an "intellectual approach" to proselytizing.

In 1867, Allen dove into what would become his greatest love: journalism. He founded a Chinese-language monthly called the *Globe*. With his colleague, the British missionary Timothy Richard, he made the *Globe* the flagship of their Society for the Diffusion of Christian and General Knowledge Among the Chinese—an organization aimed at introducing the Chinese to the latest developments in the West.

The *Globe* had an electrifying effect on China's intellectual elite. From its pages, many Chinese first learned about democracy, socialism, economics, and world affairs. In an admonition that Chinese Communist leader Deng Xiaoping would repeat a century later, Allen advised his readers that China needed to become rich before it could grow strong. Allen and other writers implored the Chinese government to embrace reforms. Look at Japan, they wrote; in less than two decades, it has emerged as a power.

Allen and his colleagues sold Christianity as an ingredient essential to becoming a world power. To Li Hongzhang's question, "What good is Christianity?" the newspaper responded with a thirteen-part series emphasizing the political, social, moral, and material benefits of the faith. Only one part mentioned its spiritual dimension.

The market for the *Globe*'s essays was so vast that Chinese printers wantonly pirated them. In one city, Young John Allen found six editions of an essay he had written on the "eight bad habits" of the Chinese. The grand Chinese tradition of intellectual piracy prompted the Americans (predictably) to threaten litigation against the miscreants.

Allen and other missionaries played a central role in the demise of foot-binding. The practice had begun in the tenth century, with a favorite imperial concubine who danced with her feet squeezed into tiny shoes. It spread, allowing Chinese men to control the movements of their womenfolk. Many Chinese men found the disfigurement of the foot and thereby the woman's hips and vagina sexually thrilling.

To fight foot-binding, Allen and others shamed their Chinese contemporaries. The *Globe*'s stories described in detail the crushing of the four smaller toes, the compression of the anklebone, and the stench from the often-fatal infections that accompanied the making of the three-inch-long "Golden Lotus." They also argued that if China wanted to become rich and strong, it would need healthy women as well as men.

In his autobiography, Kang Youwei, an influential intellectual known as the Wild Fox, credited the *Globe* with changing his mind on foot-binding.

What worked best, he acknowledged, was the shaming. "I owe my conversion chiefly to the writings of two missionaries, the Reverend Timothy Richard and the Reverend Doctor Young J. Allen," Kang wrote, adding that "there is nothing which makes us objects of ridicule as much as foot-binding." It was not the last time that the loss of "international face" prompted China to change.

In 1894 in the southern metropolis of Guangzhou, Kang founded the Unbound Foot Association. Within a few years, it claimed a membership of ten thousand. He wrote to the emperor on the subject. Europeans and Americans were "strong and vigorous because their mothers do not bind feet and therefore have strong offspring," he observed. Now that China was locked in a struggle with the West, foot-binding had to be discarded, he wrote, because "to give birth to weak offspring is perilous." Eight years later, in 1902, the Empress Dowager Cixi issued an edict urging the cessation of the practice. A decade after that, Sun Yat-sen, the first president of the Republic of China, banned it outright, and eventually the custom petered out.

In April 1895, as eight thousand provincial degree holders converged on Beijing for the triennial national civil service examination, news of the Treaty of Shimonoseki broke. Allen published leaked notes of the talks. Shocked at Japan's gains, scholars submitted petitions to the Qing court calling for reforms. They organized study groups—such as the Self-Strengthening Society and the National Preservation Society—modeled on the clubs run by their missionary friends.

Three years later, in 1898, Kang Youwei wrote a series of reports to Emperor Guangxu calling for bold Western-oriented political and economic measures. Guided by Young John Allen and others, he argued that Japan should be "the model for our reform." And as the exemplar of a leader whom Guangxu could follow, Kang invoked none other than China's adopted hero, George Washington. "Washington had no one and no land, yet he managed to preserve the country," Kang wrote to the emperor in January 1898. "China has 20,000 li of land and 400 million of people!"

Emboldened by Kang Youwei, Emperor Guangxu issued a dizzying array of edicts aimed at revolutionizing China's administration. Starting in June 1898, the emperor abolished government sinecures, reformed the military and the bureaucracy, took steps to open up the economy, and embraced Western education.

Kang Youwei had also proposed that Guangxu establish an advisory council and he nominated himself to become the emperor's chief aide. Kang's ambition put him on a collision course with Empress Dowager

Cixi. While she, too, understood the need for change, she brooked no challenge to her authority. Some among Kang's cohorts suggested that Cixi should be removed. In September 1898, a band of eunuchs burst into Guangxu's chambers and imprisoned him on an island in the Forbidden City. Cixi proceeded to arrest and execute her way back to the top. Sentenced to death by flaying, Kang Youwei and his closest follower, Liang Qichao, fled to Japan.

Although the Hundred Days of Reform of 1898 was dead, the idea that China needed to embrace Western-oriented change burrowed deep into China's soil, where it contended with the opposing view—that China should exterminate the foreigners and shut its doors to the West. A showdown was coming.

●

CHAPTER SEVEN

Bible Women

On a clear morning in May 1865, Adele Fielde landed in the British colony of Hong Kong after a stormy 149-day voyage on a tea ship from New York. A friend had squeezed Fielde, suffering from a high fever, into her wedding gown, and now she waited unsteadily on deck for her fiancé, a Baptist missionary named Cyrus Chilcott. They had planned to meet in Hong Kong, marry, and then head to Bangkok to preach to Chinese there.

A rowboat approached the ship but Chilcott was not on board. Typhoid fever had struck him down, the boatmen told Fielde, who now found herself, she would write later, "in appalling desolation alone on the shores of Asia." The ship's captain advised her to return to the United States. She set out for Bangkok instead.

A farmer's daughter, born in 1839 in upstate New York, Fielde grew up in a time when the great social and feminist issues of the nineteenth century were rousing a generation. Women in the North fought slavery, and after the Civil War, they demanded opportunities. Women's colleges opened. By the time she was twenty-five, Fielde was the principal of a girls' school. Following Chilcott's death, the Baptists hired her as a missionary— one of the first single women to work as a missionary in Asia.

Because of Fielde and pioneers like her, the American missionary endeavor in China became a profoundly feminine one. Women, especially single women, would soon make up the largest share of American missionaries. Fielde's story illustrates the powerful ties that bound Chinese and

American women as the Qing fell and a Republican China struggled to its feet.

To Fielde and other pioneers like her, China offered freedom and opportunity at a time when educated American women faced limited career choices at home. American women were surgeons in China when they were denied entry into operating rooms in America. They chaired university departments when only a few of them were teaching at the college level in the United States.

Fielde and her American sisters also spearheaded the extraordinary advances that Chinese women made at this time. They helped unchain Chinese women from the home and attacked foot-binding, freeing them to move up in the world. American missionaries took the lead in educating Chinese girls and in providing them with role models for a new kind of life.

Women from other countries vied for influence in China: anarchists from Russia, revolutionaries from France. But none could match the Americans in their numbers and in defining what it meant to be a "new woman" on the cusp of a new century. Americans barged into China's classrooms, hospitals, kitchens, and bedrooms in their desire to fashion what Baptist missionary leader Lucy Waterbury Peabody called "a new woman abroad."

In Bangkok, Fielde moved into the home of her dead fiancé. Within a year, she was able to converse in the Chaozhou dialect spoken by the Chinese laborers and their families in Siam. As she gained fluency, she began to threaten the mission chief, a conservative Baptist named William Dean.

To Dean, missionary work was a battle for souls. He called himself "a warrior for God." His fellow missionaries were "reinforcements," and he vowed that he would fight for Jesus until he ended in a "soldier's grave." He wanted Fielde to stand on a street corner and harangue passersby. But Fielde, who regarded missionary work more as farming than fighting, considered Dean's war a folly.

In October 1868, she summed up the work of Dean's mission in an open letter to her Baptist colleagues back home. Over the previous thirty-four years, she reported, Protestant missionaries in Bangkok had gained eighty converts of "dubious conviction." Could they ever succeed in Christianizing Asia this way? "It cannot be done," she concluded. A new model was needed. Education was important, but so were women missionaries. And they should be single. Only then could they could focus their undivided attention on their Chinese sisters and bring the Light into Chinese homes.

Fielde's letter infuriated Dean. She had already become a sensation among the Baptist faithful back home with her dramatic report of Chilcott's death and her sensitive portraits of the Chinese in Siam. In December 1869, Dean demanded Fielde's recall. She had begun fraternizing with Presbyterians, he disclosed. She had played cards and danced "with men who have the reputation of living unlawfully with unmarried women." She was, he claimed, "a wheel out of gear."

The Baptists ordered Fielde back to the United States for a hearing. On her way, she passed through the Chinese port town of Shantou, the hometown of many of Bangkok's Chinese. There she met a Baptist missionary, William Ashmore, who welcomed her idea of paying special attention to Chinese women as a way to win Chinese souls.

On January 18, 1872, authorities from the American Baptist Mission in Boston interrogated Fielde. The Presbyterians were not devilish, and card playing wasn't a sin, she argued. And when she danced, she was no farther from God "than when on my knees in prayer." The board's executive committee didn't like Fielde and her uppity kind, but it had to consider public opinion. Fielde was all the rage among American Baptist women. Churches across the country were clamoring for her to speak, and donations were pouring in. Besides, William Ashmore had officially requested that Fielde be transferred to Shantou. A day after hearing Fielde's case, the executive committee cleared her name. By the fall of 1872, after a six-month speaking tour across America, Fielde was in Shantou.

The Shantou station in the hills above the town consisted of two large typhoon-resistant houses and a chapel. From there, Fielde traveled through nearby villages, seeking out willing women and teaching them to read. Raised in the Chinese tradition of memorization and storytelling, many proved to be quick studies. Among these women, Fielde told her American readers, was "Goldgetter," a totally illiterate forty-two-year-old who within ten months could read a hundred hymns, the four Gospels, and the book of Acts. "Speed," the daughter of a Chinese Christian, could "hold the attention of a congregation of heathen women for hours at a time." The Chinese gave Fielde a name, too: Sister Fei, or "Elegant Female Missionary."

Within a year, Sister Fei had started a school, The Path of Brightness, which constituted the first formal literacy program for women in modern Chinese history. She called her students "Bible women." Fielde broadened the curriculum to include hygiene, child care, basic medical skills, and geography, so that her missionary work began to resemble less an evangelical enterprise than an early version of the Peace Corps. "I desire to do good, but I do not wish to be pious," Fielde said. Hard-line Baptists considered that blasphemous, but they kept quiet. Back in America, Fielde was a fundraising dynamo.

The Path of Brightness started a handicrafts section, teaching women needlework so that they could support themselves. The industry grew to employ hundreds of thousands of women in southern China and transformed Shantou into an export powerhouse.

In May 1877, in Shanghai, Fielde became the first woman to address a nationwide Protestant missionary conference, speaking about "Bible women." Though a few American male missionaries walked out in protest at a woman being allowed on the dais, the conference formally backed the idea of bringing more single women to China. In a few years, more than 60 percent of the American missionaries in China would be women and more than half of them would be single.

Fielde's open letters to American churches were so popular that they were collected in a book called *Pagoda Shadows*, published in 1884. The first edition sold out in a week, and it went through six printings. In it, Fielde described Chinese dress, weddings, festivals, funerals, and medicine. She referred repeatedly to the low regard in which Chinese society held its women; the torture of foot-binding; how Chinese women became property when they married; and how they obtained power in the family only by bearing sons.

Fielde surveyed 160 of her Bible women and found that they had personally killed 158 unwanted baby girls and not a single boy. Fielde and other missionaries set out baskets beside lakes with a note: "Place your babies here. Do not throw them into the pond."

There was nothing either obvious or inevitable about America's abiding fascination with the Middle Kingdom, but American women were entranced by Fielde's China with its rich tableau of exotica and its universal humanity. Fielde had succeeded in her goal: to create a bond between American and Chinese women. When she visited America in 1882, she was again deluged with requests to speak.

While on furlough in America, Fielde enrolled at the Women's Medical College of Pennsylvania, to study surgery and obstetrics. She had concluded that China needed fewer missionaries and more doctors, scientists, and engineers. China's infant mortality rate at the time was about 50 percent. Often, simple improvements such as hot water and soap could save the life of a newborn and its mother.

Armed with a medical degree, Fielde returned to China in 1885 but she would not stay long. The long hours, the diseases, and the frustration weighed on her health and her spirit. Her heart had also moved on. Charles Darwin and the principles of modern science had trumped Baptist doctrine. And she concluded that America needed her more than China did. Fielde left missionary work in 1889 and became a nationally renowned researcher in the United States, a specialist on ants, a leading proponent of the theory of evolution, and a suffragette. When she passed away in 1916, the Northern Baptists did not favor her with an obituary. For them, she had died when she left China in 1889.

Fielde's legacy lived on. Eight years after Fielde first arrived in China, Lottie Moon, the daughter of wealthy plantation owners in Virginia, traveled to rural Shandong to teach for the Southern Baptists. Like Fielde, she violated all the Baptist rules for female conduct. She lived alone in a Chinese village. She preached to Chinese men, and she demanded that women be allowed to become ministers—a prayer that to this day the Southern Baptists have not answered. Moon died in China on Christmas Eve 1912 at the age of seventy-two.

Where the Northern Baptists had ignored Adele Fielde's death, the Southern Baptists fixated on Lottie Moon's. Starting with her first official biography, published in 1927, the claim was made that she was so in love with her Chinese converts that she gave them all her food and starved to death for China. Even though there is no factual basis for that story, the Southern Baptists launched the Lottie Moon Christmas Offering to commemorate her sacrifice. Since its inception, the campaign has raised more than $2 billion in one of the most lucrative fund-raising ventures of all time.

In 1896, two Chinese women opened a Western-style medical practice for women and children in Jiujiang, a small city on the Yangtze River in central China. Shi Meiyu and Kang Aide had just graduated from the University of Michigan's medical school, courtesy of the women's board of the Methodist Episcopal Church.

Shi and Kang would go on to found hospitals and clinics that treated thousands of women and children a year, inspire a generation of Chinese women to become physicians, and almost single-handedly create a new profession for women in China, nursing. They would be hailed as models for a new type of Chinese woman—independent, career-oriented, patriotic, and . . . single. Chinese writers sang their praises in essays, short stories, and poems. Marriage proposals flowed in from around the country. Kang Aide was pursued by—and turned down—one of China's presidents.

In the United States, Shi Meiyu was known as Mary Stone and Kang Aide as Ida Kahn. In the 1910s, heated debates raged in the dormitories of Smith College and other women's schools over who was the greatest living woman—Mary Stone of China or the social worker Jane Addams, the second female recipient of the Nobel Peace Prize, which she was awarded years later in 1931. Hundreds of Americans followed Kahn and Stone to the Middle Kingdom to devote themselves to the cause of the new China. The work they did inspiring both Americans and Chinese is another example of the deep ties uniting the two countries.

Ida Kahn was born in 1873 in Jiujiang to a family that did not want another girl. A friend suggested that instead of tossing her into a ditch, the family give the two-month-old baby to an American missionary who had recently come to town. Gertrude Howe had been raised a Quaker in a family of radical abolitionists. She had arrived in Jiujiang in 1872 as the first missionary sent by the Woman's Foreign Missionary Society of the Methodist Episcopal Church and had founded what would become the Rulison Girls' High School, one of China's best.

Most Western missionaries were happy to preach to the Chinese but lived apart. They hardly touched chopsticks, and their social and material lives revolved around the Montgomery Ward catalogue, July 4, Washington's Birthday, and Christmas. Howe was different. She mingled with the Chinese. Although unmarried, she adopted Ida and would go on to raise three more Chinese children, shocking her American colleagues, who did not allow her and her charges to live inside the missionary compound.

Mary Stone came into Gertrude Howe's life a few years later when her father, a merchant and a Christian, sent seven-year-old Mary to Howe's school. Another daughter, Anna, would follow her a few years later. Mary's father had not bound his daughters' feet. He had also decided that his daughters should become doctors.

By the early 1890s, Gertrude Howe had saved enough money to bring five of her best pupils to her alma mater, the University of Michigan. In 1892, she took them to Ann Arbor and tutored them in math, chemistry, physics, and Latin for the entrance exam. The medical school accepted Ida

Kahn and Mary Stone, the Methodists paid their tuition, and the young women graduated second and third in their class.

In 1896, the two graduates and Gertrude Howe returned to Jiujiang. Stone and Kahn were employed as missionaries at salaries higher than local missionaries but well below white ones. Hundreds of cheering towns-folk greeted their arrival, and scores lined up for medical attention even before the women had a chance to set up shop. In the first year, the pair treated more than six thousand patients and visited more than a thousand homes in the countryside. By 1901, they had raised enough money— mostly from a Chicago doctor named I. N. Danforth—to build a hospital. By 1903, Danforth Hospital was serving upward of five thousand patients a month and training hundreds of nurses, establishing the nursing profession in China.

In 1897, the reformer Liang Qichao met Kahn and wrote an essay upholding her as a paragon to be emulated by the new Chinese woman. Liang praised Kahn's unbound feet, her work ethic, and her love of China. He ignored Kahn's Christianity and described Gertrude Howe, not as a missionary but as the traveling "daughter of an American scholar-official" who had just happened upon Ida Kahn.

Liang's portrait of Kahn illustrated the reluctance among leading Chinese to acknowledge how much Western values such as Christianity had molded Kahn, Stone, and others like them. It also reflected a Chinese problem with accepting the idea that their compatriots could love both China and God at the same time. To Liang Qichao, practical Western knowledge of the type that Kahn had received could be divorced from its underpinning traditions. He anticipated the day when Kahn would have children for the motherland. That day would never come.

In the early 1900s, when large numbers of American women missionaries began coming to China, marriage was nearly universal among Chinese women. But together, American and Chinese women fashioned a new world that offered the latter the possibility of a career and an alternative to married life. Although American female missionaries were supposed to be priming their Chinese charges for a life of marital bliss with a Christian husband, the message became muddled because so many of the American women, like Howe, remained single themselves. Stone and Kahn and their Chinese sisters modeled themselves on what their American teachers, doctors, and adoptive mothers did, not what they said.

In 1919, the entire inaugural graduating class of Jinling Women's College of Arts and Sciences, an American-funded missionary school in Nanjing and the first university in China to grant bachelor's degrees to women, took an oath not to marry. "I loved to be alone, it was in general the attitude of the woman of our time," wrote Xu Yizhen, a member of that first class.

Many Chinese men were none too happy with the idea of tough-minded, self-reliant women. "The boys resent the girls' independence and refusal to fall in behind them," observed Matilda Thurston, Jinling's first president, who herself remained single after she was widowed in 1904. China's men would accept gender equality, Thurston quipped, as long as it was carried out "in proper subordination to men."

Kahn, Stone, Stone's sister, Anna, who had also returned from studies in America, and Gertrude Howe refused to subordinate themselves to men. In Jiujiang, just down the river from Nanjing, they created a special world. Mission reports described their home as a meeting place between East and West, an ideal toward which some Chinese and Americans had been striving for decades. It "fairly overflows with guests, native preachers and their wives; Chinese ladies who would not honor foreigners with their presence, officials and their retinue," read one report. A Chinese official sent his daughter 450 miles just to meet Stone, "for the inspiration she would receive."

In 1906, Anna Stone died of tuberculosis. At about the same time, Ida Kahn left Jiujiang for another city, where she and Howe would live until they died several decades later. As Mary Stone mourned her sister's death, a new American missionary entered her life.

Jennie Hughes was a red-haired American beauty. She and Stone spent the next forty years together. They shared a bed, were apparently lovers, and, as "aunties," raised five adopted children. Their relationship inspired admiration and the support of those around them, not least because Stone was clearly Hughes's equal. "The harmony—may I not say Christian love—existing between Miss Hughes and Dr. Stone," wrote Stone's benefactor, I. N. Danforth, "is something worth going a long way to see." To Stone, her relationship to Hughes was a microcosm of what a merging of America and China could be. The women called themselves "Gemini—the heavenly twins."

Like Adele Fielde and Lottie Moon, Stone was a crack fund-raiser. On furloughs in America, she would wow Methodist churchgoers across the country with her voguish slang and progressive flair. "Kipling would not have sung, 'Oh, East is East and West is West and never the twain shall meet' had he known Dr. Mary Stone!" wrote Mary Wilton in the *Christian Advocate* in July 1916. "In her, East and West have met with peculiar power."

Underlying Stone's particular allure was a serious purpose. She had studied American ideals; now she wanted Americans to practice them. The Methodists never did pay her equally, nor did they allow her to live inside the missionary compound. Every advance she made had to be wrested from the Methodists despite the hundreds of thousands of dollars she raised for them across the United States.

Stone and Hughes ultimately left the Methodist Church and struck out on their own. In 1920, they founded the Bethel Mission on the then radical principle of Chinese and American equality. The pair bought a ten-acre plot in Shanghai and built a high school, a three-story hospital, and a tabernacle. Americans employed at Bethel had a simple assignment: train Chinese nurses and missionaries and leave. As Hughes said, the time was coming when "this people called the Chinese . . . would do the work of bringing China to Jesus Christ."

Adele Fielde, Mary Stone, Ida Kahn, Gertrude Howe, and Jennie Hughes touched the lives of thousands of Americans and Chinese and hinted at the magic in the melding of the Beautiful Country and the Middle Kingdom. Reflecting that coming together, Mary Stone invariably dressed in a Western-style skirt and a Chinese top. She brought Western religion and medicine to China but insisted that the Chinese take ownership of both, preparing Chinese Christians and doctors for the day when their Western counterparts would be shown the door. Like Fielde, she insisted on the inseparability of modern science and religious faith. To that end, these women's legacy is a reminder to both peoples that the quest for modernity cannot succeed without a belief in something more.

CHAPTER EIGHT

The Door Opens and Shuts

In 1899, diplomat William Woodville Rockhill returned to Washington after a dead-end posting in Greece. A thirty-five-year-old Philadelphian who had grown up in France, fought in the Foreign Legion, run a ranch in New Mexico, and served in St. Petersburg, Constantinople, and Beijing, Rockhill was given a special job. He was to serve as Secretary of State John Hay's adviser on East Asian affairs.

That the then tiny State Department (it had a workforce of eighty-six people, many of them clerks) would even care about Asia underscored a sea change in the American attitude toward the Far East. A year earlier, the United States had annexed Hawaii. And in December 1898, at the height of the Spanish-American War, President William McKinley, moved by what he said was "Providence," had ordered the invasion of the Philippines and seized Guam. China suddenly did not look so far away.

The end of the nineteenth century was a period of excitement in America. The country had recovered from an economic downturn in the 1880s. The population now stood at seventy million, and the nation had expanded to the edge of the continent. Yankee agricultural and manufacturing exports coursed throughout the globe.

American thinkers were proud of their nation's growing power but anxious that without new markets, America's factories would overproduce and precipitate an economic collapse. Alfred Thayer Mahan, a former US Navy officer who struck up a close friendship with a young Teddy

Roosevelt, argued in *The Influence of Sea Power on History* that only a mighty navy could provide the military muscle to support increased trade and national strength. Mahan urged Americans to turn their gaze toward the Far East as the primary locus of the coming world struggle. To him, Hawaii and the Philippines were the stepping-stones to China, a "carcass" destined to be devoured, he wrote, by Western "eagles."

After languishing for decades, American trade with China had picked up, accompanied by the usual overblown enthusiasm. China in the 1890s was buying half of America's cotton exports—much of it going to Manchuria. American kerosene, wheat flour, iron, and steel also flowed to Asia. America's trade with Hong Kong doubled in 1898.

In economic terms, America and China had swapped places. At the turn of the twentieth century, China, which had once made one-third of all the products in the world, now manufactured barely 6 percent, while America accounted for nearly one-quarter of such output. America's rapturous enchantment with the idea of the China market returned. But now, instead of calling for a railroad to control commerce from the Middle Kingdom, American business, backed by Mahan, demanded a canal. The National Association of Manufacturers, founded in 1895, pushed the US government to cut a waterway through Central America to speed American exports to the Far East. The Panama Canal would be completed in 1914.

American business also lobbied the US government for help in China. In January 1898, the *Journal of Commerce*, the most prominent business paper at the time, slammed the McKinley administration for ignoring the China trade. Europeans and Japanese were blocking the sale of American goods there, and if the US government did not do something about it, the paper thundered, it would amount to "the most colossal blunder in the history of the foreign policy of the United States." Business organizations called on Washington to ensure an "open door" to China.

American businessmen and strategists were responding to a challenge. In the 1890s, Germany, Russia, Britain, France, and Japan had all appropriated more Chinese territory. From the south to Manchuria, China was being carved up. "All of Europe is seizing China," warned Henry Cabot Lodge, a senator from Massachusetts who represented New England's textile magnates. "If we do not establish ourselves in the East, that vast trade, from which we must draw our future prosperity . . . will be practically closed to us forever." Lodge and others demanded that America stop the partition of China.

It was against this backdrop that William Rockhill began to consider the future of America's relations with China. He was an unusual figure. Six-feet-four with a shock of red hair and a mustache right out of *The Three Musketeers,* Rockhill was the scholar-diplomat-adventurer of his time. Over several decades in the State Department, he would alternate bloodcurdling adventures to Tibet and translations of ancient Tibetan scrolls with hard-nosed diplomacy. After reading Rockhill's account of a journey through Mongolia, his friend the writer Henry Adams wrote to him: "It is as though I had lived on intimate terms with Marco Polo, and had Genghis Khan for dinner." Yet unlike Anson Burlingame, Rockhill admitted to no affection for the Chinese. "I have never met in my life more than one or two Chinamen who were gentlemen at heart," he admitted to a friend, "but I have got to grin and bear it." Rockhill struck terror into the hearts of his colleagues at the State Department. They called him "big chief."

Along with US business, the British government prodded the United States to do something for China. While England wanted to keep its Chinese colonies and concessions, it also sought to ensure that its merchants were not excluded from other parts of the Middle Kingdom. So Rockhill's British colleagues approached him to argue that the United States, as the only power with no territory in China, was uniquely positioned to halt the country's dismemberment. America should demand that China's ports be open to trade from all nations. All goods should be subject to the same tariffs, and all vessels should be treated equally.

Persuaded, Rockhill got Hay's permission to draw up some notes on the relationship with China. Working out of the swank confines of the recently opened Holland House Hotel on Fifth Avenue at Thirtieth Street in New York, he reiterated what had been a consistent American stance since the Treaty of Wangxia of 1842 and Humphrey Marshall's addendum a decade later: that trade should be open to all and that China's stability was in the interests of the United States. As he wrote to a British friend, he wanted the United States to make "a pledge on our part to assist in maintaining the integrity of the Empire." Rockhill called on each of the powers in China to eliminate the preferential treatment of their citizens and their nation's products within their spheres of influence. He wanted no extra tariffs on any goods anywhere in China.

Rockhill's goal here was not so much to boost America's China trade. He was actually a tepid promoter of US business in China. He earned the lasting enmity of railroad magnate E. H. Harriman when he refused to get the Qing court to open up the Forbidden City to Harriman and his entourage during a 1905 trip to Beijing. Rockhill's aim instead was to use the Open Door to protect the territorial integrity of China, which he, like other Americans, viewed as vital to long-term US interests in Asia. The ideas undergirding Rockhill's memorandum were generous, high-minded, and even somewhat protective of China, but they were also backed up by nothing more than the force of public opinion.

In late August, Rockhill sent his notes to Secretary of State Hay. On September 6, with President McKinley's approval, Hay dispatched a text identical to Rockhill's draft to the Western powers and Japan. One by one, the foreign powers agreed to an "Open Door" with China. "It was like asking every man who believes in truth to stand up," observed the American diplomat George Kennan. "The liars are obliged to be the first to rise."

In November, news of the agreement broke, accompanied by a gusher of praise. The *New York Times* declared it "a noble work of peace" and "a victory for civilization." The *Review of Reviews* called it "one of the greatest achievements ever won by diplomacy." The *Independent*, a New York magazine, credited the United States with halting the division of China.

While Americans congratulated themselves on their moral fiber, the Chinese were justifiably perplexed. As in the case of the Burlingame Treaty, the Americans had not consulted the Qing court about the new policy. But once they digested it, the Chinese assumed that if the other great powers tried to slam the door shut, America would keep it ajar. Thus was born another great expectation. America's commitment would be tested soon enough.

At 9:00 a.m. on August 15, 1900, twenty Chinese soldiers came to the door of an American missionary compound in a dusty county seat in central China and escorted two American families away. Every man, woman, and child from the township, Fenzhou, had turned out to watch the foreigners leave.

The Americans were being expelled from Fenzhou at the height of the Boxer Rebellion, a bloody antiforeign crusade born in Shandong province in response to Western land grabs and other depredations. The Boxers, so named because they held that kung fu could repel bullets, blamed China's poverty on Western goods and technology. Exterminating the foreigners, they claimed, would bolster harvests, bring rain, and tame the Yellow River, which had roared over its banks in Shandong in 1898, wiping out fifteen hundred villages. Chanting "Sha! Sha! Sha!" (Kill! Kill! Kill!), followers of the Fists of Righteous Harmony poured across northern China.

Among the Americans leaving Fenzhou were Eva Jane Price, her missionary husband, Charles, and their daughter, Florence. After graduating from Oberlin College, the couple had lived in rural Shanxi province for eleven years. Now as the convoy carrying Price and her family snaked through fields and villages, it found no welcome. At each settlement, the village chief would pay the soldiers to move on. You cannot do it here, each chief would caution the soldiers; you cannot do it here. "If the Boxers come today, I want my little Florence to go before I do," Fei Qihao, a Christian convert in Fenzhou, overheard Eva say under her breath.

The Boxer Rebellion underscored China's tortured and often violent reaction to modernity. By May 1900, the Boxers had streamed north to Manchuria and west into Shanxi and Zhili provinces. They tore up railroad tracks, ripped down telegraph wires, and burned churches. They slaughtered Westerners and Chinese Christians, including the father of Dr. Mary Stone. The Boxers blamed foreigners for China's drought. They claimed that Westerners were hiring vagrants to poison village wells and that Western ships off China's coast carried a grisly cargo of Chinese eyes, blood, and nipples.

As the rebellion gathered steam, Western envoys took little notice. In Washington, William Rockhill assured Secretary of State John Hay on June 1 that the rebellion would fizzle. "I cannot believe the Boxer movement will be very long-lived or cause any serious complications," he wrote. "The day the Chinese authorities choose to put an end to it, they can easily do so."

Instead, the Chinese authorities chose to incite the rebels, providing them with officers and arms. After experimenting with reforms, the court of the Empress Dowager Cixi had swung in a more truculent direction. The Westerners must be eliminated, Cixi declared, or at least thrown into the sea. On June 5, the Boxers cut the railroad from Tianjin to Beijing. The Qing army joined their ranks and five days later, the telegraph lines were severed. The last cable from the US legation read: "We are besieged in Peking."

The next fifty-five days were filled with hunger, fear, death, and heroism for the 435 soldiers and 3,000 foreigners and Chinese Christians trapped together in the diplomatic quarter in the capital. The besieged lived on the meat of polo ponies, washed down by champagne that had been cellared for summer parties. Dysentery raged. The stench of rotting bodies and unwashed soldiers filled the air.

On June 19, the Zongli Yamen delivered an edict to all eleven foreign ministers in Beijing, severing relations with the Western powers and Japan and declaring war on foreigners. The Qing authorities promised all the embassies in Beijing free passage out of the country. But when Chinese troops killed the German minister the following day, the Westerners decided to stay put.

Billeted at the American embassy to the south of Legation Street, fifty US Marines were tasked with stopping the Chinese from gaining access to the sixty-foot-high and forty-foot-wide Tartar Wall that loomed over the foreign ghetto. If the Chinese were able to scale it, the Westerners below would be sitting ducks. During one firefight, Private Dan Daly, a five-foot-six Irish American from Manhattan's rough-and-tumble Five Points neighborhood, found himself alone behind a low stone parapet. As the Chinese attacked in ones and twos, Daly picked off two hundred of them. For his deeds, he won the Medal of Honor, one of thirty awarded for the mission.

When the siege began, Frank Gamewell, a Methodist minister from Camden, South Carolina, had been teaching physics at a missionary school in Beijing. He ended up designing the legation's fortifications. Cruising the makeshift fortress on his bicycle, Gamewell oversaw the construction of barricades eight feet thick and ordered trenches dug twelve feet deep to defend against underground mines. Following Gamewell's plans, Western women stuffed more than 150,000 sandbags made from satin curtains, monogrammed linen sheets, brocades, and tapestries.

When the court in Beijing ordered its forces in southern China to attack foreigners there, a group of mandarins turned to Viceroy Li Hongzhang. In punishment for negotiating the Treaty of Shimonoseki, Li had been banished to the southern metropolis of Guangzhou. "Ignore the orders," Li declared. Secret negotiations then ensued between the US government and the officials. The result was the Yangtze Compact, which confined the war to northern China and saved innumerable Western and Chinese lives.

On July 3, the mandarins in the south told Secretary of State John Hay that the United States was China's only hope for stopping an all-out war. Hay responded that same day, insisting that the United States did not consider itself at war with China. In a circular to all the treaty powers, the American secretary of state spelled out Washington's interests: China's territorial integrity must be maintained. The goal, he said, remained "equal and impartial trade with all parts of the Chinese empire." As Hay wrote to his friend Henry Adams: "The thing to do, the only thing, was to localize the storm."

Hay's circular, of course, flew in the face of the facts. The United States *was* at war with China. Just hours before he had issued the note, US and

British marines and Russian sailors had conducted a lightning raid on Imperial Army positions on the Tartar Wall, killing scores of Chinese Muslim fighters. In celebration the next day, US minister Edwin Conger pulled a bullet-riddled copy of the Declaration of Independence off the wall of the embattled American legation and read it to Americans gathered around the building's front steps.

Still, it is hard today to appreciate how important keeping China whole was to the Americans. Secretary of War Elihu Root told his wife that the partition of China "would be second to no event in its effect upon mankind since the fall of the Roman Empire." Preserving China was considered essential to the fortunes of the United States. The idea that a vast Chinese market awaited America's merchants had penetrated deep into the minds of capitalist America. And the belief that only a unified China would ensure stability in Asia undergirded the thinking of Yankee strategists as well.

In Shanxi, as the Boxer menace loomed, Eva Jane Price and her husband, Charles, had wanted to escape, but those plans went awry after thieves stole their supplies. "Our hearts have grown faint one hour to be lifted again the next," Price wrote. On July 9, in the provincial capital of Taiyuan, a mob slaughtered forty-four missionaries and their wives and children. In Fenzhou, the local magistrate posted a proclamation banning the mistreatment of Christian missionaries one day, and announced his support of the Boxers the next.

Reports of the rebellion dominated newspapers in the United States, overshadowing news of the upcoming presidential election that pitted McKinley, with Teddy Roosevelt as his running mate, against William Jennings Bryan. The *New York Sun* called the upheaval "the most exciting episode ever known to civilization." On July 5, the *New York Times* reported "All Foreigners in Peking Dead."

In Washington, Chinese minister Wu Tingfang discounted that news. He arranged for the State Department to send a telegram to Edwin Conger, the US minister, through the headquarters of a Manchu general in Beijing who had opposed the siege. Conger replied, begging for "quick relief." Some in Washington doubted that the reply actually came from Conger, but when Hay asked him for the name of his sister and got "Alta" in response, the minister's identity was confirmed.

Wu Tingfang brought McKinley a personal message from mandarins in the south, placing "special reliance" on the United States to restore order and keep China whole. Meanwhile, US forces and those of seven other nations mustered along China's coast and girded to lift the siege.

It was not easy for McKinley to spare troops for China. An insurrection was raging in the Philippines, and editorial writers at home argued that the United States, in sending an army to China to fight, was sinking to the level of Old Europe. But American business had made its position clear: it was America's job to keep China open for trade, and so a military operation was required. With an election approaching in November, a probusiness presidency bowed to the interests of its favored constituency.

Still, the United States had to maintain the fiction that it was not at war with China. It called its operation the China Relief Mission. To lead it, McKinley picked General Adna Chafee, a mustachioed veteran of the Civil, Indian, and Spanish-American Wars. "What I want," the president wrote to his commander, "is the friendship of China when the trouble is over."

On August 14, the armies of eight nations closed in on Beijing. The British marines broke the siege, followed by the Russians, the Americans, and the Japanese. The imperial family, with Cixi at its head, fled Beijing on "an inspection tour" to western China. Among the 435 foreign soldiers who had been trapped inside the embassy district, nearly half had been either killed or wounded. Seven US Marines were dead.

A day after the siege of Beijing was lifted, the convoy that carried Eva Jane Price, her husband, and Florence out of Fenzhou finally reached a village where the local chief refused to pay the soldiers to move on. And there, under a cloudless sky, amid the dust of a summer racked by drought, the escorts in their red-trimmed green uniforms massacred the missionaries and their families. Hiding in a field of head-high sorghum, Fei Qihao, who had fled after two soldiers tipped him off, heard the first shots. The bodies of Price, her child, her husband, and their friends were then dumped into a gully filled with stones.

"My heart was pierced with grief as I saw the sad plight of my friends, but I could do nothing for them," Fei wrote later. In his bag, Fei carried a letter from Price to her family in Iowa. "Dear, dear Home Folks," it began. "We are all expecting to die and God is giving us grace. . . . Were I to write a whole book I could not tell of our dreadful suspense of the past six weeks." It was a letter from the dead.

No sooner had they beaten the Boxers than the foreign armies proceeded to loot. German and French forces, which had barely engaged in any fighting, launched scores of punitive expeditions, robbing, raping, and slaughtering innocent Chinese.

"Where one real Boxer has been killed since the capture of Peking, fifty harmless coolies or labourers on the farms, including not a few women and children, have been slain," wrote the American commander, General Adna Chafee. "The 'disciplined armies of Europe,'" wrote William Rockhill, whom President McKinley had sent to China to negotiate a deal, "are everywhere conducting operations such as the Mongols must have done in the 13th century."

The British auctioned off pilfered antiques outside their Beijing embassy every afternoon except Sunday. The British ambassador's wife amassed the largest stash. Next was Herbert Squiers, a first secretary at the US mission who, with his heiress wife, Harriet, had been the social center of the American diplomatic community before the rebellion. When Squiers and his family left Beijing in September, they took along a collection of looted art that filled several railroad cars. It was displayed at the Smithsonian Museum before being sold at auction.

In the midst of the havoc, Wilbur Chamberlin of the *New York Sun* got hold of a story that prompted a national conversation in the US about what Americans were doing in China. On October 14, 1900, the reporter dined at the Beijing home of William Ament, a mustachioed preacher with an uncanny resemblance to Teddy Roosevelt. Ament had recently commandeered the house from a Manchu prince named Duanfang on the flimsy grounds that the man's relatives had killed Chinese Christians. In fact, Duanfang had distinguished himself by *saving* Christians as governor of a northern Chinese province. As Chamberlin reported in a dispatch that ran on Christmas Eve 1900, Ament and a fellow American missionary, E. G. Tewksbury, had appointed themselves judge and jury and were traipsing around the Chinese countryside, expropriating not just houses but vast swaths of Chinese land to punish alleged Boxer sympathizers. Chamberlin contrasted the purported piety of the American missionary set with the pair's irreligious greed.

The writer Mark Twain had recently returned to the United States after a decade in Europe. When he read Chamberlin's report, he let fly with an article in February 1901 that excoriated Ament and all American missionaries as the front men for imperialism. Twain's essay, "To the Person Sitting in Darkness," published in the *North American Review*, was an acid indictment of all the shenanigans that accompanied Western expansion: land grabs, unequal treaties, concessions, massacres, talk of "the white man's burden" and "manifest destiny." It raised several basic questions: Why did Americans feel compelled to "save the heathens," especially the Chinese?

Shall we "go on conferring our Civilization upon the peoples that sit in darkness," he asked, "or shall we give those poor things a rest?"

Ament had acknowledged disciplining an entire Chinese village for the actions of one resident. Such punishment was appropriate, he claimed, because it was what the Chinese did. To which Twain replied that perhaps the Ten Commandments should be revised to read: "Thou shall not steal— except when it is the custom of the country." Twain had been close to Anson Burlingame and believed, like the late minister, that Americans would do best if they stopped trying to remake the Chinese and just leave them alone.

The American public, already suspicious of their country's imperialist ventures, welcomed Twain's argument. The *New York Times* backed him in an editorial. The *Boston Evening Transcript* wondered what good America's evangelists were doing in China.

Still, American missionaries remained unbowed and once again saw in war the chance to prepare China for a "blitzconversion." As Earl Cranston, a Methodist bishop, told a congregation in Denver on June 17, 1900, the Boxer Rebellion was "worth any cost in bloodshed if we can make millions of Chinese true and intelligent Christians."

In September, four hundred Western preachers gathered in Shanghai to demand educational reforms, a radical revision of the legal system, a cash payment to foreign and native Christians, and jail or exile for all participants in the rebellion, including the Empress Dowager Cixi. They wanted Emperor Guangxu, of the Hundred Days of Reform, restored to the throne and China's foreign affairs to be run by Westerners. But McKinley and his secretary of state, John Hay, were not listening. While the missionaries howled for vengeance, cotton manufacturers petitioned the president to conclude the negotiations quickly and get back to what they believed was the business of America in China—business. Since the rebellion, American textile mills had been operating at half volume. And meanwhile, the Russians were creeping into northern China, threatening a lucrative American market.

McKinley and Hay were more concerned with stopping China's partition and ensuring American profits than with transforming China into a little America. They ordered Rockhill and Conger to ignore the missionaries and parry European and Japanese attempts to benefit from the crisis. Rockhill quickly emerged as the pivotal arbiter in the Conference of Ministers, which began talks with the Qing court.

On September 7, 1901, the Manchus and the Western powers signed the

Boxer Protocol. Rockhill successfully turned aside a German demand that all Chinese officials who had supported the uprising be put to death; only four midlevel mandarins lost their heads. He also prevented the construction of an international fortress next to the Forbidden City and substantially lightened China's indemnity. In the end, China was required to pay 335 million gold dollars (about $7 billion today), 30 percent below earlier demands. America claimed the smallest share—7.5 percent. Russia and Germany together demanded almost half.

Western powers won the right to station troops in north China. The US Army would dispatch the Fifteenth Infantry Regiment to Tianjin, where it became known for its outstanding commanders, such as George Marshall and Matthew Ridgway, and for the highest rates of alcoholism and venereal disease in the service.

The US government also directed Rockhill to press the Qing to reform the way it treated Western business. The United States asked the Chinese to open their country to American investment, create a stable national currency, and protect American trademarks—the same issues that preoccupy the two nations' trade relations today. In 1903, the two countries signed their first commercial treaty.

Upon her return to Beijing, the Empress Dowager took her first train ride. Heeding the advice of Li Hongzhang and other viceroys, she once again embraced reforms and wooed the West. She cultivated a friendship with Sarah Conger, the American minister's wife. She held afternoon teas in the Forbidden City and had her portrait painted by an American artist, Katherine Carl, who became the only Westerner to live inside the Forbidden City during the empire's last days. Carl wrote a laudatory book about Cixi, describing her "unusually attractive personality," her love of dogs, and her loyalty to her staff.

Cixi dispatched delegations to Japan and the West to study how China could be changed. In 1902, she banned the practice of foot-binding. In 1905, the Qing court abolished the traditional examination system. Henceforth, a career in government would be based on a mastery of Western concepts, not of the Confucian classics. In China's schools, American principals emphasized physics, math, English, and chemistry. In Guangzhou, an old civil service examination hall was demolished to make way for a college. Opium was banned, at least on paper. And there was talk of a constitutional monarchy.

The bleak outlook of the Boxer summer gave way to an equally irrational hope among Americans that a golden age of Christian reforms had arrived. Harlan P. Beach, an American missionary who had proselytized in China for twenty-five years, summed up the excitement. He and his colleagues, he wrote, could "scarcely believe our senses."

After the Boxer talks ended, Li Hongzhang stayed in Beijing to rest. On November 7, 1901, he died at the Shenlian Temple, his residence in the center of the capital. He was seventy-eight.

On September 14, 1901, a week after the signing of the Boxer Protocol, William McKinley died after having been shot by an anarchist assassin on September 6. Theodore Roosevelt, who referred to the Chinese as "poor trembling rabbits," became president. Among Asians, he favored the Japanese. Only they could stand up to the Russians, he believed.

With the rebellion over, Secretary of State John Hay felt that the Chinese were not grateful for the deal his government had helped negotiate. "We have done the Chinks a great service," he huffed, "which they don't seem inclined to recognize."

There were reasons why the Chinese were not as appreciative as Hay would have liked. While Americans worked to keep China's door open, the United States had shut its own door to the Chinese. Here was a nation the Chinese had trusted, that had claimed to be in China's corner; now it was murdering, expelling, and banning Chinese.

In September 1903, a Chinese military attaché was out for a stroll in San Francisco when he was accosted by two police officers. Colonel Tom Kim Yung pulled out his papers, but the officers disregarded them. They punched the colonel in the face, fastened him to a fence by his queue, and eventually hauled him off to jail, where he was held for assaulting a police officer. Released later that night, Tom brooded over the indignity and the next day, September 14, gassed himself to death in his room at the consulate. His funeral a week later was the largest ever held in San Francisco's Chinatown.

On the evening of Saturday, October 11, 1903, US immigration authorities conducted a sweep in Boston's Chinatown, rounding up more than 250 Chinese. Only 5 were found to be illegally in the United States. Caught up in the raid was Feng Xiawei. Returning to China, he wrote about the humiliation of living in a racist America. Two years later, he downed a vial of poison in front of the US consulate in Shanghai and died in the street. Demonstrations in his honor rocked the cities of southern China.

Chinese immigrants began looking to the home country to protect their rights. In 1903, Chen Yikan, an editor with the *New China Daily* in Honolulu, suggested that Chinese on both sides of the Pacific join together to boycott American goods. Chen called on Chinese Americans to head to China to stir up opposition to America's exclusion policy.

In 1904, the US Congress made the Chinese Exclusion Act permanent in direct violation of its treaties with China. After that, the push for a boycott intensified. On May 10, 1905, the Shanghai Chamber of Commerce passed a resolution urging Chinese not to buy American goods.

In Guangdong province, boatmen on the Pearl River refused to transport American products. Rickshaw drivers turned away American passengers. On July 18, 1905, a mob surrounded the US consulate in Xiamen in Fujian province, yanked down the Stars and Stripes, and smeared it with excrement. In September, when Alice Roosevelt, the president's daughter, arrived in Guangzhou with Secretary of War Howard Taft on a cruise of the Pacific, protesters slapped posters throughout the city satirizing her. The US consul general further inflamed public opinion when he leaned on local authorities who arrested three anti-American activists.

The boycott was the first instance of Chinese around the world mobilizing in a political campaign. Developments in America resonated with China's urban youth, many of whom had been educated in American missionary-run academies. Between July and September, thirteen thousand people published pledges in a Shanghai newspaper, *Shibao*, not to buy American things. Activists churned out handbills, poems, essays, and at least six novels supporting the campaign.

Americans' "enormous tongues sharp as knives are relentlessly licking our countrymen's flesh," read one line from a poem titled "National Indignity." When, it asked, "will the Chinese people wake up?" A novel, *The Bitter Society*, disputed the notion that America was a land of opportunity, a refrain that the Chinese Communists would adopt during their many spasms of anti-American agitation in the decades to come.

America's treatment of the Chinese reinforced the ideas of Social Darwinism, then fashionable among China's educated elite. The yellow man and the white man were seen to be locked in a battle for survival. The old view that America was a potential ally was now counterbalanced with a sense that it was a present threat.

Visiting the United States in 1903, Chinese reformer Liang Qichao took pleasure in the "yellow peril" literature popular in America at the time. To him, it constituted a backhanded compliment. White men, he wrote, "are alarmed because our race cannot be restrained." Liang envisioned a day when the Chinese would rule America and Australia, too. Whites, he observed in an essay, "About the Future of the Chinese Nation," were arrogant and disliked hard work.

On his way to the United States from Japan in 1903, Liang stopped off in Hawaii and noted with some anxiety that the United States had turned the islands into a coal depot for the US Navy and a stepping-stone to Asia. Liang predicted that America would soon challenge Britain and Japan for dominance in the Far East. The Chinese needed to wake up. The rise of the United States, he wrote, opens "a new strategic era for China, Asia and the world." Liang was in Vancouver when President Teddy Roosevelt gave a speech on May 13, 1903, at the Mechanics' Pavilion in San Francisco, announcing America's intention of becoming a Pacific power. To thunderous applause, Roosevelt declared that "before I came to the Pacific Slope I was an expansionist and after having been here I fail to understand how any man . . . can be anything but an expansionist." Liang, however, was convinced that China, not the United States, should rule that vast ocean.

Liang's reaction combined alarm at America's rise with distress at China's phlegmatic response to the challenges from abroad. In the eyes of educated Chinese, the Beautiful Country was growing into a disruptive young power. A century later, many Americans would be writing the same thing about China.

Liang believed that for China to regain its lost glory, the nature of the "Chinese character" had to change. But, as he visited Chinese communities in twenty-eight American cities over the course of seven months, he turned away from the idea of constitutional monarchy or democracy as the remedy for China's ills. Liang became disenchanted with his fellow Chinese. They were too insular, loyal only to their families, not to a state. "We have a village mentality," he complained, "not a national mentality." Democracy in China, he predicted, would mean "national suicide."

What the Chinese needed, he wrote, was someone to rule them with "iron and fire to forge and temper our countrymen for twenty, thirty, even fifty years. After that we can give them the books of Rousseau and tell them about the deeds of Washington." With sadness, Liang abandoned his dream of a constitutional monarchy. "The Chinese people can only be governed autocratically," he declared; "they cannot enjoy freedom." Liang's views would find echoes in generations of Chinese who visited the United States and concluded that the Chinese were ill equipped for the freedom and responsibilities of the West. Soon after he returned from America, Liang looked elsewhere for inspiration. He began, he said, "to dream of Russia." He would not be the last to do so.

In Beijing, William Woodville Rockhill, now the US minister to China, demanded that the Qing court halt the anti-American boycott. On August 30, 1905, the authorities in Beijing banned further anti-American activities. Rockhill then turned his attention to Washington. The United States needed to mollify the Chinese. In October, President Roosevelt promised to moderate the behavior of US immigration officials. "We cannot expect China to do us justice unless we do China justice," the president told an audience in Atlanta. But Rockhill wanted a more substantial act of amity, something that would again bend the course of Sino-American history. He would get it soon enough.

Rockhill's influence was not confined to China proper. He also ushered in a century of American involvement in Tibet. In 1904, the thirteenth Dalai Lama, the spiritual and temporal leader of the Tibetan people, fled Lhasa following a British military expedition to the Tibetan capital launched in part to root out Russian influence. Just as they were in other parts of Asia, the British and the Russians were competing on the Roof of the World. The Dalai Lama, advised by an agent of the czar, escaped to Mongolia.

Thubten Gyatso was of peasant stock, born south of Lhasa in 1875. In 1878, he was recognized as the reincarnation of the recently deceased twelfth Dalai Lama and, after being schooled in Tibetan Buddhism, he took power in 1895.

From Mongolia, Thubten Gyatso searched for a Westerner to whom he could plead his case. In 1908, he learned that Rockhill had been posted to Beijing and spoke Tibetan. The Dalai Lama wrote to the American minister and asked him to intercede with the Qing court on his behalf. Their correspondence prompted Rockhill to take a five-day trip on foot and mule train to the sacred Wu Tai Mountain to meet the Dalai Lama on June 19, 1908, in the first official American contact with a Tibetan leader.

Rockhill had expected to find a disengaged aesthete with a "faraway meditative look." Instead, he was taken with the Tibetan leader, describing him in a report to President Roosevelt as "quick-tempered and impulsive" but also "cheerful and kindly" and "a most thoughtful host." Still, despite his warm feelings, Rockhill discouraged the thirteenth Dalai Lama from pursuing Tibetan independence or even autonomy from the Qing. Rockhill argued that China needed to stay whole. He advised the Dalai Lama to travel to Beijing and, as he wrote Roosevelt, "submit to his sovereign's command." He told the Dalai Lama that "Tibet is and must remain a portion" of the Qing empire.

Rockhill helped smooth the way for the Dalai Lama's visit to Beijing in September 1908 when the Tibetan leader was brought in on a special train and given an enormous welcome, with trumpeters, drummers, and a throng of bronze-skinned Tibetan monks. There, officials at the Qing court insisted that Tibet be governed, like any other Chinese province, by an official dispatched from Beijing. Chastened, the thirteenth Dalai Lama returned to Lhasa.

In 1911, China's Republican revolution erupted. By the following year Chinese forces had pulled out of Lhasa and the thirteenth Dalai Lama led Tibet as a de facto independent state until he died in 1933, buried upright in a vault filled with salt. Four years later a new Dalai Lama, named Tenzin Gyatso, was discovered in Qinghai province. He would have his own troubled story with the United States.

The Boxer Rebellion of 1899–1901 coincided with the emergence of the United States as an Asian power. The rise of America marked the addition of a new player in the relationship between the Beautiful Country and the Middle Kingdom to add to the merchants, missionaries, and adventurers who had dominated the story so far. This new player—the government of the United States—assumed the role of the guardian of China. Editorial cartoonists churned out a slew of images of a benevolent Uncle Sam protecting a shuddering Chinese sage against portly Europeans and high-collared Japanese.

But those at the center of a rising America, such as Secretary of State John Hay, knew that the US would have trouble filling this self-appointed role. Keeping China's door open, Hay predicted, would depend on America's willingness to defend China, and such will was in short supply. "We do not want to rob China ourselves," he wrote, "and our public opinion will not permit us to interfere, with our army, to prevent others from robbing her." This gap between America's tender concern for China and its reluctance to bleed to protect her would bedevil the relationship for decades.

The Boxer Rebellion also pitted those in America who sought to transform China against those who sought stability above all. The White House came down on the side of a stable China. More than eighty years later, in 1989, the United States would adopt a similar position after another massacre, this one also in Beijing.

●

CHAPTER NINE

Hot Air and Hope

The first Asian battlefield of the twentieth century was Manchuria.
After the signing of the Boxer treaty, Russian troops did not pull out of
China; they merely moved into China's northeast, sparking fears that
St. Petersburg, which had in the seventeenth century fleeced the Qing
court out of territory the size of California, was eyeing more.

Viceroy Yuan Shikai, who had replaced Li Hongzhang after his death
as the main driver of China's foreign policy, asked the United States to
negotiate Russia's complete withdrawal. But President Teddy Roosevelt
declined. Looking on from its colony in Korea, Japan watched as Russian
engineers built railroads in Manchuria and Russian settlers moved into
Chinese towns.

Tokyo had used China's Boxer indemnity to fund a massive military
buildup, and on February 8, 1904, Japanese forces launched a surprise
attack on the Russian fleet at Port Arthur, beginning the Russo-Japanese
War. In March 1905, Japanese and Russian ground troops clashed in what
was then the largest land battle in modern history. On May 28, the Japanese navy demolished the czar's fleet in a similarly titanic naval operation.

In Washington, Teddy Roosevelt rooted for Japan. He was a fan of
Bushido, the Japanese way of war, and had held jujitsu exhibitions in the
White House. "The Japanese interest me and I like them," he wrote a friend.
Japan, he said, was Asia's "natural leader." Wall Street supported Tokyo as
well, bankrolling its war effort to the tune of $200 million. A key reason

for both Roosevelt and American bankers was a shared aversion to Mother Russia. Roosevelt feared the czar's meddling in the Far East. Wall Street, led by financier Jacob Schiff, opposed Russia's mistreatment of the Jews.

Three days after the scuttling of the czar's navy, the Japanese, with Russian concurrence, requested that the American president intercede to end the war. In Beijing, Minister William Rockhill told the Chinese that although they were not invited to the peace negotiations, the United States would look out for their interests. The talks were set for the Portsmouth Naval Shipyard in Kittery, Maine.

With the Treaty of Portsmouth, Japan took Russia's commercial, mineral, and railroad concessions in the southern half of Manchuria, restricting Russia to the north. Roosevelt had entered the talks hoping to see Japan and Russia "locked in a clinch, counterweighing each other," as he put it. But the treaty finished Russia as an expansionist power in Asia for thirty years. Instead, the Land of the Rising Sun was born as a great Asian power, with Teddy Roosevelt as midwife.

Yuan Shikai and the Chinese press were livid as Japanese troops, businesses, and immigrants flowed into Manchuria. "It is truly as if our country were a guest whose affairs were to be managed by these nations which make arrangements together," one Chinese editorial remarked. For his performance in Portsmouth, Roosevelt was awarded the Nobel Peace Prize, a dubious honor when viewed from the vantage point of history.

As the US government tried to balance Japan and Russia, it also sought to mollify the Chinese. The Roosevelt administration understood that if America wanted to maintain influence in China, it needed to expunge the sins of American racism. Luckily for Roosevelt, some Chinese agreed.

In 1902, Liang Cheng, a graduate of Yung Wing's Chinese Educational Mission, was dispatched to Washington as Chinese minister to the United States. Before being yanked back to China in 1881, Liang had starred on the Phillips Andover Academy baseball team. When he met with President Roosevelt soon after his posting, the president asked Liang who had been the best player on his team. Dropping any pretense to Chinese modesty, Liang claimed the honor and the president guffawed. "From that moment the relations between President Roosevelt and myself became ten-fold stronger," Liang wrote.

A jovial rotund man with a handlebar mustache, Liang Cheng was the Chinese catalyst for the Boxer Indemnity Scholarship Program, the most consequential undertaking to open Chinese minds to Western learning until the US restarted the effort in the 1970s. Cultivating Yankee politicians and reporters, Liang helped engineer a program to fund the education of more than thirty thousand Chinese men and women, turning out Nobel laureates, rocket scientists, linguists, writers, philosophers, diplomats, military officers, economists, and historians. The plan served as a model for the US government's Fulbright Program, and, as its graduates returned to China to work, it cemented intellectual bonds between the Americans and the Chinese and ineradicably altered the course of China's modernization.

Naturally, the scheme came with Yankee strings attached. The Americans refused to allow the Chinese government to manage the money, and Teddy Roosevelt used the program to sidestep the Chinese request to pour US funds into China's economic development and defense. Still, China profited profoundly from the exchange. In the years before the Communist revolution of 1949, the US-educated scholars, scientists, and artists in China made up the backbone of the country's scientific and intellectual elite and served as the conscience of their nation.

Liang's first goal in Washington was reducing China's Boxer Indemnity. He tried to convince Secretary of State John Hay to let China pay in silver, not gold. Hay refused, though he did let a tidbit slip. He revealed to Liang that when the United States asked China for $25 million as its part of the Boxer Indemnity, it had inflated its claim as part of a plan to convince all the European powers to lower theirs. But when the Europeans had refused to budge, Hay had declined to lower the US fee.

Liang worked the halls of Washington. He gave interviews and speeches and badgered Hay. When Hay died in 1905 and Elihu Root took his place, the Chinese minister continued to lobby Root and other Americans, too.

Liang's push came at a good time. The 1905 Chinese boycott against America had worried the State Department. From Beijing, William Rockhill pushed his government to use Boxer funds to educate Chinese and soothe anti-American passions. Liang liked the idea and roped in American missionaries, including Arthur Smith, whose book *Chinese Characteristics* was for decades the most popular one on China in the West. On March 6, 1906, Smith lunched with Roosevelt at the White House. What better use could be made of the Boxer Indemnity than to educate the Chinese? he asked. It would show the Chinese that not all Americans hated them. And, predicted University of Illinois president Edmund J. James, in a confidential report to the president, it would guarantee America's "intellectual and spiritual domination of [China's] leaders."

In 1908, Congress set up a $14 million fund. In addition to providing scholarships, the money built Tsinghua University in Beijing, which would become one of China's premier centers of higher learning. The first fifty students came to America in 1909.

While America had now committed to educating China's best and brightest, it also continued to smooth Japan's rise in Asia. On November 30, 1908, Secretary of State Elihu Root signed a document with Japanese ambassador Takahira Kogoro that formally recognized Japan's special interests in Manchuria. In exchange, Tokyo vowed to slow Japanese immigration to the West Coast of the United States, solving a growing political problem for the White House. Roosevelt congratulated himself on the Root-Takahira Agreement calling it part of his plan "of constant friendliness and courtesy toward Japan."

In 1909, William Howard Taft became president, and US policy on China changed again. With his secretary of state, Philander Knox, Taft promised to "smoke out" Japanese and Russian influence in Manchuria. Unlike Roosevelt, Taft and Knox did not view Japan as a "Yankee brother." It had become a threat.

As part of what would be called "dollar diplomacy," Knox pushed financier J. P. Morgan and others to establish a firm called the American China Development Company to do business in China. Knox then convinced the Western powers and Japan to allow the company into an international banking consortium that controlled loans to the Qing court. The idea was that if American companies could get their share of projects in China, the US government would be able to keep the Open Door at least ajar. The problem was that the American China Development Company did little development. While Europeans and Japanese poured tens of millions into China, the only major loan the Americans floated was a paltry $7 million for a central China railroad project that the Americans walked away from. Yankee businessmen were simply not that interested in the China market. In the early years of the twentieth century, US exports to China dropped below its exports to Africa, and American sales to Manchuria, once so promising, collapsed. "What difference does it make whether the 'door' is open or shut," quipped William J. Calhoun, America's minister to China in 1910, "if we are not disposed to go in or out of it?"

US money would build a mere thirty-eight miles of Chinese railroad track, compared with hundreds of miles bankrolled by British, German, French, Russian, and Japanese funds. Diplomat William Rockhill complained that American capitalists simply wanted to trade the rights to Chinese projects as if they were stocks. He was correct. J. P. Morgan sold his stake in the Chinese railroad project to investors in Belgium for a handsome profit.

As it sputtered in China, US trade and investment boomed in Japan. In 1912, America became Japan's number one trading partner. Wall Street issued more than $100 million in new loans to Tokyo. In a Christmas greeting to President Taft that year, Willard Straight, who had first served as a diplomat in Manchuria and had once been bullish on China, seemed deflated. "I trust that someday we shall have something to show," he wrote, "besides hot air and hope."

The deaths of Cixi and Emperor Guangxu at the end of 1908 touched off a struggle over China's future. On her deathbed, the Empress Dowager had appointed two-year-old Puyi as China's emperor. But others wanted more than a new occupant of the Dragon Throne. One of those people was a medical doctor named Sun Yat-sen, known to his comrades as "the American."

Sun Yat-sen was the only major Chinese leader to ever pierce the invisible membrane between East and West and be truly conversant with both worlds. Where other Chinese politicians, such as the Communist Zhou Enlai, excelled at manipulating Westerners, Sun came closest to embracing their values. Of all China's leaders, he was America's greatest fan. He even fraudulently obtained a Yankee passport. So it is the greatest irony that Sun received so little support from the United States.

Sun was born in Guangdong province in November 1866. At the age of thirteen, he sailed to Sandalwood Mountain, as the Chinese called Hawaii, where his older brother, Sun Mei, ran a vegetable farm and a shop. Sun Yat-sen was put to work in the store and enrolled in school. Sun soaked up the basics of Christianity, democratic thought, freedom, and equality. He may have been born in China, but he would claim Hawaii as his spiritual home. "It was here," he told an audience in Honolulu, "that I came to know what modern, civilized governments are and what they mean."

Sun fell so hard for American culture that he asked his brother for permission to be baptized. Of Hawaii's fourteen thousand Chinese at the time, only five hundred were Christian. Sun Mei did not want his brother added to the flock, so he sent him back to China for rehabilitation. In his native village, Sun and a friend went to a temple and lopped off the arm of a temple god. After village elders ran him out of town, Sun ended up at the

College of Medicine in Hong Kong where he was baptized by an American pastor, Charles Hager. Hager christened him Yixian, pronounced "Yat-sen" in Cantonese. It meant "the fairy of tranquility."

Things, however, were anything but tranquil. In the lab at the College of Medicine, Sun dabbled in explosives and detonated a bomb on a Hong Kong street. Despite his extracurricular activities, he graduated at the top of his class in 1892. Sun started referring to himself as "a little Hong Xiu-quan," in honor of the Taiping leader. Two years after graduating, Sun was in a Methodist church in Shanghai when he met a man who would become his most steadfast sponsor.

Charlie Soong was the patriarch of another Chinese family firmly tied to the United States. In 1878, then fifteen-year-old Charlie journeyed to the United States to work for his uncle in Boston, where he met boys from the Chinese Educational Mission. Inspired by them and bored with his apprenticeship in a Chinatown curio shop, Soong stowed away on a US government vessel. The captain engaged him as a cabin boy and eventually Charlie moved with him to North Carolina. During a revival meeting on October 31, 1880, at the Fifth Street Methodist Church in Wilmington, Soong felt the spirit and was baptized Charles Jones Soon; he would later add the "g." The Methodists found a place for Soong in the home of North Carolina textile magnate and philanthropist Julian Carr, who sent his protégé to Trinity College, later renamed Duke University.

Soong found himself attracted to American girls, and they returned his interest. His letters are filled with details of various young women—Ella, Annie, Eula, and Rosamond. Short and swarthy with sensuous lips and a steady black-eyed gaze, he was known for his "exceptional sprightliness," in the words of one classmate. Like many Chinese in the United States, he was the brunt of racist pranks, but Charlie persevered, remaining, according to classmate Jerome Dowd, "very amiable."

In 1882, Charlie was tossed out of one house, after apparently tangling romantically with his host's daughter. He transferred to Vanderbilt University in Tennessee, where he studied to become a preacher. Soong did not impress Vanderbilt's Southern Methodist patriarchs. George B. Winton, the acting dean, called him a "harum-scarum little fellow, full of life and fun, but not a very good student." Still, the elders ordained Soong a deacon and sent him back to China. He landed in Shanghai on January 13, 1886, and went to work for none other than Young John Allen.

Allen took a dim view of Soong's hucksterish drive. He called Soong "terribly spoiled" and predicted that he would come to no good. With a Saint Nicholas beard that earned him the nickname "the great mandarin of the Methodists," Allen was happy to hobnob with China's high and mighty, but he was not about to grant any of his Chinese employees a salary equal to that of a white man. He dispatched Soong to nearby Suzhou as a native preacher at about one-third the pay of American missionaries.

Like many Chinese returning from America, Soong felt trapped between two worlds. He chafed at the idea of trading in his three-piece suit for a traditional Chinese cap and a gown. He hated his new queue. "I felt more homelike in America than I do in China," he confessed to an American friend.

When Soong bumped into another one of Yung Wing's graduates, his life changed again. The man introduced Soong to Ni Guizhen, a preacher's daughter descended from a prominent Ming dynasty official. Ni had studied the piano, spoke some English, had not bound her feet, and believed in God. The two married in the summer of 1887, and Soong was ushered into the ranks of Shanghai's elite.

In 1890, the first of six children was born to the couple. Their three glamorous daughters, Soong Ailing, Soong Qingling, and Soong Mayling, and their three sons, led by the number-crunching Soong Tse-ven, known as T. V. Soong, would become China's most famous family in the twentieth century.

Miffed at Young John Allen's efforts to shortchange him, Soong left the ministry and went into business. By 1894, the year he met Sun Yat-sen, he had abandoned his youthful vision of saving China through the word of God and had embraced revolution.

Sun Yat-sen and Charlie Soong had both studied abroad, tasting, as the Chinese said, "Western ink." They were both Hakkas and Christians, and they believed that for the Han Chinese to rid themselves of the Manchu occupation they needed an American-style revolution. Backed by Soong, Sun Yat-sen began to agitate for violent change.

On a moonless night in November 1894 in a bungalow on the border of Honolulu's Chinatown, twenty Chinese men placed their hands on a Bible and vowed to drive away the Manchus, "recover China for the Chinese, and establish a republic." The Revive China Society, founded in Hawaii, was China's first modern revolutionary organization. Sun Yat-sen passed the hat among his compatriots and collected $2,000.

Silver from Charlie Soong and overseas Chinese funded the first republican rebellion in China's history, the Canton Uprising of October 1895. Hatched in the Holy Church Bookstore at the front of an American Presbyterian chapel in Guangzhou, the rebellion fizzled when word of the plot leaked out. Qing authorities rounded up most of the conspirators and put them to death. Others escaped with American help.

Sun Yat-sen absconded to Hong Kong, thence to Hawaii and Europe with a $100,000 bounty on his head. In October 1896, Manchu diplomats kidnapped him in London. But as they readied to spirit him back to China, Sun escaped and wrote a book about the affair. On a trip to New York, he cowered in an elevator shaft on Canal Street to evade Cixi's assassins. Sun switched aliases the way others changed hats. He slunk into Japan as "Mr. Aloha from Hawaii."

Mentions of Benjamin Franklin, Thomas Jefferson, Andrew Jackson, and that great Confucian sage George Washington peppered Sun's speeches. Abraham Lincoln's "government of the people, by the people, for the people" became his mantra. The ideals of Progressive-era America—a democratically elected president, equal opportunity, female enfranchisement, the rule of law, and the separation of powers—became his ideals.

One of America's leading Progressives, Henry George, inspired Sun's economic policy, which was based on property taxes. A self-published book on the power of consumers by an obscure Brooklyn dentist named Maurice Williams also influenced him. Even Sun's proposed system of government melded China and the United States. Three of its branches, the executive, legislative, and judicial, were American born; the other two, the Examination Yuan (to select virtue) and Control Yuan (to stamp out vice), hailed from Confucius. Sun selected an American to write his first biography.

Still, like Liang Qichao, Kang Youwei, and other Chinese students of the West, Sun Yat-sen rejected a wholesale adoption of American values. American ideas should be used in China only to make China strong, not because they were inherently good. Sun took issue with the notion that men and women are born free and that the government's power should be limited. "The rights of the people are not born of Nature but are rather created and fostered by the circumstances of time and the trend of events," he declared.

Sun also held that the Chinese needed a period of tutelage under a benevolent dictator (himself) before they would be ready for the rigors of real democracy. "Only the Party has liberty. Individuals cannot have liberty," he told members of China's Nationalist Party, or Kuomintang, which grew out of the Revive China Society. Still, unlike China's Communists,

Sun always held up the promise of representative democracy even though it had to wait.

Sun issued a constant stream of appeals to the US government and individual Americans for assistance in his crusade. He promised Americans otherworldly interest rates on "revolutionary bonds," monopolies, and other sweet deals if they would invest in his dream of turning China into a republic. In New York in 1904, Sun spelled out his views on America and China in a self-published pamphlet: "The True Solution of the Chinese Question: An Appeal to the People of the United States." He told his American readers that "we intend to model our new government after yours. . . . We should look to America."

Sun appealed to Americans to set aside their fear of China and the odious "yellow peril" claptrap that threatened to weaken what he believed to be the natural affinity between China and the United States. "Above all," he wrote, "you are the champion of liberty and democracy." In a reference to the French marquis who aided the American Revolution, he concluded, "We hope to find many Lafayettes among you."

Sun Yat-sen's stable of American Lafayettes left something to be desired. A federal judge named Paul Linebarger, who had been posted to a court in the Philippines, left the bench to handle Sun's public relations. And then there was Homer Lea.

Born in Colorado in 1876, Lea was raised in Los Angeles. He was a sickly child with a prominent hunchback, the result of a fall as a baby. Like many Americans of his time, Lea broke with the violent racial hatred of the previous generation. Instead of repulsing him, Chinatown's exoticism drew him in.

Dropping out of Stanford University in 1900, Lea surfaced in China during the Boxer Rebellion. Back home, he hatched a scheme with exiled reformer Kang Youwei to train an army of Chinese Americans to overthrow the Qing. Military academies sprang up in twenty-one cities, and hundreds volunteered. Lea called his charges the Chinese Imperial Army and outfitted them in altered US Army kit.

Money rolled in from Chinatowns across the country. Lea's cadets marched in the sixteenth annual Tournament of Roses Parade in January 1905. "They swung up the street like West Pointers, perfect alignment and cadence, rigid as German dragoons," reported the *Los Angeles Times*.

Lea shared his scheme for a republican revolution in China with some American businessmen, who welcomed the prospect of a lucrative financial relationship with a new China. Sun Yat-sen encouraged them, pledging that his China would funnel all its trade through Yankee merchants if they contributed to his cause. Lea's coconspirators sought backing from Wall Street, but there they struck out. "I am ready to do business with any established government on earth but I cannot help to make a government to do business with," Wall Street financier J. P. Morgan told one of Lea's accomplices during a meeting in February 1909.

Lea held to the view—championed by Issachar Roberts—that what China needed was an American-style revolution. Instead of a "blitzconversion" to Christianity, however, he wanted China to become a republic. A republican China, allied with the United States, would turn the Middle Kingdom into a bulwark against what Lea believed to be the greatest Asian threat to America: Japanese imperialism. At a time when many Americans were still enamored of Japan, Lea bucked the trend, predicting war in his 1909 best seller, *The Valor of Ignorance*, between Japan and the United States. After meeting with Sun in the spring of 1910 at Lea's cottage in Long Beach, Lea pledged the royalties from the Japanese edition of his book to Sun's cause. Sun promised Lea lucrative economic concessions and a position in China's new government.

On October 10, 1911, revolutionaries launched another uprising to overthrow the Qing in the Yangtze port city of Wuchang, next door to Hankou. This time, officers in the Manchu army refused to crack down, and the rebellion spread.

While this tumult was electrifying China, Sun Yat-sen was in a hotel room in Denver on another fund-raising mission. There he received word of his likely election as China's first president. Sun found Lea in Wiesbaden, Germany, and ordered him to head to London to plead with the British for financial support for his new China. But no senior British official would meet with Lea. To the British, Sun was no revolutionary; he was, a Foreign Office report declared, "an armchair politician and a windbag."

Lea cabled officials in the Taft administration, requesting American assistance, but he got no response there, either. Lea and Sun met in France. The French were also unmoved. Before he departed Marseilles for Hong Kong, Sun introduced Lea to his supporters as "the greatest military theorist under Heaven."

Christmas Day 1911 found the pair in Shanghai. Lea told a reporter that he expected to be named chief of staff of the new Republican Army, prompting US officials to warn him that he risked imprisonment if he violated American neutrality laws. Lea brushed it off. "How could I just sit there and do nothing?" he asked one reporter. On January 1, 1912, Sun was sworn in as the provisional president of the Republic of China in the viceroy's office in Nanjing. The Qing dynasty was finished and Pu Yi became its last emperor. Lea was the only Caucasian to witness the event.

On February 11, as Lea was inspecting Republican Army troops, he suffered a stroke and fell off his horse. Three days later, he boarded a ship back to the United States. By October 1913, he was dead at age thirty-six. Republican China did not forget him. In 1969, Lea's ashes were interred in a military cemetery in Taiwan.

The Republican revolution ushered in another period of Chinese enthusiasm for the West. China adopted the Gregorian calendar, ending the imperial system of calculating time based on the emperor's reign. The new minister of foreign affairs wired a message to Chinese diplomats around the world: when in doubt, he advised, dress like an American.

Long viewed as a threat to Chinese culture, Christianity suddenly became a tool that China could use to recapture its greatness. On a tour of China soon after the revolution, the American evangelist Sherwood Eddy discovered a country abruptly enamored of Jesus Christ and trusting that, through him, China would gain salvation not only in the next life, but in this one as well. In just six days in the sleepy provincial capital of Fuzhou, Eddy addressed thirty thousand people. Government schools were canceled and exams delayed to allow students to soak up Eddy's message that Christianity and progress went hand in hand. When missionary John Leighton Stuart, the head of the newly formed Yenching University, attended a session of the new provisional National Assembly in 1912, he counted that 90 percent of the assemblymen were Western educated (mostly in America) and one-quarter were Christians.

China, which had spent the past forty years trying to run from the family of nations, was now sprinting straight toward it. "We are fighting for what Americans fought for," wrote Wu Tingfang, the former Qing minister to the United States who had joined the Republican forces.

American missionaries and businessmen welcomed the revolution. In May 1912, Huang Zhiji, a leading Christian from Fuzhou, was sent to the General Conference of the Methodist Episcopal Church in Minnesota to lobby for American support. He told a packed gathering that China's goal was to "establish in Asia a second United States." The audience jumped to its feet and broke into "My Country 'Tis of Thee." The convention urged the Taft administration to recognize the Republican government.

Americans were again taken with China's prospects. At a time when forward-thinking Yankees at home were rallying for women's voting rights, in China they pushed for female education and for democracy. Helping China was no longer exotic. It was the right thing to do. To travel there was, in the words of Margaret Speer, a graduate of Bryn Mawr and a professor at Yenching University, "no big deal." China, she wrote, was "opening up, people coming and going, more contact so that it was far away but never struck me as being dangerous." The president of the Remington typewriter company wrote the State Department asking, "Now that China has become a Christian country, how soon will it be before English becomes the national language?"

Sun Yat-sen may have been the president in Nanjing, but power was in the hands of Yuan Shikai in Beijing. While working as Li Hongzhang's military commander, Yuan had built the Beiyang Army into the most potent force in China.

Having no troops, Sun was forced to agree to Yuan's terms that China be united under a Beijing government and that Yuan would lead it. In February 1912, less than two months after becoming China's first president, Sun stepped down. On March 10, 1912, Yuan Shikai was sworn in as the second provisional president of the Republic of China.

In China's first-ever national parliamentary elections, held in the winter of 1912–1913, Sun's Nationalist Party won a majority of seats. After two millennia of imperial rule, China's first experiment with democracy had begun. Song Jiaoren, an expert on the American Constitution and a cofounder of the Kuomintang, was in line to become China's first democratically elected premier. On March 8, the provisional senate adopted Song Jiaoren's constitution, which granted broad powers to the parliament, limited presidential authority, and made every citizen, including Yuan Shikai, equal before the law.

At 10:40 p.m. on the night of March 20, 1913, as Song Jiaoren waited in Shanghai Railway Station for a train to Beijing to take up his post, an assassin gunned him down. Accused by his Nationalist foes of ordering Song's slaying, Yuan responded by issuing a plea for Christians in America to pray for China. Woodrow Wilson, the newly elected twenty-eighth president of the United States, took the bait and hailed China's Republican revolution "as the most significant, if not the most momentous event of our generation." Secretary of State William Jennings Bryan sent Yuan an encyclopedia on Thomas Jefferson, along with the "hope that this 'awakening' might produce a United States of China." On May 2, 1913, the United States became the first nation to grant Yuan's government full diplomatic recognition.

American officials were aware that Yuan was unhappy with China's provisional constitution and wanted more power. US officials and American visitors to China had suggested to Yuan that he engage an American legal expert to rewrite the document. Charles Eliot, president emeritus of Harvard, recommended Frank Johnson Goodnow, the first president of the American Political Science Association and a professor at Columbia University.

Goodnow was a rising legal scholar in the United States. Americans had already come to China as missionaries for God, science, and education. Now Goodnow was a missionary for American law. Arriving in Beijing in May, six weeks after Song's murder, he discovered a China where, he claimed, people "do not even know what law is." What China needed, he said, was a government where the top man would not be hampered by "vexatious restrictions" on his power. A dictatorship would do just fine. Goodnow's opinions represented an enduring strain in the American view of China—that it was a nation too backward to deserve the fruits of democracy. Decades later, many Americans would look to Communism instead of a monarchy as the cure for China's ills.

Goodnow fashioned a constitution that handed Yuan the clout he desired. He gave the president responsibility for foreign policy, declaring war, and the national budget. He reduced the legislature to an appointed body. Freedoms of speech and of association were not protected. Goodnow called Yuan a "progressive conservative," the right man at the right time for China. The alternative was not Sun Yat-sen, he concluded; it was chaos. Other prominent Americans agreed. In November 1912, Harvard's Charles Eliot told a conference at Clark University that he supported a Chinese dictatorship. Yuan should be a despot, Eliot said, because "it is necessary that it should be so."

In July 1913, the leaders of seven southern provinces, angry at Song's assassination and opposed to Yuan's tyrannical drift, rebelled against the president, beginning what the Chinese call the Second Revolution. American military officers advised Yuan's Beiyang Army, and US and British officials winked when Yuan dispatched troops into the International Settlement in Shanghai to root out the rebels.

Some worried that America was being too one-sided in its support of Yuan. In Shanghai, Consul Amos Wilder warned that "the underdog today may be the fellow-on-top tomorrow." He was almost fired for his remarks.

By September, Yuan's forces had crushed the Second Revolution, and Sun Yat-sen had fled China again, this time to Japan. On October 10, 1913, Yuan was sworn in as China's president. In his inauguration speech, George Washington's was the only foreign name he mentioned. He called Washington his "model" and said that he had accepted America as his "guide."

Yuan was no Washington. A month after taking office, he outlawed the Kuomintang and hounded its members from parliament, which he stacked with his allies. In May 1914, the parliament rubber-stamped Goodnow's constitution. In December, Yuan further lengthened the presidential term to ten years, with no term limits. "I must confess that on the whole I approve of what has been done," Goodnow wrote to the trustees of the Carnegie Endowment for International Peace on May 18, 1914. "An Asiatic people that has always had an autocratic government" deserved such a constitution, he said. Feeling that his work was over, Goodnow left China to assume the presidency of Johns Hopkins University in Baltimore.

Unsatisfied as merely president, Yuan sought to found a new dynasty. In July 1915, Goodnow returned to Beijing and provided Yuan with a memorandum sanctioning the restoration of a monarchy. China was too backward, Goodnow argued in "Republic or Monarchy?" for anything else. In August 1915, when Yuan announced his plans to call himself emperor, Goodnow publicly praised the idea. A monarchy was "better suited than a republic to China." Yuan bought space in Western newspapers touting Goodnow's memo. The *New York Times* reported that "urged by Goodnow," Yuan would ascend to the Dragon Throne. The US legation in Beijing was firmly behind the restoration. So was American business. John Van Antwerp MacMurray, on his first posting as an American diplomat to Beijing, stated that "if Chinese find it possible to reinstitute their traditional form of government . . . so much the better."

Liberal Chinese were crestfallen. Writing from Cornell University in *Outlook* magazine on September 1, 1915, Hu Shih, who would go on to become one of China's leading intellectuals, challenged Goodnow's notion that the Chinese were unequipped to handle democracy. "The only way to have democracy is to have democracy," he argued. "Government is an art, and as such it needs practice. I would never have been able to speak English had I never spoken it."

For China, there would be no practicing. On December 12, 1915, Yuan declared himself emperor. Numerous provinces rebelled, defying US legation predictions that the opposition was, in diplomat John MacMurray's words, "giving no evidence of any likelihood of serious resistance."

Only Yuan's health curtailed his reign. He died of kidney failure on June 6, 1916.

Goodnow refused to speak to reporters when he returned to the United States the second time. But his hometown newspaper, the *Baltimore Evening Sun*, had him pegged. It ran a cartoon depicting the professor as a carpenter helping Yuan dismantle China's infant republic.

Western historians have downplayed Goodnow's role, portraying him as the naive but generally harmless dupe of a would-be potentate. But Chinese constitutional scholars argue that as an American, he occupied a privileged place in providing the intellectual cover for Yuan's coup. Though far from blaming Goodnow for the political chaos that followed, these scholars, taking Hu Shih's lead, note that if the goal of Americans who backed Yuan's dictatorship was stable governance in China, they failed to achieve it. Yuan's gambit ended up indelibly tarnishing the office of the Chinese president. From 1916 until 1928, eight presidents, twenty premiers (one man served five different times), and twenty-four cabinets would attempt to govern China as dozens of wars flared.

The chaos touched off by the Republican revolution prompted many Chinese scholars to turn away from democracy. Kang Youwei had once invoked George Washington in urging Emperor Guangxu to embrace constitutional reforms. Now, in arguments that would be echoed decades later by China's Communists, Kang declared that representative government was a dead end for China. Mimicking America, he warned, "would be like a blind man riding a horse to the edge of a deep pit at midnight."

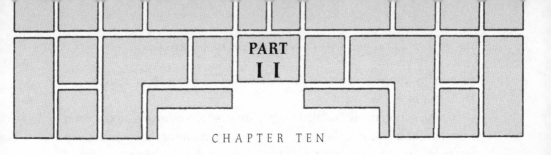

American Dreams

In 1902, China rediscovered America. The Qing court sent its first group of government-sponsored students to the United States since the Yung Wing mission. Three years later, Chinese students finally gained entry to West Point. The first group of Boxer Indemnity students came in 1909. By the 1920s, the United States was hosting more Chinese students—one-third of them women—than all the nations of Europe combined. For the next four decades, China would send more students to America than any other country except Canada. Chinese students were present on almost every campus of every major university in the nation.

In China, American missionaries had assumed responsibility for educating its populace. From the late nineteenth century on, Americans founded more than a dozen universities and scores of elementary, middle, and high schools. By 1911, more than half the missionaries in China had given up preaching in favor of teaching.

In America, Chinese students confronted a society transforming as rapidly as their own. Americans were bidding good-bye to the rigid strictures of Victorian morality just as the Chinese were challenging the principles of a dying society and state. To the Chinese, America represented opportunity. As Wu Tingfang, who served as China's minister to Washington at the turn of the twentieth century, wrote, arriving in the United States had a convulsive effect on the Chinese traveler. When a Chinese voyager "sets foot on the soil of the United States," Wu wrote, "for the first time in his life, he feels he can do whatever he pleases without restraint. . . . He is lost in wonderment."

China's students were filled with a hunger for knowledge and a determination to transform their country. Even the name of the main Chinese fraternity—the Society for the Fulfillment of Life's Ambitions—reflected their drive. "I have a country to save," wrote law student John C. H. Wu. "I have a people to enlighten. I have a race to uplift. I have a civilization to modernize."

The American emphasis on student participation—in the choirs, dramatic groups, newspapers, and debating clubs—inspired the Chinese. To C. Y. Chin, writing in 1913 in the *Chinese Students' Monthly*, one of several magazines founded by Chinese students, these voluntary groups were "the training camp of a hundred desirable traits of citizenship." The Chinese saw freedom of association as a source of American strength. Though generations of Americans have thought of Chinese as more "communal" than Americans, the Chinese viewed themselves as excessively individualistic and as poor team players. "Most of us are perhaps first graders in the school of cooperation and should have enough sense to admit it," wrote student Wan L. Hsu in the *Chinese Students' Monthly*.

Wellington Koo, who studied at Columbia from 1906 to 1912, typified the way many Chinese students dove into American life. He served as coxswain on the rowing team and acted in Dramatic Society productions. He represented Columbia in debates, won a seat as a student representative in his junior year, and as a senior, became the editor in chief of the *Columbia Daily Spectator*. Koo was typical in another sense. In 1904, when he left for America at sixteen, his family had already arranged a marriage for him. But, as they tasted freedom, Koo and his classmates rebelled against the dictates of Confucian China and became determined to seek a more fulfilling relationship with a lover or spouse.

In 1908, in the middle of Koo's undergraduate studies at Columbia, his father demanded that he return to Shanghai for his wedding. Koo agreed on two conditions: that his bride-to-be unbind her feet and that she study English. His father consented, but when Koo arrived home, he discovered that neither promise had been kept. The wedding ceremony went ahead.

Returning to America, Koo parked his bride with an American family in Philadelphia and referred to her as his sister. Koo's "sister" unbound her feet and improved her English, and after a year, she and Koo agreed to an amicable divorce. Koo then pursued a relationship based on love, seasoned with political ambition. He married the eldest daughter of Tang Shaoyi, a graduate of Yung Wing's Chinese Educational Mission, who would soon become China's premier. In 1912, Koo cut his studies short to return to China for a post in government, beginning a lifelong career in public service.

In short stories and plays, Chinese men grappled with the temptations of America and the challenge of leaving the old society behind. In 1915, P. C. Chang, two years into graduate work under the philosopher John Dewey at Columbia, penned a play, *The New Order Cometh*, about two Chinese students in the United States who fall in love. When the boy tries to break off his engagement to a girl in China, her father, whom Chang called the "old order," refuses to agree. But the jilted fiancée, the "new order," consents and finds another man. *The New Order Cometh*, starring a cast of Chinese students, played to rave reviews in New York and New Haven. Chang also wrote the first English version of the story of *Mulan*, staged at the Cort Theatre on Broadway in 1921.

For Chinese women studying in America, the tensions between America's opportunities and China's patriarchal culture were enormous. In 1907, the Qing court decreed that women could become teachers, although it restricted them to kindergartens and lower elementary schools. A career in medicine was also permitted, thanks to Mary Stone and Ida Kahn. But even with the Republican revolution of 1912, the overriding goal of female education remained, as education minister Tang Hualong announced in 1914, "to make good wives and virtuous mothers."

Influenced by their sisters in America, Chinese women pushed back. In 1917, the topic of the annual essay competition for women at the *Chinese Students' Monthly* was "home life." Just one year later, however, it was "professional careers opened to girl students." In 1922, D. Y. Koo became the first Chinese woman to major in banking, at New York University. Grace Li, the daughter of ex-president Li Yuanhong, transferred from Wellesley College to Columbia University to study political science with the aim of becoming a senior government official. Writing in 1923, D. Y. Koo argued that limiting women to medicine and teaching deprived them of free choice. What was wrong with a business major? Koo returned to China and started a bank for women.

In 1913, a twenty-one-year-old Chinese student at Cornell University met a woman named Edith Clifford Williams. Hu Shih had recently dropped agriculture as his major in favor of philosophy and literature. After three years in the United States, courtesy of a Boxer Indemnity scholarship, he still thought that arranged marriages were best for Chinese. Before he left China, his mother had promised him to the family of a girl from his native village.

Like many of his male Chinese classmates, Hu held that education should prepare "a woman to be a good mother and a good wife." But after meeting Williams, he confessed to his diary, "I believe that the highest aim of education for women should be to help women to develop into free and independent beings." This was revolutionary, and not just for China.

Arriving in the United States at the age of eighteen, Hu Shih would mature into the father of China's renaissance and one of the most important Chinese thinkers of the twentieth century. And Williams, a modern artist from upstate New York, would be his muse. Over the course of their relationship, the pair exchanged more than three hundred letters (unearthed in Beijing only in 1997) and together probed the spiritual and philosophical divide between China and the United States. Though he stood barely five feet five inches, Hu Shih had a remarkable way with women. America and China were littered with his lovers, but Williams occupied a special place in his heart.

Born into a prominent family of educators in Ithaca, New York, Williams—or Clifford, as she was known to her friends—became part of the bohemian mix that gravitated toward New York City in the early decades of the new century. She cropped her hair close and sported a tan when other white women strove to protect their pale complexions. She painted one of the earliest abstract paintings by a woman. In Manhattan, she defied convention by living alone. She called Hu "Friend by the River." He called her "Miss Williams."

Williams tested Hu as he struggled to reconcile the certainty that China needed Westernization with the pull of traditional culture. In 1914, Hu Shih cofounded the Science Society of China, which devoted itself to bringing the scientific method to his country. (The word "science" in Chinese, *kexue*, was barely four years old at the time.) In September 1915, Hu, interested in social reform, left Ithaca for New York City to begin graduate work under philosopher John Dewey.

Hu Shih spent the summer of 1916 in the city, spending much of the time in Clifford's Washington Heights walk-up while she was back in Ithaca nursing her ailing father. Hu Shih shared his thoughts with Clifford about a new way of writing in Chinese. He believed that Chinese writers should mirror modern life and use the language of the people, not of the classics. Clifford urged him on.

Clifford was also experimenting—with avant-garde painting. In the spring of 1917, Hu attended the First Exhibition of the Society of Independent Artists, held at Grand Central Palace on Forty-Sixth Street and Lexington Avenue. Two of Clifford's paintings were in the show. "The thing that impressed me most is the spirit of experiment," he wrote. That year, surrounded by Clifford's abstract art in her uptown Manhattan flat, he penned his first collection of poems written in spoken, not classical, Chinese. He called them "Experiments." He would also write what became a heralded letter to China's *New Youth* magazine calling on Chinese to follow him and also write in *baihua*, or "plain speech."

To understand the convulsive nature of Hu's call for a literary revolution, imagine that Americans wrote in Latin while speaking in English—and that suddenly someone stood up and said, "Let's write in English!" Authors across China took up their pens and began writing the way they spoke. The change to *baihua* released a burst of creative energy among young Chinese. Now, urged on by a Chinese student in New York, they could speak directly from their hearts. This intoxicatingly new way of communicating gave them the confidence to challenge their elders and to dream of a New China.

A literary revolution may have been part of the American curriculum but a political one was not. Unlike Japan and Europe, the American educational system did not churn out Chinese radicals. (The one notable exception was Sun Yat-sen.) The key was money; American scholarships, both from the Boxer Indemnity and from missionary grants, were generous enough to allow the Chinese students to focus on their studies.

America trained builders and reformers. Starting with Yung Wing's group, Chinese who returned home after graduating founded modern professions and institutions: the diplomatic service, mining, engineering, the navy, the telegraph office, architecture, the sciences, and medicine. One American-trained engineer, Zhan Tianyou, literally punched a hole between China and the outside world, supervising the excavation of a railroad tunnel beneath the Great Wall. While more Chinese studied in Japan, about twenty times more Chinese received doctoral degrees from American universities than from Japanese or European ones. Chinese students became "vocally anti-Japanese after they returned to China, while most US-educated Chinese students become pro-US," noted a report by the Japanese Diet. "Pro-US" was a relative term, though. And continuing the cycle of Sino-American relations, the United States was about to disappoint the Chinese once again.

*　*　*

Woodrow Wilson entered office in 1913 committed to aiding China and to bolstering American influence there. "I feel so keenly the desire to help China that I prefer to err in the line of helping that country than otherwise," he told his cabinet in an early meeting. Wilson had a cousin who was a missionary in China, and the president had heard the American educator John Leighton Stuart, the dean of Yenching University, China's largest Christian institution, preach at his church in Washington. Wilson was moved, he said, by "the most amazing and inspiring vision" of a "great sleeping nation suddenly cried awake by the voice of Christ."

In his passion for China, Wilson differed from his predecessors. Theodore Roosevelt and William Howard Taft had sought to guarantee stability in China by working with other foreign powers. Wilson wanted the United States to aid the Chinese directly. He pulled the United States out of an international banking consortium that controlled China's customs revenues and much of its economy. He believed the best way to secure China's future was not by convincing imperialist powers to be gentlemen but by spreading democratic and Christian ideals in the Middle Kingdom. But Wilson's honeyed talk about saving China bumped up against his nation's unwillingness to do much else, leading to a yawning gap between Chinese hopes and American action.

As his minister to China, Wilson chose an academic, Paul Reinsch. Reinsch embodied a curious combination of early-twentieth-century American impulses. A professor of political science at the University of Wisconsin, he was a Midwestern Progressive who opposed European imperialism even as he wanted America to expand its influence overseas. He believed that America was different from Old Europe. Throughout his tenure as Washington's man in Beijing, Reinsch schemed to get US businesses to invest in China and engaged in bare-knuckles diplomacy in the face-off between America and its new rival, Japan.

Reinsch arrived in Beijing in early November 1913. By the end of that month, he was meeting with Yuan Shikai and his lieutenants. One after another, the men begged Reinsch for American assistance in building industry and railroads, managing China's rivers, exploring for oil, and minting a national currency. They assured him that in return, China would model itself after the United States.

What the Chinese were proposing, Reinsch reported to Washington, was more than an informal entente. China was ready to hand over to America "more far-reaching opportunities than had been offered to any other nation" at any time. Here was America's chance, he declared, to establish itself as the dominant influence in China, to demonstrate the superiority of American enterprise, to expand American markets and enrich US business.

But Washington and Main Street just weren't interested. Reinsch tried and failed to help Standard Oil, which was already selling vast quantities of kerosene in China, to build an integrated petroleum industry there. He struck out on a gambit to have Bethlehem Steel construct China's naval fleet. And he bombed with a plan for American engineering firms and the American Red Cross to undertake a conservation project along China's third-longest river, the Huai. His great accomplishment—a joint Chinese-American bank—went belly-up.

The reasons for these failures were varied. Japan bribed Chinese officials to scuttle some deals. Conservative Chinese bureaucrats failed to implement others. But more important, US business, which had stronger links with Europe and Japan and better prospects at home, was not willing to take a chance on China. "The man in the street regards China as a heathen land, full of revolutions and capable of defaulting on its bonds," Willard Straight, a former diplomat and executive with J. P. Morgan, told Reinsch. America's disinclination to bet on China exasperated that nation's officials. "The common experience in China has been that American financiers are too slow," Finance Minister Cao Rulin complained to Reinsch in June 1918. "They never come to the point."

On the diplomatic front, Reinsch found himself at loggerheads with Washington. In January 1915, Japan ordered China to accept Japanese control of Manchuria, Inner Mongolia, and Shandong and Fujian provinces. The Twenty-One Demands, as they were called, also commanded China to employ Japanese advisers at all levels of its government and military. Reinsch campaigned against the demands in the US press but Washington ordered him to pipe down.

In the spring of 1917, Japan dispatched Viscount Ishii Kikujiro to Washington to discuss China with the new secretary of state, Robert Lansing. The result was the Lansing-Ishii Agreement, which again acknowledged Japan's "special interests" in China, including Manchuria. Reinsch, who learned of the agreement from his Japanese counterpart, viewed the American inaction on the Twenty-One Demands, coupled with Washington's recognition of Japan's interests in Manchuria, as a green light for Japanese aggression.

Nonetheless, Reinsch did have some success. He pieced together an arms embargo on China to dilute Tokyo's influence over Chinese warlord factions. He convinced Wilson to rejoin the international banking consortium to stop Japan from using loans as a way to buy Chinese acquiescence to Japanese land grabs. Like Anson Burlingame in the 1860s, he almost single-handedly convinced London to alter its policy in China—in this case away from facilitating Japanese control of Asia toward a realization that Japan had become a menace to Anglo-American interests.

Reinsch also secured China's entry into World War I. In February 1917, after the United States severed relations with Germany, Reinsch dangled the prospect of a $100 million aid package for currency stabilization, agricultural development, railroads, and ports if China would contribute one hundred thousand troops to the war effort.

Beijing returned with its own demands: it wanted full participation in any peace conference plus financial assistance. The cable was down between Washington and Beijing, but Reinsch agreed to the terms anyway. On March 14, 1917, China severed ties with Germany. Six months later, it declared war. But the Americans furnished no aid. "While millions upon millions were paid to the less important of the countries of Europe, not a cent was forthcoming for China," Reinsch griped.

On January 8, 1918, President Woodrow Wilson addressed a joint session of Congress about the European conflagration known as the Great War. With an Allied victory imminent, Wilson promised his audience a new world order. No longer would secret treaties and backdoor deals decide the fate of nations. Trade would be free, along with navigation on the seas. Wilson even seemed to vow that colonial peoples would win the right of self-determination. And he put his weight behind the creation of a League of Nations to guarantee independence for all countries, large and small. Around the world, Wilson's Fourteen Points were greeted with wishful anticipation. "A Messiah," was how the novelist H. G. Wells described the American president. The Chinese agreed.

Chen Duxiu, dean of letters at government-run Peking University and the future founder of the Chinese Communist Party, wrote that Wilson was poised to transform international affairs. He was, Chen raved, "the number one good man in the world." Chen translated America's national anthem for the readers of his magazine, *New Youth*.

Liang Qichao dropped his skepticism about America and declared that the imminent Allied victory augured a "new age." A *datong*, or Great Harmony, straight out of Confucian philosophy, was coming, and America was the spark. Despite decades of disappointment, China was putting its trust in America again.

Although China never dispatched any troops, it contributed more than two hundred thousand laborers to the Allied cause. In Beijing in 1918, President Xu Shichang, the third president to lead China after Yuan Shikai died in 1916, called on his countrymen to "help realize the consummation of President Wilson's scheme for world peace." Now that it was on America's side, China had high hopes that it would win a fair deal.

World War I proved to be a windfall for the Chinese economy. Consumed by war, the European powers could no longer supply China's markets with consumer goods, so Chinese industrialists began making things themselves. China's textile industry boomed. The number of factories in China increased tenfold. Overseas, the demand for Chinese raw materials rose. Americans once again became transfixed by the potential of the China market. US businesses lobbied Washington to exempt them from federal income taxes on their China profits. That demand was codified in the China Trade Act of 1922.

For America, the war marked its emergence as a world power. The United States joined the war well into its third year and, after nineteen months and mobilizing four million men, Germany sued for peace.

After the Armistice went into effect on November 11, 1918, the US Committee on Public Information, a wartime propaganda agency, collected all of Wilson's wartime speeches into one volume and translated it into Chinese. It was a hit. By the time peace talks began in 1919, many Chinese students could recite Wilson's Fourteen Points by heart. A Shanghai daily reprinted one Wilson speech and appended a simple comment: the president's words were "a beacon of light for the world's people." Another paper, echoing the late Qing dynasty scholar Xu Jiyu, noted that in three thousand years of Chinese history, not once had a Chinese visionary come up with an idea for permanent peace. Leave that to the Americans, it said.

Wilson's ideals even induced China's warlords to lay down their arms. Talks between the Nationalists who ran the south and a group of military leaders from the north were scheduled in Shanghai. The Chinese had pinned their hopes on Wilson and his envoys to not only erase decades of foreign humiliation but to end their civil war. Reinsch was asked to moderate. On Armistice Day, the government in Beijing declared a three-day holiday, and sixty thousand people marched in a victory parade. "Make the world safe for democracy" read the signs as students thronged outside the US legation near Qianmen Street, chanting "Long Live President Wilson!" As he listened to the happy uproar, Reinsch felt uneasy. Wilson's principles had "found a deep response throughout China" and "entered deeply and directly into the hearts of the Chinese people," he wrote to his president. Should those hopes be dashed, he warned, the consequences would be dire. "Instead of looking across the Pacific towards a Chinese Nation sympathetic to our ideals," he predicted, the United States would one day "be confronted with a vast materialistic military organization under ruthless control."

On November 26, 1918, two weeks after the armistice, Wellington Koo, now China's thirty-one-year-old minister to Washington, called on President Wilson. Wilson said that he was delighted that Koo, too, was going to Paris for the peace talks, and that he wanted Koo to keep in close touch with the American team. Koo told Wilson that China and its people loved him and that he "had given expression to the ideals of the world." Koo left the meeting feeling that America was on China's side.

The Chinese team arrived in Paris with an ambitious agenda, challenging the full gamut of unequal treaties that had been imposed since the end of the Opium War in 1842. They wanted extraterritoriality abolished. They wanted the freedom to impose their own tariffs and to use the revenue as they saw fit. And they sought the return of Shandong province, which the Japanese had seized from the Germans during the war.

Disappointments set in early. At the preliminary discussions in January 1919, Japan was awarded five votes; China got two. And while the Japanese delegation took its seats near the front of the Hall of Mirrors in the Palace of Versailles, the Chinese were shunted to the back, squeezed between Ecuador and Bolivia.

On January 28, 1919, when the Shandong case came before the council, Koo requested a restoration of Chinese control over the province, the birthplace of Confucius and the "cradle of Chinese civilization." Koo affirmed China's desire for a new world order free of secret treaties and the belief that "might makes right." The whiz-kid diplomat wowed the assembly. Koo "spoke in perfect English, and in a cool, lucid and logical argument which carried the members of the Council right along with him," wrote Edward T. Williams, a State Department expert on East Asian affairs attached to the US peace commission. In contrast, Koo's Japanese opponent "stumbled" in his presentation, Williams wrote.

Americans and Chinese mingled throughout the conference. Ray Stannard Baker, Wilson's press secretary at Versailles, found the Chinese "much more open, outright, and frank than the Japanese." American officials advised Chinese delegates on their speeches and petitions. Secretary of State Robert Lansing, generally no friend of the idea of self-determination, assured Koo of American support on strategic grounds. The Japanese imperial juggernaut was worrisome, and it needed to be stopped. Wilson seemed to share that conviction, too.

The Chinese may have had right on their side, but Japan had might. At Versailles, Tokyo revealed the existence of confidential agreements between Japan and the government of Duan Qirui, a Chinese warlord, who had promised to cede Shandong to Japan in exchange for a loan. Britain and France also acknowledged that they had agreed to back Japan's postwar occupation of Shandong province in order to get Japan into the war.

Meeting privately in April 1919, the Big Three—the United States, Britain, and France—decided that Shandong would go to the Japanese in return for an oral assurance that Japan would one day hand it back to China. "Thus," Edward T. Williams told his diary that night, "China was betrayed in the house of her friends."

Wilson's decision was based on his desire to save his beloved League of Nations. If Japan had lost Shandong, he feared, it would have walked out of the conference. But Wilson's move was also part of something larger— an often confusing and inconsistent pattern of American responses to a beleaguered China. American rhetoric perennially championing the underdog led the Chinese to expect real American support, but that support never materialized. The one thing Americans agreed on with regard to China was that China was not worth a drop of Yankee blood.

Still, most of the American delegation was shocked by Wilson's decision. General Tasker Bliss, chief military liaison to the Allies during the war, sent the president a terse note, declaring, "It can't be right to do wrong even to make peace," and threatened to resign. "I am ashamed to look a Chinese in the face," wrote Edward T. Williams. "My one desire is to get away from here just as soon and just as fast and just as far as I can." Within two weeks, Williams had left the State Department.

News of the Shandong decision reached China on May 2. Writing from Beijing, Reinsch reported that commoners and officials alike felt "utterly helpless." He predicted the rise of "a violent anti-Foreign movement." What was left for China, he asked, but "cynical hostility to Western civilization?" What's more, the failure in Versailles threatened negotiations aimed at ending China's civil war.

A day later, students in Beijing held a mass meeting. They deluged the delegation in Paris with telegrams, urging it to walk away from the treaty.

They declared a Day of National Humiliation. On Sunday, May 4, three thousand students from thirteen colleges in the capital gathered in front of the Gate of Heavenly Peace in the heart of the city to protest China's betrayal. At two o'clock, they marched toward the nearby diplomatic quarter with signs demanding "Give Us Back Shandong!" From that day on, Tiananmen Square would be the locus of the nation's political consciousness.

Student representatives were dispatched to the US legation, but Reinsch was not there. The students left a petition: Wilson was a liar, it read; his promise was an illusion. Protests spread across the country. In Paris, Chinese students heckled American speakers. Stephan Bonsal, Wilson's interpreter, feared that someone could try to kill the president.

The fury sparked by Versailles kindled the May Fourth Movement, a mobilization of Chinese students and intellectuals aimed at a wholesale transformation of Chinese politics, society, and culture. The movement would also profoundly change China's view of America. Historians have debated whether the United States "lost" China at the end of World War II, but it clearly lost a part of China in 1919. "Throughout the world like the voice of a prophet has gone the word of Woodrow Wilson strengthening the weak and giving courage to the struggling," read a pamphlet by the Shanghai Student Union. The Chinese, it said, "looked for the dawn of this new Messiah, but no sun rose for China. Even the cradle of the nation was stolen."

The hope that Wilson's principles would serve as a bridge between China and the rest of the world vanished. And as Reinsch had predicted, Versailles caused "a revulsion of feeling against America" for the very reason that "the Chinese had entertained a deeper belief in our power, influence and loyalty to principle." Reinsch quit his post in disgust.

As Reinsch had feared, the crisis also delivered a fatal blow to American efforts to end China's civil war. Betrayal in Versailles discredited the Beijing government of President Xu Shichang. The Nationalist regime in the south pulled out of talks. For the next eight years, political confusion reigned. In the Hall of Mirrors in the Palace of Versailles, the only two empty seats at the end of the talks were China's. It was the only participating country that did not sign the treaty.

In the long history of Chinese disappointment with the United States, America's failure to stand up for China at Versailles occupies a central place. The Chinese had applauded Wilson's promise of self-determination and equality among nations. But when Wilson broke that promise, he sent the Chinese on a quest for alternative ideologies. The Soviet Union was quick to respond. On July 25, 1919, the Soviet government renounced all special privileges that had been won by the czarist regime. Although many of the Soviet promises were never fulfilled, the Karakhan Manifesto, promising equality between Moscow and Beijing, led many Chinese to Marx and Lenin. In a poll taken at Peking University in 1923, asking who the greatest man in the world was, Lenin won with 227 out of 497 votes. Wilson limped into second place with 51. As Li Dazhao, one of the founders of the Chinese Communist Party, declared, in China, World War I was won "by Lenin, Trotsky and Marx rather than by Woodrow Wilson."

Nothing demonstrates the truth of his statement better than the career of Mao Zedong. In 1919, Mao was a twenty-five-year-old teacher living in the Hunanese capital of Changsha, raptly following the Versailles negotiations. He had studied Benjamin Franklin's contributions to science. He was a fan of George Washington, admired Theodore Roosevelt, and, starting in 1915, read a little English each morning, a habit he would retain until late in life. In a letter to a friend in 1916, Mao had predicted that China and America would one day join forces to counter Japan. "We attack the Japanese army. The US attacks the Japanese navy," he wrote. "Then Japan would be defeated in no time." Like many of his countrymen, he had been inspired by Wilson and had placed his hopes in the United States. In the weeks following China's betrayal, Mao founded a student association, organized a student strike, and established a journal, the *Xiang River Review*. In it, he poured scorn on the Western powers, including America, calling them "a bunch of robbers" who "cynically championed self-determination."

By the fall of 1920, Mao had fastened onto another Western remedy for China's ills. He called it the "Russian extremist party." In September, he formed the Russia Studies Society, followed by a Communist study group. In December, he wrote to a friend declaring his faith in Marxism and violent revolution. In June 1921, Mao went to Shanghai to attend the first national congress of the Chinese Communist Party.

●

CHAPTER ELEVEN

Mr. Science

Americans may have stumbled in their quest to persuade the Chinese to believe in God and the United States, but they succeeded brilliantly in convincing the Chinese to follow them elsewhere—straight into the American temple of science. Around the time of the May Fourth Movement, American pragmatism and the Western scientific method took root in China, and the new American missionaries traded Bibles and black robes for microscopes and lab coats. Turning from China's soul, Americans sought to colonize China's brain.

A potent combination of American money and American scientists and educators helped drive one of the most dynamic periods in modern Chinese intellectual history. Starting in the 1910s, the Chinese packed into less than three decades a whirlwind of institution building, research, investigation, and discovery. When the Republican era began in 1911, China had three barely functioning national universities, thirteen small American missionary colleges, several European colleges, and no modern research institutions. By 1937, the country boasted fifty-six colleges, sixteen sponsored by American organizations; twenty-three professional schools; scores of modern scientific research institutes; one of the best medical schools in the world; and a flourishing academy of science—the Academia Sinica. Despite its fractious political landscape and brushfire wars, for a generation China enjoyed an unparalleled openness and freedom—due in part to the United States.

American-funded institutes in China created the fields of medicine, biology, paleontology, botany, chemistry, mathematics, physics, and geology. Americans and American-trained Chinese dominated the media, social sciences, public policy, and diplomacy. Modern Chinese architecture and city planning were all born in the intersection of the Beautiful Country and the Middle Kingdom.

Leading the charge was the Rockefeller Foundation. The patriarch of the Rockefeller dynasty, John D. Rockefeller, had made millions in China selling oil and kerosene, which by 1914 constituted half of America's exports to China. Rockefeller had grown so rich by the mid-1910s that his net worth surpassed the US federal budget. Advisers urged him to create a philanthropic foundation. Rockefeller assigned this job to his son, John Jr.

John Jr. and his wife, Abigail, were captivated by Asian culture. The Rockefellers' collection of Oriental antiques would form the core of the Asian holdings of the Metropolitan Museum of Art in New York. Their Oriental gardens in New England and the Hudson River Valley were a testament to Abigail's fascination with Asian themes. The family bought so many antiques that one leading dealer, Yamanaka and Company, opened an outlet in tiny Northeast Harbor on Maine's Mount Desert Island, where the family summered.

In 1915, the Rockefeller Foundation purchased a twenty-five-acre parcel of land in central Beijing that had once been the home of a legendarily venal Manchu aristocrat. In Chinese, the place was known as Yu Wangfu—the Palace of Prince Yu. Chinese would soon be calling it You Wangfu—the Oil Prince's Palace—as the Rockefeller Foundation poured $8 million into the site.

On September 15, 1921, the Peking Union Medical College opened its doors. Green tiles evoked the grandeur of the nearby Forbidden City; Chinese motifs decorated the buildings. Modeled after the Johns Hopkins University School of Medicine, it was the Rockefeller Foundation's first major overseas investment. By the time the Communists seized the hospital in 1951, it had received tens of millions of dollars of Rockefeller money and served as a laboratory for ideas on health and welfare that would spread around the world.

Peking Union was a home to leading Western medical scholars. Davidson Black and Edmund Vincent Cowdry established the department of anatomy. Cowdry would go on to the University of Chicago. Black would study the remains of Peking Man, one of the world's greatest finds of the human ancestor *Homo erectus*. (The fossils vanished during World War II.)

PUMC, which would grow to encompass fifty-nine buildings, was just the brightest star in a constellation of Rockefeller-supported projects in China. In the years before the Communist revolution, the foundation would donate more money to China—in excess of $50 million—than to any other foreign country. It funded dozens of other hospitals, spearheaded the study of parasitical diseases, bought X-ray equipment, and helped the medical missionary Mary Stone establish nursing as a profession for women. It sent hundreds of Chinese doctors to the United States for advanced training and endowed a project to classify all Chinese plant species. PUMC researchers specializing in traditional Chinese medicine isolated ephedrine from the Chinese plant ma huang, the most significant discovery in that field during the twentieth century.

Another organization devoted to building a new China was the YMCA and its sister the YWCA. The two Ys held lectures on health and science and launched hygiene and literacy campaigns using Yankee showmanship, brass bands, and street theater to publicize the message. The Ys also became a central cog in the American effort to bring sports to China.

Basketball arrived in China in 1895 in Tianjin and soon spread to almost every province, courtesy of the Ys. Max Exner, the YMCA's first educational director in China, noted that "wherever athletes go, the queue falls into disfavor because of the hindrance it presents." By the 1930s, hoops had become China's officially designated national pastime. Baseball caught on as well and held on through the early days of Communism when the People's Liberation Army used it to boost morale.

Americans were impelled to do things in China that they would not dare to try in the West. China was so old and yet so malleable. The word "plastic" pops up again and again in American statements about China during the first few decades of the twentieth century. China is "plastic" in the hands of "strong and capable Westerners," announced Woodrow Wilson in 1914. "China has become plastic after centuries of rigid conventionalism," declared Selskar M. Gunn, a vice president of the Rockefeller Foundation, in May 1933. For American scientists in all fields, China was ripe for experimentation. Its crises presented opportunities for Americans with ideas. A similar attitude persists today. At its core, the notion that mobilized hundreds of Americans to come to China was a belief that America had the right stuff to help that country build a modern, independent nation similar to the United States. China was a place, often *the* place in the minds of many Americans, to which the high-minded principles of the United States could be transplanted.

The leading exponent of this sense of America's destiny in China was America's great pragmatist philosopher, John Dewey. In the fall of 1918, Dewey was on leave from Columbia University when he decided to take a trip to Asia. His wife, Alice, had been devastated by the death of a son in Italy, and the famed philosopher thought that time in a different environment would help her recover.

Dewey went first to Japan. Then, invited by his former student, Hu Shih, to voyage across the Yellow Sea, the Deweys landed in China on May 1, 1919, three days before the May Fourth Movement erupted. "We are going to see more of the dangerous daring side of life here, I predict," Dewey wrote to his surviving children. "We are very obviously in the hands of Young China. What it will do with us makes us laugh to anticipate."

The Deweys had planned to stay for a few weeks, but Dewey was so taken by the volcanic energy bursting from "Young China" that he ended up dallying for more than two years, traveling to eleven provinces and giving more than two hundred lectures, many of them translated by Hu Shih, before tens of thousands of people. Dewey's lectures were turned into best-selling books. Even Young China's Communists adored him. Chen Duxiu, one of the founders of the Chinese Communist Party, said that Dewey embodied "Mr. Science and Mr. Democracy"—the twin mascots of the May Fourth Movement.

With the exception of Karl Marx, note the historians Susan Chan Egan and Chih-p'ing Chou, no other Western thinker has had such a deep influence on modern China as John Dewey. What he brought to China was a way of thinking immersed in the scientific method. Hu Shih boiled down Dewey's philosophy into two sentences: "Your hypothesis should have guts! Your proof should be done with a careful heart." In a culture fond of idioms, this one took hold and was quoted by dockhands, students, and egghead intellectuals alike. The Chinese called Dewey Du Wei, or Dewey the Great.

Dewey's argument that there was a pragmatic experimental approach to confronting problems appealed to a nation on a desperate search for a way out of its economic, social, and political binds. What was required was not a new ideology, he said, but "a step forward here, a bit of improvement there." Progress, he said, was "piecemeal, not all at once." It was a "retail business, not wholesale."

Dewey's pragmatism washed over the world of intellectual Chinese like a breeze. In one provincial capital, more than a thousand unticketed middle school students broke through a phalanx of armed police and jammed into an already-packed hall to hear Dewey speak. If he had been lecturing in the United States, quipped an American professor, "we might imagine a thousand American college students tramping over a squad of policemen to get out of a hall." Many saw his focus on real problems and his search for practical solutions as a way for China to face the future while saving treasured parts of its past. Dewey warned against the uncritical adoption of Western ideas (including his own) just as he cautioned against the blind denial of Chinese tradition. He disapproved of Chinese students' tendency "to welcome any idea so long as it was new."

"More Study of Problems, Less Talk of 'Isms'" was the title of Hu Shih's most famous essay, a paean to Dewey's step-by-step methods for addressing social ills. It upset Hu Shih that so many Chinese were rushing to embrace Marxism, anarchism, Fascism, and capitalism as *the* answers to China's woes. Instead, like Dewey, Hu Shih wanted specific issues solved, not big questions asked. "We don't study the standard of living of the rickshaw coolie," he wrote, "but rant instead about Socialism." When Hu Shih's youngest son was born in 1921, he named him Sidu, or Remembering Dewey. On October 19, 1919, Cai Yuanpei, the chancellor of Peking University, celebrated Dewey's sixtieth birthday with a banquet honoring him as "the Yankee Confucius."

Dewey was gripped by China's potential and by the sense that everything was up for grabs. Children as young as fourteen were leading movements for political reform and shaming merchants and politicians into joining them, he observed. He implored his audiences to focus on China's economy. Fix that, he said, and China's problems could be unscrambled. "China remains the country nearest his heart after his own," his daughter Evelyn wrote.

Dewey noted a strong pro-American bent in his audience. Resentment toward Japan, he wrote, had contributed to a "pathetic affection for America." This was dangerous, he wrote, because it would lead only to disappointment. "China in her despair has created an image of a powerful, democratic, peace-loving America" that was prepared to save her, Dewey said. But that America did not exist.

Despite his disappointment with America over the Paris peace treaty, Mao Zedong modeled a "self-study university," called the Xiangtan Society for the Promotion of Education, on Dewey's ideas. He stocked Dewey's books in a bookstore that he ran. "Dr. Dewey of America has come to the East," Mao wrote. "His new theory of education is well worth studying."

When Dewey traveled to Changsha to speak in October 1919, Mao transcribed his lectures.

Mao ultimately rejected Dewey's gradualism for the explosive violence of Marxist-Leninist class struggle and the idea that Communism offered China the solution to its quest for modernity. Mao understood the threat that Dewey's moderate ideology posed to the founding of a totalitarian state. Once he seized power, he would spend decades trying to snuff it out.

With the May Fourth Movement, Chinese intellectuals launched themselves on a crusade to transform their countrymen. They were convinced that something was rotten with being Chinese and searched for evils inside what they called their "national characteristics." Here again, they drew inspiration from Americans.

The most influential treatise on the Chinese in the late nineteenth century was written by an American. Arthur H. Smith was a missionary who fought on the side of the Union during the Civil War and in 1872 moved to China to preach for the Congregationalist church. He stayed in China for more than half a century. Like most American missionaries, Smith was not short on self-regard. He gave himself the Chinese name Ming Enpu, or "Bright, Broad Benevolence." In 1894, Smith wrote *Chinese Characteristics*, and it became the most widely read book on China in the world for more than thirty years. In it, Smith divided the traits of the Chinese into twenty-six categories including "face," politeness, disregard for time, disregard for accuracy, an absence of nerves, and an absence of sympathy. Predictably, he concluded that the only way to "save" China was through Christ. Smith's message that there was something wrong with the Chinese would later be labeled as racist by Western scholars. But it struck a chord with the May Fourth generation as they searched for the root of China's ills.

Smith's book became a primary source for Lu Xun, China's greatest modern writer, as he set out to dissect China's weakness. Lu Xun read *Chinese Characteristics* in a Japanese translation while he was a student in Tokyo in the early 1900s. In his diary, Lu Xun called it "a master text" and observed that it "offers insights that would lead us to analyze, question, improve and transform ourselves." In 1921, Lu Xun was stirred by Smith's take on the Chinese concept of "face," or self-respect, to write the most famous modern Chinese novella, "The True Story of Ah Q." The tale about a part-time laborer who spends his days rationalizing everyday defeats until he is finally executed for a petty crime constituted the paramount disquisition of Lu Xun's generation on what was wrong with the Chinese.

That it had been inspired by an American missionary constituted yet another example of the intellectual cross-pollination between the two sides.

Ideas from America prompted other Chinese to tackle more practical tasks. Building on the work of Adele Fielde with her Bible women, Americans and Chinese began teaching more Chinese to read. In 1918, after finishing his bachelor's degree at Yale University, Jimmy Yen, a native of Sichuan, set sail from New York for France. He and seventy Chinese compatriots had formed a YMCA group to aid the two hundred thousand Chinese workers who had been dispatched to Europe as part of China's contribution to the Great War. These laborers worked in munitions plants and on farms, repaired roads, and dug trenches to free French and British soldiers to fight.

In Boulogne, Yen wrote letters for homesick workers and organized activities to divert them from whoring, gambling, drinking, and fighting. He asked whether anyone wanted to learn how to read. His first class was a success. Of forty students, all trench-diggers, thirty-five passed, earning diplomas as "Literate Citizens of the Republic of China." Soon, three thousand Chinese were studying using a textbook Yen had written, the *People's 1000 Character Literacy Primer.*

Working among his countrymen in France, Yen vowed to devote his life to "the pent-up, God-given powers of the people." Literacy for all Chinese became his goal. The only way a democracy could succeed, he argued, was if people knew how to read. "China can never become a truly representative government if the great masses of her people are illiterate," he wrote.

Yen returned to the United States after the war and earned a master's degree at Princeton. Like many Chinese students in the New York area, he spent weekends in Manhattan at the welcoming home of Huie Kin, the pastor of the Chinese Presbyterian Church on East Thirty-First Street, and his wife, Louise, the daughter of a Dutch American manufacturer. There, Yen, a wiry man with an engaging smile, met Alice Huie, the family's second daughter. In September 1921, the two married and moved to China.

Yen discovered a China much different from the one he had left. Just three months before his marriage, the Chinese Communist Party had been founded in the French Concession in Shanghai. Marxist-Leninist ideas had begun coursing through the minds and magazines of Young China. Leftist Chinese pamphleteers, searching for a new bogeyman to blame for China's ills, switched from the Manchus and the Qing dynasty and took aim at the West.

When the World Student Christian Federation announced in February

1922 that it would hold its eleventh conference in Beijing, students in Shanghai, guided by the Communists, founded the Anti-Christian Student Federation, touching off a new wave of riots against religion. Christianity, which had so recently been accepted as a savior for China, was on the outs again, and American influence faced a new test, not from Japan but from the Soviet Union.

Yen recognized the threat of Communist ideology, its facile class analysis, its eagerness to assign blame, and the appeal of violence. He still looked to the United States as a model. Americans were not better people than Chinese, he wrote. But they possessed a "doctor who can treat their soul to cure them." That doctor was Jesus Christ.

Yen started his first major literacy campaign among the urban poor in Changsha, the capital of Hunan province. But, as a son of rural Sichuan, he was drawn to the countryside, where the vast majority of China's four hundred million people lived. He found a spot in Hebei province called Ding county, the site of a floundering rural reform project, and decided to make his life there. Years before Mao Zedong fixated on the peasantry to power his revolution, Jimmy Yen had identified the countryside as the key to changing China. With funding from the YMCA, Jimmy and Alice Yen moved to Ding county, where Yen founded the Mass Education Movement. He pleaded for help from American-educated Chinese and persuaded experts in agriculture from Cornell and Ohio State to join him. Some dramatists from Columbia and a Harvard political scientist showed up, too.

The Yen household formed the heart of a community of thirty experts and their families. Alice founded a school for their children. For the first time in Chinese history, a large group of intellectuals had relocated to the countryside to help China's weakest link. Yen drew up a ten-year plan for improving literacy, agriculture, health, and the local economy. The going was tough. The farmers laughed when Yen, sporting his *1000 Character* handbook, said that he had come to teach them to read. They scowled when he told them that he wanted to educate their wives and daughters, too.

As part of citizenship training, he published a book on China's national heroes. Taking a page from the YMCA playbook, he used the drama troupe to educate farmers about health, farming techniques, and hygiene. He avoided politics but cultivated China's high and mighty, convincing the wife of a former premier to lobby for donations on his behalf. By the mid-1920s, as anti-Christian feeling rose, he distanced himself from the Y, although American churches continued to fund his project. He ran literacy programs for competing warlords and persuaded most marauding potentates to leave Ding county alone. When police ransacked Yen's headquarters in 1928 and arrested his closest adviser, Chen Zhusan, Yen went to bail him out of jail and found Chen teaching the *People's 1000 Character Literacy Primer* to the prison guards.

Yen, as was typical of the Chinese graduates of American schools, was a reformer. His belief in the "retail" theory of social change ran deep. Henry Ford donated $10,000 to Yen's cause, telling him that "you go about the mass education of people the way I go about the mass production of cars." And, if imitation is the sincerest form of flattery, China's Communists flattered Yen. In their literacy campaigns, Mao and his men embraced Yen's techniques. However, instead of Yen's *People's 1000 Character Literacy Primer,* they used a different study guide. It attacked bureaucrats and capitalists and replaced Yen's Christian fellowship with class warfare.

The American failure to aid China at the Paris Peace Conference became an issue in the 1919 US presidential campaign. The Republicans had used the Shandong fiasco as an excuse to reject American participation in the League of Nations; now they wielded it as a cudgel to retake the White House.

At campaign stops, Warren G. Harding and his Republican Party surrogates cited the "shameless," "damnable," "inexcusable" "rape of helpless China" to discredit the Democrat candidate, James M. Cox, and his thirty-seven-year-old vice presidential running mate, Franklin Delano Roosevelt. Harding won the election and entered the White House wanting at least to appear to care about China.

When Harding suggested a focus on Asia at the world's first disarmament conference, scheduled for 1921, China's corps of young, mostly American-educated diplomats jumped at the chance. Faced with a rising Japan, Harding and his secretary of state, Charles Evans Hughes, sought a balance of naval power in the Pacific as a way to head off a costly arms race. Hughes also wanted a resolution of Sino-Japanese tensions to give China breathing space to get its political house in order.

Japan "approached the meeting somewhat in the mood of a naughty child called to the teacher's desk for a reprimand," wrote John B. Powell, the most clear-eyed American journalist writing in Asia at the time. Japan knew that America would try to counter its schemes to control China. Still, Tokyo also saw the conference as a chance to cement its place as a great power and slow the arms race. Defense expenditures were eating up half of Japan's budget. Fearing that its days as a superpower were numbered,

Britain also supported the talks. London was seeking to avoid a precipitous collapse in the Far East, angling for a managed decline instead.

The Washington Naval Conference convened at the Daughters of the American Revolution Hall on Seventeenth Street Northwest on November 21, 1921. In his opening remarks, Secretary of State Hughes dropped a bombshell by volunteering to halt the construction of sixty-six naval vessels. "The delegates stared at each other in wonderment," John B. Powell wrote. The arms race, Hughes thundered to explosive applause, "must stop!"

China was represented by Alfred Sze, Cornell's first Chinese graduate, and Columbia's Wellington Koo, the silver-tongued veteran of Versailles. Sze and Koo presented a list of Chinese demands. China wanted to set its own tariffs, to arrest foreigners who committed crimes in China, and to see foreign troops leave its territory. China asked for the return of Shandong province from the Japanese, the annulment of Japan's Twenty-One Demands, and the end to any special Japanese rights in Manchuria. In short, China wanted to accomplish in Washington what it had failed to do at Versailles.

Though they did not obtain US support to raise the Shandong issue at the conference itself, the Chinese did win an American agreement to help facilitate talks with Japan on the sidelines. For thirty-six sessions, Koo and the Japanese negotiated over Shandong as the Americans looked on.

When the conference ended in February 1922, the United States, Britain, and Japan had agreed that no new battleships would be constructed for a decade. For existing battleships, a ratio was set. For every five battleships in the US and British navies, Japan would get three. It was the modern world's first strategic arms freeze. China won Shandong back from Japan and two smaller territories from France and Britain. It secured the right to increase its tariffs, which led to a healthy bump in revenues, and for the first time, the Western powers promised to consider allowing China to run its own railroads.

A Four-Power Treaty obligated the United States, Japan, Britain, and France to consult in the event of a crisis in Asia. And in a Nine-Power Treaty, the powers promised to respect China's territorial integrity, to assist China in maintaining "an effective and stable government," and to safeguard the Open Door. The American press called it "the Chinese Charter of Liberty" and crowed that America had expunged the guilt of Versailles. For the first time ever, Chinese diplomats, with the help of the United States, had persuaded the main Asian powers (except the Soviet Union, which had not been invited) to agree with America that keeping China whole was in the best interests of the world.

The Americans thought they had solved the central dilemma of their Asian policy. They had found the formula that, in the words of Woodrow Wilson's former adviser Edward House, would "leave the door open, rehabilitate China, and satisfy Japan." Jacob Schurman, the new US minister in Beijing, declared that the conference would usher in (yet another) "new era" in Chinese history. Secretary of State Hughes was triumphant. "We are seeking to establish a Pax Americana maintained not by arms but by mutual respect and good will," he declared.

By 1920, after several more years in exile, Sun Yat-sen had returned to Guangzhou to establish a government in China's south, far from the warlords who ran Beijing. In March 1921, Sun sent a congratulatory note to Warren Harding on his election. He told the American president that the success of democracy in China would depend on the actions of the United States, which he described as "the Mother of Democracy and Champion of Liberalism and Righteousness."

John MacMurray, now running the State Department's Asia desk, made sure that Harding did not get Sun's note. He also stopped representatives of Sun's Nationalist Party from attending the Washington Conference. Official America still looked on Sun as a "troublemaker," "a disreputable character," and a man of "grandiose schemes."

There were still a few dissenting views among Americans who considered US policy shortsighted and thought that as nationalism was remaking China's political landscape, Sun Yat-sen should be cultivated instead of shunned. A. B. Ruddock, an interim minister in Beijing, reported that Sun was clearly more inclined toward the United States than other Chinese leaders. Following Sun's second inauguration as president of the rump Republic of China in Guangzhou on May 5, 1921, Consul Ernest B. Price praised Sun for "supporting the principle and cause of democracy." Still, official US policy continued to back the warlord governments in Beijing. In Washington, the view first enunciated by Frank Goodnow prevailed. China was not ready for democracy, and it needed a compliant ruler to enforce all the Western-imposed treaties.

When Sun was compelled to flee Guangzhou again in June 1922 because of a local uprising, most American diplomats sneered at his troubles. Sun sought protection in the International Concession in Shanghai. There a sole portrait adorned the wall of his study—one of Abraham Lincoln.

Rejected by living Americans, Sun found succor in their ideals and pictures of their heroes. In a 1922 interview with the *Saturday Evening Post*, Sun complained that America had offered him nothing. But like so many Chinese, he still hoped for a miracle. He begged the *Post*'s readers to "help us get the recognition by the United States, for that will mean victory."

Later that year in Shanghai, representatives of the Communist International, or Comintern, saw an opportunity to pull Sun Yat-sen into the Soviet camp. Communist agent Adolph Joffe offered Soviet financial and military aid to the Kuomintang on the condition that it would allow the 123 members of the newly established Chinese Communist Party to enter the Nationalist ranks. On January 15, 1923, Nationalist forces recaptured Guangzhou; two weeks later, Sun and Joffe released a manifesto announcing that Soviet weapons, ammunition, and cash would be flowing to southern China and that the Nationalist Party would be reorganized along Marxist-Leninist lines. On March 2, Sun Yat-sen again took the reins of power.

By June, Sun's offers to Americans of monopolies, sweet business deals, and high interest rates on his revolutionary bonds were gone. In a statement sent to the US consulate in Guangzhou, he blasted the United States for its support of the northern government. In August 1923, he sent a trusted lieutenant, Chiang Kai-shek, along with a team of Communists and Nationalists, to Moscow to study the Soviet system. Later that fall, Mikhail Borodin, another Cominterm agent, fresh from undercover work in America, arrived to advise Sun, distribute weapons, and reorganize the Nationalist Party. Borodin was technically in China as a correspondent for the Soviet news agency, later officially known as TASS. While he trafficked in revolution, his way of life was thoroughly bourgeois; his children attended the Shanghai American School.

In September 1923, facing a financial crisis, Sun's government announced that it would seize customs duties from the port of Guangzhou. Those duties were normally collected by the China Maritime Customs Service, which was run by Westerners. Diplomats in Beijing vowed that they would block the move; after all, the money was earmarked for the Boxer Indemnity, which China was still paying off. The US government ordered four destroyers to steam into Guangzhou Bay.

On December 16, Sun presided over an anti-American rally as the ships took up positions in the harbor. A day later, he released a letter, "To my friends, the American people," that sounded like the lament of a spurned lover. "When we first waged the revolution to overthrow dictatorship and the corrupted government, we had America as our model, and we hoped we could have the help of our American Lafayette to achieve our goal," he wrote. Instead, the United States dispatched warships to threaten an attack. "Has the nation of Washington and Lincoln denied its faith in freedom and taken to repressing people of other countries who struggle for freedom?" he asked. The warships left without firing a shot.

In 1924, Vasily Blyukher, the former commander of Soviet Far Eastern Forces, arrived in Canton to open the Whampoa Military Academy and plan a military campaign to unite China. By October, the Soviets had furnished more than eight thousand rifles, hundreds of machine guns, and scores of artillery pieces to the Nationalist army. Chinese Communists took positions throughout the Kuomintang government and military. Two men were placed at the helm of Whampoa: as chief, Sun appointed Chiang Kai-shek, freshly back from three months in Moscow; for deputy political commissar, he turned to Zhou Enlai, who, with the looks of a silent film star and the silkiness of a Parisian intellectual, would dazzle generations of Americans in his role as the top "barbarian handler" of the Chinese Communist Party. To lead the Nationalists' propaganda bureau, Sun picked another Communist: the Hunanese firebrand Mao Zedong. By the end of 1924, more than a thousand Soviet military and political personnel were in southern China, and the Comintern was funneling tens of thousands of dollars a month to its new friends in Guangzhou. The cognoscenti in the region started calling each other "comrade."

As chief propagandist of the newly reorganized Nationalist Party, Mao foreshadowed his later missives to the party faithful by blaming imperialism for China's woes and reserving special opprobrium for the United States. America was a problem for China, Mao wrote in August 1923, because so many Chinese liked it. The Chinese, he wrote, had "a superstitious faith in the United States." These naive people did not know, he wrote, that "America was actually the most murderous of hangmen." Even though he remained personally fascinated by the Beautiful Country, Mao would spend decades trying to purge a fondness for the United States from the minds of his fellow Chinese.

In Shanghai, journalist John B. Powell watched Sun's tilt toward the Soviets with alarm. He placed the blame for it squarely on Washington and the American legation in Beijing for their inability to see that a new day was dawning and that China's demands for fair treaties, sovereignty, and control of its borders had to be met with sympathy, not gunboats. Washington, Powell wrote, "continued to grant diplomatic recognition to the most reactionary elements in China . . . while ignoring Dr. Sun Yat-sen and his Kuomintang associates who were developing a more modern nationalist form of government." He faulted the United States and Britain for permitting the Nationalists to come under Russia's spell.

Despite decades of disappointment with the United States, Sun surrounded himself with Americans and American things as his life drew to a close. In the late winter of 1925, he traveled to Beijing for a last attempt at a negotiated settlement with the warlords of northern China. He was a sick man. He sought the best medical care available in China—at the American-funded Peking Union Medical College. But his liver cancer was too advanced. On March 12, 1925, at 9:30 a.m., he died. No sooner had Sun passed away than the Communists claimed him as their own. Comintern agent Mikhail Borodin arranged for a phony set of Sun's last words praising Lenin to be drawn up. They ran in *Pravda*, but everyone knew it was a fake.

Starting in the 1910s, American money and ideas helped usher in China's age of openness. Civil society developed, literature blossomed, Chinese universities grew in size and influence, and Chinese scientists collaborated with some of the keenest minds in the world. But, while private American initiatives supported the best China had to offer, the US government seemed stuck in a time warp—backing a series of warlord governments in Beijing. America's inability to recognize the wave of the future in China opened the door to a country that would grow into its biggest foe: the Soviet Union.

●

CHAPTER TWELVE

Fortune Cookies

From the 1900s on, Americans feasted on a spicy stir-fry of Chinese fantasy, sex, murder, sleuthing, art, and food. In books, magazines, gardens, and restaurants, on farms, movie screens, and after 1920, the airwaves, Chinese things entered everyday American life as never before. America's transition to a manufacturing powerhouse created a yearning for "authentic" places and emotions. The Middle Kingdom filled the role as a wiser, more exotic civilization than the well-oiled if somewhat antiseptic one that Americans were forging.

Once seen as germ-infested slums, America's Chinatowns became tourist attractions. When the bubonic plague struck San Francisco in 1900, city and state authorities mulled the idea of leveling Chinatown, which they blamed (unfairly) for the epidemic. But when earthquake and fire hit the city six years later, such was the need for tourist dollars that city fathers worked with the Six Companies to rebuild Chinatown in its original style. The city's Chamber of Commerce would soon promote the neighborhood as "the chief jewel in San Francisco's starry diadem of tourist attractions."

In New York City, a flashy ex-boxer named Chuck Connors proclaimed himself mayor of its Chinatown and gave tours, escorting rubberneckers to a fake opium den while his sidekicks splayed themselves upon beds. Each year around Christmas, Connors and his Chinese girlfriend, Pickles, hosted a midnight Chinatown Ball where the color line was crossed in all directions. "Chinamen dancing with white girls, negro women waltzing with white men," was how the *New York Times* described the ball in 1903.

Anti-Chinese prejudice remained strong, even though by 1920 the number of Chinese in America had dropped to about sixty thousand, the lowest point in half a century. In a 1927 social survey, only 27 percent of respondents were willing to accept Chinese as fellow workers, and a mere 11.8 percent as friends. But exotic China appealed to Yankee romantics in ways that would have shocked earlier generations.

Gouverneur Morris IV, the great-grandson of a Founding Father, churned out mass-market short stories in his spare time while working as a California bank executive. His most famous, "The Incandescent Lily," published in 1914, tells the tale of Chudder, a strapping East Coast WASP with a passion for rare plants. Chudder journeys to China on behalf of Harvard's Arboretum, finds a rare lily in a hidden valley along with an alluring Chinese princess, and steals the lily but dumps the girl. Penny novel readers lapped it up.

Readers got more substantial fare in the short stories of Edith Maude Eaton, the daughter of a British businessman and a Chinese woman from Shanghai. Growing up as a Eurasian child in upstate New York, Eaton braved whispered insinuations, outright insults, and fights with class-mates because she was a mixed child. Neither East nor West, she was "a stranger," she wrote, in her own home. She took the pen name Sui Sin Far, the Cantonese name for narcissus, signifying love for a homeland she would never see.

Sui was an early literary avatar of the belief that, for better or worse, the Chinese and American cultures were locked in a permanent embrace. In her landmark short story, "Mrs. Spring Fragrance," published in 1912, she tells the tale of a young Chinese American couple navigating the treach-erous shoals between Chinese tradition and the brash immodesty of the United States. They succeed, but other characters in her oeuvre were killed or committed murder as they tumbled into the chasm of the cultural divide.

China could also be cuddly. *The Story About Ping*, published in 1933, cap-tivates American children to this day. Written by Marjorie Flack with illus-trations by Kurt Wiese, a salesman in China during World War I, this tale of a lost duckling depicts China not as a world of alluring royals or priceless flora but as a place where family values reign. Like Chang and Eng, the show-boating Siamese twins, Ping captured the American imagination. Starting in the 1950s, Captain Kangaroo read the story aloud once a week for seven-teen years on television. *Sesame Street* ran an animated version in the 1970s.

And in the 2008 film *Kung Fu Panda*, the hero's daddy is a goose named . . . Ping. Meanwhile, Tyrus Wong, who immigrated to America from China when he was nine, created Bambi for the Disney animated classic in 1942.

At the beginning of the twentieth century, China reached Americans through their stomachs. From the 1910s to the 1930s, Chinese food spread throughout the United States and became a mainstay of American gastronomy. Chop suey led the way.

A stir-fried dish of vegetables, noodles, and scraps of meat, chop suey has no ancestors on mainland China. Some believe that it emerged from railroad camps in the West as Chinese laborers slapped together leftovers. Others credit a visit to the United States by Viceroy Li Hongzhang in 1896. Li's cook rifled through the cabinets of the Waldorf Astoria's kitchen, where Li was staying, and whipped up the dish there. White Americans had viewed the dish with horror and believed that it contained rats. But in the 1890s, their tastes underwent a change.

In a guidebook to Chinatown published in 1898, Lucien Adkins, a New York gourmand, described enticing friends to try the dish. One bite, Adkins reported, and the novice is hooked, and "soon there are times when the gnawing hunger for chop suey, and for nothing else, draws him to dingy Chinatown alone."

In 1908, the *Boston Daily Globe* advised its readers to try Chinese themes for weddings and anniversaries. In New York, Chinatown sprawled next to the Lower East Side, forming a bond between Jewish taste buds and Chinese stir-fry. Sundays? Christmas? The breaking of the fast after Yom Kippur? American Jews flocked to Chinese joints. They were always open and did not discriminate. Neither did Chinese clubs. Jewish performers Eddie Cantor and Isidore Baline, later known as Irving Berlin, both made their debuts in Chinatown.

Chinese restaurants were the place, the *Chicago Tribune* wrote in 1914, where "the $12 a week clerk" takes "the $6 a week sales girl." What were its secret ingredients, the *Tribune* asked? "Novelty, excitement, change." A report from the American Chemical Society in 1919 advised Americans, especially children and invalids, to eat Chinese food for their health. Just a few decades earlier, Americans had been told that the Chinese harbored virulent bugs. By the 1920s, Americans could barely recall a time when Chinese food was not a staple. It had become so American that Louis Armstrong named his first composition, written in 1925, "Cornet Chop Suey."

Chinese immigrants became the most widely dispersed minority in the United States. By 1930, 30 percent of America's counties had at least one

Chinese resident. Many opened eateries. Today there are forty-one thousand Chinese restaurants in the United States, more than all the McDonald's, Burger Kings, Wendy's, Domino's, and Pizza Huts combined.

While Chinese food tempted American taste buds, its flora remade America's landscape. Many of the seeds arrived courtesy of Frank Meyer, a Dutch immigrant with a passion for hiking. In 1905, the US Department of Agriculture sent Meyer to China, where he would spend thirteen years as an "Agricultural Explorer."

Meyer's exploits fending off bandits and villains while on the hunt for an agronomic gold mine were the stuff of legend in the US press. In China, Meyer felt like a zoo animal. In each town, a crowd of men and boys would surround him and gape. "Loneliness hangs always around the man who leaves his own race," he wrote. He favored Buddhist and Taoist monks, whose temples served as sanctuaries for rare plants.

On his journeys, Meyer found a disease-resistant variety of spinach that saved the American spinach-canning industry. He collected twenty pounds of hemp seeds and wondered "what use the American public can make of this hashish." Varieties of asparagus, clover, oats, thirty kinds of bamboo, and the hardy yellow rose that grows from New England to the prairie states were among his finds. The Meyer lemon formed the basis of the lemon juice industry in Florida. The Siberian elm now provides a windbreak from Canada to Texas.

Meyer's most important contribution was the humble soybean. Before he went to China in 1905, US farmers grew eight varieties. Meyer added forty-two more, propagating an agricultural exporting powerhouse. Surveying Meyer's cornucopia, USDA official Walter Swingle declared China America's "chief agricultural creditor."

Meyer spent years wandering through China's rural areas, sleeping in fleabag hostels, braving brigands and disease. In all he collected more than two thousand plant species and varieties and sent them home. He often worked alone, had no friends, and suffered from bouts of depression. On June 1, 1918, at the end of his fourth expedition to China, he fell off the back of a riverboat on the Yangtze, a suspected suicide.

Other adventurers in the Middle Kingdom kept armchair explorers equally enthralled. To his contemporaries, the life of the botanist explorer Joseph Rock seemed like something straight out of "The Incandescent Lily." His catalogue of 493 varieties of rhododendron transformed American gardens, and a spectacular peony bears his name. But it was his encounters with bandit kings and Tibetan warriors, his travels through a "weird fairyland of the mountains," and his creation of a real-life version of the mysterious Orient that made his name.

Born in Vienna, the son of a butler to an Austro-Hungarian count, Rock was both a serious scholar—his work on the Naxi people of Yunnan province saved their language from extinction—and a spinner of outrageous tales. In practically every story he wrote for *National Geographic* between 1922 and 1935, he falsely claimed to have been "the first white man" to discover valleys, mountains, peoples, kings, and rivers across western China. Nonetheless, his reports from among China's "noble savages" raised intriguing questions for his readers in a modernizing America. "Here people live and die without the slightest knowledge of the outside world," he wrote about the Mosuo people of Yunnan province. "How oppressive to be buried alive in these vast canyon systems! Or are they happier for it?"

Rock's adventures provided rich material for Western journalists, poets, among them Ezra Pound, and novelists. His reportage probably inspired the cult classic *Lost Horizon*, a 1933 novel by British writer James Hilton about a harmonious, monastic land named Shangri-La, where no one ever aged. In 1949, after the Communist revolution, when Rock was forced to leave Lijiang, the picturesque mountain village in Yunnan province where he had made his home, he wrote mournfully, "I want to die among those beautiful mountains rather than in a bleak hospital bed all alone."

By the turn of the twentieth century, huge quantities of Chinese porcelains, bronzes, and paintings began to flow into private American collections and the nation's museums. Initially funded by men whose families had enriched themselves in the China trade, these collections were supplemented by a motley crew of diplomats, adventurers, missionaries, businessmen, dealers, and self-appointed experts. War and political chaos turned China into a smugglers' paradise. Road building, funded by the American Red Cross, disinterred graves packed with ancient pottery and ceramic guardians of the underworld.

Chinese and Japanese art fascinated wealthy Americans who dabbled in Eastern religions, too. The Rockefellers had a deep appreciation for Chinese art; Lucy Aldrich, the sister of John Jr.'s wife, Abigail, fancied herself a Buddhist as did New Englanders Billy Bigelow, the scion of a China trading family, and Ernest Fenollosa, an expert in Japanese art. Bigelow and Fenollosa built the Boston Museum of Fine Arts into one of the world's great repositories of East Asian art.

In Beijing, many of the American dealers congregated in the courtyard house of John C. Ferguson, a former Methodist missionary who had left the church to establish a university and run a Chinese newspaper. Ferguson leveraged his connections with Chinese literati to collect antiques. In the early years of the twentieth century, he spent hundreds of thousands of dollars of other Americans' money buying treasures. He landed the Metropolitan Museum of Art's first large cache of Chinese paintings, several more than one thousand years old.

Chinese literature also influenced American tastes. In the first two decades of the twentieth century, American poets and their editors staged a rebellion. Frustrated with the fusty language of the Victorian era, Ezra Pound, Harriet Monroe, T. S. Eliot, and Amy Lowell vowed to purify the art form. At the same time that Hu Shih was in America mustering the courage to launch his literary revolution in China, these American writers looked to Chinese verse to aid them in a parallel revolt.

Ezra Pound was born in 1885 in the American West but grew up in a Philadelphia suburb, in a home interested in missionary work and China. His parents donated money to the Chinese mission. As a young man, he was drawn to the Asian art just appearing in American museums.

In 1913, Pound met Mary McNeil Fenollosa, the widow of Ernest Fenollosa, of the Boston Museum of Fine Arts, and fell into a discussion of Chinese and Japanese art. Mary had read Pound's poetry and suggested that he become literary executor of her husband's estate. Among Fenollosa's papers, Pound found notebooks filled with poetry from the Tang and Song dynasties rendered into literal English. In these translations, Pound discovered an economy of language and a clarity of meaning that could serve as a model for a new American poetry. Pound selected fourteen poems and rewrote them. The result—*Cathay*—was published in Venice in 1915.

Cathay was a founding text of Anglo-American modernism. Appearing during World War I, its themes spoke to the times: long separations, perilous travel, soldiering, and exile. Men read its poems—including Li Po's "Lament of the Frontier Guard"—on the frontlines. T. S. Eliot called Pound "the inventor of Chinese poetry for our time" and dedicated his masterpiece, "The Wasteland," to his fellow American expatriate. Pound's rendering of the Chinese into sparse, simple images inspired Ernest Hemingway. Carl Sandburg noted that reading *Cathay* made one "realize the closeness of the Chinese soul as a next-door human neighbor." Owning *Cathay*, wrote the classical scholar Robert Fitzgerald, "you need no porcelains."

Some detractors mocked Pound for his ignorance of Chinese and for the literary license he took with the ancient verse. Arthur Waley, a British Sinologist, lambasted the poet for his many linguistic inaccuracies. Pound responded that Waley may have known Chinese, but his "bungling" English left a good deal to be desired.

In an editorial in the magazine *Poetry*, the editor Harriet Monroe called Pound's work "the beginning of a search for the Chinese magic" that would save American verse. Western impressionist painting had already found "the regenerative influence of Oriental art," she wrote. Now it was literature's turn.

It wasn't all high culture, however. China to many Americans also meant fun. The 1920s witnessed the beginnings of an American craze for mah-jongg, the Chinese game of tiles, courtesy of an enterprising executive from Standard Oil. Mah-jongg occupied the centerpiece of bridesmaids' brunches and charity luncheons. There were mah-jongg-themed movies, recipes (mah-jongg chicken salad), a ballet, and a mah-jongg shawl. The game was popular among Jewish matrons in the north and the country club set down South. Americans even gave Chinese names to games that had nothing to do with China. In 1928, the Pressman Company renamed a German board game Chinese checkers, and it also took America by storm.

As moving pictures seized hold of the American imagination, Anna May Wong, a laundryman's daughter born in Los Angeles in 1905, became the first nonwhite star in the United States. Wong was modeling at ten. At seventeen, she played the lead role in a Technicolor feature. That year she also dodged her father's attempt to marry her off to another laundryman. By nineteen, she was plotting against a bare-chested Douglas Fairbanks, America's top action star, in his production *The Thief of Baghdad*. She went to Europe and dazzled audiences there. And unlike so many stars of the time, she survived the transition to the talkies and then to television, performing in English, German, and French. Her Chinese name was Yellow Frosted Willow—Huang Liushuang.

On the screen, Anna May Wong smoldered with a leggy sensuality and, at five feet seven inches, towered over many of her costars. With her large eyes, full lips, and lithe body, she danced—or rather shimmied—and she knew that she drove men wild. "I danced once before," went one of her most memorable lines, "but there was trouble, men, knives." She appeared in fifty-five movies and remains the most influential Asian American actor to grace the silver screen.

Wong certainly faced racism. She was saddled with Chinese female stereotypes, bouncing between treacherous and tragic. Death scenes became her forte. Directors used a dizzying array of methods to dispatch her. She was impaled, shot by a firing squad, plugged point-blank, and killed by her own hand (seven times). "I died so often," Wong said. "Pathetic dying seemed to be the best thing to do." (All this female carnage wasn't just a Chinese thing, however. Greta Garbo didn't make it out of most of her films alive.)

Wong was the first star to sport bangs. In 1934, the Mayfair Mannequin Society of New York voted her the "world's best dressed woman." Four years later, *Look* magazine called her the "world's most beautiful Chinese girl." Rumors of prodigious liaisons littered the gossip columns, but her most serious affair probably ended because California law prohibited whites and Asians from marrying. Nonetheless, in fertile US soil, Anna May Wong planted a commanding image of a sexy, alluring, and powerful Asian woman.

In the country of her ancestors, Anna May Wong ignited conflicting passions. When she visited China for the first time in February 1936, thousands flocked to the Shanghai docks and crowded along the Huangpu River to catch a glimpse of the American star. A month later in Hong Kong, a mob shouted "Down with Anna May Wong, the stooge that disgraces China!"

Wong was too hot for the Confucianist prudes and the equally prissy Chinese Left. She was held up as a warning to Chinese womanhood and branded an imperialist toady. Her star power defied traditional Chinese views of propriety even as her beauty, talent, and charisma stirred her fans. A Nationalist diplomat was even partially responsible for Wong's losing what would have been her greatest role, as O-lan in the 1937 movie version of Pearl Buck's *The Good Earth*. T. K. Chang, a Chinese consul based in Los Angeles, argued that Wong was not "Chinese" enough for the part; so a white woman, Luise Rainer, who would go on to win an Academy Award, played the role in "yellow face" instead.

All the Chinese harrumphing about Wong underscored the challenge that American society posed to China. The West, especially America, had played a key role in liberating Chinese women from foot-binding and a life of illiteracy. But now, Western influences were extending into ever more private realms. Wong embodied the enticing mix of threat and appeal that America has always represented to the Chinese. Faced with a freewheeling American sex symbol, and an ethnically Chinese one at that, Chinese critics reacted with profound unease.

If the American portrait of Chinese women swung between vixen and victim, its depiction of Chinese men was equally at odds with itself. In one corner crouched the dastardly Fu Manchu; in the other slouched the huggable Charlie Chan. Fu Manchu was the product of Sax Rohmer, a British author, and represented the apex of "yellow peril" literature, popular in both the United States and the UK in the early twentieth century. But it was Hollywood that turned him into an international sensation.

An agent of a secret society, the Si-Fan, whose tentacles penetrated from the English countryside to the White House, Fu Manchu was an Oriental wizard, an expert in chemistry, medicine, engineering, botany, zoology, and hypnotism. A Superman, as one wag put it, with a heart of coal. Fu Manchu underscored the extent to which anti-Chinese racism was founded upon a fear of Chinese smarts. Like Bret Harte's card-sharking Ah Sin, Fu Manchu bested Americans at their own game. But he did not occupy center stage alone. In the battle to become the leading Chinese man, another significantly more approachable individual vied for the role.

Earl Derr Biggers always claimed that it was a newspaper brief about an opium bust that inspired him to conjure the character of Charlie Chan. A Harvard man from small-town Ohio, Biggers was working on his second novel in the Reading Room of the New York Public Library in 1924 when, leafing through back copies of a Honolulu paper, he chanced upon "an item to the effect that a certain hapless Chinese, being too fond of opium, had been arrested by Sergeants Chang Apana and Lee Fook, of the Honolulu police." With that, Sergeant Charlie Chan entered Biggers's novel, *The House Without a Key*.

That Biggers was inspired by Chang Apana, a diminutive Chinese police officer born in a Hawaiian village, is an intriguing instance of cultural mixing. Biggers met the real Chang only after his Charlie Chan had become famous. But Chang's legendary police work gave Biggers the muse he needed to create a character who became the most recognizable Chinese folk hero in US history.

Biggers's Charlie Chan spawned an industry—four novels, forty-seven movies, a comic strip, a card game, a board game (the forerunner of Clue), a radio serial, and a 1970s TV series with a dog named ChuChu and a young actress named Jodie Foster voicing one of Chan's ten children. Chan embodied the stereotype of the wise, industrious, somewhat asexual Chinese man, despite his many offspring. Wrote Biggers of Chan: "He walked with the light dainty step of a woman."

Like all great fictional detectives, from Columbo to Hercule Poirot to Philip Marlowe and Sherlock Holmes, Chan is idiosyncratic. His sentences want for subjects; his verbs do not agree. "Relinquish the firearm, or I am forced to make fatal insertion in vital organ belonging to you," was one line.

The first three Charlie Chan films received scant notice. It was not until 1931, when Warner Oland, a Scandinavian who claimed Mongolian ancestry, played the role for Twentieth Century Fox Film Corporation in *Charlie Chan Carries the Day*, that the detective finally got his proper due. The film was a hit, keeping Fox afloat during the Depression. "Charlie is more than a detective," opined *Film Daily*, "he is a witty philosopher, and in this characterization Oland is at his best."

Biggers died of a heart attack in April 1933; Chang Apana followed him to the grave eight months later. But Charlie Chan survived. Oland acted in fifteen more Chan movies, alternating between the soft-spoken copper for Fox and the dastardly Fu Manchu for Paramount Pictures.

While American academics in the 1980s labeled Chan the creation of a racist America, Chinese in the 1930s hailed him as the first Chinese character portrayed positively in the West. When Oland arrived in Shanghai on March 22, 1936, he was mobbed by journalists and feted nationwide. He remained in character throughout his stay. "Visiting the land of my ancestors makes me so happy," Oland announced in Mandarin. Chinese studios made a series of Chan knockoffs with actors who mimicked Oland, creating a bizarre cultural loop-the-loop, as the historian Yunte Huang has noted, of a Chinese actor imitating a white actor portraying a Chinese character created by a Caucasian.

Pearl S. Buck influenced more people on the subject of China than anyone since Marco Polo. Her eighty books and countless articles and speeches were translated into 145 languages—more than those of any other American author. Sixty-five of her books were best sellers. Fifteen were Book of the Month Club selections. Published in 1931, her most popular work, *The Good Earth*, the first mass-market pocket-sized paperback in America, sold four million copies. It spun off a Broadway play and a Hollywood movie and earned Buck more than a million dollars. Her writings on China made her the first American woman to win both the Pulitzer Prize and the Nobel Prize for Literature.

Building on some of the more positive stereotypes that already existed, Buck created a new China for Americans—less exotic, more authentic, and tethered to the land. Her transformation from a missionary who despised the "heathen Chinee" into their greatest advocate had a profound effect on American society writ large.

Born in 1892 and raised in China, Buck was the daughter of mission-aries Absalom and Carrie Sydenstricker, ascetic Southern Presbyterians who had been stationed in China since 1880. In 1911, she entered Randolph-Macon Woman's College in Virginia, where she was known as "the freak who could speak Chinese." After graduation, she returned to China, and married the agronomist missionary John Lossing Buck, who was assigned to a village north of the Yangtze River in central China.

Buck lived the isolated life of a missionary wife in rural China. She scolded the Chinese for venerating their ancestors and for other "sins." In letters to friends and family, she complained of her "constant contact with the terrible degradation and wickedness of a heathen people." The Chinese, she pronounced in one missive, "are all thieves." She condemned the infanticide that many women practiced. She pronounced herself unwill-ing, in a letter to her brother, "to have China considered as even a semi-civilized country. . . . She is a country given to the devil."

In 1920, Buck gave birth to a daughter, Carol. It was a difficult delivery, and she was forced to have a hysterectomy. Carol suffered from phenylke-tonuria, a genetic disorder, and became mentally impaired. The couple left the countryside and moved to Nanjing, where they both worked at the American-built Nanking University. Pearl began teaching English litera-ture, and slowly, more slowly than many missionaries, she came to accept the idea that China needed modernization more than conversion.

In March 1927, Buck and her husband were in Nanjing when National-ist and Communist troops attacked the city as part of the Kuomintang's attempt to unite China. The soldiers targeted Westerners, beating scores and killing at least six. Buck and her family were saved by her family's washerwoman who hid them in a small hut while soldiers looted their home.

Following the attack, Buck and her husband left China for Japan. They had wanted to return to the United States, but missionary boards in America, fearful that fleeing missionaries and their tales of woe would hurt dona-tions, declined to pay for passage across the Pacific. As Adele Fielde had forty years before, Buck turned away from the church and found another passion: in her case, writing.

Buck's first novel, *East Wind: West Wind*, was published in 1930. In it, she explored a mixed marriage between a Chinese man and an American woman and their efforts to persuade their parents to recognize their love. Sales were disappointing. Sui Sin Far had already plowed those fields.

In her next novel, Buck portrayed a new China. Not fast-changing or reforming, it was a nation beyond the reach of history. Buck wanted to call the novel "Wang Lung," but her publisher, Richard Walsh, balked. It sounded too much like "one lung," he quipped. The book, he wrote, was written "not as a story of Chinese life, but as a novel of the soil." He suggested *The Good Earth*. The title stuck.

Published in March 1931, *The Good Earth* follows a Chinese farming family as it weathers a series of crises. Wang Lung and his homely but hardworking wife, O-lan, start a family, work the land, but are forced off their farm into the city to beg. They ultimately return to the land triumphantly after Wang happens upon a small fortune. True to her new views, Buck brushes aside Christian missionaries as irrelevant; O-lan uses a Christian tract to mend Wang Lung's shoes. The novel closes with Wang Lung on his deathbed and his children plotting to sell his beloved land.

To American audiences, *The Good Earth* was both a vivid portrait of faraway China and a very American tale: an up-by-the-bootstraps parable about the values—modesty, thrift, and closeness to the land—that had made America great. *The Good Earth* married the Protestant work ethic with Confucius. As Dorothy Canfield Fisher, one of the judges who chose the novel for the Book of the Month Club, put it, "most oriental novels, you know, are for Americans really only curiosities, travel books of the mind," but Buck's novel "makes us belong to the Chinese family as if they were cousins and neighbors."

The book's success led to a dramatic makeover of Buck's identity. She sold herself as a hybrid—more Chinese than American. She sold the book as a hybrid, too, a melding of American literary realism with tales from a seventeenth-century Chinese classic, *The Water Margin*. "By birth and ancestry I am American; by choice and belief I am a Christian," she wrote, "but by the years of my life, by sympathy and feeling, I am Chinese." Most striking, however, was Buck's about-face on China. The novel ignores many of the social ills that had disgusted her a few years earlier. There is no mention of infanticide, mass starvation, or political chaos. There's no challenge from the West, and no need for Western technology. There is just timeless China.

Buck's new China was just as much of a fantasy as the heathen China she had battled as a missionary's wife in Anhui. It was Fu Manchu in reverse. Where they had once belonged to the devil, Buck's Chinese now could do no wrong. "I was a white child in a land of brown people, and they were all kind people, at least to me," she wrote.

In 1934, Buck returned to the United States with her daughter, divorced

John Lossing Buck, and married her editor, Richard Walsh. She then devoted herself with a missionary's zeal to a new cause—racial equality.

The Good Earth was also a hit in China, where pirated editions abounded. Throughout the 1930s and 1940s, it was translated into Chinese at least eight times. One translation went through twelve editions. No other book by any foreigner had ever before been so popular. Chinese critics praised the novel's depiction of China; many said that Buck, an American, had produced the first accurate account of rural life. Leading liberals Lin Yutang and Hu Shih loved it, but so did Mao Dun, a future minister of culture in Communist China. Never before had Chinese readers met characters like Wang Lung and O-lan.

Still, some Chinese critics were uncomfortable that Buck, an American, was revealing a country the West had never seen. It triggered a sense of shame and dismay, a feeling that China had somehow "lost face" because a foreigner had described it as poor. In the New York Times, in January 1933, Jiang Kanghu, the founder of the Chinese Socialist Party, criticized Buck's focus on China's common people instead of the cream of Chinese civilization. "They may form the majority of the Chinese population," he wrote of Wang Lung and O-lan, "but they are certainly not representative of the Chinese people." Responded Buck: "If the majority in any country does not represent the country, then who can?"

The Good Earth and the 1937 movie version have provided generations of Americans with their primary understanding of traditional China. Eight decades since they appeared, both remain a fixture on junior and senior high school syllabi. It was hardly inevitable that "this simple story of a Chinese farmer," as the movie called it, would appeal to so many Americans. But neither was there anything inevitable about America's deep fascination with the Chinese. The opening of the film version depicts China as a nation of "vast promise." It could just as well have been written today.

America's feelings about the Chinese have never been monochromatic. Racism mixed with respect; prejudice vied with a preference for China's art, food, and people. But from the 1920s, a trend was clear. Mainstream Americans embraced an increasingly positive view of China and the Chinese. Fu Manchu crept away. Evolving as Japan intensified its attacks on China, these images would prove crucial to China's cause. Books and movies like The Good Earth, films about Charlie Chan, and those starring Anna May Wong gave names and faces to the Chinese on the eve of global conflagration.

CHAPTER THIRTEEN

Up in Smoke

In 1881, when tobacco baron James B. Duke learned of the invention of a machine to roll cigarettes, his first words were, "Bring me the atlas." When he came to the legend "Pop: 430,000,000," he stopped. "That is where we are going to sell cigarettes," he said. Before him was a map of China.

The story may be apocryphal, but Duke indeed created a market for massive tobacco sales in China. When his company, the British American Tobacco Company, or BAT, started doing business there in the 1890s, only a few people smoked. By 1933, the Chinese were puffing on a hundred billion cigarettes a year, more than any other nation except the United States.

British American Tobacco prospered by turning itself into a Chinese company. Carolina farm boys peopled its executive ranks, but the real work was carried out by hundreds of Chinese merchants and shopkeepers. "We were called salesmen, but actually we did no selling," wrote James Lafayette Hutchison, a BAT man from North Carolina who arrived in China in 1911 and stayed until the 1930s. "Interpreters and dealers took care of that end."

In addition, BAT beat the competition by, well, beating them. Nowadays, American businesses complain about Chinese business practices: intellectual property rights rip-offs, unfair competition, and price-cutting to win market share. But the Chinese did not invent these tricks. They had a model in James Duke's BAT.

The history of American tobacco in China is entwined with the story of opium. In the late nineteenth century, American missionaries led a movement to stop opium smoking in China. They wrote the 1906 Qing law banning use of the drug. They convinced Theodore Roosevelt and his successor, William Howard Taft, to hold conferences regulating its sale.

Thanks to missionary pressure, the United States and other Western powers joined with Japan and China in 1912 to sign the International Opium Convention, the first drug-related covenant in modern history. Legislation to prevent the export of raw opium and to limit the use of its derivatives were drawn up for the first time.

In China, as opium use slowed, the British American Tobacco Company filled the void. In 1915, the Life Extension Institute of New York, a supporter of medical missions, noted that BAT was distributing tens of millions of cigarettes for free with "the avowed purpose of planting the habit" in opium's wake. BAT's agents ventured deep into the Chinese countryside, doling out cigarettes at temple fairs, just as opium dealers had once passed around their drug.

BAT began its operations in China in 1902, the year it was formed in a merger between Duke's American Tobacco Company and the Imperial Tobacco Company of England. The Americans dominated BAT; Duke appointed twelve of the eighteen positions on the board and held two-thirds of the stock. He had based the company in London simply to avoid US antitrust regulations.

In 1905, Duke sent James Thomas, the son of a North Carolina tobacco farmer, to Shanghai to build one of the first global businesses in China. Thomas had been selling cigarettes since he was nineteen. In 1899, he moved to Singapore and India to open markets there. "As a missionary of this new American industry," Thomas wrote, "I went out to the East."

Thomas's strategy in China mirrored Duke's in the United States, notes business historian Sherman Cochran. In China, BAT snapped up competitors and introduced mass production and mass distribution. From the beginning, BAT benefited from taxes even lower than those in the United States. The company could make the same cigarette in both countries, sell them for 40 percent less in China, and still turn a higher profit. In 1902, the Qing attempted to tax BAT at the going rate for foreign goods—about 5 percent. But BAT convinced the Qing authorities to grant it the status of a "native" industry and tax it at 1 percent.

In 1923, Mao Zedong lambasted the government for easing up on the cigarette tax. "If one of our foreign masters farts, it is a lovely perfume,"

Mao wrote in one of his first published esssays. "Isn't it true that the Chinese government is a country house of our foreign masters?" The low taxes encouraged BAT to invest so much in China that it became one of the country's largest investors. The company's cigarette plants stretched from Shanghai up the Yangtze River to Hankou, and to Shenyang and Harbin in the northeast. In Shanghai, BAT operated out of a thirty-acre site in the Pudong section of town. BAT's factories there employed more than thirteen thousand Chinese workers. Nationwide, BAT made twenty million cigarettes a day. And Thomas, at $100,000 a year, made more money than any other foreign executive in Asia.

Thomas's genius was that he saw China not as a national market but as a series of regional ones. And in everything, he relied on Chinese knowledge. He engaged a battalion of Chinese artists and calligraphers to adapt BAT's message to local tastes. They churned out scrolls, handbills, wall hangings, window displays, even a small rug that cushioned the floor of a rickshaw.

Tang dynasty concubines; imperial generals; an immortal white serpent; Shanghai cigarette girls with come-hither looks; China's New Woman as a social activist—all were fodder for BAT's advertising mill. BAT's annual calendar was a nationwide smash. BAT posters covered the walls of temples, the sides of ferries, even the cliff face of the Three Gorges on the Yangtze River. That stunt got Thomas into hot water, and he was forced to apologize publicly: "It is not the policy of the Company," he wrote, "to spoil the beautiful scenery of the Yangtze Gorges."

The company built the single largest and most expensive advertising device in China, a 130-foot-tall tricolor clock sign in Shanghai touting Ruby Queen cigarettes, then the world's second most popular brand. BAT's movie studios cranked out films trumpeting the virtues of smoking. It was modern, sophisticated, and good for your health, BAT claimed. Within a few years, the ritual exchange of a cigarette had become a habit among Chinese men.

BAT did more than sell its product; it grew tobacco. By 1917, Chinese farmers were producing 8 million pounds of bright tobacco a year. Twenty years later, the harvest yielded 125 million pounds. Ever reliant on Chinese know-how, BAT ditched American chemical fertilizers after one growing season, switching to cheaper Chinese nightsoil instead.

BAT benefited from the low taxes and cheap labor that would lure American businesses to China decades later. In the United States, Duke replaced workers with machines; in China, BAT hired brigades of laborers to perform those same tasks. Like the outfits that would turn China into the "factory of the world" in the 1990s, BAT employed mostly female workers, who took home less than fifty cents a day. "We have an abundance of good, cheap and efficient labor which works eighteen hours a day without the assistance of labor unions," Thomas bragged in 1915. He sounded like an American investor in 1990s China.

BAT's leading salesman was Wu Tingsheng, the son of a Christian preacher from Zhejiang province, just south of Shanghai. Wu was educated at Young John Allen's Anglo-Chinese College in Shanghai. At the age of twenty, he met Thomas, who was struck by the young man's ambition and gift of gab. The two men started hawking cigarettes together on the streets of Shanghai. Wu was embarrassed by the peddling, but Thomas told him the Biblical parable of the mustard seed—great things coming from a humble start—and he embraced the work.

Wu became BAT's troubleshooter. He purchased a government sinecure and hawked BAT cigarettes while on official business. He helped Thomas break out of the treaty ports and into the Chinese interior, where the Chinese consumer lived. Under Chinese law, BAT could own warehouses and land only in the ports along the coast and up the Yangtze River. So Thomas and Wu formed a joint venture called Union Tobacco Company. As it was technically a "Chinese" firm, Union could own land anywhere. While Wu was working for BAT, he also took a post as adviser to the Beijing government as its leaders mulled the prospect, following a Japanese precedent, of nationalizing the tobacco industry. (Unsurprisingly, Wu persuaded them not to.)

Wu helped Thomas weather BAT's first crisis in China—the 1905 anti-American boycott. The company was a major target of the campaign. In Shanghai, posters showed a dog smoking a cigarette. "Those who smoke American cigarettes are of my species," it said. Chinese newspapers dropped BAT's ads, and Chinese ships refused to transport its cigarettes. At the beginning of the boycott, there were four Chinese cigarette firms; by the end, there were twenty.

With Wu's assistance, BAT drove the competitors out of business. The company slashed prices and snatched back market share. By 1907, BAT was booming again. By 1915, it was selling 1 billion cigarettes a month. From 1915 through the 1920s, with the exception of one year, the United States exported more cigarettes to China than to the rest of the world combined, increasing from 1.25 billion in 1902 to 12 billion in 1916. BAT was so convincing at getting the Chinese to light up that by 1916, Chinese smokers consumed four-fifths as many cigarettes as Americans. "We have made big progress in China," Duke said in 1916, a year when his firm made almost $4 million in profit in China, the equivalent of about $90 million today.

One Chinese tobacco company did survive. Started by a family of Chinese immigrants with relatives in Japan, Hong Kong, and Thailand, Nanyang Brothers tried to capitalize on China's growing nationalism to boost sales and stay afloat. As China's economy boomed during World War I, Nanyang set up a cigarette factory in Hong Kong and used its family connections in Guangzhou to sell to the Cantonese.

BAT fought back. It undercut Nanyang's brands. BAT agents bought up thousands of Nanyang cigarettes, held them in damp warehouses until they moldered, and then released them onto the market for free. BAT hired armies of young men to rip down Nanyang posters. At a time of intensely anti-Japanese feeling (Tokyo had just issued its Twenty-One Demands), BAT posters fingered Nanyang Brothers as stooges for the Japanese. One of Nanyang's founders, Jian Zhaonan, was, indeed, a Japanese citizen; he even had a Japanese name. BAT sued Nanyang for trademark infringement in Hong Kong and won. Duke's company dispatched fake customers to public spaces to bad-mouth Nanyang's products. It paid reporters to write negative reviews.

But Nanyang survived, helped by a national movement to "buy Chinese." The company donated to the Nationalist government of Sun Yat-sen in Guangzhou, hitching its star to the Kuomintang, and worked aggressively to prove its Chineseness. It paid workers at BAT's plants to strike. Chinese firms would revisit all these tactics in the early decades of the twenty-first century in their battle with Western multinationals.

From Guangzhou, Nanyang moved north, establishing distribution centers in Shanghai, Hankou, and Tianjin, but BAT fought on. When Nanyang put a rental deposit on a factory site in Shanghai, BAT bought the building. Nanyang's chief problem was that it relied almost exclusively on the Cantonese, whereas BAT hired anyone with talent. And where BAT tweaked its advertising campaigns to appeal to China's regional differences, Nanyang was a one-trick flag-waving pony. Patriotism worked in Guangzhou, but it floundered elsewhere. "None of the people in the interior know what 'national goods' are or why they are significant," founder Jian Zhaonan complained to his brother Jian Yujie in October 1917. When Nanyang found competent staff, BAT poached them. When Nanyang tried to grow tobacco in central China, BAT lured away all but one of its leaf specialists.

In 1917, Thomas offered to buy Nanyang. He told Jian Zhaonan that he wanted to create a Sino-American duopoly to block other foreign firms from selling into the China market. Nanyang would remain separate on paper, but secretly BAT would hold more than half its stock. He and Jian would continue to spar publicly, Thomas said, and never let on that they had merged. Jian liked the idea, and at the end of February 1917, he wrote to his brothers urging them to align themselves with Duke.

Brother Jian Yujie dismissed the idea of being taken over by "the foreign devils." "Our company's goods really have won the respect of our people and glory for our nation," he wrote. "If we are lured astray then surely we shall be reviled and spat on by our own society." The battle, he noted, was not between companies but between races. Nanyang was more than a cigarette company, he told his brother; it was a symbol of China. Merging with BAT would violate patriotic principles. What Nanyang should do, he argued, was operate only in areas where it was appreciated. "It is better," he wrote his brother, "to be a chicken's beak than an ox's ass."

Jian Zhaonan reacted strongly to these concerns, in a way that reflected many of the tensions that marked China's response to America. He called his brother a "hidebound bigot" for opposing the sale. The choice facing Nanyang was stark: merge or be crushed. What Chinese companies needed was profit, not xenophobic passion. "The principal thing which has enabled people to bring prosperity to the world and its societies and to generate power and wealth," Jian wrote his brother, "is money." That was the antidote to Nanyang's and China's ills, and that was what BAT was offering. But Jian Yujie remained unconvinced and Jian Zhaonan's untimely death in 1923 ended all talk of a merger.

By the mid-1930s, BAT had invested more than $200 million in China. It employed more than thirty thousand people, and about two million Chinese farmers grew tobacco for its cigarettes. Even through the Second World War, it continued to sell. But in the Communist revolution, BAT met its match. In 1952, the Communists seized all BAT's assets and shut the firm down. They expropriated Nanyang Brothers, as well.

The story of British American Tobacco's rise in China shows that not all American businesses were reluctant to enter the Middle Kingdom and that for at least some firms, the China market was more than an illusion. But BAT's extraordinary success is of greater significance than that.

Today, China is the largest cigarette market in the world, with more than three hundred million smokers and lung cancer rates among the highest in the world. Tobacco sales, dominated almost entirely by domestic brands, account for more than 10 percent of government revenues. The opium scourge, in which Americans were also involved, is memory. But the tobacco industry and the afflictions it causes stand strong, with roots in the relationship between the United States and China.

Other Americans soon learned that in China business, like politics, is local. And no one understood this more clearly than Cornelius Vander Starr. "Neil" Starr was born in Chicago in 1892, the son of a railway engineer who died when his son was just two years old. The family moved to Fort Bragg in Northern California, and from the age of twelve, Starr was working. He wrapped cigars, swept out a Baptist church, opened Fort Bragg's first ice cream parlor, passed the California Bar, and bought real estate. In 1918, he enlisted in the US Army but maintained a sideline business laundering his platoon's clothes. Once World War I ended, he took a job in Japan with the Pacific Mail Steamship Company but got tired of working for a boss and drifted to Shanghai.

Shanghai at the time was "the headquarters for American get-rich-quick operators and adventurers," wrote John B. Powell, the leading American journalist in the city. The International Settlement became, Powell wrote, the "base of operations for salesmen of fake jewelry, worthless stocks, patent medicines, dangerous drugs." American women ran several of the city's most profitable brothels, and the madams cruised the shopping district along Bubbling Well Road, according to a contemporary report in *Cosmopolitan*, in "carriages heralded by runners and drawn by blooded horses with jingling, silver-mounted harness."

Starr fell in with one of the leading American entrepreneurs, a fellow Californian named Frank Raven. Raven had come to China in 1904 and landed a job as a surveyor for the British- and American-run Municipal Council. He bartered inside information about the city's development plans for a piece of a real estate company that, acting on Raven's tips, snatched up land parcels before the council publicized its intentions. By 1919, when Starr joined the firm, Frank Raven's real estate and banking business was estimated to be worth a staggering $70 million.

That year, Starr took over Raven's flagging insurance operation with two clerks in two rooms at the corner of Nanjing and Sichuan Roads. He called his little business American Asiatic Underwriters. This company, started by a twenty-seven-year-old American to serve the Chinese market, would eventually grow into the global insurance behemoth American International Group, or AIG.

For Starr and his colleagues, selling insurance in China was not, in the words of a *Fortune* magazine profile, "the dull, routine-ridden affair that is so typical of this profession in America." He and his coworkers carried handguns and fought off kidnappers. Starr, in the words of C. J. Smith, his longtime colleague and friend, was "working all the time, scheming, travelling incessantly."

Soon after American Asiatic opened shop, a string of warehouses off Shanghai's Suzhou Creek burst into flame, destroying hundreds of thousands of silkworm cocoons. American Asiatic was on the hook for huge claims. Gathering his clients at a banquet, Starr offered to make good on a third of each of their losses before they even filed a claim. With that he turned the fiasco into a PR triumph.

Starr had two revolutionary insights that set him apart from his mostly British competitors in China. One was that the Chinese consumer was worth his time. The second was that it was Chinese workers who would make his company great. Starr's Anglo competitors called him a buccaneer. Like the early American traders in Guangzhou, another Yank was rocking their colonial boat.

Starr rejected the white notion that the Chinese were more inclined to dirty tricks than Anglo-Saxons. "Chinese fraud is no more to be feared than Western fraud," he said. His support of the Chinese rankled Western bigots in Shanghai. The Rotary Club expelled him when he predicted that the era of foreign privilege was coming to an end.

Life insurance had been sold in China since 1850, but mostly to foreigners. In 1921, Starr started Asia Life Insurance—the first Western insurance business specifically targeting Chinese citizens. In Chinese, it was called Youbang Baoxian, or Friendly Federation Life Insurance, capitalizing on the warm feelings that many Chinese had for the United States. Starr's salesmen blanketed the Yangtze River valley and the big cities and county seats of central China with ads. Business boomed.

Where many Westerners saw only chaos and warlords when they looked at China, Starr saw opportunity and progress. He noticed, as *Fortune* magazine put it years later, "that the standards of living and hygiene of the Chinese middle classes are improving, with a consequent decline in the death rate." More than 40 percent of Starr's Chinese clients were outliving actuarial tables, which meant big profits for Neil Starr. Within a decade of starting his business, he had opened offices and agencies in fourteen cities in China and Southeast Asia.

Starr served as the Asian agent for American insurance companies; at one time, he represented twenty-six. His profits grew so great that he soon began to buy his American clients. In 1926, he opened American International Underwriters. It was the first case of an American company headquartered outside the United States starting a subsidiary back home.

Starr didn't limit himself to insurance. He bought two English-language newspapers and started a Chinese-language one, reflecting a decades-old American interest in the Chinese press. After Japan invaded China in 1937, Starr's Chinese-language paper, known in Chinese as *Damei Wanbao*, or the Big American Evening News, played a key role in reporting news of the war. *Damei* broke the story of a competition among Japanese soldiers to kill the most Chinese and detailed Japanese massacres of Chinese. While extraterritoriality protected *Damei* from censorship, it couldn't protect its editors from Japanese thugs. Big American's offices were bombed and three of its editors were assassinated.

Starr was routinely threatened himself and began riding around town in a bulletproof limousine. When he moved his operations to New York in 1939, he offered his Chinese staff a berth on a passenger ship and a job if they came along. Those who couldn't speak English had a place in the company kitchen.

Starr wasn't the only American to get involved in China's press. While missionaries Young John Allen and Elijah Bridgman stumbled into journalism in the service of the Lord, by the early 1900s, American reporters were coming to China in the service of truth, a scoop, or the chance to make their mark on history. Over the next century, American journalists would change the way Americans thought about China. They would change China, too.

The first great American newspaperman to land in China was Thomas Franklin Fairfax Millard, who would found several newspapers and magazines and mold a generation of American reporters. Millard had been the drama critic at the *New York Herald* before he discovered a flair for war reporting. He despised colonies and disliked imperialists, particularly the British. He had covered the Boer War in South Africa and made it to China in time for the Boxer Rebellion.

Millard wanted to help China become a modern, independent nation. He blasted the American chamber of commerce types and other Yankees who sought to preserve their colonial privileges. He called on the United States to declare a Monroe Doctrine for Asia wherein the United States would ensure that no one picked on China as it modernized. Millard's journalistic successors would embrace his belief that it was America's duty to support China against the rest of the world. They would disagree, however, on which Chinese to back.

A tiny man, known for his impeccable taste in clothes and a volcanic temper, Millard hated bullies, and in China, he found one: Japan. In a series of influential books starting in 1916, Millard argued that the Japanese threatened the rest of Asia and American interests as well. He spent much of his career—as a writer, editor, publisher, and adviser to the Kuomintang—trying to counter what he believed was the peril from Tokyo.

Based in Shanghai's swanky Astor House Hotel, Millard launched the English-language *China Press* in 1911 and *Millard's Review of the Far East* six years later. His tone marked a break from that of Shanghai's dominant, British-run English-language paper, the *North China Daily News*. When a massive flood inundated large swaths of northern China in 1911, the British press ignored it. The *China Press* gave the event front-page coverage and led a donation campaign. Millard believed—correctly—that there was a market for news about China. Among his early investors was Wu Tingfang, the former Chinese minister to the United States and soon to be Nationalist bigwig. Half of Millard's readers were English-speaking Chinese. The *China Press* landed scoops of international importance: the 1911 rebellion that touched off the Nationalist Revolution; details on the negotiations between Sun Yat-sen, Yuan Shikai, and the collapsing Qing; and the first interview with Sun Yat-sen after he returned to China in late 1911.

Millard was a graduate of the University of Missouri, and as the *China Press* grew, he tapped the old-boy network for an editor, John B. Powell, and a reporter, Carl Crow. Powell had never seen a transoceanic telegram before he received Millard's job offer. Crow, who was covering murders and general thuggery in Texas, did not know whether he should sail across the Atlantic or the Pacific to get to Shanghai. The pair formed the nucleus of what would become the Missouri Mafia, more than fifty graduates of the School of Journalism who dominated China's American press corps for years.

Crow arrived in Shanghai in 1911. Born in 1883, the son of a schoolteacher, he had started in the news business at sixteen as a printer's apprentice. Like many Americans who caught the China bug, Crow was spellbound by the place. On his second day in Shanghai, he took a stroll. "I found myself on a crowded street with no English signs and no white faces," he wrote. "There was no one who even remotely resembled the people with whom I had lived from the time of my birth."

In 1912, Crow married Mildred Powers, who had come to Shanghai as the representative of the Singer Sewing Machine Company. Crow served as a US government propagandist during World War I. Later, he was a hostage negotiator, a police sergeant, an informal adviser to governments in China and the United States, and an author. In 1918, with the files on China's rich and famous that he had amassed during a stint writing pro-American publicity during World War I, Crow opened Carl Crow Incorporated and set out to remake the ad business in China. Shanghai was already a city of three million. New department stores were opening; new fashions had hit the streets. Knives and forks were stylish. Perms, bobs, and bangs, lipstick, silk stockings, and a suffragette movement—all were signs of an emerging New China.

Crow and two Chinese colleagues, K. C. Chow and art director Y. Obie, began to buy billboard space up and down the Yangtze River valley. Within a few years, Crow owned space on fifteen thousand billboards in sixty cities across China's heartland. Any firm that wanted to advertise—other than giants like British American Tobacco or Standard Oil—had to do it through him. He grew fat, literally, on the profits of China's advertising market, later founding China's first women's fashion magazine and issuing China's first glossary of automobile terms and its first book of poker rules. Like Neil Starr, Crow invested in his Chinese employees. With painter T. K. Zia, he created the sexy Shanghai girl, one of the indelible images of 1920s China.

To Crow, China "was a land of unremitting industry." He rejected the American missionary belief that the country was drenched in sin. "If it is true that the devil can only find work for idle hands," he wrote, "then China must be a place of very limited Satanic opportunities." By the mid-1930s, Crow had twenty-five large accounts. Carl Crow Incorporated moved to more spacious digs in an office decked out like a New York ad agency, with black furniture, linoleum floors, and English prints on the walls.

Crow published his first book, a China travel guide, in 1913. His biggest seller came out in 1937: *400 Million Customers: The Experiences—Some Happy, Some Sad—of An American in China and What They Taught Him.* Appearing six years after *The Good Earth*, the book portrayed a modernizing China, where people hankered after change. The writer Dorothy Canfield Fisher praised the book as "one of the most convincing and life-like descriptions of Chinese life we have ever had." It earned Crow a National Book Award and fan mail until his death in 1945.

The very American idea that the customer is always right influenced Chinese businesses as well. K. P. Chen was born in Jiangsu province in 1880 into a family of merchants that had fallen on hard times. By the age of twelve, he was working in a brokerage firm and studying English in night school. By nineteen, he was fluent. In 1904, Chen's father-in-law paid for him to go to America as a member of a provincial delegation to the St. Louis World's Fair. There at the Granville Hotel, he met Sun Yat-sen.

Other Chinese guests in the hotel were so petrified that a "revolutionist" was in their midst that they refused to come downstairs for breakfast. Not Chen. "I was young and I was curious," he wrote. Sun spent two hours with Chen, spelling out his Republican program. "I was just nobody," Chen wrote. "Why should he waste so much time on me?" Chen had saved $1,000 to use for tuition in the United States, of which he gave Sun $5.

In 1906, he was accepted to the Wharton School of Finance and Commerce at the University of Pennsylvania. Upon graduation, he interned at an American bank for a year and returned to China in 1910. After being fired from a Chinese bank for refusing to reveal the names of its account holders to a Chinese warlord, Chen founded his own bank with several partners, also returned students from the United States, in June 1915.

Chen started the Shanghai Commercial and Savings Bank with less than $50,000. His competitors called it "the little Shanghai bank." By 1926, Chen's bank was no longer little. It handled more foreign exchange transactions than any other private bank in China and was China's fifth-ranked commercial bank. Inspired by the American way of doing business, Chen focused on the customer. He established China's first "dollar savings accounts" for small depositors. He lent to industrialists when other Chinese banks favored merchants. He preferred long-term relationships and long-term profits; his competitors ran after a quick buck. Despite grumbling from the Westerners who monopolized China's railway industry, he founded a travel agency and sliced into their profits. He established a fund at his bank to send up-and-coming managers to the United States for training.

Chen was a patriot, but he broke ranks with ultranationalist Chinese who wanted to expel Western businesses from China. He believed that Western competition was essential to making China great. He argued that China's institutions would improve only by vying with Western banks for customers. Chen's ideas on the importance of American business practices to improving China would resurface again and again.

Americans were great fans of K. P. Chen. Hans Morgenthau, the secretary of the Treasury during World War II, called Chen "everything that a story-book Chinese businessman should be and most of them ain't!" *Time* magazine described him as "of average height, moderately fat, bespectacled, careful." Chen had no hobbies, *Time* said; he just "works 24 hours a day."

With insurance, cigarettes, newspapers, advertising, and banks, American and American-trained entrepreneurs, missionaries, and scientists sought to remake the Middle Kingdom in America's image. Like America's diplomats, they, too, hoped for a strong united China. The problem, however, was that for most American businessmen, this China remained a dream. Throughout the early twentieth century, American trade and investment with China barely budged. America was important to China; from the 1930s on, the United States was China's number one trading partner. But China's market was not important to the United States. After the early 1800s, trade with the Middle Kingdom never exceeded more than 2 percent of America's total for decades. And China was littered with bad American investments, huge losses, and dashed hopes. From his perch in Shanghai, Carl Crow watched a string of American pharmaceutical and cosmetic company executives who had come to China with "rosy daydreams in which a private yacht occupies the foreground and a country estate can be seen in the middle distance." Many had cut huge deals with Chinese partners only to find, on returning home, that those "fat orders" had disappeared.

●

CHAPTER FOURTEEN

The Soong Dynasty

On May 30, 1925, just over two months after Sun Yat-sen died, British police in the International Settlement of Shanghai fired on Chinese students who were protesting the killing of a Chinese worker at a Japanese textile mill. At least nine demonstrators died. Boycotts and marches followed.

The Soviets used the May Thirtieth Movement to agitate for open season on Westerners across China. Communist Party founder Chen Duxiu stressed that America was no exception. Anyone, he declared, who "advocates that America is China's friend is a traitor to the Chinese nationalist movement." On street corners, young Communists sermonized against "imperialistic foreign devils." In June 1925, a general strike against all foreign firms was called in Guangzhou. Chinese working for Westerners were ordered to stay home. Pamphlets similar in tone to the 1860 antimissionary screed, "A Record of Facts to Ward Off the Cult," circulated on Guangzhou's streets. Up the coast in Shantou, where Adele Fielde had spent decades teaching women to read, Chinese who were found aiding Westerners were beaten. The Masonic Hall, where Fielde had taught, was looted. In Wuzhou, near Guangzhou, an American hospital was attacked.

Hundreds of Russian operatives moved throughout southern China, directed by Mikhail Borodin. He hadn't created Chinese nationalism or its particular strain of anti-Western bigotry, but he gave it a focus—the West and especially Britain and the United States. As American reporter George

Sokolsky wrote at the time, "Borodin turned Chinese nationalism Communistic and utilized anti-Christianity as a weapon to drive American cultural influence out of China. He almost succeeded."

By 1926, Chiang Kai-shek had emerged as the leader of the Nationalist Party. Born in 1887 in Zhejiang province along the coast, Chiang had lost his father, a salt merchant, as a boy. A boyhood tutor described him as "wild and ungovernable." In his twenties, Chiang studied at a Japanese military academy, returned to China, dabbled in Shanghai's stock market to raise money for the Republican revolution, and became a denizen of Shanghai's underworld. Along the way, he collected three wives and one son. But as he rose through the ranks of the Kuomintang, he tamed his wild side and began a daily regime of meditation and readings. Like Mao Zedong, Chiang believed that he had been chosen to play a leading role in China's future. "I will cultivate a glorious stature so as to be illustrious throughout the world," he vowed.

The idea that Chiang was a closet Fascist has been a foundational myth promoted by left-wing American academics. It helped explain why a man known as the Generalissimo deserved to lose the civil war to the Chinese Communist Party in 1949. But Chiang was far more than the venal villain in the passion play of US-China relations. He was, for one thing, notes the historian Jay Taylor, his own worst critic. In a diary that he kept from 1918 until a heart attack in 1972, he described himself variously as "wicked," "extravagant," "lascivious," "ruthless and tyrannical," and "full of sorrow and indignation." Chiang was clearly an autocrat. But he was also an impassioned patriot, a die-hard foe of imperialism and, on the issue of economics, despite his close ties to America's right wing, a socialist.

In the mid-1920s, northern China was still controlled by a handful of warlords. Some leaned toward Japan; some favored the United States and Britain. Chiang was eager to fulfill Sun Yat-sen's dream to unite his country. On July 9, 1926, he spoke to one hundred thousand soldiers of the National Revolutionary Army gathered at the Whampoa Military Academy, readying his men for war.

To pay for his campaigns, Chiang relied for decades on American-trained bankers. Two of them, T. V. Soong and H. H. Kung, ultimately became his brothers-in-law. While the Soviets and then the Germans furnished Nationalist China with military advice and materiel, American-educated Chinese raised Chiang's revenues and secured his loans. The tradition continues; China's Ministry of Finance is staffed by dozens of American-educated bankers today.

In popular accounts, written with more venom than veracity, Soong and Kung have been portrayed as privileged, corrupt, and money hungry—wily Chinese bamboozling Americans while their country burned. The reality is more complex. The two were enormously successful in bankrolling Chiang's wars, increasing China's revenues, allowing a Chinese government to take control of its finances for the first time in almost a century, and creating a national currency.

Nonetheless, if finances were key to the rise of Chiang Kai-shek, they were also crucial to his fall. The central problem was Chiang's inability to grasp the consequences of using his government as a printing press to churn out endless reams of cash. He also looked to America as a piggy bank; the Americans would dub him "Cash My Check."

Although forever bound by family ties and their training in the United States, Soong and Kung disagreed about how to manage China's economy. Soong believed that China needed to cut military spending and grow the economy. That stance regularly threw him into conflict with Chiang Kai-shek, who would fire him, then call him back, several times. In contrast, Kung bent to Chiang's wishes and embraced the disastrous idea that China could print its way out of debt. Kung's wife, Soong Ailing, was undeniably corrupt. Even before the Second World War, she was implicated in a scheme to skim money from a program to buy American planes. Kung himself was probably corrupt, too. But it's unclear how deeply T. V. Soong's fingers dipped into the Nationalist cookie jar.

T. V. Soong was tall and proportionately broad. He combed his black hair back in a pompadour and favored glasses with tortoiseshell frames. When discussing matters of state, he would slouch in a leather chair and dangle his legs over one arm. Although he'd graduated with a degree in English from Harvard in 1915, he was a whiz at mathematics, taking courses in economics at Columbia University while he worked on Wall Street. Soong spoke English like a Boston Brahmin and used it to correspond with his father, Charlie Soong, and other Chinese friends. He wrote his speeches in English and had major documents that needed his attention translated from the Chinese. Having spent his formative years in America, Soong exhibited a "Yankeefied drive and impatience," noted American diplomat John Paton Davies, that grated on many Chinese. He was stalked by dark moods and constipation.

Chiang Kai-shek viewed his brother-in-law's can-do spirit as both an opportunity and a threat. When Soong helped establish China's air force, Chiang took steps to ensure that Soong did not control it. When Soong turned China's Salt Administration tax collection force into an army with modern weapons, Chiang worried that he was plotting a coup. In 1934, Soong was ousted as finance minister and replaced by his more malleable brother-in-law, H. H. Kung. To Arthur Young, an American who advised China's ministry of finance throughout the war years, Chiang's turn to the pliant Kung had enormous consequences. "Soong could have done better during the war," said Young.

While Soong brooded, Kung was all backslaps and bonhomie. Rotund like a teddy bear, he favored Cuban cigars and dispensed more gifts—to warlords, out-of-favor politicians, and gangsters—than Santa. After graduating from Oberlin College in 1906, Kung returned to China to run a missionary school but soon tired of proselytizing and went into business. He became an agent for British American Tobacco and Standard Oil, hawking cigarettes and kerosene. When Yuan Shikai cracked down on the Republican revolution in 1913, Kung joined the exodus of Chinese republicans to Tokyo. There he met Sun Yat-sen and the family of Charlie Soong. In 1914, he married Charlie Soong's first daughter, Soong Ailing. A year later, Sun Yat-sen divorced his village wife and eloped with Charlie's middle daughter, Soong Qingling, ending his friendship with Charlie Soong. Soong Qingling was barely twenty; Sun was forty-eight.

In June 1917, T. V. Soong returned to Shanghai from Harvard and a stint at the International Banking Corporation. It wasn't easy coming home. He preferred American food to Chinese. He pined for his friends at the fraternity that he had started, called the Flip Flop Club. By 1923, T. V. Soong was in Guangzhou, where Sun Yat-sen appointed him general manager of the newly founded Central Bank of China.

As the Kuomintang prepared to unite China, Soong employed New York smarts and Chinese muscle to raise money for Chiang's Northern Expedition. At the time, Standard Oil of New York dominated the energy business in China. In 1926, Soong offered Standard Oil a deal under which its taxes would be increased significantly above the old tariff of 5 percent in exchange for something close to a monopoly in Nationalist territory. John MacMurray, the US minister in Beijing, fought the idea. Like many American diplomats, MacMurray opposed the Nationalists and was wedded to the old system, under which Westerners set China's tariff rates and disbursed its revenues.

Standard Oil turned Soong down. Soong then blocked Standard Oil's sales in southern China and seized its stocks in Guangzhou. Pro-Nationalist labor unions struck Standard Oil's warehouses and distribution centers, shutting down the business from Shanghai to the south. MacMurray wanted American gunboats to teach the Nationalists a lesson. But Standard Oil ignored the American minister and took Soong's deal instead. The strikes stopped. And Soong adjusted Standard Oil's taxes after the oil company agreed to pay in advance. Imports of Standard Oil fuel jumped 40 percent in 1926 alone. Meanwhile, labor action continued to shutter British competitors. By 1927, Soong had collected $3.5 million from Standard Oil, enough to pay for a large part of the Northern Expedition.

Soong next set his sights on British American Tobacco. For years, the Nanyang Brothers had cultivated the Nationalists in Guangzhou, urging them to help Chinese businesses battle Western firms. Figuring that he could appease the Chinese business community and squeeze more revenue from the Americans, Soong slapped a 40 percent tax on all foreign cigarette brands in southern China. In exchange for an agreement not to hike taxes, BAT counteroffered to pay almost $4 million up front. With that, two American firms, BAT and Standard Oil, had become China's largest taxpayers.

Soong Mayling, the baby of the Soong family, was born in March 1898 in Shanghai. By that time, her father, Charlie Soong, had become a successful businessman. Mayling was raised in a house in the Hongkou section, far from the putrid slums of the inner city. The family led a hybrid existence. Charlie, imbued with an American do-it-yourself spirit, raised his own vegetables. The Soong home boasted the latest Yankee gadgets—running water, gas heating, and kerosene lights. At night, the family gathered around the piano where Mayling's mother, Ni Guizhen, would play Stephen Foster ballads and the Southern anthem, "Dixie."

Ni kept a Christian home: no alcohol, cards, or dancing allowed. "I must ask God first" was her response to requests. For a Chinese mother, she was revolutionary. Her feet were not bound, and she kept the crippling rags away from her daughters. Nor would they be cloistered like the girls in other families. Her daughters received an education equal to that of their brothers. The girls attended Shanghai's elite McTyeire School—founded by Young John Allen. T. V. Soong and his brothers went to St. John's College—the finest school for boys.

In 1903, Charlie Soong sent his first daughter, Ailing, to the United States to Wesleyan Female College in Macon, Georgia. In 1907, when it was

Qingling's turn, Mayling, barely nine, insisted that she be allowed to tag along. Mayling and Qingling went first to New Jersey to stay with a family and "became Americanized so fast we hardly remembered they were Chinese," wrote Dorothy Jaegels, a neighbor. A year later, the pair headed south to Wesleyan Female College. Mayling dabbled with cosmetics—which the straitlaced Southern Methodists considered risqué—and commented freely on the strangeness of Americans. "She will never learn to watch her tongue," fretted big sister Qingling.

Qingling graduated in 1913, and Mayling brought her southern lilt north to Wellesley College in Massachusetts to be near her brother, T. V., at Harvard. Just fifteen, Mayling refused to admit that she was Chinese. She called herself a "hot Confederate." Southern fried chicken was her favorite dish, and she showed so little ethnic pride that her friends at Wellesley found it hard to imagine that she would ever return to China. Like her father, she was drawn to Westerners of the opposite sex—an attraction that would complicate her life. As a student, she exhibited flashes of brilliance. She also sank—like T. V. Soong—into depression and would sometimes lock herself in her dorm room for days. At Wellesley, she majored in English literature and philosophy.

As Mayling neared the end of her senior year, the question of what to do next weighed heavily. "The only thing Oriental about me is my face," she told a friend. She considered staying in America, but her family called her back. She graduated in June 1917 as a Durant Scholar—Wellesley's highest academic honor. She wept as her train pulled out of Grand Central Terminal bound for Vancouver and a ship home. She was nineteen.

In Shanghai, Mayling moved into her parents' newish home in the leafy French Concession. It boasted a sprawling garden, a tennis court, and a croquet pitch. She and big brother T. V. occupied the entire third floor. She studied Chinese, tutored her younger brothers in English, and raised money for famine victims. Mayling missed the freedom and the bustle of the United States. "I just feel my mental powers getting more and more dulled every day," she lamented in a letter to an American friend. She hated Chinese music and retched at the smell of garlic. "I have not yet assimilated the things . . . Oriental," she confessed. She wanted a career. Her sisters—both married—schemed to set her up with a man. She fell in love with at least two Westerners, according to her biographer Laura Tyson Li, but her mother nixed those liaisons. "Our family is so conservative and puffed up with family pride over keeping 'pure' the family blood that they would rather see me dead than marry a foreigner," Mayling complained.

She longed to find her place in a world that promised more opportunities for women than it actually provided. She served on Shanghai's film censorship board and was given a position on the city's foreign-dominated Municipal Council, where she fought against child labor. She was the president of the American College Club and on the board of a hospital. And she perfected a weapon that she would wield for the rest of her life. She found that her combination of southern gentility, New England polish, and Oriental allure held remarkable sway over Western men.

"I go to the managers of the banks personally and look them in the eye and literally the money rolls in!" she gushed to an American friend about her fund-raising efforts for the YWCA. Mayling always brought along a Western female chaperone from her church, but she did the talking. She wore her finest clothes. "To be well dressed means that a large contribution will be assured," she confided, "for the men would be ashamed to give any sum too small to buy my shoes with at least!"

In December 1922, Mayling met Chiang Kai-shek at a Christian revival meeting at Sun Yat-sen's home. Chiang was a junior military aide to Sun. After that, there is no record of any contact between the two until 1926. The story is told that once Chiang took the reins of the Nationalist army, Mayling's eldest sister, Ailing, fastened on him as a likely prospect for Mayling. "He was the only revolutionist in China who could make the revolution stick," wrote the American journalist and family friend George Sokolsky. Chiang Kai-shek was the perfect match for the ambitious Mayling.

Pouring up from southern China, as the Taipings had three generations earlier, Chiang's armies rolled over their warlord foes. On July 11, 1926, two days after his speech at the Whampoa Military Academy, Chiang and his men marched into Changsha, the capital of Hunan province, just four hundred miles north of Guangzhou.

By January 1927, Nationalist forces had captured the industrial center of Hankou on the Yangtze River. Throughout southern China, whipped up by Communist agitators, Nationalist soldiers looted Christian missions and menaced foreigners. Missionaries fled with "their clothes, their skins, and little else," wrote Phil Greene, a surgeon at the Yale-in-China hospital in Changsha. Greene, his wife, Ruth, and their four children left Changsha, crammed onto a tugboat. One boat arriving in Nanjing from Hunan held 158 people aboard a vessel built to hold thirty.

The American press seized upon the Nationalist campaign as another sign of hope for China. The *Baltimore Sun* said that the Nationalist troops represented "a spirit as fine as anything that animated the revolutionary troops of George Washington." Downplaying the significance of Communist infiltration, the *New York World* gushed that "Chiang's army is as red as Washington's at Valley Forge."

But on the ground, Westerners worried that another Boxer Rebellion was at hand. "You feel as if you were living in a madhouse," wrote Alice Tisdale Hobart in *Harper's Monthly*. "The refugees from Changsha were all doctors and teachers. . . . There is something shattering about it all—their life work destroyed." Hobart considered herself lucky to be living in relative safety in Nanjing. Still, she predicted, "our turn will come."

The Nationalists marched into Nanjing, the old capital of the Taipings' Heavenly Kingdom, on Thursday morning, March 24, 1927. Nationalist troops shot a British consul and killed Nanjing University vice president John E. Williams when he balked at handing over his watch. Goaded by Communist agents, Nationalist forces looted foreign homes and killed foreigners. Fifty-two Westerners sought protection in the Standard Oil compound on a hill overlooking the Yangtze River. Nationalist soldiers massed by Standard Oil's door. Alice Hobart's husband, Earle, walked outside and offered them tea. Huddled indoors, Alice Hobart thought, "In five minutes I shall be a widow." But the soldiers held their fire.

A short time later, another contingent of Nationalist troops attacked. From the roof of the Standard Oil house, US sailors signaled US and British gunboats on the Yangtze. American and British artillery shells thundered around the perimeter of the house, and the Chinese troops fled. The Westerners then sprinted to the banks of the Yangtze, shimmying down sixty feet of bedsheets to waiting boats below. After helping others to safety, Earle Hobart took the leap, breaking his ankle.

Like Pearl Buck, Alice Hobart found her views on China transformed by the Nanjing Incident. Alice had moved to China in 1910 to teach and had married Hobart, an up-and-coming salesman for Standard Oil of New York. By 1927, she had already written two books and had become an ardent admirer of American big business and a booster of America's role as enlightener of the Chinese. But face-to-face with murderous xenophobia in Nanjing, she found herself doubting that America's beneficence had done anything for China.

Despite her husband's heroism in protecting Nanjing's foreigners, Standard Oil forced Earle Hobart to resign. The couple returned to the United States, where Alice completed what would be the greatest book of her career: *Oil for the Lamps of China*, a novel about Stephen Chase, an American oil trader, his frail wife, Hester, and their Chinese associates.

Hobart's title paid tribute to the munificent contribution that US business thought it was making to China's modernization. It conveyed the image of an enterprising oil company exporting kerosene to China so that every home and every mind would be illuminated—literally and figuratively—by light from the United States. But, like her real-life husband, the book's hero, Stephen Chase, is betrayed by his company and by the new China as well. In the novel's climax, Chinese who had worked loyally with the Americans are incinerated by the very American import—kerosene—brought to open Chinese minds. "This thing called progress," Hobart wrote, "was upon China now." However, it was not "like the bright flame of a lamp illuminating the darkness." Rather it was "more like some gigantic man seeking to be born, tearing and destroying the womb in the agony of birth." Published in 1933, *Oil for the Lamps of China* became a best seller, second in sales only to Pearl Buck's *The Good Earth* among American works on China at the time.

Hobart and thousands of Americans like her had expected China to take Western ideas and technology and go in one direction, but it was careening in another. Dashed hopes for China's republican revolution dismayed America's apostles of business and the Lord. Once believing that they could do everything—feed, clothe, cleanse, build, teach, and transform China—America's missionaries now reckoned that they had accomplished nothing. "We cannot evangelize China. We cannot cure China's multiplying diseases. We cannot educate her multiplying millions or feed them," announced Frank Gamewell, the American missionary-builder who had masterminded the defense of the foreign legation during the Boxer Rebellion and now led Methodist efforts in China. Whereas the Boxer fiasco had precipitated a surge of American passion to change China, the Northern Expedition had the opposite effect. In 1925, there had been 8,300 Protestant missionaries in China, the most ever and most of them American. After the campaign, thousands of them sailed for the United States, never to return.

Just as one group of Americans lost faith in the Middle Kingdom, a new brand of Yankee embraced a different dream for China. Rejecting the piecemeal "retail" reforms advocated by John Dewey, Young John Allen, and Jimmy Yen, Americans of a progressive bent now sought "wholesale" change. In the tradition of Issachar Jacox Roberts, they championed a new kind of "blitzconversion" of China. But instead of a Christian nation, these Americans envisaged a socialist one.

In the late 1920s, the old convictions of the China mission—that the Beautiful Country was the proper model for the Middle Kingdom—gave way to unease. Capitalism wobbled and Russia beckoned. "We are much less sure of our traditional convictions," observed American Lydia Johnson, a YWCA worker in Tianjin. "Not only is the atom proving capable of being split, and time itself challenged by Mr. Einstein, but we are beginning to question seriously the time-honored bulwark of our economic structure, the capitalistic system and 'rights' of private property." Johnson noted that "our 'rugged American individualism' . . . is being held up for critical examination." Not just by Americans but by the Chinese as well.

In early 1927, as the National Revolutionary Army moved north, the left wing of the Kuomintang, along with the Communists and Stalin's agent Mikhail Borodin, established a new government in Hankou, an industrial center on the Yangtze five hundred miles upriver from Shanghai. A tribe of American reporters and political activists, many of whom had witnessed the Bolshevik Revolution in Russia, descended on the riverside metropolis. Bill Prohme and his fiery-haired partner, Rayna, led the charge.

Bill and Rayna had moved to China in 1924 from California, stopping first in Beijing. Rayna had taken a job editing the Beijing *People's Tribune*, a leftist paper, run by Eugene Chen, a smooth-talking half-black lawyer from the Caribbean. To the Prohmes, the Middle Kingdom offered an escape from the middle-class existence of home. China attracted the Prohmes on an individual basis much as it drew the Rockefeller Foundation on an institutional one. It was an arena where Americans were free to experiment and to witness a transformation that had been completed back home. "I want to see what happens to a people when their friendly family world suddenly becomes strange and bewildering," Rayna wrote as she prepared for her adventure.

In Beijing, Bill and Rayna sheltered Communists. Rayna wrote editorials haranguing the warlord government. When word circulated of a plot to kill her and her husband, Rayna laughed it off. "Wouldn't it be fun if we were arrested and the American Legation would have to send its marine guard to rescue us?" she chuckled to a friend. But when the American legation made it clear that the shield of extraterritoriality couldn't block an assassin's bullet, they left the capital for the south.

In the spring of 1927, Eugene Chen, now foreign minister of the government in Hankou, appointed Rayna as the new government's international press representative. She handled press appointments for Mikhail

Borodin and served as personal secretary to Soong Qingling, the widow of Sun Yat-sen. Rayna worked out of a building in the old German Concession. Borodin lived on the third floor. The Comintern offices were on the second. Other American radicals soon arrived: Anna Louise Strong, a Soviet acolyte who would promote revolution from China to Russia and back for decades, and Paul Blanshard of the *Nation*.

English was a bond among these fellow travelers, and after work, Borodin, Eugene Chen, Sun Ke, the Columbia University–educated son of Sun Yat-sen, and Soong Qingling, whom the Americans all called Suzie but who referred to herself as Rosamonde, would gather at the Prohmes' apartment to talk politics and sing "The Internationale." It was, veteran American correspondent Randall Gould observed, "more like an excited lot of college freshmen than a real revolution."

Earl Browder was another member of the Chinese American fraternity. He had cut his teeth as a labor organizer in the American Midwest and was in the middle of a two-year stint in China before he would lead the Communist Party of the USA. Browder was not very impressed with Borodin and other Comintern agents, who lived like grandees, with chauffeurs and big American cars, while fomenting revolution on the side. At Browder's first meal in China, he theatrically refused to eat anything but bread and water in solidarity with the Russian peasants who had paid his way. Such contradictions did not bother Rayna. She was starstruck. Borodin, she wrote, "has impressed me more than any person I have met in a long time, as a man, a personality, a social force." As for Suzie Soong, who would captivate a generation of American writers, Rayna wrote, "she is a marvelous person."

One of the most trenchant observers of the blossoming American journalistic obsession with Chinese revolutionaries was Milly Bennett, born Mildred Jacqueline Bremler in San Francisco in 1897. Bennett belonged to a generation of pathbreaking women journalists who wandered the globe in the 1920s and 1930s reporting on rebellions and wars.

Bennett noted with wry amusement the unthinking wonder of the American journalist crowd, "bowled over" by Soong Qingling, with her idiomatic American English, the scandalously romantic saga of her marriage to Sun Yat-sen, and her brave opposition to the autocratic Generalissimo Chiang Kai-shek. One American reporter, Bennett noted, "came away from his interview with Mrs. Sun Yat-sen pronouncing her 'the most beautiful woman in the world.'" American reporters, she wrote, "come to Hankow to observe the unorthodox doings and they go away in a dither of hero worship." Among journalists and academics of the American left, the hero worship of China's radicals would continue for years.

Two days after the Nanjing Incident, on March 26, 1927, Chiang Kai-shek came to in Shanghai to calm fears about an impending massacre of foreigners. Shanghai's better-informed Westerners had begun to understand that Chiang, whom many had dubbed "the Bolshevik General" due to his earlier stay in Moscow, was no Bolshevik at all. They also realized that Chiang Kai-shek's relations with the Communists and left-wing Nationalists close to Soong Qingling were anything but good. The Kuomintang's left wanted to expel Westerners from China and follow the Soviet Union. Chiang believed that the West's support was crucial if China was to modernize.

Chiang arrived in Shanghai to find the Communists leading a provisional government in the city. As he plotted to unseat them, Chiang reached out to his old friends in Shanghai's underworld. His forces also needed the services of an American. In early April 1927, Stirling Fessenden, the stuffy Maine-born chairman of the Municipal Council, was called to a meeting in the French Concession with the French chief of police and a top gangster named Big Eared Tu.

Big Eared Tu asked the French for five thousand rifles. From Fessenden, he requested approval to use the International Settlement as a base from which to ambush Communist strongholds. The French provided the weapons, and Fessenden allowed the gangsters free passage. Fessenden was "taking a desperate chance," as he later told journalist John B. Powell, but he believed that a Communist takeover had to be avoided at all costs.

On April 12, Nationalist troops and underworld hit squads went after the Communists. Hundreds were executed, hundreds were arrested, and thousands fled the city. Fessenden wasn't the only American involved in the bloodshed. T. V. Soong's contacts at Standard Oil got into the act. In February 1927, as tensions simmered, Standard Oil's Shanghai office had advanced Chiang's operatives $350,000. When Chiang's forces began to root out radicals from the General Labor Union, which had helped the Communists seize Shanghai, A. C. Cornish, Standard's agent in Hankou, slipped Chiang's men the names of Communist operatives. In late 1927, Henry Everall, who ran Standard's operations in north and central China, wrote to headquarters in New York that the firm's cooperation in eliminating Communists had put Standard in a better position than other foreign companies in China. The liquidation of Communist labor organizers had done much for "stability," he said.

The clampdown in Shanghai shocked the Communists not because of its brutality but because of its swiftness. After all, Stalin had advised Borodin that when it came to Chiang, he should: "Utilize to the end, squeeze out like a lemon, and then fling away." But the Generalissimo had struck first.

On July 14, Rayna published Soong Qingling's "Appeal to the Chinese People," in which she accused Chiang Kai-shek of abandoning her husband's principles. Qingling yearned for a real revolution, Rayna wrote, not "merely a change in government." Four days later, Soong Qingling and Rayna slipped out of Hankou on a sampan. Two weeks after that, Borodin fled as well. Soon they were all bound for Moscow on a special train.

On November 20, 1927, in Moscow, a blood vessel exploded in Rayna's brain, and she was dead by nightfall. At her funeral, she was eulogized for her selfless devotion to China's cause. What John Reed had been to Soviet Russia, Rayna Prohme was to China, her eulogists claimed. One person called her China's Lafayette. In 1935, reporter Vincent Sheean dedicated a best-selling memoir, *Personal History*, to Prohme. Hers, he wrote, was "a marvelously pure flame." But after that Rayna Prohme was forgotten.

Chiang Kai-shek required more than underworld muscle to unite China. He needed the support of China's elite. With Soong Ailing acting as matchmaker, he was offered the backing of Shanghai's wealthy on three conditions: that he appoint her husband H. H. Kung prime minister and her brother T. V. minister of finance and that he marry her youngest sister, Soong Mayling. Chiang agreed and told his wife, Jennie, that he needed this "political marriage" to save China. He packed her off to the United States, where she attempted suicide and wrote a damning memoir, published after both she and Chiang had died.

Chiang and Soong Mayling wed on December 1, 1927, in Shanghai, first in a private Christian service at the Soong family home, followed by an opulent Chinese ceremony at the Majestic Hotel. "Our wedding is more than a celebration of our happiness," Chiang told his followers; "our marriage today is the foundation of the Revolution."

There was something about Mayling—her verve, her energy, her charisma, her Americanness—that Chiang Kai-shek needed to succeed. For Mayling equally, Chiang was the vehicle through which she could realize her Yankee-inspired dreams. Burning inside her, she wrote, was "a passionate desire to do something for my country. Here was my opportunity."

Chiang's marriage to a devout Methodist sparked another wave of expectations among the missionary crowd, which had so recently lost faith in China. In Washington, Stephen Porter, the Republican chairman of the House Foreign Relations Committee, shepherded through a resolution calling for a new relationship with China, one based "on mutual fairness and equity." The United States, Porter argued, should unilaterally agree to do away with its privileges in China as an example to the rest of the world.

The American press fawned over the couple. The announcement of their engagement made papers nationwide. There were some titters about Chiang's shady past and the fact that his ex-wife had surfaced in the US. But by the time Chiang and Soong Mayling actually married, the couple received nothing but Yankee acclaim. The ceremony, wrote Edna Lee Booker, the Shanghai correspondent for the New York–based *International News Service*, was "impressive, very beautiful, a bit exotic . . . with its touch of the East and the West." China had found its leader.

CHAPTER FIFTEEN

Opportunity or Threat

As the ideological battle between the Chinese Communists and the Kuomintang sharpened in the late 1920s, political assassinations, kidnappings, and disappearances became routine. But there was one thing on which both extremes of China's political spectrum could agree: the United States had become a threat.

The problem for China's politicians was that despite political disappointments at Versailles and a deafening drumbeat of anti-imperialism at home, the Chinese remained broadly predisposed to Yankee influence, and not simply in education. American culture was flourishing in China, especially in its greatest city, Shanghai.

Shanghai's nickname—"Paris of the East"—was a misnomer; the city, the most polyglot metropolis in Asia, was more of a mix of Manhattan and a frontier boomtown. Though the British directed much of the economy, Americans owned the power and phone companies, ran the best schools, and dominated entertainment and the arts. In Shanghai, there were "radio and jazz bands, cocktails and correspondence schools, night clubs and cabarets, neon lights and skyscrapers, chewing-gum and Buicks, wide trousers and long skirts, Methodist evangelists and the Salvation Army," reported journalist Edgar Snow, who moved there in 1928. The Yanks cast a long shadow. The year Snow moved there barely two thousand Americans lived in a city of more than two million people. That didn't stop Snow from declaring, however, that Shanghai "has become Americanized."

Babe Ruth (Beibei Luosi in Chinese) visited in December 1934 at the head of a barnstorming team. American adventurers, scam artists, playboys, and sportsmen, dramatic troupes and circuses, movie stars and musicians— all beat a path there. By the early 1930s, the neoclassical British buildings that lined the Bund along the Huangpu River were making way for American-inspired art deco palaces. Films starring Douglas Fairbanks, Charlie Chaplin, and the Keystone Cops beat out anything the Europeans could offer. In 1935, more than 350 American movies were shown in China— more than 90 percent of all films. (By contrast, today's China allows in only 34 foreign films a year.) The Chinese churned out a stream of copies: Chinese Westerns, Chinese romances, Chinese slapstick. Chinese directors invariably had kung-fu stars don cowboy hats. Hollywood shaped the Chinese sense of what's funny and what's romantic, too.

The arrival of Duke Ellington's first recordings in the 1920s touched off a craze for American music and a Great Harmony of sorts in the melding of American jazz with Chinese folk tunes. Black American musicians became a fixture in Shanghai's clubs. The Depression in America was still in full swing back home, and American jazz bands jumped at the chance to cross the Pacific for a long-term gig. Working in Shanghai beat "looking for jobs in such ridiculous places as hot-dog stands" in America, wrote trumpeter Buck Clayton, whose band, Buck Clayton, and the Harlem Gentlemen, held court at the swanky Canidrome Ballroom throughout 1935.

Clayton teamed up with a Chinese musician named Li Jinhui to bring a jazz sensibility to Chinese folk songs. The result, known as *shidaiqu*, or "modern melodies," was a hit. Critics from the Left and the Right lambasted Li's compositions for their romantic content and decidedly nonrevolutionary vibe. The Nationalists and Communists both called them pornographic. Regardless, the foot-tapping arrangements lodged themselves in the minds of the Chinese and set the foundation for modern Chinese music—Cantopop and Mandopop. In 1967, during the Cultural Revolution, Red Guards branded Li a "corruptor" of public morals; he died of a heart attack during a beating that year.

American values worried Chiang Kai-shek. Though he modeled China's new capital, Nanjing, on Washington, DC, Chiang was less inclined toward American ideals than Sun Yat-sen. Challenged by warlords and the Communist Party, he had little use for the American concepts of personal freedom or democracy. He valued loyalty above all.

In his views of America, Chiang shared something with Mao Zedong, who loathed the way many of his compatriots admired the United States. As Chiang told American reporter Lewis Gannett in 1926, "Thinking men in China hate America more than they hate Japan." Japan talked to China in terms of ultimatums. "She says frankly that she wants special privileges," Chiang said. "We understand that and know how to meet it." But the Americans, he said, "come to us with smiling faces and friendly talk" but do nothing to help China. "Because we have been deceived by your sympathetic talk," Chiang said, "we end by hating you most."

Where Sun Yat-sen was clearly inspired by Abraham Lincoln in formulating his "Three People's Principles," Chiang linked those concepts to Confucius. "There is nothing in European and American political thought that surpasses" the Confucian classics, he declared. Chiang would denounce liberalism and Communism with equal intensity.

The Communist Party had also fixed its sights on American liberalism. By the 1920s, the party's cofounder, Chen Duxiu, who had once branded Woodrow Wilson "the number one good man in the world," had lost his affection for the American Way. When he learned that US immigration officers had detained a group of Chinese students at the US border, he exulted. Let those Chinese suffer, he sneered, because "it is public knowledge that almost every single American-trained student opposes revolution, worships money, and idolizes the United States. The fewer such Chinese the better."

A string of Communist Party congresses starting in 1922 identified the United States as one of the main enemies of China's revolution. It was a formidable opponent, the party noted, because so many Chinese were passionately pro-American. The party spilled vast quantities of ink trying to convince Chinese not to be hoodwinked by America's promises. In a 1929 policy paper, the Communists charged that American missionary, health, and education activities were "only a disguise of liberalism." Anyone who doubted that, said Chen Duxiu, "is a traitor."

Mao Zedong's youthful dalliance with American ideals was over as well. In the 1920s, he applauded a string of terrorist bombings in the United States that touched off America's Red Scare. To him, American liberalism was an "extremely harmful tendency" that "disrupts unity, undermines solidarity, induces inactivity and creates dissension."

This change of heart was not merely political. With the dawn of the 1930s, influential Chinese began to take a more jaundiced view of American culture, too. American women in particular came under increased scrutiny. Once an ideal, they were now portrayed as extreme. This transformation was charted, for one, in the pages of *Linglong* magazine, China's most popular women's weekly in the 1930s—a combination of *House and Garden* and *Cosmopolitan*. Its entertainment section ran the usual stories of stars and films. But most noticeable was the focus on American excess.

Linglong's second issue in 1931 featured the actress Clara Bow—the It Girl of 1931. "She's so hot even her clothes have come off," read the caption. Next to Bow, the editors ran a photograph of a Shanghai beauty—Miss Zhou Ming. Zhou sat demurely on a bench with clothes covering everything but her face and hands. The message was clear. America may be an advanced nation, but it lacked morality.

As China modernized the question was, how fast? The writer and poet Sophia Chen, a friend of Hu Shih, who had fled an arranged marriage to attend Vassar College, spoke of a broad anxiety that social changes "too much, too soon" were threatening the foundations of Chinese culture. Chinese writers came up with a new storyline for America; it was too free, too loose, too wild. An article in 1934 reported on an American kissing competition; the winning couple smooched for three hours and two minutes. "The strangeness of Americans is clear from this," *Linglong's* editors opined. Chinese couples, it advised, should kiss "in moderation."

Hu Shih battled this anti-American tilt. Writing in 1930, he pleaded with the nation's young not to heed "the fools who've never been abroad who drone on 'Look to the East! Look to the East! The Western way won't work!'" Only by acknowledging that the West surpassed China "in its material wealth, political system, morality, knowledge, music, art and physique," he wrote, would China have any hope. Hu Shih's critics called him a traitor. When a US-educated Chinese political scientist named Chen Xujing seconded Hu Shih's position with a passionate call in 1933 for the "wholesale Westernization" of Chinese society, he was likewise criticized.

Mao, Chiang, and others feared American liberalism because, like other aspects of American culture, it was so well received. Though China's liberals have been airbrushed from China's modern history, in fact from the 1920s to the 1940s, a group of several hundred men and women, many educated in America, became the conscience of their nation in opposing the tyrannical ideologies of the Communists and the Kuomintang, resisting Japanese imperialism, and advocating democracy. Some of China's greatest writers and thinkers embraced the promise of American democracy. One of them was Lin Yutang.

Born into a family of poor Christians in rural Fujian province, Lin was a top student who spent his high school years in Shanghai at the American-run

St. John's College and then won a half scholarship at Harvard. Following a stint helping Jimmy Yen teach reading to Chinese workers in Europe, Lin returned to China to pursue a career as a writer.

In a 1924 essay, Lin created a word in Chinese, *youmo*, to sound like the English word "humor." In promoting his neologism, Lin was trying to carve out a place where the Chinese could debate their country's future with a smile. In the face of increasingly violent demands for ideological purity from both ends of the political spectrum, Lin advocated something revolutionary: tolerance. His magazines (he would be involved in more than six) welcomed all types of writers—socialists, Marxists, anarchists, liberals, Confucianists, his most ardent supporters, and his fiercest critics—as long as they were civil. And much to the chagrin of the Communists and the Kuomintang, the magazines were popular.

In his essay titled "On Humor," Lin noted that it was not that laughter did not exist in Chinese literature and culture. It was that it had been marginalized and underappreciated. In China, he wrote, "the serious becomes too serious and the non-serious too vulgar." He founded China's first two humor magazines: *The Analects Fortnightly* and *This Human World*.

Lin launched his magazines in the middle of a momentous battle over how China's best and brightest should serve the nation. Like Hu Shih, he believed that China should adopt the values of the liberal West. Lin disagreed with the notion that the struggle for "national salvation"—to which both the Communists and the Nationalists laid claim—justified sacrificing individual rights or a civil society.

He poked fun at Communist orthodoxy and at the censorship of the Kuomintang. He described himself as a man on a "tightrope." His highwire act was risky. When he fingered a warlord general involved in opium smuggling, secret agents shadowed him. Nationalist thugs assassinated two of his colleagues with whom Lin had founded the China League for the Protection of Civil Rights.

The Communist-controlled League of Chinese Left-Wing Writers attacked Lin, too. His problem, one leftist writer argued, was that his magazines encouraged people to think, when, given China's plight, such publications should instead drive people to hate. Essays "must be daggers, spears must be able to kill," the writer claimed. To the leftist art critic Hu Feng, Lin was "China's Nero, who would fiddle while the country burned." (After the Communist revolution, Hu would spend thirty-five years in the Communist gulag for questioning Mao Zedong.) In 1936, Lin left China for the United States.

In America, Lin authored two back-to-back best sellers about his home-land. *My Country and My People*, published in 1935, was the first popular nonfiction book about China written by a Chinese. Two years later came *The Importance of Living*, one of America's first self-help books, a witty antidote to the dizzying pace of 1930s America.

Lin presented the Chinese as a global model minority. He sketched a portrait of an approachable, unthreatening people, of an old and great culture different from the West but worthy of respect. His tone was almost apologetic. He treated white fears and prejudices as if they were the prod-ucts of rational thought. He dwelt on China's artistic, literary, and phil-osophic heritage, suggesting that China was superior to the West and that the Chinese were more intelligent than other ethnic groups, but in such a gentle way that American readers lapped it up. He censured Amer-icans for their racism and the Chinese for their absence of "public citizen-ship." He noted that Confucius's teaching made for strong families but was disastrous for society at large, as "the family became a walled castle outside which everything is legitimate to loot."

Back in China, others took up his torch. In 1919, Luo Longji was a Boxer Indemnity student at Tsinghua University during the May Fourth Move-ment. He led protests, prompting three deans to resign. Luo then went to America, and earned a PhD in political science at Columbia. Returning to China, he joined Hu Shih and Lin Yutang on a magazine called *Cres-cent Moon*. Luo challenged the dictates of the Nationalist and Communist Parties, which demanded that individuals sacrifice their freedom for the greater good. He countered that a free society would always be stronger than one that stifled expression.

In the 1930s and 1940s, Luo became the most active politician in China besides Chiang and Mao. He edited newspapers, organized protests, formed political parties, participated, when he was allowed to, in national conferences, and dodged assassins, when he was not. The questions he raised—among them whether China could recapture its greatness if it limited freedom—continue to vex China's leaders today.

Luo was equally critical of the Kuomintang and the Communists. In September 1929, he blasted the Nationalists for violating the ideals of Sun Yat-sen. Why, he asked, was it considered "rebellious" to want a constitu-tion, which China did not have, or "a cover for nefarious plotting" to dis-cuss human rights, which China also lacked? For that effrontery, he was arrested and jailed for several months.

Writing about the Communist Party the next year, Luo asked, "What magic does the Communist Party have to make everyone completely selfless?" Like most American-educated Chinese, Luo preferred the arduous process of evolution to the bright flameout of a revolution. What he really wanted was for Chiang Kai-shek to embrace reform and create an attractive alternative to the Communists. The first steps, he argued, would be to allow freedom of thought and end the Nationalists' one-party rule. Luo agreed with the argument—advanced by Liang Qichao and other thinkers—that China needed a "new people." But he rejected the contention—promulgated by both Chiang Kai-shek and Mao Zedong—that such a transformation could occur only under a dictatorship.

Chiang Kai-shek may have been reluctant to embrace American ideals, but by the late 1920s, he became increasingly interested in cultivating American support. Ever since the death of Sun Yat-sen, the Nationalist Party had placed little faith in the United States. Germany had become the Nationalist regime's principal supporter.

But in May 1928, as Chiang's armies headed north from the Yangtze Delta to extend Nationalist rule, they clashed with Japanese troops in Jinan, the capital of Shandong province. On May 3, Japanese forces slaughtered thousands of Chinese civilians and executed a team of Chinese negotiators. Chiang wrote in his diary that Japan would soon become China's chief enemy. This realization compelled China's leader to follow in the footsteps of his predecessors and resume the search for a special relationship with America. Chiang dispatched a string of diplomats and politicians to Washington to improve ties.

The Nationalists found Calvin Coolidge, who had entered office in 1923 after the unexpected death of President Warren Harding, in a receptive mood. After the Nanjing Incident in 1927, British officials had called for the execution of the commanding general along with his division commanders as punishment for the death of the six foreigners. At the US legation in Beijing, John MacMurray agreed. But in Washington, Frank Kellogg, Coolidge's secretary of state, noted that Chiang Kai-shek had apologized. Chiang was "apparently a leader of the Moderates" and should be encouraged, not chastised, Kellogg said. President Coolidge agreed, telling reporters that during a revolution, accidents happened.

On June 4, 1928, Japanese army officers assassinated Zhang Zuolin, the reigning warlord in Manchuria, as he rode in his private train through the northeast. Zhang had been on the verge of declaring loyalty to the Nationalist government, and the last thing the Japanese army wanted was a united China. The Nationalists redoubled their efforts to woo the United States. Officials from all the party's factions descended on Washington, seeking money, better ties, and American advice. Within a year, of the sixty-odd foreign advisers in Nanjing, thirty-two would be American; only two were Japanese.

In June 1928, Chiang's forces took Beijing. With the city of the Yellow Emperor in their hands, the Nationalists issued a statement: China was unified, and the government now wanted to wrest control of its customs revenues from the Westerners and the Japanese, who had controlled them for more than seventy years. Secretary of State Kellogg instructed Mac-Murray in Beijing to negotiate a new treaty. MacMurray opposed the idea.

MacMurray had been a longtime opponent of the Kuomintang, fearful of the party for encouraging what he called "furious anti-foreign feeling." He believed that the best way to deal with China's nationalism was to send in the gunboats. Kellogg, on the other hand, wanted America to cultivate China's Nationalists. He saw a new treaty as the way to restore China's faith in America and block "Communist activities inspired from Russia." He also sought to keep America ahead of Britain in the hearts of the Chinese.

In July, Nationalist finance minister T. V. Soong traveled to Beijing and with a reluctant MacMurray, he hammered out a new treaty with the United States. On July 25, 1928, the United States, the first power to recognize Republican China, became the first to agree to grant it control over its customs revenues. Eleven other nations followed suit within a year.

In 1928, Herbert Hoover was elected the thirty-first president of the United States. He was the first American president to have been to China before he entered the White House. Hoover had moved to China in 1899 as a twenty-five-year-old engineer, working for a British mining firm. He was appointed manager of the vast Chinese coal complex in Kaiping near Tianjin. When the Boxer Rebellion erupted a year later, Hoover volunteered as a scout for the US Marines as they lifted the siege of Tianjin. After the upheaval, the Chinese government sought to place key assets in the hands of British or American companies out of concern that Germans, Russians, and Japanese would seize them as part of the indemnity. Hoover transferred ownership of the Kaiping mines to his employer, Bewick, Moreing, and Company. But when the Chinese government asked for the mines back, the firm rejected the request. The deal put Hoover well on his way to becoming a millionaire, although a lawsuit by the Chinese government, which exposed this escapade, caused him considerable embarrassment later on. In another example of the intertwined destiny of Americans and Chinese, Hoover invested his China profits wisely and in 1919 made his first donation of $50,000 to Stanford University. That gift laid the foundations for the Hoover Institution on War, Revolution and Peace, still the most influential conservative think tank in the United States.

Hoover's secretary of state, Henry Stimson, was considerably more pro-China than his boss. Like his predecessor Kellogg, Stimson believed that the United States should become the first Western nation to treat China as an independent country. When the Nationalist government announced in 1929 that it wanted an end to the unequal treaties, Stimson thought the time had come. From Beijing, MacMurray again proposed dispatching the US Navy to scare the Chinese into submission, earning himself the nickname "America's gunboat minister" in the American press. Stimson cabled MacMurray that "the hour may already have passed" for that type of action. MacMurray resigned from his post in October 1929.

By the late 1920s, the Nationalists had partial control of eleven out of twenty-eight provinces. Chiang Kai-shek was keen to continue the battle to unite China, fighting both warlords and Communists while simultaneously seeking to keep the Japanese at bay. On the ground, German and Soviet officers trained China's army, but a ragtag band of Depression-era American stunt pilots, engineers, and salesmen taught the Chinese to fly. While official Washington juggled its support of China with its unwillingness to provoke Japan, unofficial America joined the fight on the side of Chiang Kai-shek.

The most famous Chinese aviator of the day was Zhang Weiqiang. Zhang had learned to fly in the United States, and in 1928, he bought a plane similar to Charles Lindbergh's *Spirit of St. Louis* and shipped it to China. In the fall of 1928, he barnstormed across the country, calling himself "the Lindbergh of China" and his plane "the Spirit of Canton." For a nation racked by political chaos, his flights—direct from Guangzhou to Hankou (600 miles in nine hours) and Beijing to Nanjing (660 miles in ten hours)—were a welcome diversion. (Charles Lindbergh himself showed up in China with his wife, Anne, landing their Lockheed Sirius 8 in the middle of Nanjing's Lotus Lake on September 19, 1931.)

Zhang rose to the top in the Nationalist government's newly created Aviation Department. He was keen to build a modern air force to use against the Communists, who had fled into the mountainous countryside in Fujian and Jiangxi provinces after the 1927 massacre in Shanghai. In September 1929, Zhang approached the Chance Vought Company and contracted to buy a dozen Corsair fighter-bombers—modern planes with a top speed of 158 mph—for about $1 million in gold.

The request was well timed. As the Depression rolled across the United States, shuttering factories and tossing millions out of work, the Commerce Department was eager for any deal that would save jobs. But the State Department agreed to the sale only if all the weapons—the machine guns and bomb racks—were removed. State Department officials were worried that selling weapons to China would endanger relations with Japan.

At an impasse, the US bureaucracy kicked the decision up to Herbert Hoover in the White House. Hoover authorized the sale—weapons included. And with that, the floodgates were opened. China's arms imports from America tripled in a year. From 1930 to 1934, China bought 478 tons of smokeless gunpowder—mostly from the DuPont Company in Delaware. United Aircraft Exports Company added one million rounds of ammunition, bombs, and other equipment for the planes. For the next decade, China would be American aircraft manufacturers' biggest foreign customer.

The arms sales underlined growing American support for the Nationalist government. But Hoover was clear; the United States would not challenge the Japanese as Tokyo sought to extend its control over Manchuria. Nothing Japan did in China's northeast, Hoover said, imperiled the "freedom," the "economic," or the "moral future" of the American people. As the newspapers of William Randolph Hearst editorialized at the time: "We SYMPATHIZE. But it is NOT OUR CONCERN."

Still, Americans did more than sell China warplanes; they were at the center of China's first aviation revolution. On St. Patrick's Day 1931, an American construction engineer with a toothbrush mustache and gray-blue eyes landed at the port of Shanghai and began a decades-long adventure that would remake flight in China.

William Langhorne Bond was a thirty-seven-year-old veteran of trench warfare in World War I. His last job had been building roads in the American South. Like most Americans, he'd been gripped by Charles Lindbergh's transatlantic adventure in 1927.

Bond had come to China at the behest of George Conrad Westervelt, who was married to Bond's first cousin and managing a joint venture—the China National Aviation Corporation, or CNAC—between the

American plane manufacturer Curtiss-Wright and the Chinese government. Westervelt, who had supervised the construction of more than fifteen hundred planes for the US Navy in World War I, had arrived in China in December 1930 to study its civilian aviation. Here was a terra nova as vast as the United States, with obvious needs for planes, airports, and pilots. By the time Bond showed up, Curtiss-Wright had already sunk half a million dollars into a 45 percent stake in the Chinese venture. CNAC had inaugurated service from Shanghai up the Yangtze to Nanjing and then on to Hankou.

But CNAC was in free fall. According to the writer Gregory Crouch, overbearing American managers had alienated most of the Chinese staff. The airline was running at a loss. That was where Westervelt and Bond came in. One of their first moves was to fire Harry Smith, CNAC's operations manager, who was known for his rants against the Chinese. Bond took his place. In his first meeting with CNAC's American personnel, Bond was blunt. The whoring and drinking had to stop, and the Yankees were to treat their Chinese colleagues with respect.

As chief engineer, Bond hired Wong Tsu, a Beijing-born graduate of MIT, who had helped launch an aviation giant when he designed the first commercially viable plane, the Model C seaplane, for Bill Boeing in 1916. Wong's Model C saved Boeing's business, another example of the back and forth between China and America. The *Seattle Times* called Wong "a proficient birdman" and a mechanical genius. When Wong left the United States to return to China, Boeing cut him a check for fifty dollars.

CNAC's stable of pilots was a collection of American barnstormers, a German who had flown with Baron von Richthofen during World War I, and several ethnic Chinese, including Moon Fun Chin, who was born in 1913 in a mud hut in a hamlet outside Macao and grew up in Baltimore. Like Bond, Chin had followed Lindbergh's flight. In Maryland, his parents paid for flight school. When the Depression hit, Chin returned to China to search for work. He would go on to become one of the most decorated civilian pilots in US history.

In March 1933, Pan Am bought out Curtiss-Wright's interests in CNAC and announced plans to link San Francisco and Shanghai. With a battalion of Douglas DC-2s, CNAC finally began to make a profit. In 1935, CNAC carried nearly twenty thousand passengers, more than fifty times the total in 1929.

Then, on November 22, 1935, taking off from the waters off Alameda Island, the *China Clipper* inaugurated the first transpacific commercial flight, island-hopping its way from the Golden Gate across Hawaii, Midway, Wake, and Guam to Manila Bay. Twenty-two passengers paid $675 per ticket; one hundred thousand letters crammed the cargo hold. Within days, two more four-engine planes—the *Philippine Clipper* and the *Hawaii Clipper*—joined the team. Within a month, Pan Am was crossing the Pacific every week. From Manila, Pan Am connected China to the outside world via Hong Kong and Guangzhou. The world had just gotten smaller. And China was the lure.

Born in Nebraska in 1889, Floyd Shumaker was an early flyboy with the US Army Air Service. Arriving in China in 1929 as a representative of the Aviation Corporation of America, owned by the Douglas Aircraft Company of Santa Monica, California, Captain Shumaker drew up a 133-page report urging the Nationalists to reorganize their air force along American lines. He advised Chiang to build a series of airfields near the new capital, Nanjing, from which his air force could strike almost anywhere in China. Shumaker, of course, recommended using Douglas bombers; they could fly nonstop for eight hours on a full tank of fuel.

By February 1930, Shumaker had become an adviser to the Nationalist government. Later that year, as Nationalist forces moved north to challenge recalcitrant warlords, Shumaker directed Nationalist air operations from the front. In July, a report from the US consulate in Tianjin identified "an American named Shumaker" as having bombed a railroad bridge over the Yellow River. Shumaker's reasoning for the sortie was typical of many private Americans who wanted to lend the Kuomintang a hand: the Chinese were having a hard time finding people who could do the job themselves.

Another Yankee, Robert M. Short, came to China as a Boeing representative and was also engaged as an adviser. In the spring of 1931, Short was training a squadron of Nationalist fighters in "bandit suppression," the term of art for anti-Communist operations. Then, in September 1931, the Imperial Japanese Army grabbed most of northeastern China, rolling over the Korean border and up from Port Arthur.

At the State Department, Henry Stimson advocated a tough response, including economic sanctions, but President Hoover wanted none of it. Trade with Japan, which ran a close third behind trade with Canada and Europe, was important to the economy. And besides, Hoover noted, imposing economic sanctions without the will to back them up with force would be like "sticking pins in tigers." Wall Street also backed the Japanese regime. In the early 1920s and 1930s, J. P. Morgan floated almost $100 million in

Japanese bonds freeing Tokyo to engage in military adventures. Morgan's chief, Thomas Lamont, argued that Japanese investment in Manchuria would accrue to China in the end.

Domestically, American politicians envisaged a trade-off between Tokyo and Washington. The 1924 Immigration Act had barred all Asians from becoming naturalized US citizens, closing off decades of Japanese immigration to the United States. But Japan's population had doubled in fifty years. Some American officials realized that Japan needed an outlet for its people. Better to have them head to Manchuria, the thinking went, than to America's West Coast.

On January 7, 1932, Stimson issued to Japan and China what became known as the Stimson Doctrine. He informed both sides that the United States would not recognize territorial changes executed by force. At the same time, under no circumstances would the United States deploy troops to defend Chinese territory. Stimson encouraged the League of Nations to censure Japan, but when asked whether he would add America's voice to any league proceedings, he shied away, worried that the "China baby" would be dumped, he wrote, in America's lap.

On January 28, 1932, three weeks after Stimson issued his nonrecognition statement, Japanese bombers attacked Shanghai, hitting the entire city, except for the International Settlement, and killing hundreds of civilians. The young Chinese air force could do little in defense. On February 18, 1932, Japan announced the founding of a new country, Manchukuo, consisting of Japanese-held territory in northeast China. On March 27, 1933, Japan formally withdrew from the League of Nations, with its foreign minister Yosuke Matsuoka proclaiming it "a day on which Japan set the world on the road to the establishment of a true and real peace." Japanese troops intensified their attacks on Kuomintang positions throughout northern China.

This time the American press championed the Chinese. Reporting from a hospital ward filled with wounded Chinese women, Victor Keen of the *New York Herald Tribune* accused the Imperial Japanese Army of "irresponsible hysteria or merciless racial hatred." President Hoover dispatched US Marines to Shanghai but only to protect American lives and property. His bottom line was that America had no dog in this fight. US correspondents disagreed. "Surrounded by Marines from California, Texas and Virginia, I watched the Japanese bomb the defenseless city," wrote Reginald Sweetland in the *Chicago Daily News*. The United States should have done something, American reporters insisted.

On February 20, 1932, weeks into Japan's assault on Shanghai, Robert Short was flying alone over the city in America's newest fighter biplane, a Boeing 218 P-12 prototype. He was there to witness Japanese air strikes. But when he spotted three Japanese fighters preparing to strafe a defenseless section of the city, Short attacked, downing one plane, killing its pilot, and forcing the other two planes to flee. On February 22, Short took to the air again. Japanese bombers appeared with an escort of fighter planes heading for the railroad station in Suzhou, where a refugee train from Shanghai had just arrived. Short flew into the teeth of the bomber formation. He killed the pilot of the lead bomber, and the Japanese turned tail. But as Short circled for another run, Japanese fighters trapped him and fired. In full view of the refugees in the station, Short's Boeing burst into flames and spun to the ground. The Chinese proclaimed Short a national hero and brought his mother, Elizabeth, and brother, Edmund, over from Tacoma, Washington, for the funeral. More than one million mourners filled Shanghai's streets. T. V. Soong called Short's courage and sacrifice "electrifying."

With American assistance, the Nationalist government established a Central Aviation School and inaugurated its own aeronautics industry. In 1932, it diverted $11 million from naval development to build up air power. That spring, T. V. Soong asked the United States to dispatch a mission to train Chinese pilots. The US State Department opposed the plan, and the War Department passed a special order banning army personnel from traveling to China to offer advice. So Soong and Nationalist adviser Arthur Young proposed a scheme for an unofficial mission staffed by volunteers. The Commerce Department supported the idea because it guaranteed more sales.

Ultimately, the State Department agreed to a "civilian" mission. Colonel John Jouett, the commander of training for the Army Air Corps, led the team. Commerce Department officials quietly agreed to Chinese requests that their pilots be schooled in bombing, gunnery, observation photography, and close air support—not generally in the syllabus of a civilian flight school. Jouett's team of fourteen arrived at the Central Aviation Academy in Hangzhou on July 8, 1932. By September, classes for the first fifty pilots had begun. In all, almost four hundred men would graduate from the academy by the time Jouett left China in 1936. They formed the nucleus of China's air force.

Jouett's efforts were just one aspect of the Commerce Department's plan to corner the China market. In 1933, it sent famed stunt pilot and speed ace Jimmy Doolittle to Shanghai to demonstrate another new biplane fighter, the Curtiss Hawk II. Doolittle dazzled crowds in Shanghai, buzzing the city's rooftops at two hundred miles an hour with his 700 horsepower Wright Cyclone engine. After Doolittle's "raid," the Chinese ordered seventy-two Hawks. By mid-1935, the Nationalist air force had five hundred aircraft, most of them American. Finance Minister T. V. Soong realized that the Nationalist government could save millions if it built its own planes. And again, he looked to the United States.

In April 1933, Curtiss-Wright, Douglas, and Boeing banded together to form the Central Aircraft Manufacturing Company of China and set up a factory near the flight school in Hangzhou. William Pawley, a flashy American, ran the plant. Born in South Carolina and raised in Cuba, Pawley had already made and lost a fortune before he came to China in 1933. He had sold fruit, flipped properties during a Miami land boom, and then fixed on aviation as the flight path to riches. He established Cuba's first airline and founded the All-American Air Races at Miami Municipal Airport in 1930. "Shifty as the devil" was how James McHugh, a US Navy intelligence officer, described the man.

In China, Pawley had started with CNAC but left the firm after Pan Am bought out Curtiss-Wright's share. He cultivated Soong Ailing and her husband, H. H. Kung. Thanks to kickbacks to Soong Ailing, Pawley ended up brokering 90 percent of American plane sales to China. Shipping aircraft in kits from the United States was cheaper than exporting them whole. The Hangzhou plant saved China some money and made Pawley a lot more. Over the next decade, Central Aircraft would build and repair $30 million worth of Chinese planes, earning Pawley an average of $1 million a year.

On April 17, 1934, Japan's chief of intelligence, Eiji Amau, issued what would come to be called the Amau Doctrine. Japan announced a "holy war" against Communism and declared that any foreigners assisting China were to obtain Japan's permission first. Amau directly criticized the Americans for "supplying China with war planes, building aerodromes in China and detailing military instructors or military advisors to China."

In October, Prime Minister Koki Hirota piled on more demands: China was to abandon its policy of playing one barbarian against another; Japan and the Nationalists were to enter an alliance to suppress the Communists; and the Chinese government was to recognize Japan's puppet state of Manchukuo in China's northeast.

At the State Department, Asia Hand Stanley Hornbeck advised the new secretary of state, Cordell Hull, that it would be best if America did not provoke Tokyo. President Franklin Delano Roosevelt had been in office for a little more than a year, and facing the Depression, the last thing he wanted was to hurt the profitable trade with Japan. American citizens, Hornbeck argued, should be ordered to stop aiding China's military. Sales of military hardware should be halted, too. China, Hornbeck wrote, should "stand on its own feet." With that, America's flyboys left China, Colonel Jouett's mission ended, and even Madame Chiang Kai-shek's American pilot had to return home.

At a time when Americans were wringing their hands over Japanese landgrabs in Manchuria, a piece of American legislation did almost as much to enfeeble China as the Imperial Japanese Army. On June 19, 1934, President Roosevelt signed into law the American Silver Purchase Act, which directed the US Treasury to buy silver until the price tripled. This obscure decree, long since forgotten, had no effect on the US economy, already reeling under the shock of the Depression. The annual American output of silver amounted to a piddling $32 million, dwarfed by peanuts and potatoes.

But Roosevelt needed the votes of the senators and representatives from the silver states—Nevada, Utah, and Montana. In exchange for a multibillion-dollar subsidy to America's mining interests, Roosevelt won their support for his New Deal. Still, the law claimed a casualty: China.

Senator Key Pittman, a powerful Democrat from Nevada, had argued that increasing the price of silver would make China's currency and therefore American exports to China rise together. His Democratic colleague, Senator William King of Utah, talked up the "great China market" that would be unleashed by a bump in silver's price.

In the United States, silver was just a commodity, but in China, it was cash. China had been on the silver standard for centuries. That was why the United States had minted the US trade dollar in the 1870s in an earlier failed bid to boost the China trade.

As soon as the Silver Act passed, silver flowed out of China in record amounts. In two years, 645 million ounces of silver—half of China's holdings—exited the country, most of it bound for the US. Within a year, the price of silver had doubled, and the value of China's currency followed suit. But America's exports to China didn't budge.

In China, credit tightened, interest rates tripled, industry and commerce slowed, and bankruptcies spread. Exports of raw silk, China's biggest cash crop, plummeted. More than half of China's cotton mills closed. A US policy designed to bolster a tiny interest group back home brought China's economy to the brink of collapse.

Worse, America's silver policy benefited Japan. As soon as the law was enacted, Japanese banks began smuggling huge quantities of silver out of China and selling them at a profit—to the United States. The windfall bankrolled Japan's naval buildup—a perverse consequence of a plan that had been marketed as a boon to both America and China. Flush with cash, Japan in 1934 gave notice that it would abrogate the naval arms control treaty negotiated in Washington in 1922.

T. V. Soong, H. H. Kung, and their longtime economic adviser Arthur Young appealed to the United States for relief. Circumventing the State Department, they found a friend at the Treasury Department. Chagrined at the damage to China's economy, Treasury Secretary Henry Morgenthau told colleagues that he felt like "a Japanese agent." Morgenthau's Treasury Department would push the United States to take actions that Secretary of State Hull and his advisers opposed. The sole Jewish member of Roosevelt's cabinet, Morgenthau believed that democracy was destined to fight a war with Fascism in Germany and Japan and that America had better bolster nations, like China, on the frontlines.

In late 1934, China approached Washington about sending T. V. Soong to the American capital to negotiate a way out of its silver mess. The State Department opposed the trip; Soong was openly anti-Japanese, and Tokyo would protest. "This, of course, is typical State Department philosophy," Morgenthau wrote angrily. "Don't do anything that might offend anyone!"

With the State and Treasury departments at loggerheads over how to proceed, China took the initiative. On November 3, 1935, the Nationalist government announced a currency reform program that took China off the silver standard. It was a bold move and another example of how events in America forced change in China. The new program mandated that all silver be handed over to the government's currency reserve board. For the first time in China's modern history, the entire country had a single currency, the *fabi,* that would be managed by a central bank.

Japan saw the reforms as a threat. If they succeeded, they would mark a major step toward China's financial independence. Japanese banks in China refused to relinquish their silver and Tokyo demanded that China immediately halt the reforms.

On November 13, Alfred Sze, China's minister to Washington, rushed to Morgenthau's office to report that Japan's Yokohama Specie Bank had begun buying huge amounts of US dollars in China, attacking the under-pinning of the *fabi*. China needed to sell the United States one hundred million ounces of silver and get its hands on greenbacks to stabilize its new currency. The crisis presented Morgenthau with an opportunity. He sent Sze out of the room and called President Roosevelt. "The Chinese are desperate," he said. Could the Treasury buy fifty million ounces of Chinese silver? Roosevelt agreed. "The only reason for doing this," Morgenthau later told Sze, "is that everybody seems to be against you."

The American silver purchase doubled China's foreign currency reserves. Morgenthau suggested that Kung or Soong come to Washington to discuss silver in more detail. Bending to the State Department's concerns, the Nationalists sent top banker and Wharton grad K. P. Chen instead. Within a year, China would receive almost $100 million from the United States in exchange for silver. The American purchases replenished China's foreign exchange reserves, stabilized the *fabi*, and helped China weather the economic storm.

Morgenthau's purchases of Chinese silver committed the United States government to the success of one of Nanjing's most significant reforms and involved Washington more deeply than ever in East Asia. They underscored a shift in the American government's view of China and Japan. For the first time since World War I, there was a realization that the policy of nonintervention in East Asia was leading to the demise of American influence and was facilitating Japan's rise. The State Department's program of avoiding confrontation with Japan was failing because Tokyo showed no limit to its desire to dominate China. Even the department's main China expert, Stanley Hornbeck, had begun to evolve; he supported Roosevelt's push for a massive naval buildup. At the time, Morgenthau reflected in his diary "that fifty years from now the fact China was not gobbled up by Japan and again becomes a strong nation may be the most important thing we did here." He spoke too soon.

In the early 1930s, China's two leading political parties moved away from American ideals even as Chinese society continued to be inspired by the United States. Neither the Communists nor the Kuomintang believed that American freedom had any role to play in the building of a new China. At the same time, as Japan annexed more Chinese territory and attacked its cities, China's government, as it had in the past, looked to America and Americans for help. And Americans again tried to navigate between their tender feelings for China and their reluctance to get sucked into a war.

CHAPTER SIXTEEN

A Red Star

Like earlier Chinese leaders Yuan Shikai and Sun Yat-sen, China's Communists looked to Americans to tell their story—to both the rest of the world and to the Chinese themselves. Given the persistent, sometimes inexplicable, respect accorded America in China, nothing served the Communists better during the 1920s and 1930s than the Good Housekeeping seal from a Yankee scribe.

Internally, the Chinese Communist Party continued to insist that the United States was an enemy, even more devious than the Japanese. Following Japan's seizure of Manchuria in 1931, the party's Central Committee claimed that the United States was plotting to occupy the Yangtze River valley and Fujian province with a hundred thousand troops. In January 1933, the Central Committee accused the United States of angling to enslave Asia. Bizarrely, in the midst of the Japanese onslaught, the United States, according to Party Central, was the worst imperialist aggressor.

That said, the Communists had no problem using American writers to their advantage. To ensure that they controlled the message, the Communists had loyal agents vet the Americans first. One of their chief operatives was Agnes Smedley, another reporter from Missouri.

Born in 1892, Smedley claimed, in her semiautobiographical novel, *Daughter of Earth*, to have grown up poor and oppressed. It wasn't true. Like so many other American advocates for China's revolution, Smedley, the daughter of an itinerant farmer and coal mine worker, had not been raised in poverty. As a young woman, she embraced radical politics in America. During World War I, she worked for the German government on a plot to stir up a rebellion in British India. In 1928, Smedley crossed the Manchurian border from Russia and, according to her biographer, Ruth Price, was recruited that year into the International Liaison Department, the intelligence wing of the Communist International. For the next eight years, she worked for both the Comintern and the GRU, Soviet military intelligence. She wrote for the *New Republic* and the *Nation* on the side.

Smedley's newspaper coverage hewed to the Soviet line, which, following Chiang Kai-shek's slaughter of the Communists in Shanghai, sought to undermine the Kuomintang and replace it with a Communist regime. In vivid prose, she focused on the corruption and venality of the Nationalist regime and claimed that the Communists enjoyed broad popular support. When Soviet plans to foment an uprising in southern China failed, she moved to Shanghai, where her apartment became a center for the black arts of Soviet spycraft—a courier safehouse, a dark room for microfilmed copies of secret materials, and a radio transmitter linked to Moscow.

Though Smedley and her comrades denounced extraterritoriality, her Yankee nationality shielded her from Nationalist prosecution. From 1930 to 1934, Smedley was a lover of and a key aide to Richard Sorge, a famed Soviet agent. She nicknamed him "Handsome Hercules" and became the single most successful recruiter for his spy ring. During this time, she wrote two books on the Communists, praising their Spartan lifestyle and incorruptibility. One book, *China's Red Army Marches*, was a novelistic account of the revolutionary government that Mao Zedong and his army chief, Zhu De, had established in Jiangxi province in the early 1930s, even though Smedley had never been there.

China's Red Army Marches was banned by the Nationalists. But the Communists translated it into Chinese and circulated it on university campuses, where it served as a recruiting tool. How could the Communists be dangerous, many asked, if an American had given them the thumbs-up?

Smedley worked with Sun Yat-sen's widow, Soong Qingling, to cultivate American writers and convince them of the righteousness of the Communist cause. One of their recruits was Harold Isaacs, the son of a wealthy New York real estate magnate. Isaacs had come to Shanghai in 1930. He was a whirlwind of energy and enthusiasm, and Qingling, still young, was drawn to him, as she would be attracted to other American male writers. Isaacs was a regular guest at Soong's residence on Rue Molière in Shanghai.

Isaacs started writing for John B. Powell, but Soong and Smedley soon set him up as the editor of a newspaper called the *China Forum*, headquartered in Shanghai's French Concession to escape Nationalist censorship. The Comintern funded the *Forum*, and Communist agents plied Isaacs with scoops. Isaacs devoted himself to exposing Shanghai's underbelly in tough-guy tabloid prose, with a staff manned by underground Communist Party operatives.

On the night of February 21, 1931, Isaacs's sources handed him an exclusive. Twenty-four Communist Party activists had been arrested and then taken from the Longhua Garrison, a Nationalist prison in Shanghai, and forced to dig their own graves. Some had been shot, others buried alive. Among them were five writers. After Isaacs ran the story, Smedley launched a PR campaign to commemorate the Longhua Martyrs. She drew up a petition and convinced leading American writers—James Thurber, Sinclair Lewis, and Langston Hughes among them—to sign it, marking the first time that Western intellectuals had criticized Chiang Kai-shek's regime.

For Isaacs, the story was too good to check. He believed, as he wrote, that the Nationalist government had "no parallel in history except perhaps the invasions and slaughters staged by the Huns in the fourth and fifth centuries." Like Baptist missionary Issachar Roberts, he had found the devil in China and was determined to root him out.

The problem was that the story was only half true. Yes, the Nationalists had executed Communist Party members, but they were actually doing the bidding of another faction of the Communist Party. The Longhua Martyrs had been meeting in a hotel in Shanghai's International Settlement to discuss an alternative to the Communist Party leadership imposed by Joseph Stalin. Stalin's spies had gotten wind of the meeting and tipped off Shanghai's British-run police, knowing that the British cops would hand the participants over to the Kuomintang. What looked like a clear-cut human rights case was a factional squabble, too.

Smedley's success on the Longhua Martyrs case helped make China the first foreign country of interest to America's nascent human rights movement. Roger Baldwin, who founded the American Civil Liberties Union in 1920, had been appalled by the Soviets' persecution of writers. But his attempts to lobby for Russians in Stalin's gulag ran into the pro-Soviet sympathies of America's left wing. When Chiang Kai-shek's regime began executing leftist political dissidents, however, Baldwin and Smedley found it easy to provoke outrage.

The first poster girl of an American international human rights campaign was a Chinese woman writer, Ding Ling. In the spring of 1933, Smedley sent Baldwin reports about Ding, who had disappeared in Shanghai and was believed to be a prisoner of the Nationalist regime. Baldwin became convinced that Ding's case represented a compelling opportunity for the ACLU to expand its purview overseas.

Baldwin organized rallies on Ding's behalf in New York, San Francisco, and Chicago and masterminded a march in Washington headlined by leading American writers. Smedley helped with the translation of Ding Ling's stories—"Miss Sophie's Diary" and "A Certain Night," which details the Nationalist crackdown on dissent—and Baldwin got them published in the *Nation*, the *New Republic*, and the *Daily Worker*.

Within the ACLU, Ding's case sparked a debate. Do civil rights cross borders from East to West like textiles? Are democracy and freedom of speech national or universal ideals? Some, like the novelist Theodore Dreiser, argued that Americans had not just a right but a *responsibility* to insist that China—and other countries—treat their citizens according to American values. Others, such as free speech advocate Norman Hapgood, said that they did not wish to impose US thinking on China or anyplace else.

When the Nationalists, under international pressure, freed Ding Ling in 1937, she fled to the Communist base in northwestern China. Within five years, she had fallen afoul of Mao for questioning the Marxist-Leninist tenet that art must serve the revolution. In 1957, the Communist government declared Ding Ling a "rightist," and persecuted her for decades until she was freed from hard labor in 1978. But after Ding Ling disappeared in "the Red Zone," the American Left no longer bothered with her case.

The greatest foreign conscript in the Communists' war with Chiang Kai-shek was Edgar Snow. Snow's writing on Chinese society and the Chinese Communist Party influenced generations of Americans and, as important, generations of Chinese. If Frank Goodnow was key to burnishing the image of Yuan Shikai, Snow was even more crucial to a Communist campaign to transform Mao Zedong from a bandit king into, as Snow put it, a "rather Lincolnesque figure" who "may possibly become a very great man."

Snow was an early advocate of the idea that China's Communist revolution was inevitable and not actually the result of decades of Japanese aggression. He peddled the notion that China's Communists were less totalitarian than their Soviet brethren. And he helped create the cult of Mao, not just in China but also in the United States, portraying the Great Helmsman, just when he needed it most, as a Robin Hood battling China's Prince John, Chiang Kai-shek.

Snow's Mao was a rebel with a cause. The puritanical Communists had banned tobacco, but Mao chain-smoked. Their attention to physical exercise gave them ramrod-straight posture, yet Mao slouched. Crew cuts were compulsory; Mao's hair cascaded over his collar. To Snow, Mao was an Apache chief, a rusticated philosopher-king.

An altar boy and an Eagle Scout, graced with Irish good luck and looks, Snow was born in Kansas City in 1905, the son of a printer who loved books and recited Shakespearean verses over the din of the printing press. Snow grew up with literary ambitions inspired by the works of Mark Twain and Jack London. He attended the University of Missouri's School of Journalism and then drifted to New York, where he wrote for an ad agency. In early 1928, he made $800 in the overheated stock market, sold his shares, and set off for Shanghai, stowing away on a freighter out of Hawaii. He predicted that he would be away for nine months. "Adventure! Experience!" he wrote to his parents of his impending journey.

Like many of his Missouri classmates, Snow first docked in Shanghai at John B. Powell's *Weekly Review*. He and Powell would become great friends but disagreed violently about whom to back in China. Powell supported Chiang; Snow would choose Mao. In 1928, early into Snow's stay, he won a plum assignment when Sun Yat-sen's son, Sun Ke, the director of China's railroads, offered him free passage on the rails. Snow spent a month in Manchuria and wrote about Japan's industrial buildup, predicting correctly that the Japanese would soon start a war. He visited the scene of a famine in northern China and discovered human flesh for sale in local markets.

Snow used the *Review* to blast the policies in British buildings that banned Chinese from taking the white man's elevator, and he demanded that Shanghai's Western-owned shops welcome Chinese customers. The British secret police opened a dossier on him. He traveled to Southeast Asia and India, hobnobbed with anticolonial leaders, read Marx, and concluded that Socialism was the panacea for what ailed China.

The *Chicago Tribune* hired Snow as a stringer. Pretty soon he was writing for fifty American newspapers, including the *Saturday Evening Post*. In 1931, he met an aspiring American writer, Helen Foster, known as Peg. Inspired by Snow's prose, Foster had traveled to Shanghai to try her own hand at journalism. Snow asked her out.

In letters to his family, Snow said that he found China "pitiable" and that the country needed a "crusader," to save it. The "stench and decay, the misery and sufferings and national agonies" cried out for a "Great

Redeemer," he wrote. Already Snow had begun to be entranced by the Communists. He told his father that they possessed "a vigor and enthusiasm" that would carry them to victory. Like others before him, Snow fell under the spell of Soong Qingling. In 1932, he profiled her for the *Herald Tribune*. In the interview, Qingling condemned Chiang Kai-shek for violating the legacy of her late husband, Sun Yat-sen. During frequent meetings at the Chocolate Shop, an American hangout in the heart of the International Settlement, Soong introduced Snow to writers such as Lu Xun and Agnes Smedley. "I met the thoughts and sentiments of China at its best," Snow wrote of his visits to Soong's residence on Rue Molière.

Soong Qingling used the affable American to publicize her views. He in turn employed her words to flesh out his own position that China needed the single-mindedness that only the Communists possessed. In a September 1932 dispatch, he quoted her as saying that the Nationalist Party had become a "moribund institution doomed to extinction." Soong thinks, Snow wrote, "that the Chinese Communist Party is the only real revolutionary force in China today."

Soong blessed Snow's budding romance with Peg Foster. To celebrate the couple's wedding on Christmas Day 1932, Soong gave them an American coffee percolator and threw them a Chinese banquet. In early 1934, Edgar and Peg moved to Beijing. Snow wrote and taught journalism at Yenching University, run by the veteran missionary John Leighton Stuart. Beijing in the 1930s was dirt cheap for an American couple who had steady work writing and teaching. Edgar and Peg partied on the roof of the Peking Hotel and owned a Mongolian racing pony and a white greyhound named Gobi.

Xiao Qian, a Yenching student who became a frontline war correspondent noted for his keen eye and graceful prose, remembered Snow as different from other Western professors. Snow didn't employ "'the teacher talks, the students listen' approach to teaching," Xiao wrote. Snow lacked, Xiao wrote, "the natural superiority of white people" and was unusually optimistic about China's future. "This type of foreigner was rare in China," observed Xiao, who under Communist rule suffered because of his friendships with Americans.

Snow lectured on the growing Fascist menace in Europe and Japan. Fascism and Communism were both antidemocratic, he told his students. But the Communists could be forgiven because their goal—a classless society—was honorable. The dictatorship of the proletariat, Snow declared, was just a transitory evil along the way.

The Communist underground—more active at Yenching University because it was an American school and therefore protected from Nationalist secret police—noticed Snow and Peg and their progressive views. Groups of patriotic students gathered at the Snows' sprawling courtyard home in Beijing's northwestern suburb, and Snow began passing messages between them and Soong Qingling.

In the spring of 1935, Edgar and Peg suggested that the students organize a march on the anniversary of the May Fourth Movement. They promised to write about it, too. Peg penned anti-Fascist poems and leaflets for the students. When hundreds demonstrated on May 4, Snow and Foster joined their ranks. It was intoxicating to Snow, this sense that he, an all-American kid from Missouri, could make history. "Now I know why people like . . . Tom Millard and other newspapermen mixed up in China's internal affairs in the past," he wrote. China was a canvas on which Americans could freely draw.

The next month, Japanese officials attempted to force China to recognize a second protectorate in the north alongside the Japanese puppet-regime of Manchukuo. Snow's students fanned out to universities across Beijing. In meetings at the Snows' residence, underground Communist Party members Yao Yilin and Huang Hua, both of whom would end up as senior officials in the Communist hierarchy, were elected leaders of the movement, while a young agent from the Comintern, David Yui, arrived to give direction and advice.

New Japanese depredations could not have come at a better time for the Communist Party. Forced out of Jiangxi in the south by Chiang's forces, the party was on the brink of annihilation. Its Red Army had just completed the legendary Long March—an eight-thousand-mile retreat during which 90 percent of the participants died or were killed by Nationalist forces. In October 1935, Mao and several thousand beleaguered followers had trickled into Shanxi province in northwestern China. With Chiang preparing a final campaign against them, the party had been searching for a way out.

Hope for the Chinese Communists arrived in the person of a courier from Moscow. He carried news of the Comintern's new policy. In Moscow, Stalin, under intensifying pressure from Adolf Hitler's rise in Germany, had decided that Fascism, not Western capitalism, was now enemy number one. In December 1935, Chinese Communist Party leaders gathered at Wayaobao in northern Shanxi to follow Stalin's lead. Mao's new policy called for a united front with the Nationalists against the Japanese and an alliance with the United States. Just a few years earlier, America had been a foe.

On December 9, 1935, Snow and Foster joined a march of thousands on government headquarters in central Beijing. A second demonstration erupted three days later. Protests mushroomed nationwide, calling for the establishment of a united front to fight Japan. Stunningly, Japan dropped its demand that China recognize another Japanese-dominated government in North China, granting the Communists a huge moral victory over their Nationalist foes. "We sparked a rebellion," Snow claimed. "It is a charming irony," Peg would write later, that Japan "had to retreat when faced with two little anti-Fascist Americans living on fifty dollars a month—but armed with a piece of the truth."

Snow's service spearheading one of the Communist Party's most successful propaganda triumphs further elevated his profile. When asked to recommend a foreign journalist to come to the Communist redoubt in Shanxi province to tell the party's story, Soong Qingling named Edgar Snow. On a mid-June evening in 1936, Snow boarded the midnight train to Xi'an, the legendary terminus of the Silk Road.

In early July, Snow and George Hatem, an idealistic American doctor from Buffalo who had been treating prostitutes in Shanghai for venereal disease, slipped out of Xi'an and headed for Communist-held territory. After a two-day walk across porous battle lines, the men reached the walled city of Bao'an, just north of the famed future Communist stronghold, Yanan. In Bao'an, they were met by a bearded Zhou Enlai, the commander of the East Front Army. Zhou welcomed Snow as a "reliable" journalist, "friendly to the Chinese people." Other leading Communists gathered around. Bugles blew, and a crowd, assembled for the occasion, shouted, "Welcome to the American journalist to investigate Soviet China!" Soon Snow was spending hours in Mao Zedong's cave, carved out of the yellow soil of the northern China countryside. Snow recorded Mao's story, and his highly massaged account remains the basis of the party's officially approved story of Mao's life—an indication of the Chinese Communists' deep and still abiding respect for the power of the American pen.

Snow was bowled over by the Communists. The Reds "go about remaking the world like college boys to a football match," he gushed to his diary. "Every house rings with singing at night, laughter and good humor." The

Communists possessed a "personal dignity" that Snow had never seen before in China, except perhaps at the Chocolate Shop in his tête-à-têtes with Soong Qingling. They were "cheerful, gay, energetic and loyal—the living spirit of an astonishing crusade of youth." These were "better" Chinese, Snow reported. Like many Americans, Snow had found a China he could believe in, and his expectations were boundless. Compared with Nationalist-controlled China, Soviet China was "a contrast of life and death, a living force and a dead one, a young and growing culture, and an old, disillusioned, spent and diseased one."

It is understandable why the Communists were so appealing to Edgar Snow, a child of the American heartland. Though technically atheist and fiercely opposed to missionaries, the Chinese Communist Party used the Christian movement as a model. Like the American missionaries, the Communists employed street theater to get their message out. Moderate reformer and Christian Jimmy Yen inspired their literacy campaigns. From the Rockefeller Foundation, they swiped the idea of the "barefoot doctor." And Mao Zedong's emphasis on revolutionary transformation mirrored the Protestant conviction that spiritual renewal was the Middle Kingdom's only hope.

Occupying center stage in this spectacle was, of course, Mao himself, the forty-three-year-old revolutionary. Mao, it is sometimes alleged, was reluctant to reveal details of his personal life. Snow convinced him to open up, drawing his attention to the compelling narrative surrounding George Washington. In fact, Snow was pushing on an open door. His interviews with the Communist leader came at a time when the party, aided by Stalin's minions in the Soviet Union, was turning Mao into a cult figure.

Snow was an eager scribe. He depicted Mao in down-to-earth, human terms. Mao was "plain speaking and plain-living." He had the "simplicity and naturalness of the Chinese peasant" but was also a classical poet and a student of philosophy. The meetings between Mao and Snow in July 1936 were Mao's first lengthy encounter with an American, and throughout, Snow noted, he expressed "the liveliest curiosity about the United States." Mao had studied the War of Independence and the Civil War and wanted to know whether America was ripe for a Communist revolution.

Mao told Snow about his early life, describing a troubled relationship with his autocratic father and a close bond with his mother. As a young man, Mao had flirted with various political ideologies—including democracy and anarchism—before settling on Marxism-Leninism. He regaled Snow with tales of revolutionary bravado from Jiangxi province and on the

Long March. He capped off his story with self-serving accounts of internal party struggles and his rise to power.

Snow accepted Mao's claim that the Chinese Communists were independent of the Soviets—a fable that grew to be hugely influential with Americans. In fact, Mao and his Soviet paymasters downplayed their connections as part of a plan to attract liberal Chinese and Westerners, like Snow, to their cause. "We are certainly not fighting for an emancipated China in order to turn the country over to Moscow!" Snow quoted Mao as saying.

After interviewing Mao, Snow hit the road with the Red Army. He noted that, in contrast to Nationalist troops, Red Army soldiers did not loot, did not pillage, and did not rape. Women, Snow reported, "look upon the soldiers as their friends and protectors." At the entrance to one town, a bugler waited as Snow entered through a gate in the massive city walls. Troops lined the streets and saluted as he passed. "I felt," Snow wrote, "like a generalissimo with his prick out." The party used Snow's visit to boost morale. In stop after stop, a large banner proclaimed: "WE ARE NOT ISOLATED. WE HAVE THE SUPPORT OF INTERNATIONAL FRIENDS!" That meant Snow.

Back in Bao'an, Snow interviewed other Communists. He played tennis with Otto Braun, a Comintern representative, and taught the wives of revolutionary leaders how to play gin rummy. He dined in Zhou Enlai's cave, enjoying dishes cooked by Zhou's wife, Deng Yingchao. By the time Snow left, the Communists were calling him comrade. One commander bade him farewell with tears in his eyes. As he passed out of Bao'an on October 12, the Red Academy was holding an open-air lecture. The cadets rose up in unison and shouted "Long Live Comrade Si-nuo!"—Snow's Chinese name. "I felt," Snow wrote, "that I was not going home, but leaving it."

Snow's scoop was sensational, captivating Americans and Chinese alike. Powell's *Review* in Shanghai published his first article; the *Herald Tribune* ran thirty. He held a press conference at the US legation in Beijing. *Life* magazine paid him $1,000 for seventy-five pictures. And then Snow wrote a book. He had fiddled with titles, including *I Went to Red China*. But Peg convinced him that Mao, not Edgar Snow, should anchor the tale. It was like getting the story of the American Revolution from George Washington at Valley Forge, she told him. "It's a classic. It's priceless," she said.

Published in 1937, *Red Star Over China* was a monumental work of literary imagination, detailing travels in a magic, forbidden land—a mix of

Joseph Rock and "The Incandescent Lily," with real-world impact. In its *Boy's Life* depiction of Soviet China, the historian Charles Hayford has noted, *Red Star* was as American as Huckleberry Finn, one long prose poem to the previously unknown Chinese Communists. Snow made the parallel even more obvious, quoting Mark Twain to describe Mao as possessing "that calm confidence of a Christian with four aces." In Snow's eyes, the Red Zone was a place that any American would understand, a place where political purges, executions, and ideological rigidity were nowhere to be found. "Ed, now, this is just too idyllic," a friend, Harry Price, who taught economics at Yenching University, remarked after reading a draft. "Well," Snow replied, "I'm just telling you what I saw."

But Snow did care what others thought and took pains to edit his work when friends in the Communist Party questioned his conclusions. The Communist Party of the United States (CPUSA) refused to sell Snow's first edition in its bookstores, alleging that he had exaggerated Mao's independence from Stalin's line. Pat Toohey, the CPUSA's representative to the Comintern in Moscow and a staunch Stalinist, declared it "Trotsky poison." Snow apologized and begged the party to lift the ban. "I would destroy the entire third part of the book and rewrite it to the satisfaction of the CPUSA for future editions," he wrote to Toohey. Zhou Enlai demanded cuts as well. Also falling by the wayside was any mention of the moderate reformer Jimmy Yen, whom Snow had praised in the book's first edition. Snow continued revising; finally, by the third edition, he had mollified all the various Communist factions involved.

Among the Chinese, *Red Star* surpassed Pearl Buck's *The Good Earth* in impact. Appearing under various titles, *A Trip to the West, Impressions of a Foreign Journalist on His Visit to the Northwest*, the book was a hit, particularly on college campuses. Central to its impact was the notion that China's transformation into a Communist state followed the logic of history. Just as Snow's American predecessors in China had predicted that China would one day become Christian, Snow confidently forecast what he called "the dynamic necessity" of Communism's advance. And for the Chinese, the prognostication was all the more reliable because it came from a red-blooded Midwestern Yankee.

Red Star was how many students and intellectuals in Chinese cities first learned of Mao Zedong and the Communist Party and it inspired a stream of young intellectuals from the cities to migrate to the party's revolutionary base. Li Maocai, a student at the time, described the book as "like a fire that starts the power generator." Writing in the magazine *Hwa-*

mei, she reported that, after she and her classmates had read the book, "What I saw could be described as a miracle: in the dark-blue night sky, the whistling arrows with their fiery feathers have sounded the horns of truth." Snow's words, she declared, "are flowers of our nation!" Zhou Enlai summed up the party's feelings about the book and Snow. "To us," he said, "Snow is the greatest of foreign authors and our best friend abroad." Snow understood his role. He was the medium, he wrote, through whom Mao "had his first chance to speak to the world—and, more important, to China."

●

CHAPTER SEVENTEEN

New Life

By the mid-1930s, China was at last partially unified for the first time since the fall of the Qing dynasty in 1911. The warlord period was drawing to a close. Despite a worldwide depression, a collapse in exports and foreign aid, and record droughts and floods, much was being accomplished in China. To be sure, clashes with Japan and domestic rebels, including the Communists, shook the state's foundations. A huge military budget sapped resources from education and infrastructure, health, and economic development.

But the economy was growing, and the Chinese were enjoying a period of unparalleled freedom, despite the intermittent terror imposed by Chiang Kai-shek's police. In foreign affairs, Republican-era diplomats had pulled off a stunning feat. China's mainly American-trained diplomats had taken an empire and convinced the world to recognize it as a nation. Compared with the Ottoman and Austro-Hungarian Empires, which collapsed around the same time, it was an amazing achievement. The Republican era was a period of great hope in China and suggested to the world and to the Chinese people what a modernizing and relatively free Chinese state might look like. And from the beginning, Americans and American ideas played a significant role.

From the new capital, Nanjing, Chiang's wife Mayling spoke out for women's rights; she badgered parliament to enact a civil code to protect married women from philandering husbands. Minimum ages were established for marriage. Mayling also fought extraterritoriality, arguing in her gracious southern lilt that it was unfair for Westerners to be able to evade Chinese law in China and expect that Chinese obey Western laws abroad.

She became her husband's chief translator and adviser. She taught him English, although he rarely spoke it in public after he asked the British ambassador to give him a kiss when he had meant to say "good morning." In late August 1929, Mayling apparently had a miscarriage, and she would never have children. "She sits alongside the Generalissimo and tells him what to do, and he does it," reported Clarence E. Gauss, a long-serving US diplomat in China. "She issues instructions and they are obeyed."

Though he continued to fulminate against Western influence, Chiang littered his ministries with American advisers: Arthur Young at the finance ministry, Colonel Jouett in the air force. August Vollmer, the town marshal of Berkeley, California, trained a generation of Chinese police. Paul Monroe from Columbia Teachers College almost single-handedly reformed China's elementary school education. American scientists and doctors held sway across a vast array of disciplines.

American papers nationwide covered Chiang's baptism as a Methodist on October 23, 1930. The *Chicago Daily Tribune* credited Madame Chiang with molding a new, clean-living, God-fearing president. New York's *Herald Tribune* put the story on its front page. Chiang's baptism, the paper reported, highlighted the Generalissimo's belief that "Christian faith includes many principles which are vitally linked with the regeneration of the Chinese nation."

George Shepherd was not an American by birth. Born in New Zealand in 1894, he had sold hardware in his home country before heading to the United States where he became an evangelical Christian. He studied at Moody's Bible Institute in Chicago and set off to China to preach with the fundamentalist Plymouth Brethren in 1917. In 1921, Shepherd married an American physician, Clara Sargent, a graduate of the University of Michigan, who pulled him away from saving souls and pushed him toward saving China. In 1925, Shepherd joined the Congregationalist mission, which was dedicated to modernizing China, spent a year at Harvard, and returned to China to take up a post in rural Fujian province. There he became one of the first Americans to confront the Communist challenge on a daily basis.

Before they fled to northwestern China, the Communists had established a breakaway government in the mountains of Jiangxi bordering

Fujian province. In the late 1920s and into the early 1930s, Communist attacks would roust Shepherd out of his parish in Shaowu village in the mountains of Fujian province four times. In the process, he evolved into a new type of American evangelical. Along with Jimmy Yen, Shepherd would lobby passionately for missionaries to stop worrying about China's cities and start fretting about its countryside.

From 1931, when Shepherd wrote "The Unmet Rural Challenge" for the missionary publication the *Chinese Recorder*, he argued that China's rural poverty and the inequitable distribution of land would one day bring the Nationalist government to its knees. If a Communist revolution succeeded in China, he warned, it would be on the backs of the rural poor. Shepherd lambasted American missionaries and the "city-minded outlook bred by Christian institutions." Why was the church faltering in China? he asked. Because it ignored the majority of China's four hundred million souls, who labored in rice paddies and wheat fields every day.

Shepherd worked closely with Zhang Fuliang, a Shanghai-born son of a blacksmith, to counter Communism in Shaowu. Zhang had graduated with a master's from Yale's School of Forestry. He had married Harriet Huie, the sister of Jimmy Yen's wife, Alice. In 1929, China's National Christian Council named Zhang its chief rural secretary. Inspired by his brother-in-law Jimmy Yen's work in Ding county, Zhang urged Chinese Christians and Western missionaries to help improve living standards for China's farmers. "Go to the country!" he proclaimed in articles for missionary publications.

Shepherd and Zhang viewed China's rural challenge as a huge opportunity for the church. Returning to Shaowu after one Communist assault, Shepherd found his church destroyed and all his records gone. For him and other Americans, he wrote, such destruction signaled the beginning of a new era in the West's relations with China. The days of special protection for Westerners were over. The church needed to inaugurate a new type of relationship with the Chinese—one of equals. Zhang agreed.

Like many American missionaries who confronted the Communists, Shepherd was ambivalent about their program. He resented their intrusion into his fiefdom and abhorred their cruelty. But he admired their tenacity, and he acknowledged their egalitarian aims. In his annual letter to donors and the National Christian Council in 1932, he asked whether Christianity had what it took to compete with Communism in its "crusade against the entrenched evils of society." A year later, after having fled from another Communist assault, he noted that many Christians had joined the Communist movement. Despite the rising threat from Japan, Shepherd understood that Moscow represented a deeper challenge. "We can no more ignore it than we can the sun and the moon," Shepherd wrote. "Shall Christ or Marx win?"

Zhang and Shepherd drew up a five-point program for rural reconstruction in the Min River basin that stretched from Fujian's capital in Fuzhou toward the province's border with Jiangxi. They chose Lichuan, a small county seat in the mountains along Jiangxi's border with Fujian, as their headquarters. Jimmy Yen advised them. Visiting Ding county, Shepherd was inspired by Yen's work and called it "the only answer to Communism that has yet appeared." In November 1933, Shepherd and Zhang established the Jiangxi Christian Rural Service Union. Shepherd put his wife in charge of the health division and called for a crash program to attract educated Chinese youth into the area to help. To raise funds, Shepherd and Zhang traveled through the Yangtze River valley, visiting merchants and bankers in Shanghai and Kuomintang officials in Nanjing. Shepherd had not been up the Yangtze in seven years. Roads now linked the region's growing cities, and the government and the Christian church were working together, he wrote, to build "a peaceful and prosperous countryside."

In Jiangxi province, after four attempts, Chiang's armies, following a German plan, finally succeeded in dislodging the Communist forces from Shepherd's stomping grounds. In the fall of 1934, more than one million Nationalist troops forced the Red Army on its historic Long March retreat to northwestern China. Jiangxi and Fujian were cleansed of Communists, but they desperately needed attention and development.

Soon after he pushed the Communists out of Jiangxi, Chiang Kai-shek announced a crusade to renew his revolution and China's spirit. The New Life Movement would later be scorned for its Fascist overtones and silly campaigns; it was anti–fruit flies, anti–tooth decay, and anti–anything above the knee. But at root, the campaign stemmed from a realization by Chiang and Soong Mayling that China's Republican revolution was flagging and required an infusion of Western, specifically American, inspiration. *Time* magazine called it "a big dose of the castor oil of Puritanism."

As Chiang declared in 1934, what China needed was "an integrating force." In England and the United States, churches served that purpose. In Russia and Italy, it was "the dominant party." The problem in China, he continued, was that its dominant party, the Nationalists, had "lost public respect." So who could replace it? Christian leaders, he answered, because they "are already up to the standards of the New Life Movement."

Chiang ordered teachers, students, military officers, and the police to study the organizational tactics and modernizing mission of the American Protestant church, particularly the YMCA. "Western church leaders in our midst ought also to be utilized," he said. "Their attitude toward life is sane and sensible." He noted that he was not "urging that we become foreignized, that we eat foreign food, wear foreign clothes and live in foreign houses, but rather that we live the rational sane life that the Movement and its principles called for."

The New Life campaign underscored that even after decades of disappointment, many Chinese still believed that Western society was worthy of imitation. Maybe it could do without American democracy, but China required American values. The fact that Chiang believed that the YMCA, of all organizations, would be able to mend China's fragmented society was an example of his monumental expectations of America. "Amazing" was how Shepherd described Chiang's outreach. "Think of it," he wrote to his missionary comrades in America, "Chinese leaders have already turned from communism and Russia to the Christian church." Would the church, Shepherd asked, let China down?

Chiang launched the New Life Movement in Nanchang, the capital of Jiangxi province, from which the Communists had recently been expelled. He offered a large swath of territory recovered from the Communists to Christian missionaries for reconstruction. American churches were slow to welcome the opportunity. The board of the Episcopal Church in New York refused to allow one of its leading Chinese ministers to head the project. "Suicidal" was how Shepherd termed that decision. Didn't these Americans know history? Sun Yat-sen had turned to Mikhail Borodin after the United States and Britain let him down, Shepherd wrote. "I don't need to go into details on the cost of that folly."

Despite Shepherd's warnings, things moved slowly in Lichuan. In April 1935, the mission took stock. It had planted ten thousand trees, introduced new types of vegetables, and conducted a study of village industry. But its school was poorly attended. And only two families had sought out the mission's doctors for help with a birth, even though infant mortality was high. No one had been converted to Christianity.

Chinese volunteers came but did not stay. Shepherd and Zhang Fuliang were dismayed that so many Chinese, educated in American schools in China, seemed to look down on country living. Many church leaders voiced their support, but when asked to actually do something in Lichuan, the missionary organizations in China responded feebly. Shepherd tried to get the authority to force landowners to cut their rents or sell their land to groups of farmers. But the Kuomintang never backed this plan because landowners remained a bulwark of Nationalist rule.

As the New Life Movement spread nationwide, it took on the trappings of both Christianity and Confucianism. It embraced the Christian notion that social change happens one man and one woman at a time. "Salvation from within" was the movement's motto. The cross was always "in the background of the New Life movement," said Soong Mayling. At the same time, an organization known as the Blue Shirts, who modeled themselves after Hitler's Brown Shirts, terrorized China's cities as they enforced the New Life's rules. Some places banned mah-jongg; others outlawed dancing and drinking. Some forbade public displays of affection. And others stopped funeral bands from blaring the Chinese favorite "A Hot Time in the Old Town Tonight." Soong Mayling had to give up smoking her mentholated cigarettes in public.

In late 1935, Chiang Kai-shek and Mayling invited Shepherd to spend a Sunday with them in their country retreat. During the visit, Chiang asked Shepherd to direct the movement. Shepherd was flabbergasted. "The New Life Movement is their answer to the needs of modern China and they are requesting a Christian missionary to be at the heart of it," he wrote to his colleagues in the United States. When he protested that the burden would be too great, the couple calmed his fears. "You know the needs of our people," responded Mayling. Shepherd's thoughts naturally turned to another Westerner who had wanted to change China, too: the Comintern agent Mikhail Borodin. "What would Borodin do with a chance like this?" he wondered.

By March 1936, Shepherd had moved to Nanjing and taken up a post as an adviser to the New Life Movement. His job was to breathe new life into the campaign even as the tensions between its American-inspired Christian message and its Fascist tendencies threatened to tear it apart. Shepherd was tasked with pushing the New Life Movement into rural areas, but he was also expected to tighten links between the government and the Christian community. As he prepared to resist Japan, Chiang concluded that he needed all the Western friends he could get.

The autumn of 1936 was a period of confidence and consolidation for the Nationalists. Chiang's attitude toward Japan was hardening, and his popularity was rising. In November, John B. Powell's *China Weekly Review* reported that "we to our great joy have at long last found our Leader."

Stalin's policies toward China had also changed, further strengthening Chiang's hand. From vowing to toss Chiang out like a "squeezed lemon" in the 1920s, Stalin had morphed into a friend of the Kuomintang. He had directed his Communist minions, now holed up in northwestern China, to begin negotiations with the Generalissimo over the creation of a united front to fight Japan. Still, Chiang remained obsessed with the possibility of wiping out his Communist foes.

In 1936, he dispatched a warlord-playboy-opium-addict named Zhang Xueliang, who had ruled Manchuria before the Japanese occupied it in 1931, to Xi'an to deliver the final blow to the Reds. In December, Chiang traveled to Xi'an to oversee the final push. But when Chiang arrived in Xi'an on December 11, Zhang took him hostage and demanded that he end his war against the Communists and form an alliance with them against the Japanese. In Bao'an, Mao Zedong celebrated Chiang's capture. On December 13, the Chinese Politburo called for Chiang's execution. But Stalin countermanded his Chinese comrades. He ordered the Communists to let Chiang live.

Mao dispatched his trusted lieutenant Zhou Enlai to Xi'an to help with negotiations. For the next thirteen days, Chiang's life seemed to hang in the balance, along with China's fate. Soong Mayling went to Xi'an to save her husband, and on Christmas Day, Chiang was freed to universal acclaim. Confident that Stalin, with whom he had been in secret negotiations for more than a year, would support China in its fight with Japan, Chiang agreed to form a united front with the Chinese Communist Party. Edgar Snow grudgingly acknowledged that the national joy at Chiang's release confirmed that his standing surpassed "that of any leader in modern Chinese history."

The Xi'an Incident was front-page news in the United States. Coast-to-coast, American newspapers covered each wrinkle of the affair. Chiang was reported dead; he was alive, then dead, then alive. The *New York Times* ran fourteen stories on the kidnapping, seven on the front page. The *San Francisco Chronicle* published twenty-one. Central to the drama was Soong Mayling, who alternated in the American media's imagination between "the pretty, doll-like wife" described in the *Boston Daily Globe* and the "powerful figure" depicted in the *New York Times*.

Once freed, Chiang placed Zhang Xueliang under house arrest where he would languish for more than fifty years, before moving to Hawaii, where he died in 2001. Chiang fulfilled his promise to end his war with the Communists. He began remitting thousands of dollars a month to the

Communists and allowed them to resume trade, telegraph, and postal services. Chiang was torn about the united front. He had spent years trying to crush the Communists, but he desperately needed military assistance, and as of 1935, the Soviets, with their new policy of battling Fascism, were the only ones offering him aid. "I am choosing between two evils"—Russia and Japan—he told his diary.

With US dollars from Chiang's treasury and from the Comintern in Moscow, the Communists bought a fleet of American buses and trucks and started a bus service from Xi'an to their headquarters in the countryside, opening the way for thousands of young Chinese to join the revolution. The Communist Party issued a confidential communiqué predicting that the united front strategy would allow it to increase its influence "thousands of times." It was right. While many in America at the time saw Chiang's release as his apotheosis, it actually marked the start of his decline. It meant, as Chiang wrote, that he would have to wait to wipe out the Communists. He would never get another chance.

The Xi'an crisis bred in Shepherd a new sense of loyalty and urgency: loyalty to Chiang Kai-shek as the only one who could save China from a triple threat—Japan, the Communists, and Fascist elements within his own party—and urgency that now was the time for well-meaning Americans to stand with their Chinese friends. The only alternative to Chiang, Shepherd wrote, was "chaos"—a word many Americans have used over the decades to justify their support for various Chinese regimes.

In the spring of 1937, more American Christians got onboard Chiang's bandwagon. Addressing the Methodists on Good Friday, Chiang emphasized the role that the Bible, faith, and prayer had played in helping him cope with his kidnapping. The *Chinese Recorder*, the main magazine of the American missionary movement, crowed that such an attitude "would have been unthinkable twenty or so years ago." It showed, the *Recorder* said, that the American church was still relevant to China and "that the Christian faith, being adventurous, meets the needs of adventurous people."

The hour was propitious for China and for Christianity. Christian groups across the ideological spectrum reexamined their reservations about Chiang and the New Life Movement. In May 1937, the *Chinese Recorder* devoted a whole issue to the campaign. Shepherd authored one essay, enthusing that it marked the opportunity of a generation. "May the church take care that it does not let the New Life Movement down!" he wrote.

Other American missionaries began to rally around Chiang. George A.

Fitch, the YMCA representative in Nanjing, was shocked that American writers like Edgar Snow and Agnes Smedley were so intent on criticizing the Nationalists. "Some of our best papers," he wrote soon after the Xi'an Incident, "have persisted in referring to General Chiang as Dictator and as having won his position by the ruthless slaughter of countless thousands of Communists." Fitch called these accusations "unjust and absurd." A fault line was opening up between Americans over China; it would have momentous consequences for both nations later on.

On July 7, 1937, Japanese forces encamped north of Beijing launched a search for a Japanese private who had wandered off base. Clashes between Japanese and Nationalist forces erupted around an overpass with eleven arches known as the Marco Polo Bridge, or Lugouqiao. Despite the reappearance of the missing soldier, the Japanese widened their assault. By the end of the month, they had taken Beijing. Chiang Kai-shek told his diary: "This is the turning point for existence or obliteration."

On August 14, Carl Crow was at his desk in Shanghai, writing to the Colgate toothpaste company to report that sales had jumped 60 percent despite increasing competition and Colgate's high price. He was bullish on China. The place was changing even faster than when he had first arrived in 1911. Then his office exploded.

Shrapnel ripped through the air. Crow peered out his shattered windows to see mayhem on the streets below. The big guns from the Japanese cruiser *Idzumo*, anchored just off Shanghai's Bund, flared red as they pulverized Chinese sections of the city. Black Saturday had begun. Before it was over, thousands of civilians would die, many killed by errant Chinese bombs. "The usually gay city of Shanghai," Crow would write, "was a city of the dead with more corpses on the streets than coffins could be provided for." Like Millard and Powell, Crow was a fierce opponent of Japanese imperialism. Realizing that he could not stay in Shanghai, he closed down his firm and left "with the suit I'm wearing, a suitcase and an overcoat." His vision of a commercially prosperous China, with himself as its biggest booster, had vanished.

By October 1937, after the bloodiest battle in Asia since the Russo-Japanese War of 1904–5, Crow's Shanghai had been transformed from Asia's great metropolis into a charred ruin where wild dogs, fattened on human flesh, roamed in packs. Withering Japanese assaults had gutted the best of Chiang Kai-shek's German-trained divisions; Chinese casualties were estimated at three hundred thousand.

Medical missionaries Mary Stone and Ida Kahn had been in Shanghai during the invasion and followed Crow to America. Gone as well was their dream of a nation that was Chinese, Christian, and equal to the West. They left for Pasadena, California, where they lived quietly until they passed away in the 1950s. In Ding county in Hebei province, the Japanese onslaught roared through Jimmy Yen's rural reconstruction station. Yen fled south to Changsha in Hunan province. Communist and Nationalist forces vied to show which was more patriotic, but Yen worried that both sides would devalue human life. "New tyrannies must not take the place of the old," he warned.

Japan's invasion of China aborted China's American-inspired modernization. During the first half of 1937, China's trade had jumped 40 percent over the first half of 1936. By 1937, China had paid off 80 percent of its debts to Western creditors. The Nationalist government had extended railway lines, dredged harbors, improved river navigation, strengthened flood control, developed air transportation, and built sixty thousand miles of roads. Businessmen had begun to invest in manufacturing. In the spring of 1937, Nelson Johnson, who had been elevated to an ambassadorship the previous year, noted that Chiang's government had been "pushing its program of economic reconstruction on all fronts . . . accelerated to a marked degree by the fact and fear of Japanese encroachment." But then that encroachment turned into an invasion.

Japan's aggression set the stage for the Communist takeover of China. No other event was more critical in sealing China's fate. Chinese and Americans would battle this occupation together. And as they had in the past, many Chinese would again look to the United States to save their country, while Americans would expect China to do more to protect itself. Both would be disappointed.

So much of what Republican China had accomplished was due to the influence of American-educated Chinese. They helped cement a new value system and a new worldview. The Chinese Communist Party spent decades trying to demolish this work and to bury the stories of the men and women who performed it. But the influence of American-educated Chinese endures.

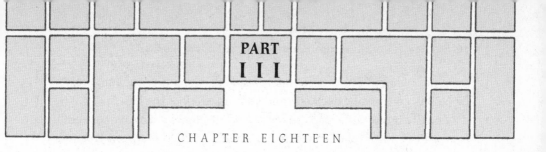

CHAPTER EIGHTEEN

Bloody Saturday

In 1935, the State Department asked the former US minister to China, John MacMurray, who had returned to the diplomatic corps in 1933, for suggestions on how to respond to Japanese aggression in Asia. "America's gunboat minister" set down his thoughts in a historic memorandum: "Developments Affecting American Policy in the Far East." Scanning the East Asian scene, MacMurray found his culprit: China. The Middle Kingdom's relentless attempts to rid itself of unequal treaties, reestablish sovereignty over its territory, and regain control over its revenues was roiling the Pacific and raising the risk of war, he argued. The Chinese, impelled by "the hysteria of their elated racial self-esteem," declared, had brought the crisis on themselves.

MacMurray predicted that the United States was headed for conflict with Japan if it did not accommodate Tokyo's interests. Manchuria was indispensable to Japan, whereas China's sovereignity was "an almost negligible factor" to the United States. He called on America to withdraw its military forces from China and cease meddling in the region's problems. He acknowledged that this would be difficult because of America's "rather romantic conception" of its ties to China.

If war between America and Japan did erupt over China, MacMurray predicted, in a line that would go down as one of the most prescient in American diplomatic history, "Nobody except perhaps Russia would gain from our victory." The Soviet Union would fill the power vacuum created by Japan's collapse, he declared, and seek "mastery of the East."

Equally important, MacMurray saw scant hope for a closer collaboration with China. If the United States would "save" China from Japan, he wrote, America might "become the 'Number One' nation in the eyes of her people," but it would also become "the most distrusted of nations" in the eyes of China's government. China's leaders, he wrote, would "thank us for nothing."

State Department officials immediately classified MacMurray's memorandum, and it did not resurface until after World War II, when the celebrated American diplomat George Kennan hailed it as "prophetic." MacMurray's analysis reflected a decidedly unromantic view of America's options in Asia. According to MacMurray, the opportunities that China presented were overhyped, America's ties to China were more emotional than rational, and China's leaders would never sincerely embrace American values or friendship. Expectations of a shared future with a like-minded China were the stuff of fantasy, MacMurray wrote. Did China, he asked, have to be the "sun" around which all of America's relations in the region were merely "planetary?" This question remains relevant today.

As Japan ratcheted up the pressure on China in the 1930s, many Chinese and Americans worked to counter MacMurray's realism through public relations campaigns, clandestine operations, and official schemes to unite the Beautiful Country and the Middle Kingdom. Much of the effort aimed at depicting China as a budding democracy and an ally worthy of Yankee aid. The campaigns tried to convince Americans that China was keen to be transformed—again—into a younger version of the United States by American know-how, weaponry, and ideas. These projects resulted in some of the most complex and striking examples of Sino-American collaboration since the two nations first met in 1784. And they ended up inflating American hopes for China—and China's expectations of the United States—to unprecedented levels.

On August 13, 1937, a forty-three-year-old Texan with something to prove was at the Nanjing Military Academy as Generalissimo Chiang Kai-shek, his wife, Soong Mayling, and a collection of Chinese generals drew up plans to battle the Japanese in Shanghai. "They are killing our people," Mayling sobbed. "What will you do?" asked the Texan, Claire "Old Leatherface" Chennault. "We will fight," she answered defiantly.

A former US Army Air Corps stunt pilot, Chennault suggested bomb-

The Americans, with the rest of the Western powers, traded with the Chinese out of a small encampment on the banks of the Pearl River in Guangzhou. (Lamqua, *View of the Hongs at Canton, 1825–35*, ca. 1835; M3793, photograph by University of Tokyo Institute of Oriental Culture)

Wu Bingjian, known to Western traders as Howqua, or Houqua, was the world's richest merchant in the early eighteen hundreds, thanks to tea, money-lending, and a little opium. (Lamqua, *Portrait of Houqua, 1825–50*; Peabody Essex Museum, M23228, photograph by Mark Sexton)

Warren Delano, shown here in a photograph taken before January 1862, was a China trader and the grandfather of American president Franklin Delano Roosevelt. (Courtesy of the Franklin D. Roosevelt Presidential Library and Museum)

Yung Wing was one of the first Chinese educated in the United States and spearheaded a Chinese government program to educate Chinese in the US. (Ca. 1900; The Connecticut Historical Society)

Wong Chin Foo, in the only confirmed photograph taken of him (early 1870s), was one of the first Chinese to demand civil rights for Chinese in America and the first to publicly use the term Chinese American. (Reproduced with permission from Special Collections/University Archives, Bertrand Library, Bucknell University, Lewisburg, Pennsylvania)

Chang and Eng Bunker were Siamese twins who grew rich performing as circus freaks. They bought a Southern plantation and are shown here circa 1865 with their wives, the sisters Sarah and Adelaide Yates, and two of their many children. (*Chang and Eng with Family*, Ronald G. Becker Collection of Charles Eisenmann Photographs, Special Collections Research Center, Syracuse University Libraries)

Bret Harte's poem captured the racism experienced by many Chinese in America. It was set to music (shown here in a handbill circa 1870) and turned into a Broadway hit. (Lester S. Levy Sheet Music Collection, Sheridan Libraries, Johns Hopkins University)

Ulysses S. Grant visited China in 1879 and met with Viceroy Li Hongzhang, who asked Grant to negotiate with Japan on China's behalf. (Library of Congress)

PUTTING HIS FOOT DOWN.

UNCLE SAM (to the Powers)—Gentlemen, you may cut up this map as much as you like, but remember that I've here to stay, and that you can't divide me up into spheres of influence!

This cartoon, from *Puck* magazine, August 23, 1899, shows Uncle Sam "putting his foot down" to prevent China from being carved up by European powers. (Library of Congress)

The Workingman's Party, with its plank against Chinese immigration, became a political force in the Western United States in the late nineteenth century. (Historical Society of Pennsylvania)

Mary Stone and Ida Kahn were two medical missionaries who were educated at the University of Michigan in the 1890s and practiced medicine in China. (United Methodist Archives, Drew University)

Young John Allen, shown here circa 1900 with colleagues, spearheaded a movement to bring modern education and science to China. (Young John Allen Papers/Stuart A. Rose Manuscript, Archives, and Rare Book Library, Emory University)

In China, American women were given more opportunities than at home. Here, Elizabeth Reifsnyder, a surgeon, is shown removing a massive tumor, circa 1885. (Boston Medical Library in the Francis A. Countway Library of Medicine, Harvard University)

Buck Clayton, an influential jazz musician in 1930s China, worked with Chinese musician Li Jinhui to give traditional Chinese melodies a modern flair. (Used with permission of the University of Missouri–Kansas City Libraries, Dr. Kenneth J. LaBudde Collection, LaBudde Special Collections)

The British American Tobacco Company was at the forefront of creating an image of the sexy Chinese woman in the 1920s. (Collection of Agnes Tabah)

Anna May Wong, a Chinese American actress, was the first nonwhite star in the United States. She captivated audiences around the world. (Library of Congress)

Cornelius Vander Starr, shown here with a Chinese client in 1922, founded his first insurance company in China. It grew into the giant AIG. (C. V. Starr East Asian Library, Columbia University Libraries, with permission from the Starr Foundation)

Homer Lea, circa 1902, was an American aide to Sun Yat-sen who tried to raise an army in America to overthrow the Qing dynasty. (Reproduced with permission from the Homer Lea Research Center)

Sun Yat-sen was the one Chinese leader who pierced the membrane between China and America. He is shown here in 1924 after publicly denouncing the United States. (Library of Congress)

Chiang Kai-shek is shown here with the Soong sisters—(*from left*) his wife, Mayling, Ailing, and Qingling—following his release after being kidnapped in Xi'an in 1936. (Library of Congress)

The American writer Edgar Snow, shown here in 1936, was enormously influential in creating an image of Mao Zedong (*right*) as a moderate reformer. (Edgar Parks Snow Papers, University Archives, University of Missouri–Kansas City, with permission from Lois Wheeler Snow)

Pearl Buck, in a 1932 photograph, remains one of the most important writers on China. (Library of Congress)

ing Japanese warships on the Huangpu River. Chiang asked the American to lead a counterattack. Chennault stayed up until 4:00 a.m. shaping the next day's mission. "Unknowingly," Chennault acknowledged in his memoirs, "we were setting the stage for Shanghai's famous Black Saturday." At 6:00 a.m., Chennault was airborne over Shanghai to supervise the city's defense. His plans went quickly awry. Chinese bombs missed the Japanese destroyer *Idzumo* and hit populated areas. A single shell killed hundreds of civilians.

Black Saturday marked the catastrophic start of a gripping tale of cooperation between China and the United States. Just as Frederick Townsend Ward had commanded Chinese and foreign forces against the Taipings in 1862, Chennault would lead bands of foreigners and Chinese against a sworn enemy of the Chinese government. Initially, Chennault fought the Japanese with little help from his own country; American diplomats threatened him with arrest, and American military officers ignored his advice. Later, he would gain worldwide renown as the founder of the American Volunteer Group, known as the Flying Tigers, a band of hotshot pilots who would amass a spectacular combat record against the Japanese.

Chennault's journey to China began on a chilly day in Miami in January 1936. At the All-American Air Races, as Chennault, John Luke Williamson, and Billy McDonald, known as the Three Men on the Flying Trapeze, looped the loop and wowed the crowd, Chinese colonel Mao Bangchu looked on. Aircraft manufacturer William Pawley had brought Mao to America to help him recruit trainers for China's fledgling air force to replace those led by the departing colonel Jouett. Pawley threw a party on a yacht in Miami Harbor and introduced Mao to the Three Men. Mao offered to double their army paychecks if they came to China. McDonald and Williamson agreed. But Chennault, whose dream was to revolutionize the US Army Air Corps, declined the offer.

At the time, American air power strategists believed that it was possible to bomb opponents into submission. Chennault, then a lowly captain, championed a different approach that envisaged using fighters, backed by an early-warning ground intelligence system, to obliterate bombing formations. A year before the Miami show, Chennault had published a book—*The Role of Defensive Pursuit*—criticizing then brigadier general Henry "Hap" Arnold for promoting unescorted bombing runs. Arnold responded: "Who is this damned fellow Chennault?" and ensured that no one in the army corps would listen to the craggy-faced maverick from Commerce, Texas.

Stymied by the brass and burdened by ill health (he was deaf in one ear and suffered from recurring bouts of bronchitis, thanks to three packs of cigarettes a day), Chennault was grounded by army flight surgeons in the winter of 1936. Meanwhile, his air-show buddies wrote from China that if Chennault ever wanted to try out his new theories, China was the place. When the Chinese sweetened their offer to $12,000 a year, Chennault took it. On the morning of May 1, 1937, hours after retiring from the air corps, he left for the Far East, beginning an eight-year adventure.

Chiang Kai-shek's decision to challenge the Japanese in Shanghai, along China's central coast, and not on the North China Plain, reflected the influence of the German military advisers who had trained Chiang's army since 1934. Northern China was uniquely suited to Japan's tanks and artillery. Shanghai's terrain, crisscrossed by creeks and tenements, nullified that advantage. Chiang also picked Shanghai because it was an international city, with settlements run by the British, the Americans, and the French. A great battle in Shanghai would unfold under the noses of Westerners, who would tell China's story to the world.

The Battle of Shanghai erupted in the second week of August 1937. Westerners in the International Settlement did as they had always done: they gawked. Anglo-American guests at the swank Park Hotel, wrote correspondent Edgar Snow, gazed out the windows of the top-story dining room, "while contentedly sipping their demitasses" and gauging "the marksmanship of the Japanese batteries."

As Chiang's armies battled, American newsmen again took China's side. Carroll Alcott, a radio journalist from South Dakota, visited Chinese soldiers on the frontlines while Japanese artillery shells rained down around them. He found them unfazed, huddled in do-it-yourself caves, cooking rice and vegetables over a charcoal brazier.

Writers and photographers were not shy about goosing the story for effect. On August 28, 1937, H. S. "Newsreel" Wong took a picture of a blackened Chinese baby at the Shanghai South Railway station just after a Japanese air raid. Editors named the picture "Bloody Saturday," and it became the most celebrated symbol of the conflict. There was China mewling helplessly for a Western savior. Questions were raised about the authenticity of the image when another photograph surfaced showing a man, probably Wong's assistant, carrying the infant. Wong seems to have staged the shot.

No matter. By October, more than fifty million Americans had seen "Bloody Saturday"—in movie-house newsreels, in the pages of more than eight hundred newspapers, and in *Life* magazine. Anti-Japanese sentiment in the United States grew. Even American isolationists, such as Senator George W. Norris of Nebraska, branded the Japanese "disgraceful, ignoble, barbarous and cruel." The small but growing pro-China lobby slapped the image on its fund-raising material. And the Japanese Imperial Army slapped a $50,000 bounty on Wong's head. (He died peacefully at home in Taiwan in 1981.)

Still, few in America had any stomach for war with Japan. Secretary of State Cordell Hull moved to block the Nationalists from hiring American pilots. American officials in China forced four of Chennault's American aides to return home. Clarence E. Gauss, the consul general in Shanghai, tried to have Chennault arrested. But in Nanjing, Ambassador Nelson Johnson looked the other way. Whenever his superiors in Washington pressed him about Chennault's whereabouts, Nelson reported that the Texan was "somewhere in the interior" even though Chennault and Nelson lunched together regularly.

Kuomintang officials complained that the United States was obstructing China's ability to fight. Soong Mayling told Johnson that it was "unneutral" for the United States to deprive China of flight instructors, considering that American planes made up 90 percent of China's air force. By September 1937, Hull had softened. Americans could advise the Chinese, he determined, but they could not fight. Chennault flouted those rules, shooting down (he claimed) thirty-seven Japanese planes.

China's endless woes and Japan's insatiable drive for territory worried the US president. Franklin Delano Roosevelt hailed from a family of China traders. His grandfather Warren Delano had spent many profitable years in Guangzhou, swapping opium for tea and silk. Roosevelt's mother, Sara Delano, lived for several periods in the family's residence known as Rose Hill in Hong Kong. At Hyde Park, FDR was raised among Chinese furnishings and blue-and-white porcelain; the clang of a bronze gong acquired in China in 1863 summoned the family to dinner.

Roosevelt had started his political career believing that America needed to extend its empire, but he had grown into a foe of imperialism. In particular, he opposed the foreign penetration of China. As assistant secretary of the navy under Woodrow Wilson in 1913, FDR drew up war plans against Japan. He was taken with Wilson's belief that Japan should not be allowed to dominate China. A year after Roosevelt was elected president in 1932, he told his advisers that he wanted to renounce all of America's unequal treaties with China, but State Department experts, including John MacMurray, convinced him not to go too far too fast.

China would loom large in Roosevelt's plan to establish a new world order after World War II. A strong, democratic China would stabilize the Pacific, counter a resurgent Japan, and tamp down Soviet expansionism in the region, Roosevelt believed. A democratic China would inspire the colonies of Asia to seek independence and embrace free trade. It would be one of the "four policemen" along with the United States, Great Britain, and the USSR, that would guarantee a permanent peace.

There was something of Anson Burlingame, America's first minister to the Qing court, in Roosevelt's quest. Like Burlingame, Roosevelt recognized China had shortcomings; he spoke of it as "still in the eighteenth century." But, as one of the president's favorite films, *The Good Earth*, said, China was a nation of "vast promise." And American help could give it the boost it needed. As Roosevelt told one of his closest foreign policy advisers, Sumner Welles, treating China as a peer was the best means of avoiding "a fundamental cleavage between the West and East in the years to come."

Roosevelt faced the same challenge that then secretary of state Henry Stimson had confronted under President Herbert Hoover: Could he protect China without fighting Japan? In the early 1930s, Japan continued to be America's largest Asian market. Airplanes, weapons, and scrap metal to make into shrapnel flowed from the West Coast to the Land of the Rising Sun.

By the fall of 1937, the Japanese Expeditionary Force had seized Shanghai. Halfway across the world, Benito Mussolini's troops had annexed Ethiopia. In Germany, Adolf Hitler, flouting the Treaty of Versailles, was rearming. Japan and Germany signed the Anti-Comintern Pact vowing to fight Communism. Fascist victories compelled Roosevelt to take on the powerful isolationist sentiment in the United States. In a speech in Chicago on October 5, 1937, he urged Americans to stand up to the "epidemic of world lawlessness." He warned that neutrality would not protect the United States and called for an "international quarantine of the aggressor nations." Henry Stimson followed Roosevelt's speech with a letter to the *New York Times* urging an embargo on war materiel to Japan. That was front-page news, along with Stimson's claim that China was fighting for American interests in East Asia.

US editorial writers blasted the speech and pooh-poohed Stimson's rallying cry. The Veterans of Foreign Wars and other isolationist groups gathered twenty-five million signatures against war. Calls for Roosevelt's impeachment were mooted in Congress. "It is a terrible thing to look over your shoulder when you are trying to lead," Roosevelt remarked, "and find no one there."

At the Nine-Power Treaty Conference in Brussels in October 1937, US delegate Norman Davis told the British and the French that America had no intention of responding to Japan's attacks on China. Wellington Koo, now China's ambassador to Paris, demanded sanctions against Japan, but the Americans reminded Koo that the Nine-Power Treaty lacked enforcement provisions. When Japan refused to consider mediation over its Chinese landgrabs, the diplomatic architecture constructed at the Washington Naval Conference fifteen years earlier collapsed.

While America fiddled, other nations stepped into the breach. On August 21, 1937, the Soviet Union and China signed a treaty of nonaggression, once again opening the floodgates for Soviet military assistance to the Kuomintang. Given Japan's alliance with Germany against Communism, Stalin was more than happy for China to tie up the Japanese military and spare the Soviet Union an assault from the East. For the next three years, under Operation Zet, the Soviets would furnish China with millions of dollars' worth of warplanes, bombers, tanks, antiaircraft batteries, ammunition, and trucks. Soviet army pilots battled the Japanese over China's skies. Up until Pearl Harbor, financial support from Moscow constituted more than 80 percent of China's foreign aid.

Japanese forces took Beijing in August 1937. In next-door Tianjin, Japanese bombers pulverized American-inspired Nankai University, the brainchild of Columbia graduate Zhang Boling. On November 9, after losing some two hundred thousand men around Shanghai, Chiang's forces retreated up the Yangtze to defend the capital in Nanjing.

Japan's forces converged on Nanjing from three directions—almost half a million men, two hundred tanks, backed by seemingly unlimited air power. And so, on the morning of December 7, Chiang Kai-shek rose at 4:00 a.m., said his prayers, and fled the doomed capital with Soong Mayling, flying halfway up the Yangtze to the industrial center Hankou. Government ministries had already decamped even farther west to Chongqing, a sprawling city built on hills at the confluence of the Yangtze and Jialing Rivers in Sichuan province. "Broken hearted," Chiang wrote in his diary. The Generalissimo vowed that his troops in Nanjing would fight to the last man. But his battle plan collapsed as thousands of Chinese soldiers retreating from Shanghai streamed through the city, prompting Nanjing's defenders to run as well.

On November 17, 1937, fifteen Western missionaries, businessmen, and educators formed the International Committee of the Nanking Safety Zone. A German businessman, John Rabe, was elected to head it. The American majority on the committee, considering Rabe's membership in the Nazi Party and Japan's recent pact with Hitler, hoped that he might have some sway with the invaders.

On the evening of December 12, as the first wave of Japanese forces closed in on the capital, the Chinese commanding general slipped out of town, leaving the city's fate in the hands of the Western committee. George Fitch, an American born in Suzhou and the head of the Nanjing YMCA, was appointed chief administrator of the refugee zone centered in the northwest corner of the city. Rabe appealed to Japanese forces not to attack the zone; they agreed, as long as no Chinese soldiers were there. The committee designated one of the refugee centers for women and children; it was at Jinling Women's College and was led by an American named Minnie Vautrin.

Minnie Vautrin, who would come to be known as China's Goddess of Mercy, was born in 1886 to a struggling farming family in Secor, Illinois. Her mother died when she was six, and Minnie helped her blacksmith father raise a younger brother. An ace student, Minnie took odd jobs, including a stint as a door-to-door saleswoman for the *Encyclopedia Britannica,* to pay her way through high school and then the University of Illinois Urbana–Champaign. There, like thousands of other Midwesterners, she joined the Student Volunteer Movement for Foreign Missions and embraced the idea of saving the world through social work and education. When she graduated in 1912, she volunteered to be a missionary in China and was dispatched to Hefei, a central Chinese backwater, where she founded the region's first school for girls. She took a Chinese name Hua Qun—or "Hua of the Flock."

After six years in China, Vautrin returned to the US, earned a master's degree at Columbia Teachers College, and then went back to China in 1918 as the interim president of Jinling Women's College in Nanjing. The new job forced her to decide between marriage and China. Like many American women in the mission field, she chose China, broke off an engagement, and remained single for the rest of her life. Vautrin held that Americans had a moral duty to guide China to a place of peace, stability, and righteousness.

She pushed Jinling's students to descend from their ivory tower and be of practical use to their homeland as teachers of the poor.

In the mid-1920s, when the Chinese government ordered that all schools were to be run by Chinese, Vautrin stepped down as president of Jinling to work under Wu Yifang, one of Jinling's first graduates and the first woman president of any Chinese university. Vautrin was in Nanjing, cowering in an attic with a group of other foreigners, when Nationalist troops attacked the city in March 1927. After the Nanjing Incident, she left with other Westerners but soon returned, defying US consular orders that Americans stay away. A year later, Vautrin's ailing father asked that she come home to care for him. Once again, she chose Jinling.

As dean of students, Vautrin was known as a bit of a scold. At night, she roamed the campus, breaking up make-out sessions between visiting young men and Jinling's women. She was vacationing at the beach in Qingdao, China, and preparing for another leave from China when the Marco Polo Bridge Incident erupted in July 1937. She canceled her furlough and rushed back to Nanjing. "Men are not asked to desert their ships when they are in danger," she told her diary, "and women are not asked to leave their children." On August 15, as the Japanese began bombing Nanjing, the US embassy ordered all Americans to leave. Again, Vautrin stayed, administering to wounded Chinese soldiers who were transported into the city in boxcars.

As the Japanese closed in, Vautrin convinced Wu Yifang to leave the city to establish a Jinling campus in Sichuan province, far from Japanese guns. In her diary, Vautrin predicted that the Japanese would spare Nanjing. Having been in the city in 1927, she was more concerned about the possibility of marauding Chinese troops. "Let's see how correct I am," she wrote. She festooned the Jinling campus with American flags, betting that they would keep the refugees safe. Japanese bombing runs ignited fires throughout the city. On December 8, as Nanjing burned, Jinling took in its first refugees. "Tonight I look 60 and feel 80," wrote Vautrin. She was fifty-two.

On December 12, the last remnants of the Kuomintang army fled the city. That same day, Japanese bombers attacked the American naval warship *Panay*, which was anchored on the Yangtze and loaded with refugees. Three American sailors and scores of Chinese civilians were killed. Although the Japanese claimed that the attack had been unintentional and sent a formal apology to Washington along with an indemnity of

$2.2 million, US code breakers had intercepted Japanese communications and learned that the pilots had been under clear orders to sink the ship. Not wanting to tip off Tokyo that America had broken its codes, Roosevelt accepted the apology.

A day after that attack, just before dawn, the Japanese entered Nanjing, and Vautrin and the other Westerners began hearing reports of atrocities. Japanese soldiers walked through the Jinling campus searching for men and found four. "They took them to our west hill, I heard the shots," Vautrin wrote. Other soldiers hunted for victims to rape: girls as young as eleven, women as old as sixty. On December 16, Vautrin wrote that there had been at least one thousand rapes in the city. "These Japanese are wild," she told her diary, "there is nothing they won't do; if they want to kill, they kill; if they want to rape, they rape." That night Jinling housed four thousand refugees; it had planned for half as many. On December 18, Japanese troops ordered Vautrin to leave the campus at the point of a gun. She refused. "This is my home, I cannot leave," she said.

Vautrin appealed to the Japanese consulate to rein in the troops. The consulate posted military police officers to the Jinling campus, but the MPs themselves began to rape. On Christmas Eve, with nine thousand women and children packed on campus and a quarter of a million refugees in the safety zone, a Japanese officer arrived at the school and demanded that Chinese prostitutes be rounded up to service his men. The idea, Vautrin wrote in her diary, was to "start a regular licensed place for the soldiers then they will not molest innocent and decent women." Vautrin found twenty-one prostitutes. The officer wanted a hundred. Refugee women pleaded with Vautrin not to let the Japanese pull the other seventy-nine from a pool of "the decent girls," Vautrin wrote.

Vautrin's Chinese colleagues worshiped and resented her at the same time. Cheng Ruifang had worked with Vautrin for years at Jinling and wondered to her diary why an American was so important to the safety of the Chinese. On December 16, when a delegation of Japanese soldiers came to Jinling, Vautrin invited them for tea and cakes. "I hated Miss Vautrin for thinking that treating the soldiers nicely would make them behave better," Cheng told her diary. "The more she complains, the more bad things they do." When the refugees began calling Minnie "Guanyin," the Buddhist goddess of mercy, Cheng was jealous. Still, she acknowledged somewhat acidly, "If Miss Vautrin was not here, it would not work either."

The tiny foreign community continued to push back at the marauding Japanese. Japanese soldiers shoved Miner Searle Bates, a former Rhodes scholar and an administrator at Nanjing University, down a flight of stairs after he inquired about a student who had vanished. Bates wrote of witnessing countless atrocities. It had been, he wrote, "Christmas in Hell."

"To have to stand by," declared YMCA chief George Fitch, "while a thousand women kneel before you crying hysterically, begging you to save them from the beasts who are preying on them is a hell I had never before envisaged." Fitch and others began documenting Japanese war crimes. On the winter's solstice, American doctor Robert Wilson wrote, "This is the shortest day in the year, but it still contains twenty-four hours. . . . I could go on for pages telling of cases of rape and brutality almost beyond belief."

Four American reporters were in the city as the massacre began. Arch Steele was the first to get word out. Slipping to the waterfront on December 15, he boarded the USS *Oahu* and wired his story to the *Chicago Daily News*, where it ran with the headline "Japanese Troops Kill Thousands." Steele observed that the Japanese could have taken the city without firing a shot; instead, "they chose the course of systematic extermination." The last thing he saw as he left Nanjing, he reported, was a group of three hundred Chinese being mown down before the city walls. "It was like killing sheep," he wrote.

Steele's reports, and those of Charles Yates McDaniel of the Associated Press, Arthur von Briesen Menken of Paramount News, and Frank Tillman Durdin of the *New York Times*, shocked the American public. Durdin compared the barbarity to "vandalism in the Dark Ages in Europe." And these reporters had left before the real killing began.

By late January 1938, the Japanese occupiers had ordered the refugee camps closed, but Vautrin and others argued that the city was still not safe. Vautrin taught the refugee women handicrafts and schooled their children. "The tragedies that come to us each day!" she wrote on March 17. "I pray I may not become hardened and indifferent."

By May 1938, Jinling's refugees had departed. Still Vautrin was reluctant to leave. She felt that her charges, in fact, all of China, could not go on without her. Finally, the Jinling board ordered her to return to America. Racked with guilt, she boarded a steam liner bound for Vancouver. In the middle of the Pacific, she considered jumping overboard. Back in America, she was committed to the Psychopathic Hospital of the State University of Iowa, and given hormone shots and an antidepressant called Metrazol that caused seizures.

Vautrin felt that she had failed China. "At a time when the whole world is in such travail and agony, I am sorry to be on the side lines, helpless and a burden," she wrote to her colleagues. On May 14, 1941, left alone in the apartment of a friend in Indianapolis, she turned on the gas jet of the kitchen stove and ended her life. She was fifty-five years old. The United Christian Missionary Society called Vautrin "a casualty of the war." She was buried in Secor, Illinois. Her tombstone is engraved with four Chinese characters, "Jinling Yongsheng," "Jinling Forever."

On January 3, 1938, weeks after Nanjing fell to the Japanese, *Time*, the most influential news outlet in the United States, declared Chiang Kai-shek and Soong Mayling "Man and Wife of the Year." In their cover portrait, Chiang held a fedora and Mayling wore a simple dress, both exuding dignity and defiance. "Through 1937 the Chinese have been led—not without glory—by one supreme leader and his remarkable wife," the magazine enthused. "Under this man and wife the traditionally disunited Chinese people—millions of whom seldom used the word 'China' in the past—have slowly been given national consciousness." *Time* predicted that the pair would write "a great page of history." China's fight against Japan was front-page news.

The man behind the *Time* cover would become one of Chiang's greatest patrons and one of the most influential voices in US-China relations—media titan Henry R. Luce. Luce was born in 1898 in Shandong province, where his missionary father, Henry W. Luce, was teaching at the Dengzhou Boys' School. Henry, freshly graduated from Yale, and his wife, Elisabeth Root, believed that China needed Western education, not evangelism. Calvin Mateer, the great advocate of schooling for the Chinese and Dengzhou's founder, baptized their firstborn son, who, like his father, was known as Harry.

Luce grew up with other missionary children behind the mission walls. While his contemporary, Pearl Buck, had Chinese friends, Luce had few and never spoke much Chinese. Still, he was a precocious learner. At four, he was giving sermons in the mission courtyard. At ten, he had exhausted his mother's capacity to teach him and was sent to a British boarding school. By fourteen, he was attending the elite Hotchkiss School in Connecticut, where he was nicknamed "Chink."

Luce was a top student; he founded a magazine at Hotchkiss and at Yale joined the *Yale Daily News* and the exclusive undergraduate secret society Skull and Bones. He gained a reputation as the most vociferous anti-Communist on campus. Though he had been raised far from America, Luce was passionately patriotic. From his first visit at the age of eight, he had been mesmerized by America. In 1920, Luce won Yale's DeForest

Prize for oration. His topic was the global responsibilities of the United States, foreshadowing what he and his publications would one day call the American Century. "America is power," he declared, "and it sits astride the globe."

After graduation, Luce landed a reporting job in Baltimore. By day, he covered the city; by night, he and his Yale classmate, the magnetically cool Briton Hadden, planned a news magazine. By the end of 1922, capitalizing on Hadden's connections, the two had raised about $100,000. For names, they toyed with "Facts," "What's What," and "Destiny," until Luce came up with *Time*. The first issue came out on March 3, 1923, and a publishing empire was born.

By 1937, despite the Depression, *Time*'s circulation had surpassed six hundred thousand. By 1941, *Time* and its sister publications, *Life* and *Fortune*, were being read in almost four million households—the broadest reach in American media history. Luce's magazines had always covered China but had portrayed it more as a basket case than as an opportunity. *Time* chronicled Japan's invasion of Manchuria in the early 1930s as a dispute between two tyrannies—Japanese imperialists against Chinese warlords. It referred to Chiang Kai-shek as "Dictator Chiang" and interpreted his kidnapping in Xi'an as proof of China's disarray. "Chaos and disorder are 'normalcy' to China," read one article. (Even as late as June 26, 1939, *Time* was still referring to the war in China as inconsequential, "a matter of yellow man killing yellow man.")

In 1932, Luce returned to China for the first time in twenty years. He had left the land of his birth at the start of the Republican revolution and had missed the anti-Christian riots and protests of the 1920s. Now, like many other Christians, he rediscovered a China that was full of hope. He was taken with T. V. Soong and Soong's predictions of great economic and political progress. To Luce, Soong's prophecies augured the fulfillment of his father's dreams of drawing China into the modern world. And Chiang Kai-shek struck Luce as the man to do it. The Generalissimo would grace *Time*'s cover ten times, more than FDR, Stalin, or Churchill, and the same number as Mao Zedong.

As *Time* grew, and after Hadden's untimely death in 1929, Luce evolved from private businessman to a public figure. He quipped that he believed in God, the United States, and the Republican Party, though not necessarily in that order. Still, he was not a predictable conservative. He had a restless intellect that drove him to support "liberal" ideas, most particularly racial integration—a cause also dear to Pearl Buck.

Like many China Hands, Buck and Luce clashed over how to configure the Sino-American relationship. Luce was convinced that the road to a modern China passed through the United States. He also believed in the Great Harmony, the ultimate commingling of China and the United States, but his merger would be on America's terms. China was destined, he believed, to be an Asian America, a pupil of the United States.

Buck's version of the Great Harmony involved a future built on co-operation, patience, and political moderation, not on Americans instructing the Chinese on how to live. Buck used Luce as the model for the character of William Lane in her novel *God's Men*. Lane qualifies as the most villainous personality in all her oeuvre, a megalomaniacal magazine mogul who wants to control the world. Luce ordered his writers never to say anything nice about Buck again. *Time*, which had once praised her novels, now mocked her "soggy prose."

April 29, 1938, was Japanese Emperor Hirohito's thirty-seventh birthday. To honor him, Japanese forces planned an assault on Hankou. Chennault had worked well with the Russians and the Chinese so far; Chinese fighters had shot down more than forty Japanese bombers in the skies over Nanjing.

Chennault prepared a surprise for the Japanese. The night before Hirohito's birthday, Chinese and Russian fighter aircraft flew out of Hankou in an ostentatious departure, circling the city for all to see. As expected, Japanese spies reported the withdrawal but failed to notice that at sundown the fighters returned, skimming in along the treetops. The next morning, the Japanese launched a massive bombing run, but the Russians and Chinese surprised them. When the smoke cleared, thirty-six of thirty-nine Japanese planes had been lost in the biggest pre–World War II battle in aerial history.

Chennault continued to experiment with fighting techniques. Noticing that he could tear the aluminum siding from the Japanese planes with his bare hands, he convinced his men to ram the aircraft in midflight to sheer off their wings—a tactic that the Russians later employed against the Luftwaffe in World War II.

On October 27, 1938, Hankou fell. The Nationalist army had lost 255,000 men, but by inflicting 107,000 casualties on the Imperial Army, it had halted Japan's advance. Soong Mayling dispatched Chennault to Kunming in China's southwest. She wanted him to establish a Chinese air force training academy. "Old Leatherface" never flew another combat mission, but he would go on to make history.

In September 1938, Xiao Bo, a chubby Chinese major who worked for China's spy chief, Dai Li, approached a balding man named Herbert Yardley on a street in Queens, New York. Yardley was the father of American cryptography and had cracked Japanese codes during the Washington Naval Conference in 1922. When the US government shut down its Cipher Bureau in 1929, tossing Yardley out of a job, Yardley wrote his memoirs, *The American Black Chamber*, which revealed that the United States had broken the codes of nineteen other countries. Herbert Yardley was the Edward Snowden of his day.

A pirated translation of Yardley's book had surfaced in China and caught the eye of spies employed by Dai Li, who sat at the helm of the Bureau of Investigation and Statistics of the Military Affairs Commission, or Juntong. Dai Li's organization specialized in assassination, clandestine operations, dirty tricks, and sabotage in support of Chiang Kai-shek's regime. Xiao Bo, Juntong's man in Washington, offered Yardley a job, and in November 1938, traveling as "Herbert Osborn, an exporter of animal hides," he arrived in Chongqing.

In mid-1939, working with Chinese cryptographers, Yardley broke the code of the Japanese air force. Coupled with a ground detection unit set up by Chennault, this decoded information would provide Chennault's pilots intelligence they needed to down Japanese planes and would also form the basis of a first-rate air warning system against Japan's air raids on Chinese cities.

Like Frederick Townsend Ward, Yardley was an American adventurer. To Dai Li's delight, he had no affection for the preachy, patronizing approach of the missionaries and "Old China Hands." At a banquet in 1939, Yardley gave an eloquent defense of assassination, to which Dai Li responded, "Gan bei!" (Bottoms up!) But Yardley presented the Chinese with other problems. He organized orgies and kept a "comfort" cottage for his mistresses. He turned his bedroom in a rat-infested Buddhist temple over to lusty diplomats and journalists looking for privacy. "I wanted to know how many foreigners are frauds in their sex life," he wrote.

In Chongqing, Yardley was a denizen of a demimonde of Eurasians, Westerners, returned Chinese students, journalists, and spies. He took a twenty-three-year-old American reporter, Theodore White, under his wing, teaching him poker; Yardley would go on to write a best-selling introduction to the game. White was eternally grateful for another of Yardley's lessons: "how to behave in an air raid."

Yardley was in Chongqing when Japanese bombers carried out their infamous raid of May 5–6, 1939. He watched men burn alive in raging fires and homes collapse on pregnant women. "Here a child's head lay in the gutter," he wrote, "there pieces of human bodies." He chanced on an old man sitting on a curb, moaning. "What does he say?" Yardley asked his interpreter. "He says he wants to go home," she replied. The old man struggled to his feet. His whole left side was torn open, revealing a still-beating heart. "He took one step," Yardley wrote, "and fell dead." Yardley left China in early 1940. With his help, the Nationalists had set up two hundred radio operations that would intercept more than two hundred thousand secret Japanese radio transmissions over the course of the war.

Herbert Yardley, Henry Luce, Minnie Vautrin, and Claire Chennault represented America's mission in China as Japan began nine years of unrelenting aggression against the Middle Kingdom. It was a place for adventurers, entrepreneurs, true believers, and people with something to prove. But China wanted more. Ever since the Opium War, China had sought the full backing of the United States government against its foes. In its life-and-death struggle with Japan, it would be compelled to seek it again.

●

CHAPTER NINETEEN

Little America

On October 31, 1936, months before the Japanese invasion of China, Hilda Yan was in the VIP section of the stands at Longhua Airfield in Shanghai for a celebration of Chiang Kai-shek's fiftieth birthday. Just two years earlier, Yan had set aside her life as a Shanghai socialite and mother of two to serve as the hostess of China's embassy in Moscow, where her uncle Yan Huiqing was ambassador. From there she moved to Geneva, where she became her nation's first female representative to the League of Nations and battled child labor. Now back in China, Yan was looking for opportunities. And here was one literally bearing down upon her.

In the skies above, a stunt pilot executed a brilliant series of airborne acrobatics, soaring to a great height and then steering the plane into a power dive headed straight toward the stands where the cream of Shanghai's high society watched with a mixture of horror and amazement. A short distance from the dignitaries' heads, the pilot pulled up, and the aircraft thundered into the blue. The crowd went wild. When the plane finally came to a stop on the airfield, the cockpit popped open—and out jumped a woman. It was movie star turned aviator Li Xiaqing. At that moment, Hilda Yan decided that she, too, would learn to fly.

Yan and Li became fast friends. They shared much in common: both had recently divorced and were living the difficult life of a modern Chinese woman, navigating the perilous shoals between East and West. Li had been an actress since her youth and had played the role of the Chinese woman warrior, Mulan, in the first cinematic adaptation of the story. After earning her pilot's license, she had volunteered to enter combat training in the Chinese air force but had been turned down.

Following Japan's attack in 1937, Li went to California to drum up support for China. Hilda Yan was already on the East Coast at flight school. The two stayed in touch. What better way to raise awareness of China's plight, the pair decided, than a barnstorming tour across the United States?

That two Chinese women would hatch such a plan is an indication of the faith the Chinese had in the people of the United States. The pair served as warriors in a battle for US hearts that China launched as the conflict with Japan intensified. While the Nationalists and the Communists competed to bend the minds of America's elite, Hilda Yan and Li Xiaqing along with a host of others appealed directly to the American people to get them on China's side.

American missionaries, American-educated Chinese, and the Yankee press subjected Americans to a barrage of images designed to convince them that Chinese society was emulating the United States and deserved America's support. Sun Yat-sen was described as "the George Washington of China," Chiang Kai-shek "the Lincoln of China." Money-man T. V. Soong was its Alexander Hamilton. "Like our own America," ran a newsreel that played in movie theaters nationwide, "China is a vast and beautiful country. . . . Our common struggle has brought its people close to our hearts."

Even China's Communists, who just a few years earlier had vexed missionary George Shepherd and his colleagues, were now worthy of praise. Their social reforms, the anti-Communist *Missionary Review of the World* now acknowledged, were "compatible with the aspirations of all progressive people." The *Catholic World*, long vigilant against the Red Threat, opined that Mao's Communists blended "Chinese common sense and Chinese individualism" and credited them with protecting freedom of speech, assembly, and religion.

In Chongqing, the Kuomintang set up a Ministry of International Information and hired Americans to tell China's story. Fresh out of Harvard with a degree in Chinese studies, Theodore White got his first job writing propaganda for the Republic of China. White's greatest creation was the legend of a Chinese Amazon based on a news item he spied in a Chinese newspaper about a woman who had tossed a hand grenade into a movie theater, killing a few Japanese. White embellished the tale, turning her into a guerrilla chief. Her given name was Huanghua, which means "yellow flowers" in Chinese, but White opted for the more mellifluent "Golden Flowers" instead. When American newspapers demanded a picture of the heroine, the Ministry of Information issued a photograph of a Chinese woman toting six-shooters. With that she became "Pistol Packing Miss Golden Flowers." A few years later, as a correspondent for *Time*, White was asked to revisit the story. Only then, he observed, did "I confess my role as father of a fraud."

The Chinese used other methods to tug at American heartstrings. After the first live panda cub arrived in America in 1936, courtesy of American explorer Ruth Harkness, Soong Mayling understood the allure of the cuddly beasts and packed off two more—Pan-dee and Pan-dah—to the Bronx Zoo. So began decades of panda diplomacy.

The Communists got into the act, backing left-wing Chinese students in their efforts to rally progressive Americans to China's side. They founded organizations such as Hands Off China, the All-American Anti-Imperialist League, and the American Friends of the Chinese People, which received cash and direction from Moscow. By the 1930s, at least fifty Chinese students had joined the Communist Party of the United States.

The Kuomintang established its fabled lobbying organization—the China Lobby—in May 1938 when former missionary Frank Price and his brother Harry, a financial adviser to the Nationalist government, formed the American Committee for Non-Participation in Japanese Aggression. Participants ranged from Communist agent and writer T. A. Bisson to former secretary of state Henry Stimson. The group's main goal was a trade embargo against Japan, which the committee predicted would end the war.

To stage-manage propaganda operations, the Kuomintang sent to New York P. C. Chang, the Columbia University thespian who had adapted the story of *Mulan* into English for the Broadway stage. Chang was a master at making Chinese culture palatable to Western tastes. In 1930, he oversaw a wildly successful tour of the US by Peking Opera star Mei Lanfang. Just a few years earlier, one American witness had described Peking Opera as "an excruciating din" from which "the visitor rushes out into the night to cool his throbbing brain." But Chang cut down on the noise and added more dance moves, and Hollywood fawned over Mei when he played to sold-out crowds in Los Angeles. The party dispatched Earl Leaf, a United Press photographer who would later become one of the world's first paparazzi, renowned for his candid shots of Marilyn Monroe. In Washington, the Chinese pressed American missionaries to flood Capitol Hill to argue China's case with their representatives. YMCA missionary George

Fitch presented film of the Nanjing massacre to the House Foreign Affairs Committee on March 22, 1938.

The funding for these operations came from Nationalist China. Even after Congress passed the Foreign Agent Registration Act in June 1938, obliging lobbyists representing foreign countries to register with the State Department, the Nationalists continued to funnel unreported cash to their American friends. In October 1939, Japan acknowledged twenty-three agents in the United States; Nationalist China, which was bankrolling dozens, did not admit to a single one. Other Americans joined the effort to turn decades of growing receptiveness to Chinese culture into a political force. The most intriguing group was the International Committee for the Promotion of Chinese Industrial Cooperatives, the brainchild of Peg Snow, Edgar's wife.

In 1938, Peg came up with the idea that what China needed to replace its bombed-out industry was a network of cooperatives. Scattered around the country, they would be too dispersed for the Japanese to wipe out. They would be worker-owned and would supply China with many of its war needs and, perhaps most important, teach Chinese the virtues of self-reliance and democracy. The Snows, along with Rewi Alley, a friend from New Zealand, and several other foreign and Chinese associates, formed the Chinese Industrial Cooperatives and nicknamed the organization Indusco. Old friends from Shanghai, Soong Qingling and the writer Lin Yutang, agreed to headline its fund-raising campaigns.

Backed by a $2 million seed loan from T. V. Soong, Indusco grew into a force for change in China. At its peak in the early 1940s, it boasted more than three thousand cooperatives employing three hundred thousand worker-owners churning out, as *Time* magazine reported in April 1940, "gloves, caps, greatcoats, padded clothes, gauze, tents, field cots."

Like Americans in the past, the Snows looked to war as an opportunity to transform China. Indusco was a way to remake Chinese society from the ground up. "Lawrence brought to the Arabs the destructive technique of guerrilla war," Edgar Snow wrote. But Indusco "was to bring to China the constructive technique of guerrilla industry." *Time* magazine predicted, "If China ever succeeds in becoming truly democratic, it will be because the crankshaft has been turned over by democratic self-starters like Indusco."

China's supporters in America raised millions for Indusco. Snow tapped the Hollywood crowd, enlisting actor John Garfield as one of his fund-raising frontmen. Indusco's motto, "Gung ho," means "working together" in Chinese. But in English, it signified a wholehearted devotion to a cause. Gung ho caught on with US Marines in the Pacific and entered the American vernacular from there.

Indusco also became an important source of funding for the Communist Party. In his memoirs, Chen Hansheng, a Communist agent based in the United States during the early years of the war, estimated that Communist agents inside Indusco diverted $20 million to the party and that a significant portion did not go into industrial development—but to buy arms.

Arriving in the US in December 1937, Hilda Yan commuted between her flight classes at Roosevelt Field on Long Island and the embassy in Washington. She spoke about China's plight to the Woman's Club of Chevy Chase, the American League for Peace and Democracy, and other groups. Yan, the *Washington Post* reported in January 1938, "is at the center of interest wherever she appears." On November 10, 1938, she received her pilot's license. A month earlier, Li Xiaqing had landed in San Francisco.

By New Year's 1939, Yan and Li were in New York City, preparing to fly, separately, to dozens of cities to raise money for China and appeal to America to stop trading with Japan. They planned to end their trip together at the World's Fair in New York. The American press dubbed Li "China's First Woman of the Air," and Hilda "China's Amelia Earhart." (That was somewhat morbid as Earhart had vanished over the Pacific two years before.) Notable figures, including Helen Keller, Eleanor Roosevelt, and Elizabeth Arden, signed up as supporters.

On March 23, 1939, the pair took off together from Floyd Bennett Field in New York's Jamaica Bay in a Stinson Reliant SR-9B monoplane with "Spirit of New China" emblazoned on its underwings. They landed at Camden Airfield in Philadelphia, taxiing into the maw of a giant publicity machine. The next day they flew to Washington, where they were garlanded with roses and feted at a gala dinner at the Chinese Lantern near Union Station.

On April 3, Hilda got her own plane—a Porterfield 35-W two-passenger monoplane—and the women split up. Campaigning through the South, Yan addressed overflow crowds in churches and converted dance halls. On Monday, May 1, as she flew from Mobile to Birmingham, Alabama, she lost her way. Following railroad tracks, she made for the capital, Montgomery, but overshot the airport and landed in an oat field. When she tried to take off again, she flew into a stand of trees and nosedived to the earth with a thud. She was knocked unconscious and suffered cuts on her face.

Yan's crash propelled her to coast-to-coast fame. Telegrams and calls flooded in from around the country and even from China, via the four-year-old transpacific radio-telephone, at thirteen dollars a minute. Alabama governor Frank M. Dixon stopped by her room at the Prattville General Hospital. News photographers recorded her every move. By the time she was released ten days later, she had become a hero.

Li Xiaqing, meanwhile, was roaring from coast to coast. In three months, she hit forty-two cities. In Miami Beach, she posed in a swimsuit and high heels. In Los Angeles, she landed a bit part in a movie. She mingled with football players and starlets and partied with the A-list. T. K. Chang, the Nationalists' envoy in Los Angeles, managed her fund-raising. Though Chang had pooh-poohed Chinese women's portrayal as sex kittens on the silver screen and lobbied against prominent roles for the sultry Anna May Wong, he urged Li to show some leg and swap her sex appeal for funds for China.

Yan and Li ended their American adventure at the New York World's Fair, where October 10—Nationalist China's independence day—was proclaimed China Day. Over the next few weeks, six hundred cities nationwide threw "rice bowl" dinners to raise money for refugees and the war wounded. Bandleader Artie Shaw composed a special arrangement of the Republic of China's national anthem; schoolchildren competed in essay contests on China's plight. On November 9, the United Council for Civilian Relief in China took over New York's Hotel Pierre for a fund-raising ball. Chinese dress, which had become all the rage since Japan's assault on China, dominated the affair. In homes across America, parents told their children to clean their plates because people were starving in China.

In the summer of 1938, Chiang appointed American-educated writer Hu Shih as China's ambassador to Washington. China's leading liberal intellectual was a reluctant envoy. He had spent decades criticizing the Nationalist regime. But now that Japan was eviscerating his country, Hu viewed the job, he told his old friend Edith Clifford Williams, as "a kind of military draft."

Like the two women pilots, Hu was tasked with turning America's growing sympathy for China into concrete action. He crisscrossed the country speaking on his homeland's behalf. "China is now at Valley Forge," he told one group of Americans, "but I hope she will soon be at Yorktown!" Hu's addresses were not limited to the war. He discussed philosophy, art, and education. He sang old Cornell songs with prominent alums and hobnobbed with top reporters. He counted leading jurists Felix Frank-furter and Louis Brandeis among his friends.

Hu arrived in Washington, according to historians Susan Chan Egan and Chih-p'ing Chou, with his personal life in turmoil. He had deposited his wife and eldest son in China and had continued a relationship with Edith Clifford Williams. He had also taken up with an American who was simul-taneously having an affair with his old teacher, John Dewey. From China, a third lover wrote him of her plans to join a Buddhist convent since Hu Shih had "gone West," meaning that he had chosen American women over her. Three months into his post, Hu suffered a heart attack; he would bed his nurse, as well.

Hu Shih lived at Twin Oaks, an eighteen-acre estate almost the size of the White House in the heart of Washington's Cleveland Park neighborhood. There he rode herd over a veritable global village. Hu's butler was Belgian, and all five servants were European refugees. Even the food was continen-tal. The embassy's hostess, a Chinese graduate of an American university, helped Hu Shih work to make the establishment welcoming to all.

One of the Kuomintang's chief goals in Washington was to get more financial assistance. Hu's sole condition for taking the ambassadorial post was that he be excused from negotiating such aid. So in the summer of 1938, Secretary of the Treasury Henry Morgenthau suggested that China send his friend, the banker K. P. Chen, back to the United States to discuss how America could help.

Cordell Hull's State Department continued to worry that too much support for China would anger Japan. But Morgenthau ignored the depart-ment's concerns and cobbled together aid packages for China. He once waited until Hull was aboard a ship and out of reach to sign one deal. In all, Morgenthau arranged for four loans to China, worth $170 million. Hu Shih called them "life saving infusions." But they meant more than that. The United States as a government and a world power was moving—albeit slowly—toward championing China's cause.

To his minders back in Chongqing, Hu counseled patience. "Although they often dilly dally in the face of a crisis," Hu Shih wrote to the Genera-lissimo, "when we are in the worst straits, the Americans always give us a hand."

Despite the loans, continuing trade with Japan contributed to the sense that the US was letting China down. From 1937 to 1939, the United States sent more than $437 million worth of cotton, oil, scrap iron, and other strategic materials to fuel Japan's war machine—more than triple what it sold to China. Medical missionary Walter Judd, who returned to the United States in 1938, brought home the connection between US business and Chinese bloodshed in speeches in which he described removing American shrapnel from the mangled bodies of Chinese civilians.

Soong Mayling shared this profound disappointment at America's failure to stop its weapons trade. In a "Message to the Women of America," she wondered whether American inaction in China signaled "the death knell of the supposed moral superiority of the Occidental." America's silence "in the face of such massacres" did not qualify, she wrote, as "a sign of the triumph of civilization."

On July 1, 1938, Washington took the first step toward cutting its arms trade with Japan. The State Department notified US aircraft manufacturers that it opposed the sale of planes and aeronautical equipment used in attacks against civilians. In early 1939, the Roosevelt administration announced its intention to abrogate the 1911 commercial treaty with Japan, clearing the way for a total embargo.

Still Chiang Kai-shek was impatient with the Americans and with his ambassador, Hu Shih. In December, he decided to send Soong Mayling's brother, T. V. Soong, to the United States as his personal representative to shake things up. Hu Shih's performance, Chiang declared, was "not satisfactory."

T. V. Soong's return to America marked a shift in China's approach to the United States. The Generalissimo and his brother-in-law believed that China did not have the luxury of being genteel in its quest for guns, money, and an embargo on Japan. Washington couldn't be trusted to do the right thing, as Hu Shih maintained; it had to be compelled.

Whereas Hu Shih had once returned $60,000 in Kuomintang lobbying funds to the party, Soong wired the American capital like a Washington insider. He wheedled access to classified cables and put Roosevelt's relatives and friends on China's payroll. "You make too many speeches and don't attend to business," Soong scolded Hu Shih. Of the Americans, Soong boasted, "I can handle those boobs."

Soong hosted Washington worthies—Supreme Court Justice Felix Frankfurter; naval officers; lobbyists; and FDR's relative, the columnist Joseph Alsop—at his home with his wife, Laura, and his three Americanized daughters. He was a master poker player and lost just enough to keep Washington's high and mighty coming back for more. "I was helpless for the first six months here in Washington," he wrote to Chiang Kai-shek, "but in the past two months I began to get the knack." He would become one of the most successful lobbyists ever.

In July 1940, Henry Stimson was sworn in as secretary of war and joined with Morgenthau to press for a total cutoff of trade with Japan. There were dissenting voices. Chief of Naval Operations Admiral Harold Stark argued that blocking Japan from buying oil would prompt an attack on the Dutch East Indies or the United States. Secretary of State Hull and Army Chief of Staff George Marshall agreed. Though the United States was rearming at a frantic pace, its military still ranked nineteenth in size world-wide, between Portugal's and Bulgaria's.

As American officials squabbled, back in China, things were only getting worse. Also in July, with the Battle of Britain raging in the skies over the south of England, Japan demanded that London close the Burma Road, a key supply artery that stretched from the port of Rangoon into Yunnan province in China's southwest. Not wishing to chance a simultaneous attack on Britain's Asian outposts, Winston Churchill shut the road down. On September 23, 1940, Tokyo's troops flooded into Indochina, halting French rail shipments into China. Now the sole link to China was through Soviet Russia. But the Russians, worried about a Japanese invasion, would not allow anything through.

On the evening of September 25, Roosevelt approved another loan of $25 million to China. In mid-October, Chiang Kai-shek told Ambassador Nelson Johnson that he was outraged that the United States had agreed to allow Britain to close the Burma Road. China would seal a separate peace with Japan, he warned, if the United States did not pony up—a threat he would repeat throughout the war.

Nelson Johnson sympathized with China's plight. "This thing," he wrote of Japanese bombers thundering up the Yangtze River valley, "is beyond all description in its brutality." But he, too, agreed that America's meager interests in Asia did not justify spilling Yankee blood. What the US should do, Johnson argued, was live up to its promises. He noted that Chiang and other Nationalist leaders bitterly repeated the American slogan, "All aid short of war," wondering where the aid was. "Failure of the United States . . . to afford timely aid" to Chiang, he warned, "may in the end result in Communist ascendancy in China."

By the summer of 1940, most of the Soviet military advisers and pilots had left China as Stalin turned his attention to Europe. Chiang had fewer than forty fighters and forty bombers to counter Japan's air force of almost one thousand warplanes. "Japanese bombing goes unchallenged and the people are filled with disquiet," Chiang told Ambassador Johnson. Moreover, after a short sharp battle in 1939, the Japanese and the Soviets negotiated a neutrality pact—signed in 1941—that allowed Japan to turn all its attention to China and Southeast Asia.

Chiang needed more than cash from the United States. He wanted weapons, too. In the fall of 1940, Chiang sent Claire Chennault to Washington to petition for lethal aid. Chennault was more than happy to have a break from China. In October 1940, a Japanese air raid on Kunming had pulverized his house; he had barely escaped in his car.

In America, Chennault and T. V. Soong worked on a secret proposal for a "special air unit" that would protect China in its hour of need. The men huddled at Soong's house in Chevy Chase and at the apartment of China's financial adviser, Arthur Young, in Washington. It was all supposed to be hush-hush. But most of the discussions were conducted at a near-shout because Chennault was almost deaf.

The group came up with a shopping list: 350 fighters, 150 bombers, 10 transport planes, and 350 American "flight instructors." Soong passed the list to FDR on November 25. Behind the scenes, Henry Morgenthau supported the program, peppering Roosevelt with memos and running rings around the far more cautious Secretary of State Cordell Hull. In the White House, Roosevelt adviser Lauchlin Currie also backed the plan.

On November 30, Japan installed a puppet regime in Nanjing. Chiang again appealed to Roosevelt and again threatened to surrender. In early December, Roosevelt approved the special air mission. America's first covert overseas military operation—the Flying Tigers—was born.

Later that month, Chennault found one hundred P-40 fighters at a Curtiss manufacturing plant in Buffalo. The planes had been earmarked for the British, but London had rejected them as out of date. "Buy what you need and send me the bill," Soong told Chennault. The planes were to be broken down and reassembled in Burma at a facility run by aviation investor William Pawley. He would make half a million dollars on the deal.

Next Chennault and Pawley had to figure out a way around US laws that prohibited Americans from fighting for another country. Secretary of the Army Henry Stimson leaned on Chennault's old nemesis, General Henry "Hap" Arnold, now the commander of the Army Air Corps, to let Chennault poach army pilots and mechanics. Secretary of the Navy Frank Knox was more welcoming. Pawley arranged to have one of his companies, Intercontinent, cut the men's paychecks. For the first time in US history, a private corporation would be used to carry out US policy in a war in which America was not a belligerent. It would be a model for CIA operations, several involving Pawley and Chennault, in the years to come.

Much of the credit for establishing the Flying Tigers, even the legendary name, has to go to T. V. Soong. After the war, Soong wrote to a friend that he had understood the need to find "a significant emblem for this Chinese-American adventure." He nixed an eagle as too American and a dragon as too Chinese. He recalled the Chinese expression "adding wings to the tiger"—*ruhu tianchi*—thus the Flying Tigers. Artists from the Walt Disney company came up with a logo—a winged big cat bounding through a V-for-Victory sign.

In January 1941, Roosevelt dispatched the first of many special envoys to China. White House adviser Lauchlin Currie was, in the words of diplomat John Paton Davies, "a brisk, little, rimless-bespectacled Harvard economist who had been acquired by Roosevelt as a special assistant." Currie knew nothing of China but typical of what Davies called "the helter-skelter Roosevelt administration," he would play a big role in Asian affairs.

FDR wanted Currie to gauge China's fighting power. During a three-week visit to Chongqing, Currie spent twenty-seven hours with the Generalissimo, met with Chiang's cabinet and generals, American-educated students, and, in a secret rendezvous at the British embassy, with the Communist representative in Chongqing, Zhou Enlai. Currie returned to America overwhelmed by China's problems. The economy was a mess, Chiang's government was suppressing dissent, and China's Western-leaning intellectuals were, he reported, "disillusioned, discontented and discouraged."

When Currie passed along FDR's hope that the Nationalists and the Communists would be able to unite to fight Japan, Chiang argued that the Communists listened to the Soviets, not the Chinese people. Currie left Chiang with the uneasy feeling that in its zeal to defeat Fascism, the United States would look to China's Communists not as a probable enemy but as a potential friend. This strikingly different perspective on the Chinese Communist Party would plague Chiang Kai-shek's relationship with America throughout the war.

In a report to the president, Currie suggested that Roosevelt frame his discussion of China's fate "in the same terms now used toward England," the country with which the United States had maintained its longest and deepest ties. Chiang Kai-shek, he advised, should be treated as "an equal or an ally." He suggested that no strings be attached to US aid until after the war. And echoing Christian missionaries, he argued that America should "guide China in her development as a great power in the post-war period."

Currie's proposals were a counterweight to John MacMurray's argument for American disengagement from the East Asian mainland. Currie advocated not only supporting China in the war against Japan but also flooding the country with American experts in economics, politics, transportation, and the military. Needed at the top of this American pyramid, Currie said, was a "liberal adviser" to guide Chiang's hand.

As Currie saw it, the goal of American support for China was not simply to use the country as quicksand to entrap the Imperial Japanese Army. That's what the War Department wanted. Currie set for America the far more ambitious objective of "political, social and economic reforms" that would make China strong. Once again an American saw war in Asia as a way to open the Middle Kingdom to American influence. Currie's expectation—which Roosevelt echoed—was that China would emerge from the fight an ally and friend. "China is at a crossroads," Currie wrote. "It can develop as a military dictatorship or as a truly democratic state. If we use our influence wisely we may be able to tip the scales in the latter direction."

However, as it would in a myriad of other ways, the White House talked big on China but acted small. For political adviser, Chiang had wanted William Bullitt, the plugged-in ambassador to France whose ties to Roosevelt would have guaranteed the Generalissimo a hearing at the highest levels of the US government. Instead, he got Owen Lattimore, a China-born academic who knew Mongolia better than Massachusetts Avenue. To make matters worse, Lattimore, though not a Communist, was sympathetic to the cause. He would later publish a glowing account of a visit to the Soviet gulag.

Currie's plan was redolent of Roosevelt's romantic notion of the role America had to play in China—as its big brother on China's road to modernity. The problem was that although FDR and Currie shared the aim of elevating China into the rank of a world power, many others thought this was a pipe dream. Winston Churchill described Roosevelt's long-range hopes for China as "the great American illusion" and fumed to his foreign minister Anthony Eden that it was an American "affectation to pretend that China is a power." When Roosevelt cautioned Churchill that 425 million Chinese should not be overlooked, Churchill sneered, "425 million pigtails."

One of Currie's responsibilities was to figure out how to supply China, so he sought out William Langhorne Bond. Bond had remained at the helm of the China National Aviation Corporation, which despite the war continued to limp along. In 1938, a Japanese fighter had downed one of CNAC's planes and killed fifteen passengers in the first ever attack on a civilian airline. Japanese bombers had destroyed CNAC aircraft on the ground. CNAC's mechanics patched together one damaged DC-3 with a wing from a DC-2, and called it a DC-2½.

As Japan pushed the Nationalists back into the mountains of Sichuan province, Bond deduced that Tokyo planned to cut China off from the outside world. The Burma Road would be severed, he predicted, and Hong Kong would go as well. Bond told Currie that China would survive only if the United States helped construct an air bridge to India.

The flight from northeastern India into southwestern China was considered the most treacherous in the world. The western escarpment of the Himalayas, which rise as high as twenty-three thousand feet, divides the two nations. Three rivers cut ten-thousand-feet-deep trenches through this heavily forested land. Freak winds, torrential rain, and fog buffet the zone. Turbulence routinely flipped planes on their backs. Below were the Japanese, "wild tribes," and "head hunters," as the US Army put it. It was over this forbidding terrain—called the Hump—that Bond proposed to jury-rig a lifeline to China using CNAC's planes. Currie returned to the White House, singing the praises of Bond's plan.

The doggedness of yet another private American and the talent of his Chinese and American pilots turned the Hump into China's salvation. CNAC began flying the Hump in April 1942. The US Army Air Corps was dragged kicking and screaming into the operation. But for almost two years, from 1943 until late 1945, the Hump provided Nationalist China with 80 percent of its supplies. As was true of many other American endeavors in China, the operation served as a model for future enterprises. The men who managed the Hump later ran the 1948 operation to break the Soviet blockade of Berlin.

On March 15, 1941, President Roosevelt addressed the White House Correspondents' Association ball at the Willard Hotel in Washington and vowed to turn the United States into an "arsenal of democracy" against the dictatorships menacing the world. Four days earlier, he had signed a Bill Further to Promote the Defense of the United States, which launched the Lend-Lease program under which Washington would furnish its allies with food, oil, warships, warplanes, and ammunition.

Following Currie's recommendations, Roosevelt singled out two countries for their heroic efforts: Britain and China. "China, through the Generalissimo, Chiang Kai-shek, asks our help," Roosevelt declared. "America has said that China shall have our help." Roosevelt's speech put China on par with Great Britain in American minds. The reality proved to be different. The United States provided its allies with more than $50 billion (more than $800 billion in today's dollars) in Lend-Lease supplies. Of that, Britain received more than 60 percent while China got 3 percent and Russia, which was not even mentioned, collected more than six times China's share. The gap between what the Chinese believed America had promised and what the United States delivered would be a source of destructive friction between the two countries for years.

On March 31, 1941, T. V. Soong presented the White House with China's first military wish list. China wanted supplies to equip a modern air force and thirty infantry divisions, a new railroad connecting China and Burma, the expansion of the current Burma Road, and transport aircraft to open up William Langhorne Bond's air bridge. If these requirements were met, Soong vowed, China would be able to take the fight to Japan in two years. A day later, Soong set up a new company—China Defense Supplies—to move military equipment from the United States to China. True to his reputation as a Washington operator, he appointed Roosevelt's uncle, the Hong Kong–born Frederic Delano, honorary chairman. David Corcoran, the brother of Roosevelt fixer Tommy "the Cork" Corcoran, was the CEO. William Bullitt, back from Paris, was an adviser, as was the columnist Joseph Alsop. None of these men registered as agents of a foreign government.

As Lend-Lease aid trickled toward China, US advisers flowed toward Chongqing. Daniel Arnstein came to China to ram the aid through the Burma Road. Arnstein controlled the second-largest fleet of taxis in New York and was famous for breaking strikes—and strikers. He figured that his bull-in-a-china-shop ways would do just fine in China. All the country needed, he argued as he readied to leave the United States, was a little Yankee ingenuity. "It's as simple as ABC," he told a reporter. "The idea is to go over there and install American methods of moving freight. . . . They work here and they'll work in Burma."

Lend-Lease supplies arrived by ship at the Indian Ocean port of Rangoon on Burma's southern coast. From there, they moved inland by rail to Lashio in Burma's northeast, where they were offloaded onto trucks and mule trains and hauled into China along a 736-mile road to the southwestern city of Kunming. Running through one of the most formidable jungles in the world, the Burma Road was barely a footpath at some points. Within one 40-mile stretch, it tumbled down and rose up ten thousand feet. From the air, it resembled a coiled rattlesnake; at no point along its serpentine course could a driver see more than an eighth of a mile ahead. The May to September rainy season reduced the roadbed to a malarial mud track. During the dry season, dust plagued motors and lungs.

But the most onerous obstacles were man-made. In Rangoon, British colonial customs officials slapped high duties on Chinese cargo. Once the stuff passed Lashio near the Chinese border, sixteen separate government agencies had responsibility for the thoroughfare. And none kept records. Trucks of one hauling company could not be repaired by mechanics from another. Of the approximately three thousand General Motors vehicles belonging to the Chinese government, fewer than half were in working order. The trucks were not equipped with jacks, so changing a flat tire could take up to a day. For every three tons of cargo that left the port of Rangoon for the road, only one actually made it to Chongqing, the other two-thirds vanishing on the black market.

"Intolerable" was the most frequently used adjective in Arnstein's thirty-five-page report on the road. "The only goddam way to get that goddam job done was to blast your goddam way through it," he told the *New Yorker*, which ran a two-part profile of him in 1942. The magazine reported that after Chiang Kai-shek adopted Arnstein's proposed fixes—round-the-clock customs services, clearer lines of authority—traffic on the road quadrupled. Chiang asked Arnstein to stay in China and run the road as a private concession, but Arnstein needed to get back to his cabs. "If I'd had the time, I'd have done it for nothing as a personal favor to the Generalissimo and the Madame," Arnstein told the *New Yorker*. "She's a honey."

In July 1941, Army Chief of Staff George Marshall agreed to Currie's suggestion that a team of officers head to Chongqing to help the Nationalists determine what they needed to fight. Unlike the British, who were planning their own defense, the Chinese, Marshall believed, required an American to tell them what to do. Marshall picked Brigadier General John M. Magruder to lead the American Military Mission to China, the first American military adviser unit officially assigned to another country.

A World War I combat veteran, Magruder had served two tours in China as an attaché in the 1920s.

Magruder had a low opinion of the Chinese military. In April 1931, he had concluded that the Chinese were not fit for war. In an article for *Foreign Affairs*, he remarked that "the Chinese have no military history worthy of scientific study," and he declared that they were essentially pacifists who excelled as "artists and actors rather than soldiers." He contended that while he could turn twenty thousand Turks into a "first class fighting machine," the same could not be accomplished with the Chinese. "Eagles grow in time from the puniest eaglets," he sighed, "but . . . doves snap ineffectually at hawks."

Magruder's team of fifty officers arrived in China on October 10, 1941, and his reports to the War Department reflected his bias. He contended that Chiang Kai-shek was stockpiling US equipment to battle the Communists, not the Japanese. He believed that tales of Chinese heroism in the battles for Shanghai, Changsha, and elsewhere were "entirely without foundation," despite the deaths of hundreds of thousands of Nationalist soldiers and a large number of Japanese. Over time, Magruder's unfounded views spread from the American military to American reporters, diplomats, and historians. France's collapse within six weeks of the first Nazi assault was never used to build a case about the weak-kneed nature of Gallic manhood, but China's strategy of trading space for time against Japan's mechanized war machine served as proof of the Kuomintang's fundamental flaws.

Magruder urged his superiors to use the promise of American aid to force China to follow American orders. Army Chief of Staff Marshall backed him, but the White House did not see the need. As Currie wrote Marshall in the fall of 1941, the Chinese were so dependent on the United States that "it is not anticipated that any difficulty of non-cooperation will be experienced." This disagreement represented a critical divide in US-China policy. Should America compel China to follow its rules, or should it lead by example and count on China to tag along?

In any case, very few American weapons were being shipped to China. By October 1941, six months after FDR had announced the Lend-Lease program, the United States had yet to send a single gun to China under the deal. The 100 P-40s for the Flying Tigers had been obtained outside of Lend-Lease and paid for with Chinese money. A subsequent order for 66 bombers and 269 fighters approved in July 1941 was never filled. When a large cache of weapons finally did make it to Rangoon aboard the USS

Tulsa for transshipment to China, British forces commandeered it. Marshall had also excluded China from talks between Britain, the Netherlands, and America on the defense and security of the Pacific. Chiang adviser Owen Lattimore told Washington that the Generalissimo felt that "the democracies regard [China] as inferior and of not being worthy of being considered an ally." He was right.

By early 1941, the Flying Tigers had an official name, the American Volunteer Group. Recruiting at airbases around the United States, William Pawley and his representatives offered pilots $600 a month (triple what many were making) and a rank equivalent to lieutenant, along with $10,000 in life insurance, a bounty for each downed Japanese plane, and six months' salary in case of death. By the middle of 1941, recruiters had identified one hundred men for the group's first squadron; ninety-nine would sail.

None of the contracts mentioned combat; the mechanics' contract didn't even use the word "aircraft." Among the volunteers, some were fleeing bad marriages, others ugly pasts. But most were like Frank Losonsky, a twenty-year-old grease monkey who listed "money, a subsidized trip to the Orient, and the promise of adventure" as his reasons to go to China. As the first group mustered to leave the United States in June 1941, their passports listed an array of bogus professions—ranchers, radio announcers, acrobats. Claire Chennault's job title—"executive"—came closest to the truth.

The American Volunteer Group set up its first training camp in an airfield outside Toungoo, a British colonial outpost 130 miles northeast of Rangoon, to be close to the planes and equipment arriving by ship at the Burmese harbor. Pawley had moved the Central Aircraft Manufacturing Corporation from Hankou, which had fallen to the Japanese, to the Burmese town of Loiwing. There, carved out of the jungle miles from civilization, Pawley established an aircraft assembly plant for a thousand Chinese workers, supervised by American managers, with electricity, running water, and a nine-hole golf course.

At Toungoo, Chennault told his men to forget what they had learned in the United States. Some of his men were talented aviators; others were duds. One pilot crashed three planes in the first week. On September 8, 1941, the Flying Tigers lost their first man—during a practice dogfight that turned into a midair crash. By December 1941, the Flying Tigers had sixty trained American pilots and sixty flight-worthy warplanes. The Chinese said that AVG, the acronym for American Volunteer Group, stood for "America, Very Good!"

On July 24, 1941, Japanese troops seized the airfield and naval base on Cam Ranh Bay in French Indochina and surged toward Saigon. Two days later, FDR declared an oil embargo against Tokyo and froze Japanese assets in the United States. America had been supplying 80 percent of Tokyo's oil. Great Britain followed with its own trade ban.

Chiang knew that behind the scenes, Tokyo and Washington were trying to avoid a war. In November 1941, Japan made a final offer to reduce its troop strength in Indochina if the United States resumed trading with Japan. The Japanese indicated that they planned to occupy large swaths of China for a "suitable period," interpreted to mean as long as twenty-five years. In Washington, Secretary of State Cordell Hull showed the deal to Ambassador Hu Shih and to the representatives of the British, the Australians, and the Dutch. Only Hu Shih voiced opposition. Chiang Kai-shek railed at the Americans and even convinced Winston Churchill to weigh in on China's behalf.

On November 26, Hu Shih visited the White House to demand that any deal with Japan include a full withdrawal from China. "For the first time in his diplomatic life, the soft-spoken scholar is reported to have lost his temper," *Life* magazine wrote a few weeks later. "He reminded the President of his many, freely given pledges to China." Following the visit and Churchill's intercession, the Americans rejected the Japanese proposal.

Negotiations with Japan collapsed, and two weeks later, on December 7, 1941, Japanese bombers attacked the American naval base at Pearl Harbor in an assault that lasted less than two hours, killed more than twenty-four hundred people, and destroyed eighteen American ships and more than three hundred planes. On the morning of the attack, Hu Shih had met with Roosevelt. He had just returned to the Chinese embassy when he received a call: "Hu Shih," the president said, "the Japs have bombed Pearl Harbor. I want you to be among the first to know."

Many voices joined in promoting the idea that China was an ally deserving of American aid. Missionaries, American-educated Chinese, politicians, writers, moviemakers, and reporters all helped create an image of the Middle Kingdom as full of earnest people who wanted to live like Americans and who were fighting America's fight. The flip side of this effort was the demonization of Japan, propelled along by the sneak attack on Pearl Harbor. If the Chinese were America's favorite allies, the Japanese became its most reviled foes. Whenever Roosevelt listed America's allies to Congress, "the brave people of China" always drew the loudest cheers. A February 1942 poll showed that 62 percent of Americans favored concentrating the war effort on Japan, while only 25 percent preferred focusing on Hitler.

This herculean effort to glorify China, undergirded by decades of a growing American fascination with the Middle Kingdom, had repercussions. Americans expected that the United States would support China to the bitter end. Many opposed the decision to focus on Europe first. These feelings only sharpened with time, forcing Roosevelt and his generals to search for a way to appear to help China without actually expending the blood and treasure needed to do the job. In the end, the Roosevelt administration settled on a renowned American general as the answer.

●

CHAPTER TWENTY

Burmese Days

At 1:00 a.m. on December 8, 1941, an aide woke Chiang Kai-shek to deliver the news that the United States had been attacked. The groggy Chinese president dictated a letter to Roosevelt: "To our new common battle we offer all we are and all we have to stand with you until the Pacific and the world are free from the curse of brute force and endless perfidy." To his diary, Chiang called America's entry into the war "an opportunity of a thousand years" and welcomed it with an assault on Japanese forces around Changsha, the capital of Hunan province.

Following Pearl Harbor, in an unprecedented acknowledgment of America's importance to China, Chiang appointed T. V. Soong as China's foreign minister and he kept him in the US capital. "No matter what," the Generalissimo wrote him, "we should stick with the Americans."

Soong would stay in Washington for the next two years, while Ambassador Hu Shih was recalled. The *New York Times* saw Hu's departure as a mistake. Soong's hardball tactics had made enemies in Washington, and even though he would not admit it, he profited from Hu's walk-softly approach. It was a "great relief," Hu wrote his friend Edith Clifford Williams, "to be a free man and to have leisure to sleep!"

By the time the United States entered the war, China was a spent force. Fighting continued and hundreds of thousands were still to die, but Chiang's government was incapable of an effort remotely comparable to what the Americans, Soviets, and British would mount. Even in the best of times, the Generalissimo never had complete control of China. Now half of his nation was occupied by the Japanese, and in the northwest, the Communists held sway.

Still, Roosevelt held on to the myth that China would become a power and that Chiang Kai-shek, whom he referred to as "Shang," was firmly in charge. The problem was that the only way to realize this dream would have been to make China a decisive battlefield of the war, build up the Nationalist army, land hundreds of thousands of American soldiers on China's coast, and retake it from the Japanese, as America would do in Europe against the Nazis. But that approach—considered in early Allied councils—was discarded quickly in favor of an island-hopping strategy in the Pacific.

With China as a sideshow, Americans who favored impractical initiatives and held naive viewpoints exerted enormous influence on US policy. Up to twenty different American bureaucracies had a stake in China during the war, and like rats in a cage, they competed ferociously for the morsels doled out by the War Department. The US Army, the US Army Air Force, the US Navy, and the British all battled one another for funds and materiel. State Department officials fought each other and all the military branches. America's fledgling intelligence agencies—the Office of Strategic Services and the Naval Group China—spent so much energy plotting against one another, it's remarkable that they had any left to battle the Japanese. "Every shade of opinion in the Embassy tended to pull in a different direction, and animosity between those shades became very bitter," observed John Melby, an American diplomat who served in Chongqing during the war. No wonder the China-Burma-India Theater, which Roosevelt established to fight the Japanese, was known as Constant Bickering Inside. "Everything seems to go wrong," FDR said in October 1943 about his China policy. "But the worst thing is that we are falling down on our promises every single time. We have not fulfilled one of them."

At root, the issue was this: Roosevelt's political goal of turning China into one of the Four Policemen ran headlong into the military strategy to first win the war in Europe and then win in Asia via the Pacific. FDR dreamed of using the war to forge a strong China, but in the face of fierce competition for resources, the US could only keep the Nationalists on life support. This life support allowed China to trap half a million Japanese troops. But it never did much more.

While the United States pursued victory elsewhere, Chiang Kai-shek strove to use this "opportunity of a thousand years" to make his country rich and strong and remain atop China's political pyramid. To do this he needed America's support in fighting the Japanese. But he never got it. Chinese forces, when they were used, fought for the Allies outside China—in Burma.

At the beginning of the war, the Nationalists and Great Britain were in a similar spot. To survive, they had to ally with a stronger nation. Winston Churchill bent America to his strategic needs. Chiang Kai-shek failed to do the same.

Within weeks of Pearl Harbor, the United States and Britain met for the Arcadia Conference in Washington, laying out the Allies' war plans. Counter to Chiang's wishes and to American public opinion, which had been enraged by Japan's sneak attack, the Allies agreed that the liberation of Europe would come first. They established the Combined Chiefs of Staff and the National Munitions Control Board, which set the goals for the war and distributed the weaponry to achieve them. Though Chiang assumed that China would participate in both councils, no invitation came.

The Allies, Chiang observed, viewed China as "only useful as a distraction to drain Japan's military power." Still, he scolded himself for expecting more. "Self-interest is the primary driver of international relations," he noted in his diary. "If you think this is strange or feel let down because it does not live up to your standards, you are just being foolish."

During the Arcadia Conference, President Roosevelt created a special theater for continental Asia and nominated Chiang Kai-shek to command it. He instructed the War Department to dispatch a high-ranking US officer to serve as Chiang's chief of staff, lead US troops in the region, and supervise China's Lend-Lease supplies.

The War Department's first choice for the job was Lieutenant General Hugh A. Drum, a decorated sixty-two-year-old combat officer and a veteran of the the Spanish-American War and World War I. But when Drum surmised that the United States had no intention of dispatching a combat contingent to China, he declined the offer. Army Chief of Staff George Marshall's next pick was an old friend, Joseph Stilwell. The two men had served together in the Fifteenth Infantry Regiment in Tianjin, and Marshall had brought Stilwell to Fort Benning, Georgia, as Marshall launched a revolution in army tactics. Marshall praised Stilwell as "exceptionally brilliant." The army had rated him number one among its forty-seven major generals. He also spoke decent Chinese.

From the moment Stilwell arrived in China, he became a hero. Lionizing Stilwell was a way for Washington to free itself from its bind in China. Stilwell became living, breathing proof of America's commitment to China at a time when most of its men and materiel flowed elsewhere.

Joseph Stilwell was handed an impossible task. While the White House viewed his mission as facilitating China's rise, the War Department's far less ambitious goal was to keep China in the war. Briefing Stilwell before he departed, Secretary of War Henry Stimson implied that China would be used as a jumping-off point for an offensive against Japan and hinted that Stilwell would get ground troops. Marshall, however, vetoed that idea. Stilwell would spend the next four years pleading for American troops to fight the Japanese in China. But Marshall had no troops to give. Stilwell told his diary that he felt like "the goat sacrificed as a burnt offering."

Despite enormous personal bravery, Stilwell was also uniquely unsuited to his job. Though he had gained fame in US field exercises for speed, surprise, and spirit, before he arrived in China the largest unit he had led into battle was a platoon; his specialty was intelligence and instruction. "Stilwell never commanded a company, battalion, or regiment," wrote Haydon L. Boatner, an army general who served with him throughout the war. "He just did not have the staff and senior command training nor the breadth of military view required of a senior commander."

Moreover, Stilwell was also assigned the delicate diplomatic mission of ensuring that American, Chinese, and British forces were heading toward the same goal. That was hard for him. He looked down on the Chinese and despised the British so much that he often appeared, as one British officer wrote, to be "fighting the War of Independence all over again." There was a reason that Stilwell's nickname was "Vinegar Joe." He was well known for his acid tongue.

Stilwell had already served three tours in China. He was there for the Republican revolution in 1911–12 and returned in the mid-1920s to learn Chinese and then again as a military attaché in the 1930s. Although he had traveled throughout China as a military intelligence officer, in Beijing he lived the life of a cosseted Westerner. He collected ivory fan handles and a robe worn by the Empress Dowager and made his home in a Beijing courtyard built for a Qing dynasty viceroy. K. P. Chen, the American-educated banker who negotiated loans for China with Henry Morgenthau, observed that "the ease and luxury of the decadent life in Peking" engendered in Stilwell and others like him a sense that they were better than their

Chinese hosts, particularly educated Chinese. "Whenever Chinese showed resentment to this insufferable Occidental superiority complex," Chen wrote of Stilwell and his colleagues, "they quickly became irritated and violently anti-Chinese." Stilwell insisted that he loved the "common man in China," but Chen said that Stilwell actually meant "Chinese people who obey and please."

In a 1929 lecture on the "psychology of the Oriental," Stilwell accused the Chinese, who at the time were devouring Western ideas, of possessing "a conservative complex . . . whose inertia is simply enormous." He reserved most of his bile for the Nationalist Party and Chiang Kai-shek. On the eve of the Nationalists' battle for Shanghai in 1937, he predicted that the Nationalists would never fight. Once they began battling the Japanese, he declared that they were saddled with an "inherent distaste for offensive combat." What the Chinese needed, he argued, was American leadership to forge China's military into an army capable of attack. And he was the man to provide it.

Where he bad-mouthed the Kuomintang, Stilwell idealized China's Communists as the only force capable of standing up to the Japanese. It was as if Stilwell had burdened the Nationalists with his prejudices while bequeathing the Communists his dreams. And this was despite no real evidence that Communist forces ever offered more than token resistance to Japanese aggression; after all, Nationalist forces suffered 90 percent of Chinese casualties in World War II and exhibited great bravery in battles around Shanghai and Hankou and their multiple defenses of Hunan's capital, Changsha. "Those Reds may be bandits, as Chiang says," Stilwell wrote in the 1930s, "but they're masters of guerrilla warfare."

In the first week of the Pacific War, Japanese planes and warships sank 80 percent of Anglo-American naval strength. On December 23, the islands of Guam and Wake fell to a Japanese assault. Hong Kong surrendered on Christmas. By January 2, 1942, the Japanese were driving toward Manila. After the sinking of the HMS *Repulse* and the HMS *Prince of Wales*, the pride of the British fleet, the British capitulated in Singapore on February 15. Soon, Java was in Tokyo's hands, exposing the United Kingdom's "white dominions" of Australia and New Zealand to the Japanese. For Americans desperate for good news from the front, the lone bright spot was in China.

On December 20, 1941, ten Japanese heavy bombers raided Kunming and Chennault's Flying Tigers took to the air. When the smoke cleared, four Japanese bombers had been shot from the sky in what an Associated Press bulletin called a "swift, decisive clash." Three days later, the Japanese turned on Rangoon, and the Flying Tigers, hampered by the British refusal to set up a ground intelligence network, still managed to shoot down six bombers. On Christmas Eve, Japanese bombers again swarmed over Rangoon. A single squadron of Chennault's pilots climbed above them and bagged fifteen bombers and nine fighters, losing only two P-40s. "It was like shooting ducks!" enthused squadron leader James Howard, a China-born son of missionary parents.

Over the next six months, in the skies above Rangoon, eastern China, and Vietnam, the Flying Tigers downed what writer Daniel Ford estimates to have been 115 planes and killed four hundred Japanese airmen. Chennault had proved his detractors wrong. In the service of a foreign government thousands of miles from home, he had shown that aggressive pursuit tactics could overwhelm enemy bombing formations. China had again served as a petri dish for an American experiment. Chennault made his men repaint the noses of their planes after each sortie to make the Japanese think that they had more aircraft than they actually did. Japanese broadcasts estimated that the Flying Tigers had 500 planes; by this time, they had fewer than 50.

Chennault's reputation attracted pilots looking for action. Among them was Robert L. Scott, who, at the age of four, had witnessed the death of a stunt pilot at a 1912 air show in Macon, Georgia, and dragged his mother by the hand to see the dead pilot in the cockpit. From that point on, he recalled, all he had ever wanted to do was fly. Scott bought his first plane at thirteen, attended West Point, and at the age of thirty-four, joined the Tigers. "Scotty" earned a reputation as "a one-man air force," in the words of *Life* magazine. He was credited with thirteen Japanese kills. His 1944 autobiography, *God Is My Co-Pilot*, was a best seller and was made into a movie.

Burma was an accidental battlefield of World War II. Japan had not planned to conquer it, and Chiang was more worried about a Japanese assault into southern China from Indochina than an attack from the southwest. Britain had concentrated its forces on Singapore, leaving Rangoon virtually undefended. It was only on February 9, 1942, that the Japanese Imperial General Headquarters, gripped by victory fever, ordered Japanese forces to march into Burma's jungles. Japanese ground forces moved up the Kra Peninsula from Malaya into Thailand. Wearing sneakers and shorts, lugging backpacks and disassembled heavy weaponry, they crept into Burma along jungle paths, ambushing British colonial forces, who kept to the main roads.

In Washington, Britain's losses in Burma raised fears that China would be cut off. T. V. Soong and Chiang Kai-shek lobbied for more American aid, requesting $1 billion from the United States and Britain. The Americans offered $500 million. At the Treasury department, Morgenthau tried to impose conditions, proposing that the money be used to pay China's troops "so that while the boys fight, they get their money and if they don't fight, no money." But Soong appealed to the White House and got the conditions removed. As Secretary of War Henry Stimson told the House Foreign Affairs Committee on February 3, the loan was a chance "to play for the highest stakes in the Far East. . . . If America refused to take this chance she would not deserve to win the war." The loan passed without debate; it would cause enormous problems between the two countries later on.

On February 9, Stilwell met with Roosevelt and asked whether the president had a message for Chiang Kai-shek. "Tell him we are in this thing for keeps," FDR said, "and we intend to keep at it until China gets back ALL her lost territory." As Stilwell's biographer, Barbara Tuchman, noted, countries do not normally promise to win back their allies' territory, but Roosevelt felt an obligation to China.

Stilwell left the United States on February 13 for the three-week journey to China. Halfway to his destination, in Cairo, he took up his pen as the Allied defeats snowballed. "The world is crashing," he wrote. On March 7, the Japanese seized Rangoon. The next day, Stilwell met Chiang Kai-shek in Chongqing. In their first meeting, Stilwell argued that Burma could be saved by an attack; Chiang responded that Rangoon's fall, a lack of artillery, insufficient gas for his tanks, and long lines of communication would doom any assault. Chiang proposed instead "defense in depth," under which Chinese and British forces would fall back to Mandalay in northern Burma and hold an east-west line across the country with the idea of building a road from India for China's resupply. "Going on the offensive should not be a guiding principle so far as Burma is concerned," he warned Stilwell. The British agreed. Once Rangoon had fallen, London's priorities switched to defending India.

Stilwell insisted on an offensive. But no one knew how many Japanese troops were in Burma. "No plan, no reconnaissance, no security, no intelligence, no prisoners" was how US Army Major Frank Merrill described the strategic situation there. When Chiang asked how the Chinese could attack if they did not know where or whether the Japanese were reinforcing, Stilwell answered: "Let's go before they build up."

Stilwell ordered two divisions of Chiang's best soldiers south toward

Toungoo to strike the Japanese. "I have a hunch," he told his diary, "the Japs are weak." His hunch was wrong. The Japanese quickly surrounded Chiang's forces and blocked their retreat into China. Then the Japanese themselves attacked, and on April 29, they seized Lashio, the last town on the Burmese side of the Burma Road, and took Mandalay as well. Now only one obstacle stood between the Japanese Imperial Army and China's soft southwestern underbelly: the Salween River. If the Japanese could cross it and storm the Nationalists' supply depot in Kunming, China would probably be theirs.

Claire Chennault and his Flying Tigers flew to the rescue. The Burma Road had become a Japanese parking lot: trucks, tanks, supply vehicles, infantry soldiers, and refugees jammed the nine-foot-wide serpentine thoroughfare. Chennault recognized an opportunity. He had his engineers reconfigure the P-40s to carry bombs and hit the cliffs above the road, sending tons of dirt into the gulch. For twelve days, from April into May 1942, the Flying Tigers strafed the Japanese, stopping them in their tracks.

Inside Burma, chaos reigned, and now it was Chiang Kai-shek's turn to err. With thousands of Chinese troops cut off from China, Stilwell called for a withdrawal west to India. General Du Yuming, the commander of China's Fifth Army, balked at the orders, concerned that China's forces would be sacrificed to protect the British as they, too, fled. Hoping to get his best troops back into China, Chiang backed Du's decision. But Du and other commanders proved incapable of maneuvering their forces through Japanese lines. Thousands starved to death, died of fever, or were picked off by the Japanese in a gruesome death toll that far surpassed the number of men lost in Stilwell's misguided assault.

Instead of organizing a retreat, Stilwell decided to walk out of Burma into India himself. From May 6 to May 20, Vinegar Joe led a motley group of some one hundred American soldiers, British commandos, Indian and Malay cooks, Burmese nurses, and a British Quaker ambulance unit through the rain forest. Two Chinese divisions followed him. In Chongqing, Chiang was astounded that his American commander, who could have flown out of the battlefield to oversee the withdrawal, had opted to hoof it through the jungle. Stilwell "has abandoned my 100,000 soldiers in foreign jungles and headed off to India," Chiang wrote in his diary. "Could it be that because of the battle, his nerves have given way?"

In America, Stilwell's fiasco was spun into a victory by officials desperate for good news from the front. "Invading Jap Force Crushed by Stilwell" ran one headline. Arriving in New Delhi on May 24, Stilwell was lionized in defeat. Jack Belden, a correspondent who had accompanied Stilwell on his march, sang his praises in articles for *Time* and in a book, *Retreat with Stilwell*, published a year later. *Life* magazine put Stilwell on its cover. "I claim we got a hell of a beating," Stilwell told a news conference on May 24. "We got run out of Burma, and it is humiliating as hell. I think we ought to find out what caused it, go back and retake it."

American newspapers universally praised the blunt-talking general. In the words of Theodore White, Stilwell was "wholeheartedly democratic, with no tolerance for corruption, duplicity or the niceties of diplomatic small talk." That may have been true, but highlighting Stilwell's personal exploits also became a substitute for committing America to China's fight. At the height of the battle for Burma, Army Chief of Staff George Marshall did not allow the US Tenth Air Force, based in India, to go into action, preserving them for India's defense.

In reports to Washington, Stilwell blamed Chiang Kai-shek and the British for his failures. He started referring to Chiang in his diary as "Peanut," another sign of his lack of respect for his ostensible commander. (Stilwell called Roosevelt, stricken with polio, "Rubber Legs.") Stilwell attributed the Burmese disaster to flaws within the Chinese character. "Through stupidity, fear and the defensive attitude," he wrote, "we have lost a grand chance to slap the Japs back at Toungoo."

In fact, Stilwell's gambit in Burma exhibited recklessness and an inflated self-confidence born of his sense of himself as a superior white man among the heathens. He based his most significant decision—to attack—on a "hunch" about Japan's weakness without intelligence on the enemy's intentions or troop strength. Then, with defeat imminent, a well-managed retreat would have meant that more of Chiang's troops could have been saved—but Stilwell disappeared into the jungle.

Chiang Kai-shek faulted Stilwell for the disaster. He noted that the price for his alliance with America was that "I am compelled to yield to the US." Increasingly, Chiang sensed that his country was little more than a minor attraction for the Allies and that events in China were important more to boost American morale at home than to further the war effort in Asia. As the fight unfolded in Burma, another event reinforced this view.

On April 27, two days before the Japanese seized Lashio, flyboy Jimmy Doolittle returned to China at the head of sixteen US Army Air Force B-25B Mitchell medium bombers. Taking off from the USS *Hornet* aircraft carrier

BURMA circa WWII

BHUTAN

Ledo

to Ramgarh, India

Myitkyina

Imphal

INDIA

Loiwing

Lashio

Mandalay

Burma Road

Toungoo

Rangoon

Moulmein

Bay of Bengal

N

Kunming

CHINA

INDOCHINA

THAILAND

0 Miles   200
0 Kilometers   200

© 2016 Jeffrey L. Ward

deep in the western Pacific, Doolittle's men struck Tokyo and other cities
in the first US air raid on Japan. Too heavy to land back on the *Hornet* (they
could barely take off), the lumbering aircraft headed for China. US officials
had given Chiang Kai-shek a week's warning of the plan.

Chiang had opposed the raid, fearing that it would spur Japan to overrun his airfields while his best forces were trapped in Burma. He pleaded
for time to finish the Burma campaign, but the Americans would not wait.
To appease the Generalissimo, they promised that China could keep the
bombers after the mission.

The Doolittle Raid was a smashing success—for American self-esteem.
The attack led the papers from coast to coast. FDR awarded Doolittle the
Medal of Honor. But to Chiang, it represented another broken promise.
None of the aircraft landed intact. Fifteen crashed in China and one in

Russia. Eight of eighty airmen were captured by the Japanese. The Chinese rescued the rest, including Doolittle, except for the crew in Russia.

What followed was an orgy of Japanese retribution. More than 200,000 Japanese troops attacked cities and towns along China's east coast in the largest and most sustained Japanese operation since 1939. Chiang poured 300,000 troops into the region in a desperate attempt to defend the air bases and his people. The Japanese beat him back, killing 30,000 Chinese troops and an estimated 250,000 civilians. "The Japanese slaughtered every man, woman and child in these areas," Chiang wrote to Marshall. He felt more deeply than ever that the United States did not value his nation and its sacrifices.

From India, Stilwell warned the War Department that it was making a strategic mistake in not sending US ground troops to China. Japan needed to be fought and beaten in China, he said. Reconquering Burma became his obsession. With Burma free, he wrote in June 1942, he could supply and train China's army and open up the coast for an American landing that would then sweep Japanese forces from the Asian mainland and bring the Japanese home islands to their knees. Stilwell proposed establishing a training camp in India for the two Chinese divisions that had successfully retreated there.

Stilwell's bosses, including George Marshall, did not share his views. In a June report, a US Joint Intelligence Committee dismissed China's strategic importance, noting that the Chinese army "has so many inherent weaknesses that it will not be able to stage a major offensive." Marshall approved the training mission, however. It would not require many American troops. In addition, there were already 45,000 tons of Lend-Lease supplies in India slated for China that could be provided to the trainers. More important, it meant that an even larger quantity—145,000 tons—could be transferred elsewhere. To Marshall, training China's army in India was a cost-effective way of showing American commitment to China's cause.

Defeat in Burma was a huge blow to the Nationalist Chinese government and contributed to its eventual collapse. Chiang lost more than a third of his Western-trained troops, together with their heavy equipment. It would be two and a half years before the air route over the Hump carried a tonnage equal to the modest amount that had trickled in over the Burma Road at the end of 1941.

More broadly, the disaster set the tone for an emerging view of Nationalist China promoted by Stilwell, the US government, and American reporters. According to this narrative, the Americans were engaged in a benevolent effort to save China, but their altruism was stymied by Chiang Kai-shek's unwillingness to fight. Stilwell trafficked in this notion to make up for his shortcomings. The American press adopted it because it absolved their Yankee hero of any blame. The Roosevelt administration encouraged it because it justified a China policy of neglect.

Chiang understood this, and it enraged him. Between Pearl Harbor and July 22, 1942, 80,000 Nationalist troops had been killed or wounded; US casualties worldwide were less than half that. How could this mean that he was reluctant to fight? They are "contemptuous and blacken our name," Chiang wrote about the American officers surrounding Stilwell. "They are lukewarm about helping us. Thinking about this angers and pains me."

For Chiang, the experience of losing some of his best men in Burma in an operation he had questioned, watching the Americans keep their air power in India, and braving Japanese retribution for the Doolittle Raid on China's east coast punctured his American dream. "Now I know that the alliance is just empty words," he told his diary, "and I don't exclude America from this." Still, he continued to hope for better days.

●

CHAPTER TWENTY-ONE

Dangerous Liaisons

China's Communist Party went through its own cycle of views on America, usually tied to Moscow's party line. In the early 1930s, the party's Central Committee issued circulars referring to America as an enemy and casting it in the role of Japan's enabler. When Stalin switched gears in late 1935 and declared Fascism the greatest threat, Mao Zedong fell into line, calling for a united front with Chiang Kai-shek to counter the Japanese. Liu Shaoqi, one of China's top Communists, even acknowledged that the US was helping China against Japan. But as Stalin sought to make nice with Hitler, the party shifted again. In August 1939, Mao backed the Soviet Union's nonaggression pact with Germany and accused Roosevelt of being no better than Hideki Tojo, the prime minister of Japan. The Communists accused America of plotting to hand China over to Japan.

When Japan and the Soviet Union signed a nonaggression pact in April 1941, Mao privately praised the accord because it meant that Japan could devote more troops to crushing Chiang Kai-shek, thereby paving the way for Communism's victory in China. On March 15, 1941, as Roosevelt vowed to turn America into an "arsenal of democracy" and aid China in its fight against Japan, China's Communist press labeled him a "warmonger."

Then on June 22, 1941, Germany invaded Russia. The Soviets ordered China's Communists to cooperate with the Nationalists and stop criticizing the United States. Roosevelt, a "warmonger" in April, became an "enlightened bourgeois politician" in June.

After that, Mao directed his followers to contact Americans and tell them the party's side of the story. Zhou Enlai, the Communist representative in Chongqing, informed John Paton Davies, a State Department officer on Stilwell's staff, that Communist troops would be proud to follow Stilwell, and in August 1942, he requested that the United States dispatch an official American delegation to Communist territory in northwestern China. Zhou wrote to Lauchlin Currie, lobbying for an equal share of Lend-Lease supplies. American dignitaries traveling to China were now routinely praised in the pages of the party's *Liberation Daily*.

Communist documents make it clear, however, that the praise was tactical. Aid from the United States and Britain must be "utilized . . . to the fullest extent possible," one memorandum issued in late 1942 read, but only the Soviet Union was a genuine ally. As Mao had written in one of his most important essays, "On New Democracy," "all imperialist powers are hostile to us." Only the Soviet Union could be trusted.

As war enveloped China, a new group of Chinese scholars and writers ventured to the United States, once again finding inspiration there as they sought to change their own country. Visiting in 1943 and 1944, the anthropologist Fei Xiaotong labeled the United States "a paradise." "Above there is heaven, below there is America," he wrote. Fei focused on a feature that has since become a Chinese obsession: America's capacity for reinvention. In the 1930s, Chinese visiting the United States saw an America on its knees, with its economy in a ditch and its self-confidence flagging. But Fei found a nation on its way back. He credited America's tradition of self-reliance with fostering a culture of change. People were not afraid of failure, he wrote, and that gave them the tools to overcome it.

In 1945, Fei published a book in China about his visit to the United States. In it, he explored issues that Chinese writers would return to again and again. How did America innovate? Why was religion important? How could America meld so many cultures into its own? Fei argued that China needed to embrace the American spirit to enter the modern world. Chinese lived as if they were passengers on a ferry, he wrote. They needed to take control of the boat. Chinese values were those of acceptance, not creation. "A people so poisoned are as paralyzed—not dead, yet not alive," he wrote.

In America, Fei hustled for money for China's social sciences. He sought grants and joint projects between Americans and Chinese. He called himself a "promoter" and declared that he embodied the American spirit of enterprise. "I am in fact more American than Chinese," he claimed in 1943. "In China such a personality . . . is too disturbing." Like Hu Shih, Fei drew close to American women. He enjoyed, he wrote, the "motherly care" of these women, who seemed to reflect in their tenderness toward him an American instinct to dote on China as on a needy child.

Fei praised Americans' support of the war effort, contrasting it to the way so many Chinese dodged the draft. He was struck by the industriousness of American women, who had populated factory floors as men joined the fight. Back in China, the Left and the Right attacked Fei's book for glorifying America. When one Westerner lauded Fei for his "absence of national prejudice and national hatred," the Communists took that as proof that he was a foreign spy.

Still, America's constant pursuit of the next new thing exhausted Fei. He bemoaned the life of the elderly in America. To bring up children only to "watch them fly away like swallows," he wrote, "is just too cruel." He pitied Americans for inhabiting a world, he wrote, "without ghosts." He had grown accustomed to the spirit of his dead grandmother padding through his family's ancestral home. But Americans, he wrote, didn't read ghost stories; they had Superman. They didn't dwell in the past; they had the future.

Unable to sustain China militarily, the White House launched a campaign to bolster it politically. In October 1942, the Roosevelt administration announced that America would abolish extraterritoriality. Somewhat unwillingly, Britain followed suit, but Churchill put his foot down when Roosevelt suggested that Britain agree to return its colony Hong Kong to China after the war.

In China, the news broke on October 10, China's National Day, and was hailed by both Nationalists and Communists. Chinese writers drew a parallel between China's rocky path to sovereignty and the American Revolution. The Communist *New China Daily* cheered "the young America" for "gathering freedom loving people from around the world." Chiang Kai-shek ordered a three-day holiday and commissioned a song with the colorless title "Abrogating the Unequal Treaties."

A month later, Madame Chiang Kai-shek left China for the United States. Soong Mayling had not been to America since 1917. Landing at Mitchel Field on Long Island, she was met by Roosevelt adviser Harry

Hopkins. During the long ride into New York City, she talked about the need to give Asia priority in the global war.

Madame Chiang's adventure in America ushered in what Arch Steele of the *Chicago Daily News* called "a period of dreamy unreality" about Nationalist China. As she waved to adoring crowds, kissed babies, and lectured Congress, Soong Mayling found a nation enthralled with China and the Chinese. On February 17, 1943, she arrived in Washington after a prolonged stay at Presbyterian Hospital in New York for the treatment of various ailments. From the start, the American press was enraptured. She "was as attractive as her photographs would indicate—and then some," gushed the *Washington Post*.

On February 18, Soong Mayling became the first private citizen and the first woman to address Congress. In the House, Texas congressman Sam Rayburn introduced her as "one of the outstanding women of all the Earth." The Chinese were fighting for the same cause as the Americans, she told her audience. Defeating Japan was as important, if not more so, as beating the Nazis, she said. Soong Mayling's message underscored more than a century of Chinese expectations of the United States. Stop telling us that you like us, she said, and start proving it. She challenged Americans to pony up more aid.

Eleanor Roosevelt told her diary that as she watched Mayling come down the aisle in the Senate, escorted by tall white politicians, she "could not help a great feeling of pride in her as a woman." It was a deep illustration of the warp and woof that bound the US to China—a Chinese woman, raised in Shanghai and the American Deep South, educated in New England and steeled in wartime Chongqing, returning to the United States to inspire American women. As *Time* magazine observed, "Tough guys melted."

However, Roosevelt administration officials were alarmed at her eloquence. And the Combined Chiefs were so rattled by Mayling's argument that they feared she might derail their strategy of focusing on "Europe First." During a February 19 joint press conference, Mayling scolded the president for America's failure to live up to its promises to China of support. "We can't fight with bare hands," she said. After the press conference, Roosevelt turned to his aides and mumbled, as one story goes, "Get rid of that bitch."

Leaving Washington, Mayling toured five cities. She addressed thousands at Madison Square Garden in New York and in the Hollywood Bowl in Los Angeles. The coverage was glowing. Newspapers held poetry-writing competitions; elementary schools drowned her in letters. During her eighteen days on the road, the leading newspapers in New York, Boston, Chicago, San Francisco, and Los Angeles ran 178 stories, 45 on the front page, along with the complete text of the speech she made in each city.

Her mix of intelligence and sex appeal, cosmopolitan wattage, and Asian refinement worked wonders. In her, the *Los Angeles Times* pronounced on March 31, Americans had found "a human demonstration that the ideologies of Orient and Occident are not irreconcilable nor even very widely separated." The American press referred to her as China's Queen. If Chiang was the Generalissimo or the more familiar Gissimo, she was, as *Life* called her, the Missimo.

Lauchlin Currie complained to diplomat Jack Service that Mayling was, Service wrote, "appealing over the head of the president by going directly to Congress, stirring up a lot of sympathy for aid to China, really attacking the whole strategy of war." Saying that he wanted "to build a backfire" to counter her message, Currie set up meetings between Service and *Washington Post* columnist Drew Pearson, who began questioning the "shotgun" marriage between Washington and Chongqing. "I was Lauchlin Currie's designated leaker," Service told E. J. Kahn of the *New Yorker* years later.

Currie gathered information on Mayling's charities, and the FBI opened an investigation into Soong family corruption. Currie urged other American reporters to begin questioning the Kuomintang. In early 1943, Theodore White of *Time*, who had earlier been so intimately involved in buffing the Nationalists' image, broke the story of a massive famine in Henan province and accused the Kuomintang of bungling the relief effort. "I ran around screaming, in almost insane fashion, 'People are dying, people are dying,'" White wrote in his memoirs.

In Chongqing, Chiang Kai-shek feared that his government's relationship with America was headed for a fall. "After my wife's visit to the White House," he predicted to his diary, "I'm certain that it's American policy just to make use of us without any sincerity." Chiang's instincts were right. Washington was beginning to sour on his government. It had some help along the way. Although the Kuomintang's China Lobby has gotten the bulk of attention for pulling strings in Washington, the Chinese Communist Party may actually have done a better job. Communist operatives played a key role in convincing American policy makers of the rot within the Kuomintang. One such agent was Ji Chaoding.

The scion of a family of Shanxi bankers, Ji Chaoding, like T. V. Soong, was a numbers man. He graduated from the University of Chicago, earned a PhD in economics from Columbia in the 1920s, and, after meeting Zhou Enlai in Europe, joined the Communist Party of the United States. Ji spoke perfect English. Sidney Rittenberg, an American Communist who lived in China for decades after the Communist revolution, called him "the best revolutionary propagandist of the lot." In the 1930s, Ji took a job in New York at the Institute of Pacific Relations, a Rockefeller-funded think tank. With the American scholar Owen Lattimore, Ji edited the institute's influential journal *Pacific Affairs*. Under pseudonyms, Ji wrote articles attacking the Kuomintang. Under his own name, he conducted studies of China's economy.

Ji gained access to the Roosevelt administration via his University of Chicago classmate Frank Coe, who by the 1930s had landed a job at the Treasury Department. Coe introduced Ji to Secretary of the Treasury Henry Morgenthau, FDR's chief financial adviser Harry Dexter White, and Solomon Adler, another Treasury Department official. US intercepts of signals traffic from the Soviet embassy have shown that White, Adler, and Coe cooperated with Soviet intelligence throughout the war. Historian Stephen MacKinnon has concluded that Morgenthau's growing cynicism about China owed much to the influence of Ji Chaoding.

Ji was close to many American reporters and influenced their work. One of them was a former China missionary named T. A. Bisson. In July 1943, Bisson wrote a hugely influential article for the *Far Eastern Review* arguing that there were two Chinas. One was "Feudal China," backward-looking, corrupt, and passive in the face of the Japanese. That was Nationalist China. The other was "Democratic China," active against the Japanese, modernizing, and ready to lead the nation into the future. This was Communist China. Bisson argued that Mao Zedong wasn't a Marxist-Leninist and that what he was achieving in his fortress in northwestern China was "the essence of bourgeois democracy." Bisson was more than a reporter. Messages from the Soviet embassy decrypted after the war identified him as a source of confidential US government reports. Mainstream publications picked up Bisson's message. Hanson Baldwin, a military affairs reporter for the *New York Times*, rejected the then popular view of the Nationalist army as competent and its soldiers as brave. Writing in *Reader's Digest*, Baldwin called Nationalist soldiers "poorly led and incapable of using modern weapons." As he put it, "Missionaries, war relief drives, able ambassadors and the movies have oversold us" on China.

* * *

Soon after Washington's renunciation of extraterritoriality in January 1943, Pearl Buck spearheaded a campaign to end the American ban on Chinese immigration. She and her old nemesis, Henry Luce, organized the Citizen's Committee to Repeal the Chinese Exclusion Act. As expected, labor unions, historic foes of Chinese Americans, opposed any change. But this time, the need to keep China in the war trumped anti-Chinese bigotry. The *Washington Post* editorialized that failure to repeal the law would only aid "Jap propaganda."

In congressional testimony on May 20, 1943, Buck argued that Chinese deserved to be allowed into the United States. Chinese devotion to family and the land, she declared, represented a form of "natural democracy" that Thomas Jefferson could have understood. Frances Bolton, a Republican congresswoman from Ohio, called the Chinese "the most individualistic race in the world." An ad in the *New York Times* read: "The Chinese saying is 'all around the four seas all men are brothers.' Our saying is 'all men are created free and equal.' Let us prove by our acts that we mean it."

Worried about a backlash, Buck arranged it so that no Chinese testified before Congress. Echoing Anson Burlingame's treaty negotiations with Secretary of State William Seward, Buck believed that she could represent Chinese interests well enough. To collect the votes to repeal the law, Representative Warren G. Magnuson wrote the new bill so that only 105 Chinese would be able to immigrate each year. Americans seemed satisfied; 60 percent of those polled supported repealing the law, but 75 percent said that they still wanted a cap on Chinese immigration.

The Chinese army in India made its home in the hill country nine hundred miles north of Calcutta in a town called Ramgarh. There, at a converted World War I POW camp, 250 American officers backed by 500 senior enlisted personnel trained three divisions of Chinese troops for more than a year in everything from grenade throwing to bayoneting, engine maintenance to tank driving. Stilwell appointed Brigadier General Haydon L. Boatner as commander of the camp.

The US goal, according to an army publication, was "the creation of a modern fighting force which could stand toe-to-toe with the Japs and slug it out to victory." For most of the Chinese recruits, it was the first time they could eat as much as they pleased. On average each soldier gained twenty pounds. Three hots and a cot constituted, as one wrote, "a meat pie from heaven."

Boatner, who had a master's in Chinese history from Harvard and spoke the language fluently, maintained that, if not handled delicately, cultural differences could scuttle the operation. "You are taking up a very, very difficult assignment," he told his trainers. "It will tax your initiative, ingenuity, tact and spirit of cooperation to the utmost." Boatner developed three simple rules for avoiding problems: "Tell the Chinese the truth, the whole truth and nothing but the truth. Be American but not too American, let the Chinese be Chinese but never too Chinese. And never get mad at a Chinese officer in the presence of others." Boatner recognized something that Vinegar Joe Stilwell had overlooked. The Chinese had already been fighting for a decade, so the onus was on the American trainers to prove themselves worthy of emulation.

US Army officers had to choose which battles to fight. When Chinese officers beat their men, they did not interfere. But Boatner stood his ground where money was involved. Traditionally, Chinese commanders distributed pay to their men and pocketed a portion. Boatner decided that in India, the United States would pay Chinese soldiers directly. He fired the camp's first Chinese commander when he refused to agree.

The Chinese responded to the Americans with attitudes that persist to this day. Sergeant Qiu Feng called the Americans "open, unsophisticated." To Private Deng Shuyi, they were "less complicated . . . and easygoing." Zhou Wenxing, a conscript, remembered that the Americans taught marksmanship differently from his Chinese platoon commander. The Americans didn't sweat posture, he wrote, "so long as you could shoot!" The Americans taught the Chinese baseball and tap dancing and organized bridge tournaments. The Chinese found them childlike in their desire to have fun.

But it was Yankee women who made the deepest impression on the Chinese, whose memoirs are filled with paeans to American nurses. Private Hu Dongsheng recounted "an unforgettable encounter" with a nurse from Seattle named Jenny, who tried out some of her Chinese on him. As another soldier, Liu Shuying, wrote: "Often in my mind were the beautiful images of nurses."

Inside China, relations between Yanks and Chinese floundered. The Americans griped about Chinese personal habits, their thunderous throat-clearing and public defecation. Writing from Xi'an, American diplomat Edward Rice noted that almost all of the American soldiers he knew were "bitterly critical of China and the Chinese."

The Chinese view of the Americans could be equally tortured. As K. P.

Chen remarked in notes to himself during the war, "The Chinese and Americans are not on happy terms with each other." His countrymen, he wrote, "resent the Americans and want to push them out of power, yet at the same time they are scared of the Yankees when they are face to face with one." Chen reminded himself that he needed to be vigilant when confronting America's incessant protestations of support for China. "Our minds, benumbed with this sugar-coated talk, think that every American is a friend of China," he wrote. "There are plenty of unreliable ones."

At the operational level, Joseph Stilwell had a clear vision for what he wanted to do with China's forces. He wanted to train two armies, the X and Y forces, to retake Burma—X from India and Y from China. The problem was that Washington's promises of support always fell short. A key reason, starting in 1942, was the success of the US Navy in the South Pacific, five thousand miles from Chongqing.

In May 1942, at the Battle of the Coral Sea, the US Navy halted a major Japanese advance for the first time. A month later, at the Battle of Midway, the navy sank four of the six big Japanese aircraft carriers that had participated in the attack on Pearl Harbor just six months earlier. From Midway, the Allies began their island-hopping campaign, launching their first assault, on Guadalcanal, in August. By early 1943, American soldiers, sailors, and marines had opened the way north to Japan.

The US victories ended plans for an American landing on China's coast. Still, despite China's shrinking tactical importance, Roosevelt demanded that China be included in the war. So military planners came up with another idea—turning China into a giant Allied air base from which to attack Japan. In a memorandum on the first anniversary of the Pearl Harbor attack on December 7, 1942, Army Chief of Staff George Marshall backed the idea of lifting the siege of China but not as a way to help China's army, as Stilwell had wanted. Rather, China would be employed to support the emerging Allied strategy in the Pacific. Pointing to the successes of Claire Chennault, the craggy-faced commander of the Flying Tigers, Marshall noted, "Already the bombing attacks, with very light US casualties, have done damage out of all proportion to the number of planes involved." The idea would not be to fight the Japanese *in* China but to fight the Japanese *from* China.

This new strategy would have consequences for the Nationalist government. Enormous resources would pour into constructing air bases in China, limiting the flow of material that could have been used for China's defense. With their sights set on the speediest course to victory, Washington's strategists would leave the Nationalist army in the lurch.

Washington's turn to airpower as a solution for China favored Claire Chennault. The loser was Stilwell. Vinegar Joe had argued that China needed an army of well-trained infantrymen to roll back Japan's occupation. "It's the man in the trenches that will win the war," Stilwell is reported to have declared. To which Chennault replied, "Goddammit, Stilwell, there aren't any men in the trenches." In this battle, Chiang Kai-shek favored Chennault. Like many Chinese, Chiang was taken with the magic of American technology. To him, airpower represented a way out of the morass of an ill-led infantry, dominated by warlords and hacks.

Beaten on the battlefield and in the bureaucracy, Stilwell refused to cooperate with Chennault and became increasingly insulting during meetings with Chiang Kai-shek. He urged his superiors in Washington to speak to Chiang in "sterner tones." On March 8, 1943, in a letter to Marshall, Roosevelt declared that Stilwell's way of dealing with the Generalissimo was "exactly the wrong approach." Roosevelt disagreed with threats and slapping conditions on American aid to Chiang. "All of us remember that the Generalissimo came up the hard way to become the undisputed leader of four hundred million people," Roosevelt wrote. "He is the chief executive as well as the commander-in-chief and one cannot speak sternly to a man like that or exact commitment from him the way we might do from the Sultan of Morocco."

But Stilwell continued to resist the idea that Chennault should be given a separate command or that airpower might benefit China. Finally, Chennault and Stilwell were called back to Washington in the spring of 1943 as Roosevelt and Churchill gathered again to set strategy for the next stage of the war.

Arriving in America, Stilwell and Chennault, who were barely on speaking terms, were hailed as heroes. A *New York Times* editorial on April 30 spoke of Stilwell's "unequaled fitness for his post." Stilwell, the *Times* continued, "makes no blunder. . . . He is on equal terms with the Chinese: from the Generalissimo down they all like him." The *Times* hoped that "he gets what he wants."

Stilwell did not get what he wanted. Asked to make his case for building a new Chinese army and why Chennault's airpower scheme was unworkable, Stilwell could barely speak. Roosevelt thought he was ill. Marshall said that his friend "sat humped over with his head down and muttered something about Chiang not fighting."

Stilwell actually had a cogent argument. In reports, he worried that Chennault would become a victim of his own success. Chennault's newly named Fourteenth Air Force was proving so adept at harassing the Japanese, Stilwell warned, that they would launch a large-scale ground offensive to destroy Chennault's airfields.

Roosevelt sided with Chennault and ordered that the Fourteenth Air Force be given priority over Stilwell's army retraining plan. The Allies also agreed to reconquer Burma, but they did not agree on how. Chiang promised that his forces would fight in Burma, but only if there was an amphibious landing to reopen the port of Rangoon.

Stilwell did not take his defeat lying down. With the help of his political assistant, John Paton Davies, he briefed reporters on China, including a meeting at the home of Eugene Meyer, the owner of the *Washington Post*. There he painted a picture of Chiang Kai-shek as incompetent and of the Communist Party as the true Chinese patriots. As historian Jay Taylor has noted, it was unprecedented for an American general and his State Department aide to undermine a wartime ally.

As 1943 unfolded, FDR began to take an increasingly negative view of Vinegar Joe. To Harry Hopkins, he noted that Stilwell "hated" the Chinese. China's foreign minister T. V. Soong lobbied to have Stilwell removed, and by October, Roosevelt, urged on by Hopkins, had agreed. Soong and Hopkins worked out a program that would replace most of the older officers in the Chinese army with Westernized recruits. In addition, at almost every level, the plan partnered an American officer with a Chinese.

Roosevelt and Churchill met again in August at the Quadrant Conference in Quebec, where they sketched out plans for the Normandy invasion. Chiang again was not on the invitation list. The conference further detailed Allied plans to use China as an air base. Since 1939, the Boeing aircraft company had been working on a long-range bomber called the B-29 Superfortress. American air strategists, following the long-held tradition of using China for their experiments, backed the plan to base the B-29s in China to bomb Japan.

At Quebec, the Allies set up a new command in Asia called the South East Asia Command, under Lord Louis Mountbatten. Churchill was intent on having a voice in Asia's future. American officers joked that the South East Asia Command really stood for Save England's Asian Colonies.

From China, Chiang viewed the events with alarm. Miffed that he had been denied an invitation to another strategic conference, he blasted the "inequality" of "international society." Chiang's sense of powerlessness intensified in October when Mountbatten came to Chongqing. Mountbatten had gotten wind of T. V. Soong's plot to unseat Stilwell. Mountbatten informed Chiang that without Stilwell, China's armies in India would be under British command. This only heightened Chiang's concerns that the British were angling to use his men to save their empire. In response, Chiang reversed his decision to have Stilwell replaced. Vinegar Joe may have been unfit for command, but at least he wasn't British.

Returning to China, T. V. Soong reacted badly to the scuttling of his plans. "Are you the chief of an African tribe that you should change your mind so capriciously?" he shouted at the Generalissimo. For his impertinence and because of Chiang's fear that Soong was scheming to replace him, he was placed under house arrest until early 1944.

In late 1943, Chiang Kai-shek finally secured an invitation to a strategic gathering set to take place in Egypt in November. The Cairo Conference would be the first—and only—gathering to grant an Asian leader equal billing with Roosevelt and Churchill.

At dawn on November 21, 1943, Chiang and Soong Mayling landed in Cairo. The conference opened the next day at the Mena House Hotel, with its striking views of the pyramids. Soong Mayling was the only woman in attendance, and as she shifted her legs beneath her cheongsam skirt, British field marshal Lord Alanbrooke detected a "suppressed neigh" from the younger officers. The British were unhappy that Chiang had been invited. Churchill suggested that the couple go see the pyramids. But Roosevelt insisted that the Generalissimo and Soong Mayling take part.

From the start, it was clear that the British did not like the idea of an amphibious assault on Burma. Lord Mountbatten presented a plan that limited the fighting to the north. Roosevelt demanded, however, that the port of Rangoon be opened.

On Thanksgiving Day, Roosevelt confided to Chiang that Churchill was his "biggest headache." Britain, the president said, "simply does not want to see China become a power." Roosevelt again committed to an amphibious operation in Burma and promised to arm ninety divisions of Nationalist troops. The Generalissimo agreed to base the B-29 bombers in China. He also bowed to Roosevelt's demand that he form a coalition government with the Communists, under two conditions: that the United States ensure that Russia would not occupy Manchuria and that Britain hand back Hong Kong. Chiang noted that the talk was "exceedingly satisfactory" and that FDR treated him "like an old friend." He was pleased that the Cairo Declaration had promised that "all Chinese territory obtained by Japan shall be retuned to China."

The Generalissimo called Cairo "an important achievement" of "his revolutionary career." With, he wrote, "a stroke of the pen," issues that had troubled China for decades were seemingly erased. His country was promised the return of Manchuria, Taiwan, and Penghu Island. And Korea would gain independence; the implication there was that it would again come under China's sway. Chiang had also made his point: China would participate in yet another massive battle outside its borders on the condition that the Allies do what they had promised. He did not want to fight alone.

China was now in the club, and, indeed, Roosevelt had stage-managed the event to signal China's rise. In his diary, Chiang praised Soong May-ling; she had worked twelve hours a day, charming and finagling China's way into an important agreement. Chiang even thought that she had gotten Roosevelt to agree to a $1 billion loan, though that promise would evaporate.

Nonetheless, Stilwell continued to plot against Chiang. In Cairo, Roosevelt met one-on-one with Vinegar Joe once for twenty minutes. Stilwell complained about the Generalissimo and later claimed that FDR had hinted that he would not oppose Chiang's assassination. Returning to China, Stilwell directed his aides to come up with a workable plot. A plan was hatched that involved faking a midair engine failure and giving Chiang a faulty parachute. As Stilwell told his diary a few months later, "The cure for China's trouble is the elimination of Chiang Kai-shek." It was the first time that American officials had mulled the assassination of a third-world leader, but not the last.

From Cairo, Roosevelt and Churchill went to Tehran to confer with Joseph Stalin. There, the Allies pulled the rug out from under Chiang Kai-shek. Stalin demanded that the United States and Great Britain focus all their energies on the Normandy landings in Europe. Hitler had to be dealt with first. In exchange, the Soviet leader promised that three months after Hitler's defeat he would attack Japan's forces in China. Stalin also expressed support for Roosevelt's idea of a United Nations.

Stalin's guarantees drove China's strategic stock to an all-time low. Roosevelt and Churchill's commitment to Operation Overlord, the full-scale assault on the beaches of France, meant no amphibious operation in Burma. And once Stalin promised to flood Manchuria with the Red Army, what China could do for the war no longer mattered.

On December 7, the second anniversary of Pearl Harbor, Roosevelt and Churchill informed Chiang of the canceled amphibious assault. FDR offered him two options: go ahead with a limited campaign in northern Burma or wait a year for an attack by sea. Chiang had felt the change coming, given, he told his diary, British "treachery."

Chiang reacted in typical fashion. He threatened Roosevelt with "a sudden collapse of the entire front of China" and demanded a $1 billion loan. (He wouldn't get it.) Chiang wanted one thousand planes and a doubling of the tonnage over the Hump or else he might surrender. Chiang noted that in their declaration from Tehran, Roosevelt, Churchill, and Stalin had mentioned only Germany. From that, Chiang warned, the Japanese would conclude that the East Asian mainland no longer figured in Allied strategy and they would be tempted to attack. Chiang told the Allies that Japanese troops were already massing in Manchuria and heading south. Stilwell accused Chiang of crying wolf. But Vinegar Joe was wrong again. Another disaster, code-named Ichigo, was about to unfold.

•

CHAPTER TWENTY-TWO

The Rice Paddy Navy

When US Navy captain Milton E. Miles was hunting for volunteers to team up with Nationalist spies and guerrillas in late 1942, one of his main conditions was a lack of familiarity with China. "The less our recruits know about China," he wrote, "the less they have to unlearn." Miles wanted his men "slightly crazy," he wrote, and he rejected any "Old China Hands."

Miles's aversion to the old way of looking at China—and his support for the Nationalist government—made him unique among the Americans who flooded Chongqing during World War II. It would color his outfit, known as the Sino-American Cooperative Organization. SACO (pronounced, with grim relish, "Socko"!) became the most notorious joint operation between the two governments during the war.

Miles's unit ultimately grew to twenty-five hundred men from the armed services, the US Narcotics Bureau, the FBI, the Departments of Corrections and the Treasury, the Secret Service, and the New York State Troopers. These operatives trained tens of thousands of Chinese guerrillas to destroy Japanese supplies and ammunition and establish a network of weather stations critical to US Navy operations in the Pacific. Weather reports from China were indispensable in the planning of the attacks on Iwo Jima and Okinawa, and advance notice of a storm allowed hundreds of US bombers to take off unobserved on a massive raid on Tokyo.

SACO frogmen blew up Japanese freighters in Xiamen, and American and Chinese teams manned a string of coastal lookout stations on China's southern coast. SACO's Yangtze River Raiders, led by a US Navy lieutenant and kitted out in Chinese peasant garb, prowled Dongting Lake, blowing up Japanese ships and sabotaging railroad bridges.

But if, in the words of State Department adviser and historian Herbert Feis, the US operation in Chongqing during the war was a "circus in six or so separate rings," Miles's "rice paddy navy," as it was called, was the freak show. Even the navy's official history calls it "most bizarre." In teaming with Chiang Kai-shek's top spy, Dai Li, Miles involved himself with hit men and torturers who often seemed more committed to battling Communism and Western liberalism than to fighting the Japanese.

Of the many American operations in China, SACO would be the most divisive. Oscar P. Fitzgerald, a naval historian, wrote that "SACO guerrillas killed more Japanese and destroyed more enemy material with a smaller expenditure of men and supplies than any other forces in the Far East." By contrast, William "Wild Bill" Donovan, the first chief of the Office of Strategic Services, reported to Roosevelt in 1944 that "no intelligence or operations of any consequence have come out of SACO."

Still, in the tradition of China serving as the proving ground for American initiatives, Miles's operation became a model for US Cold War collaboration with security services around the world. American officials ignored gangland-style tactics and repression in the interest of battling a common foe. SACO also turned into a touchstone for American views on China. American liberals and left-wingers were scandalized by Miles's association with Dai Li, whom Stilwell dubbed "China's Himmler." And China's Communists used SACO's story as a prop in their decades-long campaign against the United States.

Milton Miles enlisted in the navy at seventeen at the start of World War I and earned his sea legs aboard ships that plied China's coasts during two tours in the 1920s and 1930s. His comrades dubbed him "Mary," after the silent film star Mary Miles Minter. Miles took command of his first ship, the destroyer *John D. Edwards,* in 1939 on the Yangtze River Patrol, which had been deployed on China's great inland waterway since 1854. Far from Washington's prying eyes, he developed into "an officer who loved to kick 'the book' out the window and get things done," wrote his colleague Navy Lieutenant Commander Charles G. Dobbins.

From aboard the *Edwards,* Miles witnessed Japanese operations against the Chinese. When a Japanese naval vessel ordered Miles to vacate one battle zone, Miles hoisted a pennant inscribed with "What the hell" and the symbols "???!!!***." They would become SACO's emblems.

Miles became a loyal supporter of the Nationalist regime and worried that Russia had designs on China. Miles represented a strain of American thought that tried to place China in context. He had a lot of sympathy for China's Nationalist revolution and regarded its excesses with forbearance. Miles was wary of Britain's reach as well. Like Americans in the nineteenth century, he saw huge opportunities for the United States in the Middle Kingdom, as long as other powers were kept at bay.

Back in Washington in the early 1940s, Miles joined a group of officers interested in China, including some of the navy's top planners. After Xiao Bo, the Chinese intelligence operative who had brought code-breaker Herbert Yardley to China, read an interview about Miles's adventures in China, he tracked him down and gained access to the group.

When the Japanese hit the US fleet in Pearl Harbor, Admiral Ernest King, the chief of naval operations, ordered Miles to return to China. At the time, naval planners were considering the idea of an amphibious landing on China's coast. "In the meantime, do whatever you can to help the Navy and to heckle the Japanese," King advised. Xiao Bo had suggested a joint intelligence operation, to which King and FDR agreed. Dai Li was going to be Miles's partner; their joint operation was dubbed the Friendship Project.

Miles flew over the Hump to Chongqing in April 1942 as the Japanese completed their seizure of Burma. Several days later, he met Dai Li. The Chinese spy chief was a slightly built man of five feet seven inches with a big smile that revealed gold bridgework, but what struck Miles most was "the lively snap of his wide-open and piercing black eyes."

Dai Li set Miles up in a mansion, the former residence of the mayor of Chongqing, known in English as the "Fairy Cave." It came equipped with a bomb shelter and several Chinese agents who served as Miles's translators as well as Dai Li's spies. Dai Li gave Miles a Chinese name—Mei Lesi, or "Winter Plum Blossom, Enjoy the Here and Now."

Miles requested a tour of the Chinese coast, which would entail sneaking into Japanese-occupied territory. On May 26, Miles, Al Lusey, a radioman with the Office of Strategic Services, and a dozen Chinese operatives set off on a fifty-one-day odyssey through four southern provinces. Traveling in the back of trucks and sleeping on sampans, Miles was impressed with how easily Dai Li's teams passed through Japanese territory. The trip persuaded Miles that he would have ample opportunity to "heckle" the Japanese, and he wrote that he began to entertain "wider plans than any that had previously entered my head." At Pucheng, in the northwest corner of Fujian province, Miles's team met up with Dai Li. On the morning of June 9, Japanese bombers attacked the town. As Dai Li and Miles cowered in a rice paddy, the general turned to Miles. "Mr. Winter Plum Blossom," he said, why doesn't the United States arm and train fifty thousand of my guerrillas? "What a situation," Miles wrote later. He had been in China for barely a month, yet here he was, riding out an air raid in a rice paddy with China's top spy, who was offering a partnership in a fifty-thousand-man army. Dai Li extended his hand. Miles shook it.

Radioman Al Lusey cautioned Miles that Washington really should be involved in the plan. Miles wasn't concerned. "Naval officers are supposed to make decisions," he wrote. "They don't ask Washington what to do in a storm, or whether or not to attack the enemy." Within a year, American money, weapons, and personnel would be flowing into Dai Li's headquarters in a place called Happy Valley, in the suburbs of Chongqing.

The deal that Dai Li sought with Miles was this: Juntong would help the navy set up its observation posts around China. In exchange, the Americans would provide Juntong with training and equipment, such as radios and tommy guns. Dai Li wanted to focus on the dark arts of demolition and spy work, which seemed to be more relevant to internal security than to fighting Japan. Americans at the embassy weren't happy that Miles had agreed to give the Chinese operational control of the mission. But Miles thought it appropriate that the Chinese take charge. "It's their country," Miles wrote. "And it's their secret service, too." Miles and Admiral Ernest King wrote each other frequently about the proper way to treat an ally, especially one as sensitive to slights as the Chinese. US Army officers and State Department officials had little patience with Miles's approach.

"Mary" Miles also continued the American tradition of freelance action in China. As a military officer, he was technically under General Stilwell's command, but Stilwell knew little of what Miles was up to. In an environment where no one was really in charge, Stilwell's political aide, the diplomat John Paton Davies, noted that Miles "played with appropriate thin-lipped taciturnity the role of man of mystery."

Work soon began on a compound for the Americans of the Naval Group China. By the time it was finished, it included barracks for eight hundred men, office buildings, lecture halls, classrooms, warehouses, garages, laboratories, doghouses, and lofts for one hundred homing pigeons. SACO established nine training camps around China. It set up weather stations in the Gobi Desert. Other camps specialized in industrial demolition, guerrilla warfare, and espionage. In all, SACO would train close to one hundred thousand Chinese fighters. Joint operations with American advisers began in mid-1944.

SACO forces worked with Chennault's Fourteenth Air Force to mine harbors and rivers up and down the Chinese coast. Miles provided Chennault's pilots with a mine that could be dropped into the water by a passing plane. They sank seventy-four Japanese ships. To avoid them, Japan's merchant fleet ventured farther into the Pacific, where the US Navy chewed it up. In October 1943, American mines blew up a freighter in the Indochinese harbor of Haiphong, blocking the port until the end of the war.

Miles's most controversial training camp was Camp Nine, established in 1944 and led by Charles Johnston, a Treasury Department narcotics agent. Johnston gathered an array of American law enforcement officers specializing in everything from forensics to interrogations. Over the Hump, Johnston flew in motorcycles and fingerprinting equipment, arms, ammunition, and medical supplies. Embassy officials alleged that the United States was now involved in strengthening the Kuomintang's internal security apparatus. Miles was touchy about the criticism and hinted darkly to John Paton Davies that if it continued, someone might find himself with a knife in his back. "People disappear in China," he observed.

Davies wrote that he didn't know how many of Miles's stories were true. At least one, involving Miles's claim that SACO provided intelligence leading to the dramatic sinking of three Japanese vessels at a Chinese port on January 23, 1945, turned out to be fiction.

SACO wasn't the only American intelligence operation in China. The Office of Strategic Services also established a network of spies but kept it outside the control of the Kuomintang. When OSS chief "Wild Bill" Donovan visited China in November 1943, he told Dai Li that the OSS planned unilateral operations in China. Dai Li warned him that he would shoot any American operatives working outside the SACO umbrella. Donovan slammed his fist on the table and shouted: "For every one of our agents you kill, we will kill one of your generals!" Donovan established several secret bureaus, one of which used Chennault's Fourteenth Air Force as cover.

In mid-October 1944, US Marine Corps brigadier general Lyle Miller came to China to try to sort out the OSS battle with the US Navy and with the Nationalist Chinese. In meetings with Dai Li, the two seemed to be making headway. Then, on the evening of October 22, Dai Li threw a banquet in

Miller's honor. Rising to make a toast, Miller launched into a rant. He demanded Chinese "sing-song girls." He joked about Chiang Kai-shek's latest girlfriend, called China a "fifth- or a sixth-rate" power, and maintained that if not for America, China would already be under Japanese rule. "You Chinamen must open your eyes and stop sleeping like that idiot over there," Miller said, pointing to a guest who had succumbed to the grain alcohol. In a report to Washington, the OSS described only the printable version of Miller's diatribe, adding that "very grave diplomatic relations have arisen." What's worse, it appeared that Miller had not been drunk.

It's easy to discount Miller's tirade as that of a frustrated American under the influence of Chinese hospitality. But Miller summed up what many Americans in China thought by the mid-1940s. The split between the Americans who supported Chiang and those who hated him had intensified. And in an environment where China mattered less and less to Washington, those who despised the Kuomintang were gaining the upper hand.

In December 1942, soon after the end of the Cairo Conference, Vinegar Joe Stilwell began to realize his dream to reconquer Burma. Starting in the Indian town of Ledo, at the end of a railway spur in northwestern India, thousands of mostly African American troops began turning an ancient dirt footpath into a two-lane 271-mile all-weather road to the Chinese border. Burma's strategic significance had shifted according to the whims of Allied planners. Now, retaking Burma was deemed critical to ensuring that the B-29 bases in Chengdu got what they needed to decimate Japan.

Crossing terrain known as the ancestral home of the leech, drenched by an annual rainfall of two hundred inches, stricken with malaria, bombed and strafed by Japanese warplanes, the American engineers wielded bulldozers and dump trucks against a jungle so thick that it was impenetrable to sunlight. By January 20, 1943, work was around the clock. One American engineering battalion cleared the forest, while the battalion behind it graded the road. On February 28, roadwork had reached the Burmese border, forty miles from Ledo. Troops posted a sign: "The Road to Tokio."

In March, the monsoon set in. The British withdrew Indian construction gangs, thinking that the Americans would also give up. But they kept digging, even when heavy equipment sat marooned in mud for weeks, when avalanches unleashed thousand-pound boulders and the fog grew so thick that airdrops of food halted, and the men survived on hardtack and fetid water. The African American soldiers worked and slept in mildewed clothing. Boots and uniforms rotted in the damp.

The Chinese Army of India provided protection for the black engineers.

As they moved deeper into Burma, they passed hundreds of skeletons at every water hole—the remains of the Chinese soldiers who had died trapped in Burma in 1942. The Chinese moved forward secure in the knowledge that there were no Japanese troops in the region. According to the army's official history of the campaign, Stilwell's intelligence section had told Chinese officers that enemy positions were "insignificant."

But as in Toungoo in 1942, Stilwell had it wrong again. Five Japanese divisions were waiting in the jungle. On October 20, 1943, a Chinese company was raked by enemy fire. And this was not just any enemy; it was the Eighteenth Division of the Japanese Imperial Army, the same outfit that had stormed Singapore. An "intelligence and reconnaissance failure" was how the army's official history described the affair.

The Japanese attack forced Stilwell to speed up his plans to recapture Burma, but his partners were uncertain. Still smarting from the decision to cancel the amphibious assault to open up the port at Rangoon, Chiang Kai-shek had not yet agreed to send reinforcements from China into Burma. The British were skeptical, too. In January 1944, Admiral Louis Mountbatten, the chief of the South East Asia Command, proposed delaying the campaign until the Normandy invasion was over. Mountbatten dispatched his American chief of staff, General Albert Wedemeyer, to Washington to argue that even if Stilwell's Burma adventure succeeded in linking China to India, the Ledo Road would not be in operation until 1946 and therefore would contribute little to the war.

Stilwell sent Brigadier Haydon L. Boatner, the chief of staff of the Chinese Army of India, and diplomat John Paton Davies to Washington to lobby on his behalf. In the American capital, Davies and Boatner planted stories with *Time* magazine, accusing Mountbatten of unwillingness to fight the Japanese. Stilwell's backbiting prompted London to demand that Vinegar Joe be recalled. Revealing Allied disagreements, Mountbatten declared, "gives our strategy away." Stilwell's job was saved in the end by London's concern about bad PR. Noted John Dill, Churchill's representative in Washington, "Stilwell, as built up by the American press, is something of a hero." The American public would blame Britain if their hero lost his command.

Meanwhile, Stilwell in Burma was the happiest he had been in months. "We are in tiger and elephant country," he enthused to his wife, Winifred. Writing of the Chinese and the British, he observed, "The jungle is a refuge from them both and I am leaving the shoveling of manure to a couple of my boys." Indeed, for a nine-month stretch from December 20, 1943, until September 6, 1944, Stilwell spent only four days in Chongqing.

But events at the front also began to turn against Vinegar Joe. Starting in February, Japanese forces launched two counteroffensives along the Indian border. As in 1942, the Japanese assault threatened to cut Stilwell's forces off from their home base. At Imphal, on the Indian border, the Japanese surrounded sixty thousand British troops. Outfoxed again, Stilwell complained to his diary: "This about ruins everything."

Stilwell now desperately needed Chiang's forces to move into Burma from China to relieve pressure on his hasty offensive. On March 27, Chiang wrote to Roosevelt saying that he would not dispatch his forces from Yunnan across the Salween River. China needed those troops, he argued, because the Japanese were preparing another offensive inside China. FDR responded a week later, announcing that further American aid to China would become "unjustified" if Chiang did not send his armies into Burma. On April 13, Marshall ordered Stilwell to stop all Lend-Lease material going to the Yunnan force and divert it to the B-29 Superfortress program in Chengdu. At that point, Chiang Kai-shek caved in. On April 14, two divisions of Chinese troops moved into Burma. With Chennault's planes providing close air support, the Y force inched west toward the Chinese Army of India.

At that point, Stilwell and the Chinese Army of India were stuck in the Hukawng Valley. And Stilwell knew that if he did not make it to Myitkyina, 150 miles and a mountain range away, before the monsoon season began, the liberation of Burma would have to wait another year. So Stilwell decided to make a mad dash to Myitkyina, the most strategic Japanese outpost in northern Burma. In so doing, he made all the mistakes that he had once pinned on Chiang Kai-shek.

Stilwell employed a relative—in this case, his son—in a critically important position as his chief intelligence officer. His forces were continually surprised by the enemy's location and size. He supplied his troops with a fraction of the food they needed to survive. He hid his plans from both his allies, in this case Mountbatten and Chiang. And he sent men ill equipped to fight into the heat of battle; the Japanese massacred one company of Americans who had not used weapons since basic training.

For the sprint to Myitkyina, Stilwell chose the only American combat troops deployed to the Chinese theater—a regiment of about three thousand volunteers known officially as the 5307th Composite Unit (Provisional) and by history as Merrill's Marauders, after their commander, Frank Merrill. The Marauders had already fought through five hundred miles of jungle and had lived on K rations since early February.

Most of them were suffering from dysentery, and their bodies were pock-marked with festering sores, courtesy of Burma's hand-sized leeches. No matter, on April 27, Stilwell ordered them into the jungle again. And after a stunning eighteen-day trek across the Kumon mountains, the Marauders retook Myitkyina airfield on May 17, 1944.

Stilwell released the news that Myitkyina had fallen, again burnishing his credentials as an American hero. But the news was premature. The Yanks had only taken the airfield; the town was still in Japanese hands. Only seven hundred Japanese soldiers remained—unbeknownst to Stilwell's slipshod intelligence work. Still, when offered a British division, Stilwell turned it down. He wanted Americans to finish the job. And as he scoured hospitals and rear-echelon encampments for Yankee soldiers, five thousand Japanese reinforced the town's defenses.

By then, the Marauders had been in the bush for more than three months. They'd had one hot meal since March and had received no mail. British medics flown into the Myitkyina airfield declared 90 percent of them unfit for combat. The Japanese held out until August 3, ordering a retreat not because of Stilwell but because the British, led by then major general William Slim, had broken the siege of Imphal to the west.

The African American servicemen in Burma shared an affinity with the mostly white Marauders. Black soldiers pitied their plight. "We were at the bottom of the barrel and they had finally reached it," recalled Private Clyde Blue, a truck driver from Chicago. When the Marauders' operational commander, US Army colonel Charles N. Hunter, complained about Stillwell's atrocious handling of his men in a letter on May 27, 1944, Stilwell's only response was that Hunter's missive was strongly worded. Writing of Stilwell's actions in Burma, army historian Scott R. McMichael observed, "Seldom have American soldiers been treated so heartlessly." At the end of the mission, only two hundred of several thousand Marauders were on their feet. The rest, wrote John Paton Davies, were either "dead, hospitalized at Ledo, or convalescent and close to mutiny."

While Stilwell was in Burma, the Japanese launched Ichigo, or Operation Number One, the largest Japanese ground invasion of the entire war.

With its shipping pulverized by the US Navy, Japan sought to cut a land corridor through China to move goods, oil, and food from its occupied territories in Indochina to its home islands. The Imperial Army also wanted to overrun Chennault's bases. In October 1943, Chennault's men had sunk five thousand tons of Japanese shipping. In November, they tripled that toll. On Thanksgiving Day 1943, Chennault masterminded a raid on Japan's colony of Taiwan, destroying forty-two aircraft in twelve minutes.

On April 17, 1944, Japanese troops, the first of two waves of half a million men, crossed the Yellow River and rolled south across the Henan wheat fields. In mid-May, the Japanese swept down on Luoyang, a key transport hub on the river. Chiang Kai-shek appealed to Stilwell to use the B-29 Superfortresses, which were now in Chengdu, against the Japanese, but Stilwell turned him down.

Luoyang fell as the Nationalist army lost twenty-one thousand men. Chennault again pleaded with Stilwell to use the long-range bombers to hit Japanese troop trains and bridges. Again, he was rebuffed, this time by the War Department. "Instructions understood," Stilwell replied to General "Hap" Arnold, the Army Air Force chief. "And exactly what I had hoped for." At the State Department on May 15, China desk officer John Carter Vincent accused the Nationalists' news agency of overstating the size of the Japanese assault. "It is not clear that the over-all Chinese strategic position would be drastically affected," Vincent concluded.

On June 5, Chiang pleaded for Lend-Lease supplies for China's defense. On June 7, Marshall ordered Stilwell not to divert any material destined for the B-29 program without approval from the Joint Chiefs of Staff. Marshall stressed that "the early bombing of Japan will have a far more beneficial effect on the situation in China than the long delay in such an operation which would be caused by the transfer of these stocks to Chennault." US strategy was clear; helping the Nationalist army was not a priority. Using China as a springboard for an attack on Japan was.

In late June, Japanese forces smashed into Hubei province south of Hankou and were heading toward Changsha, the capital of Hunan province, which the Nationalists had heroically defended twice before. Other Japanese units pushed south of Guangzhou and were moving toward Hanoi. Chennault's air fields in Jiangxi and Guangxi provinces were threatened.

Chennault's Fourteenth Air Force, trying to defend a battlefront a thousand miles long, was in a bind. Old Leatherneck had 500 planes but 350 of them were either protecting the B-29 airbases in Chengdu or were in Burma fighting for Stilwell. In eastern China, Chennault's pilots flew four missions a day. Within weeks, nearly half the pilots of three squadrons had been killed or taken prisoner. Chennault pleaded with Stilwell to support a local Chinese commander who had earned a solid reputation as a seasoned fighter. Again, Stilwell refused. "Let him stew," Stilwell wrote in his diary.

* * *

The US Army mission to use China to bomb Japan was called Operation Matterhorn. From the start, Matterhorn was plagued by a lack of planes; of the first ninety-seven B-29s manufactured by Boeing only seventeen could fly. What's worse, the decision to base the mission in the southwestern Chinese city of Chengdu put Matterhorn at the dead end of a twelve-thousand-mile logistical train.

Neither Stilwell nor Chennault wanted Matterhorn. Chennault had asked that the B-29s be put under his command and used primarily to bomb Japanese forces in China. He was ignored. Unfathomably, command of the B-29s in China remained on the other side of the globe.

FDR wanted bombing to begin in January 1944, but bottlenecks delayed the first sortie by half a year. When it finally occurred, on June 5, 1944, the Superfortresses found their target—a railroad crossing in Thailand—obscured by fog and no damage was done. On June 15, the B-29s launched their first strike on Japan. Sixty-eight took off, bound for the Imperial Iron and Steel Works on Kyushu Island. Only one bomb landed near the target, and the steel mill wasn't even scratched. Nonetheless, in America, the press hailed the raid as "historic." On June 16, the front page of the *New York Times* read: "Yawata Industry Heavily Damaged; Japanese 'Pittsburgh' Bombed Accurately."

The War Department's spin couldn't alter the facts. Matterhorn was a flop. In all, B-29s would take part in only ten attacks from the air bases in Chengdu. And the mission took a massive toll on China's defense. Equipment and gasoline were diverted as Japanese forces gobbled up huge swaths of Chinese territory. After the war the US Strategic Bombing Survey concluded that "aviation gasoline and supplies used by the B-29s might have been more profitably allocated to an expansion of the tactical and anti-shipping operations of the 14th Air Force." In other words, Chennault would have done a better job. In December 1944, the Joint Chiefs ordered the B-29s transferred to the Mariana Islands, which had fallen to the United States.

On July 4, 1944, as the Japanese advanced, George Marshall concluded that China's government faced imminent collapse. The time had come, Marshall announced, for the Allies to take drastic action in China. He proposed that "all the military power remaining in China must be entrusted to one individual." And that individual was Joseph Warren Stilwell. Two days later, FDR wrote to Chiang demanding that the Generalissimo hand over the command of all his forces to Vinegar Joe.

Chiang stalled. He accepted FDR's demand in principle but argued that the details needed to be worked out, particularly the Americans' desire that Stilwell lead not just Nationalist but also Communist forces. Appointing an American to command China's armies would be fraught with risk. Nationalist China had been founded on the idea that China would no longer be subjugated to the West. Now the United States was preparing to place a Westerner on China's highest military perch. Japanese and Communist propaganda crowed at the possibility, charging that Chiang was nothing but the white man's stooge. Some thought that the idea would never fly. John Paton Davies accused Roosevelt of "naive optimism" in believing that the Chinese would submit to a foreigner. It was, Davies wrote, as if Washington had found another Frederick Townsend Ward.

To strengthen Stilwell's case, Marshall took the remarkable decision of engineering Stilwell's promotion to full general, making him one of only five Americans holding that rank. Stilwell's image as a hero was of strategic importance to Washington. His fourth star served as proof to Americans and Chinese that the United States was supporting China to the utmost. Chiang Kai-shek reluctantly accepted Roosevelt's ultimatum. In his hour of need, the Generalissimo could not risk a rift with the United States. Still, no further move came until August 8, when Hengyang, the second-largest city in Hunan province, fell to the Japanese.

Chiang told Washington that he wanted to withdraw his forces from Burma to protect his strategic rear. The Ichigo offensive was bearing down on the American air base in the scenic town of Guilin, and Chiang worried that once Guilin fell, the Japanese would break through to Yunnan province and take Kunming. Stilwell and Chiang met and clashed over strategy; Vinegar Joe wrote that he was "appalled" that Chiang would consider pulling his forces out of Burma to defend his own country. After the meeting, Stilwell fired off a cable to Marshall, calling Chiang "a crazy little bastard." The Generalissimo, Stilwell alleged, was about to cause a complete reversal in Burma. In reality, nothing of the kind occurred.

Marshall drafted a letter on the president's behalf. Far more insulting than anything he had sent to Chiang Kai-shek before, Roosevelt's missive arrived on the morning of September 19. Stilwell read it, noted that it was "hot as a firecracker," and took a jeep to Chiang's residence on the outskirts of Chongqing that afternoon. Chiang was already meeting with Patrick Hurley, another of Roosevelt's envoys, and T. V. Soong, who had been restored to favor. Documents on the table before them attested to the fact that Chiang was deep in discussions over the move to appoint Stilwell commander of China's armies.

Stilwell asked to see Hurley alone and showed him the message. "No chief of state could tolerate such an insult as this letter," Hurley later recalled telling Stilwell. "Joe, you have won this ball game," he said and urged Stilwell not to read the telegram to Chiang. But Stilwell was determined. He presented the cable to Chiang and asked a Chinese officer to read the Chinese translation. "I have urged time and again in recent months that you take drastic action to resist the disaster which has been moving closer to China and to you," Roosevelt began. FDR commanded Chiang to keep his troops in Burma and grant Stilwell "unrestricted command of all your forces." If Chiang refused, Roosevelt warned, there would be no land opening to China and even the Hump would be closed. "For this you must yourself be prepared to accept the consequences," Roosevelt said. The letter was patronizing and insulting. Stilwell watched as "the harpoon hit the little bugger in the solar plexus and went right through him," he wrote. Chiang ended the meeting. Alone with T. V. Soong, the Generalissimo burst into tears. It was, Chiang told his diary, "the most severe humiliation I have ever had in my life."

For an alleged China Hand, Stilwell had violated the most basic tenet of civility as laid out by his comrade and sometime competitor Milton "Mary" Miles: he had disgraced a senior Chinese official in front of his subordinates. There was no way Chiang could allow Stilwell to remain in the country. T. V. Soong hypothesized that Stilwell had engineered the event to ensure that he would not become commander because he knew that he was not up to the job.

When Hurley informed Stilwell that Chiang was angry and hurt, Stilwell laughed. He commemorated the event with a poem to his wife:

> *I have waited long for vengeance*
> *At last I've had my chance*
> *I've looked the Peanut in the eye*
> *And kicked him in the pants.*

It continued in that vein for five stanzas.

Chiang demanded that Stilwell be recalled to the United States. He blamed China's predicament on Stilwell's obsession with Burma. It was not he but the United States and Britain that had reneged on the promise of an amphibious landing at Rangoon, he noted. And in response to his pleas for weapons to fight off the Ichigo offensive, he said, Stilwell had only released "60 mountain rifles, 320 anti-aircraft guns and 506 bazookas." The two campaigns in Burma had drained off his best troops. "We have taken Myitkyina but we have lost almost all of East China," he wrote to Roosevelt, "and in this General Stilwell cannot be absolved of grave responsibility." Chiang told the Americans that he would accept another American as his "field commander," but Roosevelt was not interested. Instead, the War Department named General Albert Wedemeyer, who had helped plan the Normandy invasion and was now Mountbatten's deputy in Southeast Asia, to Stilwell's old position as one of Chiang's chiefs of staff.

Roosevelt had decided to distance himself from Chiang Kai-shek. Engaged in a tough reelection campaign, which the Gallup polling agency predicted would be close, FDR could not afford to be held accountable for failure in China, especially now that the war in Europe had hit a snag, and the Japanese were fighting fiercely in the Pacific.

The War Department marked Stilwell's recall with a short press release and asserted that the general "had no public statement to make." But in Chongqing, Vinegar Joe sat down with American reporters, including Brooks Atkinson of the *New York Times,* to vent. On October 31, 1944, the *Times* ran a front-page story headlined "Stilwell Break Stems From Chiang Refusal to Press War Fully." Atkinson contended that Stilwell's ouster "represented the political triumph of a moribund, corrupt regime that is more concerned with maintaining its political supremacy than driving the Japanese out of China." Chiang, the *Times* claimed, just wouldn't fight, and so Stilwell was forced out. FDR personally approved the story's publication. On November 7, Roosevelt won a fourth term.

Later that month, Guilin and its US air base fell to the Japanese. But for Tokyo, Ichigo was hardly a crowning victory. The Japanese ran a few trainloads of supplies north from Indochina toward Manchuria, but Chennault's air force continued to make life difficult, taking out bridges and railroad junctions.

Ichigo's main beneficiary turns out to have been Mao Zedong. As Japanese forces pushed the Nationalists out of eastern China, Communist operatives expanded southward, deep into territory once controlled by Chiang Kai-shek. By the end of the Japanese offensive, the Communists had extended their territory by hundreds of thousands of square miles. That, in the end, was the legacy of Ichigo and the failed strategy to use China as an unsinkable aircraft carrier from which to bomb Japan.

●

CHAPTER TWENTY-THREE

The East Is Red

The Nationalist regime of Chiang Kai-shek began to lose the war for American hearts and minds in 1942. When Henry Morgenthau's Treasury Department loaned China $500 million in February of that year, China's finance minister, H. H. Kung, set aside almost half that amount to buy up Chinese currency as a way to control inflation already reaching 100 percent. But Kung's plan to issue Dollar Savings Certificates and Allied Victory US Dollar Bonds turned into a scam to enrich himself and other friends who possessed US dollars. The Nationalist financial adviser, Arthur Young, called it "a missed opportunity." That was an understatement. On December 18, 1942, Morgenthau could only acknowledge that the loan had done nothing to tamp down prices; the only beneficiaries, he told Roosevelt, were "insiders, speculators and hoarders." Kung's gimmick cost him China's best friend in the US government.

China's unwillingness to adjust its exchange rate with the dollar further enraged Morgenthau. On the black market, the Chinese currency continuously dropped against the greenback, but the Nationalist government stuck to a twenty-to-one exchange rate and forced the US Army to pay its fees according to the government-set rate. China didn't seem to understand, Arthur Young told his diary, that "US$80 for a simple chair is unreasonable."

The most outrageous pricing of all came in 1943 when 375,000 Chinese laborers built eight runways near the Sichuanese capital of Chengdu for the B-29 Superfortresses. Accomplished by hand, it was a phenomenal feat of engineering. The price tag was phenomenal, too: $150 million, worth more than $2 billion today.

Chiang's ideology also alienated the Americans. In 1943, the Generalissimo published *China's Destiny*, his vision for a new China. Written in the stilted prose of semiclassical Chinese, the book was required reading for all Kuomintang members, memorized in schools and universities, and replaced the writings of Sun Yat-sen as the Bible of Nationalist China.

In it, Chiang blamed Westerners for famines, stock market panics, the breakup of the Chinese family, selfishness, and drug use. He castigated Christianity—even though he was a Methodist—and lambasted Western education—even though his wife had been schooled in the United States. To accomplish the task of modernizing China, Chiang, in a companion volume called *Chinese Economic Theory*, advocated a state-run economy. He criticized capitalism and individualism and touted Confucian morality as the answer to China's ills. "Make friends with the ancients," he advised.

Chiang's book fell flat among the influential American China watchers who read Chinese. (English translations did not appear until 1947.) John K. Fairbank, a Harvard scholar working as an analyst for the OSS, warned that the US would support Chiang "at our peril." Philip Jaffe, a China watcher based in New York, dubbed it the Chinese version of *Mein Kampf*.

Many American readers compared Chiang's manifesto unfavorably with an essay by Communist leader Mao Zedong—"On New Democracy"—that had appeared in 1940. Writing in the folksy style popularized by Hu Shih, Mao vowed to create a new nation and a new culture. This appealed to Americans who sensed in Mao the type of disruptive awakening they believed China needed. Moreover, unlike Chiang, who rejected a market economy, Mao vowed that his China would tolerate capitalists. It mattered little what Mao really planned; he made his Marxism palatable to any taste.

In 1944, Chiang's minions intensified their crackdown on liberal politicians, throwing dozens in jail. In April, reports of a Nationalist operation in America to monitor Chinese students surged through the American press. The *New York Times* called the campaign "totalitarian." When a Chinese government spokesman defended the program, he only made matters worse. The Chinese government was not indoctrinating its people, he claimed, it was merely teaching them table manners. The US press guffawed in disbelief.

Even Soong Mayling, the longtime darling of the US press, got the cold shoulder. When she came stateside in 1944 for medical treatment, American newspapers ruminated about the ruinous state of her marriage. Her visit to the White House was framed as a courtesy call by a sad-sack supplicant, no longer China's "queen."

So many influential Americans were souring on the Nationalists that Nathaniel Peffer estimated in the *New York Times Magazine* in May 1944 that "a majority would favor our shifting our support from Chungking to the Communists." Mao's chronicler Edgar Snow used his bully pulpit in the *Saturday Evening Post* to urge a new policy toward China. "Sixty Million Lost Allies" read the headline on Snow's article in June 1944. He wanted America to embrace the Red Army and dump Chiang Kai-shek. Snow painted a utopian picture of the Red Zone—democracy, free universal education, happy peasants—and a hellish one of Nationalist China, where corruption and incompetence reigned.

It was no longer just journalists who were taking up the Communists' cause. As early as January 23, 1943, Jack Service, a second secretary at the US embassy in Chongqing, had appealed to the State Department for permission to visit the Communist stronghold in Yanan. In a controversial cable, Service blamed the Nationalists for violating the terms of their united front with the Communists and questioned the logic of continuing American aid to Chiang Kai-shek. He charged that the Kuomintang was hoarding American military equipment to use against the Communists at a later date.

Service suggested that the US government recognize the Communists as a partner in the fight against Japan. He floated the idea of giving the Communists "a proportionate share of American supplies sent to China" and proposed that the United States dispatch an American envoy, ideally a foreign service officer trained in Chinese, to the Communist-controlled areas. He was nominating himself.

Two weeks later, senior State Department official Stanley Hornbeck warned that an official American mission to the Red Zone would poison America's relations with the Nationalists. It would be, he wrote, "both vicious and stupid" to support both sides in what he believed to be an inevitable civil war. He pleaded for "intelligent skepticism" about reports that the Communists were fighting the Japanese.

How much the Chinese Communists actually fought the Japanese during World War II is subject to debate. The official history of the People's Liberation Army claims that Communist guerrillas battled continuously against the Japanese. However, in January 1940, Zhou Enlai told Stalin that China had suffered more than one million casualties, of which forty thousand, or about 4 percent, were Communists. The rest were Nationalists. Mao Zedong authorized only one major offensive against the Japanese, the Hundred Regiments Campaign, in the fall of 1940. It ended in defeat.

In his wartime diary, Petr Parfenovich Vladimirov, a Russian wire service correspondent who doubled as a Soviet adviser at Mao's headquarters, noted that Mao gleefully celebrated each of Chiang's defeats. The Communists, he wrote, "have long been abstaining from both active and passive action against the aggressors."

The Americans on Stilwell's staff, however, believed that the Communists were fighting. The Communists, John Paton Davies wrote in January 1944, sustained "the most cohesive, disciplined and aggressively anti-Japanese regime in China." Even though he was a Republican, Stilwell was also enamored of the Communists, calling them the "only visible hope of relief from crushing taxation, the abuses of the Army and Dai Li's Gestapo."

By 1944, officials in Washington generally agreed that the United States should reach out to the Communists. In late June of that year, Vice President Henry Wallace came to Chongqing to press the case, urging Chiang to allow an American mission to the Communist redoubt in Yanan. Chiang reluctantly agreed. "For twenty years the Communist bandits and the Russians have been plotting against me, but now the British and the Americans were plotting with the Communists," Chiang wrote in his diary. "This is like world imperialism ambushing me!"

The Americans assembled a delegation of officers, enlisted men, and two American diplomats, including Jack Service, to travel to Communist-held territory. Led by Colonel David B. Barrett, a chubby Chinese-speaking assistant military attaché at the Chongqing embassy, the delegation was known formally as the United States Army Observation Group to Yanan. Everyone else called it the Dixie Mission; the Red Zone was rebel country, after all.

On July 22, 1944, Barrett and the first part of his team landed in Yanan, a sleepy town set in a treeless valley in northern Shanxi province. Communist Party chairman Mao Zedong and Zhu De, leader of the Red Army, met them at the airfield. In the *Liberation Daily*, Mao called the Dixie Mission "the most exciting event ever since the war against Japan started." Previously, the Chinese Communist Party had been merely a domestic irritant to Chiang Kai-shek. Now, as the American plane rolled to a stop in a ditch at the Yanan airfield, China's Communists had become an international challenge to Chiang's regime.

Mao's goals in the talks, according to a report by Vladimirov, the Soviet political adviser, were to secure diplomatic ties with the United States and cadge as many weapons from Washington as possible. Mao had nonetheless assured him, Vladimirov wrote, that "no matter what form the contacts with the Americans will take, our revolution will eventually turn against the imperialists." Vladimirov reported that Mao viewed the talks as part of the game against Chiang, not as a function of the war with Japan. "His calculations are simple," Vladimirov wrote, "whenever Chiang Kai-shek suffers a defeat, the [Communist] Special Area benefits."

Mao wooed the Americans, hinting at the bright future of Sino-American trade and discounting Soviet influence. "Chinese and American interests are correlated and similar," he told Service in a wide-ranging discussion in August 1944. "They fit together, economically and politically. We can and must work together." Mao urged Service to persuade America to provide the Communists with arms and promised that his party would be a better ally than Chiang Kai-shek. "We would serve with all our hearts under an American general," he said, "that is how we feel toward you." Mao carped about the Russians. Stalin would not support China's Communists, he complained. He had pinned his hopes on the United States.

The Americans arrived in Yanan just after a brutal party rectification campaign had left scores dead as Mao consolidated his position at the top of the party. The Americans had no idea what they had missed. American intelligence on the Communists was laughable. As late as June 1945, the Office of Strategic Services identified Mao's ruthless internal security chief, Kang Sheng, as an "intellectual." Kang swaggered around Yanan in Russian boots, accompanied by a large dog, but to the Americans, he was all but invisible. They thought that the organization he ran, the Social Affairs Department, was in charge of scheduling dances. They also believed that the Agricultural Department focused solely on crops; it actually doubled as the site of a radio transmitter linking Yanan to Moscow.

Barrett's team was struck by the Communists' vigor and popularity. Jack Service, who did the bulk of the political reporting, called the party's leaders "modern" and "Western" and compared them favorably with the has-beens in Chongqing. Service took seriously Mao's remarks that "what China needs most is democracy, not socialism" and that foreign capital would be welcome in China after the war. Service did not realize that Mao's charm offensive had been carefully calibrated with Stalin to veil the party's radical intentions and attract Chinese liberals and even the US government to its side. Though Mao talked publicly of the need for "genuinely free general elections," he was busy suppressing deviant thinking and nurturing his cult of personality. When Service asked Mao whether he was afraid of democracy, Mao scoffed. "We are not even afraid of the Japanese occupation of half of China's territory, let alone the democratic influence of the United States," he said.

Mao directed the party's propaganda organs to again alter their portrayal of the United States. "American Imperialist" was dropped and replaced with *you bang*, or the "friendly federation." On July 4, 1944, the party mouthpiece, *Liberation Daily*, celebrated Independence Day with an editorial by Hu Qiaomu, Mao's ideological shaman. July 4, Hu wrote, was "a holiday for the great fight for freedom and democracy." He lavished praise on presidents Washington, Jefferson, and Lincoln, extolled America's "immortal acts" during the war, and ended the elegy with "Long Live Democratic America!"

Stalin played his part in this game, soft-pedaling any connections with the Chinese Communists even as he bankrolled their operations with a monthly stipend of American dollars and gold. In a June 1944 meeting with Averell Harriman, the US ambassador to Moscow, he described Mao and his band as "margarine Communists." America's diplomats were taken in. As Stilwell's political adviser, John Paton Davies, wrote in a cable, "Politically any orientation which the Chinese Communists may once have had toward the Soviet Union seems to be a thing of the past."

In a secret directive, "On Diplomatic Work," issued on August 18, 1944, the Chinese Communist Party hailed the Dixie Mission as a victory in its battle for China. Mao reminded party members that the Soviet Union was China's most reliable friend. In cultivating America, the goal wasn't an alliance, he said, but to "neutralize" the role America would play in the upcoming civil war.

On a personal level, Mao used the Dixie Mission to gratify his lasting obsession with the United States. US Army resupply planes flew dozens of American films into Yanan, which Mao watched feverishly, an interpreter at his side. He took in Henry Fonda, Betty Grable, Charlie Chaplin, and more. Many in Mao's rank and file shared the chairman's curiosity about the United States. "Does everyone in America have a car?" the Communists asked Sidney Rittenberg, an American from South Carolina who would join their movement. Hsiao Li Lindsay, the Chinese wife of British radio operator Michael Lindsay, recalled that at soirees, the Americans were kept on their feet dancing. "I think it was the Americans who felt shy instead of the young Chinese women," she wrote. Still, when one GI made a pass at a girl, Zhou Enlai intervened.

Service had vowed not to be taken in by "the spell of the Chinese Communists," but it was hard to resist. The Communists flattered him, calling him "*zhongguo tong*," or "the man who knew China." In Yanan, Service felt as if he had "come into a different country." Unlike in Chongqing, where everyone griped constantly about Chiang, he observed, "Mao and the other leaders are universally spoken of with respect." This was a sign of the party's popularity, he argued, not the result of its having just spent two years terrorizing those who dared to think otherwise. "There is no feeling of restraint or oppression," Service wrote. "There is no hesitation in admitting failure." The program in the Special Area, he declared, "is simple democracy . . . much more American than Russian in form and spirit."

Yanan had no beggars, no desperate poverty, and an absence of the "spooning couples seen in parks or quiet streets in Chungking." To Service, this brave new world was a welcome change and not a chilling harbinger of the totalitarian regime that Mao would unleash upon a quarter of humanity. Service did note a "uniformity" in the way people thought, but it did not trouble him. His view differed markedly from that of Vladimirov, who wrote that the party's purge had led to an "oppressive, suffocating atmosphere."

Service was convinced that the Communists understood that capitalism would be good for China. He believed that the United States, rather than the Soviet Union, would be "the only country" to help China modernize. He was not alone in this view. The term "so-called Communists" began popping up with increasing regularity in State Department reports out of Chongqing.

Service was the ultimate China Hand. Born into a missionary family in China in 1909, he routinely expressed his love for the country and was one in a long line of Americans who believed that he could mend China if only everyone would listen. "I felt I had a special kind of linkage and insight," he wrote in his unpublished memoirs. "Was this a seed of hubris? Possibly." During the war, with his American wife in the United States, Service took up with a Chinese actress. "I was in love with China and with the hopes and aspirations of my young intellectual friends," he later wrote. "It was not surprising perhaps that I made this more personal by falling in love with a Chinese woman."

Service reacted to the Red Zone as if it were the fulfillment of the century-old missionary dream for a spiritually rejuvenated China. "It was the same kind of optimism that motivated my father," he wrote of the Communists. Mao, he wrote, "was a missionary convinced of the value and eventual success of his mission." Yanan reminded him of an American revival camp, with the same tinge of "smugness, self-righteousness and conscious fellowship." To him, Yanan was "the most modern place in China."

In September 1945, John Paton Davies arrived in Yanan for talks with Mao and other Communist leaders. A year older than Service, Davies had also been born in Sichuan to missionary parents. He believed that a civil war in China was unavoidable and that America needed to befriend the Communists because they were going to win. Weeks after his visit, he wrote: "The Communists are in China to stay and China's destiny is not Chiang's but theirs." Davies wagered that if America aided the Communists, they could be changed from hard-line Marxist-Leninists to friends of the United States.

Davies's bet hung on his conviction that the Reds were not all that red; he called them pragmatists and ideological "backsliders." He also held to the notion that like all other Chinese, they could not say no to America. He was wrong on both counts. "I obviously underestimated the commitment of the Chinese Communist ruling party at the time to ideology and the dexterity with which Mao and company manipulated it," Davies acknowledged later in life.

Within weeks of landing in Yanan, Barrett, the Dixie Mission chief, recommended that the United States supply arms and equipment to the Communists. Otherwise, he warned, "the chances of civil war would increase and Mao would revert to his close alliance with the Soviet Union." The Office of Strategic Services, which had agents on the team, also pushed cooperation and began flying in radio sets. Eventually, fourteen thousand pounds of American radio equipment would make it into Yanan.

There were, of course, practical reasons to supply the Communists, chief among them the need to rescue American pilots who had been shot down by the Japanese over Communist-held territory. Many of these pilots—a total of sixty—were saved by the Eighth Route Army, known in Chinese as the Balu Jun and to the Americans as the Balus.

From Chongqing, Ambassador Gauss passed Service's and Barrett's starry-eyed reports on to Washington but attached a rider: "Recent Chinese Communist claims of military achievement against Japan seem to have been exaggerated." Vladimirov was even more dismissive. When Mao sent a telegram to Moscow on July 19, 1944, claiming that the Communists had enjoyed a string of successful operations against Japan, Vladimirov informed Moscow that Mao had inflated the figures. "The Eighth Route Army and the New Fourth Army have actually folded up military operations since 1941," he reported. Years later, Barrett acknowledged that he, too, had been "unduly impressed with the Communists." He pleaded "naiveté."

The warm feelings many Americans harbored for China's Communists came from many sources, but the master at wrapping Chinese Communism into an attractive package for American consumption was Zhou Enlai. "He was one of the smoothest liars in the world, but you couldn't help but like him as a person," recalled Henry Byroade, a US Army officer who had extensive dealings with the Communists. Based for much of the war in Chongqing, Zhou and his pulchritudinous assistant, Gong Peng, undertook one of the most successful PR operations in the world.

Born in 1898, Zhou hailed from a family of aristocratic scholar officials. He was educated in Tianjin at Nankai Middle School, run by the American-educated Zhang Boling, was the editor of the school newspaper, starred in student plays—many directed by American-educated playwright P. C. Chang—and finished at the top of his class. Zhou studied overseas, first in Japan and then in France, where he joined the Communist Party. At twenty-six, during the first united front between the Communists and the Nationalists, he was appointed deputy political commissar of the Whampoa military academy, run by Chiang Kai-shek. Later, he led the *teke*, or Communist secret police, famed for its brutal liquidation of Communist turncoats and Nationalist spies. No one on the Nationalist side, wrote correspondent Peggy Durdin, "could touch Chou En-lai in persuasiveness or in intellectual charm."

Gong Peng was living proof that Edgar Snow's message about Mao Zedong had gotten through to China's best and brightest. Born into a Christian family in Anhui, Gong had known Edgar and Peg Snow when she was a student in Beijing during the 1930s and had been transfixed by the slideshows Edgar gave when he returned from his trip to the Red Zone. She translated parts of *Red Star Over China* and circulated it among her classmates. In 1938, she herself headed to Yanan and by 1940 was working in Chongqing as Zhou's chief liaison to the Western press. Peggy Durdin called her "the most impressive public relations figure I ever met."

Zhou's persuasiveness was legendary. *Time*'s Theodore White ranked him with Stilwell and John F. Kennedy as "the three greatest men I met . . . in whose presence I had near total suspension of disbelief." White called

Gong Peng the most beautiful Chinese woman he had ever encountered, a real, live "Pistol Packing Miss Golden Flowers." So when a group of American correspondents arrived in Yanan a few months after the Dixie Mission, they, too, were predisposed to favor the Communists.

For many of these journalists, being in Yanan was a near-religious experience. John Roderick of the Associated Press described Mao's wife, Jiang Qing, one of the great tyrants of the twentieth century, as "the plainest of plain Janes" and compared her unadorned wardrobe favorably to Soong Mayling's seductive cheongsams. Brooks Atkinson of the *Times* praised the Communists' plays, and photojournalist Harrison Forman even found a way to laud the unbending cultural orthodoxy that Mao demanded of his followers. "The Communists take their culture seriously," Forman observed in his book *Report from Red China*. In prewar Shanghai, he wrote, poets, painters, playwrights, and novelists pursued art for art's sake, but "far-seeing Mao Zedong observed this and decided that it was no good." Arch Steele of the *Herald Tribune* capped the religious metaphor: "A trip from Chungking to Yenan," he wrote, was like going "from hell to heaven." The leftist American belief that Communism provided an answer for China fit neatly within the American missionary tradition. Like the Taipings of the mid-1860s, the Communists promised a "blitzconversion," not to Christianity but to socialist modernity.

Against this tide of alienation from Chiang's regime and temptation by the Communists battled one of China's greatest liberals: Lin Yutang. Lin returned to China in 1943 for only the second time since moving to America in 1937. In China, he found himself backing the Nationalist regime and forgiving Chiang Kai-shek most of his sins. Back in America, he set down his thoughts in a book, *The Vigil of a Nation*. Pearl Buck and her second husband, Richard Walsh, who was Lin's editor, cautioned him that his pro-Nationalist stance would hurt sales. "People will wonder at you because you now so wholeheartedly support the government you once criticized," Walsh wrote.

Published in late 1945, *The Vigil of a Nation* was sympathetic to Chiang's plight as the leader of a fractious country ravaged by Japanese aggression and a Communist insurgency. Lin praised Chiang as a farsighted "humanist" and pleaded for patience with the Kuomintang. He pilloried the Communists, detailing Mao's bloody purges, his rule by terror and secret agents, "the farce of packed popular elections," and the party's total domination of thought. He called the Red Zone a "totalitarian dictatorship" devoted to class struggle and a crusade against religion, family, and tradition. He described Communism's defenders in the United States as useful idiots and saps.

Some Americans greeted Lin's book with derision. On NBC's *American Town Meeting of the Air*, the old Soviet spy Agnes Smedley, with whom Lin had cofounded the China League for Civil Rights, asked him why he didn't just admit that "he got a big fat check in American dollars from the Chinese government." Helen Snow accused him of wanting to start a civil war. Phillip Jaffe, the editor of the left-wing *Amerasia*, devoted an entire issue in March 1945 to an attack on the book, denouncing Lin as an "apologist for the Chinese government" and the book as "dangerously provocative."

In a review in the *Nation*, Lin's old friend Edgar Snow seemed to shed the last vestiges of objectivity, calling the Communists the most democratic administration in China. Snow implied that Lin had no right to speak for China—that was better left to white Americans who were more objective. Lin had written a book, Snow wrote, "with such unexpected smallness of faith in a man's people, so full of mischief, and so lacking in dignity and pride."

In a rebuttal in the *Nation* the following month, called "China and Its Critics," Lin acknowledged that American public opinion was not on his side. China's Communists had become "America's sacred cow." He had been a longtime critic of the Nationalists' political oppression, but Chiang's depredations were a garden party compared to the regimented thinking imposed in the Red Zone. Throughout the war, Lin noted, leftist newspapers were able to publish in Nationalist territory, books and magazines routinely attacked the Generalissimo, and demonstrations organized by the Communists and other political parties were tolerated off and on.

Lin made an important point about American "China Hands." Though many of them could speak Chinese, few could read it. They never bothered to check Communist Party documents and relied instead on "what the communists say . . . to foreigners on a conducted tour." When Mao was carrying out the Yanan Rectification campaign, journalists like Snow hadn't bothered to read his writings. "To study Chinese events of the past years without studying Chinese writings is to go blindfolded," Lin declared.

Lin had once described himself as a man on a tightrope, teetering above totalitarians on one side and authoritarians on the other. Now he had jumped and had chosen Chiang Kai-shek. Knowing that a civil war loomed, he called on America to provide Chiang with the weapons he needed to win. Any attempt to piece China together with mediation, he said, would be "naive."

As Hu Shih had once asked Frank Goodnow, Lin asked his old American friends why the Chinese didn't deserve freedom. "Liberty for Americans is their life blood, but for Chinese, what does it matter anyhow?" he wrote to Pearl Buck. "The consigning of 500 million to totalitarian rule does not even arouse a ripple of phlegm. . . . I have no country to return to. I suppose Edgar Snow and Agnes Smedley think I am a fool not to jump into the Communist heaven."

The Chinese Communist Party's success in convincing most of the State Department diplomatic corps that it was patriotic, moderate, and willing to fight Japan had a significant effect on the outcome of China's civil war. It weakened support for the Kuomintang and enticed Americans to believe that the Communists were an acceptable alternative to Chiang Kai-shek. As World War II drew to a close, it also reinforced the notion that the Communists would be responsible members of a coalition government and not dedicated to seizing absolute power later on.

●

CHAPTER TWENTY-FOUR

Keys to the Kingdom

Stilwell's replacement, Lieutenant General Albert Wedemeyer, disagreed with Vinegar Joe's basic premise about Chiang Kai-shek and his men. "Far from reluctant to fight," Wedemeyer wrote, Chiang and the Nationalist army had shown "amazing tenacity and endurance in resisting Japan" with only "a trickle of aid" compared with what Britain and Russia had received.

Taking up command in November 1944, Wedemeyer broke with Stilwell's my-way-or-the-highway approach and sought compromise with all his partners: the Chinese, the British, and the brass in Washington. Chiang had wanted to pull all his troops out of Burma to protect Chongqing and Kunming, but Wedemeyer convinced him to leave half his men there. Wedemeyer even cajoled Washington into using its B-29 Superfortresses on Japanese troop trains along the Yangtze River. By December 1944, Japan's Ichigo offensive, which had started with such a bang, had ended with a whimper.

Albert Coady Wedemeyer was an ironic choice to replace Stilwell. Author of the Victory Plan, the basis for the "Europe First" strategy of World War II, and one of the architects of the D-day landings, Wedemeyer had studied in Germany in the 1930s and was one of the world's experts on German military tactics. But in 1943, Winston Churchill had engineered his removal from Europe as punishment for having forced the Normandy invasion down the throats of an unwilling British military. The army's foremost authority on German tactical operations was sent to Ceylon to serve as deputy to British admiral Louis Mountbatten on the South East Asia Command.

A Nebraskan, born in 1897, Wedemeyer was a smooth talker and a consummate diplomat who prided himself on his strategic vision. Stilwell called him "the world's most pompous prick." The Chinese were more generous. Banker K. P. Chen remarked that, unlike Stilwell, Wedemeyer, who had also served in China with the US Army's Fifteenth Infantry Regiment, possessed "remarkable presence of mind as to what to say and what not to say." Wedemeyer's own words have done his image more harm than good. His memoir, *Wedemeyer Reports!*, published in 1958 while the debate over "who lost China" still raged, is the work of a bitter man.

Wedemeyer adopted a low-key approach toward the Chinese. With Chiang Kai-shek, he played the role of confidant. As he wrote to Marshall soon into his assignment: "I have been uniformly careful to massage his ego and place myself in an advisory position so that he will not lose face." He was blunt with Chiang, but never within earshot of other Chinese.

Stilwell's staff had always shunned the Thursday morning meetings held by the Chinese military, considering them, Wedemeyer wrote, a "tea drinking, time consuming farce." But Wedemeyer turned them into a joint staff meeting. In the beginning, the Chinese were reluctant to contribute but they soon began to express themselves. Chiang Kai-shek started showing up, and within weeks, a modern war room had taken shape.

Wedemeyer built on Stilwell's program for modernizing the Chinese army. By 1945, more than three thousand American officers, airmen, and enlisted men were sprinkled throughout thirty-six divisions of the Chinese army down to the regimental level. When the Chinese attacked, Americans were there with them, advising on tactics, calling in air and artillery strikes, and ensuring that the wounded received treatment and the soldiers were fed.

Wedemeyer understood that while being sensitive to Chinese customs made sense, pretending to be Chinese was a bad idea. Soon after taking over, he met with Wei Lihuang, the commander of the Y Force, and urged him to attack into Burma and link up with the Chinese Army of India. When Wei refused, Wedemeyer pointed out that he and Chiang had agreed that Wei must fight, and he warned that he would confiscate Wei's American equipment if he did not. Then he turned his back and left Wei's tent.

Brigadier Frank Dorn, Stilwell's closest aide, who had accompanied Wedemeyer, backed out of the tent, bowing like a Chinese scholar. When Dorn told Wedemeyer that he had insulted Wei by turning his back on him, Wedemeyer responded that he had lived in China before and that "if the cupped-hands, bow-out-backwards method had been successful, perhaps I would not have been ordered to China to succeed Stilwell." Wedemeyer commanded Dorn to drop the China act; Americans made bad Chinese. Wei subsequently attacked and the Chinese opened the Ledo Road on January 28, 1945, in what the *New York Times* called "a smashing climax to China's first real offensive of the war."

Like many American and British officers in the theater, Wedemeyer viewed Stilwell's obsession with the Ledo Road as a waste of resources. He predicted correctly that by the time the Ledo Road was connected, it would no longer be needed. In July 1945, the last full month of World War II, only six thousand tons made it overland into China while seventy-one thousand were flown over the Hump. The main thing that Stilwell's Chinese troops accomplished in Burma was to regain a lost colony for Britain.

Wedemeyer did not publicly criticize Stilwell until after the war. In a letter from China to his father-in-law, Lieutenant General Stanley Dunbar Embick, Wedemeyer vented privately that Stilwell had made "a botch" of the job, spending too much time in Burma "commanding a few battalions," and had neglected his responsibilities as a theater commander. Stilwell never gave Chennault any direction, he said, resulting in an almost complete breakdown in coordination between air and ground forces. And he had failed to control the numerous American bureaucracies, including the battling spy agencies that vied for a piece of the China pie. "When I tried to determine where all of the Americans were in China, and what they were doing, it was such a jumbled mess that even today," Wedemeyer wrote long after he had assumed command, "I have not yet received that information."

Still, the combination of American advisers and Chinese firepower led to some success. In June 1945, the Japanese threw eight divisions at western Hunan province with the aim of thrusting all the way to Chongqing. Some twenty Chinese divisions along with two hundred bombers from Chennault's Fourteenth Air Force stopped the assault. As usual, Chiang Kai-shek tried to go behind the backs of the American advisers attached to Nationalist units, but Wedemeyer, unlike Stilwell, who would have thrown a fit, talked him out of it. "Using honey for my part instead of vinegar," Wedemeyer wrote, "I discovered Chiang was eminently willing to accede in planning in which he had primarily an onlooker's part." Soon after the successful defense, Wedemeyer and his Chinese colleagues began to plan an offensive—a Nationalist push to the coast.

Support for a united China was deeply embedded in the psyches of American strategists, businessmen, and missionaries. The concept that a stable, sovereign China was in the best economic and strategic interests of the United States had taken root in the 1800s. Now, deep in the Second World War, Americans redoubled their efforts to fend off a civil war and to keep China whole.

In November 1944, Clarence Gauss, the American ambassador to China, retired and was replaced by Patrick Hurley, Roosevelt's envoy, who stayed on in Chongqing. When Roosevelt had first sent Hurley to China in July 1944, he had directed him to try to improve relations between Stilwell and Chiang. He had failed. So FDR promoted him, radioing Hurley that "your intimate knowledge of the situation there both from the military and diplomatic stand-points . . . eminently qualifies you to be Ambassador to China." Had Roosevelt deliberately tried to wreck his China policy, he could scarcely have done better.

State Department officials considered Hurley senile, ignorant, and superficial. He mangled Chinese names. He called Chiang Kai-shek "Mr. Shek" and Mao Zedong "Moose Dung." Hurley viewed bringing Communists and Nationalists together as "not much different from persuading Republicans and Democrats to accept bipartisanship at a time of national crisis," wrote the diplomat John Paton Davies. He was in for a rude shock.

Hurley was by nature an optimist. Like many Americans fresh off the boat in China, he thought that he could accomplish anything, including a peace deal between Chiang Kai-shek and Mao Zedong. He also bought the Russian line that China's Reds were "not in fact Communists," as Soviet foreign minister Vyacheslav Molotov assured Hurley during one of Hurley's trips to Moscow.

On November 7, 1944, Hurley flew to Yanan to cut a deal with Mao Zedong. Standing at the door of the arriving plane, he let out a Choctaw war cry—John Paton Davies called it a "prolonged howl"—to the bemusement of Zhou Enlai and other Communist officials waiting for him at the airstrip. After much "pulling and tugging" with Mao, Hurley later wrote, he came up with a five-point plan that put the Nationalists and the Communists on an equal legal basis in a coalition government and allowed the

Communists to keep their army intact. American military supplies were to be shared. In return for these extraordinary gains, Mao had only promised to pledge loyalty to Chiang Kai-shek.

The Communists had gotten everything they wanted in exchange for a pledge. Hurley was pleased with his work and signed it—twice—along with Mao. For good measure, he tacked the American Bill of Rights onto the end of the deal and promised Mao that the US government would fully back the agreement, too.

T. V. Soong was appalled. "The Communists have sold you a bill of goods," he remarked when Hurley returned to Chongqing. Hurley did not understand that Chiang's shaky position atop a pile of competing warlords and opportunists would not survive the introduction of a Western-style democracy. Especially, Davies noted, when one of the participants—the Chinese Communist Party—was dedicated to using a coalition government to seize total power.

Chiang's response was that he would legalize the Communist Party only if its forces were incorporated into his army. And Mao had to hand over control of his armies first. Hurley showed the counterproposal to Zhou Enlai, who rejected it. On December 8, Hurley sent Colonel Barrett to Yanan to negotiate with Mao. The Communist leader threatened to release details of the earlier deal to the press. Hurley was livid. So was Mao.

US embassy officials were increasingly pessimistic about their ability to prevent a civil war. On November 15, Davies again urged Washington to try to "capture politically" the Communists rather than watch them "go by default wholly to the Russians." On January 4, 1945, Davies warned that "the future balance of power in Asia and the western Pacific" was at stake. Davies and his colleagues began quietly cultivating the Communists without informing Hurley. On one trip to Yanan, Davies and several US military officers met with Zhou Enlai to discuss an OSS-sponsored project for joint US–Chinese Communist sabotage operations against the Japanese. The Americans raised the prospect of a school for dirty tricks, enough equipment to supply twenty-five thousand guerrillas, a radio network across northern China, and one hundred thousand Woolworth one-shot pistols. Hurley learned of the talks and demanded an explanation. Davies said that he could not respond, since the offer was a military secret. Hearing this, Hurley "became a little rough" in his language, Hurley later wrote.

On January 10, 1945, OSS officer Ray Cromley, a former *Wall Street Journal* reporter, sent Wedemeyer a cable informing him that Mao and Zhou had proposed that one or both of them head to the United States for talks with Roosevelt about an alliance against Japan. Mao had never been out of the country, and now he wanted to go to America. Zhou requested that Hurley be cut out of the communication. "I don't trust his discretion," Zhou said.

Wedemeyer shared the cable with Hurley, who erupted. On January 14, Hurley wrote to FDR and complained that the secret negotiations were sabotaging his efforts. The message shook Washington, as did a follow-up cable from Wedemeyer, acknowledging that "unauthorized loose discussions by my officers employed in good faith by General Hurley could have strongly contributed to the latter's difficulty in bringing about a solution to the problem."

In early February, open rebellion hit the embassy in Chongqing. With both Hurley and Wedemeyer on their way to Washington for consultations, the political officers drew up a report arguing that the US policy to promote a unified China "did not necessarily mean that China should be united under the Generalissimo." In the cable, Jack Service accused Hurley of presenting an "incomplete and non-objective" view of China and of censoring reports from Chongqing. Service again advocated supplying arms to the Communists, arguing that this would have the dual benefits of hurting Japan and forcing the Nationalists and the Communists to unite. It would "hold the Communists to our side," he wrote, "rather than throw them into the arms of Russia." All the political officers in the embassy signed the document. "They'll say we're all traitors, that when the cats were away the mice began to play," quipped George Atcheson, the normally by-the-book chargé.

The embassy's China Hands timed the cable to arrive in Foggy Bottom just as Hurley landed in Washington. He called it an act of disloyalty and predicted that, if its recommendations were adopted, it would result in the overthrow of the Nationalist government. At the State Department, however, China desk officer John Carter Vincent supported the rebel diplomats and when Hurley visited, he found himself "put on the carpet" for his views. Hurley's ace in the hole was his direct access to the president. Roosevelt declared that no arms would be provided to the Chinese Communists without Chiang Kai-shek's approval. In time, Hurley would have all the China Hands who disagreed with him drummed out of the Chongqing embassy.

The break between Hurley and his staff foreshadowed one of the most divisive political battles in the history of American foreign policy—the blame game over "who lost China?" Hurley laid the responsibility for his failure to unite China on the shoulders of Davies, Jack Service, and the other American diplomats who he claimed had subverted his efforts to bring peace. It was American perfidy that "lost" China, Hurley would allege.

Hurley may have been persuaded that his staff was to blame for his failure to unite China, but in February 1945 a far more forbidding factor emerged. Roosevelt, Churchill, and Stalin met at the Black Sea port of Yalta in Soviet Crimea, the second gathering of the Big Three since the start of the war. Though the conference focused on Europe, Roosevelt wanted Stalin to formally commit to attacking the Japanese army and participating in the United Nations.

FDR had a blind spot when it came to Joseph Stalin. He regarded him as an ally and did not seem to comprehend the extent of Uncle Joe's guile. As Roosevelt told Churchill, "I think that if I give him everything I can and ask him for nothing in return, noblesse oblige, he won't try to annex anything and will work with me for a world of democracy and peace." Roosevelt clung to that idea until the day he died.

Stalin's price for attacking the Japanese was high. He wanted to restore the influence Russia had lost in East Asia at the Portsmouth Conference with Roosevelt's cousin, Teddy, forty years before. Stalin demanded a lease on the Port Arthur naval base at the tip of China's Liaodong peninsula. He laid claim to the Chinese Eastern and Southern Manchuria railroads and insisted that Mongolia stay "independent," which meant that it would fall under Russian control. Soviet troops should occupy half of Korea after the war, he said. And he demanded that FDR sell the deal to Chiang Kai-shek. In addition to attacking the Japanese in Manchuria, Stalin also promised to sign a treaty with the Nationalist government to bolster Chiang Kai-shek.

As in the past, no Chinese leader was involved in the discussions concerning China's fate. That made Chiang Kai-shek worry more. "The influence of this conference on China will be great," Chiang predicted in his diary. "I hope Roosevelt isn't plotting with Churchill and Stalin against me." The prospect plunged him into gloom. The Yalta deal, concluded secretly on February 11, 1945, allowed Russia to step into Japan's shoes in northeast Asia. In the space of a week, Roosevelt and Churchill had ceded to Stalin the privileges that China had spent fifteen years trying to deny Japan. The stage was then set for the Soviets to bend the course of China's revolution and Korea's future as well.

Roosevelt based his deal with Stalin on the faulty assumption that the Soviet Union would cooperate with the US in a postwar world and not act like an imperial power and carve out an empire. Robert Sherwood, a presidential speechwriter, understood that in Yalta, Roosevelt had broken all the agreements he had made with Chiang Kai-shek in Cairo, but he defended the president as being "tired and anxious to avoid further argument." Roosevelt hoped, Sherwood wrote, that "when the time came to notify the Chinese, he would be able to straighten the whole thing out."

The Yalta agreement cannot be explained simply as a case of American treachery or as the result of a vast Communist conspiracy. A dying Roosevelt was trying to save American lives. Generals George Marshall and Douglas MacArthur had insisted on a Soviet entry into the Asian theater because they believed that the United States would have to invade Japan, with an expected death toll of 350,000 American boys. No one knew whether the Manhattan Project to make a nuclear weapon would succeed. For Chiang Kai-shek, Yalta's terms were hard to take. Throughout the war, Chiang had pleaded with his allies to dispatch one million Western ground troops to China. He had wanted Americans; he would get Russians. And China would be forever changed.

On February 3, a day before he entered the conference hall to shake hands with Churchill and FDR, Stalin told Mao about the Red Army's imminent return to Asia. On receiving this news, Mao ordered Zhou Enlai, who had gone to Chongqing at Hurley's request for more talks, to terminate negotiations.

The news from Yalta emboldened Mao. Where just a few weeks earlier he had been offering to travel to the United States, now he called on party members to prepare for bloodshed in the struggle against America and Chiang Kai-shek. He coined the term *ChiangMei*—combining Chiang's last name with the first character for the United States. This was the party's new foe. Mao informed party members that massive Soviet aid would soon arrive. "If it fails to come, I will let you have my head," he declared. He stressed the central role that the Soviet Union would play in China's revolution. Though China's Communists needed to keep this secret, Mao cautioned, "there should be no mistake who is our leader. It is Stalin."

During the Seventh Congress of the Chinese Communist Party that spring, Mao demonstrated his fealty to Uncle Joe's totalitarian system. He assumed the chairmanship of all the party's ruling bodies, concentrating his power as never before. A new constitution enshrined "Mao Zedong

Thought" as its guiding principle. So, even as he voiced his support for democracy to US diplomats, among his Communist comrades, Mao had taken another step toward turning himself into a living god.

FDR, for his part, did not deem it necessary to tell Chiang Kai-shek what he had decided in Yalta. Chiang and Hurley had to discover it for themselves. Returning to Washington, Hurley struggled to uncover the outlines of the secret pact, visiting FDR twice before the president finally owned up to the arrangement. Hurley was stupefied. The concessions violated the principles of the Atlantic Charter, which mandated that territorial adjustments accord with the wishes of the affected peoples.

Roosevelt's team had in fact started having second thoughts about Yalta. Stalin had installed a puppet government in Poland and would soon violate his agreement to hold elections there. In Moscow, Ambassador Averell Harriman announced that Stalin's goal was the "establishment of totalitarianism." Still, though US officials understood that Stalin sought mastery of Europe, they were slow to see that he had similar designs on Asia.

In Washington, Hurley had just begun his battle with the China Hands. On April 2, 1945, following a meeting with Roosevelt, he held a press conference and declared that the United States would support only the central government of China. In the face of all evidence to the contrary, he pronounced himself optimistic that the Communists and Nationalists were "drawing closer together." He then used FDR's vote of confidence to purge the China Hands from the embassy. Davies was lucky; he had already left for Moscow. Service was recalled to Washington and reassigned, as were several others.

Hurley flew to London and Moscow to try to wrest pledges from Churchill and Stalin that they would abandon their territorial ambitions in China after the war. In a conversation with Churchill, he noted that if Britain kept Hong Kong, the Soviets could make a case for Manchuria. Churchill was dismissive and called Washington's China policy "the great American illusion." Stalin also refused to give up his privileges in Manchuria. But he reiterated his support for Chiang's government and promised not to back the "radishes," as he called the Chinese Communists, claiming that they were red only on the outside. American diplomats in Moscow tried to warn Hurley that he was being duped. As George Kennan observed, "There was ample advice to him which he showed no desire to tap."

Hurley returned to China to break the news of the Yalta deal to Chiang. China, Chiang wrote after he had been briefed, had been "sold out" and its war of resistance had been "in vain." It was an insult that China's sovereign rights had been given away once again. On April 12, 1945, amid all the horse-trading and backroom deals, Roosevelt died. In the preceding weeks, he had sent Chiang a series of telegrams urging him to make peace with the Communists, clearly hoping to solve that problem before the Soviets invaded Manchuria.

The passing of the American titan worried Chiang Kai-shek. For all his foibles, big plans, soothing words, and fickle promises, Roosevelt had shared with Chiang Kai-shek a vision of a strong China allied with the United States. His successor, Harry Truman, was an unknown. Would America now be swayed more by the British, who seemed intent on keeping China weak? Or by the American Left, which fancied Mao's men over Chiang's? Was Truman, Chiang asked, "sincere"?

●

CHAPTER TWENTY-FIVE

The Beginning of the End

Jack Service arrived in Washington on April 12, 1944, the day Roosevelt died. With his family in California, the gregarious Service sought the company of reporters interested in Asia. He met regularly with Philip Jaffe, a Ukrainian-born editor of *Amerasia*, a journal of Far Eastern affairs. Like Jaffe's other sources, Service provided *Amerasia* with classified reports.

In January 1945, the Office of Strategic Services, followed by the FBI, placed Jaffe under surveillance after his magazine ran, almost verbatim, the text of a secret OSS memo on British policy in Southeast Asia. The OSS broke into *Amerasia*'s Manhattan office and found piles of government documents, including those authored by Service. The FBI bugged Jaffe's office and put a tail on him. Service got roped into the investigation when he was taped at a Washington hotel telling Jaffe about "very secret" military information—presumably the plan to provide lethal aid to China's Communists.

Jaffe had connections with a wide group of leftists. He met with Soviet officials and Earl Browder, general secretary of the Communist Party of the United States. Several of his associates on the magazine, including Ji Chaoding (who was married to Jaffe's cousin) were Soviet plants or members of the Communist Party.

On June 6, 1945, the FBI dropped a bombshell, arresting six people for unauthorized possession and transmission of government documents.

Among them was Jack Service. "FBI Seizes Six as Spies, Two in State Department" read the headline in the *New York Times*. *Time* magazine called it the "biggest State-secrets case of the war." Recalling the incident years later, Service pronounced himself "overwhelmed with disgrace and shame." The Cold War was approaching. The Soviets had just announced their plans to occupy one-third of Germany. In America, the hunt for Communist spies had begun.

Service argued that it was routine for government officials to leak reports to journalists as background material. He had, after all, been authorized to do so by none other than Lauchlin Currie, the point man on China in Roosevelt's White House. For that reason, Currie, worried that he might be implicated, turned to FDR's old friend and Washington fixer, Tommy Corcoran. Corcoran promised Attorney General–designate Tom C. Clark that he would ease his confirmation through the Senate if Clark, according to historians Ronald Radosh and Harvey Klehr, went easy on Jack Service.

In August, a grand jury cleared Service of any wrongdoing by a vote of twenty to zero. Three of the six arrested were indicted. Jaffe pleaded guilty to "conspiracy to embezzle, steal and purloin" government property, paid a $2,500 fine, and avoided jail. Service won sympathetic treatment in the American press. At the *Washington Post*, Drew Pearson called his arrest "America's Dreyfus case," after the Jewish captain in the nineteenth-century French army who was falsely accused of espionage. Pearson explained Service's story as part of "the intense cut-throat rivalry between" the Nationalists and the Communists. "The USA is backing the wrong horse in China," Pearson wrote.

The *Amerasia* Affair was the first chapter in the bitter aftermath of America's entanglement in wartime China. Service, a thirty-five-year-old diplomat, became a lightning rod in the hunt by anti-Communist senators Joe McCarthy and Pat McCarran to root out those who "lost" China. The Communist *Liberation Daily* blasted Washington for Service's arrest, saying that it highlighted the deep division in the US between those who "acknowledge the Chinese people's great democratic force" and Yankee reactionaries. The paper singled out Hurley, calling him "the puppet master," with Chiang Kai-shek the puppet. The editorial was another sign of a shift in the party's view of the United States. Now that Stalin was riding to the rescue, Mao no longer needed to play nice with the Beautiful Country.

A few weeks before Service's arrest, on May 28, 1945, a team of five OSS men had parachuted behind Japanese lines near the town of Fuping in Hebei province. The Spaniel Mission, named for a team member's dog, was supposed to carry out sabotage operations against the Japanese. Instead of welcoming the Americans, however, Communist forces locked them up.

The Americans had landed on top of a Communist secret. Communist troops and those of the Japanese-installed puppet government had been cooperating, not battling, over vast expanses in China. As the OSS team wrote in an after-action report: "The amount of actual fighting being carried out [by the Communists] has been grossly exaggerated." It was Communist policy "to undertake no serious campaign against the Japanese or Puppets." The Communists imprisoned the Spaniel Mission for four months, leaving Wedemeyer and the OSS chief, "Wild Bill" Donovan, in the dark as to the team's fate.

Other OSS missions worried the Communists as well. One was run by Thomas Megan, a hard-drinking Catholic missionary from Iowa who had worked in northern China since 1926 and was known as "the Fighting Bishop." Megan's spies—the Little Brothers of St. John—unmasked eight Japanese double agents and unearthed details about Japanese troop movements, which Chennault's Fourteenth Air Force exploited with murderous efficiency.

Megan's extensive network weakened the Communist Party's greatest bargaining chip with the Americans—access to Japanese-occupied territory in northern China. And it challenged the Communists' claims. Megan and his peasant bands were fighting the Japanese while the Communists kept their powder dry. It was no wonder that in 1940, at the height of the war, the Communists captured and tortured Megan's predecessor, a Belgian monk named Vincent Lebbe. He died soon after he was released.

On July 7, 1945, the Communist Party issued a directive to study what it called the Fuping Incident and called for a boycott on cooperation with the United States. It ordered Red Army units to bar Americans from the front lines. "As soon as [US troops] enter our zones," the order said, "you must disarm them, block their communications." Megan's guerrillas were mentioned by name as a threat to the party.

Secure in the knowledge that Soviet aid was coming, Mao authorized his propaganda organs to again attack the United States. It was in 1945, wrote the *Liberation Daily*, that "the Chinese Communist Party finally became deeply convinced that the United States was a hostile, imperialistic country."

On August 6, 1945, the United States dropped an atomic bomb on Hiroshima. On August 8, a day before a B-29 Superfortress unleashed the second nuclear attack, on Nagasaki, one million men from the Soviet Red Army invaded Manchuria in a blitzkrieg-style offensive that crushed Japan's forces there. Washington cheered the news of the Soviet invasion. "Think of the kids who won't be killed!" President Truman wrote to his wife, Bess. On August 15, Japan surrendered.

The end of the war in the Pacific interrupted China's battle plans. Wedemeyer, who had been preparing an operation to punch through to China's coast, fretted that Nationalist China was not ready for victory. His OSS chief for China, Colonel Richard Heppner, put it succinctly: "We have been caught with our pants down." While his country celebrated, Chiang agonized. "Everybody takes this as a day of glory. I alone feel great shame and sorrow," he told his diary. He worried that Stalin and Mao would "plunge China into chaos and anarchy." If his government used military means to solve the Communist problem, the outlook would be "bleak," he acknowledged, because Russia would enter the conflict on Mao's side. But, he asked, what other choice did he have?

Chiang had sent his son Chiang Ching-kuo and T. V. Soong to Moscow to negotiate a treaty based on Yalta's terms. The Generalissimo was incensed at the Truman administration's refusal to push the Soviets for a better deal. "This is an insult," he told his diary. "I didn't acknowledge Yalta; I didn't take part. I don't have responsibility for it, so why should I carry it out. They really do think China is their vassal."

On August 14, a day before Japan's surrender, China and Russia signed a treaty. The Soviets assumed control of Mongolia. The czarist special rights in Manchuria, which Russia had lost to Japan in 1905, were restored. Moscow promised that any aid would "be entirely given to the Nationalist Government as the central government of China." Everyone was clear, however, that Stalin's agreement to recognize only Chiang Kai-shek was a weak reed on which to secure the stability of China. A US intelligence report concluded, "There is nothing in the treaty which specifically obligates the Soviets to exclude the Chinese Communists from Manchuria."

Indeed, Chinese Communist troops from the Eighty-Eighth International Brigade, led by Soviet officers and wearing the uniforms of the Soviet Red Cross, had spearheaded the USSR's charge into the northeast. The Soviet Red Army then looked the other way as more than one hundred thousand other Chinese Communist fighters slipped into the region from the south. On August 12, Mao wrote that the "political implications" of the Soviet invasion were "beyond any measurement." Two days later, he refused Chiang's invitation to peace talks in Chongqing. Mao thought he could take over China quickly—or at least the strategically crucial northeast.

Runaway inflation helped undo the Nationalists. As the end of the war approached, prices, which were already jumping upward at 10 percent a month, started rising even faster. Arthur Young, the longtime economic adviser to the Kuomintang, told the story of a Chinese couple who had saved for years for their son's college education. When he reached eighteen, their nest egg was enough to buy him a cake.

At the US Treasury Department, Morgenthau had soured on Chiang Kai-shek's regime, with some justification. China's minister of finance, H. H. Kung, was clearly incompetent. Then there was the advice Morgenthau was receiving from his closest advisers on China—Harry Dexter White, Frank Coe, and Solomon Adler.

During the 1950s, Senator Joe McCarthy and his followers alleged that White, Coe, and Adler conspired to prevent the United States from helping the Nationalist government tamp down inflation, leading to China's economic collapse and Communism's rise. In the 1980s, American historians argued that those allegations were false.

Since then, decrypted Soviet signals traffic from the Russian embassy has shown that White, Coe, and Adler had, indeed, collaborated with the Soviets. The Russians gave them code names—Jurist, Peak, and Sachs—and the troika shared intelligence with their Soviet handlers.

Harry Dexter White was a senior aide to Morgenthau and one of the architects of the International Monetary Fund and the World Bank. In the 1940s, while at Treasury, he hired eleven men who would cooperate with the Soviets, including the department's wartime representative in China, Solomon Adler, and Frank Coe, the director of the Treasury's Division of Monetary Research. White also helped Ji Chaoding, the undercover Communist agent, land a job inside the Nationalist Ministry of Finance as the personal assistant to Finance Minister H. H. Kung.

McCarthy's allegations against White, Coe, and Adler concern $200 million in gold that the United States was to provide to the Kuomintang as part of an effort to lower inflation. Morgenthau agreed to China's request for the gold in July 1943. But White, Coe, Adler, and Ji Chaoding argued against transfers. They maintained that pervasive corruption within the Nationalist government and its failure to adopt financial reforms meant that an infusion of gold would do little to control prices.

Morgenthau agreed to slow gold shipments. So did the War Department, which was focused on accomplishing its B-29 Matterhorn mission and wanted nothing heavy—including gold—taking up space on flights over the Hump. As a result, by July 1945, two years after Morgenthau had approved the transfer of $200 million in gold to China, only $29 million had made its way to Chongqing. Hyperinflation had set in, reaching more than 1,000 percent a year. At that point, Morgenthau, feeling that he had been misled by his advisers, reversed himself, telling White and others that they had put him "in an absolutely dishonorable position, and I think it's inexcusable."

McCarthy's charge that White, Coe, and Adler manipulated US policy was an exaggeration. Many other players, including Morgenthau himself and the War Department, were involved. But the three men were clearly a factor in weakening official American support for the Kuomintang.

During the McCarthy hunt for American Communists, Adler and Coe left the United States and ended up in China—Coe in the late 1950s and Adler in 1962. White, who was accused of being a Soviet spy, died in August 1948, three days after denying charges of Communist affiliation before the House Un-American Activities Committee. Adler maintained that he moved to Beijing because of his "unshakable faith in the cause of socialism." There, he helped translate Mao Zedong's writings into English. Coe worked for a Communist Party intelligence agency, writing propaganda heralding the success of the disastrous Great Leap Forward and reports on political developments in the West. Coe died in Beijing in 1980, Adler in 1994.

As World War II neared its end, American confidence in the riches of the China market returned. At the Thirty-first National Foreign Trade Convention in 1944, officials predicted that China's economy represented "the greatest area of future possibilities in the world." The Sino-American Industrial and Commercial Association, a business group started in 1943, had close to four hundred members by the end of the war. Lobbying the State Department, the group advocated whole-scale privatization of China's state-owned firms and low tariffs, especially on American goods.

The US Department of Commerce estimated that China's international trade would hit $1 billion, with the United States accounting for a quarter. Writers such as Randall Gould urged Americans to make Shanghai into an American city, just as Hong Kong had become British. In August 1945, a survey of American business leaders found many eager to resume operations in China. "We're all straining at the leash," said an executive from Chase National Bank.

US officials urged Americans who had lived in China's commercial capital of Shanghai, including those who had spent the war in Japanese internment camps, to pick up where they had left off. Channeling Caleb Cushing's mission in 1844, the Americans touted the idea that now, finally, the United States would replace Great Britain as the dominant commercial power in the Pacific.

General Wedemeyer encouraged Americans to take advantage of the opportunities presented by peace. He convinced Chiang Kai-shek to order all cars, as of January 1, 1946, to drive on the right side of the road. The stated reason was safety; US military vehicles were killing Chinese pedestrians at an accelerating clip. But the result guaranteed a bigger market for American automobiles. Wedemeyer convinced Chiang to reject a British offer to build China's navy and used his influence to cancel a planned sale of British aircraft frames to the Nationalist air force.

Wedemeyer called for massive US financial and military assistance to China. Under his plan, China would not be permitted to purchase weapons from any foreign powers without consulting the United States, and US representatives would supervise "the development of Chinese commercial aviation, communication and navigation systems." American influence would be cemented.

The Navy, War, and State Departments debated Wedemeyer's proposal. At State, John Carter Vincent attacked the idea. The United States should get involved only if China became "unified and democratic," he argued. Wedemeyer disagreed. Like generations of Americans before him, he believed that China needed a strongman leader, "a benevolent despot or a military dictator," as he wrote in a cable to the War Department on August 17, 1945. Neither the Nationalists nor the Communists were angels, but Chiang Kai-shek, he wrote, was the least bad of the bunch. The State Department ignored his advice.

In November 1945, Wedemeyer moved the headquarters of the China Theater to Shanghai. Thousands of American troops, Seabees, and merchant marines streamed through the city. On the Bund, in the shadow of the Hong Kong and Shanghai Bank building, the Cathay Hotel, and other crenelated symbols of Britain's colonial imprint, a simple wooden shack attested to America's intrusion onto British turf. "US Navy Hamburger Stand" read its sign. At one point that autumn, of the ninety ships anchored in Shanghai harbor, eighty-five were American. "My boy," one enthusiastic Yankee businessman told *Time* magazine for its November 26, 1945, edition, "Shanghai is due for the biggest boom in history." By the year's end, the United States had become China's biggest trading partner. American goods made up nearly 60 percent of China's imports, while 40 percent of China's exports went to the United States.

None of this, however, meant that Chiang's government was ready to welcome American capitalism. In *China's Destiny*, Chiang had already vowed that his country would follow neither the American nor the Soviet model. The economy would be mixed, with the government controlling key sectors and private business making up the rest. A Western economy was "founded on lust," Chiang wrote. His China would measure economic success by the benefits that accrued to the nation, not to individuals.

In the end, American businesses would see their dream of the China market dissipate like fog under a blazing sun. And Chiang's government, expecting a huge injection of American cash and technology, would get neither capital nor know-how. Once again both sides would be disappointed.

One reason for this was America's muddled message. Ever since the days of the Rockefeller Foundation in China, some American economists had championed the idea of a planned economy for the country. When T. V. Soong told FDR in 1943 that China's postwar plans were for a "strongly socialist" economy, Roosevelt responded, "I am exceedingly glad to hear that." And when the president dispatched Donald Nelson, the former head of the American War Production Board, to China in 1944 to help the Nationalists boost production, Nelson and his assistants agreed that the Chinese government should control a major share of the economic pie.

Nelson promoted big government-backed projects similar to the New Deal's Tennessee Valley Authority. At his bidding, the Bureau of Reclamation dispatched engineers to draw up plans for the damming of the Yangtze, planting an American seed that would bear fruit six decades later in the Three Gorges Dam. Yet simultaneously, State Department officials advocated cutting the government's participation in the economy. Nelson's advocacy of a state-controlled economy emboldened Chiang's advisers to stiff-arm the State Department. So, plans for joint US-Chinese oil exploration ran aground, for example, because the Chinese would not allow the Americans to own a majority in the concern. Chiang's economic advisers announced that vast areas of the economy—energy, mines, and railways— would be closed to American investment.

Negotiations on what would be formally known as the Friendship, Commerce and Navigation Treaty and Protocol between the United States of America and China dragged on for three years before it was finally signed in November 1946. On paper, the treaty welcomed American capital, but American CEOs were reluctant to invest. Samuel Broers, the president of Firestone Tire and Rubber, hesitated to put a dime into China because he was not sure whether Firestone would be able to control its business there. James Fullam, an executive at the ITT Corporation, worried that Nationalist bureaucrats would shut down the ITT-owned Shanghai Telephone Company.

As the war ended, the Nationalist government moved to put even more of the economy into its own hands. By 1947, the National Resources Commission, the government's bureau of state-run industries, controlled one-third of all mines, almost half the cement production, two-thirds of electricity generation, 90 percent of iron, steel, and sugar production, and all of China's oil wells. And these were supposed to be free-market partners of the United States.

Muddled policy was not confined to the economy. In the days following Japan's defeat, as Soviet troops spread throughout Manchuria and welcomed the Chinese Communists, the Truman administration took a series of contradictory steps that exemplified America's confused approach to China.

On August 11, 1945, President Truman announced the end to all military "assistance except that required to support the reoccupation mission" in China. All programs "designed only to strengthen the Chinese Army," Truman ruled, would be shut down. Six days later, General Douglas MacArthur, now the supreme commander of Allied Forces in the Pacific, issued General Order Number One, instructing Japanese forces to surrender only to the Chinese Nationalist army, except in Manchuria, where the Soviets held sway.

On the heels of MacArthur's order, the Joint Chiefs directed Wedemeyer to move Chiang's armies, which were mostly in the southwest, to Nanjing and Shanghai so that they could be deployed north on US Navy ships. Wedemeyer called it "the largest troop movement by air in the world's history." He was not exaggerating.

The massive air- and sealift placed the United States on the side of Nationalist China as civil war loomed. The United States provided additional support to Chiang when it dispatched two divisions of US Marines to occupy major cities, railway hubs, and ports in China's north. And yet simultaneously, the Joint Chiefs warned Wedemeyer not to "prejudice the basic principle that the United States will not support the Central Government in China in fratricidal war."

Wedemeyer was squeezed between his orders. He had to help National-ist forces resume control of the country. But the US government had for-bidden him to meddle in the civil war. "It is impossible to avoid involvement in political strife or fratricidal warfare under present cir-cumstances," Wedemeyer complained, "yet I am admonished to do so by my directive." After consulting with Wedemeyer in Washington, Tru-man reversed his policy in the fall of 1945 and agreed to train and equip thirty-nine divisions of ground troops and fifteen air squadrons and to establish a US military advisory group in China. But there was a catch: in the event of civil war, when the Nationalists would need the help, the aid would stop.

Wedemeyer urged Washington to focus on China. On August 14, he told the Joint Chiefs that he viewed Asia as "an enormous pot, seething and boiling." If Washington did not seize the initiative, the steam from that cauldron "may readily snuff out the advantages gained by Allied sacrifices in the past several years." He believed that the key to stability in Asia resided in Washington and Moscow. The United States and the USSR had to cut a deal over China. United pressure from Stalin and Truman consti-tuted "the only sure method of avoiding a civil war between the Com-munist and Central Government forces with all of its potentially explosive consequences."

Washington responded to Wedemeyer's entreaties by leaning on Chiang to begin talks on a united government. Chiang had already invited Mao to Chongqing in early August, and Mao had rejected him twice, but Stalin reined in his disciple and ordered him to the talks.

In his memoirs, Mao's Russian translator, Shi Zhe, reported that Mao was "very distressed and even angry" about going to Chongqing. But Sta-lin, meeting with Mao's deputy, Liu Shaoqi, in Moscow explained his rea-soning. The negotiations in Chongqing were a smokescreen, he said, to give China's Communists time to mobilize their troops.

On August 27, 1945, Patrick Hurley flew to Yanan to escort the fifty-two-year-old Communist Party boss on his first airplane ride. Soon after Mao left for Chongqing, a representative of General Rodion Malinovsky, the commander of the Soviet Red Army in Manchuria, arrived in Yanan. Lieu-tenant Colonel Dmitri Belorussov told his Communist friends that Soviet forces in the northeast would look the other way if the Chinese took Com-munist insignias off their uniforms and occupied areas other than those already held by Stalin's army. Chinese military commander Zhu De spoke of a "unique opportunity" for the Communist cause. As the Eighth Route

Army's orders put it, the USSR "takes an indulgent attitude toward our activity in the Northeast as long as we don't cause diplomatic difficulties."

Wedemeyer, meanwhile, made a series of suggestions to Chiang. He had urged on the Generalissimo a "liberalized policy with reference to freedom of speech and writing." He told Chiang that he should move his troops into northern China but not go into Manchuria. If Chiang's forces pushed north of the Great Wall, Wedemeyer warned, they would ultimately be cut off. As for Manchuria, he told both Chiang and Washington, the best way to deal with it would be to place it under a trusteeship, policed by the Soviets, the Americans, and the British.

Wedemeyer worried that Chiang had "a lack of appreciation" for the challenges of holding China's northeast. Chiang was so impatient to seize it that he sent his forces north without winter clothing. Wedemeyer halted at least one troop movement to wait for shipments of US Army surplus from Alaska. What Chiang should do, Wedemeyer argued, was regain control of northern China below the Great Wall and strengthen his position in the South. In his reports to Truman, Wedemeyer discussed his belief that Chiang would not be able to unite China for many years. In contemplating a partitioning of the Middle Kingdom, Wedemeyer had hit on perhaps the single best way to deal with the Chinese Communist threat. But he was also going against more than a century of American belief in the idea of a united China.

Naturally, Wedemeyer's ideas found no purchase in the Truman administration; Chiang also rejected the trusteeship idea because as a Nationalist he wanted foreigners to stop meddling in China. As tensions mounted, Chiang moved his forces farther into the northeast.

On August 20, 1945, an OSS captain named John Birch led a team of thirteen officers into Shandong province. The Americans were scouting for landing strips that could be used to repatriate American prisoners of war held in Japanese camps in China. Thousands of Allied POWs had been discovered in China in the weeks after the war, many of them starving to death.

John Birch had come to China in 1940 with the World Fundamentalist Baptist Missionary Fellowship and evangelized in Hangzhou before it fell to Japanese troops. As the Japanese seized cities up and down the Yangtze Delta, he had fled inland. In April 1942, when Jimmy Doolittle and his team parachuted over China after bombing Tokyo, Birch helped save them and steer them to safety. Doolittle told Chennault about Birch's heroism, and Chennault took Birch on as a first lieutenant of the Fourteenth Air Force. Birch established twelve intelligence cells from the Yellow River to

Beijing. He earned praise from the US military as "one of the outstanding intelligence officers in our organization."

In Shandong, Communist Chinese troops discovered Birch and his team and demanded that they hand over their weapons. Birch declined. "Peace has come to all the world and still you make trouble here. Why?" Birch asked. Surrounded by Communist troops, Birch asked to speak to a commanding officer but none stepped forward. Finally, one Communist officer ordered the Americans to drop their weapons. But when Dong Qinsheng, a Nationalist officer accompanying Birch, moved to hand over his firearm, the Communists shot him in the leg. Then they fired on Birch.

Birch's body was later found, arms and feet bound, on a cinder pile in a railroad yard. To hide his identity, the Communists had mutilated his face. "The job was so thorough," read a US Army report, "that nothing but bone was left." What the Communists committed on August 25, 1945, the army declared, was "murder."

Birch's execution sent shock waves through Wedemeyer's command. Though some Western historians have argued unconvincingly that Birch's death was an isolated incident, the late Chinese scholar Ren Dong-lai, citing internal party documents, showed that following the Fuping Incident, Mao's party had ended all cooperation with the United States and had adopted a hostile policy toward US military activity in China.

Wedemeyer suppressed news of Birch's death as he sought a working relationship with the Communists. No major American newspaper reported it. Birch's parents were told that he had been killed "as the result of stray bullets fired by Communist forces," and he was therefore denied a Purple Heart. Details of his death were finally revealed in September 1950 in the Senate as part of the battle over who "lost" China.

John Birch is commemorated as the first casualty of the Cold War. Thirteen years after his death, a group of anti-Communists in the United States founded the John Birch Society, which grew into one of the most influential conservative groups in America. It's another illustration of the enigmatic connection between these nations that an American missionary and spy killed in China inspired a political movement in the US.

Mao spent most of August 1945 in Chongqing as he and Chiang went through the motions of hammering out a peace accord. At root, however, the issue of who would control the Communist army was never settled— and never would be.

While the two old enemies made nice in Chongqing, their forces readied for battle. Two days after the talks began, Wedemeyer's transport planes airlifted Nationalist troops to Nanjing and Shanghai. From Shanghai, the US Navy transported Chiang's forces north, but Soviet forces in Manchuria refused to allow the US ships to dock at Dalian. And when five hundred Nationalist officials arrived in the Manchurian city of Changchun, the Soviets would not let them leave. Mao noted that the Soviet occupation of the northeast was "the golden opportunity that occurs once in a thousand years."

On September 18, Mao declared that "we must stop civil war and all parties must unite under the leadership of Chairman Chiang to build modern China." Chiang was conciliatory, too. The two sides issued a vague statement about establishing a democracy and a united army, but once back in Yanan, Mao told his comrades that it was "a mere scrap of paper." To the Soviet representative, he confided that civil war was "virtually inevitable." On October 19, the Chinese Communist leadership decided to "go all out to control the entire Northeast."

On November 12, Chinese Communist forces took over Changchun from the Soviets. Eight days later, Yanan instructed its forces in the northeast "to pretend that the Chinese Communist Party has no connection with the Soviet Union." The purpose of this policy, it said, was to "neutralize the United States" and ensure that America would not throw its strength behind Chiang Kai-shek.

On November 28, 1945, the Communist Party's "Directive on the Strategy of Struggle Against the US and Chiang" laid out Mao's tactics for the next four years. The Communists sided with the Soviets, it said, but to fool America and China's moderates, they needed to keep their distance from their Soviet comrades "in appearance" while cooperating with them "in substance."

The Second World War saved the Chinese Communist Party. In 1937, when hostilities erupted, the party had dwindled to forty thousand members, and it controlled barely any turf. By the time World War II ended, the Communists boasted more than one million members, an army of more than nine hundred thousand, and territory that stretched over one-third of China. The Soviet Union, the party's chief ally, had occupied China's strategic northeast and was funneling weapons into the party's armory and money into its accounts.

The party's challenge was to ensure that America not enter the civil war on the side of Chiang Kai-shek. To do that, Mao Zedong, Zhou Enlai, and other senior Communists courted the United States and gave American diplomats the impression that they would welcome American investment, ideas, and influence in the New China. For decades, some American scholars argued that Mao was serious and that America lost a chance with the Communists in 1945. But more recent research by historians such as Chen Jian has all but demolished this notion. All along, Mao was committed to siding with the Soviet Union in the approaching Cold War. There really was no lost chance for the United States in China.

For the Generalissimo, paradoxically, if Japan had held out longer, the Nationalist regime might have been saved. But when Japan surrendered, Chiang's armies were unprepared for victory. While the United States continued naively to hope for peace in China, Mao, Chiang, and Stalin girded for war.

●

CHAPTER TWENTY-SIX

Mission Impossible

On November 26, 1945, barely an hour after assuring President Truman that he would be returning to China, Patrick Hurley announced his resignation as ambassador, alleging, in a scathing letter that he read aloud at the National Press Club, that State Department officials were siding "with the Communist armed party and at times with the imperialist bloc against American policy."

At a cabinet meeting that day, Truman was livid. "See what the son of a bitch did to me," he exclaimed. Responding to allegations of Communist infiltration from Hurley and other prominent Republicans, Truman ordered an investigation of federal employees, resulting in the formation of Loyalty Boards throughout the government. The president also called George Marshall, who was six days into retirement as army chief of staff, and ordered him "to go back and finish the job in China that Hurley left."

In November 1945, George Catlett Marshall, the architect of the Allied victory in World War II, was a five-star general and a national icon. Truman called the sixty-five-year-old hero "the great one of the age." Five days before Marshall's plane touched down in Shanghai on December 20, 1945, Truman issued a statement explaining that America's goal was "a strong, united and democratic China." This required the Nationalists to end their monopoly on power and institute "a broadly representative government." The Communists should be allowed to enter the government on the condition that they somehow merge their units into the Nationalist army.

It is truly amazing that Truman could believe that Marshall, one man with a puny staff, a limited understanding of China, and no army, was going to stop Chiang Kai-shek and Mao Zedong from continuing a decades-old war for control of China. But Americans had always thought that they had a special way with the Chinese, and the ill-fated Marshall Mission fit neatly with the American expectation of a "blitzconversion" of China, in this case into a multiparty democracy with a free press, an independent judiciary, and a united army. In reality, Marshall's mission was doomed from the start; he was supposed to forge a democracy, but not one that would ultimately threaten Chiang Kai-shek's rule. As Chiang observed of American diplomats and their schemes, "They talk a great deal but really do very little, even to the extent of making a bold beginning but then settling for a weak conclusion."

When they heard that Marshall would mediate, the Nationalists were worried. Yan Xishan, a liberal-minded warlord in central China, predicted that Marshall's intervention would simply give the Communists time to gain strength. For their part, Mao and Zhou Enlai were elated and, true to Yan's analysis, welcomed the effort as a chance to prepare for war.

The Communists did their best to impress Marshall with their eagerness to cooperate. Their spies planted bogus intelligence to convince the Americans that they were serious about peace. In 1946, Communist agents infiltrated the office of an OSS officer in the US Consulate in Shanghai. The operatives plied the officer with phony reports attesting to the party's commitment to peace, according to a 1981 memoir by Zhang Zhiyi, the former head of Communist intelligence in Shanghai. US analysts took these reports seriously. "Our successful disinformation strategy," Zhang wrote, "gained us half a year more time for our armed forces to train and prepare."

Like Stilwell, Marshall had served in China, commanding the Fifteenth Infantry Regiment in Tianjin in the 1920s. Marshall had inherited a dislike of Chiang Kai-shek from Stilwell as well as the belief that the Communists were the ones actually fighting the Japanese. Colonel Ivan Yeaton, who had replaced David Barrett as the chief of the Dixie Mission to Yanan and then served as Wedemeyer's chief intelligence officer, recalled briefing Marshall on the Chinese Communists, stressing that contrary to much State Department reporting, they were not "agrarian reformers" but "pure Marx, Lenin and Mao." Marshall did not seem interested. "If he had heard a word I said," Yeaton wrote in his memoirs, "he did not show it."

Many of Marshall's contemporaries thought that he had embarked on a fool's errand. On the day Marshall arrived in Shanghai, Wedemeyer escorted him to his room at the Cathay Hotel and told his old comrade that nothing could stop a civil war. Marshall responded angrily: "I am going to accomplish my mission and you are going to help me."

If Marshall's goals—a peaceful, united, democratic China—were pie-in-the-sky, the Nationalists and Communists were more practical. Chiang Kai-shek looked at the mission as yet another American fantasy to be tolerated as long as the US continued to stake him enough money and weaponry to crush the Communist bandits. The Communists viewed the endeavor as providing an array of opportunities. They could use it to enter a coalition government on an equal footing with the Nationalists and wait to seize total power at a later date. Or they could employ it to prepare to fight. Marshall's mission to China did not lay the foundations for peace; it set the parameters for war.

Japan's defeat generated another wave of pro-American feelings among many Chinese and a belief in America's ability to solve China's problems. US Marines, sailing into Tianjin, were welcomed by bands, smiles, and posters reading, "Hail to Our Glorious Allies and Cooperators." In Beijing, when locals said they were *ban Mei shi* or "doing things the American way," it meant they were doing them the right way. The *Ta Kung Pao* greeted George Marshall's arrival to China with a simple headline: "The Morning Sun Is About to Rise."

Marshall's first weeks went swimmingly. By early January 1946, he had convinced Chiang to call off an offensive in northern China to cut Chinese Communist forces in Manchuria off from their forces south of the Great Wall. A truce was set for January 10, 1946. On that same day, the Nationalists, Communists, and representatives of smaller liberal parties met in Chongqing. There Chiang promised to protect civil liberties, release political prisoners, abolish press censorship, and legalize political parties. The representatives drafted a new constitution modeled on the US Constitution and celebrations broke out nationwide. Never before in Chinese history had an assembly of freely competing political parties been convened. On mainland China, it would be the first and only time.

By February 1946, the Nationalists and Communists had settled on the outlines of a deal to merge their armed forces. At the American embassy, the doubters began to believe. "When he pulled off the cease fire which nobody really thought he could do, we suddenly had this kind of wild hope that maybe the great man can do it," recalled embassy staffer John Melby.

In a memo to Truman, Marshall argued that the US Marine divisions that had deployed to accept the Japanese surrender should leave so that the Soviets would be forced to pull out, too. "We must clear our hands out here as quickly as possible," he told Truman on February 9, 1946. But while the marines sped up the repatriation of some four million Japanese troops and civilians from China, the Russians in Manchuria passed weapons to their Communist friends. Chinese historian Yang Kuisong has estimated that the Soviets provided enough weapons to equip several hundred thousand Chinese troops. This benefaction, Yang has concluded, tipped the balance of power in the northeast.

Flush with his initial success, Marshall returned to Washington in March to report to the president. At that point, Melby noted, "We all had a sense, the minute he left, that this thing was going to blow up." And blow up it did. The Soviet Red Army had delayed its pullout from Manchuria for almost six months. By March 1946, however, the Russians quickened their withdrawal. American intelligence officials estimated that Soviet troops stripped $900 million worth of industrial equipment from the northeast. "They'd tear out the light switches," recalled US Army officer Henry Byroade, who witnessed the aftermath of the Red Army's heist. As the Soviets left, China's Communists moved in. Stalin turned Shenyang, Manchuria's capital, over to the Communists, and at the end of April 1946, the Soviets handed them Harbin, the northernmost big city. Meanwhile, in southern Manchuria, Nationalist forces were rushing in to fill the vacuum left by the Russians' departure.

On March 5, Winston Churchill traveled to Fulton, Mississippi, with President Truman to deliver the famous speech warning that an "iron curtain" was dividing Europe and calling for an Anglo-American alliance to oppose Soviet expansionism. Truman ordered Secretary of State James Byrnes not to "play compromise" with Stalin any longer: he now wanted America to "rehabilitate China and create a strong central government."

Moscow prodded China's Communists to take the gloves off. The leadership of China's Communist Party directed Zhou Enlai to return from Chongqing to Yanan, ending talks with the Kuomintang. On March 15, it observed, "In Manchuria the conflict . . . will now begin." By the time Marshall returned to China on April 18, full-scale civil war had erupted. On April 20, the headline in the *New York Times* read, "Marshall's Efforts Fail."

In July, Marshall engineered the appointment of John Leighton Stuart to replace Patrick Hurley as US ambassador to China. Marshall had passed over Wedemeyer in favor of a candidate who knew both Nationalists and Communists on intimate terms. Born in Zhejiang province to missionary parents, Stuart could speak with both Chiang Kai-shek and Zhou Enlai in their local dialect. From 1919 to 1941, he had presided over Yenching University, turning the Beijing institution into China's greatest university. He had taught and protected underground Communist Party members for years. After Japan's seizure of Beijing, Stuart refused to fly the Japanese flag over the Yenching campus and spent almost four years in a Japanese internment camp.

Stuart was the consummate friend of China. In the 1910s, he had battled with fundamentalist Christians, arguing that Americans should educate the Chinese more and proselytize them less. Presbyterian authorities in the United States had accused him of heresy, but he'd beaten the charges. Stuart had been an early advocate of tearing up the unequal treaties with China, calling on the United States in 1925 to take the lead with "an act of aggressive good will." He supported the Nationalist revolution from its earliest days and had grown close to Chiang Kai-shek. The American government hoped that Stuart's feel for the culture and his deep ties with many on both sides of the Communist-Nationalist divide would bring about a miracle.

John Melby, who observed Stuart from his perch as one of the US embassy's experts on Communism, found him more Chinese than American. "Dr. Stuart knows nothing and cares less about how the American Government works, nor does he really know too much about America in general," Melby wrote. As fighting intensified between Chinese factions, Melby wrote, Stuart watched "a lifetime going down the drain."

For the next two years, the Communists and Nationalists battled for the strategic northeast. Marshall warned Chiang Kai-shek time and again that even though his forces appeared to have the upper hand, the circuitous lines into the region—hundreds of miles of railway and bad roads—meant that his armies risked being cut off.

But other Americans were always willing to help out. In 1946, Claire Chennault, along with legendary fixer Tommy Corcoran, founded a new airline to provide airlifts for the United Nations relief agencies in China. Civil Air Transport, as it was called, soon began shuttling more than aid. It transported Nationalist reinforcements and ammunition into cities surrounded by Communist troops. Within a few years, the Central Intelligence

Agency would purchase the operation for $2 million, change its name to Air America, and use it in clandestine operations throughout Asia.

America's official response to Chiang's increasingly perilous situation was, as usual, confused. In December 1945, Truman had told Marshall that if negotiations collapsed, the United States would support Chiang Kai-shek. But on July 2, 1946, then acting secretary of state Dean Acheson informed Marshall that if full-scale civil war erupted, the United States would stop backing the Nationalists and leave China. There was no mention of Truman's earlier commitment to Chiang.

Then in the summer of 1946, the Truman administration agreed to transfer millions of dollars' worth of military equipment to Chiang's forces. But on July 29, Marshall slapped an arms embargo on the Nationalists that would last ten months. Chiang Kai-shek could be forgiven for being perplexed. "Even when we offer to pay cash for American weapons, their State Department still refuses to issue an export license," he complained.

In January 1947, Marshall ended his mission and left China to become Truman's secretary of state. In a public statement, Marshall blamed both sides for his failure. John Leighton Stuart did not agree. As Marshall readied to leave, Stuart met with him one last time. The United States, Stuart told Marshall, should "have either given sufficient aid to the National Government . . . or we should have withdrawn." Instead, the Americans had opted for "a hesitating, half-hearted form of continuing assistance," which guaranteed Chiang's defeat.

Most biographers have treated the failure of the Marshall Mission as a blip in a career of untarnished success. But Marshall's defeat in China had a deep effect on his later work in Europe with the Marshall Plan and in fashioning a strategy to confront Communism. Never again would the general advocate a negotiated power-sharing agreement with a Communist regime. With diplomat George Kennan, he would become an architect of a containment strategy that involved massive support for anti-Communist governments that endured for more than thirty years.

As the Marshall Mission fizzled, the Chinese Communist Party upped its attacks on America. Like Chiang Kai-shek, Chairman Mao was disenchanted with the United States. He had hoped that the Americans would end up facilitating his revolution by peaceful means. Now he understood that he would have to fight for it. "We made mistakes in our work during the previous period," he told party members in 1947 as the civil war blazed.

"It was the first time for us to deal with the U.S. imperialists. . . . We won't be cheated again."

The US Marines deployed to China to accept the Japanese surrender were an easy target. Communist newspapers claimed that the marines were the advance guard of a new foreign occupation. Starting in June 1946, party cells at universities across the country were ordered to protest the US military presence in China. The nation's students responded enthusiastically, organizing a "U.S. Forces Get Out of China Week."

The marines wanted to leave, too. They had been hailed as heroes, but they had worn out their welcome. American servicemen had brawled in cafés, beaten up rickshaw pullers and money changers, and fought with Chinese police. In Shanghai, between September 1945 and January 1946, there were four hundred traffic accidents involving US Army vehicles. Admiral Charles M. Cooke, the commander of the Seventh Fleet, bemoaned his men's lawlessness, lamenting "crimes of gang violence," including "knifing and blackjackings" of Chinese. "Even our friends think we are bums and bullies and ruffians," reported the *Stars and Stripes*.

The American troops felt trapped between the Nationalists and the Communists and lashed out at innocent Chinese. Marine Lieutenant Richard C. Kennard, who had admired China as a "real civilization," soon felt that he and his men were "only sticking around in a hell hole" where "the inhabitants live like pigs." Communist troops took potshots at his positions, while Nationalist troops just "stood around," expecting the marines to do all the work. The *North China Marine* asked the question on everyone's mind: "When are we going home?"

Communist accusations against the United States took on the hyperbolic fanaticism that would characterize anti-American propaganda for the next half century. The Communists falsely accused the US Army Air Force of strafing their positions in the northeast and charged the navy with plotting to seize in perpetuity the port of Qingdao. On July 29, 1946, Communist forces ambushed a marine convoy of relief supplies headed to Beijing as it drove through the village of Anping, fifty miles northwest of Tianjin, killing three marines and wounding eleven others. The *Liberation Daily* claimed that the marines had fired first and demanded an American apology and compensation. Internal Communist reports acknowledged, however, that their men had set the trap. "On July 29, when U.S. vehicles arrived, our forces opened fire first," read one report, "but we should not admit this in negotiations."

In September 1946, another week of demonstrations erupted on campuses across China. On September 29, the Central Committee issued a general directive to its underground operatives. "The movement should turn to a new direction," it said. "It should publicize the atrocities of the U.S. military." So began a nationwide "Anti-American Atrocity Campaign." Communist papers falsely claimed that sixty thousand American troops remained in China, when there were fewer than ten thousand.

Then, on Christmas Eve 1946, the Communists got the atrocity they had been waiting for. A nineteen-year-old Peking University student named Shen Chong was grabbed in downtown Beijing by two US Marines, who took her to an open field, where one of them, Corporal William G. Pierson, allegedly raped her. On December 30, eight thousand students marched in Beijing to protest the purported crime. A day later, the Central Committee of the Chinese Communist Party ordered underground operatives to take control of this issue to demand not only justice but a US withdrawal. In Shanghai, thousands of demonstrators at Fudan University shouted, "Go home!" One poster read: "Japan Was Not as Bad." Pierson was tried in an American military court, convicted, and sentenced to fifteen years in prison and a dishonorable discharge. The verdict was overturned after he returned to the United States.

The Shen Chong case gave the Communists ammunition as they angled to turn public opinion against the United States. Earlier in 1946, when the terms of the Yalta agreement were formally revealed in China, student protests had focused on Soviet depredations in Manchuria, including hundreds of rapes. But thanks to the Communist campaign, an anti-American movement had replaced anti-Soviet fury. Mao was ecstatic. Great progress, he said, had been made in "the nationwide struggle against imperialism and feudalism."

CHAPTER TWENTY-SEVEN

A Third Force

In February 1947, the British told the Americans that they could no longer afford to aid the royalist government in Greece, which was struggling to avert a Communist takeover. Turkey, too, was in danger of becoming a Soviet satellite. Truman stepped into the breach, telling Congress on March 12 that the United States must help "free people who are resisting attempted subjugation." In addition to military aid and advice, the Americans readied a massive program to rebuild Europe—the Marshall Plan.

Truman's announcement rekindled Chiang Kai-shek's hope that America would come to his rescue and that the president now viewed China's civil war as part of a global rivalry between the US and the USSR. Chiang's ambassador, the veteran diplomat Wellington Koo, worked the halls of Congress, arguing that China deserved military assistance as much as Greece and Turkey. He entreated Henry Luce and other friends of the Nationalist cause to write positive stories about the Kuomintang.

But Marshall, now secretary of state, told Congress on February 20 that for America to roll back the Communists in China, the United States would have "to take over the Chinese Government." It was too big a task. Asked what a Communist China would mean for the United States, he replied that it would be too weak to constitute a threat. His State Department colleagues agreed. In a joint cable, Acheson and John Vincent Carter predicted that instead of Communism in China, a new era of warlordism would set in.

For the Truman administration, the Truman Doctrine, whereby the

United States committed to assisting anti-Communist regimes worldwide, did not apply to China. As the president told his cabinet in March 1947, giving China more aid would be "pouring sand into a rat hole." But Chiang still had friends in America. In May 1947, congressional pressure forced Marshall to lift the arms embargo that he had slapped on Chiang's regime nine months before. Still, no one on either side of the US political divide advocated spilling American blood to stop the Communists' rise.

In July 1947, Marshall sent Albert Wedemeyer, who had left China in April 1946, back to China to report on the situation. It was a shrewd move; Marshall calculated that Wedemeyer, an ardent anti-Communist, would agree that Chiang was finished and thus help ward off the China Lobby.

On August 22, 1947, after interviewing scores of officials and traveling the country, Wedemeyer addressed a joint meeting of the State Council and other senior Nationalist leaders in Nanjing. He "excoriated them for practically every public—and even private—vice ever known," John Melby wrote. One senior Nationalist official wept at the criticism. Wedemeyer called on the Nationalists to institute "drastic, far-reaching" changes. "Promises will no longer suffice," he said. "Performance is absolutely necessary." Back in the United States, Wedemeyer argued, contrary to Marshall's bet, that the fall of the Republic of China directly threatened the security of the United States and that Washington needed to double down on the Generalissimo. He advocated a massive aid program to save the regime, reiterating his proposal to turn Manchuria, now almost completely controlled by the Communists, into an international trusteeship. The scheme would have amounted to the partition of China into a Communist north and a south run by Chiang Kai-shek. The State Department suppressed his recommendations.

Still, in Washington, the wind was shifting in the direction of the Kuomintang regime. Campaigning for the White House in the fall of 1947, Republican candidate Thomas Dewey blasted Truman's China policy. Republicans, who had taken over Congress in the midterm elections of 1946, threatened to hold up Truman's aid package for Western Europe unless he did something for Chiang Kai-shek. In February 1948, Truman reluctantly approved more than $400 million in economic assistance and $125 million in military aid for China. The State Department did fend off Republican attempts to deploy American advisers with Nationalist combat units as the United States was doing in Greece. And it also dallied on the aid. It wasn't until November 16 that the first supplies under the China Aid Act began arriving.

With the aid package approved, Wellington Koo allowed himself a bit of optimism. "China in 5000 years of her history has had many crises, some worse than this one," he told his diary. The year 1948, he believed, was no worse than 1938; one just needed "faith." But "faith" in the Nationalists was in short supply. Defeat piled atop defeat as the Communist army, equipped with a hodgepodge of Japanese, American, and Soviet weaponry, seized most of China's north.

The end of World War II forced China's American-educated liberals to make a difficult choice between two illiberal parties. For years, China's "Third Force" had struggled barehanded against the two armed camps— the Communists and the Nationalists—arguing that a free society would make China strong. Pleading for a peaceful settlement between Chiang and Mao, the Third Force, consisting of several thousand mostly American-educated intellectuals, adopted the role of the nation's conscience.

Throughout World War II, the Third Force had concentrated in Kunming, where China's three great universities—the US-funded Tsinghua University, Nankai University, founded by American-educated Zhang Boling, and Peking University—had decamped to avoid the Japanese. There, in a city known for splendid scenery and devastating poverty, the Third Force waited.

But as the war ended, instead of cultivating China's conscience, Chiang Kai-shek cracked down. In October 1945, he ousted Long Yun, the warlord in Yunnan province who had sheltered the liberals. Next, agents of his archconservative adviser Chen Lifu moved in. In December, Chen's hit men were suspected of killing four students in Kunming during a demonstration against civil war. In June, Nationalist thugs assaulted a coalition of students and intellectuals who had come to Nanjing to appeal for peace. On the evening of July 11, 1946, soldiers in Kunming gunned down Li Gongpu, a leading member of the liberal Democratic League. Four days later, the poet Wen Yiduo was shot to death as he finished giving a eulogy for his murdered friend.

Truman was flabbergasted, telling Chiang that to Americans, the Kuomintang appeared more interested in relying on "force, military or secret police rather than democratic processes" to run China. The American press was scathing as well.

For years, Theodore White's China reporting for *Time* had been given a positive spin at the behest of Henry Luce. Now White wanted to set the record straight. In 1946, he and journalist Annalee Jacoby came out with the best seller *Thunder out of China*. The faults of the Nationalist party, they wrote, "were that its leadership was corrupt, its secret police merciless, its promises lies, and its daily diet the blood and tears of the people of China." As the Pulitzer Prize winner George Weller told readers of the *Saturday Evening Post* in June 1947, "Let's quit kidding ourselves about China." The Kuomintang, he argued, was a spent force.

Of course, for all the nasty authoritarianism of the Nationalist regime, it paled in comparison to what awaited China's intellectuals under Mao Zedong. Throughout the war, most of the members of the Third Force voiced their opinions freely. The Communist press published in Nationalist-held cities and ran searing attacks on Chiang. Nonetheless, the Kuomintang's spasmodic crackdowns and assassinations played into the Communists' hands. Mao positioned his party as the guardian of human rights and the guarantor of democracy. "What China needs most is democracy—not socialism," Mao told the *Christian Science Monitor*.

In December 1945, the Communists and the Democratic League, the largest coalition of liberal groups in China, agreed to work together to overthrow Chiang Kai-shek. At the center of the agreement was the American-educated Luo Longji, the league's secretary general and a longtime advocate of democracy. Luo's decision to throw his lot in with the Communists would be a fateful one for a man who had earned his PhD at Columbia University and championed American-style political campaigning with gusto since his days as a student firebrand at Tsinghua University in the 1910s.

As the Nationalist government tightened the screws on liberal dissent, Luo's disappointment grew. Nationalist thugs tried twice to kill him. His house was bombed. His friend Wen Yiduo was assassinated. American diplomats hid Luo in a Shanghai hospital. Luo lobbied the US embassy to cut its support for Chiang Kai-shek, arguing that the Communists would stop fighting and a peaceful solution could be reached. Still, Luo was torn by the league's decision to throw its lot in with the Communists. He told diplomat John Melby that the Communists would tolerate even less freedom than the Nationalists, but he believed that they would feed people faster than Chiang's tottering regime. American diplomat Raymond Ludden noted that Luo was "badly frightened at the prospect of a Communist victory." Nonetheless, when the Communists won, Luo stayed in China.

In April 1945, delegates from fifty nations gathered in San Francisco for the founding conference of the United Nations. Emphasizing the world-wide shock at Nazi concentration camps and the intensifying Cold War with the Soviets, the State Department convinced other nations to include a special commission on human rights in the UN Charter.

Although it was a founding member of the UN, the Nationalist government of China played a passive role at its birth. Chinese diplomats were present at all the meetings but were generally ignored. When the UN formed its Human Rights Commission, consisting of eighteen member states, the Nationalist government appointed a non–party member, P. C. Chang, to represent China as the commission's vice-chairman.

The life of playwright professor P. C. Chang had taken an unexpected turn since he had been sent to the United States in the early 1940s to manage China's campaign for American hearts and minds. He had joined the Foreign Ministry of the Nationalist government and had served as ambassador to Chile and Turkey.

But it was Chang's work in the drafting of the UN's Universal Declaration of Human Rights that was to cap the life of a man born in China and educated in America. Marrying Western belief in the primacy of the individual with Chinese concern for the greater good, Chang personified the dream of the Great Harmony between China and the United States.

More than any other participant in the two-year odyssey to write the declaration, Chang pushed the committee to make it truly universal. He urged his colleagues to study Confucian thought and incorporate its teachings into the document. "In intellectual stature he towers over any other member of the committee," wrote John Humphrey, the first director of the UN Secretariat's Division on Human Rights. But Chang could be diplomatic, too. He was, Humphrey wrote, "a master of the art of compromise."

The story of Chang's labors, along with those of the Lebanese Christian Charles Malik and the Indian feminist Hansa Mehta, demolishes the notion, circulated later in Asia and backed strongly by the Chinese Communist Party, that the Universal Declaration on Human Rights represents Western political values incompatible with those of the rest of the world.

In early 1946, Chang joined the UN's commission for its first meetings in London under the leadership of Eleanor Roosevelt. FDR's sixty-two-year-old widow brought Chang, Malik, and Humphrey back to New York in the spring of 1946, where they huddled over tea at her apartment on Washington Square and at an old gyroscope factory in Lake Success, New York, which doubled as the UN's temporary headquarters.

Chang's relationship with Malik was a stormy one. Malik hailed from a newly independent Lebanon. He was a Christian philosopher and placed God at the center of his moral universe. Chang was a secular humanist who didn't concern himself with divinities. From the start, Malik insisted on including either "God" or "nature" in the document to show that a higher power had endowed humans with rights. Chang argued that a great many people in China "had ideals and traditions different from the Christian West." So God and nature fell by the wayside.

Chang introduced the Chinese idea of *ren* into the declaration. The Chinese character for this concept combines a person with the number two and thus depicts the idea that humans are social animals. *Ren* appears in Article 1 of the Declaration, translated as "brotherhood." Chang believed the foundations for a truly universal principle on human rights lay somewhere between Confucius and the European Enlightenment. A declaration on human rights was not simply about the rights of the individual, Chang argued. It was also about the individual's obligations as a social animal to society. It was Chang's fight for *both* individual rights *and* individual responsibilities that gave him a unique voice in the fashioning of the historic document.

Chang labored without direction from his government as the Kuomintang crumbled. On December 10, 1948, he addressed the third meeting of the UN General Assembly in Paris. In the face of Mao's juggernaut and the collapse of the Nationalist army, he lamented that force was deciding China's future and criticized the Communist "tendency to impose a standardized way of thinking and a single way of life." On that same day, the United Nations passed the Universal Declaration on Human Rights.

Chang continued to work on the Human Rights Commission until he retired in 1952. Diplomats from the Soviet bloc attacked him as an American stooge. They hated the declaration because it legitimized outside interference in their nations' internal affairs—a position China still maintains. Chang believed that the declaration should be used "to build up better human beings, and not merely to punish those who violate human rights." As he told the commission: "Sweep the snow in front of your own door. Overlook the frost of another's roof tiles." Suffering from heart disease, Chang died in 1957. Like many of China's towering liberals, he and his work to fuse the traditions of East and West have been forgotten on mainland China.

Harry Truman's election in 1948 came as a shock to Chiang Kai-shek, who had banked on a Dewey victory. ("Banked" in more ways than one: Nationalist operatives had funneled money into the GOP's campaign.)

Chiang fired off telegrams to the president, blaming the Soviets for all his troubles and begging for aid. "If we fail to stop their advance now," he wrote on November 9, "then the democratic countries would lose all of China."

That month, Chiang sent Soong Mayling on another voyage to America. This trip, her third in a decade, was even less productive than her voyage in 1944. The American press treated her like an unwanted guest. "Madame Chiang's Trip Believed a Mistake," declared the *Los Angeles Times*. In Washington, no one of significance met her upon her arrival.

When Truman finally did see her, it was for tea with his wife and daughter—a social call, not an audience befitting the Missimo. "No other emissary or leader of a major and friendly foreign power has been received so coolly as the petite and personable wife of China's Generalissimo," the *Chicago Daily Tribune* reported on December 11.

In January 1949, Truman appointed Acheson to replace Marshall as secretary of state. Acheson wasn't interested in Asia. As Dean Rusk, who had served with Stilwell in China and then joined the State Department, said, Acheson "did not give a damn about the little red-yellow-black people in various parts of the world." During his tenure in Foggy Bottom, Acheson traveled to Europe eleven times but never crossed the Pacific. The president shared Acheson's indifference. Not a page in his memoirs focuses on China in 1949. Still, it was in Asia that the two men faced their greatest challenge.

With his forces rattled by defeats and riddled by defections, Chiang resigned as president of the Nationalist government on January 21, 1949, and was replaced by a warlord named Li Zongren. Peace talks began with the Communists but, when Li refused Mao's demand for a total surrender, the Communists resumed their advance. The Communists took the capital, Nanjing, in April 1949. On April 25, Mao's soldiers attacked the US embassy in Nanjing and barged into Ambassador Stuart's bedroom at 6:30 a.m. to announce that "all this will belong to the people."

From Nanjing, the Nationalist government fled to Guangzhou, then back to the wartime citadel of Chongqing and then to Chengdu. Behind the scenes, Chiang Kai-shek and Li Zongren vied for control of what remained of Nationalist China. Chiang's son Chiang Ching-kuo organized the transfer of $200 million in gold from Shanghai to the island of Taiwan, which the US had returned to Nationalist rule in October 1945. More than two million civilians, military personnel, and government officials fled the mainland for the island as well.

Meanwhile, the Communists started detaining Western diplomats. In November 1948, Communist agents incarcerated Angus Ward, an American consul in the Manchurian city of Shenyang, to stop him from filing reports about Soviet support for Mao's forces. During a brutal winter and a sweltering summer, without electricity, heat, or running water, Ward and his staff lived on cockroach-infested bread and the occasional bottle of vodka. The Communists were so intent on suppressing the natural friendliness of the Chinese toward Ward and his crew that "passers-by were even arrested for waving greetings," Ward recalled. Before they released him thirteen months later, the Communists charged Ward with opposing the revolution and "world peace."

Communist Party documents reveal that Ward's incarceration and the beating and harassment of other American diplomats were hardly the random acts of local zealots. They were part of a policy to sweep Americans and American influence from Chinese soil. "We Chinese have no further need for you knaves," declared a poem in a Communist-run Shanghai evening paper. "Imperialists beware. All is not well with you anymore."

On November 10, 1948, a Communist party directive ordered all Western diplomats in Communist-held areas stripped of their status and treated like ordinary foreigners. Mao announced that the party would abrogate China's international agreements, shut down foreign-owned newspapers and radio stations, and take over foreign trade.

Eliminating American influence would become critical to establishing Mao's "people's dictatorship." The only way to guarantee the party's victory was to show America the door and embrace a self-imposed isolation that would allow his revolution to do its work. Mao shared these views with Anastas Mikoyan, an Armenian Marxist whom Stalin sent to Mao's new headquarters in Xibaipo in Hebei province in January 1949. The United States was interested in ties with his government only to "subvert the new order from within," Mao declared. "The later the U.S. and other Western countries recognize us the better because our house is still very dirty, and only after we have cleaned our house can we properly host guests." The Communists did send feelers out to Washington, but documentary evidence from China and Soviet archives suggests that this was simply part of the Communist strategy to "neutralize" America by encouraging the false hope that a Communist China would welcome US friendship and investment.

The Communist overtures bolstered Secretary of State Dean Acheson's view that it would be possible to extricate the United States from Chiang Kai-shek's embrace and find an arrangement with Mao. He asked some of Chiang's American friends to suggest that the Generalissimo flee into exile. Acheson along with others in the State Department entertained the notion that America's magnetic influence over China would turn Mao into someone like the independent-minded Yugoslav revolutionary Josip Broz Tito, who was distancing himself from Moscow.

How to entice Mao was the problem. The State Department urged American businessmen and educators to stay in China, and while other nations moved their representatives to Guangzhou with the Nationalists, Ambassador John Leighton Stuart remained in Nanjing to maintain an open channel with the Communists.

On February 3, 1949, during a meeting of the National Security Council, Acheson called for the suspension of all aid to the Nationalists. Three weeks later, he met with the GOP leadership in Congress and mused that with a house half-collapsed, the proper course was to "wait until what is falling down falls." The Republicans stormed out of the room, and both houses of Congress rang with maledictions blasting Truman, Acheson, and State Department officials for their betrayal of Chiang Kai-shek. "This blood must not be on *our* hands," declared Senator Arthur H. Vandenberg, an influential Republican from Michigan. If Truman stopped military aid now, Vandenberg warned, it would be America that "gave China the final push into disaster." Acheson faced trouble within the administration as well. The Joint Chiefs of Staff and Secretary of Defense Louis Johnson did not particularly like Chiang Kai-shek, but they wanted to keep Taiwan free from Communist control. Truman decided not to formally halt military aid to Chiang Kai-shek but told Acheson to delay the aid "without formal action."

As criticism of America's China policy mounted and Nationalist China trembled, Acheson seized on an idea that his underlings had been suggesting for months. Why not publish a record of America's support for China during the war and use that to convince the naysayers of the inevitability of a Communist victory and the futility of continuing to support Chiang Kai-shek? As John Melby, who was assigned to write much of the report, said, the goal was to "call off the dogs from the China Lobby."

On August 5, three days after John Leighton Stuart left China for the last time, the Truman administration published a report titled *United States Relations with China: With Special Reference to the Period of 1944–1949*. The White Paper, as it came to be known, contained more than one thousand pages of analysis and State Department documents, accompanied by a fourteen-page letter, which ended up being the most controversial part. The basic thesis was that, despite decades of American goodwill toward China and Chiang Kai-shek, Nationalist "ineptitude" and the loss of a "will to fight" had doomed Chiang's regime. Assistance to the Kuomintang had been "pursued vigorously," but now, given all Chiang's failures, only a "colossal," all-out "commitment of our armies" could save China. The Communist victory, which had yet even to be proclaimed, "was the

product of internal Chinese forces." The United States had been an innocent bystander at a train wreck. The only hope the document offered was
the prediction that "the democratic individualism of China" would one
day resurface and that America would be ready when it did.

The China Lobby poked holes in the paper's claim to be a full record of
State's relations with China by publishing documents revealing the department's flirtation with the Communists. Others pointed out that the White
Paper glossed over years of broken American promises. The *New York
Times* called it a "lawyer's brief" and termed America's China policy "a
sorry record of well-meaning mistakes." In a three-part series in September 1949, columnist Walter Lippmann asked, if Chiang Kai-shek had been
so hopeless, why had Washington given him $3 billion?

The White Paper appeared to be an attempt to pave the way for dump-
ing Chiang and improving ties with Mao, but it failed. Eleven days after its
release, due in part to a congressional groundswell of support for Chiang,
the State Department announced that it had no intention of withdrawing
recognition from Nationalist China.

In China, the White Paper touched off a hysterical outburst in the
Communist press. While in America the report was attacked on the grounds
that the United States had done too little to save Chiang Kai-shek, in Beijing it was cited as proof that America had done too much. Anti-American
diatribes were ubiquitous for weeks, including five from Mao, the most
famous of which he entitled "Farewell, Leighton Stuart!"

The White Paper, Mao wrote, was "a bucket of cold water" that should
sober up those "who believed that everything American is good and hope
that China will model herself on the United States." It marked another
chance to generate the virulent anti-American sentiment that was so crucial to his success. Given the warm feelings that many Chinese still harbored for the United States, Mao faced a daunting challenge. But Acheson's
bluster about "democratic individualism" provided the justification Mao
needed to urge his followers to uproot America's "fifth column in China"
and obliterate "the short-sighted, muddle-headed liberals."

As the danger of American military intervention receded, Mao used
the White Paper to gin up what he called the threat of an American "spiritual
invasion," led by "enemies without guns." Persistent conflict with the West,
particularly with America, would serve as a pillar for Mao's new state. Once
its best friend, America now became China's worst enemy.

On June 30, 1949, Mao declared that China would seal an alliance with
the USSR and "lean to one side." An accord with Moscow was necessary to

destroy Chinese illusions about their deep friendship for and expectations of the United States.

The proclamation of the People's Republic of China (PRC) on October 1, 1949, sent shock waves through an America already rattled by the Soviet Union's detonation of an atomic bomb in September. In November, the second trial against alleged Soviet spy Alger Hiss opened in America. In December, Mao Zedong visited Moscow, the first time he had ever left China. In February 1950, Mao signed the Sino-Soviet Treaty of Friendship, Alliance and Mutual Assistance, formalizing China's entry into the Soviet bloc.

Normally, the collapse of a foreign government would have registered barely a ripple on the American political scene. But the explosive combination of America's expectations for China, its growing anti-Communism, and a Republican Party desperate for an issue turned it into a momentous affair. Following Dewey's surprise defeat in 1948, the Republicans had seized upon Communist subversion as a club to wield against Truman. With Chiang's toppling, they had an unambiguous example of the duplicity of their Democratic foes.

The China Lobby was made up of strange bedfellows. Some members, like Henry Luce, believed passionately in America's mission in China. As he told John Melby, the missionaries and their kids "had made a lifetime commitment to the advancement of Christianity in China. And now . . . you're asking us to say that all our lives have been wasted." Others saw China's civil conflict as a proxy war against the Soviet Union. Chiang's fall was a tragedy not because it locked 450 million Chinese behind the Bamboo Curtain but because it strengthened Moscow. That was why Taiwan was important. Occupying a vital position just off China's coastal shelf, the island was, as James Lilley, a CIA officer born to missionaries in Shandong, put it, "the cork in the bottle," plugging up China's access to the western Pacific. Still others, such as New York financier Sonny Fassoulis, were in it for the money. Fassoulis profited handsomely from deals with Chiang's regime. For two decades, this coalition ensured that Chiang would get continued aid and that the United States would neither recognize the People's Republic of China nor allow it into the United Nations.

Partly because of the China Lobby, US policy makers were at a loss as to how to deal with China. In October 1949, while the Truman White House was publicly distancing itself from Chiang's collapsing regime, the fledgling Central Intelligence Agency, through Chennault's Civil Air Transport, funneled loads of cash—sometimes in big wicker baskets—to anti-Communist forces in China's south. At all times, an official CIA history recounts, the Chinese were told that the cash came from "wealthy American interests" and not Uncle Sam.

Meanwhile, Acheson was convinced that it was time to walk away from Chiang Kai-shek. Weeks after Mao declared the founding of the PRC, he gathered what he believed to be the brightest minds on China to formulate policy toward Mao's revolution. Overwhelmingly, the experts called for coming to terms with Mao. John K. Fairbank, of Harvard University, urged the administration to recognize China and ally itself with what he argued were the forces of the future in Asia. Echoing Frank Goodnow, Fairbank argued that democracy and freedom were out of reach for the average Chinese. "A man will think of food before he thinks of free speech," he had written in the September 1946 edition of the *Atlantic*. "Communists could seem good in China, though bad in America." Other participants went even farther. Owen Lattimore, still a State Department consultant, maintained that the United States should leave Korea to the Russians as well.

At the conference, John Leighton Stuart found the discussion "discouraging and disconcerting." He had been devastated by the Communist victory in China and now felt that his government, on the advice of "naive and unsuspecting" American diplomats and scholars, was ready to throw the Nationalists under a bus. In Washington, the State Department banned him from speaking to the press. US officials censored his speeches to Protestant congregations. Then on November 30, 1949, as he returned by train to Washington from visiting friends in Cincinnati, Stuart, grieving China's fate, was found unconscious in the men's bathroom. He had suffered a massive stroke. Hospitalized for a year, he would never work again. Stuart moved in with the family of his longtime secretary, Philip Fugh, who nursed him until he died in 1962.

In December 1949, Chiang Kai-shek and his son Chiang Ch'ing-kuo were in Chengdu, trying to organize its defense as the Communists closed in. On the morning of December 10, father and son boarded an aircraft named "May-ling" and flew to Taiwan. By this time, President Li Zongren had gone to the United States for medical treatment, where he denounced Chiang as a "dictator" and "usurper." In March 1950, Chiang again had himself declared president of the Republic of China. He would never return to mainland China again.

In America, John Leighton Stuart and Congressional Republicans were not the only ones who opposed the abandonment of the Nationalist regime. In a remarkable document written for the White House in the winter of

1948, George Kennan's team at the State Department's Policy Planning Staff analyzed the future course of US relations with China with extraordinary precision. The need to modernize would ultimately force China to seek economic ties with the West, it stated. Though China would remain "suspicious" and even "hostile" to the United States, Beijing would one day distance itself from the Soviets as the Russians devolved into their traditional role of imperialist predators. Kennan counseled patience and advised the United States and Japan to trade with China to nurture "the germs of friction between a Chinese Communist regime and the Kremlin."

But Kennan also understood that losing Taiwan to the Communists would impair America's position in Asia. The CIA and the Joint Chiefs of Staff argued that giving the Communists an island smack in between America's allies Japan and the Philippines would provide them with a platform from which to stalk the US Navy. At the same time, keeping Taiwan out of Mao's clutches would also block any possibility of better ties with the mainland.

President Truman wavered as these two impulses—to court Mao and to save Taiwan—battled back and forth within his administration. On January 5, 1950, Truman announced that the United States had "no desire to obtain special rights or privileges to establish military bases on Formosa [Taiwan] or to detach Formosa from China." No more aid would be given, he said, "in the civil conflict in China." On January 12, Acheson gave a speech to the National Press Club placing both Taiwan and South Korea outside the US defensive perimeter. But within weeks, the US military pushed back. On January 25, 1950, Omar Bradley, chairman of the Joint Chiefs of Staff, gave off-the-record testimony to the Senate Foreign Relations Committee about the dangers of a Communist takeover of Taiwan.

On February 9, 1950, Joseph McCarthy, a forty-one-year-old junior senator from Wisconsin facing a tough reelection battle, rose before a group of Republicans in Wheeling, West Virginia, to allege that in his hands he carried the names of scores of Communist Party agents working in the State Department. McCarthy claimed that China had not fallen because of Chiang's incompetence, but because spies at the very highest levels of the US government had facilitated Mao's rise. McCarthy's allegations prompted Senate hearings; among those McCarthy named were Jack Service and Owen Lattimore. McCarthy absurdly identified Lattimore as "Moscow's top spy" and "the architect of our Far Eastern policy." China was at the center of McCarthy's witch hunt to rid America of "Commie symps." Using the loss of China to stoke fears of a new Yellow Peril, McCarthy unleashed the most damaging political campaign in America's modern history.

Owen Lattimore went toe-to-toe with McCarthy. He put the word "McCarthyism" into general usage and argued in his memoirs, *Ordeal by Slander*, that anyone accused of being a Communist was by definition an innocent victim. "A tide of fear has swept Washington, undermining the freedom of the nation," Lattimore declared.

While Senator Millard Tydings, a Democrat from Maryland who chaired the Senate hearings, agreed that Service had been "extremely indis-creet" in passing documents to *Amerasia* (and in taking a Chinese lover), his committee cleared both Service and Lattimore of disloyalty. McCarthy had been responsible, Tydings said, for "perhaps the most nefarious campaign of half-truths and untruth in the history of this Republic." But McCarthy wasn't done.

As the senator homed in on Acheson's China Hands, the secretary of state moved quickly to mend fences with the Republicans. Acheson offered up Walton Butterworth, the head of the Far Eastern section, as the first sacrifice, replacing him with Dean Rusk, the son of a Georgia sharecropper, a former Rhodes scholar with good relations across the aisle. Rusk brought in a prominent Republican, John Foster Dulles, the grandson of the Qing dynasty's lobbyist, John W. Foster, as a special adviser.

Rusk had served on Stilwell's staff in World War II and had inherited the general's contempt for Chiang Kai-shek. But he felt that permitting Taiwan to pass into Communist hands would cause an even greater blow-back in public opinion than the one McCarthy was stirring up.

In John Foster Dulles, Rusk found a partner, and the pair set out to lobby for more support for the island. Rusk peppered Acheson with reports suggesting that the rump Nationalist government on Taiwan was not, as the CIA had claimed, on the verge of collapse. Dulles argued that America could not in good conscience hand over seven million people to the Communists.

In Taiwan, the China Lobby moved stealthily to help Chiang Kai-shek. In January 1949, as Washington mulled ending aid to the Kuomintang, two American intelligence officers landed in Taipei with the blessing of General Douglas MacArthur, the top army officer in Asia, to survey the island's radar needs. Then in early February, MacArthur arranged for Charles M. Cooke, the former commander of the Seventh Fleet, to visit Taiwan.

Cooke arrived in Taipei as an accredited correspondent for the

International News Service, with a side business selling fertilizer. He soon gained access to Chiang's inner sanctum and suggested hiring retired US military officers to advise the Nationalists. In March, Cooke and Chiang established the Special Technician Program. Soon, more than thirty former American officers had taken up positions in Chiang's army, navy, and air force headquarters. Once again, the Chinese had found a slew of Frederick Townsend Wards. Over the next six months, Cooke would transfer millions of dollars in military hardware—aircraft spare parts, artillery shells, and armored cars—to the Kuomintang.

China's Communist revolution had an enormous influence on the United States. It was a significant factor in the US decision to rearm following World War II. It stoked a new Yellow Peril in America and contributed directly to the rise of McCarthyism. Here was a nation that Americans had considered as America's ward. And now, as longtime China correspondent Jack Belden wrote in his 1949 book *China Shakes the World*, "There they are, vibrant, vital and vigorous, . . . a new force, a terrible force in an ancient world."

Was America responsible for the fall of the Republic of China? The answer has to be no. China was not America's to lose. As the *Washington Post* editorialized in 1954, "China was lost by the Chinese to some other Chinese." But America played a role in the collapse of Chiang Kai-shek. Washington's decision to treat China as a sideshow in the Pacific war denied Chiang's armies the training and materiel they needed to secure their country once the war was over. American support for a postwar coalition government was a mistake. This error was rooted in the unwillingness of the US government to contemplate a division of China, based on the century-old belief that a united Middle Kingdom was in the best interests of the United States and on the mistaken notion that China's Communists were not Marxist-Leninists.

To many Americans, Mao's call for a "continuous revolution" would make China a continuous threat. The chairman's focus on the "intermediate zone" of oppressed non-Western nations as the fulcrum of history shifted America's primary battlefield of the Cold War away from Europe to Asia. From June to August 1949, Mao's lieutenant Liu Shaoqi visited Moscow. He and Stalin agreed that the "revolutionary situation" in Asia was ripe for exploitation. China's duty, Liu declared, would be to incite "Eastern revolution." So, by the middle of 1950, as China and America faced off, all the two nations needed to start a conflagration was a spark.

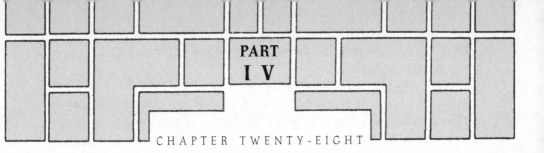

CHAPTER TWENTY-EIGHT

Hate America

At 4:00 a.m. on June 25, 1950, a fusillade of gunfire ripped through the predawn calm along the thirty-eighth parallel on the Korean peninsula. Thousands of troops from the Korean People's Army, equipped with Soviet weapons and T-34 tanks, advanced into South Korea. By the end of the month, Communist forces had captured Seoul. By July, they had seized most of the South.

Within thirty-six hours of the first shot, President Truman ordered the deployment of US troops to South Korea. The United States rammed two resolutions through the UN Security Council, condemning the invasion and slapping sanctions on North Korea. Truman sent the Seventh Fleet into the Taiwan Strait, derailing the Communists' plan to take Taiwan. A few days later, eight C-47 transport planes flew across the Pacific, bringing the first batch of what would eventually balloon to $1 billion in military aid to French forces in Indochina. Truman avoided calling Korea a war. He described it to the White House press corps as a "police action."

On June 30, a lightly armed task force of fewer than six hundred men from the US Army's Twenty-Fourth Infantry Division landed in South Korea; it was quickly outgunned. After World War II, America had demobilized at lightning speed. From a wartime high of twelve million men, US forces had shrunk to one and a half million. "The Army," said Omar Bradley, the chairman of the Joint Chiefs of Staff, who had led the invasion of Germany, "could not fight its way out of a paper bag." North Korean forces trapped more than one hundred thousand US, South Korean, and other allied troops on the southeastern tip of the peninsula, around the city of Pusan. American commanders told their men to "stand or die."

On June 29, 1950, the Central Committee of the Chinese Communist Party issued a directive to all propaganda agencies to portray the American entry into the Korean War as "not scary at all but favorable for the further awakening of the Chinese people." In early July, Mao created the Northeast Border Defense Army, transferring to Manchuria the troops that he had been mustering for an assault on Taiwan. China also increased its support of Communists in Indochina, slipping advisers and guns to the Viet Minh.

On August 4, at a Beijing meeting of the Politburo, the party's highest decision-making body, Mao argued that China had no choice but to support North Korean leader Kim Il-sung. If the North Koreans lost, he warned, the United States would become "more arrogant and would threaten us." By the middle of August, a month before the US Army broke out of its encirclement, the Communists had decided that China must join the fight. Still, as Zhou Enlai told the Central Military Commission, according to research by historian Chen Jian, China had to appear as if it were defending itself. Only this would ensure the success of a crucial political campaign that he and Mao were planning to accompany China's entry into the war. By August 22, 1950, the Northeast Border Defense Army had deployed three hundred thousand men along the Yalu River dividing China and Korea.

Then, on September 15, General Douglas MacArthur pulled off one of the greatest flanking maneuvers in modern warfare, landing seventy-five thousand troops at Inchon on the west coast of the Korean peninsula behind North Korean lines. Within two weeks, American troops had recaptured Seoul and cut off the North Korean army. A day after MacArthur's masterstroke, Stalin asked Mao to send troops to North Korea. Mao replied that China would respond when the Americans moved across the thirty-eighth parallel.

Truman knew that the failure to pursue total victory would open his administration to yet more charges of being soft on Communism. Midterm elections were approaching, Republicans were baying for Communist scalps, and John Foster Dulles was demanding that the United States "obliterate" the thirty-eighth parallel. Communism's rollback would start in Korea, Dulles and others vowed.

Washington gave MacArthur ambiguous orders. He could move north of the thirty-eighth parallel as long as Soviet or Chinese Communist forces were not present in large numbers. US troops were barred from provinces directly bordering China. Air and naval operations against Manchuria or Soviet territory were banned. But as American diplomat Averell Harriman later observed, "Psychologically, it was almost impossible not to go ahead and complete the job." On September 30, the first South Korean units crossed the thirty-eighth parallel. On October 7, the US Army's First Cavalry Division followed.

China *had* warned the United States not to enter the North, choosing as its messenger K. M. Panikkar, India's first ambassador to Communist China. From late September to early October, Chinese officials told Panikkar that if US troops invaded North Korea, China would be forced to intervene. The CIA suggested that the Chinese were bluffing. Secretary of State Dean Acheson called the warnings "mere vaporings of a panicky Panikkar." Some in Washington counseled caution. Top diplomat George Kennan urged the United States to push the North Koreans out of South Korea and then leave Korea and "the mess" the French were making of Indochina as well. But a mix of American hubris, the lust for victory, and politics at home drove the United States deeper into China's trap.

General Matthew Ridgway, who had led airborne operations in Europe during World War II, noted that MacArthur was so intent on winning in Korea that he "simply closed his ears" to the growing presence of Chinese troops in Korea. MacArthur, Ridgway wrote, was like Custer at Little Bighorn, "with neither eyes nor ears for information that might deter him from the swift attainment of his objective." It didn't help that MacArthur's intelligence chief, Major General Charles Willoughby, was a bigot who had no respect for Chinese soldiers. Willoughby thought that no "Chinaman" would dare take on the mechanized might of the US armored cavalry.

Mao's choice as commander of the Korean operation was Peng Dehuai, a Red Army officer who had served with the chairman since the 1930s. Peng's forces were named the Chinese People's Volunteers at the suggestion of Huang Yanpei, an educator and follower of Sun Yat-sen who argued that creating an unofficial arrangement—"volunteers"—would reduce the risk of a formal war with America. On October 19, the Chinese People's Volunteers crossed the Yalu River into North Korea. That day, US forces took the North Korean capital, Pyongyang.

On October 15, 1950, four days before China crossed the Yalu, Harry Truman met MacArthur on Wake Island in the mid-Pacific. With the midterm elections nearing, Truman's political advisers reckoned that a meeting with the hero of Inchon (Truman called him "God's right hand man") could help defang the Republican Right. Truman expressed concern that the Chinese were about to enter the war, but MacArthur assured him that they would not. "If the Chinese tried to get down to Pyongyang, it would be the greatest slaughter in the history of mankind," the seventy-one-year-old general declared. MacArthur predicted that North Korean resistance would crumble by Thanksgiving and that the Eighth Army would be home by Christmas. MacArthur estimated that the Chinese could provision fifty thousand troops in Korea. (He would be off by a factor of thirty.) After his brilliance at Inchon, the general was about to commit what the late writer David Halberstam called the worst military miscalculation of the twentieth century.

On November 21, US forces, ignoring Washington's orders to stay out of provinces abutting China, reached the Yalu River. David Barr and Edward Almond, commanders of the Seventh Infantry Division and X Corps, stopped to urinate in its waters. The Americans put the number of Chinese in North Korea at less than a hundred thousand. There were three times as many.

On November 25, the Chinese struck across a vast front, sending American and South Korean forces reeling. That same day, as the Americans fought back, another story in the tangled destiny of China and America unfolded when a US air strike on Peng Dehuai's headquarters killed Mao's son Anying. We will never know, but this single act of violence arguably led to one of America's most enduring legacies in China, blocking Mao from establishing a Red dynasty in China, as would appear in North Korea with the Kims. For several days after he learned of Anying's death, the chairman ate little and was unable to sleep. Mao ordered that Anying's body stay in North Korea. On January 4, Seoul fell again, this time to the Chinese People's Volunteers.

When General Walton Walker was killed in a road accident on December 23, Ridgway took his place as commander of the Eighth Army. He arrived in Korea just after Christmas to find an army in retreat. Unlike MacArthur, Ridgway had no contempt for his opponent. He studied Chinese tactics and realized that the United States had an advantage: technology. Ridgway's war combined artillery, close air support, and airborne intelligence. His men called it "the meat grinder." Now it was Mao's turn to be arrogant. He pressed Peng Dehuai to send the Volunteers deeper into South Korea. Peng warned Beijing against "unrealistic optimism." Food became a problem, then fuel. By January 25, Peng's offensive had literally run out of gas.

As the Chinese People's Volunteers forded the Yalu River in October 1950, the Communist Party crossed another Rubicon, launching a nationwide political campaign against the United States. Hating America became one of the key pillars of the Communist revolution and remains one of its most nettlesome legacies today.

It was clear from the struggle's name—"The Great War to Resist America and Assist Korea"—and its slogans—"Defend our nation! Defend our home! Defeat American arrogance!"—that the United States stood directly in the party's sights.

Communist operatives used the war as justification to root out American influence in universities, charities, businesses, churches, scientific research institutions, cinemas, and most important, in Chinese hearts and minds. A party directive ordered that feelings of admiration and respect for the United States must be redirected into "hate America, despise America and look down on America," with the goal of "encouraging national self-confidence and self-respect"—forever joining the yin of hating America with the yang of loving China. Mao wanted the movement to penetrate into every family, factory, and farm in China and to cure "three diseases": *kongmei bing* (the disease of fearing America), *chongmei bing* (the disease of worshipping America), and *meimei bing* (the disease of flattering America).

Communist propaganda outlets churned out an endless stream of overblown invective. America was "thoroughly dark, thoroughly corrupt, thoroughly cruel," wrote the *South China Daily*. It was, the *Daily* said, "a living hell ten times, one hundred times, one thousand times worse than any hell that can possibly be depicted by the most gory of writers." Posters portrayed Truman and MacArthur as serial rapists, bloodthirsty murderers, and savage beasts.

The few American missionaries left in China were natural targets for the Communists, who charged them with allegations straight out of "The Record" from the 1860s. In March 1951, the *People's Daily* claimed that an American-run missionary orphanage in Nanjing had killed hundreds of children. In April, it alleged that "those murderous [American] gluttons" in Guangzhou had slaughtered four thousand orphans. Francis Xavier Ford, a sixty-year-old bishop from Brooklyn who had lived in China since 1918 and supported Chinese guerrillas throughout World War II, was accused of espionage and beaten to death on February 21, 1952. In between beatings, party thugs in a Guangzhou jail forced Ford to undress in front of his assistant, a Maryknoll nun named Joan Marie Ryan, to bolster the Communist claim, also echoing "The Record," that missionaries specialized in sanguinary orgies. Ryan was forced to sign a document saying that Ford had died of old age.

In highly Westernized Shanghai, Communists attacked the city's first love—American movies. In November 1950, the Shanghai newspaper *Wen Hui Pao* ran a series of essays by readers describing how Hollywood had wrecked their lives. "If it hadn't been for American movies," lamented housewife Wang Ruiyun, "I would not have had this horrible marriage." Before the revolution, Wang wrote, she had dressed like a starlet and "hated my family for not possessing the sumptuousness of an American life." Chinese boys didn't interest her. She fantasized about being swept off her feet by an American. "He would have to be as handsome as Errol Flynn," she wrote, "and be very, very rich." In the end, she settled for a Shanghai businessman, but he lost all his money. Finally, following "liberation," she wrote, she saw the light. "I finally understood that I had ingested the poison of American films," she wrote. "American films ruined me. And I protest!"

In the fall of 1950, the party closed down 660 American-funded charities in Shanghai. The city's cafés and dance halls, gambling dens, and casinos were shuttered. Suits and ties, the uniform of the modern set, gave way to the dour blues and greens of the revolution. Returning to China after two years in Australia, Li Zhisui, a doctor who had been trained by Americans in Sichuan and who would later gain fame as Mao's physician, felt like a foreigner "with my Western style suit and tie, leather shoes, and hair that suddenly seemed long."

The Chinese were told that South Korea, backed by America, had started the Korean War. (Today's Chinese school textbooks stick to this claim.) The United States was also falsely accused of supporting Britain during the Opium War. China's state-run press depicted the American-funded Peking Union Medical College as a laboratory where American doctors performed gruesome experiments on Chinese women and children. And the post–World War II United Nations food relief program, under which tons of American grain kept millions of Chinese alive, was a US plot to contaminate China's crops.

The emerging stalemate on the Korean Peninsula bolstered the campaign at home. The Chinese were accustomed to losing to powerful armies, yet now they had battled a great power to a standstill. It was, Li Zhisui wrote, "the first time in more than a century that China had engaged in a war with a foreign power without losing face."

One of the most virulent American ideas that needed to be expunged was the pragmatism of John Dewey. Dewey's concept of a gradual, peaceful evolution toward modernity and democracy directly challenged Communist rule. Mao trafficked in violence and class struggle, executions and permanent revolution. Dewey was a self-described proponent of the "retail" theory of progress. He believed in peace.

To get at Dewey, the Communists attacked his Chinese disciples. First among them was Hu Shih, who had left Beijing on December 15, 1948, boarding the last plane that Chiang Kai-shek had sent to evacuate leading intellectuals from the city. Hu and his wife, Dongxiu, departed, but their youngest son, Sidu, named after John Dewey, refused to go.

On September 22, 1950, Hu Sidu denounced his father, declaring that he had been "conquered" by American culture and had been transformed into "a stinking bourgeois." Sidu told the readers of the *Ta Kung Pao* newspaper that in fleeing China, Hu Shih had chosen the life of a "white Chinese." Party hacks churned out more than three million words—books, magazines, and reports—on the nefarious influence of American pragmatism, exorcising what they called "the ghost of Hu Shih." Responding from the safety of New York City, Hu Shih remarked that the campaign gave him "a feeling of comfort and encouragement—a feeling that Dewey's two years and two months in China were not entirely in vain."

Rural reformer Jimmy Yen and his wife, Alice Huie, were in the United States when the Communists took control in 1949. Yen had brought his two daughters to America, while the couple's three sons had stayed behind to build the New China. The boys promised to send a snapshot of themselves after the Communist takeover. If anyone was standing, it meant that he was having problems with the new regime. When the photo arrived, all three of the Yen boys were standing. (One of them would later be driven to suicide.)

Key targets of the party were China's Western-leaning liberals, like those in the Yen family. Now that China had been "liberated," the independent thinkers that Mao Zedong had courted to defeat Chiang Kai-shek constituted a threat to Communist rule. So they were savagely repressed.

Mao used the Democratic League to lead the Hate America campaign. In October 1948, just before Mao's victory, league chairman Luo Longji had proposed that China adopt a parliamentary system and embrace a policy of "harmonious diplomacy" with both the US and the USSR. Luo wanted the league to be recognized as a legal opposition party. But war with America gave Mao the excuse he needed to reject Luo's plea.

The party believed that reducing China's liberals to the status of gofers and attack dogs was the most efficient way of breaking the spell of American ideas. After the Korean War erupted, Luo was appointed director of the China Peace Committee and was forced to churn out anti-American screeds to prove his patriotism. "America is an incurably sick country," read one. "Its final destruction is just a matter of time." American freedom, Luo wrote, was a sham. The league's paper, the *Guangming Daily*, ran testimonials by professors and other intellectuals who had converted to Communism.

Jin Yuelin, a brilliant philosopher with a doctorate from Columbia, declared himself "an instrument of American cultural aggression" who had fallen into the "bottomless pit of the degenerate philosophy of the capitalist class." Jin had been one of the first Chinese to import Western concepts of logic to China. Feng Youlan, another philosopher and a Columbia graduate, announced that his writings constituted "crimes against the people." He spent the next thirty years rewriting what had been a fabulous history of Chinese philosophy in a futile attempt to conform to the latest wrinkle in Maoist liturgy. After his reeducation, Luo Changpei, another scholar who had spent years in the US pioneering the study of Chinese linguistics, declared that "I hate myself."

In the winter of 1948, as the Communists closed in on Beijing, Fei Xiaotong wondered "if in the future we will still have the opportunity of free thought." But when the Red Army marched onto the campus of Tsinghua University on December 16, 1948, Fei was still there. After the revolution, Fei churned out a series of pro-Communist essays. "We love our present-day life," he wrote in one. "We have realized what life can mean, realized that we, with our hands and brains, can create true happiness. . . . Friends! Do I really seem the downtrodden worm?" The Communists called their method of realigning people's thoughts *xinao*. The literal translation: brainwashing.

In October 1951, Zhou Enlai subjected three thousand teachers and professors, many educated in America, to a seven-hour lecture at party headquarters, next to the Forbidden City in Beijing. China's intellectuals, he warned, were victims of "mistaken thoughts of the bourgeois class." In the audience was Wu Ningkun, who had studied English literature at Manchester University in Indiana and later at the University of Chicago.

He had arrived just six weeks earlier, abandoning a doctoral thesis on T. S. Eliot for a chance to build the New China. As he was leaving America, a physicist friend named T. D. Lee accompanied him to the dock. When Wu asked Lee why he was not returning to China, Lee replied that he did not want to be brainwashed. Wu had never heard that term before, but as he sat listening to Zhou, Lee's words came back to him. "Little did I know," Wu wrote, "that the seven hour report was nothing less than a declaration of war on the mind and integrity of the intelligentsia for the next forty years."

Many faked their devotion to Mao's campaign. Although Hu Sidu publicly repudiated Hu Shih, he sent letters to his mother, Dongxiu, entreating her to care for his father. As *Ta Kung Pao* acknowledged on March 2, 1952, American-educated Chinese remained "incapable of fostering hatred for America." Their "dreams" about the United States persisted in the face of the party's withering assault.

In Shanghai, the party's campaign against American movies faced so much opposition that Communist-appointed mayor Chen Yi appealed to authorities in Beijing to give the city more time to eradicate Hollywood's influence. Though American films were banned throughout China in 1950, they continued to be shown in Shanghai for several years. "Let the moralists be damned," Chen told party officials during a meeting on February 15, 1950, on the issue. The campaign also faced challenges in the capital, which the Communists had moved back to Beijing. A November 1950 memorandum issued by that city's Party Committee acknowledged that many movement participants "still deeply worshipped America and were afraid of America." A report from the Communist Youth League observed that even at the height of the anti-American campaign, students persisted in believing "that America's work to educate Chinese was an example of America's friendship for China." Workers expressed similar feelings. America made good machines and durable socks, read a report from the Beijing Federation of Trade Unions, so why should the Chinese despise it? In the countryside, the Union noted, "Japan is hated but America, not so much."

Even party propagandists couldn't hide their awe of the Beautiful Country. *Return from the Big Jail*, which appeared in April 1951, was one of hundreds of anti-American pamphlets published by the state-run press. The pamphlet's stated goal, it said, was to demolish Chinese "fantasies" about the United States. There was Manhattan, with "skyscrapers sixty stories high that block the sun." There was the "magnificent" Waldorf-Astoria, and there was Wall Street, "where the endless beat of the ticker tape controlled the fate of America and the rest of the capitalist world." Wasn't this what Chinese aspired to? Even China's industrial designers could not break the Yankee spell. China's first luxury car, the Red Flag, which rolled off the assembly line in 1955, was modeled after a Chrysler.

The Truman administration had not the slightest inkling of how useful a war with the United States would be to Mao Zedong. Before the conflict, Mao dominated the Central Committee of the Chinese Communist Party. After the war, Mao would dominate China and be hailed as a revolutionary hero around the world. The war provided Mao with the opening he needed to sully the United States and its many friends in China, allowing him to carry his revolution past the point of no return. "The movement to fight America and support Korea has had huge results," Zhou Enlai wrote as the campaign unfolded. "Without such an enemy, we would not have been able to mobilize such strength." Still, Hate America had its limits. Zhou told the Soviet envoy Pavel Yudin that getting people to despise the United States was one of the hardest things the party had ever done. And, for the next four decades, like a bad gene in the DNA of the Chinese psyche, China's pro-American proclivities would resurface again and again, tormenting China's Communist overlords.

CHAPTER TWENTY-NINE

Hate China

While China was undergoing paroxysms over Americans, the United States was having a corresponding convulsion: Should Americans love or hate, shelter or dread the Chinese? For some, the "Yellow Peril" had returned, updated with tanks and howitzers and a decidedly un-American ideology. "Aggressive China Becomes a Menace" reported *Life* magazine in November 1950. "Red China's Fighting Hordes" was the title of a 1952 US Army report on China's way of war. Battling the Communist Chinese, it opined, was "like dealing with mass lunacy." At the same time, mainstream American society was more welcoming of Chinese than it had ever been before. The number of Chinese in the United States doubled, and educated Chinese entered American society at the highest rungs.

The Korean War gave Senator Joe McCarthy new credibility in his hunt for Reds. Following the North Korean invasion, he charged that the advice of "highly placed Red counselors" in the State Department was proving "far more deadly than Red machine gunners in Korea." Then, just three weeks into the war, Julius and Ethel Rosenberg were arrested on charges of passing secrets on the atomic bomb to the Soviet Union. McCarthy's stock soared.

Meanwhile, in Korea, Douglas MacArthur fumed at the restrictions placed on his forces. He could not bomb inside China. He lobbied in vain for a blockade of China's coast and for "unleashing" Chiang Kai-shek's forces to attack China's south. Neverthless, Matthew Ridgway's "meat grinder" campaign was proving effective against the Chinese. Allied forces retook Seoul on March 14, 1951. A week later, Truman and Acheson were preparing an appeal to the Chinese Communists to negotiate an end to the war when MacArthur cut the ground out from under them, demanding that China pull its forces off the Korean peninsula or risk "imminent military collapse." MacArthur then sent a letter to the Speaker of the House, Congressman Joe Martin of Massachusetts, blasting Truman and Acheson for failing to understand that, if the US lost the Korean War, Europe would fall to the Russians. "There is no substitute for victory," he thundered.

Like the great majority of Americans before him, MacArthur opposed sending US ground troops into China. But he wanted to use Korea to roll back Communism in Asia. He was convinced, Ridgway wrote, that "the Chinese masses were ready to welcome Chiang back." Truman worried that MacArthur would wind up bringing the Soviet Union into the fight, with prospects for a nuclear conflict and a Russian invasion of Europe. "In the simplest terms," Truman said, "what we are doing in Korea is this: we are trying to prevent a third world war."

On April 5, Speaker Martin released MacArthur's letter to the press. Not since the American Civil War had an American general so tested the president of the United States. On April 11, Truman relieved MacArthur of his command. One hundred thousand telegrams deluged the White House, almost all opposing the decision.

MacArthur's dismissal provided Joe McCarthy with more fuel for his fire. On June 14, 1951, he broadened his assault to include George Marshall. On the floor of the Senate, McCarthy accused Marshall and Dean Acheson of "craven, whimpering appeasement" in the face of the Communist takeover of China and blamed Marshall's mission to China for the US defeat. Marshall's actions, McCarthy boomed, "must be the product of a great conspiracy, a conspiracy on a scale so immense as to dwarf any previous such venture in the history of man."

The speech bombed. The *Milwaukee Journal*, the leading newspaper in McCarthy's state, called it "garbage." At *Time*, Henry Luce, once sympathetic to McCarthy's Red-baiting, had grown tired of his relentless insistence on Communists under the bed. He told his editors that the time had come to take McCarthy down.

Still, the senator soldiered on. He was joined in his witch hunt by Pat McCarran, a Democratic senator from Nevada, who held more hearings on State Department officials. In July 1951, McCarran called Owen Lattimore back to the Senate to defend himself. Lattimore would soon be hit with seven perjury charges relating to testimony he gave on his time leading a think tank called the Institute of Pacific Relations. He would beat them all.

McCarthy continued to probe and slash at Truman, the State Department, and other enemies, real or imagined. He addressed the Republican National Convention on July 4, 1952, and won reelection to the Senate in November. But when Dwight Eisenhower, a Republican and a World War II hero, won the White House in 1953, McCarthy's value to the GOP fell. He had served the party's purposes as an attack dog, but he was not suitable to lead. To Eisenhower, McCarthy was an embarrassment. And as *Time* magazine argued in October 1951, when Luce put him on the cover under the headline "Demagogue McCarthy," his "antics foul up the necessary examination of the past mistakes of the Truman-Acheson foreign policy."

Luce had a point. By turning Lattimore and others into martyrs, McCarthy had precluded a cool-headed examination of Soviet and Chinese penetration of the US government and Chinese Communist success at affecting US policy. Lattimore's organization, the Institute of Pacific Relations, played a key role in molding American public opinion on China at a time when no fewer than eight Soviet and Chinese Communists were on its staff. IPR publications edited by Lattimore exposed Nationalist corruption and argued that the Communist Chinese would be a better partner for the United States.

While Lattimore was being persecuted, some prominent American liberals, though repulsed by McCarthy's tactics, expressed little love for the State Department's China Hands and their Communist sympathies. Writer Diana Trilling, a leading New York intellectual and literary critic, told readers of the *Partisan Review* that she found Lattimore more dangerous than a spy because he was an honest, independent thinker "whose idealism just happened to coincide with Russian realism." For Trilling, Lattimore posed a dilemma. You could not ban such thought but, she stressed, you needed to understand what he believed so you could counter it.

McCarthy's outrageous attacks were so toxic that they ended up giving anti-Communism among America's China watchers a bad name. As such, noted Richard Walker, who was a young China scholar at the time, they had the "unintended consequence of moving the center of gravity" on issues involving China to the left. Hounded out of government, the China Hands found shelter in American universities. And what emerged from those institutions, Walker argued, was an overly forgiving view of Communist China that made American Sinology "more often than not spectacularly wrong on the essentials." For example, when Walker wrote about the famine caused by Chairman Mao's disastrous Great Leap Forward in the late 1950s, basing it on interviews with refugees in Hong Kong, Harvard historian John K. Fairbank, who also had been dogged by McCarthy, deemed "extreme" his estimate of one to two million dead. In fact, more than thirty million people died. The China Hands also fostered the notion that the US government was responsible for its bad relations with Mao Zedong and that Mao's revolution was the best thing that had ever happened to China. Once ties with China were restored in the 1970s, this contributed to the sense that the United States owed China's Communists an apology.

On July 10, 1951, talks aimed at ending the Korean War began in Kaesong, the ancient capital of the Korean kingdom. US Navy admiral C. Turner Joy represented the UN forces. Senior officers of the Chinese People's Volunteers led the Chinese and North Korean teams. The Chinese, expecting a fast settlement, left their winter coats in Beijing. Two years and 575 meetings later, the two sides signed an armistice.

The Americans had started off on the wrong foot. Once US forces had retaken Seoul, Truman had gone for an armistice "at the first sign that the Reds might be ready to sue for peace," Ridgway noted. Truman called off major combat operations, stopping US forces from pushing north of the thirty-eighth parallel, a decision that Ridgway lamented in his memoirs. The goal would not have been to grab more real estate, Ridgway argued, but to keep the pressure on China to end the war. Ridgway wanted to give China the option of defeat or a deal ratifying the prewar status quo. Admiral Joy agreed. "Demonstrating our own good faith we lost the initiative, never to regain it," Joy wrote.

Mao regarded any American act of goodwill—especially an end to major combat operations—as a sign of Yankee weakness, a view his successors would inherit. So when the Americans halted their offensives, they removed the incentive for Mao to end the war. Indeed, Mao's first aim in agreeing to talks was, he acknowledged, to give his forces a breather from Ridgway's meat grinder. As the two sides prepared for negotiations, Mao fired off telegrams to Stalin asking for more weapons and more Soviet advisers so that he could plan another assault.

In negotiations at Kaesong and then Panmunjom, the Chinese placed the Americans on the south side of the table, reserved in traditional Chinese statecraft for the defeated forces, while they took the north. Joy, a hulking officer with a large head, was furnished with an undersized chair, forcing him to gaze up at his enemies like a schoolboy. Joy came to the talks with a small UN flag; the Communists responded with a larger North Korean standard, prompting the American to speculate that perhaps the tallest flagpole in the world would soon be erected.

The one-upmanship continued outside the talks. Joy arrived in a US army Chevrolet sedan, while his Communist counterparts showed up in a captured Chrysler. "They could never match us with helicopters," Joy wrote later in his salty but insightful book, *How Communists Negotiate*.

The issue that deadlocked the negotiations was the disposition of prisoners of war. In January 1952, the Americans proposed that all POWs be given a choice between returning home or moving to another country. The Chinese accused the United States of violating the Geneva Convention, which called for repatriation of all prisoners.

The Americans estimated that about 10 percent of the 170,000 Chinese and Korean prisoners would refuse repatriation—a number the Communists could stomach. But when the International Committee of the Red Cross determined that more than half wanted to stay in the free world, the Chinese and North Koreans balked at the prospect of such a wholesale rejection of their system.

Desperate to turn the world's attention from the POW issue, the Chinese issued claim after claim of American atrocities. In April 1952, Beijing alleged that US forces had waged germ warfare against China. US Air Force planes had air-dropped infected flies, mosquitoes, spiders, ants, bedbugs, lice, fleas, dragonflies, and centipedes over parts of the country, the party charged. Beijing wheeled out several captured American pilots, who confessed to the charges—after having been tortured.

An international commission was organized by the Soviet-controlled World Peace Council to investigate the allegations. Joseph Needham, a British biochemist, author of a famed study on science in China and a friend of the Communists, led the commission, which predictably corroborated the claims. The scare prompted many Chinese to don surgical masks, a habit that endures today for different reasons. However, the allegations were bogus. According to material in the Soviet archives, Lavrenty Beria, the then head of Soviet intelligence, noted that the Chinese created "false plague regions" and depicted ordinary burials as those of germ warfare victims. On May 2, 1953, the Presidium of the USSR Council of Ministers dismissed all such accusations as "fictitious" and advised Mao to cease making them. In 2013, Wu Zhili, the chief surgeon of the Chinese

People's Volunteers, admitted that the claims were false and that he had been ordered to fabricate evidence.

The POW issue took seventeen months to sort out. Finally, Mao was forced to relent. When the armistice was signed, 6,700 Chinese returned to China while 14,000 stayed away, going mostly to Taiwan. About 3,600 Americans came home; 21 American soldiers remained in China.

The November 1952 election of Republican candidate Dwight Eisenhower and his running mate, the thirty-nine-year-old Richard Nixon, alarmed Moscow and Beijing. Eisenhower's vow to rely more heavily on nuclear weapons with his New Look strategy carried an implicit threat: that Eisenhower was open to using the A-bomb again in Asia.

In his first State of the Union speech, on February 2, 1953, Eisenhower announced that the Seventh Fleet was leaving the Taiwan Strait, hinting that he was ready to let Chiang Kai-shek open another front on China. In Korea, the United States stepped up its air campaign and opened negotiations on a defense treaty with the South.

A month after Eisenhower's State of the Union speech, Joseph Stalin died. The new leaders of the Soviet Union wanted to improve ties with the West. Moscow had already curtailed the flow of arms to the Chinese. Now, it told Beijing that it wanted peace. On July 27, US Army lieutenant general William Harrison and North Korean general Nam Il signed an armistice at Panmunjom. No one spoke a word during the ten-minute ceremony. Harrison refused to don a dress uniform to face opponents whom he contemptuously regarded as "common criminals." He signed his name on the armistice document in Chinese as Hai Lisheng, "the victor standing on the sea."

Mao would achieve none of the goals he had set at the start of the war. The cease-fire line was fixed at the line of contact, and not the thirty-eighth parallel as he had demanded. US forces did not leave the Korean peninsula; about thirty thousand remain there today. And there was no discussion of Taiwan's fate or a Chinese seat at the UN.

Still, Mao Zedong emerged from the war a dashing hero and a leader of an international Communist movement once dominated by Joseph Stalin. Mao had held the strongest nation on earth to a draw, and American officials had been forced to accept representatives of the People's Republic of China as their equals. The Korean War opened the way for the People's Republic of China to emerge as a force to be reckoned with. China played a major role at the Geneva Conference in 1954 and the Bandung Conference in Indonesia the following year.

The Korean War was a violent example of how American-Chinese interactions changed US and world history. The war prompted the United States to alter the terms of the San Francisco Treaty that had ended the Pacific War with Japan. Previously, Washington had considered handing China a string of islands—the Spratlys and the Paracels—in the South China Sea that Japan had once occupied. The Americans had pondered giving Taiwan to China as well.

Instead, the treaty, signed by forty-nine countries on September 8, 1951, left the status of the island chains in the South China Sea undetermined, kept Taiwan from mainland China, and gave the US administrative control over Okinawa and the Senkaku Islands, which the US would use for military exercises. Decades later, the ownership of these territories remains a source of tension in Asia.

The Korean War also gave rise to a concept that dominated American foreign policy for decades—the domino theory. This was the conviction that if one nation fell to the Communists, others would tumble, too. To prevent dominoes from falling, the United States concluded a raft of treaties. Washington formed the ANZUS Pact with New Zealand and Australia in 1951. A year later, it signed the US-Japan Security Treaty. And in 1954, it created the Southeast Asia Treaty Organization. The Korean War was used to bolster the case for America's intervention in Guatemala, Iran, and, of course, Vietnam.

The POW repatriation issue should have been a victory for the United States, but the twenty-one defectors to China stuck in the craw of the American public. The loss of this small batch of men negated the sense of triumph over the many thousands more North Koreans and Communist Chinese who had opted to defect.

Americans searched for reasons for the men's decision and seized on one: brainwashing. Those wily Chinese had discovered a way to bend men's minds. Why else, mused journalist Edward Hunter, would Americans forsake "the highest standard of living that the earth had ever seen" and choose instead "an extremely backward, dreadfully impoverished country?"

Hunter, who served as an intelligence operative during World War II, is credited with coining the word "brainwashing" in English. He compared the process to "witchcraft, with its incantations, trances, poisons, and potions." It was "psychological warfare on a scale incalculably more immense than any militarist of the past has ever envisaged," he wrote. To Gladwin Hill, writing in the *Atlantic Monthly*, Chinese brainwashing constituted "a new secret weapon." The Chinese were all too happy to confirm American fears. What else was Mao Zedong Thought, wrote Mao's right-hand man Lin Biao, than "a spiritual atom bomb of infinite power?"

Spooked by the thought of Communists fiddling with the psyches of American boys, the CIA studied mind control as well, with occasional deadly results. The agency launched a research program in 1953, code-named MKULTRA, in which CIA researchers tested LSD and other psychoactive drugs on Americans. CIA chief Allen Dulles called it "brain warfare."

When Chinese and Americans exchanged their first batch of prisoners in April 1953, the Department of Defense worried that the Chinese had handpicked POWs who were primed to introduce the Communist virus into the United States. The men were placed in lockdown in the Valley Forge Army Hospital in Phoenixville, Pennsylvania, where the Defense Department subjected them to "political psychiatric therapy" to counteract China's black magic.

In a book on the defectors, *21 Stayed*, Virginia Pasley, a Long Island *Newsday* reporter, blamed dysfunctional families, a failure to attend church, poverty, and—in the case of Clarence Adams, an African American corporal from Memphis, Tennessee—anger at racism. Pasley argued that the failure to instill patriotism in America's youth rendered them ill equipped to resist Communism's lure. The Chinese had an advantage. They followed a single party line; they were automatons—"blue ants" or ChiComs in the parlance of the times. The belief, first born in California's gold country a century earlier, that Americans lacked the inner strength to confront the Chinese resurfaced in a new form. In the face of China's "brain warfare," *New Yorker* writer Eugene Kinkead contended that American POWs in Korea had collaborated more than in other conflicts and had died at an alarming rate from the disease of "give-up-itis."

Americans emerged from the People's Republic denouncing the United States and praising China and were widely believed to have been the victims of brainwashing. Harriet Mills was a Fulbright scholar in Beijing in 1950 when she was denied permission to leave China and charged with espionage. Her Chinese captors often kept her shackled and locked in solitary confinement, and in lengthy interrogation sessions they preyed on Mills's feelings of guilt about the privileged life she had lived as the daughter of China missionaries to get her to question her former identity and values. In 1955, she was released after more than four years in prison, describing herself to US newspapers as an "espionage agent" for the United

States and labeling Americans "warmongers." Writing in the *Atlantic Monthly* in 1959, Mills declared that the Chinese government was engaged in the "greatest campaign in human history to reshape the minds of men."

These anxieties about the mind-bending powers of the Chinese were reflected in the Cold War masterpiece *The Manchurian Candidate*, which appeared as a novel in 1959 and as a movie three years later. It's the story of a brainwashed American POW released back to the US as part of a plot to assassinate a presidential candidate so that the Communist-agent wife of the vice presidential candidate can become the power behind the Yankee throne. The film's dastardly Chinese puppet master, Yen Lo, combines the cunning of Fu Manchu with the ideology of Chairman Mao. As the lead character Raymond Shaw says of the Chinese, "They can make me do anything, Ben, can't they? Anything."

The problem with all the dark talk of historic levels of collaboration and brainwashing was that it wasn't true. An official Defense Department investigation by air force sociologist Albert Biderman determined that American POWs in Korea were no less patriotic than prisoners of other wars. He also found, as he wrote in 1957, that what was "new and spectacular" about Chinese methods was "nothing new or spectacular" at all. To break their prisoners, he wrote, the Chinese tortured them, deprived them of sleep, exposed them to intense cold, and forced them into excruciatingly painful stress positions for long periods of time. After a while, most men or women would say or do anything to get the torture to stop.

In one of the many twists of the Sino-American story, the techniques the Chinese employed against Americans in Korea became the basis for US military interrogations of prisoners following the September 11, 2001, terrorist attacks. A Defense Department description of the methods given as guidance to US forces dealing with suspected terrorists had been copied verbatim from Biderman's 1957 report. Only the title—"Communist Coercive Methods for Eliciting Individual Compliance"—had been changed.

On October 21, 1949, twenty days after Mao Zedong founded the People's Republic of China, An Wang filed a patent for an invention as technologically revolutionary as Mao's invention of the PRC was politically. Wang had discovered the fundamental process underlying the modern computer memory chip. An Wang was one of thousands of Chinese whom the Nationalists dispatched to the United States at the end of World War II to learn about American industry. Wang, who had spent the war scraping together spare parts to build combat radio equipment for the Nationalist army, won a scholarship to earn a PhD at Harvard.

An Wang completed his doctorate in 1948 and began work at the Harvard Computation Laboratory under Howard Aiken, one of the pioneers of computer development. Wang's parents were deceased, so he was freed from the guilt of choosing America over family in China. He also knew, he wrote in his memoirs, that he "could not thrive under a totalitarian Communist system." He wanted to make his own decisions about his life, an impossibility in Mao's China.

In 1949, Wang applied for a patent for magnetic-core memory, a process that would constitute the foundation of the computing industry up to the 1970s when semiconductor chips appeared. In 1951, he started a business with "no orders, no contracts and no office furniture." Wang named his company Wang Laboratories because, he wrote, he wanted "to show that Chinese could excel at things other than running laundries and restaurants." He designed equipment to help fledgling American industries—a device to determine the decay rate of radioactive waste for nuclear power plants and a machine that counted white blood cells. Ultimately, Wang Laboratories would manufacture one of the first computers designed for word processing.

Wang Laboratories sparked the development of a computer industry along Route 128 near Boston. Wang was obsessed with overtaking IBM, and he actually came close—an incredible feat for the son of an English teacher from Jiangsu province. But the company ultimately failed, at least in part, because Wang did what any good Chinese boss often does and promoted his son to run the company. Unfortunately, the results in this case were disastrous.

Like most American-educated Chinese, Wang wasn't interested in the radical politics of Mao Zedong. "As a nation we do not always live up to our ideals," he wrote about the United States, "but we have structures that allow us to correct our wrongs by means short of revolution." He and his wife, Lorraine Chiu, a distant relative of Yung Wing of the Chinese Educational Mission, became naturalized American citizens in 1955.

The couple became Americans during a period of unprecedented growth in America's Chinese community. For the first few years after the repeal of the Chinese Exclusion Act in 1943, fewer than 100 Chinese immigrated to America. But starting in 1945, Congress began enacting laws—the War Brides Act, the Chinese Alien Wives of American Citizens Act, and the Refugee Act of 1957—that transformed the face of Chinese America.

During the war, 7,000 Chinese women married Americans, the most famous bride being Chen Xiangmei, a reporter for China's Central News Agency who wed Claire Chennault and became known to Americans as Anna Chennault. With the brides' arrival in America, Chinatown's bachelor society finally gave way to a community of families. In 1900, there had been 19 Chinese men to each Chinese woman in America; by 1950 the ratio had dropped to 2 to 1. More Chinese lived in America in 1950—around 110,000—than at any time since 1880.

The original intent of the American endeavor to educate the Chinese was to arm them with Yankee technology and values and send them back to China. But as the Cold War of ideas seethed, Americans came to view Chinese minds as the kindling for an intellectual bonfire in the United States. A hundred years earlier, Chinese brawn had helped build the West. Now Chinese brains took over. Chinese men and women—An Wang; his fellow native of Jiangsu province, the architect I. M. Pei; Nobel Prize winners C. N. Yang and T. D. Lee; writers and entrepreneurs—rewarded the United States with an enormous payoff. Along with Americans and other gifted foreigners from across the globe, Chinese Americans raised the scaffolding of an advanced industrial economy in the United States.

In 1950, the State Department began finding jobs for about 5,000 Chinese students and scholars stranded in America by the Communist revolution. Over the next few years, State would dole out $10 million to 3,600 men and women, allowing them to settle in America. Meanwhile, confronting an avalanche of more than a hundred thousand visa applications from Chinese in Hong Kong and elsewhere, China's friends in the United States founded Aid Refugee Chinese Intellectuals Incorporated. From 1952 to 1959, the group helped with visas, chartered planes, loaned money, and found jobs for thousands more elite Chinese who wanted to move to the US.

Walter Judd, a Republican congressman from Minnesota, led the group. Judd had spent six years in China as a medical missionary encouraging Chinese to get an education in America and return to build China. Now, he was trying to get gifted Chinese out of China to help build the United States. Judd's colleague, the missionary-turned-journalist Geraldine Fitch, called America's programs to find talented Chinese "brains for a bargain."

A 50 percent jump in population and greater opportunities gave America's Chinese a new self-confidence. In 1943, Pardee Lowe, a graduate of Stanford University and the Harvard Business School, wrote the first book-length autobiography of an American-born Chinese. Lowe's *Father and*

Glorious Descendant charted his lifelong efforts to fit in with mainstream, white America. He made fun of Chinese names—"Sing High, Sing Low, Wun Long Hop"—and described the "uncomfortable feeling" when Chinese people addressed him by his Chinese name.

Just seven years later, when Jade Snow Wong published the first auto-biography by a Chinese American woman in 1950, the apologies were gone. In Wong's *Fifth Chinese Daughter*, Chinese culture was an asset, not an embarrassment. Wong's book sat on the best-seller lists for four months. It was a Book of the Month Club selection, won the Commonwealth Club's Medal for Non-Fiction, and was translated into dozens of languages, selling half a million copies. For more than a quarter of a century, it was the most widely read book by a second-generation Chinese writer until Maxine Hong Kingston's *The Woman Warrior* appeared in 1976. Kingston credited Wong with inspiring her to write.

Wong was born in 1922 in San Francisco. Her parents ran a sweatshop and manned sewing machines after work. The family lived in a cramped basement apartment in Chinatown. Wong's brother, favored over her and her sisters, had his own room, a pet German shepherd, and a Chinese language tutor. When he graduated from high school, his parents paid to send him to college. Jade had to put herself through school.

To earn money for tuition, Jade worked as a housekeeper and a cook for white American families. She faced racism from bigots at her mostly white school and the occasional bad attitude among her employers. But she made it into a junior college and then transferred to Mills College, the renowned women's university across San Francisco Bay. There she flaunted her ethnicity. She discovered, she wrote, that "the girls were perpetually curious" about her Chinese background. She also found that whenever she wrote about Chinese themes, she got better grades. It might have helped that one of her papers concerned *Jin Ping Mei*, a Ming dynasty novel and one of the world's great pornographic masterpieces.

Jade battled for years with her father over her life plans. Finally, she gave up trying to change him. When she entered the Wong household, she didn't talk back and she performed her usual daughterly duties. But outside, she blazed a trail, blending Chinese aesthetics with Yankee entrepreneurial chutzpah. Jade had a talent for pottery and for self-promotion, and set up a business on Grant Avenue in San Francisco, putting her studio in the display window where, with a potter's smock and traditional Chinese braids, she worked the wheel—and stopped traffic.

"Chinatown was agog," Wong wrote. "The woman in the window, her legs astride a potter's wheel, her hair in braids, her hands perpetually messy with sticky California clay, her finished products such things as coolies used in China, the daughter of a conservative family, running a business alone—such a combination was sure to fail!" It didn't. Wong's pottery won awards, was collected by more than twenty museums, including the Metropolitan Museum of Art, and her artistry was acclaimed as an example of the long-sought Great Harmony, an integration of China into the mainstream culture of the United States.

The State Department saw in Wong's book a chance to show off the success of a Chinese American to Asians gripped by nationalism and the desire to be free of colonial domination. In 1953, it arranged for the book to be translated into Chinese and several other Asian languages and sent her and her husband to Asia on a four-month lecture tour. Wong was blunt with her audiences about the latent racism in American society. But she also told them she was glad that her father had decided to try his luck in America instead of staying in China. Jade Snow Wong "could never have obtained her education, or learned her art, or started a career, had she been born on that side of the Pacific," she declared. Critics would later wince at her political incorrectness, but she was right.

While books like Pardee's and Lowe's were saluted as signs that Chinese Americans were, in the words of Helen P. Bolman, writing in the *Library Journal*, America's "loyal minority," other Chinese in America were seen as a threat. Some were treated as spies and leftists and expelled. Others were considered so dangerous that the United States prevented them from returning home. Citing an obscure 1918 law that allowed authorities to block citizens of an enemy nation from leaving America, US officials pulled Chinese scholars off ships bound for Asia to block them from aiding China's efforts in the Korean War. A total of 175 such detention orders would be issued. In March 1951, James Reston of the *New York Times* reported that the controversy over what to do with the Chinese had produced "a whole series of small interdepartmental wars in Washington."

At the California Institute of Technology, the FBI and the Immigration and Naturalization Service launched a multiyear investigation of one of the world's greatest rocket scientists, Qian Xuesen, which ended in his expulsion from the United States. As Lee Dubridge, Caltech's president, wrote to one US official about Qian's case: "This is a ridiculous situation that one of the greatest rocket and jet propulsion experts in the country is not only denied the opportunity of working in his chosen field, but by such denial is forced to return to occupied China and his talents made available presumably to the communist regime there."

At the University of Illinois, American authorities ordered sixteen Chinese students out of the country. "We are making a gift to our enemies, the present Government of China, of trained technicians, steeped in American know-how," wrote Arthur Hamilton, the supervisor of foreign students at Illinois, in a letter to the *New York Times*. The *Times* called these deportation orders "criminal."

On October 4, 1957, the Union of Soviet Socialist Republics announced that it had successfully launched the world's first satellite. The beep-beep broadcast from Sputnik, a metal ball twenty-three inches in diameter orbiting the globe, triggered a national crisis in the United States.

Barely a month later, two Chinese men, working in American labs, rode to the rescue. C. N. Yang and T. D. Lee won the 1957 Nobel Prize in Physics for proving that one of the basic laws of quantum mechanics—the conservation of parity—is violated in weak nuclear reactions. The award, the first for ethnic Chinese, reassured Americans who were concerned that the West was losing the Cold War in science and technology.

When the news of Yang and Lee's experiment first broke in January 1957, and that another Chinese researcher, C. S. Wu, a female physicist at Columbia University, had verified their results, American newspapers paid little heed. Yang and Lee were described as "Chinese-born theoreticians," and Wu was called "another Chinese professor."

It took Sputnik to make Yang and Lee heroes. *Time* ran biographies along with pictures of them and their families in front of their solidly middle-class American homes. *Newsweek* headlined its coverage "These Chinese Choose," highlighting the fact that both men had decided to stay in America. That said, American officials, *Newsweek* reported, worried that either Yang or Lee might use their trip to the awards ceremony in Sweden as an opportunity to slip behind the Bamboo Curtain. *Newsweek* called the men "prize catches for any power."

But in Stockholm, C. N. Yang "left no doubt where he stood," *Newsweek* reported. In his acceptance speech, he thanked America for educating him, and he declared that he was "as proud of my Chinese heritage and background as I am devoted to modern science." Both men returned to the United States and became American citizens. Still, their adopted country wasn't sure whether to shun them or embrace them. When C. N.

Yang moved to Stony Brook, New York, lured by the prospect of running his own lab, no one wanted to sell a home to a Chinese man.

As mainstream America came to grips with China's revolution, Chinese-language newspapers counseled their readers to be civil to white people and try to ignore bigotry. "Maintain closer contacts with Caucasian groups and rely on the friendly support of liberals," suggested San Francisco's *China Forum*. In public, remembered Chang-lin Tien, who did graduate work in Louisville, Kentucky, many Chinese "dared not speak Chinese." Tien's white professors referred to him as "Chinaman." He would go on to become chancellor of the University of California at Berkeley, the first Asian American to lead a major US university. America's Chinese in the 1950s kept quiet, Tien recalled, "as cicadas in cold weather."

The Korean War taught the Chinese a hard lesson about the deadliness of modern mechanized warfare. Although China has never released detailed statistics on its war dead, the Chinese People's Volunteers are estimated to have lost ten soldiers for every American who died. The war strengthened the hand of those in the Communist Party who argued for more advanced weapons, better technology, and ultimately, a nuclear bomb. Though Mao continued to call the United States a "paper tiger," he never again pitted troops directly against those of the Beautiful Country.

The war left a chaotic legacy in the United States. It was the first of America's limited conflicts, in which US objectives were constrained by fears of a nuclear Armageddon. And it ended, at least for a while, the sentimental attachment to the Chinese.

The trauma of actually fighting Chinese troops cannot be exaggerated. American officials, so accustomed to believing in the special relationship, were in a state of denial about China's very nature. Secretary of State Dean Acheson called it "a Slavic Manchukuo," implying that the Chinese had become Russian. The Beijing government, he claimed, "is not the government of China. It does not pass the first test. It is not Chinese."

CHAPTER THIRTY

A Cold War

President Dwight D. Eisenhower and his secretary of state, John Foster Dulles, hated Communism. Eisenhower considered it the primary enemy of his time.

As children, John Foster Dulles and his brother, Allen, who would serve Eisenhower as the first civilian chief of the CIA, spent a lot of time in the Dupont Circle mansion of their grandfather, John W. Foster, surrounded by mementos of his days as a lobbyist for the Qing dynasty. Yet neither acquired an interest in the Far East. In 1927, Allen resigned from the State Department rather than accept a posting to Beijing. And when President Truman tried to appoint John Foster Dulles ambassador to Japan, Dulles resisted what he called "exile" in Asia.

John Foster Dulles, a prominent member of the Presbyterian Church, reserved a special place in the darkest corner of his heart for the godless Chicoms. He made sure that economic sanctions applied against Beijing were even more severe than those against Moscow, a policy that became known as the China Differential. Though Americans could travel freely to the Soviet Union, Dulles did his best to cut off all contact with the Red Chinese. He blocked an American zoo from importing a Chinese panda, threatened journalists with prosecution if they went to China, and approved the indictment of a stamp dealer who sold Communist Chinese stamps. Eisenhower shared his secretary of state's distaste for the Chinese. He threatened Mao's regime with nuclear annihilation eight times.

In the 1950s, the United States government discarded the hundred-year-old American belief that a united, sovereign China was in the best interests of the United States. In fact, Eisenhower and Dulles attributed the success of the Communist revolution to the unwillingness of American strategists to contemplate China's division. Dulles argued that it would have been better if Chiang Kai-shek had abandoned Manchuria during China's civil war and gathered his forces south of the Great Wall. "The territorial integrity of China became a shibboleth," Dulles told a colleague. "We finally got a territorially integrated China—for whose benefit? The Communists."

With the help of Allen Dulles at the CIA, the Eisenhower administration launched a series of covert operations to chip away at Beijing's control over its territory. The United States began its decades-long involvement in Vietnam. Taiwan became America's "unsinkable aircraft carrier" in the Western Pacific. Dividing, not uniting, China became the goal.

Still, both Eisenhower and Dulles were more than blinkered Cold Warriors. Their approach to Red China and what was then known as "Free China," or Taiwan, was far more complex than has often been recognized. Eisenhower's threats to use nuclear weapons against China, for example, contained a healthy dose of high-stakes bluffing. In September 1958, at the height of a crisis over Taiwan, when the Strategic Air Command deployed to Guam B-47s capable of carrying Hiroshima-sized nuclear bombs, Eisenhower remarked to his generals: "You boys must be crazy. We can't use those awful things against Asians for the second time."

Both Eisenhower and his secretary of state were also tantalized by the possibility of separating Beijing from Moscow. They disagreed only on the means. Foreshadowing US policy in the 1970s, Eisenhower believed that trade with the West would reduce Beijing's dependence on Moscow and could be used to "infiltrate democratic ideas" into China. Dulles countered that the more China was forced to rely on the Soviet Union, the more Moscow would bleed. So while Dulles made sure that the United States did not trade with the Chinese Communists, Eisenhower worked to allow China to trade with other nations. Eisenhower released Japan from an agreement to restrict its trade with China. And in 1958, when Great Britain announced that it, too, would no longer comply with American-mandated limits,

Eisenhower rejected a Defense Department suggestion that the US impose special tariffs on Britain's exports to the United States.

Ultimately, Eisenhower and Dulles were limited in their flexibility toward China not because they were unyielding Cold Warriors but because China remained a domestic political issue. The China Lobby was strong, and the American public remained deeply disenchanted with the Reds. In 1953, a China Lobby spin-off group, the Committee of One Million, collected one million signatures against China's entry into the UN. Three years later, 92 percent of Americans polled nationwide said that they opposed allowing the Chinese Communists into the United Nations, and 61 percent did not support trading with the PRC.

"Our trouble," Eisenhower complained to the National Security Council, "was that our domestic political situation compelled us to adopt an absolutely rigid policy" on trade and in other areas. However, being tough on China gave Eisenhower political capital to pursue détente with the new Soviet leader, Nikita Khrushchev. If Washington couldn't lure Mao away from Khrushchev, it would tempt Khrushchev away from Mao.

Eisenhower's policies toward Taiwan were also less monolithic than they are often portrayed. Just as World War II rescued Mao Zedong, the Korean War saved Chiang Kai-shek. After the Korean People's Army poured across the thirty-eighth parallel, America decided to underwrite the Kuomintang. A formal American Military Assistance Advisory Group, led by a US general, soon replaced Charles M. Cooke's ad hoc operation aiding Taiwan's military. CIA operatives flooded the island, as did US weapons. "It was all very wonderful and an answer to a prayer," Senator H. Alexander Smith, a Republican from New Jersey, enthused about the Korean War in his diary. "The saving of Formosa was clearly God-guided."

In 1954, the Eisenhower administration concluded a mutual defense treaty with Chiang that committed the United States to a multidecade program of military and economic aid. The treaty's purpose was not to start a war but to prevent one. The United States did not want Mao to invade Taiwan, but equally, it did not want Chiang to attack China. As a condition of agreeing to the treaty, Eisenhower and Dulles forced Chiang to grant them veto power over any major military operation.

The desire to try to avoid war also led Eisenhower and Dulles to push China and Taiwan to accept the existence of "two Chinas"—just as there were an East and West Germany and a North and South Korea. Both the president and the secretary of state spent years unsuccessfully trying to persuade Chiang Kai-shek to withdraw his troops from a few specks of

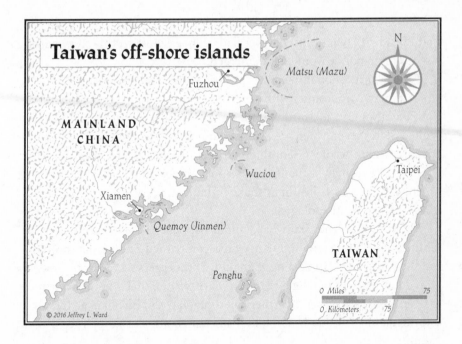

land hard along China's southern coast. Politically, those islands—Quemoy (Jinmen), Matsu (Mazu), and Dachen—constituted Chiang's sole remaining claim to be the ruler of all China. Militarily, they were a tinderbox.

In April 1954, Communist China attended its first international peace conference, in Geneva, with the United States, Britain, France, and the USSR, to discuss problems in Korea and Indochina. In the middle of the conference, the French suffered a historic defeat at Dien Bien Phu in Vietnam, sounding the death knell for their colonial enterprise in Southeast Asia.

At Geneva, the Chinese fielded a delegation of two hundred, led by the smooth-talking Zhou Enlai. They ensconced themselves in a chateau where Jean-Jacques Rousseau had once lived and served scotch, vermouth, and caviar at their first reception, which no Americans attended.

For decades, historians on both sides of the Pacific contended that at some point during the conference Secretary of State John Foster Dulles and Foreign Minister Zhou Enlai crossed paths. Zhou supposedly held out his hand, but Dulles refused to shake it. The vignette became one of the foundational myths of the Sino-American narrative. Dulles's ostentatious rejection represented yet another missed American opportunity to improve relations and implied that the United States bore sole responsibility for the sorry state of affairs between Washington and Beijing. If only Dulles and President Dwight Eisenhower had been less hostile, this story has it, a sane China policy would have emerged.

For his part, Zhou milked the tale. In 1957, complaining about America's failure to compromise with his government, he noted that "only when both parties move forward can they shake hands, but in the case of the United States, even when we extended our hand they refused to take it." Richard Nixon wrote at length about seeking, in his first meeting with Zhou on the tarmac of the Beijing airport on February 21, 1972, to make amends for Dulles's "lost handshake." That entire encounter took on the air of an American apology.

Yet, in fact, it is unclear what actually happened in Geneva. Two senior Chinese officials, Wang Bingnan, who accompanied Zhou Enlai throughout the conference, and Xiong Xianghui, Zhou's press secretary in Geneva who doubled as an intelligence officer, have written that it never occurred. U. Alexis Johnson, a senior American diplomat, and Pu Shan, a Harvard-educated aide to Zhou Enlai, told historian Nancy Bernkopf Tucker that it did.

The story of the handshake-that-might-have-been underscores a key point about the Sino-American relationship in the 1950s. There was no shortage of enmity on both sides and both sides share blame for their Cold War.

At Geneva, Dulles pressed the British to join the fight against Communism in Vietnam. To the Americans, the looming threat from China had turned the anticolonial battle in Vietnam into a struggle of global importance. But the British were not interested. Unlike the United States, Britain recognized the PRC as the legal government of China in January 1950. When it became clear that the conference would not block the rise of the Vietnamese Communist leader Ho Chi Minh, Dulles withdrew, the only time in US history that a secretary of state abandoned a Big Power conference before it ended. The British were appalled. "Dull, unimaginative, uncomprehending" was how Winston Churchill described the American secretary of state.

Geneva produced an accord on Indochina. Under that deal, Vietnam would be divided along the seventeenth parallel. Ho Chi Minh would rule from Hanoi in the north, while France and her allies would cobble together a pro-Western government in Saigon. The parties agreed that an election to unify the country would be held in July 1956.

With Eisenhower's blessing, Dulles and his brother, Allen, moved to subvert the deal. An ever-expanding CIA operation was established in South Vietnam to support Ngo Dinh Diem, a former official in the French colonial regime, whom the Americans had picked as leader in the South.

Washington's growing interest in Vietnam was a direct function of its fear of China. As the US increased its cooperation with South Vietnam, it moved to tighten the noose around Mao's China. In July, as the Geneva Conference limped to its conclusion, Washington announced its defense treaty with Chiang Kai-shek. The United States then formed the Southeast Asia Treaty Organization, grouping eight nations in Asia together in an anti-Communist bloc.

On September 3, 1954, as diplomats headed to Manila to sign the SEATO treaty, Mao's forces bombarded Nationalist forces on Quemoy Island, off the coast of Fujian province, barely a mile from the Communist-held city of Xiamen. In November, Mao ordered bombing raids on the Kuomintang-held Dachen Island, off the coast of Zhejiang province. On December 2, the United States and the Republic of China signed their mutual defense treaty. In January 1955, the People's Liberation Army landed on one of the islands in the Dachen chain. At that point, Dulles convinced Chiang to pull his forces from Dachen, arguing that they were too far from Taiwan to be adequately defended. Throughout the spring, Mao kept the pressure on, believing that somehow he would be able to scare Washington away from Chiang's side.

On March 10, 1955, as Mao's forces continued to shell the offshore islands, Dulles threatened China with nuclear war. Six days later, Eisenhower repeated the threat. "A-bombs can be used," Eisenhower declared, "as you would use a bullet." An international uproar ensued as NATO foreign ministers warned against the deployment of any nuclear device. Still, by the end of the month, talk of war with China was at a fever pitch. Admiral Robert Carney, chief of Naval Operations, told reporters that Eisenhower planned "to destroy Red China's military potential." War, he predicted, would break out in April.

Eisenhower sent Joint Chiefs chairman Arthur Radford to Taiwan to offer Chiang a deal: if Chiang would withdraw from all the offshore islands, the United States would blockade a five-hundred-mile stretch of the Chinese coast until China agreed to renounce force against Taiwan. Chiang rejected the proposal. The United States would never follow through, he told his diary. The Americans, he wrote, were "completely deceiving" and "naive and ignorant" to think that he would fall for their scheme. In

Beijing, Mao warned his lieutenants to prepare for nuclear war. He also ordered Zhou Enlai to get him out of a jam.

In mid-April 1955, Zhou traveled to Indonesia to attend the Bandung Conference, the first gathering "of colored peoples in the history of mankind," as then Indonesian president Sukarno put it. Heading to the conference, an Air India charter plane carrying Chinese Communist officials exploded over the Pacific Ocean, killing all its passengers. Zhou should have been on board but had altered his plans at the last minute. A Nationalist agent had planted a bomb in the engine well. Having cheated death, Zhou took the conference by storm.

News about the Bandung Conference hit the pages of American newspapers just as the American civil rights movement gained momentum. In 1954, the Supreme Court had ruled segregation unconstitutional. To the African American congressman Adam Clayton Powell Jr., the conference represented an opportunity for America to promote its system as an alternative to Communism. Powell urged Dulles to put together a group of observers—white, black, Asian, men and women—to show the world the power of American diversity. Dulles rejected the idea, but Powell, calling the decision an example of American "stupidity," attended anyway.

The absence of an official US representative left the field to Zhou Enlai, and American newspapers reported in detail about his accommodations—"the house of a wealthy Chinese"—his speeches, and even his moods. Peggy Durdin, who had once called him one of the most charming men alive, now referred to him as "tough and supple-witted." The Communist Chinese, she told her readers in the *New York Times*, "hate us."

Zhou was masterful, stressing China's solidarity with the developing world's struggles against colonial powers and contrasting China's support of independence movements with America's poor civil rights record. On the final day of the conference, Zhou dropped a bombshell. He offered to negotiate with the United States over the standoff with Taiwan. "The Chinese people are friendly to the American people," Zhou said. "The Chinese people do not want to have war with the United States of America." On April 24, 1955, the *New York Times* splashed his proposal across the front page, calling it "remarkable for its moderation." A week later, Mao's forces stopped shelling Quemoy.

Dulles agreed to talks with China, deputizing U. Alexis Johnson, a diplomat who had been interned by the Japanese in Manchuria during World War II, to open the negotiations. China appointed Wang Bingnan, a longtime aide to Zhou Enlai. Over the next sixteen years, representatives from the two sides would meet 136 times in Geneva and Warsaw, ending only in 1971, when Henry Kissinger visited China. Many historians and US officials have derided the talks as nothing more than organized shouting matches. The rooms in a Warsaw palace where many sessions were held contained so many bugs that a British diplomat once claimed to have picked up the negotiations on his car radio. But at several critical junctures, the continuing, if erratic, dialogue reduced the risk of war.

Mao Zedong and Chiang Kai-shek both emerged stronger from what became known as the First Straits Crisis. On the mainland, Mao used the affair, especially Eisenhower's nuclear threat, to wheedle from the Soviets a commitment to help China build its own bomb. He also forced the Americans to once again acknowledge the existence of the People's Republic of China.

Chiang got his defense treaty and a new multiyear US aid commitment. But, as usual, the Generalissimo was not happy. The signing of the mutual defense pact ended Chiang's dream of ever "recovering the mainland." He had been thrilled by Eisenhower's election, but now he told his diary that the president lacked "common sense." Disillusioned Nationalist officials who had believed Eisenhower when he vowed to "unleash" Chiang Kai-shek now quipped that the American president had instituted a "lend-leash" policy instead.

Nevertheless, the defense treaty signaled a much deeper American commitment to the island's success and to Chiang's government. American plans to replace or even assassinate Chiang were put on ice and pressure on him to democratize evaporated. When Chiang appointed his son, Chiang Ching-kuo, as security chief, the Americans raised few objections to Ching-kuo's hardball tactics, which in any case paled in comparison to the havoc that Mao's secret police were wreaking on the mainland. "We are trying to develop strength on this island, and the introduction of reforms or Western democratic ideas should be pushed only as they promise to increase the sum total of that strength," declared US ambassador Karl Rankin in a message to Washington in January 1953.

On the economic front, also gone was American pressure to privatize Free China's economy. By 1953, the Kuomintang owned 80 percent of the industry on Taiwan. The Americans supported Taiwan's policy of keeping tariffs high to protect Taiwanese businesses, even if this blocked free trade. Taiwan's first four-year economic plan was drawn up as a result of American pressure. Although Taiwan's friends in America were Yankee capitalists, they backed a government that was socialist at heart.

Employing the ideas of the rural reformer and American-educated Christian Jimmy Yen, American and Chinese experts on Taiwan's Joint Commission on Rural Reconstruction carried out one of the most successful land reform campaigns in Asian history. While Mao's followers executed an estimated two million landlords on mainland China, there was no loss of life in the Nationalists' drive to redistribute land on Taiwan.

American-educated finance officials tamed inflation. Chiang even kept his military budget in check. It helped, of course, that from 1945 to 1965, the United States gave Taiwan more than $4 billion, the largest military and economic infusion per capita at the time. But, unlike many other countries, Taiwan did not waste the aid. It resulted in the creation of a global exporting giant. From 1952 to 1982, Taiwan's economy grew an average of 9 percent a year. An island that had but a few paved roads in 1950 became the Taiwan Miracle.

Like the United States, Communist China also reaped enormous benefits from its American-educated citizens. On September 17, 1955, rocket scientist Qian Xuesen, along with his wife and their son, Yucon, and their daughter, Yungjen, boarded a ship to Hong Kong. At the dock, Qian told reporters that he was leaving the US for good. He expressed "no bitterness against the American people" for the actions of the US government. "My objective is the pursuit of peace and happiness," he said.

Back home, Qian piloted China's strategic rocket program. Two other returnees, Deng Jiaxian, a PhD from Purdue, and Zhu Guangya, from the University of Michigan, became the chief architects of China's program to build the Bomb. Xie Jialin, who had been pulled off a boat in Hawaii in 1951, was a leader in particle physics. Zhao Zhongyao, who was stopped in Japan trying to return to China, ultimately made it back with $50,000 worth of parts for China's first linear accelerator, while another researcher brought back an American oscilloscope so advanced that it mesmerized scientists from the Eastern Bloc.

Chinese educated in America built China's first satellites, designed China's first intercontinental ballistic missile and its first cruise missile, and founded the discipline of nuclear physics in China, including research into cosmic rays, particle and high-energy physics, and bubble chambers. From 1949 to 1956, 129 Chinese students and scholars from the United States went to work in the elite Chinese Academy of Sciences, where they accounted for more than a quarter of all its top slots—at a time when Soviet scientific principles were supposed to reign.

These American-trained men and women played a key role in encouraging Mao to pursue a more independent policy vis-à-vis Moscow. Qian Xuesen was appointed director of the Institute of Mechanics over a Russian-trained scientist. He was so important to China's move away from the USSR that in the 1970s, a Soviet publication theorized that his return was part of China's "clandestine bargaining with the [American] imperialists" against the USSR. Asked for his views on the generally unproductive talks with the United States in the 1950s, Zhou Enlai was frank: "We won back Qian Xuesen. That alone made the talks worthwhile." Chairman Mao wanted a nuclear deterrent. American-educated scientists, along with their European-trained colleagues, would give him one.

Despite his disenchantment with America, Qian remained loyal to the American principles of scientific education. In 1958, he helped found the elite University of Science and Technology of China, modeling it on his alma mater, Caltech. Qian's exams were dreaded because he demanded original thinking, rather than rote memorization. Even in the reddest days of China's Communist revolution, the Chinese approach to science, technology, and innovation was directly derived from the United States.

In August 1956, the Chinese government invited fifteen American news agencies to send reporters to China for a monthlong visit. In the aftermath of the Bandung Conference, China had modified its virulently anti-American stance and was seeking to improve its image in the United States.

At the State Department, however, Dulles declared that the United States would not allow US journalists to travel to China because the Chinese government planned to kidnap them. He vowed to revoke the passport of anyone who violated the ban. It was a ridiculous assertion and a heavy-handed threat, but it cowed most reporters, except for three: Edmund Stevens and Phillip Harrington from *Look* magazine, and William Worthy from the *Baltimore Afro-American*.

Worthy was one of America's first great African American foreign correspondents. He had been a conscientious objector during World War II, had covered the Korean War, and would later gain a place in American folk culture when, after he made an unauthorized trip to Cuba, Phil Ochs told his story in a popular 1964 folksong—"Ballad of William Worthy."

Worthy crossed the Chinese border from Hong Kong on Christmas Eve 1956. His reports from behind the Bamboo Curtain ran in newspapers across America. He asked, why were Americans banned from traveling to

China? Why did America not recognize the most populous country on earth? "Is it possible," he asked readers of the *Afro-American* on January 29, 1957, "that this policy stems in part from a sense of outrage that a hitherto passive nation of 'little yellow men' should stand up to the West?"

But Worthy was no useful idiot for the Communist cause. His interview with Paul J. Mackensen Jr., a Lutheran missionary from Baltimore who had been held in a Chinese prison since 1952 and repeatedly interrogated, exposed the Orwellian nature of the Communist regime. The Chinese had broken the young man, who was so racked with guilt over a catalogue of American crimes that all he could do was beg for his captors' forgiveness.

Worthy's trip touched off a debate over China. "Silly and self-defeating" was how the *Washington Post* described Eisenhower's policy of banning American journalists from going to China. In an editorial titled "Report No Evil," the *Post* cited Worthy's groundbreaking coverage, noting that "it was an illusion to think that reporting from China by American correspondents would necessarily be to the advantage of the Peiping [Beijing] government." Gallup polls released in 1957 showed that though an overwhelming majority of Americans still opposed seating the PRC in the United Nations, more than half favored allowing American reporters to travel there.

The Worthy trip and its reverberations revealed that the vast edifice opposing contact with mainland China was cracking. Even Dulles was changing. Privately, he told his aides that the time was approaching when the United States would have to treat China as it treated the Soviet Union. In August 1957, the State Department agreed to allow US news organizations to send reporters to China. But Dulles denied China the reciprocal right to send its journalists to the United States. In Beijing, the *People's Daily* blasted Dulles's proposition as another unequal treaty. "The center of the 'free world,'" the paper jeered, "isn't free."

For years many American and Chinese historians have blamed America for the sorry state of relations with China in the 1950s. Eisenhower and Dulles undeniably played their part. But this simplistic appraisal ignores how useful hostility to America was to Mao's regime. As the chairman himself told Soviet ambassador Pavel Yudin on January 8, 1955, "China is not very much interested in recognition by the US." Isolation, he declared, "gives us the chance to more freely educate our people in the anti-American spirit."

CHAPTER THIRTY-ONE

Dead Flowers

Luo Longji had done well since the 1949 revolution. Unlike many American-educated Chinese, he had not been compelled to make a humiliating self-criticism. During the Korean War, the man who had once been China's leading liberal had led fellow members of the Democratic League in denouncing the United States. In recognition of his usefulness, the Communists named Luo minister of forestry, even though he knew nothing about trees.

But by 1955, Luo's belief in freedom had begun to itch like an amputated limb. This was true of many others as well. Mao had attacked China's intellectuals in a series of political campaigns, and many were fed up. Luo believed that the dissatisfaction of China's best and brightest could be channeled into a force for good. The Third Force that had served for years as China's liberal conscience, he assured his Democratic League comrades, was not dead.

Some Communist Party leaders also realized that the party may have gone too far in suppressing what they called China's "brain workers." In late 1955, the PRC was on the verge of completing the transformation to socialism. Industry had been nationalized and private property almost fully abolished. To move to the next step, China needed people with education, but they had been cowed. On May 2, 1956, Mao announced a new policy of greater freedom in the arts and sciences. In a speech to the Supreme State Conference, he declared: "Let a hundred schools of thought contend, and let a hundred flowers bloom." Three weeks later, propaganda chief Lu Dingyi elaborated, announcing that the party now approved of independent thinking. But he stressed that there were limits. He vowed that the party would be vigilant against the mind-set that "the moon in America is rounder than the moon in China." Lu was quoting a speech that Hu Shih had made in 1947. Such a view, he said, would be erased just like "flies, mosquitoes, rodents and grain-eating sparrows." On February 27, 1957, the party released a speech by Mao—"On the Correct Handling of Contradictions Among the People"—that urged people to express their true thoughts.

Intellectuals began to stir. In March, Luo addressed a government meeting and blasted the party for wasting the lives of American-educated Chinese by assigning them jobs such as hawking cigarettes on street corners. It was worse, he noted, than the Qing dynasty's treatment of the American-educated from Yung Wing's group.

Soon it seemed as if everyone was criticizing the Chinese Communist Party. At Peking University, students set up a "Democracy Wall." In essays, on wall posters, and at public meetings, leading intellectuals, many educated in the United States, protested the numerous Hate America campaigns, the slavish veneration of the Soviet model, bans on Western literature, and the perks that party bigwigs enjoyed. Newspapers edited by Western-trained reporters circulated the criticism nationwide.

"We felt like flowers beginning to bloom," recalled Wu Ningkun, an American returnee teaching English literature in Beijing. During a lunch at a colleague's house, Wu lauded FDR's four freedoms—of speech and of religion, and from want and from fear. "You never realize how essential they are until you have lived in an environment that threatens to deprive you of them," he mused.

The anthropologist Fei Xiaotong, who had traveled to America in the 1940s, raised his voice in favor of an open debate on China's future. He labeled Stalin a dictator, called for Western-trained scientists to be allowed to participate in political decisions, and urged the lifting of all restrictions on scientific research. The Communist Party, he assured his many readers, could be trusted to tolerate dissent.

Addressing the United Front Work Department in the spring of 1957, Luo Longji questioned the rationale behind Mao's bloody political campaigns and demanded that the party apologize for its excesses. Zhang Bojun, who had studied in Germany and cofounded the Democratic League, called on the party to give the Third Force a voice in policy making. This was forbidden terrain. Luo and Zhang were advocating nothing less than the dismantling of the Communist Party's monopoly on power.

On June 11, 1957, Chu Anping, the editor of *Guangming Daily*, summed up the liberals' views of the Chinese political situation in an essay titled "Empire of the Party." "A party leading a nation is not the same thing," he wrote, "as a party owning a nation." Everyone understood the reference. Thirty years earlier, Luo Longji had used "Empire of the Party" to denounce the Kuomintang.

Mao Zedong became alarmed. In just a few months, the foundations of his revolution had shifted beneath his feet. Communism was under threat abroad as well. In October 1956, when students and workers in Hungary rose up against Soviet rule, Mao had urged the USSR to invade. And now pro-American intellectuals in his own country were sounding like the Hungarians.

On June 8, 1957, Mao announced the end of the One Hundred Flowers campaign and called on the party to "organize our forces to counter the reckless attacks of the rightists." It was necessary to silence Luo Longji and Zhang Bojun for causing "black clouds to roll across the skies of China," he thundered. What followed was a massive campaign of suppression, known as the Anti-Rightist Campaign. Mao bemoaned the lax revolutionary ardor of China's best and brightest. "They are still under the influence of bourgeois ideology, particularly ideology inherited from Americans," he explained to Russian ambassador Pavel Yudin. Mao entrusted the leadership of the campaign to one of his loyal acolytes, a diminutive revolutionary named Deng Xiaoping.

Luo and Zhang were charged with being the ringleaders of an "Anti-Party Anti-People Anti-Society Alliance." Zhang was forced to issue a lengthy self-criticism. Hoping to protect his own hide, Fei Xiaotong denounced Luo, as did one of Luo's girlfriends. On July 15, Luo addressed the National People's Congress and called himself "a guilty creature of the Chinese People's Republic." He was stripped of his posts.

The Anti-Rightist Campaign took aim once again at the subversive influence of American thinking on the minds of educated Chinese. At his Beijing university, Wu Ningkun was hauled before a "mass debate," where the details of his luncheon musings were revealed. He was labeled a "poisonous weed" and would spend the next twenty years in and out of labor camps, atoning for his pro-American sins.

In all, three hundred thousand men and women were branded rightists. Many were dispatched to labor camps, where tens of thousands died from malnutrition and disease. Mao did not ship Luo, Zhang, or Fei Xiao-tong to the gulag. He silenced them but kept them around as pathetic, living, breathing examples of ideological waywardness. Luo Longji died in December 1965, right before the Cultural Revolution, which cost the lives of thousands more pro-American Chinese. Zhang Bojun died in 1969. Fei Xiaotong held on much longer, but from 1957 until 1979, save for an article on how much better it was to grow old in China than in the United States, the man once considered one of the world's great anthropologists would not publish a single word.

In February 1956, Tibetans began rebelling against Communist Chinese rule in Sichuan and Qinghai provinces. Chinese officials had been pushing Communism down the throats of unwilling nomads and shuttering monasteries for trafficking in "backward" beliefs. Tibetan rebels in Qinghai massacred a Chinese garrison, while in Sichuan they attacked Chinese police stations and army camps. The People's Liberation Army responded with air strikes and artillery.

In the summer of 1956, CIA officers met in India and the United States with Tibetan representatives. In an operation dubbed Project Circus, the agency agreed to train Tibetans in guerrilla warfare and radio communications. An initial group of six was flown to Saipan in the Western Pacific and parachuted back into China in 1957.

Tibet was tailor-made for the CIA. Official American fascination with the region dated back to the days of William Woodville Rockhill, the six-foot-four diplomat who in 1908 had advised the thirteenth Dalai Lama to accept Chinese sovereignty. Now Americans were encouraging Tibetans to break free.

America's first contact with the fourteenth Dalai Lama, or Tenzin Gyatso, had occurred in 1942 when he was seven. That summer, the US government dispatched two intelligence officers from the Office of Strategic Services to Tibet to search for a land route into China to break Japan's blockade. The men, Brooke Dolan and Ilia Tolstoy, the grandson of the Russian novelist, carried a letter from President Franklin Roosevelt to the Tibetan leader, the first communication between an American president and the Dalai Lama. FDR followed their journey with interest, although it did not result in a new route into China. Like other Americans, Roosevelt had been drawn by the allure of the Roof of the World, brought alive by Joseph Rock's tales in *National Geographic* and James Hilton's *Lost Horizon*. Roosevelt was so taken with the idea of Tibet that he named his retreat in Maryland's Catoctin Mountains "Shangri-La." (It's known as Camp David today.)

Tibet had ostensibly been independent of Chinese control since the republican revolution of 1911. But, on October 7, 1950, tens of thousands of soldiers from the People's Liberation Army invaded Tibet. Six months after the assault, advisers to the fourteenth Dalai Lama sent two Westerners to the US Embassy in New Delhi to meet with Ambassador Loy Henderson. James Burke, a *Time* magazine correspondent, and Heinrich Harrer, a champion skier and mountaineer from Austria, told Henderson that the Dalai Lama had fled the Communist assault and was hiding in a village a few miles from the Indian border. His Holiness, wrote Harrer in his memoirs, *Seven Years in Tibet*, was unsure whether to go into exile or return to Lhasa, accept Chinese rule, and try to protect his people. "The Dalai Lama," said Harrer, according to a State Department record of the conversation, "does not know which way to turn."

Using untraceable Indian stationery with no letterhead or signature, Henderson typed out some suggestions that flew in the face of Rockhill's previous advice. The Dalai Lama, Henderson said, should choose exile. US officials promised that Washington would welcome the Dalai Lama not just as a religious figure but as the leader of "the autonomous state of Tibet."

On May 26, 1951, the Chinese announced that representatives of the Dalai Lama had signed an agreement in Beijing ratifying the Chinese occupation, even though the Dalai Lama had authorized nothing of the kind. Under the agreement, the Tibetan government ceded to China control of its defense and foreign policy. The Chinese Communists promised that if the Dalai Lama remained in Tibet, he would retain control over the region's domestic affairs. Swayed by the argument that he could do more for his people by staying in Tibet, Tenzin Gyatso spurned the American offers and returned to Lhasa to face the Chinese. Five years later, with the rebellion in full swing, the Americans got involved again.

In 1958, the US shifted its training of Tibetan guerrillas first to Virginia and then to a US Army base called Camp Hale, high in the Colorado mountains. To keep onlookers away, the CIA planted a story in the local media saying that the government was conducting nuclear tests at the site. The CIA trained about 260 guerrillas at Camp Hale. From bases in Thailand, India, and Nepal, Claire Chennault's Civil Air Transport airdropped more than five hundred tons of arms, ammunition, medicine, food, and equipment to Tibetan fighters, enough for fourteen thousand partisans.

Tibet's rebellion came to a head in the spring of 1959. In March, the Dalai Lama, fearing arrest by the Chinese authorities, fled Lhasa again. Disguised as a Tibetan soldier, the bespectacled monk sneaked out of the city with a small entourage. Outside Lhasa, CIA-trained guerrillas guided the party to safety. In southern Tibet, the Dalai Lama announced the formation of an independent Tibetan government. On March 30, 1959, Prime Minister Jawaharlal Nehru granted him and thousands of Tibetan refugees asylum in India.

US officials were elated with the Dalai Lama's flight. The State Department predicted that the "Asian impact of Tibetan developments will far exceed that of Russian intervention in Hungary." A presidential committee saw the uprising "as a windfall for the United States" and pressed to "keep the rebellion going as long as possible."

Chinese troops crushed the uprising, killing thousands of Tibetans. US-trained Tibetan guerrillas were often nabbed hours after parachuting into Tibet. But outside China, the CIA funded the Tibetan government-in-exile until the late 1960s, when President Richard Nixon decided that it was time for a better relationship with Beijing. In memoirs published in 2015, Gyalo Thondup, a brother of the Dalai Lama and a longtime CIA "asset," wrote that he regretted encouraging Tibetans to join the fight. "Had I understood how paltry the CIA's support would be, I would never have sent those young men for training," he wrote. "Mao was not the only one to cheat the Tibetans. The CIA did, too." Kenneth Knaus, a CIA officer who trained Tibetan guerrillas, was right to call them "orphans of the Cold War."

America's support of the Tibetans was part of a policy in the 1950s to do "anything we could to get in the way of the Chinese Communists," wrote Dean Rusk, who ran the China desk at the State Department in the early 1950s. Starting with the Truman administration, the CIA initiated a string of operations along China's borders. Chennault's Civil Air Transport parachuted 212 Nationalist Chinese agents onto the mainland in the early 1950s; half were killed and the other half captured. It funneled weapons and money to twelve thousand Nationalist fighters who had retreated from China into Burma. Instead of harassing the Communists, however, those Nationalist forces harassed the Burmese and turned to opium cultivation and drug trafficking.

In January 1958, Mao announced his plans for "a revolution in the technological field." China's economy, he vowed, would soon "surpass Britain and catch up with the United States." With the unveiling of the Great Leap Forward, Mao's minions radically accelerated the collectivization of the land and herded people into communes with public canteens. Food production plummeted, and tens of millions starved.

America played a key role in the Great Leap Forward, not simply as the standard against which China sought to measure its success but also as the enemy Mao used to ignite his people's revolutionary fervor. The chairman needed a crisis to arouse popular support for his plan to radically transform Chinese society. So on August 23, Mao's forces once again began shelling the Taiwanese island of Quemoy.

Mao's belligerence shocked his Russian allies. Soon after the shelling began, Soviet foreign minister Andrei Gromyko rushed to Beijing, worried that China was about to spark a war with the United States. Zhou Enlai sought to calm his fears. The attack's purpose, Zhou assured Gromyko, was to "raise the combat spirit" of the Chinese. Gromyko and Soviet leader Nikita Khrushchev worried that Mao was becoming unhinged. Just a year earlier, at the fortieth anniversary of the Bolshevik Revolution, Mao had given a speech in Moscow welcoming the prospect of a nuclear Armageddon. In the event of such a war, Mao declared, "half of mankind" might die, but Communism would win. The assembled delegates were dumbfounded. Still, Mao remained cautious when it came to America. In August, right before he ordered the shelling of Quemoy, he directed the local People's Liberation Army (PLA) commander, Ye Fei, to avoid American casualties. When Ye asked what to do if US warships opened fire, Mao repeated three times, "You must not fire back."

Eisenhower met Mao's newest provocation with a forceful response. The navy assembled the largest flotilla in American history, an armada of six aircraft carriers, forty destroyers, three heavy cruisers, and twenty other warships. On Taiwan, the US Air Force equipped its Kuomintang counterparts with state-of-the-art Sidewinder air-to-air missiles. The Strategic Air Command placed B-47s on alert on Guam, readying for a nuclear attack.

At a cabinet meeting in August 1958, senior air force officers proposed using nuclear bombs against targets near Xiamen. Air force general Nathan Twining, then chairman of the Joint Chiefs of Staff, floated the idea of nuclear strikes as far away as Shanghai. On September 4, Eisenhower and Dulles issued the Newport Declaration, announcing that the offshore islands were essential to Taiwan's defense. It was a huge victory for Chiang Kai-shek. Eisenhower followed with his eighth and last threat to use the A-bomb against Communist China.

Just as Mao's cavalier attitude toward a nuclear war had shocked his Communist comrades in Moscow, Eisenhower's eighth threat alarmed NATO and Japan. The US embassy in Tokyo warned that if the United States dropped the Bomb on China, Japan would throw American forces off its islands. Behind the scenes, Eisenhower and Dulles launched another effort to convince Chiang Kai-shek to abandon the offshore islands. They wanted China and Taiwan separated for good. Two Chinas would be better than war.

This time, however, Chiang had an ally in countering the United States. In perhaps the most bizarre twist in a decade filled with many, Chiang teamed up in 1958 with his old nemesis Mao Zedong to block the American move to divide mainland China and Taiwan. In back-channel traffic, using a Hong Kong journalist intermediary, Mao assured Chiang that he would not really invade the offshore islands and urged Chiang to stay put.

In early October, Mao told the Politburo that Chiang's forces must remain on Quemoy and Matsu. "We could shell them if and when necessary, to tighten the noose whenever tension is needed or to loosen the noose whenever relaxation is needed," he said. If the PLA took the islands, he observed, "a de facto two-Chinas situation will arise." Mao understood, according to historian Chen Jian, that as long as Taiwan was bound up with Quemoy and Matsu, it would be bound up with China.

On October 5, Mao told the PLA to stop shelling for two days. He issued an "Announcement to the Taiwan Compatriots," stressing that the Communist Party and the Nationalists agreed on at least one thing—there was only one China. Mao then declared a cease-fire to allow the Nationalists to resupply the islands. Militarily, he later explained to his comrades, "this might appear to be a joke . . . but this is a political battle." America's plans to create two Chinas, he insisted, must be defeated.

Later that month, Secretary of State Dulles went to Taipei to persuade Chiang to leave the islands. The day Dulles arrived, Mao ordered his artillery to resume firing on Quemoy. The move, Mao told his secretary Lin Ke, was to "assist Chiang" in parrying Dulles's demands. Sure enough, with Mao's guns blazing, Dulles could not order Chiang to retreat. The American secretary of state was forced to concede in a joint communiqué that the defense of the offshore islands was "closely related" to the defense of Taiwan. From October 21, Mao had his military shell the offshore islands only on odd-numbered days. "We bombard Quemoy not because we want to liberate Quemoy," Mao told Lin Ke, but because Chiang Kai-shek needed it to be shelled.

In November 1959, Mao asked Lin Ke to get him copies of three recent Dulles speeches. They concerned an American policy to encourage the "peaceful evolution" of Communist countries into governments acceptable to the West. Among the American tactics were support for opposition movements, cultural exchanges, and the spread of information. This worried Mao. "Peaceful evolution" was particularly suited to American policy toward China. After all, Americans of various stripes had been employing a similar strategy there for more than a century. What did John Dewey advocate other than "peaceful evolution"?

Mao believed that Nikita Khrushchev's embrace of peaceful coexistence with the West proved that US policies were having an effect on Moscow. Earlier in 1959, when Chinese and Indian forces had clashed along the border, the Soviets had remained neutral. In October 1959, Khrushchev, fresh from meeting Eisenhower at Camp David, had arrived in Beijing with the news that because the USSR had improved relations with the United States, it would have to scrap its agreement to help China build the Bomb. Khrushchev also asked Mao to release five Americans, including two CIA officers, Richard Fecteau and John Downey, who had been captured in Manchuria during the Korean War. Mao was livid that the Soviets were trying to make nice with the Americans.

Tensions had been building between Mao and Khrushchev ever since Stalin died in 1953 and Khrushchev had spoken out against Stalin's excesses. Mao felt that he, not Khrushchev, should assume the mantle of the world's leading revolutionary and that his radical version of a peasant-based revolution should be a model for former colonial possessions worldwide. Mao opposed the dismantling of Stalin's personality cult and, following Khrushchev's summit with Eisenhower, worried that Moscow and Washington had begun plotting against him.

The flashpoint came on October 2, 1959, when Mao's foreign minister, Marshal Chen Yi, became so enraged with Khrushchev that he began spitting at him. "You should not spit from the height of your marshal title," Khrushchev told Chen Yi. "You do not have enough spit." Khrushchev left Beijing two days later. In July 1960, thousands of Soviet experts left China. Border clashes would soon erupt as the Sino-Soviet split widened.

Mao worried that "peaceful evolution" was polluting China. In July

1959, defense minister Peng Dehuai had committed the unpardonable sin of pointing out that the Great Leap Forward was causing mass starvation and that Mao's policies had failed. What's worse, as party officials searched for a way back from the famine, Liu Shaoqi, a senior Communist official, stressed the need to study "all advanced ideas in the world, including those from America." Liu was partial to America's use of technology for higher agricultural yields. Mao felt embattled; external and internal forces were colluding against him.

At a small gathering of party leaders in Hangzhou in the fall of 1959, Mao formulated a response to Dulles's call for peaceful evolution. According to the memoirs of Bo Yibo, one of Mao's closest lieutenants, Mao told the gathering that the United States had already begun to contaminate the Soviet Union and that it would soon turn its sights on China. "The United States has adopted a more deceptive tactic to pursue its aggression and expansion," Mao told his comrades. The United States, he said, "wants to corrupt us by a peaceful evolution."

The meeting in Hangzhou was the first time that Mao mentioned peaceful evolution. He would return to it again and again in the ensuing years. Peaceful evolution was the international face of the sickness he sought to battle at home. Mao bequeathed his fear of "peaceful evolution" to his successors. Although they would renounce Mao's economic model, constant vigilance against American influence has remained a focus of party policy to this day.

In June 1960, Eisenhower visited Taipei. More than half a million people turned out to see him and gave him, the *New York Times* reported, "one of the most tumultuous receptions of his career." Mao Zedong welcomed him, too, by ordering his artillery batteries opposite Quemoy and Matsu to fire away. Eisenhower had come to Taiwan to get Chiang off the offshore islands. But now, the president, like Dulles in October 1958, was forced to assure Chiang and the people of Taiwan that there was not "the slightest lessening" of America's determination to protect them.

The American public, however, was tiring of Taiwan. Thousands of letters poured into the White House, urging Eisenhower to extract the United States from the never-ending catfight between Taipei and Beijing. Criticism of America's China policy mounted in the press. The best-selling 1958 novel *The Ugly American*, about a fictional country in Asia adept at exploiting the United States, underscored the view that Chiang Kai-shek was leading the United States down the garden path.

Democrats, out of the Oval Office for eight years, coalesced around the Taiwan issue. Dean Acheson, who had been sidelined for years due to his association with the loss of China, lambasted the Eisenhower administration. "We seem to be drifting, either dazed or indifferent, toward war with China," he warned. The offshore islands, he pronounced, were "not worth a single American life."

Stalwart members of the China Lobby began to lose their seats in Congress. In 1958, California Republican William F. Knowland, known as "the senator from Formosa," fell to Democrat Clair Engle, who called for a new China policy. Exposés of the China Lobby put the group on the defensive. One book, *The China Lobby in American Politics* by Ross Y. Koen, was so inflammatory that Chiang's agents in the United States leaned on Macmillan to withdraw its publication. Still, preview copies had circulated, and Koen's allegations—among them that Chiang's allies were smuggling heroin out of Burma—were hard to dismiss.

In November 1959, the Senate Committee on Foreign Relations released a study of American policy in Asia, arguing not just for relations with Beijing but also for recognizing the Nationalist government as the "Republic of Taiwan." The report stated what an increasing number of US officials had privately acknowledged: the "Communist bandits," as Chiang Kai-shek liked to call them, were not going away.

Once again China played a role in the presidential election. On October 7, 1960, Vice President Richard Nixon squared off for his second debate against John F. Kennedy, a dashing first-term senator from Massachusetts. Kennedy mocked Nixon as "a trigger happy Republican" because of his apparent willingness to send American boys to fight for the offshore islands. Quemoy and Matsu were "not essential to the defense of Formosa," Kennedy declared.

Nixon pounced. The islands, no matter how small, were located "in the area of freedom," he intoned. As president, he assured his audience, "I will not hand over one foot of the Free World to the Communists." It qualified as a "gotcha" moment, but it did little to help Nixon. Kennedy's charisma was too much for "Tricky Dick."

CHAPTER THIRTY-TWO

Bloody Marys

Early into the Kennedy administration, the new president assembled his team to discuss the big issues of the day. When they got to the Middle Kingdom, John F. Kennedy called to his wife, "Jackie, we need the Bloody Marys now."

There were two things about China that were enough to drive Kennedy to drink. Even more than Eisenhower and Dulles, Kennedy saw Mao's ideology of peasant nationalism as a threat to the United States. Kennedy studied Mao's strategic masterpiece, "On Guerrilla Warfare," and urged it on his aides. He believed that the unfolding battles in Southeast Asia and elsewhere in the Third World were animated by Chinese ideology. The second factor was even scarier: China was building the Bomb.

Kennedy's advisers found him fascinated by China. "He read all he could about the Chinese," wrote Ted Sorensen, JFK's longtime aide and White House counsel, noting that Kennedy was also fond of quoting Chinese aphorisms, even when they were not relevant to the situation. Searching for a way to counter Chinese influence in the Third World, the president came up with what he called the Strategy of the New Frontier, which would have America battle Marxism-Leninism using covert operatives, village pacification, helicopter gunships, the Peace Corps, and the Green Berets. In June 1961, Kennedy told the *New York Times*'s James Reston that the United States had to make a stand to "demonstrate our firmness." The place to do it in, he said, was Vietnam.

Vietnam and China were inextricably linked in the president's mind. As he noted, if South Vietnam fell, it would "give the impression that the wave of the future in Southeast Asia was China." When Kennedy took office in 1961 there were one thousand American troops in Vietnam. By the time he was assassinated in November 1963, there were sixteen thousand.

Another factor driving Kennedy to distraction was Chiang Kai-shek, who was now more than seventy years old. As reports of the Great Leap Forward famine trickled out from the mainland, Chiang saw his chance to profit from China's plight. The Generalissimo pestered Kennedy for "secret and indirect" support for an invasion. In March 1962, Chiang ordered the deployment of a massive force to the offshore islands. Though he dreamed of triggering a conflagration that would allow him to return home at the head of a conquering army, Chiang ended up pushing the United States and his nemesis, Red China, closer together, at least for a while.

In May 1962, Zhou Enlai ordered Wang Bingnan, who was on leave in China, back to Warsaw. "It seems Chiang is determined to provoke a big fight," he told his veteran ambassador, instructing him to reach out to the Americans, now represented in Warsaw by Ambassador John Cabot. "We should try to enlist the United States to curb Chiang's military actions," Zhou declared. It was an extraordinary thing for a Communist Chinese leader to say. Just a few years earlier, Beijing had teamed up with Taiwan to block US plans to separate the two Chinas. Now it was angling to use Washington to pacify Taiwan.

Chiang had alarmed the Americans as well. On June 22, Assistant Secretary of State Averell Harriman asked the British and Soviet ambassadors to pass a message to Beijing. He denied that Americans supported Chiang's adventures and advised Beijing to remain calm. The next day, Cabot met with Wang in Warsaw and vowed that the United States would "clearly disassociate" itself from any attack. Cabot said that the United States wanted the ambassadorial talks to continue even if Chiang Kai-shek sent his men into battle. Wang assured Cabot that Beijing was not seeking to settle the Taiwan problem by force. The meeting ended in a relaxed mood. In his memoirs, Wang wrote that his report "played a big role in shaping the policy making at home and Party Central was very satisfied."

That was an understatement. The Warsaw meeting was a watershed in relations between the two estranged giants. Since 1950, China had insisted that the Americans get out of Taiwan. Remove the Americans from the mix, and the Taiwan problem would solve itself. Now, China's Communists had returned to an earlier tradition of dealing with the United States—one that predated World War II. America could be coaxed into playing the role of China's enabler. This lesson would not be lost on future generations.

On June 27, 1962, Kennedy told reporters that the United States opposed the use of force by any side in the Taiwan Strait. Stunned, Chiang passed a plaintive request to the Americans via the new ambassador to Taiwan, Alan G. Kirk. "Could the United States at least not make public statements which the Chinese Communists can exploit?" it read. A day after Kennedy's news conference, China's foreign minister Chen Yi asked a British official to thank the Americans and declared that Beijing would "patiently hope for a gradual improvement in relations" with the Beautiful Country.

Gradual improvements did not come. China's defeat of Indian forces in a short border war in the fall of 1962 revived the country's image as a threat in American eyes. Secretary of State Dean Rusk declared that "the blatant aggression of Communist China on the Indian border has vast and historical significance." That fall, the Chinese condemned the Soviets for "capitulating" to the United States by agreeing to dismantle their missile installations in Cuba. The Chinese rejected a Kennedy administration offer of grain to ease the famine. And in Vietnam, the Chinese urged their Communist comrades to attack the Saigon government.

Just a year earlier, Mao had advised the North Vietnamese to focus on economic development and not go too far in destabilizing the South. But by 1962, China had donated ninety thousand rifles to South Vietnamese guerrillas, and in a March 1963 trip to Hanoi, senior Communist official Liu Shaoqi pledged more military aid. "We are standing by your side," he told his Vietnamese comrades.

To American officials, China began to loom larger as a threat than the USSR. In June 1963, the US assistant secretary of state for Far Eastern Affairs, Roger Hilsman, observed that in the Pacific the "bamboo curtain" frightened Americans more than the iron one. "In Asia," Hilsman said, "the greatest danger to independent nations comes from Communist China." The idea that China was even more alarming than the Soviets took on added currency as Kennedy grappled with intelligence indicating that China was building a nuclear weapon. Kennedy and his advisers feared that with the Bomb, the Chinese, as CIA liaison to the National Security Council Chester Cooper put it, would emerge "even more manic and hard to deal with than they are now."

Kennedy had told the *New York Times* that once China became a nuclear-armed state, the "domino theory" would no longer hold, as all of

Southeast Asia would naturally go Communist under the threat of a Maoist holocaust. "These Chinese are tough," Kennedy remarked, according to Ted Sorensen. "It isn't just what they say about us but what they say about the Russians. They . . . seem prepared to sacrifice 300 million people, if necessary, to dominate Asia."

In early 1963, Kennedy had his administration explore two options for curbing the China threat. The first was unilaterally bombing Chinese nuclear installations to set its program back while collaborating with the Soviet Union to hamper China's efforts. The second involved improving relations with Beijing to defang the Communist regime. In January, Kennedy called on Averell Harriman and two other officials—Roger Hilsman and James Thomson, a China-born specialist on the National Security Council—to explore these approaches.

With the Sino-Soviet split now past the point of no return, Kennedy and Harriman favored the concept of allying with the Soviets against the more extremist Chinese. In the spring of 1963, Harriman met with Khrushchev and floated the idea of joint military action or a unilateral American action tacitly supported by Moscow against China's nuclear facilities. Khrushchev rejected both scenarios, so Harriman suggested that Britain, the USSR, and the United States at least agree to stop nuclear tests in the atmosphere, in outer space, and underwater as a way of further isolating China as it prepared its first nuclear detonation. Khrushchev accepted the Nuclear Test Ban Treaty in July 1963. Though rising concern over radioactive fallout was the stated reason for the pact, Kennedy told the National Security Council that "the test ban treaty is important for one reason, Chicom."

At the end of July, the CIA weighed in with a major report concluding that American fears of a dangerously irresponsible China armed with nuclear bombs were misplaced. The agency predicted that, to the contrary, China would keep up its inflammatory rhetoric but proceed with caution. The report emboldened Harriman to pursue Kennedy's Plan B—exploring the possibility of better ties with the PRC.

The Sino-Soviet split helped convince Kennedy's aides that there was the potential for some type of arrangement with Beijing. James Thomson remembered attending a State Department briefing where experts argued that the split was real. "One could almost hear the snap and crackle of frozen minds undergoing rapid thaw," Thomson wrote. "For if we were no longer confronting a monolithic bloc, the policy consequences were legion in every part of the world." The opportunities were exciting, Thomson recalled, but the process of resuscitating a relationship that many considered dead was difficult. "Its origins were disorderly and even conspiratorial," Thomson later wrote. And it would take years.

Roger Hilsman suggested exchanging reporters, rethinking the trade embargo, bringing the PRC into disarmament talks in Geneva, granting the PRC a seat at the UN, and persuading Chiang Kai-shek to withdraw his forces from the offshore islands. These ideas had been floated before, but this was the first time that anyone so close to an American president had considered them all at once. Hilsman argued that opening a channel to China would affect the PRC's internal politics, and that even if China rejected US overtures, it would make America look responsible. After all, America's China policy had made it the laughingstock of the Western world. Even French president Charles de Gaulle, a diehard anti-Communist, had authorized an opening to Beijing in October 1963.

As Hilsman and Thomson worked on a speech that would unveil the administration's new thinking, Kennedy declared at a press conference on November 14 that "we are not wedded to a policy of hostility to Red China." Eight days later, on November 22, 1963, Kennedy was assassinated in Dallas. Hilsman and Thomson soldiered on with the speech. Late for a flight to Europe, Secretary of State Dean Rusk barely glanced at it, and the White House, in the chaos that followed the president's death, gave its consent on the fly. Thomson called the approval of the speech "an accident of bureaucratic politics."

Hilsman delivered the speech on December 13 before the Commonwealth Club in San Francisco. By today's lights, it's a clumsily written document, laden with Pekingology and Cold War clichés. But for 1963, it was extraordinary, representing the first time that the US government publicly acknowledged the permanence of the Communist Chinese state and raised the prospect of eventual accommodation.

There were enough olive branches in Hilsman's speech to rough out a tree, but the Americans did have a bottom line. As long as Beijing insisted on the "destruction" of the US relationship with Taiwan as a precondition to better ties, Hilsman said, "there can be no prospect for such an improvement." China had to abandon the use of force as an option for settling its dispute with Taiwan, he declared. Just a few years later, the United States would begin its new relationship with China by setting these principles aside.

Thomson sent Hilsman's speech to newspapers, China scholars, senators, congressmen, and pundits. In the Senate, South Dakota Democrat

George McGovern praised it, while the reaction from the China Lobby was muted. The speech marked a turning point. Mainstream politicians and government officials could now openly discuss a better relationship with China without fearing for their scalps. Pressure for change would grow. Academics, who had been silenced because of their connection to "the loss of China," recovered their voices. And a trickle of Americans began dribbling into China, bringing eyewitness reports to the broadest audience in two decades. Hilsman's speech had been a trial balloon, and it had floated.

The new president, Lyndon Johnson, did not take to Hilsman. Hilsman had fought in the jungles of Burma during World War II and had argued that the United States did not know what it was doing in Vietnam. Secretary of State Dean Rusk did not like him nor did the military. In March 1964, the story of Hilsman's removal landed on the front page of the *New York Times*. Johnson replaced him with William Bundy, a hard-line anti-Communist and the brother of National Security Advisor McGeorge Bundy. Harriman, too, was soon removed from all China issues. In 1964, Johnson's China policy hardened. And as Vietnam was always a function of Washington's view of China, a massive American troop buildup in Indochina would soon commence.

Fear of China's weapons and China's ideas would drive American policy for much of the 1960s. American escalation in Vietnam was entwined with its worries about China. Concern about China's Bomb prompted America to contemplate a preemptive attack on the Middle Kingdom and even to suggest to the Russians that they team up against the PRC. In the end, these worries would compel the United States to change direction, leading to a stunning rapprochement with Beijing. China was just too big to ignore.

CHAPTER THIRTY-THREE

Pictures of Chairman Mao

On the Sunday after John F. Kennedy's assassination, as a horse-drawn caisson carried his flag-draped coffin to the US Capitol to lie in state, the *Workers' Daily* in China ran a cartoon of the American president face down in a pool of blood. "Kennedy bites the dust," read the caption. In Chinese, it even rhymed.

On the surface, at least, Red China gloried in the young president's death. America was a "paper tiger," tough on the surface but rotting "day by day." The sobriquet, first attached to the United States in 1945, had stuck around for more than a decade, as had the oft-repeated assertion that America's system was headed for collapse. Mao Zedong was particularly susceptible to this misreading of American history, but he was not alone. To this day, many in China's government are astonished whenever America picks itself up after an economic crisis or a military defeat.

America, China's state-run media declared, was "a volcano about to erupt"; it was "sunset in America." The United States was "rotten to the core." When a blackout rolled across seven US states on November 9, 1965, the *China Youth Daily* crowed that it "exposed American decay and weakness."

From 1963 on, Beijing's support for North Vietnam skyrocketed. More than 320,000 Chinese soldiers served in Vietnam, according to historian Chen Jian. Chinese records claim that PLA antiaircraft forces downed

1,707 American planes and damaged 1,608 others. Its engineering units built railways, roads, bridges, tunnels, and airfields, freeing hundreds of thousands of Vietnamese to fight. American intelligence had estimated that only 40,000 Chinese troops were involved. It was off by a factor of eight.

To Mao, even more than bleeding America, the war—and the renewed threat from the US—served his revolution. The failure of the Great Leap Forward had pierced the myth of Mao's "eternal correctness." In 1959, he was removed as head of state, and Liu Shaoqi and Deng Xiaoping took control of the economy. But in 1962, Mao began pushing a new, more radical line, calling on his followers "to never forget the class struggle." He used America's snowballing entanglement in Vietnam to push more militant policies at home.

In August 1964, when Vietnamese torpedo boats may have attacked US Navy vessels in the Gulf of Tonkin, President Johnson won a resolution from Congress authorizing the use of force and ordered the bombing of targets in North Vietnam. Operation Rolling Thunder began. In response, Mao sent air force and antiaircraft units to Vietnam and launched the Movement to Resist America and Assist Vietnam. The party equated US "aggression" against Vietnam with "aggression against China." Like the Hate America campaigns of the 1950s, Resist America and Assist Vietnam would become a national theme for years.

In speeches in August 1964, Mao declared that America's new war of aggression necessitated another fundamental reordering of the Chinese economy. World War III was coming, he predicted. Chinese industry, concentrated along the coast and vulnerable to Yankee air strikes, had to be moved inland. For the next fifteen years, China committed a whopping 40 percent of its investment in infrastructure to what was known as the Third Line campaign, a massive program to move thousands of factories, research complexes, and steel mills into the mountains of western China. Millions of workers were uprooted. Families were forced to separate. The waste in lives and money was staggering—and the initial pretext was the threat from America.

Mao understood that a measure of international tension was useful to the revolution but that it could get out of hand. So even as he ginned up fear and hatred of America inside China, his lieutenants worked to ensure that the United States understood China's bottom line. From early in the Vietnam conflict, Chinese officials stressed publicly that the war was Vietnam's and not China's. On April 2, 1965, Zhou Enlai told Pakistani president Mohammad Ayub Khan, who was planning a trip to Washington, that China would not provoke a broader conflict unless it was attacked. When Khan's visit was postponed, the Chinese repeated the message to others. Only an American ground invasion of North Vietnam, the collapse of the North Vietnamese government, or a direct assault on China would pull Beijing directly into the fight, they said.

China's successful detonation of a nuclear device on October 16, 1964, amplified American fears of the Chinese. The 1950s had seen the return of the Yellow Peril in the form of a brainwashing Fu Manchu. Now China had the Bomb. President Johnson took to the airwaves, calling the four nuclear powers—the United States, Russia, Britain, and France—"sober and serious states." But China? It did not make the grade.

Americans painted a stark picture of a nuclear-armed China. Harvard scholar Morton Halperin predicted in his 1965 book *China and the Bomb* that the nuclear breakthrough marked "a milestone on China's road to world power." At a time when China's per capita gross domestic product sat south of $100 and America's had surpassed $4,000, Halperin warned that the Bomb presaged China's "eventual triumph over the United States." *New York Times* reporter Harrison Salisbury declared that a Chinese "peril stalked the world." It wasn't just a nuclear-armed China, Salisbury wrote in his 1967 book *Orbit of China*, it was a *populous*, nuclear-armed China. "On the day 2,000 million Chinese swarmed across the globe, there would be fewer than 300 million Americans," he predicted. Salisbury was convinced that China was going to take over the world.

China's Bomb, coupled with the threat of its Communism, was the central factor leading the Johnson administration to dramatically escalate US operations in Vietnam. As Johnson's secretary of defense, Robert McNamara, reported to him on November 3, 1965, the decisions to pulverize North Vietnam and pour hundreds of thousands of US troops into the region "make sense only if they are in support of a long-run United States policy to contain Communist China." On April 7, 1965, in a speech at Johns Hopkins University, Johnson explained the conflict in this way: "Over this war—and all Asia—is another reality, the deepening shadow of Communist China."

Johnson had an ambitious domestic agenda: the War on Poverty, civil rights, the introduction of Medicare and Medicaid. In a parallel with Mao, who employed the threat of America to strengthen his revolution at home, being tough on Chinese Communism gave Johnson the room to pursue his own domestic program—the Great Society. Meanwhile, fear of a broader conflict limited how the United States fought the war in Vietnam. No one in either US political party wanted a repeat of Korea. Consequently, the White House selected bombing targets with an eye to China's reaction. And it rejected the idea of invading North Vietnam.

On November 2, 1965, a Baltimore Quaker named Norman Morrison doused himself with kerosene and set himself on fire outside Secretary of Defense Robert McNamara's Pentagon offices as a protest against the war. "US Out of Vietnam" became the glue that bound together disparate campaigns for racial and gender equality, for civil rights, and against American overreach abroad. And always in the background was Red China.

As it had in the 1930s, China served as a repository for the hopes of the American Left. Mao Zedong's willingness to meet force with force was a compelling story for black nationalist groups such as the Black Panthers, who hawked Mao's "Little Red Book" on the streets of America's inner cities to raise money for their cause. In Harlem in the 1960s and 1970s, recalled historians Robin D. G. Kelley and Betsy Esch, it seemed as if everyone owned a copy of the *Quotations of Chairman Mao*.

Beijing rolled out the red carpet for a series of African American leaders. Famed black nationalist W. E. B. DuBois celebrated his ninetieth birthday with Mao in Beijing in 1959. When Robert Williams, a former US Marine, founded the Revolutionary Action Movement in the early 1960s and became one of the first black leaders to advocate a violent response to white supremacy, he took Mao as his idol. Under indictment in the United States, Williams first fled to Cuba and then in 1965 to Beijing.

The Chinese installed Williams and his family in a wing of the former Italian embassy and provided them with a cook, maids, and the use of a car. He and his wife were known as "Mr. and Mrs. Robert Williams, Representatives of the American People" and treated like royalty. Williams was given a talk show on Chinese shortwave radio and called China the "new hope of oppressed humanity." When Black Panther founder Huey Newton visited China in 1971, he declared, "I felt absolutely free for the first time in my life, completely free among my fellow men." Of course, these China fantasies were even more illusory than those of the 1930s, given the deep Chinese prejudice against dark skin. But African Americans, like so many other Americans, ignored Red China's reality and focused on its promise. This was soft power 1960s-style.

Chris Milton, a white teenager from California, personified the Left's passion for Mao Zedong and its belief that the Red Guard, the shock troops of Mao's latest revolution, were thoroughly cool. The son of American English teachers, Milton attended high school in Beijing for three years during the Cultural Revolution. Interviewed on his return to America in 1969 by the *Movement*, a counterculture magazine in Boston, he enthused about "the scene at Peking University." Describing one Red Guard leader, Milton sounded as if he was reciting a haiku. "Beautiful cat. 19 years old. Stone rebel."

In his memoirs of the 1960s, Todd Gitlin, the first president of Students for a Democratic Society, America's leading student activist organization, recalled thinking "romantic thoughts about Mao and Chou En-lai" while attending Harvard. At Yale University, Jonathan Spence, a professor of Chinese history, told his students that what Mao was doing in his Cultural Revolution was akin to closing all of America's schools, giving all of its students a railpass, and telling them to venture forth to solve America's problems. His students cheered. Tom Hayden, another SDS leader, cited Mao's adage, "Dare to struggle, dare to win" to inspire his disciples. Feminists also found a muse in the Great Helmsman and his adage "women hold up half the sky," even though Mao had unceremoniously dumped three wives.

Starting in the early 1960s, the Chinese began to dole out rare glimpses of the Middle Kingdom to a few American writers, handpicked for their loyalty to the cause. Edgar Snow was one of the first. Following World War II, Snow had fallen under suspicion of being a Communist and was questioned by the FBI. After he and Peg divorced, he remarried and moved to Switzerland in 1959. A year later, he received an invitation to return to China. Hoping to relive his dramatic "discovery" of the Chinese Communist Party in 1936, Snow spent five months on the mainland, reuniting with old friends, interviewing Zhou Enlai and Mao Zedong, and visiting more than half of China's provinces. He found a nation vastly improved from the one he had known in the 1930s. Kids in Kunming no longer sucked sugarcane laced with opium; they favored Popsicles instead. Chongqing's malarial open sewers were now covered. Life expectancy had shot up from forty to fifty-seven. But Snow was always under surveillance. Chinese minders monitored his interviews. As he wrote in his diary, "I am cordially received and given every co-operation technically correct. But no intimacy is established, no spark of human warmth established." Once he left China, however, Snow set his unease aside and in 1962 published *The Other Side of the River: Red China Today*, which clocked in at more than eight hundred pages. His main point was that he had been right all along. The Communist revolution was the best thing that had ever happened to China. Snow saw himself reprising the role he had played in the 1930s, as the American interpreter of China's Communist movement who would smooth the waters between the Beautiful Country and the Middle Kingdom.

Snow did not mention disappeared friends who had been dispatched to labor camps. Of the commune system, which critics blamed for destroying familial bonds, he wrote, it "may actually come nearer to achieving the ancient ideal of family." He lauded peasant participation in elections, even though the party picked the candidates. And he disparaged reports that China had suffered a famine. "I saw no starving people in China," he asserted. "Mass starvation such as China has known almost annually under former regimes," he declared, "no longer exists." Once again, Snow tried to prove himself a useful tool for China's Communists. This time, however, there was no payoff for the party. *The Other Side of the River* did not do well. Some questioned Snow's objectivity, while others, such as the *New Yorker*, were numbed by his recitation of facts. Snow had lost his audience, but the Communist Party hadn't noticed.

America's leftists were not the only ones exploring what a change in US policy toward China would mean for America. Even as the Vietnam War escalated, US statesmen and business leaders edged toward the view that something had to be done to pull China back into the family of nations. In March 1965, a House subcommittee chaired by Democrat Clement Zablocki, an anti-Communist Catholic from Milwaukee, recommended "limited but direct contact" with China. A year later, Senator J. William Fulbright, an influential Democrat from Arkansas, held hearings on China.

From the first day, March 8, 1966, when A. Doak Barnett, a Shanghai-born professor of political science at Columbia University, backed a new policy he called "containment without isolation," Fulbright's hearings took on a historic cast. Eleven other experts on China lined up behind Barnett, arguing that the United States should allow trade and travel. When Republican supporters of Chiang Kai-shek charged that Fulbright's witnesses were biased, he invited them to testify, too. Their arguments, however, fell flat. When Fulbright criticized the inflexibility of Washington's China policy, twelve thousand letters swamped his office; two-thirds backed his view.

Around the time of the hearings, two hundred leading Asia specialists ran full-page ads in the *New York Times,* the *Washington Post,* and the *San Francisco Chronicle* calling for formal relations with China. Prominent politicians announced that they, too, favored reconciliation. Senator Jacob Javits, a New York Republican and a member of the pro-Kuomintang Committee of One Million, resigned from the group and called for improved relations with Beijing. Vice President Hubert Humphrey appeared on *Meet the Press* and announced that he, too, wanted better ties. The Fulbright hearings had an immediate effect on public opinion. In December 1965, 67 percent of Americans opposed China's entry into the UN. Three months after the hearings, that number had dropped to less than half. China was no longer "domestic dynamite," observed the *Saturday Evening Post*. CBS broadcast a one-hour program on Chinese-American relations, along with an interview with Zhou Enlai. Academics, religious leaders, and businessmen formed organizations such as the National Committee on US-China Relations and Americans for Reappraisal of Far Eastern Policy that advocated ties with China. In February 1966, the National Council of Churches weighed in with support for relations with China.

Inside the Johnson administration, the outside chatter emboldened a group of officials who had searched for years for ways to improve ties. In the spring of 1966, Henry D. Owen, who handled policy planning at the State Department, urged the president to think more broadly about China. On the National Security Council, Alfred Jenkins noted that China's isolation was simply "too dangerous" to continue. His colleague, the China-born James Thomson, was unrelenting in his efforts. In 1967, the Johnson administration took the first steps to relax the ban on travel to China. Johnson, Thomson later wrote, appeared to be "groping for some presidential act of trans-Pacific statecraft that might somehow envelop and mute the Vietnam unpleasantness."

On July 12, 1966, Johnson gave a nationally televised address in which he became the first president to speak of the Communist regime in conciliatory terms. Not since Harry Truman contemplated recognizing Mao's China had an American president said anything friendly about the PRC. "Cooperation and not hostility," "reconciliation," and "the free flow of ideas and people and goods" were his goals with China, Johnson said. Washington even stopped using Peiping, the Nationalist formulation for China's capital, and started using the Communist-approved Peking. Hollywood got into the act, releasing *The Sand Pebbles*, a critically acclaimed drama about the US Navy's Yangtze River Patrol, in 1966. Though the movie, which starred Steve McQueen, was set in 1925, it portrayed a China in need of American support.

This 1937 photograph, entitled *Bloody Saturday*, of a baby in Shanghai during a Japanese air raid, became the most iconic picture out of China during World War II and was used, like it is in this poster, to raise money for China. (Library of Congress)

American Claire Chennault, shown here in 1944, commanded the Flying Tigers over China's skies during the war against Japan. (USAF Photo)

Li Xiaqing was a Chinese pilot who barnstormed the United States in 1938, fundraising for China. (National Air and Space Museum Archives, Smithsonian Institution)

Soong Mayling and Chiang Kai-shek at the entrance to a bomb shelter in Chongqing, the provisional capital of China, which was subjected to withering assaults by the Japanese from 1938 until the end of the war. (Library of Congress)

General Joseph W. Stilwell was a necessary American hero in the story America told itself about its actions in World War II China. This is from a *Cat-Man* comic book in October 1942. (Courtesy of the collection of Brian House)

Chiang Kai-shek, FDR, Winston Churchill, and Soong Mayling during the Cairo Conference of November 1943. (Franklin D. Roosevelt Presidential Library and Museum)

John Paton Davies, shown here in an October 1944 photograph standing next to Mao Zedong, was an American diplomat who believed the United States should support the Chinese Communists during WWII. *From left to right*: Zhou Enlai, Zhu De, John Paton Davies Jr., Mao Zedong, and Ye Jianying. (Harry S. Truman Presidential Library and Museum)

With the eruption of the Korean War in 1950, Communist China launched a campaign to turn America into an enemy of the Chinese people. This poster reads, "Resolutely cut off the bloody and criminal hand of the American aggressor that spreads germs." (International Institute of Social History, Landsberger Collection)

Jade Snow Wong's 1950 autobiography, *Fifth Chinese Daughter*, was an example of a newfound confidence among Chinese Americans. (Courtesy of the Jade Snow Wong family)

President Dwight Eisenhower was greeted to a tumultuous reception when in 1960 he became the first sitting American president to visit a Chinese territory. (AP Photo)

肯尼迪，啃泥地！ 叶春旸画

China's state-run media crowed about the assassination of John F. Kennedy. This November 1963 cartoon from the *Worker's Daily* reads, "Kennedy bites the dust." (Author's collection)

Robert Williams, shown here in 1964 with his wife, Mabel, at a Chinese commune, was one of many radical African Americans who were inspired by the Chinese revolution. (Robert F. Williams Archive, HS1104, Courtesy of Bentley Historical Library, University of Michigan)

President Nixon, here with Premier Zhou Enlai, made history with his visit to China in 1972. (Richard Nixon Presidential Library and Museum)

Deng Xiaoping celebrated the establishment of formal diplomatic relations with the United States during a 1979 trip to America. (AP Photo)

Bruce Lee, on a movie set in 1972 with basketball star, actor, and kung fu aficionado Kareem Abdul-Jabbar, became one of the most famous Chinese American actors in history. (AP Photo)

This photograph of a protester taken on June 5, 1989, became the most iconic image of the 1989 pro-democracy demonstrations in China. The protester, known as the Tank Man, disappeared and his whereabouts are unknown. (AP Photo/Jeff Widener)

Ambassador James Sasser looks out a window of the US embassy in Beijing damaged by protesters following the US bombing of China's embassy in Belgrade in 1999. (James Sasser Papers, Vanderbilt University Special Collections and University Archives)

Chinese naval pilot Wang Wei crashed into a US surveillance plane in international airspace in 2001, resulting in his death. Wang had veered dangerously close to American surveillance planes several times before, and in this photograph, provided by Defense Department officials, he shows his email address to the crew of an American surveillance plane. (AP Photo/APTN, Department of Defense)

This March 1997 cover of the *National Review*, which came out during the Asian campaign-finance scandal, encapsulated American unease with China's rise and was criticized for rehashing Chinese racial stereotypes. (Roman Genn/*National Review*)

March 24, 1997   49146 $3.50 U.S., $4.50 Canadian

CLONING DEMOCRATS —p. 22

Guns Don't Kill People — Studies Do. + Daniel D. Polsby

NATIONAL REVIEW

The Manchurian Candidates
Rich Lowry

The Illegal Services Corporation: Why Congress Still Funds the Left
Rael Jean Isaac

Facebook CEO Mark Zuckerberg, shown here greeting China's president Xi Jinping in September 2015, begged Chinese officials to end their ban on Facebook in China. (AP Photo/Ted S. Warren)

This 2011 photograph of US ambassador to China Gary Locke buying his own coffee in Seattle's airport touched off a furor in China over the corrupt and snobbish ways of China's officials. (Courtesy of Zhaohui Tang, chairman, adSage)

President Barack Obama, shown here in 2013 with Chinese president Xi Jinping, was the first American president since normalization to openly express exasperation with China. (Official White House photograph by Pete Souza)

Jacob Javits wasn't the only Republican to change his tune. In the 1960s, as he approached the end of his life, Henry Luce's mind wandered back to mainland China, the land of his youth. In speeches around the country, Luce embraced the idea of a Great Harmony between East and West. In a 1965 talk at the Commonwealth Club in San Francisco, he declared that bridging the divide between Asia and the West was more important to the future of the globe than resolving the contradictions between Communism and capitalism. The onus was on the United States to engage China, he said, and to take the first step toward establishing "one worldwide civilization." At the University of California at Santa Barbara on February 1, 1967, Luce went even further, predicting that his "American Century" would give way to a merger of East and West. Three weeks later, Henry Luce was dead.

Luce had been a patron of Richard Nixon's, and Nixon, too, was evolving. Nixon owed his success in his early career to his association with the anti-Communist crowd. But Nixon was a complex politician, a pragmatist, and hardly a fanatical member of the China Lobby. What he advocated consistently in US foreign policy was that Asia be placed on a par with Europe.

In October 1967, Nixon summed up years of cogitation in a historic piece for *Foreign Affairs* titled "Asia After Viet Nam." He lamented the fact that tiny Vietnam had "so dominated our field of vision that it has distorted our picture of Asia." He attacked the Kiplingesque notion that Asians were so dissimilar from Americans that they could only ever be of peripheral concern. He blasted talk of an alliance with Europe and Russia against the Chinese. It would amount, he wrote, to racism on a global scale. He demanded instead that the United States "come urgently to grips with the reality of China."

It was America's duty, Nixon wrote, to bring the Middle Kingdom back into "the family of nations." Leaving it "to nurture its fantasies, cherish its hates and threaten its neighbors" was too dangerous. "The world cannot be safe until China changes," Nixon wrote. And it was America's task, he said, repeating a mantra that had circulated since the nineteenth century, "to induce change." The way to do it, he argued, was to convince China that "it cannot satisfy its imperial ambitions"—in other words become rich and strong—without grappling with its domestic problems. Just like John Dewey, Young John Allen, and a host of other Americans, Nixon advised China to develop its economy first.

Nixon added a critical caveat. In reopening the Middle Kingdom to the outside world, there should be no rush to recognize the PRC, allow it into the United Nations, or "ply it with offers of trade." That would only "serve to confirm its rulers in their present course," he observed. No, the United States should adopt a policy of "firm restraint, of no reward, of a creative counterpressure" to persuade China that its interests could be served "only by accepting the basic rules of international civility."

The congressional hearings, Johnson's speech, Nixon's essay, and the backroom advocacy of more than half the White House national security team show that America's opening to China in 1971 was not—as it has often been portrayed—a bombshell decision of stupendous political risk. "Nixon goes to China" has entered the American vocabulary to describe a Hail Mary pass that could only be thrown by the right person at the right time. Chief among the purveyors of this myth were Nixon and his National Security Advisor Henry Kissinger themselves. "The only President who could conceivably do what I am discussing with you is President Nixon," Kissinger would assure Zhou Enlai.

In reality, starting in the late 1950s, America moved in fits and starts toward an awareness that it needed a relationship with the world's most populous country. Church organizations and business groups lobbied for it. Academics wrote editorials about it. Even Frank Sinatra weighed in during an interview with *Playboy* magazine in 1963, calling for "Red China" to be given a seat in the UN. "I don't happen to think you can kick 800,000,000 Chinese under the rug and simply pretend that they don't exist," Ol' Blue Eyes declared. By November 1967, the conservative editorial page of the *Wall Street Journal* had also come around, arguing that America should "nudge future generations of Chinese leadership toward moderation."

America may have been ready but China wasn't. Starting in 1966, American envoys in Warsaw detected an even nastier tone than usual emanating from China's representatives. Wang Bingnan's replacement in Warsaw, Wang Guoquan, was given to theatrical finger pointing and shouting. John Cabot described him as "loud, tendentious, . . . virtually spitting out his accusations." Wang had to act that way. His country had begun the descent into revolutionary madness called the Great Proletarian Cultural Revolution.

On October 27, 1966, China tested its first ballistic missile, a huge breakthrough for Caltech's alumnus Qian Xuesen. On June 17, 1967, China tested a hydrogen bomb. This potent combination of Maoist ideology and American-inspired science caused even more consternation at the White

House. Nine days after the H-bomb test, President Johnson met with Romanian premier Ion Gheorghe Maurer as Maurer prepared for a trip to Beijing. Johnson told Maurer that the United States had no interest in changing China or its government but that he wanted to talk about the nonproliferation of nuclear weapons and rules for avoiding nuclear war. In Warsaw, Wang Guoquan shook his fist at Cabot and called Johnson's outreach a "big lie."

In 1968, China suspended the Warsaw talks. It also brushed aside a White House invitation to Chinese reporters to cover the presidential campaign. As Wang Guoquan noted later in life, if China had not taken a wrong turn in 1966, a rapprochement with America might have happened in 1968. At the White House, Alfred Jenkins observed that China was being led by "paranoid, provincial, prophetic zealots." The best thing the US could do now was "keep relatively quiet while mainland China is trying to sort itself out."

●

CHAPTER THIRTY-FOUR

Out of Bad Things

On July 8, 1966, Mao Zedong wrote to his wife, Jiang Qing, vowing to create "great disorder under heaven." For the next decade, he would lead his country into chaos and then paralysis as he tried to root out "capitalist roaders," who, he believed, were intent on sabotaging his revolution. Mao had watched his former comrades in the Soviet Union disavow one dictator, Joseph Stalin, and then unseat another, Nikita Khrushchev. Fearful that a similar fate awaited him, he launched, in his eighth decade, the Great Proletarian Cultural Revolution to get rid of all pretenders to his throne.

Over the next ten years, Mao eliminated all but a few of his loyal lieutenants. He denied medical treatment to China's head of state, Liu Shaoqi, who died in a prison in central China on November 12, 1969. He allowed one of his most loyal followers, Deng Xiaoping, to be purged twice. He enlisted Jiang Qing and three other ultraradical revolutionaries, known as the Gang of Four, as his attack dogs and brought his country to the brink of a major conflagration with the Soviet Union.

Roving bands of students who called themselves the Red Guards persecuted millions of citizens. Once again the wheel of history turned, and once again China's best and brightest, especially those with a Western education, became targets of Maoist fervor. Hundreds of thousands of literate Chinese were publicly humiliated, imprisoned, tortured, and killed. American-educated men and women were caged in pigsties, tossed from the roofs of buildings, beaten beyond recognition, paraded in the streets wearing dunce caps, and displayed before thousands during public "struggle sessions." To escape, many of those targeted killed themselves with barbiturates, by jumping off bridges, and hanging themselves from trees.

If anyone personified the Great Harmony between China and America, it was Xiao Guangyan. Born in China, he had earned a PhD in chemistry at the University of Chicago and had been working as a researcher at Standard Oil when he and his wife, Piao Suhui, a Chinese American, decided to move to China in 1950 and help build the new country. Xiao got a research job in the northern port city of Dalian, while his wife taught English at the Dalian Maritime College. They had a daughter named Su Luolan.

On October 5, 1968, Xiao Guangyan was accused of being an American spy and thrown into prison. Red Guard contingents beat him with belts for days at a time. Xiao leapt to his death from a building on December 10. Four days later, Piao Suhui gave her daughter sleeping pills and downed a bottle herself in a mother-daughter suicide. In Shanghai, Red Guards imprisoned Li Jinhui, who had teamed up with American jazzman Buck Clayton in Shanghai to create modern Chinese pop music. The Communists fingered Li as one of three "big demons" of the Cultural Revolution, and Red Guards killed him. Murdered, too, was Chen Xujing, an American-educated sociologist who had advocated China's "complete Westernization" in 1933. Hundreds of thousands more Chinese with "bourgeois ideas" and "bad class backgrounds" followed them into the grave.

And yet, despite all this, Chinese still responded to the pull of the United States. On the streets of Beijing and other cities, Elvis Presley, known as Mao Wang, or the King of Cats, became the rage among the young and shiftless. Bowdlerized translations of Jack Kerouac's *On the Road* and J. D. Salinger's *The Catcher in the Rye* circulated, inspiring the less politically engaged. In Beijing, American teenager Chris Milton noted that the city's youth culture was peopled not only by acolytes of Chairman Mao. There were also "dudes with . . . tight pants, you know, there were some, they had little hustles," he recalled. In Shanghai, young people flocked to "underground" dances, risking arrest on charges of "hooliganism." In the jails and holding pens of the Red Guards, conversion to Christianity was often the final act of rebellion against a regime gone mad.

In late 1967, Mao Zedong obtained a translation of Richard Nixon's article in *Foreign Affairs* and concluded that if Nixon were elected to the presidency, he would reach out to China. On November 25, 1968, just weeks after Nixon won the White House, Zhou Enlai signaled that China was ready to resume the ambassadorial talks in Warsaw. In his inaugural address on January 20, 1969, Nixon obliquely referred to his *Foreign Affairs* article, declaring that America wanted a "world in which no people great or small will live in angry isolation."

Although the Chinese state-run press reacted in predictably florid fashion to Nixon's address, calling him "the jittery chieftain of US imperialism" and his nation "beset with profound crises both at home and abroad," Mao understood the reference and ordered the speech reprinted verbatim in Chinese newspapers.

For Mao Zedong, the idea of some type of relationship with America had a certain logic. Relations between China and the Soviet Union had gone from tense to deadly, and China needed protection. In March 1969, Chinese and Russian forces clashed over an island on the Ussuri River, which divides Manchuria and Siberia. US satellite photographs showed that "the Chinese side of the river was so pockmarked by Soviet artillery that it looked like a moonscape," recalled former CIA director Robert Gates.

The Chinese had also picked up credible rumors in Eastern Europe that the Soviets were weighing a surgical strike against China's nuclear facilities. In August 1969, KGB officer Boris N. Davydov revived President Kennedy's idea of an attack on China when he floated the suggestion to US diplomat William Stearman during a luncheon in Washington. This time it was the United States that balked. Stearman responded that America would view any such action "with considerable concern." On September 5, Undersecretary of State Elliot Richardson made America's opposition a matter of public record, telling an audience in Baltimore that Washington would not "let the Soviet apprehensions prevent us from attempting to bring China out of its angry, alienated shell." Henry Kissinger noted that Richardson's speech was a "revolutionary step," marking the first time that the United States publicly warned Moscow against bullying Beijing.

Faced with the Soviet threat, Mao directed a group of senior military officers to conduct an independent review of China's foreign policy. Chen Yi, Ye Jianying, Xu Xiangqian, and Nie Rongzhen were known as the Four Marshals, famed commanders during the Communist revolution. Mao instructed them to explore two questions: Who was China's main enemy, the United States or the USSR? And was war likely? They also studied whether China could play the "US card" against the Soviets, repeating stratagems it had tried since the mid-nineteenth century against Britain, Russia, and Japan.

On the surface, China's Communist propaganda agencies continued to churn out an endless stream of anti-American diatribes. The Apollo moon landing in July 1969, for example, was reported as a fake. But behind the scenes, Mao and Zhou assured the marshals that they would not be punished for thinking outside the box.

In a series of reports issued from June to September 1969, the marshals suggested that to avoid Soviet harassment, Mao should seek an accommodation with the United States. In an oral presentation, Chen Yi laid out what he called "wild ideas" about the Beautiful Country. He noted that Nixon "hopes to win over China" and use it against the USSR, so he suggested that China "pursue a breakthrough" with America and use the tension between Washington and Moscow to China's benefit. China should drop its long-standing condition that the United States first withdraw from Taiwan.

Mao's about-face would shock his nation. Li Zhisui, Mao's doctor, got an early taste. In August 1969, he overheard the chairman saying, "Didn't our ancestors counsel negotiating with faraway countries while fighting with those that are near?" Dr. Li thought his patient had gone mad. "I was aghast," he wrote. "How could we negotiate with the United States?" Mao then shared a simple truth. "The United States and the Soviet Union are different," he said. "The United States never occupied Chinese territory."

By the fall of 1969, the most violent phase of the Cultural Revolution was over. Mao ordered the Red Guards disbanded and ordered the People's Liberation Army to quell violence among various factions. The chairman then dispatched seventeen million Chinese urban youth to the countryside to "learn from the people." With his revolution curtailed, Mao's opening to America began.

Finding the right time and place to actually resume communication with Washington proved to be a challenge. Talks had been set for February 1969 in Warsaw, but Beijing canceled when the United States granted political asylum to a Chinese diplomat. In 1969, Nixon lifted the US ban on travel to China, removed the $100 limit on purchases there, and allowed foreign subsidiaries of US companies to conduct trade with China. Within a year, the State Department would approve 556 passports for travel to China, more than the total for the previous decade, but Beijing, less eager for an American tourist invasion, doled out only a handful of visas. On July 25, 1969, Nixon, passing through the US territory of Guam on his first presidential trip to Asia, unveiled the Nixon Doctrine, declaring that the United States did not want a future land war in Asia and would no longer "undertake all the defense of the free nations of the world." The United States began a drawdown of its forces in South Korea. Nixon ordered destroyers from the Seventh Fleet to stop patrolling the Taiwan Strait and began moving US soldiers out of Taiwan. On November 16, Zhou wrote: "The direction of movement of Nixon and Kissinger is noteworthy." Still, desperate not to appear too desperate, Beijing made no move.

On December 3, 1969, Walter Stoessel, the US ambassador to Poland, spotted the Chinese chargé d'affaires, Lei Yang, at a fashion show at the Yugoslav embassy in Warsaw. When Stoessel approached him, Lei Yang fled. Stoessel pursued him in vain, but he managed to buttonhole the chargé's translator and tell him that the United States wanted talks. Responding to the news, Zhou Enlai remarked to Mao, "The opportunity is coming." On December 7, China released two Americans whose pleasure boat had entered Chinese waters near Hong Kong in February.

Four days later, Stoessel and Lei Yang met at the Chinese embassy in Warsaw for an informal chat. Stoessel had suggested that he could enter the Chinese embassy through the back door, but Lei told him that the front was "eminently suitable." Mao wanted the Russians to take note. On January 8, the two men met at the US embassy. Lei arrived at the front door, the New York Times reported, in "the largest and longest black limousine in Poland, sporting silk red-and-gold starred flags on its fenders and curious tail lights, shaped like Chinese lanterns."

Still, more delays slowed the process. In April 1970, Nixon ordered US troops into Cambodia to battle the Viet Cong. On May 20, Chairman Mao attended a mass rally in Tiananmen Square where more than one million people protested the American incursion. Mao canceled talks and lambasted Nixon for his "fascist atrocities." Nixon pondered sending the Seventh Fleet back toward the Chinese coast, but Kissinger dissuaded him, arguing that Mao's statement was "remarkably bland." Actually, it wasn't. Mao was ambivalent about his opening to the United States. He had difficulty deciding whether he would rather have a continuous revolution or the protection and riches afforded by reconciliation with China's old enemy number one.

On June 18, US troops withdrew from Cambodia. On July 10, China responded by releasing James Walsh, a seventy-nine-year-old Catholic bishop who had been held in solitary confinement since 1958. In August 1970, Mao again called for Edgar Snow. Mao had always believed, mistakenly, that Snow had connections with the CIA and that reaching him meant reaching America. On October 1, the twenty-first anniversary of the PRC's founding, Mao and Snow reviewed the National Day parade from atop the Gate of Heavenly Peace overlooking Tiananmen Square. Snow was the first American to be granted such an honor.

Still, Mao let Snow dangle for almost three months before giving him an interview, another sign that he was not completely convinced about a rapprochement with America. In December, Mao met Snow and "casually" mentioned that Nixon was welcome to visit China for a chat "either as president or as a tourist." On Christmas Day, he ordered all Chinese newspapers to print the October photo of him standing with Snow on the Tiananmen rostrum. Mao was ready. But Washington didn't get the hint. "We thought he was a Communist propagandist," Henry Kissinger said of Snow. "We didn't pay any attention to him." Then, in the spring of 1971, an opportunity emerged that would electrify the world.

The Thirty-First World Table Tennis Championships were scheduled to take place in April in Nagoya, Japan, and China, after an absence of six years, was sending a team. China's world champion squad had suffered during the Cultural Revolution. Some of its greats had committed suicide; others had spent years "learning from the masses," instead of polishing their serves.

Americans had once excelled at Ping-Pong, having won the world championship in 1937. But since the 1950s, the game had been relegated to basements and frat houses. China was still the team to beat. The United States was ranked twenty-third in the world.

From the start of the games, the Chinese remarked on how curious the American athletes were about them. "Some American players were very friendly to our players at yesterday's reception and had talked a lot," read one report sent to Beijing. Early in the competition, Graham B. Steenhoven, general manager of the American delegation, noting that the English and Canadian teams had been invited to China after the tournament, told the Chinese that the US team would like to visit, too. The Chinese delegation passed the request to Beijing, but Zhou Enlai and Mao Zedong agreed that the time was not right.

In team play, the Chinese squad dominated, winning the world championship for the fourth time in a decade. But when the men's individual final rolled around, three-time world champion Zhuang Zedong withdrew because his opponent was from Cambodia, where the United States had recently engineered a coup. China would have nothing to do with a running dog of America, he announced.

An event that occurred on the morning of Monday, April 5, is still disputed. Was it a providential accident or part of a well-thought-out plan? One of the American players was Glenn Cowan, a long-haired stoner from California with a predilection for playing while high. According to one version of the event, Cowan unwittingly boarded the Chinese team bus on his way to the stadium. The other version, from Japan's *Kyodo News Service*, is that Cowan, who was sporting a US team jacket, was invited to hitch a ride.

Either way, after a few minutes of awkward silence, Cowan addressed the Chinese team through its interpreter. "I know all this, my hat, my hair, my clothes look funny to you," he said, pointing to his hippie garb. "But there are many, many people who look like me and who think like me. We, too, have known oppression in our country, and we are fighting against it." From the back of the bus, China's star player Zhuang Zedong looked on. "The trip on the bus took fifteen minutes, and I hesitated for ten minutes," he told a TV interviewer years later. "I grew up with the slogan 'Down with American imperialism,' and . . . I was asking myself, 'Is it OKAY to have anything to do with our number one enemy?'" Zhuang finally stood up, walked to the front of the bus, handed Cowan a silkscreen painting of Huangshan Mountain, and offered him his hand. "Even now," Zhuang told the writer Nicholas Griffin, "I can't forget the naive smile on his face." Arriving at the stadium, the bus was met by photographers, and a picture of Cowan and Zhuang, all smiles, flashed around the globe.

Mao, now seventy-four, had recently been diagnosed with amyotrophic lateral sclerosis (ALS) and could sleep only by downing a fistful of sleeping pills. His nurse, Wu Xujun, recalled later that when Mao heard about Zhuang and Cowan, his eyes "suddenly turned bright." Zhuang Zedong, he said, "not only plays good ping pong but knows how to conduct diplomacy." On the evening of April 6, as the pills kicked in, the Great Helmsman slumped at the table. Mumbling, he told Wu to tell the foreign ministry to reverse the order and invite the Americans to play in Beijing. "Does your word count after taking sleeping pills?" Wu asked. Mao waved his hand. "Yes, it counts, every word counts. Act promptly, or it will be too late!" At 10:45 a.m. on April 7, a Chinese official found American administrator Rufford Harrison hailing a cab in front of the Miyako Hotel. "How would you respond to an invitation to visit China?" he asked. "I was thinking," Harrison told the State Department later, "how can I avoid showing too much outward sign of joy?"

By the time the US team landed in Hong Kong, China's Ping-Pong diplomacy with the United States had become the biggest story in the world. Crossing into China on April 10, Cowan, decked out in purple bell bottoms and a floppy yellow hat, waved at Western media massed on the border. On the front page of the *New York Times*, his picture vied with reports about the Paris peace talks to end the Vietnam War. The delegation, consisting of nine players, four officials, and two spouses, was the first official American group to visit China since the revolution. On April 14, Zhou Enlai hosted the foreign teams at the Great Hall of the People in Tiananmen Square. Zhou addressed the Americans with words that would circle the globe: "Your visit has opened a new chapter in the history of the relations between the Chinese and American peoples."

As the Americans wound up their matches in Shanghai, nineteen-year-old John Tannehill had an insight into what would remain a central aspect of the Chinese response to America. He noticed that Cowan's carefree goofiness struck a chord with the Chinese crowds. Tannehill saw China as a perfect society, inhabited by "puritans . . . Plymouth Rock people." He had made the front page of the *Toronto Globe and Mail* a few days earlier when he told its correspondent that Mao was "the greatest moral and intellectual leader in the world today." But here was Cowan enchanting the Chinese. Cowan "was the exact antithesis of what the Chinese should stand for, and for some unknown reason, they loved it," he noted. To Tannehill, Cowan, with his stash of weed and hippie attire, was an American clown. To the Chinese, he was hilarious—and free.

Inviting the laughably bad American Ping-Pong team to China turned out to be the ideal way for Mao Zedong to sell his people on a resumption of ties with the US. On occasion, Chinese players deliberately lost to the Americans, playing the role of munificent hosts. This display of both Chinese dominance over and magnanimity toward the Beautiful Country clearly demonstrated China's superiority. The unwitting Americans were put in the role of supplicants; they had begged to be allowed to come to China, and China had heard their pleas. Mao would frame the upcoming visit of Richard Nixon in the same way—and Nixon was the president of the United States.

American historians have portrayed China as the passive partner in the dance with the United States. They tend to blame Washington for ignoring China in the 1950s and credit it with waking up to China in the 1970s. In reality, China's leadership needed America at that point far more than the reverse. The reasons were many, ranging from geostrategic considerations to the very basic imperative of survival.

America held the keys to four problems that China's Communist leaders had been trying to solve for decades. China wanted to become rich, strong, respected, and united. So Mao, like his predecessors, found himself looking to the Beautiful Country for solutions. Years of disastrous economic, political, social, and environmental policies had ravaged China. Mao's continuous revolution was a failure. With a surging population (it would double from 1960 to 2000), China in the late 1960s faced the prospects of another famine, even worse than the one during the Great Leap Forward. Provinces were reporting that grain reserves were down to their lowest levels since 1960. But throwing more laborers into the fields would not increase production. The country needed technology, fertilizer, and farm equipment. The Russians weren't helping. That left the United States.

Second, China felt besieged. To the north, the Soviets threatened. The Russian invasion of Czechoslovakia in 1968, followed by the rapid buildup of Soviet forces in Siberia, had stoked Mao's fear of war. To the south, India was still smarting from its defeat in 1962 at China's hands. Taiwan's forces continued to harass the mainland. And Japan was rising in the east, its economy even more miraculous than that of Taiwan. As Zhou Enlai said in 1968, "We are now isolated. No one wants to make friends with us." Mao understood that better ties with America would allow China to disarm its enemies. In that sense, Mao's move toward America echoed the decision by Yankee traders in 1783 to use China to break Britain's economic blockade of their young republic.

As for international respect, despite his allegiance to the precepts of Marxism-Leninism, Mao judged his nation according to American standards. *Ganmei* (catch up to America) was the ultimate goal he had set for his nation. In that sense, Mao's Stalinist-inspired radicalism had an ironic core. In 1949, he had proclaimed that China had "stood up," but until America recognized this fact, the Chinese historian He Di has observed, Mao's revolution would be incomplete.

Finally, in the late 1960s, Mao was no closer to the dream of unification with Taiwan than he had been in 1949. In fact, he was farther from it. The Republic of China was firmly allied with the United States, and Taiwan boasted the second-highest standard of living in Asia. Mao realized that he needed a relationship with America to draw closer to the island. The road to unification ran through Washington, not Taipei.

Evidence for the depth of China's need for the United States in 1971 remains locked in Communist Party archives. But the public record provides hints. As China prepared to make a U-turn, banners reading "Make the foreign serve China," a throwback to the Qing dynasty's idea that Western technology could make China strong, appeared nationwide. In December 1970, when Edgar Snow asked why Mao was seeking talks with the United States, the chairman declared that "American production is the biggest of any country in the world." The Soviet Union had failed as China's guide, Mao said. "I place my hopes on the American people." It was an extraordinary admission: the road to a rich China ran through Washington as well. The problem for Mao was that he had schooled his people to hate the very nation that possessed the solution to China's dilemmas. How to use the United States to attain his goals without allowing America to reseed China's soil with Yankee ideals was Mao's challenge. It continues to torment his successors.

Chairman Mao and Zhou Enlai brilliantly sold the impending rapprochement as an act of celestial benevolence, bestowing warm relations on the barbarians from the land of the flowery flag. It was an extraordinary feat. Almost immediately, American commentators began gushing about China, a dirt-poor nation still stuck in the nineteenth century, as a model for the United States, when, in reality, the reverse was true.

The fact that the Cultural Revolution in China coincided with the 1960s in the United States is another instance of the serendipity that connects the two nations. Occurring simultaneously, these two epochal movements, like the parallel eruption of the Civil War and the Taiping Rebellion in the mid-nineteenth century, yielded an immensely important legacy. They brought together the two great nations of the West and the East, triggering a convulsive economic boom that raised more people out of poverty than ever before in history. As Mao observed, "Out of bad things can come good things."

●

CHAPTER THIRTY-FIVE

Not Because We Love Them

On April 27, 1971, barely a week after the US Ping-Pong team returned to a tumultuous reception in Los Angeles, the White House received another invitation from Zhou Enlai to send a high-ranking envoy to Beijing. There was no mention of the demand that the United States first abandon Taiwan. On June 2, Zhou followed up with a second message, announcing that Mao had approved of a secret trip by National Security Advisor Henry Kissinger. That evening, Kissinger rushed into the Oval Office with the news; the missive, he gushed, was "the most important communication that has come to an American president since the end of World War II." He would travel to Beijing in July.

On the surface, Kissinger's enthusiasm arose from the administration's need for a foreign policy win after years of dead ends in Indochina, the Middle East, and Moscow. In America, public opinion was turning in Red China's favor. A May 1971 Gallup poll found that for the first time more Americans backed the PRC's entry in the UN than opposed it. Kissinger's excitement was also rooted in the traditionally vast American expectations of China. "If we can master this process, we will have made a revolution," Kissinger said. The two men toasted the occasion with a well-aged bottle of brandy.

Nixon's motives for drawing closer to China were as complex and contradictory as Mao's. On a geopolitical level, they involved a grand strategy to counter the Soviet Union and to extract the United States from the quagmire in Vietnam. Nixon had tried to schedule an arms control summit with Moscow in 1970, but the Soviets had stalled. The president bet that a US dalliance with China would change the Kremlin's mind. He also figured that China would be useful in prodding North Vietnam to agree to end the war. "Peace with honor," Nixon thought, could be had with help from Beijing.

As for the Middle Kingdom itself, Nixon wrote that it was imperative for America to "cultivate China" to ensure that it would not turn into "the most formidable enemy that has ever existed in the history of the world." Still, the president would remain torn between what American diplomat U. Alexis Johnson called his "rapturous enchantment" with China and a desire to keep the flag of US influence planted in Chinese soil—even if it was on the Maryland-sized island of Taiwan.

In his talks with the Chinese, Kissinger would make outsize promises. He would belittle America's alliance with Japan and imply that the United States was eager to dump Chiang Kai-shek and stand aside while the mainland absorbed Taiwan's by-then fourteen million people. But Nixon was more conflicted. Initially, the president heeded the caveat he had offered in his *Foreign Affairs* piece, cautioning Kissinger not to appear overeager to make a deal. "We cannot be too forthcoming in terms of what America will do," he told his national security advisor. But as time passed, the president, swept along by the euphoria of the new relationship, ignored his own advice.

Nixon's inconsistency is reflected in a rambling exchange with Walter P. McConaughy Jr., the ambassador to the Republic of China, who met with the president in Washington on June 30, 1971, just ten days before Kissinger left for Beijing. Nixon concurred with McConaughy's position that no matter what happened, it would be a bad idea for Taiwan to unite with the mainland. That would be "a disaster," McConaughy said. Nixon agreed. But Nixon also stressed that Taiwan's leaders needed to prepare for a shock as the United States improved ties with China's Communists. "Not because we love them," he added, "but because they're there." Like many Californians, Nixon had been impressed by the work ethic and the industriousness of the Chinese. "You can just stop and think of what could happen if anybody with a decent system of government got control of that mainland," he told McConaughy. "I mean, you put 800 million Chinese to work under a decent system—and they will be the leaders of the world."

As they plotted a rapprochement with China, neither Nixon nor Kissinger believed that America's tilt toward China should be permanent. "I think in twenty years your successor, if he's as wise as you," Kissinger told

Nixon, "will wind up leaning towards the Russians against the Chinese." The president concurred.

In Pakistan on July 9, Kissinger faked a case of "Delhi belly," and the White House announced that he had gone to a hill station to rest. In fact, he was on a flight to China. Arriving in Beijing, Kissinger immediately met with Zhou Enlai. In Zhou, the urbane former executioner for the Communist Party's secret service, Kissinger wrote that he had found a "soulmate." Kissinger brought a fitting gift for China's premier—a rock from the 1969 Apollo 11 trip to the moon. For years to come, Americans would describe their journeys to China in interplanetary terms.

In seventeen hours of meetings over two and a half days, Kissinger gave the Chinese the one thing he believed obsessed them—"strategic reassurance, some easing of their nightmare of hostile encirclement." To show his good intentions, he provided intelligence on Soviet military deployments. He would supply more, starting an American tradition of bringing gifts to Beijing without asking for anything in return.

In his memoirs, Kissinger dismissed China's concerns about Taiwan as "Chinese Communist liturgy." He even claimed that Taiwan was barely discussed and that Zhou assured him that the island's status would not delay the warming of relations. In reality, Taiwan played a key role in the discussions. It dominated the first part of the July 9 meeting and takes up a substantial chunk of the forty-six-page manuscript of the talks. As Zhou told Kissinger on the day they met, "Taiwan is the crucial issue."

Over the next few days, Kissinger made a series of astounding statements and promises that raised Chinese expectations about the benefits of ties with America. He started off by framing America's support for Taiwan as a historical mistake that he blamed on "public opinion at the time" and not on the American belief that Stalin and Mao planned to back violent revolution throughout East Asia.

Kissinger then announced America's intention of retreating from the Western Pacific. He committed to withdrawing the US military from Taiwan. US forces in South Korea would also wind down before the end of Nixon's second term, he said. He told the Chinese that the main reason America was interested in keeping an alliance with Japan was to ensure that it would never again turn to war.

When Zhou observed that once America pulled out of Taiwan, unification could be expected, Kissinger agreed. Taiwan's "political evolution," Kissinger said, "is likely to be in the direction which Prime Minister Chou

En-lai indicated to me." What's more, Kissinger dropped the decades-old American demand that China abandon its threat of force in dealing with the island.

Nixon had conditions for a summit, among them the release of all Americans in Chinese custody and Chinese help in leaning on North Vietnam to agree to a peace deal. Nixon also wanted to be the first American statesman to make it to Beijing. The president loathed the idea of a Democrat, like George McGovern or Ted Kennedy, beating him to Beijing.

The only condition China met was the last one. Chinese aid to Vietnam continued throughout the early 1970s. Mao waited six months after Kissinger's departure to free CIA officer Richard Fecteau. But he kept Fecteau's comrade, John Downey, the last incarcerated American, in custody until March 12, 1973, *after* Nixon had left China. The twenty-one years Downey was imprisoned made him the longest-serving prisoner of war in US history.

On the second day of talks, Kissinger added more concessions: he said that the United States would not assist Chiang Kai-shek in any assault on the mainland, and he gave Zhou a detailed road map for China's entry into the UN. He said that the United States would try to help Taiwan retain its seat, but only temporarily. At the end of the second day, Zhou and Kissinger settled on a time for Nixon's visit to Beijing—"at an appropriate date before May 1972."

When Mao heard about Kissinger's promise to withdraw US troops from Taiwan, he quipped that it would take some time for a monkey to evolve into a human being. The Americans, he said, were now at the ape stage, "with a tail, though a much shorter one, on his back."

On July 15, 1971, Richard Nixon took a helicopter from the presidential compound in San Clemente to the Burbank studios of NBC to make an announcement. It was over in ninety seconds, and, in the words of UPI reporter Helen Thomas, it "made the room rock." Nixon had sent Henry Kissinger to China, and he himself would be going there soon—all this from a commander in chief who had made battling Communism the bedrock of his political career. What were Americans supposed to think?

Americans thought it was great. *Life* magazine called the announcement "one of the great diplomatic bombshells of recent years." Nixon's allies, like Senator Robert P. Griffin, the GOP whip from Michigan, rallied to his side; even Democratic rival Senator George McGovern applauded "the president's imagination and judgment." There were a few spoilers, including the Reverend Carl McIntire, who chaired the Vietnam March for Victory committee. "It is like God and the devil having a high-level meeting," he complained.

Nixon's move once again made China the sun around which America's interests in Asia revolved. This alienated American allies in the region and created decades of concern that Washington would forsake its friends for the holy grail of good ties with the Middle Kingdom. The Nixon administration did not bother telling Japan, its closest Asian ally, of Kissinger's secret trip until minutes before Nixon's announcement. Japan's prime minister, Eisaku Sato, was reduced to tears at the news. "I have done everything they asked," he told an Australian delegation, "but they have let me down."

Most of the Taiwanese government found out about the planned summit from a news broadcast. When two American diplomats arrived in Taipei to offer explanations, Chiang Kai-shek refused to see them, ordering his son Ching-kuo to host them instead. "Our relationship with them will continue," wrote American official John Holdridge, "because they have nowhere else to go."

Preparing the Chinese for an opening to America was no easy feat for the propagandists at Party Central. Mao and his acolytes had thoroughly demonized the United States. It was the "bastion of all reactionary forces in the world," blamed for China's humiliation in the imperialist era and for keeping her divided in the Cold War. But now those views needed to be modified—and fast.

Starting in 1969, the volume of information about America in *Reference News*, the party's compilation of foreign reporting and one of the most widely circulated newspapers in China, had increased dramatically. When US official Elliot Richardson warned the Soviets against attacking China in the fall of 1969, *Reference News* reported it. When the *New York Times* broke a story of a classified National Security Council report contending that China was ready for better ties with the United States, *Reference News* ran it. When the wire services wrote of Nixon's efforts to appeal to the Chinese, *Reference News* noted the reports under the headline: "Nixon Is Trying to Curry Favor with Us."

A key message was that America was desperate for better ties. Both Mao and Zhou repeated that "it is the Americans who need something from us, not the other way around," so many times it was like a mantra. The party stressed that a rapprochement would help China confront the Soviets and win back Taiwan.

The invitation to the US Ping-Pong team was a major step in preparing the Chinese for the upcoming shift. China's state-run TV and radio covered the team's visit as if it were a moon walk. "For a long time, friendship has existed between the Chinese and American peoples," the anchor on China Central Television's nightly news told hundreds of millions of viewers. Footage showed a huge crowd smiling and waving at the American players as the US and Chinese teams marched into the stadium hand in hand.

Practically every American who passed through China—old leftists, new leftists, fellow travelers, lost souls, and Black Panthers—was given prominent play in the *People's Daily*. Nothing of consequence was written about what they said. The point was that they were Americans, and the Chinese needed to get used to them. Even Henry Kissinger was used as a prop. During one blustery day in Beijing, the Chinese hosted him for tea on a boat on Kunming Lake at the Summer Palace in front of thousands of rubberneckers. "They clearly wanted this boat ride to take place," Kissinger wrote, "and only a hurricane could have prevented it."

The party emphasized that rapprochement was a tactical maneuver in China's pursuit of its long-standing goals of becoming strong and rich. In the months before Nixon's visit, the party stressed that the United States remained a threat. Party members were directed to read "On Policy," Mao's World War II essay on the necessity of forming a united front with Chiang Kai-shek to fight the Japanese. The message was clear: reconciliation with America was a "united front" to deal with a more threatening Soviet Union. And like Chiang was then, America remained an enemy.

Throughout the country, the party explained its new policy to party members. During one study session held at the Revolutionary Committee in Pei county in northern Jiangsu province in August 1971, an official named Kong Xi assured the assembled party members that "our goal of overthrowing Nixon hasn't changed." When asked why China didn't get rid of Nixon when he came to China, the session's leaders said China was planning something shrewder: we're going to make America think, they said, that we're their friends.

By the early 1970s, Taiwan was on its way to becoming an exporting powerhouse. Within a decade, its total trade would increase tenfold. But while Taiwan's businessmen prospered in this new world of global commerce, the makers of the island's foreign policy, particularly Chiang Kai-shek, refused to change. For years, American officials had urged Chiang to accept the idea that one day mainland China would join the United Nations and that the best solution was for Taiwan to surrender its seat on the Security Council and keep its place in the General Assembly. But Chiang would not budge.

On Taiwan, the reaction to America's rapprochement with the mainland triggered anger and disappointment. Protesters attacked the US embassy in Taipei and set off bombs at a Bank of America branch. But the Nixon Shock, as it was called, did not convince Chiang's government to alter its approach on the UN question. "When asked by governments friendly to us how we would wish them to vote, we did not know what to say," Taiwan's ambassador to the United States James Shen acknowledged in his bitter memoir, *The U.S. and Free China: How the U.S. Sold Out Its Ally.* There is also significant circumstantial evidence to indicate that the Nationalists were once again coordinating their tactics with their enemies on the mainland. Neither Chiang nor Mao wanted two Chinas in the UN. They both worried that allowing two Chinas into that body would embolden those Taiwanese who sought an independent republic on the island.

The Nixon administration was also split on the UN issue. Many in the State Department supported the idea of keeping Taiwan in the General Assembly, including Nixon's ambassador to the UN, George H. W. Bush. But Kissinger called it an "essentially doomed rearguard action." As the nations of the world gathered in the fall of 1971 to vote on the issue during the sixty-first session of the General Assembly, Kissinger left again for China. In Beijing on October 21, Kissinger belittled State Department efforts to ensure that both China and Taiwan got seats in the UN, calling them "traditional policies" pursued by lower-ranking bureaucrats because he and the president had "not told them all the details of the discussions."

While he was in China, Kissinger also addressed Zhou Enlai's concerns about a nascent movement to declare an independent republic of Taiwan. Pro-independence rallies had been held in New York and Washington, and Chiang Kai-shek had alleged CIA support for these groups. Kissinger asked Zhou to pass on information on "any American, official or unofficial" who was supporting such a movement and told him that "you have our promise that it will be stopped." That was quite an undertaking. But Kissinger wasn't done. He also assured Zhou that whether or not China pursued *peaceful* unification with Taiwan, "We will continue in the direction which I indicated"—which meant that the United States would withdraw recognition of Taiwan and establish ties with China. It was an extraordinary thing to say, and it implied that the Nixon administration would look the other way if China decided to launch a military takeover of Taiwan.

Over four days of meetings totaling twenty-five hours, Zhou and Kissinger crafted a joint communiqué to be issued at the end of Nixon's trip. At one point, Kissinger complained about a recent surge in anti-American propaganda. In a tactic that all his successors would repeat, Zhou said the state-run media was just "firing empty cannons" and assured Kissinger that it did not matter. But attacking America did matter to the Communists; it was a centerpiece of their ideology. It never was "firing empty cannons." Four decades later, this remains the case.

On October 25, 1971, the UN General Assembly passed UN Resolution 2758, recognizing the PRC and ousting "the representatives of Chiang Kaishek from the place which they unlawfully occupy at the United Nations." *Life* magazine called it "a blunt foreign policy defeat" for the United States. The *New York Times* ran a front-page banner headline: "UN Seats Peking and Expels Taipei." UN ambassador George H. W. Bush was angry with Kissinger for "telling me he was 'disappointed' by the final outcome of the Taiwan vote," when Kissinger had done nothing to stand in China's way.

Returning to America two days after the vote, Kissinger told reporters that the timing of his trip and the UN vote had been a coincidence and that he had not discussed the UN issue with the Chinese. He wasn't telling the truth. To Nixon and Kissinger, China had become once again, to use missionary Sherwood Eddy's term, "the lodestar, the goal" of American policy in Asia, outshining any other territory or ideal.

The Taiwanese took their explusion from the UN in stride. The *Far Eastern Economic Review* reported that "nobody got excited the day of the UN vote. Life went on as usual." Few other nations, the *Review*'s columnist opined, "would have appeared less bloody and more unbowed after a succession of reverses such as those the Nationalists have suffered."

In responding to the defeat, Chiang Kai-shek used the same tactics he had employed to deal with the many earlier disappointments the United States had handed him. He hewed even closer to Washington. He shared his intelligence on the PRC, and he ordered his lieutenants to boost the island's economy to ensure stability.

Chiang was personally devastated by the Nixon Shock. In meetings with generals and aides, he would rail openly against Nixon. In his diary, he nicknamed the president Ni Chou, "Nixon the Clown," the Chinese equivalent of "Tricky Dick." Given Nixon's years as a card-carrying member of the anti-Communist club, Chiang felt betrayed. He would end up despising Nixon even more than Vinegar Joe Stilwell. "Nixon the Clown," he wrote in his diary, "sold out the Republic of China."

Chiang Ching-kuo, the Generalissimo's son, took a different lesson from the shock. He backed a secret nuclear weapons program because he did not trust the United States to protect Taiwan. (The United States, which had thoroughly penetrated Taiwan's military establishment, caught wind of it and shut it down.) As Taiwan's premier, Chiang Ching-kuo also improved his government's image. He brought local Taiwanese into the Kuomintang. Among them was Lee Teng-hui, fresh from a PhD in agricultural economics at Cornell University. Ching-kuo appointed Lee to his cabinet and made him responsible for agriculture. Lee would assume a historic role later on. From the tyrannical chief of security responsible for the jailing of scores of dissidents, Ching-kuo was morphing into, while not exactly a democrat, at least someone who realized that Taiwanese society, now wealthier than any other Chinese community in the world, required a more representative form of government.

American officials supported Chiang Ching-kuo's "Taiwanization." As Alfred Jenkins, an NSC staffer who would advise Nixon and Kissinger throughout their negotiations with the Chinese, put it, "We need not indicate overtly that the U.S. foresees the possibility of an eventually independent Taiwan," but Washington should work to support such a change. He noted presciently that Taiwan's fate would depend greatly on what course Chiang Ching-kuo took. If he opted for a "tight little island," Jenkins wrote, Taiwan's fate would be darker than if he chose "a relatively popular base for government." The Nixon Shock forced the Nationalists to open up.

Henry Kissinger's concessions to Chairman Mao are understandable from his and the president's perspective. Like Roosevelt at the Yalta Conference, Nixon and Kissinger believed that the geopolitical implications of their gambit with China trumped everything else—including the fate of Taiwan's fourteen million people. Their eyes were on the prize of a peaceful and productive relationship with Beijing to counter the Soviet Union and facilitate America's departure from Vietnam.

But Kissinger's promises violated Nixon's self-imposed restraints. They also broke Kissinger's golden rule. "We [Americans] like to pay in advance to show our good will," he told a radio talk show host in 1994, "but in foreign policy you never get paid for services already rendered." In Beijing, Kissinger paid in advance, and the United States got little in return.

Kissinger's commitments also raised enormous expectations in China that the United States was unable to meet. The contradictory way US officials handled the Taiwan issue—some offering it to China and others working to ensure that it remained free—created a crisis when Taiwan's American friends swung into action nearly a decade later to protect it. As the historian Nancy Bernkopf Tucker noted, the means to the laudable end of a good relationship with Communist China were "deeply flawed." They undermined US credibility and sowed the seeds of distrust in China, Taiwan, Japan, and the rest of Asia.

CHAPTER THIRTY-SIX

Tacit Allies

On Monday, February 23, 1972, Richard Nixon, accompanied by his wife, Pat, walked down the steps of the presidential plane, just landed at the Beijing airport. It was an eerie welcome. There were no onlookers, no schoolgirls with flowers. On the tarmac stood a smiling Zhou Enlai, with about two dozen officials behind him and behind them an honor guard, the first assembled in years. Temperatures hovered just above freezing. The Stars and Stripes and the flag of the People's Republic of China faced off on two flagpoles as the band plowed through the national anthems of both nations. Winston Lord of the National Security Council's planning staff looked out the plane's window and was disappointed at what he called "the strained nature of the Chinese reception." The Americans, Lord wrote, had "expected thousands of people in cheering crowds."

President Nixon was not fazed. As he descended the ramp, Zhou began to clap in that signature Chinese Communist way, the right hand sluggishly patting the left. "I returned the gesture, and then, as I reached the bottom step, I stretched out my hand to Zhou," Nixon wrote. "When he took it, it was more than a handshake. We both knew that it marked a turning point in history." Zhou played on the myth of the Dulles snub, noting to Nixon, "Your handshake came over the vastest ocean in the world—twenty-five years of no communication." Less than a year earlier, Communist Party papers had called Nixon "the world's most ferocious and cruel chieftain of imperialism." Now, a new era in relations between China and America had dawned.

Soon after the delegation arrived at the Diaoyutai State Guesthouse, Zhou invited Nixon to a meeting with Mao Zedong. The American president had come to China not knowing when, or even whether, he would see Chairman Mao. This was a timeworn Chinese tactic to keep barbarians off balance and to inspire gratitude once an actual meeting took place. Now, barely an hour into his visit in Beijing, Nixon was being summoned. The Americans recognized that the chairman was giving the visit his personal seal of approval.

Nixon's trip was one of the biggest stories of the modern age. More than two thousand reporters applied to cover the visit. The Chinese had suggested that ten slots would be sufficient, but the White House was able to convince them to increase that to eighty-seven. Nixon handpicked the journalists, weeding out those he didn't like. Twenty-two daily papers and more than a dozen magazines were represented. The three networks sent their biggest guns: Harry Reasoner from ABC, Walter Cronkite and Eric Sevareid from CBS, and John Chancellor and Barbara Walters from NBC.

Reporters dug deep into their metaphorical tool kits to describe Nixon's journey. Some returned to the past, describing the president and his team as "latter-day Marco Polos." But most looked to the stars. The Space Age had dawned, and the operative allegory was cosmic travel. "A year ago, the possibility that we'd ever see anything like this picture seemed more remote than Neil Armstrong's first footstep on the moon," remarked ABC's Howard K. Smith as Nixon deplaned. Even the president caught the bug, repeatedly comparing his journey with the Apollo 11 moon flight.

During Nixon's preparations for his encounter with Mao, Kissinger had suggested ways to bond with the chairman. According to the president's notes, Kissinger encouraged Nixon to "treat him like an emperor" and to stress that he and Mao had both achieved greatness even though they both came from common stock. "RN and Mao, men of the people," Nixon wrote to himself. Both he and Mao, his notes said, had "problems with intellectuals."

That Kissinger and Nixon would succumb to this type of flimsy moral equivalence was the start of an unhealthy trend in the way American leaders approached their Chinese counterparts. It was absurd for the president and his national security advisor to equate Mao's executions of tens of thousands of educated Chinese with Nixon's Red-baiting and haphazard wiretapping. It sent a message to the Chinese that in their desperation for better ties, the Americans were willing to set their values aside. It made the Americans seem weak. Nixon wrote that he went to China understanding that Mao would ask "Is American culture strong or weak?" But when he arrived in Beijing, he again set his own counsel aside.

In 1972, Mao Zedong was a sick man. A lifetime of smoking had ravaged his lungs. He suffered from a bronchial infection that caused convulsive coughing and from congestive heart disease. His body was so bloated that he had to be fitted with a cavernous suit for his meeting with Nixon. Throughout the summit, his doctor, Li Zhisui, waited just outside the room with a mobile respirator, donated earlier by the United States.

Mao hosted Nixon in his study at party headquarters. His hair was freshly cut and his face cleanly shaven. In his memoirs, Nixon recalled that Mao took his hand for as long as a minute, a common Chinese gesture between older men and younger boys. The meeting had been scheduled to last for fifteen minutes but it went on for an hour. Smiling broadly, Mao told Nixon, "I voted for you during your last election," and he said that he liked "rightists." Nixon responded that in America, at least, those on the Right were the only ones who could get things done.

It wasn't much of a negotiation, and the Americans recalled being befuddled by Mao, who flitted from topic to topic. He spoke about the need for the US and China to work together to oppose Russia's influence. Mao said the party would continue to claim that Taiwan was part of Communist China, but Beijing would be flexible on the timing of getting it back. He also made it clear that China would not abandon its option of using force to conquer the island and, as Kissinger wrote, "indeed expected to have to use force someday."

Watching the extravaganza on television in the hospital where he was recuperating from a heart attack, US diplomat U. Alexis Johnson was struck by the atmospherics of the event with "Nixon sitting on the edge of his chair while Mao reclined royally." The Chinese, Johnson surmised, "must have felt triumphant."

That night, the Chinese threw the Americans a welcome banquet in the Fujian Room of the Great Hall of the People. As the entourage sat down to dinner, America was just waking up, and the feast ran live on morning TV, courtesy of a satellite downlink the Americans had brought to China. At the main table, Zhou Enlai pointed to a Panda brand cigarette package and told Pat Nixon that China would present the United States with a pair of pandas. Mrs. Nixon was overjoyed, and Ling-Ling and Hsing-Hsing would soon cause "panda-monium" at the National Zoo, resuming the panda diplomacy begun in 1936 by Madame Chiang Kai-shek. (The pair of musk oxen that the Americans presented the Beijing Zoo in return failed to cause an equivalent stir. One died soon after its arrival. The other lost its hair.) Cameramen mounted chairs to capture shots of Nixon and Zhou Enlai as they ate. In his diary, Nixon's chief of staff H. R. Haldeman noted the "euphoric reporting of the banquet." The Chinese shared in the jubilation. The next day the *People's Daily* hailed the trip with three big front-page pictures. The message was clear to the average Chinese. Not even Nikita Khrushchev had warranted this kind of hospitality back in the days when China and Russia were as close as lips and teeth.

The American reporters grumbled at the lack of news. After the Nixon-Mao meeting, all they got from White House spokesman Ron Ziegler was "The president and Chairman Mao met this afternoon for one hour." John Chancellor went live with his frustration. "The American people," he announced during prime time, "are getting no real information at all."

In his talks with Zhou Enlai, Nixon showed how little America's views of China had changed since the days of the Open Door policy of 1900. Nixon wanted a prosperous China that would stabilize Asia and be open for trade. Nixon told Zhou that a continued US presence in the region would be useful to China because it would shield Beijing while the country modernized. America's security treaty with Japan would prevent Tokyo from rearming, he said, and stop it from building the Bomb.

"A strong China is in the interests of world peace," Nixon declared. "A strong China can help provide the balance of power in this key part of the world. . . . If China could become a second superpower, the U.S. could reduce its own armaments." Considering China's current rise, there's some irony in Nixon's cheerleading. Zhou laughed and said, disingenuously, that China had no plans to become so strong.

On the second day of talks, Kissinger disappeared into a Chinese villa to provide People's Liberation Army marshal Ye Jianying with a three-hour briefing on Soviet troop deployments. Kissinger stressed that the White House was happy to supply the intelligence "without reciprocity," another example of the ways the US violated Kissinger's warning not to pay "in advance."

As the two sides negotiated the Shanghai Communiqué, the Americans found that they had given China more than they had got. The US was providing China with priceless intelligence. Nixon had already reduced US troop strength in Indochina from more than half a million to less than one hundred thousand. The Seventh Fleet no longer patrolled the

Taiwan Strait. The communiqué's statement that the United States "acknowl-edges" and "does not challenge" the idea that "all Chinese on either side of the Taiwan Strait maintain that there is but one China and that Taiwan is part of China" brought Washington close to a statement in support of Taiwan's reunification with the mainland. In return, China had only removed its long-held opposition to negotiations to end the Vietnam War. Still, Beijing would continue the flow of arms to the North Vietnamese until their final conquest of South Vietnam in 1975 and America's humil-iating retreat.

In his final toast on February 27, Nixon again returned to the idea of the Open Door. Speaking in Shanghai, a city once carved up by British, French, and Japanese imperialists, Nixon declared that the American people were dedicated to the principle "that never again shall foreign domina-tion, foreign occupation, be visited upon this city or any part of China." A few months earlier, China and America had squared off as enemies in Asia, and now the American president was offering China an implicit security guarantee. Nixon was not exaggerating when he told his host, Zhang Chunqiao, one of the ultraleftist members of the Gang of Four, "This was the week that changed the world."

Nixon felt the benefits of the opening to China immediately. He arrived in Washington to a seven-point bump in his overall approval rating. The Rus-sians agreed to a summit, and in May 1972, Nixon traveled to Moscow and signed the long-awaited Strategic Arms Limitation Treaty, or SALT. That Leonid Brezhnev consented to host Nixon as the United States resumed bombing North Vietnam was a sign of the Soviet determination to restore momentum to détente.

There was progress on Vietnam, but it was slow. In October, Hanoi and the United States settled on a cease-fire. Kissinger asserted that "peace is at hand," eliminating Democratic presidential nominee George McGovern's main campaign issue. Nixon won reelection in a landslide. The Paris Peace Accords would be signed in January 1973. A month later, Kissinger returned to Beijing and the US and China agreed to open up liaison offices in their respective capitals. Writing to the president, Kissinger gushed with "raptur-ous enchantment," to use U. Alexis Johnson's phrase. "We are now in the extraordinary situation that, with the exception of the United Kingdom, the People's Republic of China might well be closest to us in its global per-ceptions," Kissinger claimed. "No other world leaders have the sweep and imagination of Mao and Chou nor the capacity and will to achieve a long range policy." Summing up his trip, Kissinger told the president: "We have progressed farther and faster than anyone would have predicted, or the rest of the world realizes. For in plain terms, we have now become tacit allies."

Kissinger wasn't the only one experiencing rapturous enchantment. A China mania was washing across the United States. Americans donned Mao jackets and Mao hats, stir-fried in woks, and wielded chopsticks. An array of American reporters, writers, academics, actors, artists, poets, financiers, and businessmen journeyed to China and brought back fantastic stories about Mao's revolution and the earth-shattering changes he had wrought. First Lady Pat Nixon posed for the cover of *Ladies' Home Journal* in February 1972 in a Chinese-style evening gown. "China," read the *New York Times* headline later that month, "It's the Latest Thing."

Americans were consumed with a blend of well-meaning solicitude and sheepish guilt toward the Middle Kingdom. Left-wing academics contended that America was wrong to have chosen Chiang Kai-shek over Mao Zedong. The Cold War with Beijing? America's fault as well.

Exhibit A of this groundswell surfaced in 1971 with the publication of historian Barbara Tuchman's *Stilwell and the American Experience in China, 1911–1945.* Tuchman's Pulitzer Prize–winning work on Joseph Stilwell was magisterial but deeply unfair. She accused Chiang Kai-shek's Kuomintang of not fighting the Japanese, even though they had. Once again Vinegar Joe Stilwell became an essential hero to the China story America told itself. He was proof of what Tuchman called America's "supreme try in China" and proof that the Nationalists got what they deserved. Once more, Stilwell became a useful prop as progressive Americans repeated the argument that now, finally, was the time to abandon Chiang's sclerotic regime in Taiwan in favor of the Red mandarins in Beijing.

With America at last cultivating China's Communists, Tuchman and other academics contended that it should have done so all along. If Washington had only come to its senses at the end of World War II, Tuchman contended in a *Foreign Affairs* essay in October 1972, "we might not have come to Vietnam." There was something profoundly paternalistic in this view because it denied the Chinese any responsibility for their affairs. Tuchman ignored Mao's decision to side with the USSR and gin up hatred of America. She held that it was all America's responsibility.

Tuchman was not the only one enraptured by Beijing. From die-hard leftists to well-meaning liberals to those securely on the right, Americans fell for China again. With their own country trapped in Vietnam and riven by drugs, the generation gap, and racial conflict, Americans found China inspirational. The US was rich but spoiled. China was poor but noble. The US was free and fractious. China was communal and harmonious. Americans dug free love. The Chinese were beyond sex. Americans worshipped individualism. China valued the collective. Americans had laws. The Chinese had morals.

In China, politically moderate Americans saw a living example of the Protestant work ethic, which America seemed to have lost. James Reston of the *New York Times* was impressed during his visit there by "the atmosphere of intelligent and purposeful work." The American Friends Service Committee, casting a wary eye at wayward American youth, reported that China's young exhibited "complete dedication" to building a better world. Banker David Rockefeller observed a "sense of national harmony" and noted that crime had been eliminated. "Doors are routinely left unlocked," he wrote. Orville Schell, a China scholar out of the University of California, Berkeley, believed that the Chinese, in opting for clothing in greens and blues, for unisex haircuts and no makeup, had rewritten the laws of nature. "The Chinese have succeeded in fundamentally altering the notion of attractiveness by simply substituting some of these revolutionary attributes for physical ones," he wrote. After a brief trip in 1972, John K. Fairbank claimed that Mao's revolution constituted "a far-reaching moral crusade to change the very human Chinese personality in the direction of self-sacrifice and serving others." Fairbank pronounced the revolution "on the whole the best thing that happened to the Chinese people in centuries." Maoism, he intoned, "has got results."

The actress Shirley MacLaine visited China in the spring of 1973 at the head of a women's delegation. Returning home after three weeks, she wrote a book and codirected a documentary, *The Other Half of the Sky: A China Memoir*. In China, MacLaine discovered that she no longer needed deodorant, rouge, or eyeliner. Unlike Americans, the Chinese, she claimed, did not obsess about their physical appearance. "Women had little need or even desire for such superficial things as frilly clothes and makeup," she wrote. "Relationships seemed free of jealousy and infidelity." The Chinese had even outgrown bickering. MacLaine's film, nominated for an Academy Award as the best documentary of 1975, was a love letter to the Middle

Kingdom. In every frame, everyone is happy. Even the woman under-going a C-section under acupuncture is happy.

Happy China became a theme. "Much of this book may sound unduly optimistic; people may seem unbelievably happy," wrote the sociologist Ruth Sidel in a foreword to her book, *Women and Child Care in China: A Firsthand Report*. But, she assured her readers, it was all true. China scholar Michel Oksenberg titled a 1973 essay "On Learning from China." In it, he argued that China could provide cures to the social ills that ailed America. Oksenberg would become the Asia director for the National Security Council under President Jimmy Carter.

On May 10, 1971, botanist Arthur Galston and biologist Ethan Signer became the first scientists to resume America's remarkable relationship with Chinese science. The two visited communes, factories, and research institutes and dined with Zhou Enlai. Galston asked the Chinese to arrange a meeting with an old friend, Loo Shih-wei, who had been one of the world's premier plant physiologists when he returned to China in 1947 from Columbia University.

Galston was taken to see Loo in Shanghai. In a January 7, 1972, feature in *Science* magazine, Galston and Signer extolled Loo's work in a peasant commune outside Shanghai. They praised China for encouraging its scientists to stay close to the needs of the people. Compared to elitist, class-riddled America, the Middle Kingdom was so much more advanced and revolutionary, the men wrote. And Loo Shih-wei was a happy man.

In reality, Communist apparatchiks had branded Loo Shih-wei a "stinking intellectual" during the Cultural Revolution. He had been beaten, forced to shovel pig manure, and banned from conducting research. Loo was working as a farmhand in the countryside when Galston wrote his name on his visa application as someone whom he would like to meet. Party authorities summoned Loo to Shanghai and set him up in his old apartment, which had long since been expropriated. Afterward, they sent him back to the farm. In 1979, Loo was allowed to visit the United States. He met Galston and told him the real story, breaking down in tears. Galston expressed shock that the Chinese could have lied to him about his friend.

Even hard-bitten reporters like Stanley Karnow found themselves disarmed by China. American journalists did not seek out dissidents, avoided questions about the military, and seemed to have an endless appetite for Potemkin villages, communes, factories, hospitals, and day care centers.

"Subliminally, perhaps we still viewed the Chinese as underdogs to whom we owe our sympathy," Karnow wrote in the *Atlantic* in October 1973, "and thus we bent over backwards to be polite."

For China, the benefits of rapprochement accrued immediately. Soon after Nixon departed, China cut a massive deal with M. W. Kellogg of Texas and its subsidiaries for sixteen fertilizer plants. At $392 million, it constituted the biggest single order of its kind. Output from these facilities more than doubled China's fertilizer production. In 1974, China's harvests finally surpassed their total in 1957. By the early 1980s, wheat productivity had increased by 60 percent and maize by more than a half. For Beijing, bettering ties with the US was more than grand strategy; it was powered by the need to feed eight hundred million Chinese.

Mao's opening to America reflected a broad understanding at the party's highest echelons that China had to expand economic ties with capitalist countries. It is important to understand that this decision predated the return to power of Deng Xiaoping, long credited with jump-starting China's leap to modernity. In 1971, while Deng still languished in the boondocks under a political cloud, China's Ministry of Fuel and Chemical Industries pushed through the 4-3 program, under which it would import $4.3 billion worth of equipment and turnkey projects, mostly from the West. China's foreign trade jumped 250 percent between 1970 and 1975. In 1972, the country opened the yearly Canton Import and Export Fair to American businessmen for the first time.

China's monumental decision to resume trading relations with the West in the 1970s paralleled the move made at the beginning of the Qing dynasty to use commerce with the European powers to heal the Chinese empire. And in many ways, Americans and Chinese picked up where they had left off as well.

Barely two weeks after Nixon left China, Tex Boullioun, a senior executive at Boeing, flew to Hong Kong and traveled overland to China to negotiate the sale of Boeing civilian aircraft to the PRC. Nixon had flown to China on a Boeing 707, and the Chinese wanted planes like Air Force One. In the 1920s, Americans had taught China how to assemble planes and fly. Starting in the 1970s, they did it again.

After rapprochement with America, a rising tide of nations—fourteen in 1971 and seventeen the following year—recognized Beijing. In January 1973, the United States and North Vietnam ended the Vietnam War, removing a hundred thousand American troops from China's vicinity. So when Kissinger returned to China in February 1973, Mao's expectations were even higher. Meeting Kissinger on the seventeenth of that month, Mao proposed an alliance with the United States to counter the Soviet threat. "We were enemies in the past, but now we are friends," he told Kissinger. "A horizontal line—the U.S.—Japan—China—Pakistan—Iran—Turkey, and Europe" could "together deal with the bastard." The United States and China, Mao declared, were "in the same trench."

This time America was the reluctant one. Nixon's visit to Moscow and Brezhnev's return visit to the United States in June 1973 had put US relations with Russia on firmer ground. As Kissinger told Nixon in early 1973, the Americans could "continue to have our mao-tai and drink our vodka, too." Mao's hopes that China could employ the United States as a cudgel against Moscow were evaporating. Washington had used China, not the other way around. Mao complained to Kissinger that America had "stood on China's shoulders" to reach agreements with Moscow.

Mao was also disappointed at the slow pace of normalization. In his meetings with the Chinese, Kissinger had promised that the process would begin after the 1974 midterm elections, leading to full diplomatic relations "before mid-1976." That probability soon fell casualty to the unfolding Watergate scandal.

On November 17, Mao gathered together Zhou Enlai and other officials from the Foreign Ministry. He warned Zhou to be wary of the Americans. He noted that China tended to go overboard when it clashed with America, but when it made up with America, it risked giving too much away. "I am of the opinion that, basically, we should do nothing with them," he said. Mao forced Zhou to undertake a humiliating self-criticism before the Politburo. On November 18, Mao directed his wife, Jiang Qing, to attack Zhou for "humiliating the country" and "kneeling down in front of the Americans." Mao reminded the party that China's move to improve ties with the United States was tactical.

In this environment, any interaction with an American became fraught. When the Ministry of Machine Building sent a delegation to the Corning Glass Works in New York in 1973 to study color television technology, the company presented the Chinese with a tiny glass snail as a memento. Jiang Qing accused Chinese officials of "a blind faith in anything foreign" and claimed that the snail implied that "we Chinese are crawling." Only after a lengthy Foreign Ministry investigation, which determined that the Americans meant no harm, did Mao force Jiang Qing to back off. By February 1974, Mao had dropped the idea of an alliance with the United States. And he rolled out his theory of the "three worlds" before the United Nations via a new representative, Deng Xiaoping.

A five-foot-tall revolutionary from Sichuan who had studied in France and Russia in the 1920s, Deng Xiaoping had been one of Mao's closest allies. In 1957, Mao had tapped him to lead the Anti-Rightist Campaign, and during the Sino-Soviet split, Deng had attacked Moscow with fervor. But after the Great Leap Forward, Deng had teamed up with Liu Shaoqi to correct Mao's mistakes with the economy and experiment with market-oriented reforms. For those "capitalist" excesses, Mao had Liu killed and Deng purged. But in early 1973, Mao brought Deng back to power to balance Zhou Enlai, whose position had been enhanced following the death of Lin Biao, a senior military officer who was supposed to take over from Mao. Lin Biao had died in an airplane crash in September 1971 after apparently attempting a coup.

On April 10, 1974, Deng addressed the UN General Assembly in New York. He attacked the United States and the USSR, accusing both nations of plotting to control the globe and oppressing developing nations, which he referred to as the Third World. America and Russia were, Deng said, "the biggest international exploiters and oppressors of today." Having fulfilled his revolutionary obligations on a Wednesday, Deng indulged his revisionist tendencies over the weekend. He ordered his minions to arrange a tour for him of Wall Street. Tang Mingzhao, then the highest-ranking Chinese at the UN, reminded Deng that the Stock Exchange was closed. "You can still look around," Deng replied. As he gazed out the car window at the Wall Street bull, Deng observed that finance was the heart of any economy. "You can only understand the outside world if you go there," Deng remarked, according to the memoirs of his translator Shi Yanhua. "America's history isn't very long; we really need to understand the history of its development," he observed. Deng might have gone to New York to give a speech for Mao, wrote Wu Jianmin, a senior foreign ministry official, but while he was there, he gathered some very un-Maoist inspiration for China's road ahead.

The Watergate scandal and Nixon's resignation postponed Washington's plans to normalize relations with China. Entering office in August 1974, Nixon's successor, Gerald Ford, proceeded with caution. To govern, Ford needed support from the GOP's right wing. Senator Barry Goldwater, the conservative eminence from Arizona, warned the White House that it would have "a hell of a fight" on its hands if it tried to recognize Beijing and drop Taipei. Ronald Reagan, the actor-governor of California, was already positioning himself to challenge Ford for the GOP nomination and Reagan had been a friend of Taiwan since the 1950s.

Ford and Kissinger, now secretary of state, tried to roll back some of Nixon's promises. Ford did not want to cut ties with Taiwan completely. The Chinese were outraged. When Arkansas senator William J. Fulbright visited China in February 1974, Foreign Minister Qiao Guanhua declared that "peaceful reunification" with Taiwan was impossible. Deng Xiaoping told a meeting of the American Society of Newspaper Editors that using force to "liberate" Taiwan would be like "removing dust from a floor with the aid of a broom."

When Kissinger returned to China in November 1974 for his seventh visit, he met Zhou Enlai for the last time. The meeting in Zhou's hospital room was purely ceremonial; Zhou was dying of liver cancer. The torch had been passed to Deng Xiaoping, whom Kissinger would privately deride as "that nasty little man."

Kissinger underestimated Deng Xiaoping. Chinese notes of conversations between the two show that Deng maneuvered Kissinger into astounding statements that Deng would use later to great effect. On November 28, Deng alleged that it was the American "occupation" of Taiwan that had prevented better ties with China. Amazingly, Kissinger agreed and acknowledged that in proceeding toward full diplomatic relations, the United States would take three steps—breaking relations with Taiwan, withdrawing its military, and annulling its defense treaty—without expecting China to take "any reciprocal measures."

In the face of Chinese recalcitrance, Ford's conditions had vanished. What's more, Kissinger praised China's position as one of "great wisdom, generosity and self-restraint." Then he added, according to the Chinese notes, "I also recognize due to the nature of this issue and our previous discussions we indeed owe you a debt."

Kissinger's obsequiousness did not play well with the State Department's China experts. It was an example, noted William Gleysteen, a China-born veteran diplomat, of "the cloyingly friendly, almost worshipful quality" of the official American attitude toward China's leaders. "It denigrated America's importance," Gleysteen recalled, "and it ground against my conviction that the Chinese needed us as much as we needed them."

To repay America's "debt," Kissinger backed a decision to offer China even more military and intelligence cooperation. He justified the move by saying that it would bolster "moderates" within the Chinese government who were dedicated to an opening to the outside world. In his discussions with the Chinese, Kissinger ridiculed Japan and framed America's attempts to improve ties with the Soviet Union as a tactic "to satisfy the softies in our own society and among our NATO allies," Gleysteen wrote. Kissinger's belittling of an ally and disparaging of détente gave the Chinese an inflated sense of their importance to the United States.

The effect of Kissinger's decision to push a military-security relationship to pay off America's "debt" to China was twofold. One, it raised American hopes that as long as the United States took steps to enhance China's power, Beijing would tilt toward Washington. And two, it cemented China's position in Asia as the sun around which US interests revolved.

Even on matters of principle, the US government bent over backward to accommodate the Chinese. In late 1974, when the People's Republic sent its first exhibit of archaeological treasures to the United States, the Chinese informed State Department officials that they would not allow reporters from nations that did not have relations with China to attend a press conference planned for the National Gallery of Art in Washington. Instead of ignoring the Chinese demand, the State Department canceled the briefing. In Beijing, George H. W. Bush, now the chief of the US Liaison Office, was angered that the State Department had caved to the Chinese. "We must not capitulate on matters this fundamental," he wrote. "We must not permit them to flaunt their way in the United States." But that's what was happening.

While Americans walked on eggshells around the Chinese, the Chinese continued to lambaste the United States. Bush was troubled by the constant stream of jeremiads against US imperialism. With Chinese officials, he tried to make the point "subtly," as he wrote in his diary on November 11, 1974, that "China is going to have to determine how much to attack us and how much not to." Bush tried to get Washington interested in the matter. But he had no traction there, either. American officials were confident that China's screeds would eventually fade away. They never have.

On the evening of April 5, 1975, the last day of the holiday when Chinese sweep the graves of their ancestors, Chiang Kai-shek suffered a fatal heart attack. His death presented a headache for President Ford. America had to bid farewell to an old friend, but the White House was so afraid of China's reaction that it did not know whom to send to Taipei. Ford chose Secretary of Agriculture Earl Butz to lead the American delegation to the funeral. But Butz, an inveterate racist, was an insulting choice. Ford finally dispatched an unwilling Vice President Nelson Rockefeller instead.

Under Ford, relations with the USSR worsened. Tensions rose during the 1973 Yom Kippur War in the Middle East, which nearly involved both superpowers. The Soviets were angry when the US tied trade with Moscow to a relaxation of Soviet emigration policies. Cold Warriors on the margins of the administration began to lobby for an even closer military relationship with China to torment the Soviet bear. In September 1975, Michael Pillsbury, an analyst with the Rand Corporation, called for selling weapons to China in an essay in *Foreign Policy*. "China is not nearly as large a security threat to us as the Soviet Union is," Pillsbury declared. The CIA weighed in with a study, coauthored by the China-born intelligence officer James Lilley, that contended that a military relationship with China would strengthen pro-American moderates in the Communist Party. Both reports received positive coverage in the US press. "Guns for Peking," read the headline in *Newsweek* on September 9, 1975.

Kissinger had already dramatically increased the quantity and quality of intelligence sharing with the Chinese. In 1974 and 1975, accompanying Kissinger to China, NSC staffer Robert McFarlane briefed the Chinese on a vast array of highly classified topics, including Soviet nuclear doctrine, its conventional forces, and Russian military aid programs. Still, the Chinese treated Kissinger rudely when he returned to Beijing in October 1975 to pave the way for President Ford's trip in December. Mao asked that Secretary of Defense James Schlesinger accompany Ford. Kissinger demurred but noted that "we have tried to suggest to you that we are prepared to advise or help in some of these problems," meaning China's defense. Mao dismissed the offer and ended the meeting.

Ford's political advisers proposed that he cancel his trip to Beijing. The president's challengers in the Republican Party primaries, like Ronald Reagan, were criticizing his China policy as appeasement. Ford went, but shaved three days off his original itinerary and added stops in Indonesia and the Philippines to show that China wasn't the only country in Asia that interested the United States.

On January 8, 1976, Zhou Enlai succumbed to liver cancer. On April 5, Qingming Day, the Chinese day of mourning for the dead, a massive rally erupted in Tiananmen Square to protest the muted government response to his death. Security forces and workers wielding clubs bloodied hundreds in the square. Radicals around Mao's wife, Jiang Qing, blamed Deng Xiaoping for encouraging the protest, and they purged him again.

On September 9, 1976, Mao, suffering from multiple ailments, died.

In October, his successor, Hua Guofeng, arrested Jiang Qing and the rest of the Gang of Four, who had spearheaded Mao's Cultural Revolution. In November, Ford lost the White House to Georgia Democrat Jimmy Carter. By the middle of 1977, Deng Xiaoping had returned to the top of China's political heap, where he would remain for twenty years until he died.

In 1972, after more than two decades, the United States and China ended their Cold War. The two nations approached each other with tremendous expectations. China looked to America to help it survive. America looked to China to defeat a dreaded foe. Americans resumed their centuries-old relationship with China with a nagging sense that they had somehow let China down. The Chinese would expertly exploit Yankee guilt in the ensuing years.

CHAPTER THIRTY-SEVEN

We Are Very Sexy People

Jimmy Carter came to office wanting to complete the normalization process with China but he was determined that "we should not kiss-ass them the way Nixon and Kissinger did." In Beijing, the new US Liaison Office head Leonard Woodcock told his colleagues, according to the writer James Mann, that "never again shall we embarrass ourselves before a foreign nation the way Henry Kissinger did with the Chinese."

Still, by the end of 1977, the Carter administration and the Chinese would relapse into earlier patterns. The relationship resumed its air of a military alliance against the Russians, with the Americans providing or facilitating the transfer of military technology to the Chinese. And the Middle Kingdom continued to receive special treatment. The White House ignored China's human rights problems even as President Carter sought to position himself as the driving force for freedom in the world. And though he had run on a platform of opposing secret diplomacy, Carter supported the tactic when it came to Beijing.

Like Woodrow Wilson, FDR, and Nixon, Jimmy Carter brought emotional baggage to the issue of the Middle Kingdom. His interest in China was kindled, he wrote in his memoirs, "when I was a small boy during the 1930s, studying about Baptist missionaries there." During World War II, as a young naval officer, Carter had visited China and, he noted in a 2013 speech, "had fallen in love with the country and with its people."

Nonetheless, there was still discomfort within the American bureaucracy with the deal that Nixon and Kissinger had worked out for Taiwan, and, in the spring of 1977, American officials again drew up proposals to boost the island's status. Leading this effort was Secretary of State Cyrus Vance, who advocated maintaining an official office in Taipei. Vance also wanted the Chinese to commit publicly to a peaceful resolution of the Taiwan issue. He argued that Washington's allies would watch America abandon Taiwan and naturally question US commitments elsewhere.

In August 1977, Vance took these ideas to Beijing, only to have them rejected in meeting after meeting. On August 24, Foreign Minister Huang Hua accused the United States of "aggression against China." Later that day, Vance met Deng Xiaoping, who reminded him that Kissinger had acknowledged that the United States owed China a debt for "occupying" Taiwan. Deng mocked Vance's proposal for a low-key State Department presence on Taiwan as "an embassy that does not have a sign on its door." He characterized Vance's approach as "a retreat." Vance's rough treatment in Beijing emboldened National Security Advisor Zbigniew Brzezinski to press the president to send him to China instead.

Brzezinski, the son of a Polish diplomat whose family had been forced into exile by the Nazi occupation, had swung full circle on China. At the State Department during the Johnson administration, he had argued against any opening to Beijing and as a scholar had maintained that America's relations with Japan were more important than potential ties with China. But now this committed Cold Warrior saw the opportunity to use Beijing as a bludgeon against the Russian bear. Like Kissinger, another European, he focused on how China could help Washington undermine Moscow, and he discounted how supporting Beijing might affect America's standing in the Far East.

"The Soviet dimension," Brzezinski wrote, "was one of those considerations of which it is sometimes said, 'Think of it at all times but speak of it never.' I, for one, thought of it a great deal." Vance countered that focusing on China as a lever against America's main enemy would backfire. China should be dealt with as part of a broader strategy in Asia, Vance said. The president initially sided with his secretary of state. But by the spring of 1978, with the Soviet Union fomenting uprisings and coups in the Horn of Africa, Angola, and Afghanistan, Brzezinski's plan to play the China card against the Russians eclipsed Vance's view.

On May 20, 1979, Brzezinski arrived in Beijing. In discussions, he dropped Vance's idea of an official US office in Taiwan and the request that

China promise to settle its problems with Taiwan peacefully. He returned to the assurances that Nixon and Kissinger had made, especially, as he put it, that "the existence of some separate Chinese entities . . . will come to an end." He informed his Chinese hosts that Carter had "made up his mind" to normalize relations according to China's formula.

To the glee of the Chinese, he peppered his visit with a string of anti-Soviet barbs. At the Great Wall, he peered north and asked, "Which side were the barbarians on?" *Newsweek* headlined its article on the visit "The Polar Bear Tamer." Brzezinski told his interlocutors that the United States would not interfere if Western European countries and Israel sold weapons and military technology to China. He expanded on Kissinger's intelligence briefings, bringing along Pentagon officials wielding satellite reconnaissance photographs of Soviet military installations. Other briefers provided the Chinese with seminars on science and technology. Brzezinski proposed a formal system of intelligence exchange and the establishment of bases in China for electronic snooping on the Soviets.

Deng Xiaoping was a lot happier with the tough anti-Soviet Polish American than he had been with the patrician Vance. Before Brzezinski left Beijing, Deng agreed to talks between Leonard Woodcock and Huang Hua to wrap up normalization. The deadline for formal recognition was set for January 1979. In his memoirs, Brzezinski claimed that he had no "special sentiment for China," only "larger strategic concerns in mind," but in reality, he, like Kissinger, had been bowled over. Brzezinski, wrote Carter after his national security advisor returned from Beijing, "had been seduced."

The next few months in Beijing and Washington were a whirlwind. At the State Department, Vance and Asia Hand Richard Holbrooke argued for congressional briefings on the normalization talks, but Carter opted for secrecy, writing later that he was leery of opening the process to scrutiny because of a concern that doing so would "arouse a firestorm of opposition from those who thought that Taiwan should always be 'one China.'"

By late November 1978, Deng Xiaoping had eased Mao's chosen successor, Hua Guofeng, from power and had taken over both foreign and domestic affairs. On December 13, he met Woodcock in the Jiangsu Hall at the Great Hall of the People, where Woodcock handed him a one-page draft of the joint communiqué to announce the resumption of formal ties. Deng accepted Woodcock's invitation to visit the United States in January. At a follow-up meeting two days later, when Woodcock reiterated that the United States would still sell weapons to Taiwan, Deng, after exploding, offered a one-word reply, "Hao" (good). It was an acknowledgment that he would not let what the Americans assured him was simply the detritus of a decades-long alliance get in the way of ties. Woodcock again let it be known that the US government believed that unification with Taiwan was inevitable.

On December 15, at 9:00 p.m. Washington time and 9:00 a.m. December 16 Beijing time, the two parties issued a nine-paragraph statement announcing that formal relations would begin on January 1. In Shanghai, radio stations played John Denver's "Take Me Home, Country Roads" to celebrate the event.

At 2:00 in the morning in Taipei, just hours before the statement was released, American officials woke up Chiang Ching-kuo to inform him that America would be severing relations with his country. Chiang Ching-kuo cried at the news. When US officials arrived in Taipei on December 27 to explain the decision, a crowd attacked their car, first pelting it with tomatoes and then smashing the windows with rocks. Deputy Secretary of State Warren Christopher suffered cuts to his face.

China's modernization and its normalization with America were inseparable. It wasn't a coincidence that on December 13, 1978, the day he accepted Woodcock's invitation to become the first Chinese leader to visit America, Deng gave the most important speech of his life to a Central Party Work Conference. Coming two years after Mao's death and the arrest of the Gang of Four, the gathering at the Jingxi Hotel in Beijing launched Deng's policies of "reform and opening up," which would change China forever. Deng pushed what he called the Four Modernizations, a program to improve China's economy, science and technology, agriculture, and defense.

During the conference, Deng directly linked normalization with the United States to his domestic agenda, according to Zhang Baijia, a historian with access to party archives. Throughout the meetings, Deng and other proponents of reform repeated a phrase—"Most of the countries in the world hope for a strong China"—directly inspired by their interactions with US officials. Though the Ministry of Propaganda still instructed China's people that America was intent on keeping China down, internally, many senior party leaders understood the opposite to be true. Ties with America would give China the security, technology, and investment to grow rich and strong.

"The American factor was, in the end, the all-encompassing factor in China's modernization," wrote Yuan Ming, a diplomatic historian at Peking

University. American science and technology would raise Chinese standards; its educational system would teach management skills; its markets would consume Chinese goods; its culture would inspire innovation and copycat businesses; and its navy would protect China's seas. Experts from all over the world, but particularly the United States and Japan, were invited to China for conferences, exchanges, and collaborations and they made indispensable contributions to China's rise as a global economic power.

In his speech to the Work Conference, Deng restored the ideas of John Dewey and the pragmatic notion that an economy must be built one factory, one railroad, one invention at a time, where "practice is the sole criterion for truth." Hewing to Dewey's "retail" theory of political and economic change, Deng urged experimentation and boldness. He called it "crossing the river by feeling the stones."

A week after the speech, Deng's ideas were enshrined at a party gathering known as the Third Plenum of the 11th Central Committee. From the lowly position as a vice premier, Deng would dominate China's political landscape for more than a decade. The decisions made then represented another turn of the wheel toward the United States as the frame of reference for modernity in China. In fits and starts, from Chiang Kai-shek, Sun Yat-sen, Liang Qichao, Li Hongzhang, Xu Jiyu, all the way back to nineteenth-century officials in Guangzhou, the United States had been a guide and a guardian for China. And now it was again. On January 1, 1979, the People's Republic of China and the United States formally recognized each other.

American influence did not flow in a single stream. Just as Deng was lobbying inside the halls of power for a modernization program fueled by US technology and capital, a restive group of poets, writers, and thinkers, inspired by American ideas, took to the streets to call for a different kind of change. In October 1978, as Deng made his bid for power, a Democracy Wall of essays, poems, and unofficial news appeared at the intersection of Chang'an Boulevard and Xidan in central Beijing. On December 5, an electrician named Wei Jingsheng pasted up a call for a Fifth Modernization—democracy—to add to the party's four. As the New York Times had noted as far back as 1881, China could not choose American technology, education, and capital and expect to shield itself from other ideas. "The virus of political rebellion" had also entered China. Deng ordered Wei arrested in March 1979 and had him sentenced to fifteen years.

Deng Xiaoping arrived in the United States on January 28, 1979, for the first state visit ever of an official from the People's Republic of China. From the outset, Deng resumed Chiang Kai-shek's old strategy of using the United States to threaten his adversaries, in this case Vietnam and its patron, the USSR. A month earlier Vietnam had sent 150,000 troops into Cambodia and routed China's ally, the Khmer Rouge regime.

At the White House welcoming ceremony, Deng became the first modern Chinese leader to spook Wall Street when he announced that "factors making for war are visibly growing." A day later, at the East Wing of the National Gallery, he blasted the Soviet Union for its "global strategy for world domination." At a private White House meeting on January 30, Deng told Carter that "China must still teach Vietnam a lesson." Carter replied that he believed an attack would be "a serious mistake," but when Deng asked for an intelligence briefing on the situation in Cambodia and for US support for Cambodian rebels and refugees, the United States agreed. "Deng got what he wanted," wrote John Holdridge, one of the architects of normalization, "a tacit U.S. endorsement of a Chinese military action against the Vietnamese."

Deng Xiaoping was the perfect amalgam to manage the two factions that had emerged at the top of the Communist Party following the arrest of the Gang of Four. On economic issues, he wanted China to grow and understood that it had to rely on America to do so. On the plane to America, the new foreign minister, Huang Hua, asked him why he was heading to the United States on his first foreign trip as China's leader. Deng responded simply. America's allies were all rich and strong. If China wanted to be rich and strong, it needed the United States.

When it came to ideology, however, Deng was a firm believer that only the Communist Party had the wherewithal to lead China into the future and that the American model would spell disaster if it was imported to China. Like many of his predecessors as far back as the Qing dynasty, Deng viewed the rough-and-tumble of American politics and its governmental structure as inapplicable to China. "There are three governments in the United States," he observed about America's separation of powers. "It is very difficult to get anything done." Deng viewed Americans' freedom as a source of chaos. So, while Deng gave hope to China's liberals, who wanted their country to adopt a market economy, he also mollified conservatives, who believed that politically China's government had to stay true to its Stalinist roots.

A day after Deng's arrival in Washington in January 1979, an Islamic revolution overthrew the shah of Iran, Mohammad Reza Pahlavi, who fled the country. The new Iranian government shut down US intelligence collection stations in northern Iran that were monitoring Soviet missile tests. Deng and Brzezinski agreed on a deal to establish a joint signals intelligence station—known as Operation Chestnut—in northwest China. With that, the US and China took the historic step of becoming intelligence partners.

While in America, Deng appealed to Yankee capitalists. He promised to import billions of dollars' worth of equipment and announced that China would need billions more in investments, too. He wanted most-favored-nation (MFN) trading status to open America's markets to Chinese goods. A 1974 law, known as the Jackson-Vanik Amendment, designed to force the Soviet Union to allow Jews to leave Russia, required that most-favored-nation trading benefits be withheld from any country that failed to permit freedom of emigration. When Carter asked whether China would allow people to leave, Deng quipped, "If you want me to release 10 million Chinese to come to the United States, I'd be glad to do so." The United States never applied the amendment to China, another instance of making the Middle Kingdom a special case.

The US media gave the vice premier blanket coverage. The *New York Times*, the *Washington Post*, *Time*, and *Newsweek* ran 127 stories on the visit. *Time*, which had named him "Man of the Year" for 1978, put Deng on the cover again on February 5. *Newsweek*, citing his fondness for spittoons, dubbed him "a larger-than-life rustic." But by far the most memorable moment of his trip was captured in a photograph at the Roundup Rodeo in Simonton, Texas, where Deng put on a ten-gallon cowboy hat and took a spin around the arena in a stagecoach. Writing later in his book *"Watch Out for the Foreign Guests!"*, Orville Schell interpreted Deng's willingness to don a Stetson as a gesture of surrender to Western values. Actually, it was just savvy public relations. Americans found the diminutive Chinese leader almost cute. The contrast to the ill-humored Leonid Brezhnev could not have been greater. As one Texan said, "I don't think this guy, Ping, is a communist anyway."

When he wasn't saber rattling, Deng fixated on American technical prowess. He toured a Ford Motor Company plant with Henry Ford III. At the Lyndon B. Johnson Space Center, he twice squeezed into the cramped cockpit of a space shuttle training ship for simulated flights. He inspected oil-drilling equipment in Houston and explored Boeing's massive plant on the outskirts of Seattle. Technology was at the center of Deng's trip. The first document the two countries signed was an agreement for the United States to bolster science in China.

In his memoirs, Carter described Deng's visit as "one of the delightful experiences of my presidency." He understood, he wrote, "why some people say the Chinese are the most civilized people in the world." The average American was charmed, too. In 1978, Gallup reported that 21 percent of Americans polled had a favorable impression of China. By 1980, the figure had more than tripled.

Two weeks after his return to China, Deng ordered two hundred thousand troops to attack Vietnam. They were easily beaten back. Hanoi did not even bother to send its best units into the fight. Still, the American decision to tacitly back China's invasion underscored the change in US policy in Asia. The US had gone to war in Vietnam to stop Communist Chinese expansion. Now it was winking at Communist China's assault on Vietnam.

Brzezinski was overjoyed at the US support for China's adventure. As the fighting raged, he convinced the White House not to cancel Treasury Secretary Michael Blumenthal's trip to discuss trade issues. "I secretly wished that Deng's appreciation of the uses of power would also rub off on some of the key US decision makers," he wrote.

The Carter administration's failure to brief congressional leaders on its normalization negotiations with China angered America's lawmakers. As a result, Republicans and Democrats teamed up to protect Taiwan in ways that went far beyond what Carter's White House had told the Chinese the United States would contemplate.

In December 1978, George H. W. Bush, Nixon's UN ambassador, declared that Carter had "capitulated" to the Communists by dropping the demand that China commit to a peaceful solution of the Taiwan problem. "For the first time in our history, a peacetime American government has renounced a treaty with an ally without cause or benefit," he wrote in the *Washington Post*.

Influential senators had asked the administration to keep Congress apprised of any changes to the mutual defense treaty with Taiwan. But the White House stiffed them. Stanley Roth, then a Senate staffer and later a senior diplomat, noted to historian Nancy Bernkopf Tucker that the White House seemed to expect "Taiwan to vanish."

In February 1979, a bipartisan congressional coalition pushed back against the White House and proposed the Taiwan Relations Act. Spearheaded by Massachusetts senator Ted Kennedy, it put China on notice that the US might respond to an invasion of Taiwan and directed the president to provide Taiwan with defensive weapons and technology.

China blasted the legislation as "an unwarranted intrusion" into its internal affairs. What the Chinese did not say publicly was that the law violated all the private assurances they'd been given—by two US administrations—that Taiwan would eventually cease to exist as a separate state. Now the United States was again placing itself between the Communists and their holy grail. In March 1979, the act passed both houses of Congress by a veto-proof margin. Carter had no choice but to sign it into law. As a further insult, through financial sleight of hand, Taiwan's friends in Congress also arranged for Taipei to keep Twin Oaks, the sprawling Washington mansion that had served as the residence of the Chinese ambassador since 1937.

Luckily for both sides, Leonid Brezhnev's Soviet Union began to throw its weight around, threatening Western Europe, meddling in Latin America, Africa, and the Middle East, and continuing a troop buildup on China's northern border. Differences over Taiwan, wrote Michel Oksenberg, who worked for Brzezinski on the National Security Council, were "shoved . . . far into the background."

In part to placate China over Taiwan, the Carter administration dropped all pretense of pursuing equally good relations with the USSR and China. The Carter administration facilitated trade, allowed exports of restricted technology, and paved the way for China's entry into the World Bank, which resulted in hundreds of millions of dollars in loans. Still, the Chinese smarted over Taiwan.

Vice presidential trips abroad are not usually historic. And in August 1979, Walter Mondale's visit to China looked to be no exception. He was greeted formally and noted immediately that the Chinese were reserved. "There was no joy," he wrote later. But on the second day of the trip, the atmosphere improved dramatically when Mondale offered the Chinese $2 billion in credits for a major hydroelectric project and announced that Congress would soon approve China's most-favored-nation trading status. "It was like somebody threw a big switch," the vice president wrote. On August 27, Mondale told Deng that "we are beginning to differentiate between you and the Soviet Union." America, he said, had entered a "gray" area in its relations with a Communist power.

Deng pushed Mondale for more high-technology imports, faster approval of most-favored-nation status, more detailed satellite photographs of Soviet installations along the Chinese border, and, for the first time, weapons. In their August 27 meeting, according to declassified transcripts released by the State Department, Deng asked for warplanes "similar to your F-15 and F-16." The two agreed that Secretary of Defense Harold Brown would become the first US defense secretary to visit China.

The United States was once again behind the idea of a powerful China. As Mondale told Deng during his trip: "We have insisted repeatedly, and I will state it again, we strongly believe in the importance of a strong China." On January 24, 1980, Congress granted most-favored-nation trading status to China, cutting tariffs on Chinese goods to the same rate offered to America's friends and allies. MFN had been reserved for countries with free market economies and basic political and civil rights, which included the right to emigrate. In 1980, China met none of these conditions, but the Carter administration pushed it anyway, arguing that the geopolitical and commercial gains far outweighed the demands of US law.

As the writer Richard Madsen has argued, there was probably a strong geopolitical and commercial case to be made for granting China most-favored-nation trading status. But the Carter administration was compelled to justify it by appealing to a higher purpose when it came to the Middle Kingdom. China deserved MFN status because Americans expected that China was on an unstoppable march toward a market economy with free and fair elections. As Representative Bill Alexander, a Carter supporter from Arkansas, told the House on January 24, 1980, the day MFN was approved, "Seeds of democracy are growing in China."

The Soviet invasion of Afghanistan on Christmas Eve 1979 boosted the emerging security relationship with China. The White House announced that it was cutting off grain sales to the Soviets, along with civilian flights, technological transfers, and consular relations. "The Chinese could barely conceal their delight," remarked Nicholas Platt, a Pentagon official who had served in the US Liaison Office in Beijing.

On January 8, 1980, Deng told visiting US defense secretary Harold Brown that the United States, Japan, China, and Europe should "get united" to counter the Soviet threat. "We must turn Afghanistan into a quagmire in which the Soviet Union is bogged down for a long time in a guerrilla warfare," Deng said. The Americans could not have agreed more.

The Carter administration was already funneling weapons to a hodge-podge of Afghan rebel groups. With China onboard, the operation snowballed into a multibillion-dollar effort. China and America both withdrew from the 1980 Summer Olympics in Moscow. In the UN Security Council, China either voted for or did not block every Afghan-related measure that the United States proposed.

For the second time in four decades, the United States and China came together in an alliance against an Asian power. In the 1940s, they countered Japan. Now they would begin a military-intelligence partnership to take down the USSR. This time the pair seemed on the cusp of accomplishing something extraordinary—not disappointing each other.

The Pentagon and the People's Liberation Army exchanged a series of visits in 1980 culminating in a September trip by William Perry, a Caltech mathematics professor who was the undersecretary of defense for research and engineering. Perry was eager to give the Chinese advice on how they could help themselves. He urged them to send PhD candidates to the United States and Western Europe. He wanted them to dispatch an army of undergraduates to focus on computer science. They would follow his advice. Perry later told writer James Mann that he opposed arms sales to China. Nicholas Platt, who was on the trip, had a different recollection. To Platt, Perry's trip "set the course for the development of military relations between the United States and China." And that included weapons sales.

Despite the Soviet invasion of Afghanistan, there were still a few voices in Washington opposed to a closer military relationship with China. In a June 4, 1980, White House meeting, Thomas Watson, US ambassador to the Soviet Union, told Carter and Brzezinski that the tilt was a bad idea and urged an "evenhanded" policy vis-à-vis the Soviets and the Chinese. "It seems to me that the Chinese have a tendency to jump around from bed to bed," Watson warned. "And I think we ought to make sure that they are lashed down to our bed before we undertake actions which we might regret later on." Brzezinski dismissed Watson's concerns. "You have to remember," he assured Watson, "we are very sexy people."

The Carter administration did not capitalize on Deng Xiaoping's eagerness for normalization to win a better deal for the United States or Taiwan. Carter's staff members, specifically Zbigniew Brzezinski, allowed their focus on battling the Soviet Union to cloud their judgment. Carter insisted in his memoirs that the United States "had been fair and honest with the people of Taiwan." But the president's sprint to establish formal diplomatic relations with China and his belief in secrecy produced what longtime CIA official James Lilley would call "a bungled, compromised agreement." The United States failed itself and the people of Taiwan, Lilley wrote, when it did not insist that Beijing drop its threat to attack the island.

The real loser in the agreement, Lilley wrote, was American prestige with its allies but also with the Chinese. "If we are as incompetent as we appear or if Peking can manipulate us so easily, how can any Chinese have any real respect for us?" Lilley asked.

The Americans did not seem to realize how much Deng Xiaoping needed the United States. Vietnam, which had swung into the Soviet orbit with the signing of a mutual defense treaty with Moscow in November 1978, was fighting the forces of Pol Pot, China's ally in Cambodia. The United States and Russia were planning a summit in May 1979, and Deng wanted ties with the United States normalized beforehand. And it was clear that Deng wanted America to play a key role in his plan to modernize China. But American officials were either oblivious to their leverage or declined to use it. As Lilley observed in a memorandum soon after normalization, "We were taken to the cleaners."

With normalization, the United States launched a wide array of programs to link virtually every US government agency with its Chinese counterpart with the aim of helping China modernize and grow. In the nineteenth century, Americans dreamed of a China stable and strong. During World War II, FDR sought to elevate China into the ranks of the world powers. Jimmy Carter picked up where they had left off.

CHAPTER THIRTY-EIGHT

China Rediscovers America

Just as Nixon's trip unleashed a long-suppressed American fascination with China, Deng Xiaoping's 1979 visit did the same in reverse. China's state-run media began to portray the US as a land of wonders. "Rich land, beautiful scenery, advanced technology, developed industry and high yielding agriculture," was how Huang Zhen, the head of the Chinese Liaison Office in Washington, described the United States in the *People's Daily*. Chinese were glued to TV images of American grandeur. Senior party officials were shaken by America's wealth. "We have wasted 30 years," Fox Butterfield, a reporter for the *New York Times*, quoted one as saying. The blitz of officially sanctioned happy talk about America was so unrelenting that the *Washington Post* worried that China had gone overboard.

Once again China turned to America for education. The Chinese government reserved its warmest treatment for American delegations of scientists and educators. When Carter sent his science adviser Frank Press to China in 1978, Deng Xiaoping insisted that he call Carter immediately to get permission for Chinese students to study in the US. When the White House phone rang at 3:00 a.m., Carter thought that Press, a geologist, was calling to tell him that a volcano had erupted. No, Press said, Deng wanted to send five thousand students to America. "Tell him to send a hundred thousand," Carter barked and went back to bed.

On December 27, 1978, four days before relations were officially established, 52 Chinese scholars aged thirty-two to forty-nine left Beijing to begin two years of study in the United States. Just like the Americans who had pierced the barrier between China and America earlier that decade, the Chinese saw their journey in intergalactic terms. "At the time," recalled Shen Xianjie, a geologist, "America was as alien to us as the moon." Little did these scholars know that they were merely the first batch of astronauts. By 1987, 100,000 Chinese would be studying in America, and by 2015, 275,000. In all, America has educated more than 2 million Chinese.

The first Chinese to arrive were astonished at the pace of American life. "As soon as I got off the flight I felt the pulse of life quicken," wrote Qian Xing, a reporter for the Xinhua News Agency. "Everywhere I feel the pressure of speed. Cars go fast, people walk fast, news is reported fast, announcers speak fast. . . . It seems as if nothing can wait. . . . Faster, faster. This is America's slogan."

From a nation of bicycles, these Chinese had journeyed to the land of the car. Chinese poets penned odes to the US highway system. Novelists waxed lyrical about flying at night, mesmerized by the lights below. Feng Yidai, who had translated Ernest Hemingway and John Steinbeck before spending twenty years in a labor camp, worried that China would never catch up. "On the road to civilization, we are walking way too slowly," he wrote. The message home was simple: we have fallen behind.

As it had before the Communist revolution, American values once again inspired the Chinese. Writing in the *People's Daily* on May 13, 1979, Zhang Yuanchun hailed American "optimism" and "pragmatism" as essential ingredients in China's pursuit of modernity. "A tidal wave" is how the writer Qian Ning described China's rediscovery of the United States. "It was as if the Chinese people were awakened from a deep, stupefying slumber. They saw a brand-new world outside."

In the spring of 1979, Fei Xiaotong, China's once legendary anthropologist, returned to America for two months for the first time since World War II. It was a bittersweet homecoming for Fei, whom Mao had muzzled during what should have been the most productive years of his life. In a Shanghai newspaper, Fei wrote eloquently about America's successes and failures, its science and race relations. As he had in the past, Fei used the United States as a mirror for his own country. He wrote about the Apollo mission to the moon and mocked the Chinese Communist Party for denying that it had taken place. "In a global battle of wits," he asked, "how could you possibly not admit that it occurred?"

Watching the 1980 US presidential election, the first since China had reopened its gates to America, state-controlled media gave the people a thorough lesson in American civics. Studying English became an obsession. The first Test for English as a Foreign Language, the gateway exam to an American college, was held in 1981. American culture went from a forbidden fruit to a public phenomenon. In 1980, a TV serial knockoff of *The Dirty Dozen*, called *Garrison's Gorillas*, took China by storm. Airing at 8:00 on Saturday nights, the show about a motley group of commandos recruited from prison to battle Germans became a smash hit. Chinese youth mimicked the actors, tossing knives and growing their hair—or so the Chinese media claimed. With ten episodes to go, China Central Television yanked the show, citing "bad effects on society." Thousands of protest letters poured in.

Outlawed for decades, American literature rushed back into style. A whole generation of young Chinese women grew up reading *Gone with the Wind*. In 1983, writer Wang Anyi spent four months at the International Writing Program at the University of Iowa, which radically changed her outlook on her mother culture. "Everything in America is the opposite of everything in our country," she told a group of students at Shanghai's Fudan University upon her return. Her time in America emboldened Wang to become the first contemporary Chinese writer to depict sex in a positive light.

The sudden reappearance of Western styles, freedoms, culture, TV, movies, and ideas intoxicated many Chinese, but it troubled Party Central. In October 1983, at the second plenary session of the Twelfth Party Congress, Deng Xiaoping attacked what he called "spiritual pollution" from the West. China's intellectuals were disseminating harmful ideas, such as individualism and liberalism. Writers were too interested in exposing the dark side of socialism. In a screenplay about a painter who returns to China after exile in America, the playwright Bai Hua dared to pose the blasphemous question: Is it possible to love China without loving the Communist Party? On college campuses, the unisex Mao jacket gave way to scraggly over-the-collar hair, bell bottoms, and filmy dresses. Deng warned the party faithful that American influences were corroding China's soul.

Hard-liners stirred up Deng's fears. "Some of our people having taken a few glimpses of the skyscrapers and freeways abroad" have concluded that "socialism is no match for capitalism," observed prominent conservative Chen Yun. The only thing to do with them, Chen argued, was "re-education." The *People's Daily* dropped its pro-American tone and ran exposés about the ugly side of life in the Beautiful Country. "Tears in

Heaven," read the caption on a cartoon of a scrawny American taking off a Mickey Mouse suit that accompanied an article on exploited workers at Disney World. Commentators, who just a few years earlier had enthused about America's work ethic and modernity, now lambasted the United States for a social system marked, as one writer put it, by "bitterness, self-ishness, deception, and greed." In China writers, editors, filmmakers, sing-ers, professors, painters, and small-time businessmen were called in by police. Books vanished from library shelves. Women caught with Western boyfriends were charged with hooliganism and shipped off to labor camps.

When party conservatives trained their sights on economic reforms, however, Deng reined them in. China would soon announce that it was opening fourteen cities along the east coast to foreign investment. Spear-heading what the Chinese called their "coastal strategy" was China's premier, Zhao Ziyang.

The son of a wealthy landowner who had been murdered by the Commu-nists in the 1940s, Zhao had joined the revolution well before his father was executed and by 1938 was a full-fledged party member. Zhao was a loyal supporter of Mao even during the Great Leap Forward. Witnessing famine firsthand, however, turned him against Maoist economics, and, following Deng Xiaoping, Zhao used his position as party boss in Guang-dong province in the early 1960s to experiment with limited market-oriented reforms.

During the Cultural Revolution, the Red Guards criticized Zhao Ziyang for walking "the capitalist road." He was purged from his govern-ment posts and spent four years working in a factory before he was called back into government. In 1975, he was appointed party secretary in Si-chuan just as China's most populous province was facing an impending famine. Zhao dismantled the commune system and allowed farmers the freedom to plant what they wanted, when they wanted. The result was a series of bumper harvests. Deng promoted Zhao to premier in 1980.

On January 11, 1984, Zhao became the first formal head of a Chinese government to visit the United States. His trip signaled the end of the anti–spiritual pollution campaign. As it described the lavish welcoming ceremonies at Andrews Air Force Base, the *People's Daily* enthused about the "tremendous potential" for China's "heart-warming" relations with the United States. Coverage of a Chinese leader in the United States gave rise to another round of effusive reports about America. There was

Zhao in Colonial Williamsburg in a horse-drawn carriage. There he was, walking arm in arm with President Ronald Reagan on the South Lawn of the White House.

Once again Chinese reporters accentuated the positive. "What is this so-called capitalist lifestyle anyway?" asked one *People's Daily* columnist. "A materially abundant life is not necessarily corrupt." And once again, American technology became China's lodestar, introduced by the newspaper's eight-part series in May 1984 on America's "new technological revolution" unfolding in a place called Silicon Valley.

On the evening of June 18, 1981, an international team of twenty missionaries led by an American who called himself Brother David set to work in a coastal town in the Philippines, packing a tugboat and a barge with 232 plastic-wrapped one-ton packages containing one million Bibles.

Hours later, on a beach in Shantou, the southern Chinese port town where Adele Fielde had once schooled China's first generation of Bible women, the two vessels were met by thousands of Chinese Christians, who unloaded their cargo and distributed the small black softcover books around the country. A patrol of People's Liberation Army soldiers appeared at the port early the next morning but found nothing but a few soggy Bibles. This operation, known as Project Pearl and led by a Pennsylvania-born ex–college football player turned evangelical named Doug Sutphen, remains the largest single Bible-smuggling mission in history.

China's opening to the outside world gave American Christians hope for another chance at the souls of the Middle Kingdom. But, just as it had been in the nineteenth century, the American church was again split between those who believed in evangelizing and those who advocated good works and education. Mainline Protestant denominations, such as Presbyterians and Episcopalians, obeyed Communist regulations that outlawed proselytizing. They focused on modernizing China. In 1980, the United Board for Christian Higher Education in Asia received $9 million from the Chinese government as restitution for the hundreds of church properties, schools, and universities that the Communists had seized after the revolution. Instead of investing that money in expanding religious studies, the board funded Chinese colleges and scholarships for Chinese students studying in the United States. When they visited China, mainline Protestant ministers engaged only with their state-sanctioned Chinese counterparts in the officially recognized and party-controlled Protestant church.

Meanwhile, an army of American evangelicals like Sutphen reached out directly to the people, following a path first blazed by Issachar Jacox Roberts. They nurtured China's underground church movement and dispensed funds, guidance, and Bibles to organizations that rejected Communist Party control. The old American verdict that Christianity in China was, in the words of one historian, "a false start, a failed endeavor," was overturned. Starting in the 1970s, these American preachers and their Chinese followers spearheaded the most successful proselytizing operation in China's history. The evangelicals' energy reflected their growing numbers and power in the United States, fueled by mediagenic, if occasionally scandal-prone, televangelists. In 1985, 35,000 American evangelical missionaries were working overseas. Many were in China.

At the age of sixteen, Dennis Balcombe, a farm boy from South Carolina, felt the call to bring Jesus to China. Eight years later, in 1969, he moved to Hong Kong, rented an office, founded the Hong Kong Revival Christian Church, and began preaching. He soon expanded into a five-thousand-square-foot space and set his sights on the Middle Kingdom. Once China began allowing Americans back into the country as tourists, Balcombe worked the same backwater southern Chinese communities that had embraced the fire and brimstone of the Taiping rebellion a century before. In places where a glimpse of a Westerner could incite a riot of rubberneckers, Balcombe donned disguises. He was once smuggled into church in a coffin. From 1985 to 1987, he took the route of thousands of other undercover American missionaries in China, working as an English-language teacher in Guangzhou and using the Bible as a textbook. He was arrested once in 1985 but released with a warning to stop proselytizing. He kept at it.

The Chinese government didn't know how to respond to the explosion of interest in Christianity. On the one hand, the American-led efforts to smuggle Bibles into China forced Deng Xiaoping to make good on a 1979 promise to Jimmy Carter to allow the Bible to be printed in greater numbers. But the Chinese Communist Party was founded on a fear of Christianity and a hatred of the American values that spread in its wake.

On the ground, Balcombe noted that the Chinese were "hungry for religion." Conversion rates, which had hovered at pitifully low levels in the nineteenth and early twentieth centuries, shot up. During Balcombe's two years in Guangzhou, he alone baptized three hundred Chinese; a hundred years earlier ten Chinese converts would have been considered a healthy crop. In 1949, on the eve of the Communist revolution, there were fewer than one million Chinese Protestant converts. Today, evangelical Protestantism is one of the fastest-growing religions in China, with the number of believers estimated at between forty and sixty million.

American preachers tried to convince the Chinese authorities that Christianity could be a force for modernization and development, repeating the argument their predecessors had made a century earlier. As Balcombe told his Chinese followers, "There's never been a revival without the word of God." When Billy Graham went to China in 1988 to meet top Communists and to pray with house-church leaders, he declared that Christianity could help China recapture its greatness. "Christians in China could be salt and light in Chinese society," he declared.

In 1982, the party issued Document 19, to date the most authoritative directive ever issued on religion in Communist China. In it, the party acknowledged that religion would continue to exist under socialism for a long time. Several months later, the party revised China's constitution, granting more freedom to believers. But as usual, the party gave itself an out. Only what it called "normal religious activities" would be protected, the party said, leaving it free to determine what qualified as "abnormal" and the right to suppress it, too.

Western scholars have often viewed the Four Modernizations, China's effort to improve its economy, science and technology, agriculture, and defense, as part of China's century-long quest to recapture its greatness. But this program was also driven by Deng's need to put his country back to work. During the 1960s, the party had handled urban unemployment by dispatching seventeen million young people to the countryside to labor with the peasants. But that endeavor had ended up costing billions of dollars, with little return. When millions of the "sent-down" youths returned to the cities, Deng turned to the United States and the developed world for investments to get them off the streets and into factories.

By far the most radical component of Deng's Open Door policy was its promotion of joint ventures and direct foreign investment. Deng knew what American capital had done in Southeast Asia, South Korea, and Taiwan and what access to the American market had done for Japan. He wanted these things for China. While the US military gave China the protection it needed to focus on the economy, American businesses and their European and Asian counterparts provided it with the money and the know-how to grow. Recalling the days of the Qing dynasty, when Howqua worked closely with traders from New England, China set up a string of export zones in the south. Now, instead of tea and porcelains, the country cranked out toys, textiles, and household goods. And again, as they had at the turn of the eighteenth century, Americans gobbled up all things Chinese.

In the fall of 1980, the Bloomingdale's department store put on a "Come to China" extravaganza, devoting all eight floors of its Manhattan flagship store to clothing, food, furniture, and tchotchkes from the PRC. Buyers from Bloomingdale's had been journeying to China since 1972 and had gathered what the *New York Times* called "the most immense variety of Chinese merchandise ever assembled under one department store roof." From the "People's Store," with its proletarian chic on the ground floor to Lucite furniture based on Ming dynasty designs upstairs, the show, the *Times* opined, was "surprisingly tasteful," notwithstanding the ultimate Chinese disco accessory, a twenty-foot-long aluminum dragon.

"Come to China" marked the beginning of a love affair between Chinese factories and the American consumer. Two-way trade started at $5 million in 1972 and climbed to $500 million by 1978. It doubled again in 1979 after normalization. In 1981, China exported more to America than vice versa and never looked back. Since then, China's cumulative trade balance with America is in the black by some $4 trillion. The wallet of the American consumer has served as the single most important foreign driver of China's rise.

American business was not immune to "rapturous enchantment" with China. US firms sought to capitalize on their historical ties to ancient China to get ahead. When Citibank started operations in China in 1983, it took the Chinese name Huaqi Yinhang, or "the bank of the flowery flag," a throwback to the name of a Citibank predecessor in the early 1900s. US trade with China historically had underperformed but American business had always focused more on China's potential than the reality of the moment. IBM chairman Ralph A. Pfeiffer Jr. sounded like a latter-day version of the English writer in the 1840s who observed that if each Chinese could be persuaded to "lengthen his shirttail by a foot," the mills of Lancashire would be "working round the clock." Except in this case, Pfeiffer mused that "If we could just sell one IBM PC for every hundred people in China, or every 1,000, or every 10,000 . . ."

The belief that China was going to make everyone rich re-emerged as a beacon for Yankee commerce. When the money-losing American Motors Corporation landed a deal in 1983 to make its Jeep in Beijing, its share price jumped 40 percent. The *Detroit Free Press* heralded the contract with the same gusto that the *New York News Dispatch* had greeted the return of the *Empress of China* to New York's harbor in 1785, calling it "one of the shrewdest industrial strokes of the decade." Armand Hammer, who had begun his career bargaining with Vladimir Lenin in the 1920s, affirmed his role as the bad boy of US capitalism by wangling an invitation to meet Deng Xiaoping during Deng's trip to America in 1979. When Hammer introduced himself, Deng responded, "You're the man who helped Lenin when Russia was in trouble. "Now you've got to come to China and help me." Hammer went.

What followed became a symbol—for a time—of how lucrative Sino-American cooperation could be for both sides. Hammer's Occidental Petroleum and a Chinese state-owned company agreed on a $650 million coal mine in Shanxi province. It was the biggest American investment in China, and it was going to be one of the largest mines in the world. "Armand Hammer," a headline in *Business Week* ran, "Still Showing Them How to Do Deals."

China's reopening coincided with a global energy crisis caused by the Iranian Revolution. Just like John D. Rockefeller's Standard Oil in the early 1900s, American oil giants bet that the combination of US technology and Chinese elbow grease would uncover huge oil deposits. As *Newsweek* reported, "The only sure thing is that China's oil reserves are vast." American roughnecks, engineers, and cash poured into southern China, looking for offshore oil. As Anson Burlingame had in the 1860s, US lawyers schooled their Chinese counterparts in the technicalities of international commercial law, passing on tough model contracts that required foreign firms to underwrite all the costs of exploration and hand over the fruit. No country had ever done this before, but it was China, so American oil companies agreed. Between 1979 and 1985, major US oil firms sank $1.7 billion into the Middle Kingdom.

But soon, one by one, the deals fizzled. The first Chinese-made Jeep Cherokee had to be pushed off AMC's assembly line in Beijing because the engine didn't work. Armand Hammer's mining venture collapsed, a victim of low coal prices, US design flaws, and China's antiquated infrastructure. None of the oil majors found significant oil reserves. American capital did end up funding a Chinese oil exploration industry that is now a global player. As for IBM, its PC business in China only took off after a Chinese brand, Lenovo, bought it in 2005.

The resumption of the China trade resuscitated an industry of American consultants who held—or at least convinced others that they held—the keys to the mandarin kingdom. Like Carl Crow in the 1920s, this new group of Americans peddled their connections to China's leadership and their insights into the Chinese mind. American firms hired aging Marxists Sidney Rittenberg and Israel Epstein as fixers to cut through red tape. Raised by his missionary uncle in Beijing, Harned Hoose dispensed Oriental wisdom from a Los Angeles mansion formerly owned by Greta Garbo and stuffed with chinoiserie. To guarantee themselves a living, the consultants sought to make the Chinese way of business as impenetrable as possible to the average executive, inserting special terms such as "face," which basically means respect, and "*guanxi*," which means relationships, into the American business lexicon.

Soon after George H. W. Bush became Reagan's vice president in 1980, his older brother, Prescott Jr., left the New York insurance business and opened up his own shop to hawk his services to US corporations seeking contracts in China. A Japanese company gave Prescott a $6 million stake in a planned $18 million golf course in Shanghai because the firm believed that the Bush name would get the project approved. "His work in China has always worried me," George H. W. Bush wrote in his diary.

Pretty soon, dozens of former American officials, Republican and Democrat alike, were also beating a path to China. Henry Kissinger, top diplomat Richard Holbrooke, former energy secretary James Schlesinger, and by the 1990s, George H. W. Bush himself, commanded huge fees for their services; Bush charged $250,000 a day. None of these officials acknowledged that this mixture of personal business and government work affected the direction of US policy toward China. But this questionable mingling gave the Chinese the impression that, as the Qing dynasty's envoy to America, Zhigang, once observed, in America "the love of God is less real than the love of profit."

For decades, the Communist Party's central ethos was one of self-sacrifice. Chinese were told that they needed to "eat bitterness" to make China strong. The opening to the West flipped that idea on its head. In 1979, families in Beijing had little in the way of appliances. By 1983, more than half had electric fans and a quarter owned tape recorders. Color TVs soon became ubiquitous, as did washing machines. Self-sacrifice was out. Materialism was in. The Chinese began to embrace an American Dream of fast food and soda, TV serials and cars.

On January 1, 1979, the day the United States and China officially normalized relations, the first Cokes since the Communist revolution arrived in China. Two years after establishing its beachhead, the Coca-Cola

Company opened its first bottling plant, celebrating the event with a gala at the Great Hall of the People featuring Aretha Franklin belting out "Coke Adds Life!" By 1989, the company had revolutionized the Chinese soft-drink industry. Qishui, China's Fanta knockoff, went the way of Peking Man, and a new generation of Chinese-brewed Coke look-alikes populated the retail landscape. Middle-aged Chinese drank Coke warm, attesting to its medicinal properties. The young guzzled it ice-cold.

In November 1987, American fast food came to China as Kentucky Fried Chicken opened its first store just off Tiananmen Square, a stone's throw from the mummified remains of Mao Zedong. On opening day, the store sold twenty-two hundred buckets of chicken, and in no time, it was bringing in more revenue than any other outlet in the KFC universe. Chinese lined up for the simple joy of clean bathrooms and well-mannered service—both rare in 1980s Beijing.

Like Neil Starr and his insurance business, KFC made itself into a Chinese company. Its first manager was an ethnic Chinese from Singapore. Unlike the burger-serving imperium McDonald's, which opened its first outlet in Shenzhen in 1990 with a Yankee menu, KFC offered soy milk, congee, a spicy chicken burger, corn-stuffed chicken nuggets, and pearl milk tea. The hot sauce was hotter than the American equivalent, and the pricing made family meals affordable.

The growing business relationship between the two countries took American officials by surprise, which was odd considering that in 1783 trade had been the original American impulse for reaching out to the Middle Kingdom. American officials had been so blinded by geopolitics that they did not understand that for the Chinese, the need for the United States far surpassed security. Modernization was their goal. As Nicholas Platt wrote, "No one who had worked on the opening to China, from Richard Nixon and Henry Kissinger on down, predicted this, much less imagined that nuts-and-bolts economics would become the center of our relationship."

Like his nineteenth-century predecessors, Deng Xiaoping sought Western science, technology, capital, and management skills, but he feared Western freedom. As he said: "Open the windows, breathe the fresh air and at the same time fight the flies and insects." The tension between the Chinese who wanted fresh air and the ones who worried about flies and insects made the United States alternately China's greatest opportunity or its worst nightmare. As the 1980s drew to a close, the party's response to the Beautiful Country careened from paranoid disenchantment to affable fascination— and back again. As time passed, this tension only grew.

•

CHAPTER THIRTY-NINE

Nobody Is Afraid of Anybody

Ronald Reagan's China policy was muddled. Henry Kissinger called it "a study in almost incomprehensible contradictions." Running for the GOP presidential nomination, Reagan declared that as president he would restore official relations with Taiwan. But, by the time he beat Jimmy Carter in November 1980, he had dropped that idea.

Reagan was an inveterate anti-Communist, but he and his administration continued the crusade to build China into a global power. Reagan's aides—particularly Paul Wolfowitz and Richard Armitage—opposed the idea of turning China into an American ally, but nonetheless oversaw even closer military cooperation with Beijing to trap the Soviet Union in Afghanistan.

During the Reagan administration, the United States and China signed their third and most controversial communiqué. On the surface, it committed the United States to phasing out its weapons sales to Taiwan. In reality, even before it was signed, Reagan had already promised Taiwan's president, Chiang Ching-kuo, that the US would do no such thing. Reagan directed James Lilley, head of the American Institute in Taiwan, America's nominally unofficial representative body in Taiwan, to assure Chiang that the United States would continue sharing intelligence with Taiwan about China's military developments and promised that Washington would not, among other things, push Taiwan to negotiate with China. Reagan also placed a secret memorandum in National Security Council files that declared the US intention to maintain "Taiwan's defense capability relative to that of the PRC." Since then, the United States has sold Taiwan billions of dollars in arms.

Soviet misbehavior continued to hold Washington close to Beijing. Starting in 1980, the US government bought $2 billion worth of Chinese weapons—assault rifles, rocket-propelled grenades, surface-to-air missiles—which the Americans funneled to the Afghan mujahideen. In 1986, China agreed to a US request, brought to Beijing by the conservative anti-Communist Republican senator Orrin Hatch, to pass US Stinger missiles to the Afghan rebels. The two countries cooperated to arm fifty thousand anti-Vietnamese guerrillas, including the Khmer Rouge. The US also backed a Chinese plan to ensure that the Khmer Rouge would retake power when Vietnam withdrew its forces from Cambodia. The White House saw its relationship with China "as the paramount interest," recalled Singaporean diplomat Bilahari Kausikan, so it "supported the return of a genocidal regime."

Beijing became an essential stop for every CIA director, starting with Stansfield Turner, who arrived there on December 27, 1980, disguised with a mustache, to negotiate the particulars of Operation Chestnut, the establishment of a listening post near the China-USSR border. It was a bizarre experience for intelligence officials from two countries that had effectively been at war since 1949. "We had to pinch ourselves to make sure it wasn't all a dream," recalled Robert Gates, then the US national intelligence officer for the USSR, who in the mid-1980s briefed the Chinese on Soviet military developments.

US arms sales to China began in 1985, with deals for six major weapons systems, including large-caliber ammunition, torpedoes, antiartillery radar, and a $500 million program to modernize the avionics of China's workhorse fighter, the F-8. That program, known as Peace Pearl, offered the Chinese a rude introduction to the Pentagon's procurement process. Cost overruns and engineering challenges marred the sale. The avionics package proved hard to install into a 1950s jet. What the F-8 really needed was a new engine, but the United States would not give China that.

Still, the Reagan administration, continuing the centuries-old US plan for the Middle Kingdom, was committed to making China strong. Beginning in 1981, the president signed three national security directives authorizing the Pentagon to sell weapons to China, approving assistance to China's civilian and strategic nuclear program, and committing the United States to China's modernization. When the United States dropped restrictions on the export of dual-use technology to China in 1982, China's imports of such technology shot up from $500 million to $5 billion a year later. American companies single-handedly created a semiconductor industry in China. "Our goal . . . is to strengthen China's ability to resist Soviet intimidation," wrote Paul Wolfowitz, the State Department's senior strategist, in June 1981. "We should let the mystique of Sino-American relations worry the Soviets," added Lawrence Eagleburger, undersecretary for political affairs, in September 1982.

After Premier Zhao Ziyang visited the United States in January 1984, Reagan, the world's best-known anti-Communist, traveled to China in April and began calling the Chinese "so-called Communists." China joined the World Bank the same month, and within two years, the Reagan administration would begin negotiations on China's admission to the General Agreement on Tariffs and Trade, the forerunner to the World Trade Organization.

On the surface, Sino-American cooperation in Afghanistan and Cambodia achieved remarkable results. In 1989, Mikhail Gorbachev, the new secretary general of the Communist Party of the Soviet Union, announced that the Russians would withdraw from Afghanistan. That same year, Vietnam pulled its forces out of Cambodia. As Michael Pillsbury, then a Pentagon official and longtime advocate of a military relationship with China, wrote, these victories bolstered the notion in Washington that China and the United States "would build on this foundation of trust and therefore become true allies forever."

By this time, few in Washington challenged the notion that it was a bad idea to base America's relationship with China mainly on security concerns. That would prove to be troublesome as the world changed in the years to come.

To many Chinese, of course, America meant more than weapons sales. In December 1972, a brilliant thirty-six-year-old astrophysicist named Fang Lizhi introduced the big bang theory to China in China's *Physics* magazine. To the true believers at Party Central, the problem with the big bang was that a universe with a definite beginning meant that a divine creator might have been involved. The party propagandists pilloried Fang for promoting "capitalist metaphysics."

Fang's essay underscored the threat that Western science and the scientific method posed to China's ruling class. The Communist Party declared that the party alone could determine truth, while Fang and a growing coterie of men and women around him held that no system, party, or individual held a monopoly on that commodity.

Fang Lizhi was a gadfly and hugely influential in China. By contending that science could not progress without freedom, he underscored the contradiction underlying the party's plan to open China to Western technology while leaving its political ideals at the door.

Born in Beijing in 1936, Fang started studying physics at Peking University at sixteen. In 1955, he joined the Communist Party. A year later, during the One Hundred Flowers campaign, he wrote a letter demanding academic freedom. In the subsequent Anti-Rightist backlash, he was booted from the party and sent to the countryside. In 1971, rocket scientist and Caltech graduate Qian Xuesen brought him back from obscurity, giving him a job as a janitor at his University of Science and Technology of China. A year later, Fang quietly resumed research. After the arrest of the Gang of Four in 1976, Fang's party membership was restored, and in 1978 he became, at forty-two, the youngest full professor in China. He was among the first generation of Chinese scientists to present papers in Europe and the United States.

Fang's interests initially aligned with those of Party Central. Deng Xiaoping had placed science and technology at the heart of his plan to modernize China, and he needed people like Fang. But as time passed, Fang strayed from Deng's script into a forbidden zone, exploring the link between Western science and Western freedom. To develop science in China, Fang wrote, Chinese needed to question authority. He rejected Marxism as useless, "composed of obsolete conclusions that have led to failure."

Despite these controversial stands, Fang was named vice president of the University of Science and Technology in 1984 and undertook radical changes in the curriculum, pushing faculty and students to look overseas for study and research opportunities. "I am going to make freedom of thought one of the administrative policies of the university," he declared. In a speech the following year, he demanded that China's intellectuals "stand up and be counted in the struggle for truth, justice, and democracy."

Fang soon ran afoul of Communist authorities. In November 1985, when a Beijing vice mayor tagged along with a scientific delegation to the United States, Fang ridiculed him for taking a scientist's place. The *Beijing Daily*, the organ of the city's party committee, attacked Fang, warning that "no science can ever replace Marxist philosophy." Fang's exit visa for a trip to Princeton University was delayed.

Returning to China in the summer of 1986 during a surge in economic reforms, Fang intensified his attacks on traditional Chinese culture and Communist orthodoxy. In a series of speeches to packed houses in universities in Shanghai, Ningbo, and Hefei, he highlighted the role of China's intellectuals as an independent force—a Third Force—for change. He credited his travels in Europe and the United States with opening his eyes. "We discovered our backwardness and were enlightened," he told students at Tongji University in Shanghai. He was speaking for a whole generation.

When party newspapers warned that Fang was advocating "Westernization," he responded that his respect for the West was founded not on the belief that "big noses are more beautiful," but on the understanding that, without learning from the West, the Chinese would never develop the "democratic and scientific mentality" necessary to become modern. Fang was optimistic about the prospects for change in China. He told students at Shanghai's Jiao Tong University that "now nobody is afraid of anybody."

At the time, many in the party's leadership believed that significant political reform was the only way forward. Deng Xiaoping's economic opening had met with opposition from vested interests in the party bureaucracy and among conservatives still loyal to the tenets of Marx, Lenin, and Mao. Starting in January 1986, the man everyone believed would be Deng's successor, the son of a farmer from Hunan province named Hu Yaobang, advocated discarding outdated theories, including Marxist ones. Hu Yaobang was known for his candor. He once had suggested that Chinese drop chopsticks for the knife and fork to stop the spread of disease. He was one of the first in China to junk the Mao suit in favor of Western attire. And when asked by a reporter which of Chairman Mao's theories were useful for China, he replied, "I think, none."

Hu was not alone. Zhao Ziyang, China's premier, also backed gradual liberalization. On August 30, 1986, the *People's Daily* quoted another leading Communist, Wan Li, as saying, "political questions can be discussed." Wan's brief statement opened the floodgates for calls for democracy, freedom, the protection of private property, and human rights.

In December 1986, students at the University of Science and Technology, encouraged by Fang Lizhi, demonstrated after the party had overturned the results of a local election. Protests spread to Nanjing, Shanghai, and Beijing. In January 1987, the Central Committee cracked down and inaugurated another attack on American values, which it called the "Anti-Bourgeois Liberalization Campaign." Fang was stripped of his party membership again and fired from his job. His speeches were distributed to local branches of the Communist Party as examples of errant thinking. But the publicity only won him more support.

Deng Xiaoping then purged his protégé and party chief, Hu Yaobang, for not cracking down severely enough on the students. Deng split the difference on his next move, appointing the relatively liberal Zhao Ziyang as Hu's replacement and moving up a conservative named Li Peng to take Zhao's place as premier. Zhao moved quickly to end the hard-liners' campaign. In a photo op organized for the Western press in November 1987, Zhao and the rest of the Standing Committee of the Politburo emerged for the first time dressed in Western suits. Zhao beamed with relaxed confidence. It was his signal that China was ready to join the world, transforming not just its economy but its despotic political system, too. When a reporter praised Zhao's double-breasted pinstripes, he smiled, pulled open the jacket, and showed off the label. "Made in China," it read.

The demonstrations in 1986 and 1987 barely raised an eyebrow in Washington. From the 1970s, the US government had adhered to three principles in reengaging with China. It did not bother with human rights. It focused on China's usefulness against the USSR. It was interested in China's leadership, not China's people.

Even the self-styled "human rights" president, Jimmy Carter, made scant mention of the issue when it came to China. The US government issued its first statement on human rights in China in 1978, praising Beijing's acknowledgment of excesses committed during the Cultural Revolution. Even that caused officials in the State Department's Bureau of East Asian and Pacific Affairs to blanch, so great were the concerns that China might take offense. When China slapped Wei Jingsheng, the electrician who called for democracy as a "fifth modernization" in October 1979, with a fifteen-year sentence, Michel Oksenberg at the National Security Council fretted that the New York Times would "make him a human rights martyr." Oksenberg's main concern, he wrote, was that Wei's imprisonment might derail the sales of advanced computers to China. (It didn't.) A Congressional Research Service report noted in 1979 that the federal government had accepted the idea that China "was not an appropriate target of human rights initiatives."

Patricia Derian, who served as the first assistant secretary of state in the Carter administration's newly created Bureau of Human Rights and Humanitarian Affairs, noted in congressional testimony in 1979 that her efforts to push for more rights in China "were stymied time and again." Not by China but by the White House.

"Set to music," she said, "the courtship of the PRC is 'Home on the Range,' where never is heard a discouraging word." A year later, Derian blasted China before Congress, at which point Deputy Assistant Secretary of State for East Asian and Pacific Affairs John Negroponte took the unprecedented step of announcing that he would "supplement" her testimony. Negroponte declared that in China "an encouraging trend has begun to emerge in the direction of liberalization."

Some Americans also held on to the old attitude that human life meant less in China than in the West and that Chinese were less concerned with rights. Even the human rights organization Asia Watch, in a report issued in 1985, declared that "the lack of intellectual freedom in China today is perceived as a problem by only a tiny minority of the Chinese people." In 1987, Roberta Cohen, a longtime human rights advocate, noted that many of her colleagues held to the "belief that the great hordes of Chinese simply are not to be judged by the same human rights standards applicable to Europeans." Frank Goodnow had argued the same thing in 1913 when he backed Yuan Shikai's plan to declare himself emperor. Among Americans, there was a sense that the People's Republic was special. When China launched its one-child policy in 1980, many Americans hailed the nation for moving to limit births. When reports emerged of forced abortions and sterilizations, no outcry came. In 1981, Steven Mosher, the first graduate student to conduct anthropological research in rural China, published an article in Taiwan about the dark side of the policy. Stanford University expelled him, apparently in deference to China. An editorial in the *New York Times* noted that Americans "found it difficult to associate the polite Chinese leaders with such brutality." No one said it better than Deng Xiaoping in February 1987: "Look at Wei Jingsheng. We put him behind bars and the democracy movement died. We haven't released him, but that did not raise much of an international uproar." The party concluded that China could suppress freedoms without fear of any reaction.

Of course, there were other points of view. Fox Butterfield, the first full-time correspondent from the *New York Times* to live in China since World War II, wrote a moving account about his time there called *China: Alive in the Bitter Sea*. It came out in 1982 and won the National Book Award for nonfiction. Butterfield provided telling details about the uses of state power to crush even the mildest dissent. Michael Weisskopf of the *Washington Post* wrote a series of devastating accounts in the early 1980s about how brutally the one-child policy was carried out. Their reporting marked a change in the American media's view of China. For almost a decade, the US press had been solidly behind the US policy to back the Chinese regime. Now it was returning to its roots—first planted by Thomas Millard and John B. Powell in 1920s Shanghai—as the defender of China's little guy, this time from a Communist dictatorship.

In the summer of 1987, military relations between China and the United States, in the words of US Air Force colonel Eden Y. Woon, appeared to be in a "very healthy state." Washington had concluded more than $100 million in arms sales. Defense Secretary Caspar Weinberger had visited Beijing twice. In 1985, General John W. Vessey Jr., the chairman of the Joint Chiefs of Staff, became the highest-ranking American military officer to travel to China since World War II. The US Navy made a port visit to its Second World War haunt in Qingdao, and the US Air Force Thunderbirds demonstration team thrilled crowds in Beijing.

But the two nations were headed for rough waters. In 1979, China had begun to sell missiles and nuclear-weapons technology to other countries. Its motivations were complex. Some in the Communist Party believed that proliferation of such weapons offered a geostrategic hedge against American and Soviet dominance. Profit was a motive, as was, in the case of Pakistan, a desire to constrain China's long-term rival, India.

In 1982, Deng Xiaoping authorized the transfer to Pakistan of a blueprint for one of China's early nuclear bombs along with 110 pounds of weapons-grade uranium, enough for two nuclear devices. No other country is believed to have engaged in such blatant proliferation. Reports in the *Washington Post* and elsewhere, corroborated by US officials, detail that China provided the uranium to Pakistan following a 1976 agreement between Mao Zedong and then Pakistani president, Zulfiqar Ali Bhutto. Two years prior to that agreement, in 1974, India had tested its first nuclear device, and Mao wanted a nuclear balance of terror between the two South Asian nations. Deng was further induced to make good on Mao's promise after Pakistan provided China with Western centrifuge technology. China's proliferation to Pakistan would reverberate around the world as Pakistani officials sold China's blueprint to Libya and Iran, and Iran passed it on to North Korea.

In 1980, war erupted between Iran and Iraq, and China's arms merchants provided an estimated $12 billion in tanks, jets, surface-to-air missiles, and small arms to both sides. China also sold Iran an antiship missile called the Silkworm, which had been developed by Caltech alumnus Qian Xuesen. In 1987, the Iranians deployed the Silkworm along the thirty-four-mile-wide Strait of Hormuz and launched Silkworms at oil tankers and at a Kuwaiti oil terminal. In response, the Reagan administration reflagged all of Kuwait's oil tankers as American ships and gave them US Navy escorts through the Strait.

US officials confronted the Chinese with evidence of the nuclear pro-liferation and the missile sales and stressed that the introduction of such weapons into the Persian Gulf was ill advised. The Chinese denied the allegations. At that point, noted Woon, writing in an academic journal in 1989, "the frustration level at the Pentagon . . . rose steadily." The United States had assumed that the relationship with China was growing closer, but China was knowingly acting contrary to US interests in a strategic region. It was a rude shock. China's refusal to even acknowledge the sales, Woon wrote, "eroded the earlier goodwill toward China felt by many in the US defense establishment. Some even questioned the basic worth of mili-tary relations with China."

The dispute over the Silkworm missiles led the Reagan administration to impose the first economic sanctions on China since normalization. In October 1987, the US government announced it would halt the export of high-technology products to China to protest the Silkworm sales. In Novem-ber, China announced that it had stopped selling missiles that a month earlier it had denied selling at all. Secretary of State George Shultz then promised to lift the export restrictions.

In 1988, after significant pressure from Washington, the Chinese agreed to a dialogue on their arms sales policy. Then, that March, another story broke: Beijing had agreed to sell Saudi Arabia an intercontinental ballistic missile with a range of fifteen hundred miles. Immediately fol-lowing the sale, the Saudi kingdom dropped recognition of Taiwan and established ties with Beijing. The deal also netted China's arms merchants $2 billion.

A few months later, reports surfaced that China had also begun to negotiate deals to sell two new missiles—the M-9, with a range of about four hundred miles, and the M-11, with a range half as long. In July 1988, the *Los Angeles Times* reported that China had agreed to sell the M-9 to Syria. That story came out on the day Shultz was traveling to Beijing, where he raised the issue. But he left with no firm Chinese commitment to cancel the deal. In December, Secretary of Defense Frank Carlucci followed Shultz to Beijing and proposed a swap. The United States would approve the use of Chinese rockets to send American satellites into orbit if China would end its missile sales. The United States had never allowed a non-ally to launch American satellites. The Chinese responded vaguely to the offer. Deng Xiaoping said that China would not sell intermediate-range missiles in the Middle East, but the Americans did not press him on whether that meant the M-9.

The United States had gone from avoiding all conditions in its negotiations with Communist China to accepting the flimsiest of promises in order to get deals done. As far back as Anson Burlingame, the first minister to the Qing court, some Americans had been arguing that China should be judged by different rules. And just as the FDR administration made China many promises that it never kept, Beijing now looked upon its deals with Washington as commitments that could be broken. Richard Armitage, for years one of the saltier senior officials in a series of Republican administrations, called the US negotiating strategy with China "teaching the dog to piss on the rug." China had vowed on numerous occasions to end its sales of missiles and nuclear technology, but every year or so, evidence of proliferation trickled out. The United States would occasionally sanction Chinese companies but generally adopted the attitude of an indulgent parent toward a wayward child.

While the Chinese government worried about how to juggle its fear of American values with its desire for American know-how, America's main assumption about China remained the same. Most officials dealing with China believed that with time the interests of the Middle Kingdom would align themselves with those of the United States. So the US government didn't concern itself with China's human rights record, nor did it make a huge issue out of China's weapons sales. Undergirding the go-softly approach was the belief, expounded by Assistant Secretary of State for East Asian and Pacific Affairs John Holdridge, that China was "not our adversary but a friendly, developing country." Americans believed that China's process of liberalization was unstoppable because the Middle Kingdom and the Beautiful Country had become friends.

●

CHAPTER FORTY

Deathsong

In June and August 1988, China Central Television aired a six-part documentary called *Heshang*, or *Deathsong of the River*. Written and directed by a group of young intellectuals, the documentary took aim at traditional Chinese culture and the Communist Party and argued that the country would regain its lost glory only if it fully embraced Western values. China's poverty and backwardness, the show contended, were not the fault of Western imperialism, as the Communist Party claimed; they arose from faults within the Chinese themselves.

"The civilization has declined!" the documentary declared. What China needed was "a brand-new civilization." This new civilization could not emerge, as had ancient China, from the turgid waters of the Yellow River. It had to come from the sea. "The sea," of course, was the United States.

Color images of Manhattan skyscrapers, the Las Vegas Strip, NASA rocket launches, and Yankee sailboats contrasted with grainy black-and-white shots of Chinese on bikes, in horse carts, and in the fields. In the first segment, "Searching for a Dream," the film laid out its thesis: only when the Chinese people embraced the American Dream would China become great again.

In its glorification of American power, *Deathsong* echoed views about America that had circulated in China since the mandarin scholar Xu Jiyu first wrote about George Washington in 1849. But *Deathsong* was more than a naive love poem to the West. Its point, stressed writers Su Xiaokang and Wang Luxiang, was that China needed to adopt Western democracy and science not to become the West but to compete with it. "To save our nation from danger and destruction, we should try to keep the foreign pirates at bay," Su and Wang wrote. "And yet to save our civilization from decline, we should also throw open our country's gates . . . and receive the new light of science and democracy." In that sense, *Deathsong* echoed the thinking of Hu Shih and other Chinese liberals of the 1930s.

Deathsong aired at a time of political ferment in China. Conservatives and liberals argued over the show. Hard-liners claimed it "vilified the Chinese people" and called for its writers to be executed, while liberals and moderates, like party secretary Zhao Ziyang, supported it. Policy experts around Zhao had suggested that the party chief consider political reforms as the necessary next step to modernizing China. On campuses across the country, Zhao's followers encouraged students and professors to hold seminars on democracy, freedom, and economic reforms. The state-run media called for separation between the party and the government—the first step in ending the party's monopoly on power. *Deathsong*'s script, meanwhile, sold seven hundred thousand copies before the year was out.

The White House was not paying much attention to the debates roiling China. Its main concern was the warming relations between China and the USSR. Soviet leader Mikhail Gorbachev was planning a visit to Beijing in May. The funeral of Japanese emperor Hirohito on February 24, 1989, gave newly installed President George H. W. Bush an opportunity to visit China before the Russian leaders. The chief objective of Bush's visit, the US embassy suggested on February 6, should be to "obtain Chinese assurances . . . that the emerging Sino-Soviet dialogue will not undercut US interests."

But the world was changing. The old logic of mooring America's relations with China to an anti-Soviet pact was increasingly out of step with the times. The USSR was opening up and mending ties with the rest of the world. "Our attitude was a throwback to the early days of our relationship, when common Soviet bashing was in vogue," wrote longtime CIA officer James Lilley, who would soon become the US ambassador to China. "We were not coping with or anticipating current realities."

And in Beijing, current realities were in flux. As part of Bush's visit, the White House directed the US embassy to organize a banquet, inviting a broad cross section of Chinese society to celebrate the strengthening ties between the two countries. Among those on the guest list were several dissidents, including the astrophysicist Fang Lizhi. When Chinese foreign ministry officials heard that Fang had been invited, they threatened to boycott the affair, but the embassy promised that Bush would neither toast Fang nor venture near his table. On the evening of February 26, however, Chinese police blocked Fang from attending the gala, leading to headlines—"The Man Who Did Not Come to Dinner," said *Time*—around the world.

The White House response was to blame the American ambassador, Winston Lord, rather than the Chinese. Even though Lord's staff had flagged Fang's invitation in several cables, "a senior White House official," later identified as National Security Advisor Brent Scowcroft, told reporters that Fang's inclusion had been a surprise. In his background briefing with reporters, Scowcroft revealed how skittish the US government had become about offending China's leadership. "Some of these things they are extraordinarily sensitive to," Scowcroft said. "Others they let go without saying a word about it. Sometimes it's hard to tell which is going to be which." Washington's eagerness to yield to Chinese sensitivities gave China enormous leverage over the United States.

On Saturday, April 15, 1989, Hu Yaobang, the former party general secretary who had been purged for being too soft on student protests in 1986–87, died of a heart attack. Through that weekend, wall posters commemorating his life went up on college campuses around Beijing. Student groups carried commemorative wreaths to the Monument for Revolutionary Martyrs in the center of Tiananmen Square. Within days, hundreds of thousands of people mobbed the square in the largest outpouring of dissatisfaction with the regime since the rally following Zhou Enlai's death in 1976.

As the spring unfolded and demonstrations spread to hundreds of Chinese cities, the Bush administration continued to focus on shoring up the strategic foundations of its relationship with China, even as that foundation crumbled beneath the weight of the changes rocking the Communist bloc. In a move orchestrated to upstage Gorbachev's visit, three US Navy vessels steamed into Shanghai on May 19, arriving a day after the Soviet leader visited the city. Also on May 19, more than one million people massed in Tiananmen Square in Beijing. The next day, the Chinese government declared martial law. "We had miscalculated on the timing and the symbolism of the visit," Lilley would later write. "What queered the Gorbachev visit were masses of demonstrators on Tiananmen square, not our ships."

The student-led demonstrations took their inspiration from many sources, but the United States played a leading role. From the movement's sound track, a rollicking rock and roll ballad from a Chinese guitarist named Cui Jian, to its symbol, a thirty-three-foot-tall statue called Goddess of Democracy—a knockoff of the Statue of Liberty—the movement had an American accent. The students and hundreds of thousands of other participants never coalesced around specific demands for American-style democracy. Most wanted lower inflation, less corruption, equal opportunity, and more freedom. But, behind those demands lay a burning desire for a new New China, a China that embraced not just the technology and investment of the West but its foundational ideas as well.

The party understood how dangerously attractive the United States was to China's younger generations. On June 1, the Ministry of State Security issued a secret report on American "ideological and political infiltration" into China. Prepared for Premier Li Peng, who became the main advocate of a violent crackdown on the movement, it accused the United States of using professors, radio broadcasts, scientific and cultural exchanges, the media, and undercover missionaries to undermine China's socialist system. Once again, the "peaceful evolution" advocated by John Foster Dulles had emerged as a bogeyman haunting the Communist state. "It is now clear," the report said, "that murderous intent has always lurked behind their protestations of peace and friendship." A day later, as senior leaders gathered to discuss the document, Li Peng declared that the only way to deal with the turmoil was to crush it by force. On the night of June 3, 1989, the People's Liberation Army attacked the protesters. By dawn on June 4, Tiananmen Square had been cleared. Hundreds had been killed.

Tiananmen was the story of the decade. As it unfolded in the spring of 1989, hundreds of correspondents descended on Beijing. The four big US TV networks, already there to cover the Gorbachev summit, swiveled their cameras toward the jam-packed square. In 1988, ABC, CBS, and NBC had aired only 44 stories total on China. In the first six months of 1989, they ran 577. NBC anchor Tom Brokaw told *Rolling Stone* magazine that no event since the 1986 explosion of the *Challenger* space shuttle had "so penetrated the American consciousness." He recalled that when he was in Los Angeles doing a story about street gangs, a member of the Crips only wanted to talk about China.

The TV coverage was riveting and surprising, with twists and turns and the spectacle of more than a million people marching for change. On May 19, CNN viewers even got to see the Party State in action when the network was yanked off the air during a live broadcast. And then, on the night of June 3, the cameras caught the bloody crackdown on videotapes that were smuggled out to Hong Kong and aired around the world. "In Cold Blood," ran the headline in New York's *Daily News*.

As Mark Hertsgaard asked in *Rolling Stone*, "Who didn't feel inspired by the lone white-shirted protester defiantly staring down an entire column of tanks the day after the massacre?" If the soot-covered baby in "Bloody Saturday" had epitomized America's feelings for China in World War II, "Tank Man" did the same for China in 1989, all the more so because he disappeared and his fate remains unknown.

The reaction in the United States was extraordinary. Since the reestablishment of links across the Pacific, Americans had been primed to expect that China was going to become like the US. As the *New York Times* had put it on February 20, 1989, "Like the bamboo shoots that emerge everywhere after a spring rain, to use a Chinese simile, democracy is sprouting again in China." And then came the crackdown, and decades, if not centuries, of American hopes for China melted in the heat from the armored personnel carriers of the People's Liberation Army. American attitudes toward China flipped overnight: a February Gallup poll before the crackdown found that 72 percent of Americans had a favorable impression of China; in August, just 31 percent checked that box. In the *Austin American-Statesman*, columnist John Kelso summed up the feelings of many: "Deng Xiaoping ain't worthy of his cowboy hat no more."

The Tiananmen Square crackdown galvanized the human rights community. Human Rights Watch Asia called on the Bush administration to withdraw its ambassador from China and revoke most-favored-nation trading status. It announced that it would devote more resources to China than to any other country in Asia, a 180-degree turnaround from a few years before. Once again, a group of Americans anointed themselves as China's conscience. Instead of Christianity, however, these secular missionaries championed the universal values enshrined in the UN Charter that China had signed. And once again, this group of Americans clashed with those who wanted stability, which in this case meant preserving the Communist regime.

A day after the Tiananmen crackdown, Fang Lizhi and his wife, Li Shuxian, requested asylum at the US embassy in Beijing. The couple sat at the top of a most-wanted list issued by Communist authorities. Embassy officials turned them away but, after phone calls with Washington, the decision was reversed. If the Chinese government needed any more proof to bolster its case that the June 4 turmoil was an American plot, here it was. After almost a year of negotiations, the couple was allowed to leave China on a US Air Force C-135 transport plane bound for Britain. They eventually settled in the United

States. The party also purged general secretary Zhao Ziyang, who was stripped of his posts and held in a Beijing courtyard house for sixteen years. Zhao became a nonperson, airbrushed out of photographs, his contributions to China's march to modernity excised from Chinese history books.

President Bush took a conciliatory approach toward the crackdown. A day after the killings, he deplored the loss of life, but he did not criticize individual party leaders. On June 5, he suspended further arms sales to China and canceled a planned military visit, but he ordered the Pentagon to complete a delivery of torpedoes, radar, and other military equipment and rejected broader economic sanctions. "Now is the time to look beyond the moment to important and enduring aspects of this vital relationship for the United States," the president told the American people.

On June 20, Secretary of State James Baker announced that the United States was suspending high-level contacts with the Chinese. But on June 30, National Security Advisor Brent Scowcroft and Deputy Secretary of State Lawrence S. Eagleburger embarked on a secret mission to Beijing "to keep open the lines of communication," as Scowcroft later wrote.

The mission was so secret that not even the US embassy in Beijing was informed, and the C-141 cargo plane that took Eagleburger and Scowcroft to China was disguised as an ordinary commercial carrier with its US Air Force markings removed. Bush wrote Deng three private letters, expressing his hope that Sino-American relations would soon recover. In one, written on July 28, he complained to Deng about the US Congress trying to cut off trade. "I will do my best," he promised China's leader, "to keep the boat from rocking too much." Bush sounded apologetic. "Please do not be angry with me if I have crossed the invisible threshold lying between constructive suggestion and 'internal interference,'" he wrote.

Bush tapped into a centuries-old American belief that China's stability was in the national interest of the United States. "We both do more for world peace and for the welfare of our own people if we can get our relationship back on track," he wrote to Deng. Bush's envoys continued to act as if the United States needed China more than the other way around. During a second trip to Beijing in December 1989, Scowcroft grasped Deng's hand and declared, according to journalist Jonathan Mirsky, who witnessed the interaction: "My president wants you to know he is your friend forever." According to the memoirs of Qian Qichen, China's foreign minister, Scowcroft explained away the sanctions as something done solely "to satisfy the demands of the American people."

The Bush administration squared off against a Right-Left coalition in

Congress that sought to punish China. Congress passed legislation mandating economic sanctions, but Bush modified it to ensure that the executive branch was given wide leeway to suspend them in the case of "national interest"—a category so broad that it allowed trade and investment to continue unabated. Weapons sales were halted, but sales of dual-use technology were not. On July 7, 1989, Bush allowed the sale of $4 billion in Boeing 757-200 jets to China, even though the navigation system was on the Commerce Department's munitions control list. In August, he allowed Hughes Aircraft Company to continue planning the launch of US-made satellites on Chinese rockets. In December, he approved the sale of three satellites to China for $300 million. In each case, he invoked "national interest." In early July 1990, two weeks after Fang Lizhi was allowed to leave the US embassy, the Bush administration stopped blocking almost $200 million in World Bank loans. China would receive more than $4 billion from the World Bank over the next two years, more than any other country.

China's friends and enemies in Washington battled over China policy. Each time Congress tried to revoke China's most-favored-nation status, the Bush administration and American businesses beat it back. Bush did occasionally try to appear "tough" with China. He signed an executive order that gave tens of thousands of Chinese students the opportunity to become American citizens. Few at the time noticed that a century after the United States had moved to block immigration from China, the US government had taken a step to further open America's door to the Chinese. And on April 16, 1991, Bush became the first American president to meet with the Dalai Lama, the exiled Tibetan leader, who had been awarded the Nobel Peace Prize in 1989.

To keep up the veneer of a normal relationship, Bush administration officials pushed parts of the US bureaucracy to move ahead with cooperative ventures, often with wild results. In 1988, the FBI and China's police had cooperated to break up a Shanghai–San Francisco drug smuggling ring that had been sending heroin to the United States sewn in the bellies of goldfish. But the case imploded when a US federal prosecutor went to China and brought back a Chinese suspect to testify in US court. Arriving in America after the June 4 crackdown around Tiananmen Square, the suspect requested a lawyer and applied for political asylum because he alleged he had been tortured by Chinese police. US district judge William Orrick then declared a mistrial and blasted the prosecutor for "reckless disregard of his obligations as a prosecutor." US authorities rejected the asylum claim but Orrick blocked the United States from repatriating him.

The Chinese government, understandably, was livid. The case was an example of the limits of the Great Harmony. As Judge Orrick wrote, it was "proof positive you can't meld the legal system in the People's Republic of China with the legal system in the United States." The Chinese suspect, Wang Zongxiao, stayed in America, stayed in the drug business, and met a gruesome end. At 3:00 a.m. on January 14, 2003, he was hacked to death in front of the Subway Café nightclub in Flushing, Queens, in a murder linked to an ecstasy ring. The Chinese did not cooperate again with US law enforcement for almost a decade.

On August 2, 1990, Iraqi leader Saddam Hussein invaded Kuwait. Once again a war—this time halfway around the world—forced the United States and China to come to grips with one another. China was a permanent member of the UN Security Council, so any action against Saddam required its acquiescence. The question was, what price would China charge?

The Bush administration ended its public ban on high-level meetings when Secretary of State James Baker met with China's foreign minister Qian Qichen in New York in September 1990, at the annual gathering of the UN General Assembly. In exchange for China's support of the Gulf War, Qian demanded that the United States lift all sanctions and invite China's new party secretary, Jiang Zemin, to the United States, or at least send Baker to Beijing. Baker balked but agreed to host Qian in Washington. Qian could meet with Bush, Baker said, on the condition that China backed the use of force to dislodge Saddam. On November 30, however, China abstained from the UN resolution authorizing force. When Baker informed Qian that there would be no meeting with Bush, Qian threatened to cancel his trip altogether. The Americans blinked first, and on December 1, 1990, Qian met with Bush in the White House, becoming the first senior Chinese official to see the president after the Tiananmen Square crackdown. Qian's photograph with Bush ran on the front page of every major newspaper in China, proving again how important American recognition was to the party's sense of its legitimacy.

In November 1991, Baker became the first cabinet-level official to travel to China after Tiananmen. In his meetings with Chinese leaders, he demanded that China abide by the Missile Technology Control Regime's limits on the export of missile technology and that China pressure North Korea to accept international nuclear inspections. He also pressed for progress on human rights. "I need concrete results—not promises, not meetings, not delays," Baker told Qian. The next day, Baker met with Li Peng for what Douglas Paal, then the Asia director at the National Security Coun-cil, described to author Robert Suettinger as "the worst meeting I've ever been in in my life." Baker and Li Peng squared off over human rights, China's missile proliferation, trade, and Taiwan. Baker wrote later that he was "appalled" by Li Peng's "surreal performance." Publicly, a State Depart-ment spokesman described the encounter as "businesslike."

On November 17, Baker met again with Qian Qichen, during which the Chinese announced they would "observe the guidelines and parameters" of the missile control regime. The Americans took that to mean that China would stop its sale of M-9 missiles to Syria and M-11 missiles to Pakistan. In exchange, Baker promised to unblock the sale of high-speed computers to Beijing. Qian also announced that China would sign the Nuclear Non-Proliferation Treaty and that China would speak with North Korea about international inspections. Qian passed Baker information on 733 dissi-dents. Several dissidents were allowed to go into exile.

One of those on the prisoner list was a man named Wu Jianmin. Dur-ing the meeting Qian told Baker that Wu Jianmin was actually attending their meeting. He was the chief spokesman of the Foreign Ministry. "Oh, so you've been released," Baker said, turning to Wu. Everyone burst out laughing. In reality, another Wu Jianmin had just begun a ten-year sen-tence for "organizing and leading a counterrevolutionary group."

Baker also came with presents. According to Qian Qichen's memoirs, he promised to support China's entry into the General Agreement on Tar-iffs and Trade and allow satellite exports to China, a huge victory for Chi-na's efforts to boost its technology.

In the fall of 1990, polls indicated that Americans disapproved of Bush's China policy by a margin of more than two-to-one. Bush and his allies argued that quiet diplomacy would maintain stability in Asia, keep trade flowing, and stave off the possibility of "losing" China once again. Punishing China would only reduce Western leverage and strengthen "hard-liners" in the Communist Party, the White House maintained. Instead, the United States should use the economic relationship to push political reform. "As people have commercial incentives, whether it's in China or in other totalitarian countries, the move to democracy becomes inexorable," Bush maintained.

This line of reasoning became central to the American argument for continued engagement with China. Washington established benchmarks for success—improving human rights, a liberalizing economy, an opening society—that were completely detached from Bush's main goal, which was simply to maintain relations with the People's Republic. What Bush sought was stability and trade, but he promised Americans China's peaceful evolution. His successors would do the same.

Not in many years had Communist China encountered the kind of domestic and international difficulties that it faced after the Tiananmen Square crackdown. The leadership, according to Chen Youwei, a former political counselor at the Chinese embassy in Washington, was thrown "into a state of near panic, hesitant and indecisive." In memoirs published in Taiwan, Chen wrote that the party's first move was to blame the United States for both the unrest and the collapse of socialism across the globe. As Communist Party elder Li Xiannian told a meeting of high-ranking Communists two days before the crackdown, the United States was waging "a smokeless world war" against China. "We had better watch out," he said. "Capitalism still wants to beat socialism in the end."

Geopolitically, China responded to the rise of what it perceived to be a revamped threat from America by turning to an old enemy for help. In April 1990, Premier Li Peng visited Moscow. Li and the Soviets agreed to reduce military deployments on their borders. A month later, Liu Hua-qing, the chief of China's navy, arrived in Russia and began negotiations to buy an advanced Russian fighter, the Su-27, heralding the beginning of a security relationship that would see China purchase more than $20 billion in Russian weaponry over the next twenty-five years.

China also hoped, Chen Youwei wrote, that the US-led effort to oust Saddam from Kuwait would weaken the United States. In August 1990, Jiang Zemin gathered members of the Politburo Standing Committee three times to discuss the crisis. The Politburo concluded that Bush's vow to roll back the invasion was nothing more than a "hegemonistic" plot to control Persian Gulf oil. Jiang ruled that China would not actively support the US-led coalition. The party believed that it was in China's interests for America to get bogged down in another quagmire, Chen wrote. This idea, that America's troubles equaled China's gain, would resurface in the future.

Saddam's ignominious defeat was a rude wake-up call for the Communist Party and especially the People's Liberation Army. The use of smart-bomb technology and the high-tech invasion that liberated Kuwait in days, not months, shocked China's generals. What the PLA called a "revolution in military affairs" had occurred while it was not looking. Almost overnight, Chinese military authorities overhauled the military budget, their weapons procurement policy, and their concept of warfare. The People's Liberation Army cut its massive ground forces while funneling the lion's share of its resources into its navy, air force, and rocket units. In PLA military exercises and expenditures, the United States became the imputed enemy, even as PLA doctrine adopted the high-tech American way of war.

The growing warmth between Beijing and Moscow emboldened Taiwan's remaining supporters in the Bush administration to lobby for their old friend. In 1991, James Lilley ended his tour as ambassador in Beijing and returned to the Pentagon, where he backed the sale of an advanced fighter plane, the F-16, to Taiwan to balance China's defense ties with Russia. Before taking up his Defense Department post, Lilley gave speeches in which he expressed publicly what many American officials had spoken of privately ever since Nixon's opening to China: Taiwan's reunification with the mainland would not be in the strategic interests of the United States. Lilley's argument was bolstered by the fact that Taiwan was moving toward democracy and that public opinion polls on the island showed only a tiny minority supporting any type of merger with mainland China.

At the same time, Bush's reelection campaign had run into problems. A smooth-talking Democratic candidate, Governor William Jefferson Clinton, from a place called Hope, Arkansas, was rising in the polls. Clinton had criticized Bush's handling of the economy as well as his China policy, accusing him of coddling "the butchers of Beijing." Then on July 29, 1992, General Dynamics, which made the F-16, announced that it would lay off fifty-eight hundred workers at its Fort Worth division. Six weeks later, Bush announced the sale of 150 F-16s to Taiwan for $6 billion—saving the jobs and, he hoped, his reelection bid.

State Department officials argued that the sale violated the Shanghai Communiqué of 1982. But they probably hadn't read President Reagan's letters to Chiang Ching-kuo, pledging to preserve the military balance across the Taiwan Strait. China's reaction was swift. It shipped parts for M-11 missiles to Pakistan, in violation of agreements with the United States to halt such sales. China found itself scanning the world for other ways to undermine the United States. In August 1991, Beijing, after having worked for decades with the United States to bring down the Soviet Union, backed the failed Communist Party coup attempt against Mikhail Gorbachev. According to diplomat Chen Youwei, China offered to fly Admiral Liu Huaqing back to Moscow to show support. With the fall of the Berlin Wall, China also tried to insert itself into German reunification talks, Chen wrote, hoping that a united Germany would emerge as a counterweight to America, but Beijing was not invited to the table. Once again, Party Central viewed America as enemy number one.

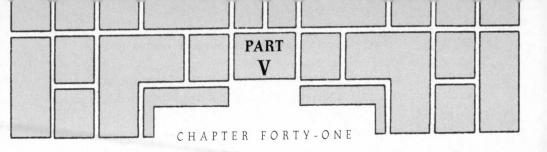

CHAPTER FORTY-ONE

Kung Fu Fighting

In 1964, after watching a martial arts competition in Long Beach, California, an ABC-TV employee invited a twenty-four-year-old recent graduate of the University of Washington to take a screen test. Two years later, Bruce Lee debuted in *The Green Hornet* as high-kicking Kato, the muscle behind crime fighter Britt Reid. Propelled by Lee's kinetic athleticism, kung fu exploded onto the pop culture scene. And Lee, the San Francisco–born son of a Cantonese opera star, became the second great Chinese American cultural icon after Anna May Wong.

With his six-pack abs and tough-as-nails vibe, Lee provided a new, self-confident image of a Chinese American male to a society that had previously pigeonholed them as dastardly and effeminate or industrious and effeminate. Lee lobbied ABC's producers for more lines for Kato and a more equal relationship with the Green Hornet. "If you sign me up with all that pigtail and hopping around jazz, forget it," he told the show's producer. Lee wasn't going to play "typical houseboy stuff."

Bruce Lee rocketed to fame at a time of enormous change for Americans of Chinese descent. In 1965, a year before *The Green Hornet* aired, Congress passed the Immigration and Naturalization Act, which removed immigration quotas for individual countries, resulting in an influx of Chinese and other Asians, along with Africans, Middle Easterners, and Latin Americans. In 1960, there were fewer than 240,000 Chinese in the United States. By 1980, the Chinese population in America had grown by

60 percent. The 1965 US Immigration Act fueled an unprecedented exploration of ethnic and racial identity that deeply affected American society.

The Green Hornet ended after one season, but Lee won praise for his role. In Los Angeles, he taught kung fu both to white stars—Steve McQueen, James Coburn, and a young Chuck Norris—and black—Kareem Abdul-Jabbar. Like Anna May Wong, Lee had setbacks. In 1970, he helped Warner Brothers develop a Chinese American Western TV serial, but the studio passed him over in favor of Anglo actor David Carradine as the star of *Kung Fu*. "The truth is I am a yellow-faced Chinese," he told a newspaper in Taiwan, "I cannot possibly become an idol for Caucasians." He was wrong.

Lee decamped to Hong Kong and in four years starred in four movies that smashed box office records and turned him into a global megastar. The films he headlined featured antiracist and anti-imperialist plots highlighted, naturally, by high-voltage fight scenes. Lee's martial prowess allowed Chinese viewers around the world to feel pride in their Chinese heritage without having to choose between Taipei and Beijing. As Lee barked to a gang of Japanese samurai that he had just overpowered in a scene from his masterpiece *Fist of Fury*, "Now you listen to me. I will only say once: We are not sick men!" He then took out an enormous Russian. Crowds in the United States and elsewhere went wild.

In America, Lee had heavyweight crossover appeal among African Americans. But in truth, Americans of all stripes flocked to see kung fu films. From late March to mid-October 1973, six Hong Kong films vied for the number one spot at the American box office. Then, at what should have been his finest hour, Lee, only thirty-two, died in Hong Kong in July 1973 from an adverse reaction to pain medication. His grave in Seattle became a shrine.

Bruce Lee was the harbinger of a new era in Chinese America. As they outgrew the confines of America's Chinatowns—by 1990, 170,000 Chinese Americans lived in LA's San Gabriel Valley alone; by 2015, there were more than 3.7 million Chinese in America—Chinese Americans became more secure of their place in the United States. In the 1930s, more than 60 percent of the Chinese in America worked as cooks, waiters, domestics, and laundrymen, and fewer than 2 percent had a college degree. By the 1960s, three out of four Chinese had white-collar jobs. In 1966, *US News & World Report* hailed the Chinese as a "model minority" capable of "winning wealth and respect by dint of its own hard work." The era of keeping quiet "as cicadas in cold weather," as scholar Chang-lin Tien had put it, was ending.

Chinese Americans began to involve themselves in political issues as never before. In 1969, the United States announced that it would return Okinawa and other islands it had occupied following World War II to Japan. Among them was a group of rocks—called the Senkakus in Japanese and the Diaoyu Islands in Chinese—that the US military had used for target practice since the war's end. In 1968, a study by the UN Economic Council for Asia and the Far East suggested that there might be oil reserves around the Senkakus. Neither Taiwan nor mainland China had claimed the islands before, but this news now touched off the first political movement of Chinese Americans in the late twentieth century.

In November 1970, Chinese students at Princeton and the University of Wisconsin founded the Protect the Diaoyu Islands Association, demanding that the islands not be returned to Japan. Chapters soon opened on campuses across the United States and Canada. On January 29 and 30, 1971, thousands of mostly Chinese demonstrators protested in six US cities against the US move. Hundreds of ethnic Chinese professors, including Nobel laureate C. N. Yang and educator Chang-lin Tien, signed an open letter that ran in the *New York Times* on May 23. As they had with the early-twentieth-century boycott of American goods, Chinese in America again fanned the flames of nationalism in China.

The Protect the Diaoyus movement galvanized the Chinese American community and gave Chinese Americans a sense that they, too, could influence American policy. Breaking with the old Chinatown organizations that supported Chiang Kai-shek, the Chinese Americans who had led the Protect the Diaoyus movement also began to lobby for better ties with mainland China.

In September 1971, soon after Nixon lifted the China travel ban, physicist C. N. Yang became the first prominent Chinese American to return to China. Zhou Enlai welcomed him with a banquet. Other scientists followed, including T. D. Lee, who had shared the Nobel Prize with Yang, and Chang-lin Tien. These Chinese Americans had a tremendous influence on their hosts' thinking, arguing that China needed to re-embrace the American way of science if it wanted to be great again. T. D. Lee briefed Zhou on US support for science and technology and on the peer-review process so essential to Western breakthroughs. Zhou became so reliant on Lee's counsel that when a Chinese physicist asked him whether China should announce that it had discovered a new atomic particle, Zhou replied that he needed to check first with T. D. Lee.

These early exchanges constituted a key factor in emboldening China to reopen intellectually to the West. It was fitting that C. N. Yang, a former Boxer Indemnity student, and T. D. Lee, educated in American missionary schools, both symbols of the early symbiosis between the Middle Kingdom and the Beautiful Country, led the way.

As he had in the 1950s, Zhou Enlai lobbied American-educated Chinese to come to China to help the motherland. Lui Lam was one of the first to go. Born in Hong Kong in the 1940s, Lam entered Columbia in the 1960s to earn a PhD in physics and joined the Protect the Diaoyus movement. Then, inspired by Chairman Mao, he dropped out of Columbia and moved to Manhattan's Chinatown to "live and learn from the masses," he wrote. Lam worked in a food cooperative, selling vegetables to poor residents at wholesale prices. After two years, he returned to Columbia and finished his degree.

In 1977, the Chinese invited Lam to China. He moved to Beijing with his wife and their infant daughter, becoming the first American-educated scientist since the 1950s to return "home." Six years later, the Chinese sent a delegation of physicists including Lam to the United States. Thousands more Chinese scientists would follow Lam, commuting from China to America and back again, in a rich transpacific cross-pollination that has continued to this day.

The Tiananmen Square crackdown of 1989 created another intellectual windfall for the United States when President George H. W. Bush issued his executive order allowing all the Chinese students in America to stay. Bush's order gave more than seventy thousand highly educated Chinese the right to work in America. Fifty-three thousand were ultimately granted green cards. For the third time in little more than a century, the United States was the beneficiary of Chinese immigration as the Chinese once again propelled leading segments of the American economy.

Throughout the 1990s, more than three-quarters of mainland Chinese studying in the US opted to remain after graduation. For several years, just about every physics major from Tsinghua University moved to America. They were following in the footsteps of their cousins from Taiwan. From 1979 to 1987, Taiwan sent 186,000 students to the United States and only 10,000 returned to the island.

Within a few years of the 1989 crackdown, Chinese and Indian immigrants constituted the largest ethnic groups of entrepreneurs in Silicon

Valley and founded some of the most successful companies. From 1980 to the present, Chinese, though barely 1 percent of the total US population, established about 20 percent of all the start-ups in the valley and created billions in wealth. Among the stars were men like Charles Wang, a Shanghai-born Queens College graduate with a heavy Brooklyn accent, who built Computer Associates into the third-biggest software company in the world. From Taiwan came Jerry Yang, who immigrated to the United States when he was a teenager, grew up near San Jose, and while in graduate school at Stanford University, cofounded Yahoo! and turned it into a $30 billion firm.

Chinese were not just good at technology, of course. Born in 1940 to a laundryman and a midwife in Stockton, California, Maxine Hong Kingston grew up during World War II and after reading Jade Snow Wong's *Fifth Chinese Daughter* became inspired to tell the world her stories, too. Kingston's first best seller came in 1976 with The *Woman Warrior,* a memoir of her childhood in America buffeted by ghosts from the old country, China. She followed that with *China Men,* which won the National Book Award in 1981. Kingston's leading characters are strong women battling racism from white society and sexism from Chinese men. Her exploration of these themes marked a break from her muse. Jade Snow Wong employed Chinese culture as a way to make the Chinese more acceptable to mainstream society. Kingston no longer felt the need to be accepted. She was part of the American fabric already, and she rejected the stereotype of the humble, hardworking, law-abiding model minority. Kingston was showered with awards and even got herself arrested, protesting the Iraq War in 2003.

In Amy Tan's *The Joy Luck Club,* a 1989 novel about four Chinese immigrant mothers and their American-born daughters, the gap between a mythical China and the reality of the United States did not drive the story. With Tan, the tension played out between the passion of immigrant mothers to raise successful children and their daughters' desires for American freedom, individualism, and stuff. Tan had moved away from a book about the Chinese to write a book about families.

There were others, too. Vera Wang made her clothing business into a global bridal-gown empire. Michael Chang became the youngest male tennis player to win a Grand Slam singles title in 1989. Maya Lin, an ethnic Chinese of Vietnamese extraction, designed the stark memorial to the Vietnam War on the Washington Mall. Award-winning cellist Yo-Yo Ma was born in France but moved to New York at the age of five, and two years later was performing for President Dwight Eisenhower and then

John F. Kennedy. In the 1890s, Gary Locke's immigrant grandfather worked as a servant in a house near the state capitol in Olympia, Washington. In 1996, Locke won the election for governor of Washington State, becoming the first ethnic Chinese governor in US history. "It took my family," he said, "one hundred years to move one mile."

By 2012, according to a survey by the Pew Research Center, Asian American households, led by the Chinese, made $17,000 more each year than the average American and 40 percent more had college degrees. Chinese Americans embraced the American Dream more tightly than other Americans. A significantly higher percentage of them than other Americans believed they could get ahead with hard work.

The Pew survey hinted at deeper truths about the interaction between the Chinese and the United States. In many ways, Chinese Americans had become emblematic of an earlier America, one where everyone worked and everyone was married. Chinese Americans didn't bear children out of wedlock, their divorce rate was less than half the national average, they rarely went on welfare, and they generally avoided many of the pathologies affecting mainstream American society. They mirrored the solid white middle-class values of yesteryear. The "model minority" had become a model for all Americans.

As China became richer, America's pull only increased. Millions of Chinese visited the United States each year. And in 2013, for the first time since the nineteenth century, more Chinese than any other nationality immigrated to the United States. Chinese money sloshed through the US real estate market. From March 2013 to March 2014, buyers from China, Taiwan, and Hong Kong spent $22 billion on homes in the United States, more than any other group of foreigners. On average, Chinese buyers paid more than half a million dollars per house, twice the US median price. "Rich Chinese have become a fixture in the public imagination, the way rich Russians were in the nineteen-nineties and rich people from the Gulf states were in the decades before that," observed the *New Yorker* in 2016. Stories of Chinese snapping up the best properties in the best school districts ran in real estate sections nationwide. Real estate agents even added a new term of art to their deal language: "the *feng shui* contingency." Before closing on a house, many Chinese buyers request that a feng shui master approve the house as part of a general inspection. The pace of rich Chinese wanting to move to America accelerated throughout the 2010s. In 2012, Chinese nationals earned 1,675 of the ten thousand EB-5 visas issued annually by the US government to foreigners who invest $1 million and employ at least ten people in the United States. Two years later, Chinese obtained 8,308 of those ten thousand slots. The US, more so than any other place on the planet, served as a magnet for Chinese.

Chinese businesses also saw a lucrative market in America. Reprising a role first played by the great Cantonese merchant Howqua in the 1830s, Chinese capital began pouring into the American economy in the early 2000s. Firms from China quickly became the fastest-growing investors in the United States. In 2015, Chinese businesses invested $15.7 billion in the United States, up thirty percent over 2014. Targets included semiconductor plants, dairies, pig farms, and oil wells. In 2012, Wanda, a real estate developer, bought the AMC Theatres chain for $2.6 billion and invested millions to upgrade the moviegoing experience of millions of Americans. In 2015, China's president Xi Jinping displaced the US president, the usual occupant of the Waldorf Astoria on Park Avenue in Manhattan, during the UN General Assembly. That's because a Chinese insurance firm had bought the legendary American hotel in 2014 for $1.95 billion. A half century earlier the "majestic" Waldorf had been featured in an anti-American screed during a Hate America campaign. Now it belonged to a Chinese firm.

In the mid-1970s, American universities, graduate programs, and law schools began phasing out special consideration in admissions for Asian Americans, and Chinese Americans in particular. In 1975, Boalt Hall, the law school at UC Berkeley, stopped giving Asian Americans preference, and the university at large followed suit in 1984, determining that Asian Americans were no longer "disadvantaged."

The policy changes did nothing to halt the rise of Asian Americans in higher education. In 1976, Asian Americans made up less than 4 percent of Harvard University's freshman class. Eight years later, they composed almost 13 percent. The increase at the Massachusetts Institute of Technology was even more dramatic, moving from 5 percent of the freshman class to more than 20 percent.

In 1996, California became the first state in the nation to overturn decades of affirmative action policies when voters passed Proposition 209, which prohibited state institutions from factoring race into admissions. The number of Asian Americans accepted into California's best state schools jumped again. Asian Americans constituted only 14 percent of California high school graduates in 2011–12, but they took 42 percent of the freshman slots at all University of California campuses and almost half at Berkeley, the most competitive school in the system. The trend was consistent nationwide. Generally considered one of the top public high schools in the country, New York's Stuyvesant High School had a student body that was 73 percent Asian in 2015. Its principal was also Chinese-born.

The more Asian Americans succeeded, the deeper their sense became that universities were holding them to higher standards than their class-mates. A case in point was that of Californian Michael Wang, the son of Chinese immigrants. Michael graduated second in his class of 1,002 at James Logan High School in Union City, aced his ACTs, sang with a choir at President Obama's inauguration, and placed among the top 150 in a national math competition—yet he was still rejected by six of the seven Ivy League colleges. In May 2015, Michael joined a coalition of sixty-four organizations in bringing a complaint against Harvard University, alleg-ing that the university made it harder for Asian Americans to win accep-tance. The suit, filed with the US Education Department's Office for Civil Rights, contended that Asians had to score far higher than whites, His-panics, or blacks on the SATs to equal their chances of acceptance. A fifty-two-year-old Chinese American author, Yukong Zhao, helped organize the coalition. As they had in the nineteenth century, Chinese Americans continued to look to America's courts to protect their rights.

It was inevitable that this awe-inspiring educational marvel would give rise to an account encapsulating the story of Chinese Americans. In 2011, Amy Chua, a professor at Yale Law School, published *Battle Hymn of the Tiger Mother*, a memoir about raising two half-Jewish, half-Chinese girls. Chua's book was marketed as a gutsy attack on overly indulgent Western parenting with its focus on buoying children's self-esteem, rather than honing their skills. Chua's op-ed in the *Wall Street Journal* in January 2011 ran under the headline: "Why Chinese Mothers Are Superior."

Tiger Mother was actually more about Chua's journey with her daughters as they battled with each other and themselves. But the message in the *Journal* article hit a nerve in the United States, where fear and admiration of the Chinese had once again come together. Looking for the secret to raising succesful kids, Americans snapped up Chua's book.

In reality, Chua's parenting had little or no relationship to how Chinese raise their children. Chua was a second-generation immigrant whose parents were not even from China; they were ethnic Chinese from the Philippines. But Chua was selling an American fantasy of the Chinese as supercompetent geniuses. In the 1950s, Americans imagined that the Chinese had discovered the secrets of the brain and how to "wash" it. In the 2000s, Americans similarly believed that the Chinese were raising superkids and looked on Chinese parenting with envy and awe.

Soon after the Tiananmen Square crackdown Americans found another way to show their high regard for the Chinese. Americans from mostly white families began adopting more babies from China than from any other country. The majority of the children were girls who were abandoned by rural Chinese families due to the "one-child" policy and a cultural disposition to favor boys. A century earlier, American missionaries had placed baskets by the sides of lakes with notes: "Place your babies here. Do not throw them into the pond." Now Americans had re-embraced that mission from halfway across the world. From 1991 until today, Americans have adopted more than eighty thousand Chinese.

By the mid-1990s, adopting a Chinese baby had become a fad among well-to-do white families. Asian babies had been popular in the United States since the Korean War, followed by the Vietnam War and the exodus of the boat people. In 2005, Americans adopted a record 7,906 Chinese. It was in that year that writer Diane Clehane adopted her daughter, Madeline. Writing in *Vanity Fair* in 2008, Clehane said that in the early 2000s she began to notice "beautiful little Chinese girls with shining black hair, dark eyes, and round faces . . . peeking out from their strollers as their Caucasian parents happily wheeled them around Manhattan." She approached mothers and asked, "Is she from China?" Invariably, the answer was yes. Clehane decided that she, too, wanted a Chinese baby.

Clehane wrote that didn't really have an answer when asked "Why China?" Was it the "one-child" policy? The fact that her mother had wanted to adopt a baby from Vietnam years ago but her father decided against it? China's prejudice against girls? A way, following the Tiananmen Square crackdown, to "do" something for China? But, at root, for many Americans, the overriding emotion was a tender, even maternal, regard for the Middle Kingdom that has been part America's cultural makeup for centuries. Clehane didn't view her act as one of simple charity, however. "I didn't rescue her," she wrote of Madeline, "we rescued each other."

The sense that China and the larger Far East could "rescue" or provide meaning for Americans continued as the twentieth century closed. Americans had always been as intrigued by Oriental mysticism just as some Chinese were enamored of Yankee middle-class values. Since the time of Henry David Thoreau and Ralph Waldo Emerson in the mid-nineteenth century, American philosophers had been taken with ideas from Asia. In the 1930s, Chinese and Tibetan exoticism beckoned to Americans when the Depression brought on a loss of confidence in the West. Fueled by the essays of Joseph Rock and the book and movie version of *Lost Horizon*, Americans dreamed of a place—a Shangri-la—where they could find refuge from the troubles of the day. The attraction continued in the 1950s, when American soldiers returned from the Korean War bringing home Asian customs, art, and wives. Some Americans trekked in India. Others, like Beat Generation poet Alan Watts, who spent a decade in Japan, wandered through the Far East. In America, many of these seekers gravitated toward San Francisco. That was where in the late 1950s, Watts met Gia-fu Feng, the Shanghai-born scion of a banking family who had graduated with a masters in business administration from the Wharton School at the University of Pennsylvania.

After the Communist revolution, Feng's parents had urged him to stay in America. He had bummed around the country and surfaced in San Francisco where he began working with Watts at the American Academy of Asian Studies. There he taught Chinese philosophy, focusing on Taoism and questions like "Are we butterflies dreaming we are men or men dreaming we are butterflies?" Feng's riddles intrigued people like Michael Murphy, a Stanford University graduate. Murphy went on to cofound the Esalen Institute in Big Sur, 150 miles south of San Francisco, in 1962. Feng frequented Esalen and embraced its message of hedonistic self-exploration through yoga, tai chi, meditation, and drugs. With his Chinese-sage beard and long black locks, Feng became a patriarch of the 1960s free-love movement. He ultimately founded his own Taoist center in Colorado, which he called Stillpoint after a line in a poem by T. S. Eliot.

The end of the '60s didn't stop the American search for a deeper meaning in Asian mysticism. In the 1980s, Tibet emerged as a topic of special fascination, a meeting point for traditional American political beliefs in the right of self-determination and the spiritual attraction of the exotic East. English-speaking Tibetan lamas began migrating to the US and, backed by wealthy donors (and no longer the CIA), they opened Tibetan monasteries across the country. Following a Chinese crackdown on antigovernment protests in Tibet in March 1989, a string of Hollywood stars championed Tibet's cause, most notably actor Richard Gere. Explaining his love of Tibetan culture in 1998, Gere declared, "I think we're hopeful that there is a place that is ancient and wise and open and filled with light." Tibet's exiled leader, the Dalai Lama, assumed mythic status in many American minds. A 2013 CNN poll found that sixty-one percent had a favorable opinion of him. By the 1990s, Americans were seeing in Tibet the attributes they had once ascribed to China. As Robert Thurman, a Tibet scholar at Columbia University, noted in a Frontline documentary, "While the American national purpose is ever greater material productivity, the Tibetan national purpose is ever greater spiritual productivity." Sounding like one of the enraptured Americans who had just emerged from China in the 1970s, Thurman noted that the West was a place of "outer modernity," while the Tibetans possessed "inner modernity."

On October 15, 1984, the body of a Taiwanese journalist and curio shop owner was found in the garage of his home in Daly City, California. Neighbors told the police that they had seen Chinese men wearing fake beards bicycling away from the scene of the crime. The murder of Henry Liu, a fifty-two-year-old writer who had revealed in a tell-all biography that Taiwan's president Chiang Ching-kuo had fathered sons out of wedlock, shocked many in the United States and Taiwan. But the tragedy also hastened the end of authoritarian rule in the Republic of China and helped spark the birth of democracy in the first Chinese community anywhere.

Chiang Ching-kuo had been president of Taiwan since 1978. He had run Taiwan's brutal internal security apparatus since the 1950s, and like his father, he brooked no dissent. But, as Taiwan's economy blossomed, a self-confident middle class had emerged on the island, demanding more freedom and a government that represented its interests. The Nationalist regime had been weakened by the loss of American recognition and the evaporation of international support. When the demands of the middle class coalesced into an opposition movement called *dangwai*, or "outside the party," Chiang's first instinct was to crack down. Martial law courts sentenced scores of lawyers, professors, businessmen, and journalists to lengthy prison sentences. In one case, following a riot in the southern city of Kaohsiung in January 1980, 152 members of the *dangwai* movement were arrested and more than forty were sent to jail. On February 28, 1980, the wife and twin seven-year-old daughters of one of those arrested were stabbed to death in their home; government thugs were suspected of the murders. In July 1981, Chen Wen-chen, a math professor from Carnegie Mellon University in Pittsburgh who had supported Taiwan's democratization, fell to his death under suspicious circumstances from the fifth floor of the library of National Taiwan University.

At a time when the United States was ignoring mainland China's human rights violations, its pressure on Taiwan was intense. Using the same tactic that Yankee missionaries had wielded against foot-binding in the nineteenth century, US politicians shamed the Kuomintang government into treating its people with more respect. American officials linked Taiwan's human rights practices to US arms sales. Leading the US charge was a Democratic congressman from Brooklyn named Stephen Solarz. Born in 1940 in New York City, Solarz had parlayed his opposition to the Vietnam War in 1975 into a congressional seat representing the liberal thirteenth district. In 1980, he became the first American official to visit North Korea since the Korean War. As chairman of the Subcommittee on Asia and the Pacific of the House Foreign Affairs Committee, he involved himself in major events in Asia. He played a key role in the ouster of Philippines dictator Ferdinand Marcos and publicized the massive shoe collection of his wife, Imelda.

Solarz used Congressional hearings to uncover an extensive network of Kuomintang spies in the United States who were monitoring pro-democracy and Taiwan independence activists. He authored an amendment to the Arms Export Control Act, banning weapons sales to countries that engage in "intimidation and harassment" of people in America. He held hearings on Henry Liu's assassination, fingering the Kuomintang. Solarz threatened to block arms sales again unless FBI investigators were given access to a leading Taiwanese intelligence official, who had been implicated in the crime. Chiang Ching-kuo consented, and in April 1985, the official, Vice Admiral Wang Hsi-ling, was convicted in Taiwan of ordering the murder and sentenced to life in prison. (He was released after six years.) Meanwhile, the State Department helped a stream of *dangwai* leaders visit the US; when they returned home, they wielded photographs of themselves with leading Americans as talismans against the Nationalist secret police.

Chiang Ching-kuo's advisers began to advocate political reform. Fred Chien, now serving as Taiwan's representative to the United States, met with Chiang in the spring of 1986 and pleaded with him to liberalize. Several months later, Chiang sent Chien a message telling him that he had been right. Democracy's time had come. Chiang understood that Taiwan's economic prosperity coupled with a democratizing political system would be assets in the republic's competition with mainland China. Taiwan would need something more than the timeworn moniker of "Free China" to appeal to the United States. In May 1986, Chiang Ching-kuo authorized Nationalist Party members to hold discussions with members of the *dangwai* movement. That year he asked his vice president, Lee Teng-hui, to draw up regulations for direct elections for the mayors of Taiwan's two biggest cities, Taipei and Kaohsiung. And when the Democratic Progressive Party was founded on September 28, 1986, becoming the first opposition party in any Chinese territory since 1949, something extraordinary happened: no one was thrown in jail.

On October 7, 1986, just a few days shy of the second anniversary of Liu's murder, Chiang announced that he would be ending thirty-eight years of martial law. In a clear signal to his key international friend, Chiang revealed his plans in an interview with Katharine Graham, the publisher of the *Washington Post*. He vowed that the Republic of China would ultimately "democratize." The *Post* treated Chiang's announcement with skepticism; its editors buried the story on page A18. But it was epochal nonetheless. "We must serve as a lighthouse of hope for one billion Chinese on the mainland," Chiang declared.

The changes that followed were extraordinary. Chiang opened up trade and travel to mainland China and lifted bans on independent organizations and speech. Taiwan's press became the freest in Asia. And in December 1986, twelve of the nineteen candidates from the Democratic Progressive Party won seats in Taiwan's legislative elections.

Chiang died of heart disease in 1988 at the age of seventy-seven. At that point, Soong Mayling, who throughout the years had had a tumultuous relationship with her stepson, attempted from her mansion in Long Island to block Chiang's vice president, Lee Teng-hui, from taking over both the presidency and the leadership of the Kuomintang. But she failed. Once China's "queen," Soong Mayling was a spent force. (She did outlive her other siblings, though, dying in New York on October 23, 2003, at the age of 105.)

In 1990, just months after the Tiananmen Square crackdown in Beijing, a massive student movement calling for full democracy rocked Taiwan. Lee had just been "reelected" by 671 members of the rubber-stamp National Assembly, and the protesters wanted a real democracy. Unlike the Communists across the Taiwan Strait, Lee did not crack down. Instead, he welcomed student representatives to the Presidential Palace and promised to hold the next presidential election by popular vote, another first for any Chinese territory in the world. The election was scheduled for 1996.

Solarz took on the role of an unofficial adviser to the Taiwanese government. From his office on Capitol Hill, he called Chiang and then Lee Teng-hui every six months to praise them for the steps they had taken and to ask for more. The development of democracy in Taiwan was the culmination of decades of economic growth and deep interaction with the West and the United States. It came as other developing nations—Turkey, the Philippines, and South Korea—also democratized. The freedoms the

Taiwanese won in the 1980s and 1990s stood as a challenge to the Chinese Communist claim that individual rights and democracy were somehow incompatible with Chinese culture. Although he had died at his home in Nutley, New Jersey, in 1957, P. C. Chang, the coauthor of the Universal Declaration of Human Rights, would have been proud.

The extraordinary success of the Chinese in America and Taiwan's march to full democracy exemplified the harmonious melding of American values with Chinese culture. Here in action was the Great Harmony that many Chinese and Americans had sought for years. But on mainland China, the political leadership viewed this merger with alarm and maintained that not only were Chinese ill suited to American-style freewheeling democracy but that it represented a mortal threat to the Chinese nation.

CHAPTER FORTY-TWO

Patriotic Education

Five days after the crackdown on the Tiananmen Square protests on June 4, 1989, Deng Xiaoping emerged to congratulate officers from the People's Liberation Army. He declared that the "biggest mistake" the party had made was "primarily in ideological and political education—not just of students but of the people in general."

Deng's statement signaled the beginning of another ideological operation—the Patriotic Education Campaign—to guide the thoughts of the Chinese people away from America. Faced with a spiritual vacuum following June 4 and the collapse of Communism in Eastern Europe and the USSR, the Chinese Communist Party turned to a resentful form of nationalism to undergird its shaky rule. This was Chiang Kai-shek's New Life Movement on steroids, carried out by a party that had just received the greatest shock of its seventy-eight-year existence.

In a letter to the Ministry of Education published in the *People's Daily* on March 9, 1991, the new party secretary, Jiang Zemin, appointed by Deng following the crackdown, declared that all Chinese students were to participate in the campaign, "even kids in kindergarten." The campaign had four points, Jiang said. In the past, China had been bullied because it had weak leaders. The worst bullies were Westerners and the Japanese. If not for the Chinese Communist Party, China would be weak and divided. And America sought to contain China and to prevent its rise. Jiang told the party that "history educational reform" was a fundamental strategy that would shield China from "the peaceful evolution plot of international hostile powers."

That year, the party issued revised history textbooks. To assure that millions of Chinese teenagers would memorize the campaign's central message, contemporary history became a topic on nationwide college entrance tests. Class struggle, once hailed by Communist historians as history's driving force, disappeared from the curriculum, replaced by nationalism. For the party, the defining issue of its history was no longer the battle with the Nationalists, but the fight with Japan, and behind it, America. Chiang Kai-shek, once the antihero of Communist history, was rehabilitated as a patriot. American support for China during World War II vanished from Chinese textbooks. It was as if China had fought the war alone.

The new enemy was Japan and the West. Mao Zedong had stressed that China was a victor in the war against imperialism. But now China played the role of victim. The whole nation, the party's Central Committee and the State Council noted in a document of August 1994, was to study China's humiliating history from the Opium War on in order to grasp the evil intent of what came to be known as "hostile Western foreign forces." The goal was to boost "self-respect and a sense of pride" and to enhance "national cohesion." As Ambassador James Lilley noted just after the Tiananmen Square crackdown, "The Chinese need a single bogeyman." And that bogeyman was the West.

In the 1990s, the party took steps to make its message more palatable to China's globalizing youth culture. The 1993 television drama *A Native of Beijing in New York* marked the emergence of commercially viable anti-American entertainment. Based on the best-selling novel by the same name, the series tells the story of Wang Qiming, a striving Chinese immigrant on his way to making a fortune in the heartless Big Apple. Wang's tale enthralled Chinese viewers and fit the needs of the post-1989 Communist Party. It simultaneously depicted the moral vacuum at the core of the American capitalist system and told a rags-to-riches story of the steely entrepreneurship that the party had embraced. In one climactic scene, Wang hires a buxom blond prostitute and showers her with dollar bills, commanding her to scream, "I love you, I love you!" In its absurdist manipulation of American materialism, the show represented the party's frustration with America, its sense of powerlessness, and its desire for revenge.

Communist Party writers embraced *A Native of Beijing* as an antidote to pro-American feelings. The show, wrote one columnist in the party-run *China Daily*, will "help those who entertain a rosy American dream to become more realistic." As the writer Jianying Zha noted, the show's operative emotion was "Screw you, America."

Running for president in the fall of 1992, Bill Clinton pledged to lead "an America that will not coddle dictators, from Baghdad to Beijing." As president, he promised to pursue a new policy toward the Middle Kingdom, one that kept tariffs on Chinese imports low but only if China's human rights record improved. Still, true to the patterns of Chinese-American interactions, the Clinton administration had a hard time imposing conditions on Beijing. By the end of the Clinton years, China had not liberalized; its human rights situation remained poor, yet the United States had ushered China into the World Trade Organization, a move that primed the already-accelerating Chinese economy with a dose of rocket fuel.

As was typical of his approach in other areas, Bill Clinton tried to marry contradictory policies. With regard to China, those policies involved America's missionary impulse to reform China and its strategic desire to keep it stable. Clinton sought trade and cooperation with China, but he also wanted it to open up politically. The Communist Party forced Clinton to choose and the side that sought stability—and commerce—won.

Clinton's hand was forced by the rise of a powerful business lobby in favor of trade with China. As they had in the wake of the Boxer Rebellion nine decades earlier, American businesses in the 1990s argued that the US should not punish China because of the way it treated its citizens; it should instead encourage commerce so that China's door would remain open to the West.

The disappearance of the Soviet Union, the Tiananmen crackdown, and the rise of China colored the 1990s. In the United States, a China mania erupted in books and articles—*China: A World Power Again* and *China as No. 1: The New Superpower Takes Centre Stage*—heralding the emergence of a new colossus. Americans were divided. Was China a threat or an opportunity? Pessimists tapped into a deep vein of fear of the Middle Kingdom. For the first time, all the elements of a new Yellow Peril—a resurgent economic power, an expanding military, a hostile ideology, and a huge population—coalesced. In 1996, historian Samuel P. Huntington's *Clash of Civilizations and the Remaking of World Order* predicted a "civilizational war" between China and the US. China, Huntington wrote, was *the* major rival to the American-led international system and the "biggest player in the history of man." Optimists pointed to China's breakneck economic development. China was the new land of opportunity, a Wild West business frontier, ready for US business to exploit. It was no threat; on the contrary, it was going to make everyone rich.

In May 1993, Clinton signed an executive order that linked renewal of most-favored-nation trading rights with human rights progress in China. On May 28, surrounded by Democratic congressional leaders, Chinese students, and Tibetan activists in the White House, the president declared, "It is time that a unified American policy recognize both the values of China and the values of America." The president said that US policy toward China was founded on "a resolute insistence upon significant progress on human rights."

In Beijing, Clinton's promise of global democratization read like a declaration of war. In December 1992, Li Peng declared that any major concessions on human rights "would shake the basis of our society." On February 27, 1994, Chinese police arrested dissident Wei Jingsheng in Beijing following his meeting with John Shattuck, the assistant secretary of state for human rights. Wei, who had already spent almost fifteen years in jail, was given another sentence of fourteen years.

When Secretary of State Warren Christopher traveled to Beijing the following month and demanded "significant progress and soon" on human rights, he got nowhere. Li Peng raked him over the coals in what Winston Lord, at the State Department, described as "the most brutal diplomatic meeting" he'd ever attended. China's human rights, Li Peng said, were "none of your business." The Chinese followed up by canceling Christopher's meeting with party secretary Jiang Zemin. Christopher told Clinton that the Chinese were "rough, somber, sometimes bordering on the insolent." Yet, even as China was clamping down on human rights, its government dangled the prospect of more profits in front of the American business community. Inside Party Central at Zhongnanhai, Deng Xiaoping was pondering his final act.

In early 1992, Deng, then eighty-seven, left Beijing on a journey to southern China. Deng and his allies were concerned that the Communist hard-liners, who had come to power after the Tiananmen Square crackdown, were mismanaging the economy. From 1989 to 1991, China's economy grew an average of less than 6 percent a year; market-oriented reforms stalled. For a poor country like China, this was unacceptable.

Deng fled Beijing in his last great political gambit to reignite China's reforms. In a series of statements in Shanghai and then in the southern city of Shenzhen, he put the party's leadership on notice that it needed to resume the transformation to a more open economy. The results were stunning. In 1992, China's economy grew by more than 14 percent. An explosion of entrepreneurial activity transformed its cities. Township enterprises pulled millions of farmers off the fields. An army of workers, many of them women, flocked to China's east coast, turning the nation into the factory of the world. In 1991, foreigners had invested only $4 billion in China; by 1993, investment surpassed $25 billion. That year alone, the Chinese signed eighty-five thousand deals with foreign partners. It was the most ferocious gold rush that China had ever seen. Once again, American businesses were obsessed with the China story. Between Deng's Southern tour in 1992 and his death in 1997, China's economy tripled in size.

In 1991, Jack Perkowski quit his job on Wall Street and moved to Hong Kong to found a venture capital fund to invest in China. A former guard on the Yale University football team and an investment banker at Paine Webber, Perkowski had already made it big in the United States. He had a capacious apartment overlooking Central Park and a sixty-five-acre farm along the Delaware River in New Jersey. He brought irrepressible Yankee optimism and a pug-nosed pugilism to the China trade.

Perkowski considered China the next big thing, and he was determined, in the words of Tim Clissold, his chief aide at the time, "to be the only guy who made it work in China." Perkowski and Clissold set off together across China scouring the industrial badlands of the Middle Kingdom for distressed factories that could be turned into gold. Over the course of nine months, Perkowski visited 350 sites. In the end, he chose automobile parts and beer as the alchemy that would make him rich.

Perkowski went back to his Wall Street associates, and over the 1993 Christmas holidays, he garnered commitments for $150 million, as he told writer Joe Studwell. Perkowski raised a total of $415 million, cobbling together the largest private equity fund any single individual had raised for Chinese deals.

Perkowski was not alone. Dozens of funds selling the China Dream emerged. Wall Street Houdini Mark Mobius came out with the Templeton Dragon Fund in 1994. AIG, founded by Neil Starr in Shanghai in 1919, returned to the Middle Kingdom with a bang—landing the first insurance license granted by the PRC since 1949 and unveiling what it touted as "the largest ever direct investment fund for emerging markets." Barton Biggs, a Wall Street visionary, emerged from a short trip behind the Bamboo

Curtain and announced, "After six days in China, I'm tuned in, overfed and maximum bullish." Following Biggs's declaration, more than $2 billion coursed through the Hong Kong Stock Exchange, chasing companies with business in China.

American companies, drooling at the prospect of a billion customers, came to China prepared to hand over the secrets to US technology in exchange for market share. Aircraft manufacturer McDonnell Douglas went so far as to provide China with state-of-the-art machine tool manufacturing capability on the condition that the Chinese use the technology solely in civilian operations. (The Chinese broke that promise.)

The Western firms that did succeed were the ones that held China to the same standards that they maintained elsewhere. But during the go-go 1990s, they were few and far between. American profit projections were as unhinged from reality as they had been seventy years earlier during the era of adman Carl Crow. In 1993, AT&T's CEO Robert Allen went to China, met President Jiang Zemin, and signed agreements for $500 million in business. McDonnell Douglas built only three planes in China before closing shop. None of AT&T's investments panned out.

Perkowski's express train to boundless wealth turned out to be a local to huge losses. Perkowski sold two breweries at a $60 million loss. His investment company, ASIMCO, was hit by every possible scam. One employee concocted a scheme to bilk ASIMCO out of $5 million. When ASIMCO sought the assistance of local anticorruption authorities, the officials demanded money to pursue the investigation and a judge wanted a green card to adjudicate the case. When ASIMCO tried to fire a manager who had transferred a swath of ASIMCO's land to another company, a bevy of protesters backed by local police barricaded Tim Clissold in a hotel room for twelve hours. Clissold was so stressed by his various skirmishes with Chinese partners—there were broken bottles, street riots, fights resulting in lost ears—that he suffered a heart attack. Clissold chronicled his and Perkowski's travails in a book he titled *Mr. China*. The pair stopped talking. The *Wall Street Journal* dubbed Perkowski's story "the most expensive business education in the world." Another reviewer quipped, "It's funny because it's somebody else's money."

Perkowski didn't lose perspective. Addressing the World Economic Forum in Beijing on April 1998, he called China "the Vietnam war of American business." He also didn't quit. He was mulishly optimistic and his pockets were deep, even after 2004, when some of his investors cashed out. He redirected ASIMCO's auto parts business, which had been founded to serve China's domestic market, toward exports. Instead of hiring from state-owned companies, he trained his own managers. Slowly, ASIMCO, which had been the punchline to the joke about overblown Yankee expectations for Chinese business, began to turn itself around.

By the beginning of the twenty-first century, ASIMCO had grown to be one of the largest automotive parts manufacturers in China, with twelve thousand employees in seventeen factories. In 2008, its sales hit $600 million, and paralleling Neil Starr and his early-twentieth-century insurance operations, Perkowski began buying American companies in his quest to create a global enterprise. That year he came out with his side of the story. Never short on brass, he titled his book: *Managing the Dragon: How I'm Building a Billion-Dollar Business in China.*

The Chinese used the lure of their market to deflect attention from human rights, betting that the American profit motive would beat out its political ideals. Each year Congress debated the most-favored-nation issue, and each year, instead of improving human rights, China committed to further opening its markets to US business. In the fall of 1993, China announced that it would reduce tariffs on almost three thousand products. That year, China's imports jumped 23 percent over the previous year. Beijing followed that with announcements that it would remove hundreds of nontariff barriers and relax regulations on currency exchanges, allowing Western firms to repatriate more of their profits. In April 1994, as another annual MFN debate was gathering steam, Wu Yi, then a senior trade negotiator, led a delegation of more than two hundred officials to the United States to, as the Chinese press put it, "shop for imports." Millions of dollars in deals were signed. Deng Xiaoping remarked that China was "too big a piece of meat" for foreign businesses to ignore. As Premier Li Peng boasted, "The number of friends is increasing and our international status is on the rise."

On May 26, 1994, Clinton abandoned the link between human rights and trade, announcing that it was no longer useful. He called his new policy toward China "constructive engagement." It would be tested soon enough.

In November 1991, the United States began pulling its forces out of the Philippines. A combination of natural disasters—the dramatic eruption of

Mount Pinatubo on June 15, 1991, burying the US Air Force's Clark Air Base under tons of mud and rubble—and the vagaries of Filipino politics forced Washington to end a military presence on the island nation that had begun in 1898.

In 1992, the same year the US Navy pulled out of Subic Naval Base, China's legislature passed a bill laying claim to the seas the United States was leaving. The "Law on the Territorial Waters and Their Contiguous Areas" seemed to assert Chinese sovereignty over virtually all of the South China Sea, with the aim of turning one of the world's most well-traveled waterways into a Chinese lake. It was no coincidence that with America seemingly in retreat, China was rushing to fill the breach. Chinese analysts called the law "China's Monroe Doctrine." Almost a century earlier the Qing dynasty reformer Liang Qichao had dreamed of excluding foreign powers from China's seas. Now China was taking steps to make it happen.

The Chinese government released a map, based on one first drawn up by the Nationalist Chinese government in 1947 with the help of the US Navy, that showed nine dashes around the totality of the one-million-square-mile South China Sea. The map stretched as far south as the southern tip of Vietnam and the coast of Borneo. One dash was just 50 miles from the Vietnamese coast; another was 24 miles from Malaysia; a third was 35 miles from the Philippines. All were well within the two hundred mile exclusive economic zone of other countries. But China was mum on the issue of whether the map meant that the sea belonged to China. Then, in 1995, China occupied the appropriately named Mischief Reef, a speck of rock 130 miles west of the Philippines' island of Palawan and more than 400 miles from China.

It wasn't only the Monroe Doctrine that had inspired the PRC. Chinese strategists looked to another American, the nineteenth-century naval theoretician and champion of American imperialism Alfred Thayer Mahan, as an inspiration for China's expansive claims. Central to this story was Liu Huaqing, a grizzled revolutionary who would emerge as the architect of a fundamental strategic reorientation by the Middle Kingdom.

Born in landlocked Hubei province in 1916, twelve years after Deng Xiaoping, Liu joined the Communist army as a teenager, participated in the Long March, and battled Nationalist forces after World War II. Liu's first encounter with the sea occurred in 1952 when he was named the deputy political commissar at the Dalian Naval Academy. Following that, he spent four years in the Soviet Union studying military doctrine.

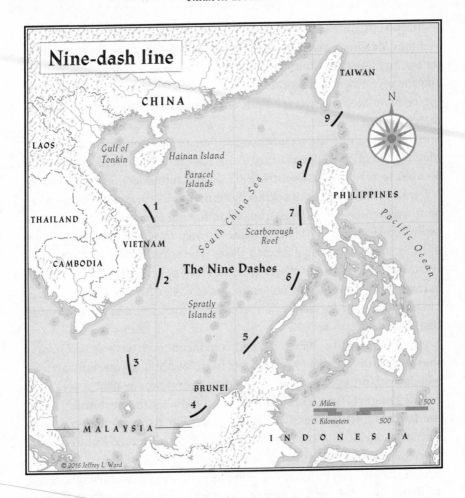

Returning from Russia, he worked with Nie Rongzhen, the architect of China's nuclear weapons program. He rejoined the Chinese navy in 1970, and when Deng Xiaoping returned to power, Liu's stock rose again. In 1982, he was appointed commander of the navy and led that service until 1987.

Liu emerged as a top Chinese military strategist just as many Chinese were turning to the West for inspiration and guidance. It was the time of the *Deathsong of the River*, the documentary that argued that China's future lay in the blue waters of the Pacific and not the scrub hills of the Yellow River plain. Think tanks called on the Chinese to embrace an "oceanic perspective" and hailed China's navy as a "strategic service." Liu was bitten by the martial version of this bug and turned to Mahan's writings for guidance.

In the late nineteenth century, Mahan supplied American presidents William McKinley and Teddy Roosevelt with the strategic underpinning for their colonial push into Asia, the seizure of Hawaii and the Philippines, and the investment in a world-class navy. Mahan argued that global commerce mandated a powerful navy, which in turn demanded more commerce to keep it afloat.

Now that China had relaunched itself on a search for wealth and power, Mahan, the man who acclaimed America's imperial adventures, would be used to validate those of the PRC. In his autobiography published in 2004, Liu credited Mahan with providing him a "theoretical weapon" as he strove to turn China away from a continental mind-set and toward the open sea. Liu wielded Mahan's greatest work, *The Influence of Sea Power upon History*, as a cudgel against those who wanted to keep China isolated. He argued that now that China was relying on trade and investment to modernize, it needed to police its seas as well. China needed to go out, Liu argued, stake its claims to the oceans around it, and back them up with a modernized navy.

By the end of the 1980s, Liu had convinced the party's senior leadership that China needed to upgrade its fleet. "Without an aircraft carrier, I will die with my eyelids open," Liu told an interviewer in 1987. A year later, Beijing bought an old Ukrainian hulk and soon began refurbishing it into the *Liaoning*, China's first aircraft carrier. For Admiral Liu, changing China's strategic culture was painstaking work. But a crisis a few years later concentrated all minds.

On the evening of March 7, 1996, Bill Clinton's Secretary of Defense William Perry hosted Liu Huaqiu, vice foreign minister of the People's Republic of China and no relation to Liu Huaqing, at a dinner in the Madison Room on the eighth floor of the State Department. Perry had prepared a statement. The Chinese, he told Liu, who had a good grasp of English, faced "grave consequences" should one of their missiles strike Taiwan. "Grave consequences" is international code for war. China was shooting rockets at the island; one had passed directly over the capital, Taipei, and splashed down in the ocean nineteen miles away. For the first time since the Quemoy and Matsu crises of 1958, China and the United States risked bloodshed.

The story of what brought China and the United States to the brink of conflict and how they drew back is one turning point in Chinese-American relations and in the way China viewed the United States. Bill Clinton had entered the White House believing that China would play a diminished role in the American imagination, but the crisis in the Taiwan Strait convinced him and many other strategists that the opposite was true. As Clinton's second secretary of state, Madeleine Albright, put it, China had become "too big to ignore."

Since taking office in 1988, Taiwanese president Lee Teng-hui had worked to improve relations with mainland China. Taiwan had abolished its "state of war" with the PRC, and trade and investment boomed. Within a few years, Taiwanese firms would become among China's top investors. Lee had also strengthened democracy in Taiwan. The opposition Democratic Progressive Party was now completely legal, and preparations were being made for the direct election of a president, scheduled for March 23, 1996. But Lee had also been pushing for more "international space" for Taiwan: he wanted membership in international organizations and formal diplomatic relations with other countries. Since normalizing ties with the United States, China had conducted a withering campaign to isolate Taiwan. When Nixon went to China in 1972, seventy-one countries recognized Taiwan. In 1994, the number was down to twenty-eight.

Lee sought to upgrade Taiwan's ties with the United States. In the spring of 1994, while heading to Central America, he had asked for US permission to spend the night in Hawaii while his plane refueled. The State Department agreed to the refueling, but skittish about China's reaction, it denied Lee's request to leave the airport. Lee was livid at what he felt to be shabby treatment from an old friend.

In late 1994, Taiwan launched a campaign to get Lee a US visa, this time to attend a reunion at his alma mater, Cornell University. The Clinton administration turned him down. On April 17, Secretary of State Warren Christopher assured Chinese foreign minister Qian Qichen that no visa would be issued. But a democratizing Taiwan had made new allies in Washington. Helped by a $5 million PR campaign, the Senate voted 97–1 to grant Lee a visa on May 3, 1994. The administration was forced to reverse itself, and as David Rothkopf, a former Commerce Department official, later told the *Washington Post*, "Christopher's credibility with the Chinese, at that moment, was over." Communist China withdrew its ambassador in protest.

At Cornell, Lee's speech on June 9, 1995, was low-key, but his appearance was a victory in itself. The bombast from Communist China was unrelenting. The Xinhua News Agency called Lee's US visa "this wanton wound" and declared that it would "help the Chinese people more clearly realize what kind of a country the United States is." Then, in July 1995, soon after Lee had returned home, the People's Liberation Army began firing missiles near Taiwan, followed by a mock invasion off the coast of Fujian, just opposite Taiwan. Soon after that, Chinese officials began threatening the United States. In January 1996, longtime diplomat Charles Freeman Jr. told the Clinton administration of a disturbing conversation he had had with a Chinese general. When Freeman predicted that the United States would protect Taiwan if China attacked it, the general scoffed. The United States was a "paper tiger," he said. America had threatened China with a nuclear attack in the 1950s, he said, "because we couldn't hit back." But now, China had its own Bomb. "So you are not going to threaten us again," the general said, "because you care a lot more about Los Angeles than Taipei." That audacious warning was followed two months later, in March, with more missile tests and military exercises in the run-up to Taiwan's presidential election.

On March 10, three days after Perry's dinner with Liu Huaqiu, the United States dispatched two aircraft carrier battle groups near Taiwan to put China on notice that its war games were out of line. It was the largest deployment of American firepower in Asia since the end of the Vietnam War. China had thought it could intimidate Taiwan's voters into voting against Lee and for candidates that favored unification. It was wrong. Lee won reelection in a landslide.

The crisis concentrated minds in Washington. Clinton administration officials summoned one of President Lee's senior advisers to a New York hotel in April to warn him to cool Taiwan's drive for more international space. Discussions with Liu Huaqiu continued. Tony Lake, Clinton's national security advisor, took him to the Virginia estate of heiress Pamela Harriman for talks on the future of Sino-American relations. One American participant described the meeting to the *Washington Post* as "tough talk in a nice room."

The tough talk presaged a return to another thread in the relationship: the American desire to turn China into a global power and a partner. Franklin Roosevelt had envisioned such a relationship with Chiang Kai-shek. Jimmy Carter had embraced the idea with Deng Xiaoping, but the Tiananmen crackdown had put it on hold. Now Bill Clinton sought something similar with Jiang Zemin. Having failed in its attempt to change China's behavior by first ignoring it and then dispatching the Seventh Fleet, the Clinton administration decided that the only way to transform China was by elevating it into the ranks of the great powers. The idea was to bind China in a web of international agreements and make it an international player with a seat at all the world's tables so that it would have a stake in maintaining the status quo—the global financial and economic system dominated by the United States. The two sides came up with a term for it: "strategic partnership."

As usual, the United States began by presenting China with gifts. The White House desisted from its annual attempt to get the UN Commission on Human Rights to pass a resolution censuring China. In exchange, Beijing released several prominent dissidents, including Wei Jingsheng, who went into exile. China also signed the International Covenant on Civil and Political Rights. But China's human rights situation did not improve.

The Clinton administration redoubled its efforts to convince China to halt its proliferation of weapons of mass destruction. China's behavior on that front had not advanced much since the 1980s. China had conducted a nuclear test for Pakistan in May 1990, had secretly sold Algeria a nuclear reactor with military applications, and aided North Korea's nuclear program, too. When the United States got aggressive, it sometimes bungled the job.

On July 23, 1993, the CIA alleged that a Chinese container ship, the *Yinhe*, was carrying the raw materials for the manufacture of chemical weapons and was bound for Iran. President Jiang Zemin personally assured Clinton that nothing of the kind was onboard. Nonetheless, Washington insisted on a search of the vessel when it docked in a Saudi port. Nothing was found and Jiang was furious that Clinton did not take him at his word.

Under the threat of sanctions, China modified some of its conduct. It had signed the Nuclear Non-Proliferation Treaty in 1992. But in January 1996, news reports revealed that China's National Nuclear Corporation had sold ring magnets, an essential component in the enrichment of weapons-grade uranium, to Pakistan. The US threatened to halt billions in trade. In May, Beijing announced that it had ended assistance to unsafe-guarded nuclear facilities in Pakistan and stopped its support of Iran's nuclear program. In exchange, Clinton revived the Reagan-era offer to let China buy US nuclear power technology.

The Clinton administration also continued efforts begun under presidents Reagan and Bush to help China build up an arms control infrastructure and train the people to staff it. With funds from the Ford and MacArthur Foundations, the Chinese created an export control system. The MacArthur Foundation poured $260,000 into the China Foundation for International and Strategic Studies, a think tank set up by the People's Liberation Army. The United States and China exchanged numerous secret visits of scientists from US weapons labs and their Chinese counterparts. On September 24, 1996, China signed the Comprehensive Nuclear-Test-Ban Treaty, which John F. Kennedy had once hoped would slow China's rush to build the Bomb.

When the Asian financial crisis hit in 1997, the US Treasury Department convinced China not to devalue its currency to make its exports cheaper, thus stabilizing the region. And, when India conducted a series of five nuclear tests in May 1998, the two sides coordinated their response.

The Taiwan crisis was a turning point for China just as it was for the US. For decades, American presidents had soothed China's leaders with the promise that Taiwan would be theirs. But when Beijing tried to intimidate the island, the United States had not only failed to step aside, it had dispatched the Seventh Fleet. Under orders from President Jiang Zemin, China shifted resources toward its navy, air force, and rocket forces, focusing almost exclusively on a potential war with America over Taiwan. The vision of Admiral Liu Huaqing, now a vice chairman on the Central Military Commission, had returned with a vengeance.

In 1996, the Chinese ordered the first of four Sovremenny-class destroyers from Russia. The ships came equipped with the most advanced antiship missiles in the world, designed specifically to hit aircraft carriers—America's strength. China's rocket scientists were also launched on a mission to develop a missile to take the giant vessels out of action. (During a parade to commemorate the seventieth anniversary of the end of World War II, in September 2015, China unveiled the East Wind DF-21D, the world's first antiship ballistic missile.)

American analysts were initially dismissive of China's naval expansion, authoring reports with snarky titles such as "People's War at Sea." When one former US Navy admiral was asked about the possibility that China might invade Taiwan, he predicted a "million man swim." But as the evidence mounted that the Chinese were altering both their military doctrine and their hardware, the American tone shifted to one of concern.

On proliferation and nuclear issues, China continued to be ambivalent about the idea that more atomic bombs and long-range missiles in more countries was a bad thing. The Chinese government had adopted a position that more headaches for America meant less pressure on China. One example was North Korea. In March 1993, North Korea announced its intention to pull out of the Nuclear Non-Proliferation Treaty rather than submit to inspections that would have revealed a substantial nuclear weapons program. The Pentagon argued that China, as Pyongyang's main source of electricity and coal, could squeeze the North to curtail its efforts to build a nuclear weapon. After years of American pressure, China relented, and Washington and Beijing worked together to encourage North and South Korea to meet.

But China's cooperation was ambiguous. Though it insisted that it was against the development of nuclear weapons on the Korean peninsula, Chinese officials acknowledged privately that their primary goal vis-à-vis North Korea was to ensure that the North did not collapse. China needed a buffer between itself and the pro-American South. North Korea was China's East Germany. If it fell, the party worried that China could be next.

As China's economy boomed and its self-confidence rose, the country's view of America soured again. Why did China need to listen to the United States now that it was on the verge of becoming a superpower in its own right? In 1996, a team of five Chinese journalists wrote a book called *China Can Say No*. It was an immediate hit, selling more than four hundred thousand copies in the first year. The book argued that China had been bullied long enough by the United States, and that it was time for China to just "say no." China had amassed a list of grudges against America. There was the *Yinhe* chemical weapons incident with Iran. In 1993, the US Congress had passed a resolution opposing China's bid for the 2000 Summer Olympics, leading, some argued, to China's loss to Sydney. In 1995, the US had granted Taiwan's president a visa.

China Can Say No depicted America as a morally corrupt nation on the decline. With the help of Japan and some "disgusting Chinese" in Taiwan, it charged, America was plotting to constrain China's rise. The chapter headings—"Burn Down Hollywood," "I Won't Board a Boeing 777," and "Prepare for War"—revealed a floridly emotional form of nationalism. China was standing up again, the writers declared. "It need not play second fiddle to anyone," especially the United States. Echoing a generation of party ideologues, the writers also contended that many Chinese were afflicted with a "pro-American psychological plague." In interviews, the writers acknowledged that they, too, had suffered from that disorder but had cured themselves by studying history. One of the writers had spent time in jail in the 1980s for his involvement in pro-democracy demonstrations; two others had participated in the protests around Tiananmen Square. But for them, those days were over.

China Can Say No fathered a whole genre of "Say No" literature—angry tracts with allegations as extreme as "The Record," China's nineteenth-century anti-Western screed. Communist Party organizations bought a copy of *China Can Say No* for every party member in Beijing. A sequel came out in 1997.

The collapse of the Soviet Union removed the ballast from the relationship between China and the United States. The two nations had come together to confront the Soviet threat, and successive American administrations had placed security at the center of Washington's ties with Beijing. Now that Russia was a shell of its former self, the relationship between China and America listed on a dangerous sea of distrust and competition.

President Clinton began his administration trying to marry America's centuries-old dream to change China with its centuries-old desire to profit from it. His results were mixed. His move to protect Taiwan, the one piece of China that embraced American values, resulted in a huge military buildup by the Communists. His idea of linking human rights and trade with China failed. Clinton then sold his new policy—"constructive engagement"—on the promise that it would benefit both America's businesses and consumers *and* China's prospects for freedom and democracy. This claim again inflated American expectations for China as a new century dawned.

CHAPTER FORTY-THREE

From China with Love

In 1944, Larry Wu-tai Chin, a recent graduate of the missionary-run Yenching University, landed a job as a translator with the US Army in China. At the army encampment, Chin roomed with a Chinese man named Wang Li. Under Wang's tutelage, Chin became a Communist.

Tall and bony (his classmates dubbed him "grasshopper"), Chin never looked the part of a spy. But his bespectacled demeanor hid the fact that Chin was an avowed gambler, a womanizer with a fondness for sex toys, and an enormously successful mole for the People's Republic of China. Chin's undercover work for China's Communists, from the 1950s through the 1980s, resulted in the deaths of Chinese who had collaborated with the United States and in one of China's biggest espionage coups against America.

Chin was just one of dozens the Communists directed to obtain classified information from the United States. Whether they did it for money, sex, love of country, or bragging rights, China's Communist agents, friends, and contacts were remarkably successful in penetrating the inner sanctums of the US government and US industry. To this day, Chinese spying on America has resulted in a windfall of classified information—from weapons secrets to corporate intelligence—flowing from one shore of the Pacific to the other.

At the end of World War II, Chin was transferred to Shanghai, where he worked at the US consulate, which housed numerous Communist spies. After the Communist takeover, Chin moved to Hong Kong and continued working for the US government. During the Korean War, he was part of a team of Chinese language experts—he spoke four Chinese dialects—who interviewed Chinese prisoners of war. I. C. Smith, who served as a senior counterintelligence officer at the FBI, wrote that on trips to Hong Kong, Chin supplied his Communist handlers with the names of collaborators. Once these POWs returned to China, these men were most likely shot.

From Korea, Chin was posted to a US installation on Okinawa, where he worked for the CIA's Foreign Broadcast Information Service, which monitored Chinese radio broadcasts. His superiors routinely gave him classified reports, which he passed on to his handlers in Hong Kong. In 1961, Chin moved to Santa Rosa, California, to work for the CIA. He also kept traveling to Hong Kong. In 1965, Chin became eligible for US citizenship. During a polygraph test at the CIA, Chin admitted to being a ladies' man and a gambler with domestic troubles. Those admissions, bizarrely, did not set off any alarm bells, and Chin was granted top-secret security clearance.

In the summer of 1970, Chin, now living in Virginia, proved his worth to China. He obtained a Presidential Review Memorandum outlining Richard Nixon's plans for a new relationship with China. The memo revealed the American bottom line on a range of subjects, including the sensitive issue of Taiwan. China, as Smith put it, "had penetrated the Oval Office itself." To get the document to China, Chin stuck it in his overcoat, took it home, photographed it, and returned it the next day. He brought the undeveloped film to a shopping mall in Toronto and gave it to a man named Li. From 1978 to March 1981, Chin made five trips to Canada. Each time, Chinese authorities transferred $7,000 into his Hong Kong bank account. In all, Chin received $140,000 from the Communists. It was not a massive sum, but he was motivated by other things.

In the fall of 1980, the CIA learned from a disgruntled Chinese intelligence officer that one of China's agents had been working inside the US government for years. At first, CIA officials contended that the spy could not have been at the CIA. They would be proven wrong. In 1983, a huge break in the case occurred when the FBI learned from the Chinese source that the spy had returned to the United States from China on a Pan Am flight on February 27, 1982. Checking the flight manifest, FBI agents found the name of Larry Wu-tai Chin.

Chin had retired from the CIA in July 1981. His service had been considered so exemplary that Bobby Inman, the agency's deputy director, had personally presented him with a career intelligence medal. A week after his retirement, according to the writer David Vise, Chin flew to Hong Kong and collected $40,000, his last payment from the Chinese. The FBI obtained warrants to follow Chin and tap his apartment and phone. They listened in as his wife discovered him in bed with another woman. They heard him urging a different lover to bring a "machine" to Washington. FBI officials thought the "machine" was an intelligence-gathering device. It turned out to be a vibrator. Agents discovered that Chin had set up an emergency escape route, using a Chinese agent masquerading as a Catholic priest in Manhattan's Chinatown.

Another break occurred in the spring of 1983. Chin was flying to Hong Kong from Washington, and at Dulles Airport, FBI agents secretly searched his bags. Inside, they found a key to room 833 of the Qianmen Hotel in Beijing. The Beijing source had revealed earlier that the spy had stayed in that exact room. I. C. Smith wrote that the CIA was reluctant to prosecute Chin. It would have had to admit that it had been duped for decades by a hostile intelligence service. On one occasion, Smith was so angered with the CIA's obsession with avoiding a scandal that he exclaimed, "My God, in a time of war, Chin would be executed for treason! He's responsible for the death of your own people!" Ultimately, the CIA agreed to a prosecution. But first, they needed to get their source out of Beijing.

By the fall of 1985, the CIA source, subsequently identified as Yu Qiangsheng, the adopted son of a former Chinese security chief, had arrived in the United States and been given a new identity. On November 22, 1985, three FBI agents went to Larry Chin's apartment in Alexandria, Virginia. There they presented him with evidence of his espionage, including the name of his Chinese handler and the room where he had stayed in the Qianmen Hotel. Chin confessed and was arrested that night. Three months later, he was convicted after a four-day trial on charges of spying and conspiracy. In court, he claimed that he was only trying to better ties between the United States and China. "When I think about what I accomplished—the improvement of the livelihood of one billion Chinese people—my imprisonment for life is a very small price to pay," he said. "It was worth it." On February 21, 1986, after an early-morning breakfast, Chin put a plastic garbage bag around his head, tied a shoelace around his neck, and died of suffocation.

The case of Larry Wu-tai Chin was only the first in an avalanche of American intelligence failures and scandals involving Chinese espionage in the United States. No sooner had the CIA got this black eye than the FBI followed it into the ring. In the summer of 1983, an FBI counterintelligence officer named J. J. Smith started a sexual relationship with a Chinese woman named Katrina Leung. Smith (no relation to his colleague I. C.) had convinced Leung to work for the FBI and aid its efforts to battle Chinese intelligence operations in the United States. Unbeknownst to Smith, however, Leung would begin two-timing the FBI, funneling information to the Chinese Ministry of State Security.

In a book on Chinese intelligence operations, writer David Vise revealed that Leung tipped the Chinese off to an FBI operation at the Chinese Consulate in Los Angeles. Intelligence officials also believe that she exposed a US plan to bug a Boeing 737 that was being refurbished for Chinese president Jiang Zemin.

Leung didn't just two-time the FBI; she two-timed Smith, bedding down with another senior FBI agent, William Cleveland, who ran counterintelligence work in San Francisco. In all, the FBI paid Leung $1.7 million for her services.

Born in Guangzhou and brought up in Hong Kong, Leung moved to America in 1970 as a teenager, attended high school in New York, and won a scholarship to Cornell University. Like many Chinese of her generation, she had her political awakening in the late 1970s during the movement to protect the Diaoyus. Leung moved from Cornell to the University of Chicago, where she earned a business degree. In Chicago, she began meeting with intelligence officials from the PRC. She married a Cornell classmate, and when he took a job as a biochemist in Los Angeles, Leung went to work for a trading house there. She came to the FBI's attention when the bureau began to investigate the firm for illegally exporting military-related technology to China.

Leung brought back reams of gossip about the internal machinations of the Chinese Communist Party. To a government starved for information about intrigue behind the walls of party headquarters at Zhongnanhai, Leung's inside track seemed priceless. In 1999, the CIA gave J. J. Smith the Exceptional Human Intelligence Collector Award. Some, however, questioned Leung's information. I. C. Smith, then working at FBI headquarters, believed that Leung's rumors about the sexual proclivities of Chinese leaders did not amount to real intelligence, "Dammit, J. J.," I. C. Smith said at one point, "where's the fucking beef?"

The FBI ignored signs that it was being taken for a ride. When Leung was taped briefing her PRC handler about the FBI's counterintelligence operations, J. J. Smith and Cleveland convinced the FBI to keep her on the payroll. When the bureau finally did investigate, the men leading the probe were on chummy terms with J. J. and Cleveland.

Finally, the FBI assigned independent-minded investigators to the case and in 2004 they broke it open. Initially, J. J. Smith, who had retired in 2000, denied that he had been Leung's lover, until the FBI showed him a video of them in a hotel room. In a low-key statement on May 12, 2004, the FBI said that Smith had been allowed to plead guilty to a single count of making false statements. He received three years' probation and was fined $10,000 although he kept his pension. Cleveland was neither prosecuted nor punished.

Under the deal with the FBI, J. J. Smith was banned from providing any information to Leung's defense, so the espionage case against Leung collapsed. Leung's lawyers negotiated a plea on related income tax issues. Like her lover, J. J. Smith, Leung was sentenced to three years' probation and fined $10,000.

Hewing to the stereotypes about Chinese women that had lingered since the days of the nineteenth-century courtesan Ah Toy in San Francisco, the media cast Leung as a "dragon lady" and a seductress. *Frontline* called its documentary on the case "From China with Love." Still, the FBI—and the rest of the US government—wasn't done bungling China cases.

In early 1995, a Chinese man walked into the US embassy in Thailand, claimed to be an official in China's nuclear weapons program, and handed over a duffel bag of documents to his befuddled American hosts. Among the files was a Chinese government memorandum describing the miniaturized W88 warhead that sits atop the ballistic missiles in the US Navy's Trident submarine. At the time, the W88 was the most advanced weapon in the US strategic arsenal, what writer David Vise called "the crown jewel" of America's nuclear deterrent.

The revelation that China had obtained the W88 touched off a massive investigation to determine the source of the leak. It was never found. The FBI and the Department of Energy fixated on one man as the sole possible suspect, excluding other promising leads. The CIA and the FBI clashed over whether the Chinese source was reliable; the CIA thought he was a double agent; the FBI disagreed. And after three years, the probe collapsed amid charges of prosecutorial misconduct and allegations that the US government was guilty of ethnic profiling. As in the McCarthy era, Americans once again allowed their emotions to get in the way of an understanding of the challenge China presented to the United States.

In May 1996, the FBI began to focus on Wen Ho Lee, a Taiwanese-born computer scientist who worked at Los Alamos National Laboratory in the weapons design department, as the source of the W88 leak. The FBI had reason to suspect Lee. He had appeared on the bureau's radar in the early 1980s when he was taped offering to help another Chinese researcher find out why the government was investigating him for leaking secrets to China. Also, twice in the 1980s, Lee had visited China, where he had met with leading Chinese nuclear weapons designers, but he had neglected to inform US lab authorities about the meetings. When one of those designers, Hu Side, came to Los Alamos on a visit in 1994, he embraced Lee, touching off another probe. Lee then informed investigators that Hu had asked him for classified information about the W88.

As pressure mounted within the FBI and the Department of Energy to find the source of the leak, Lee became the sole suspect. As a subsequent report by the attorney general's office put it, instead of trying to figure out how China got the W88, the FBI zeroed in on Lee and his wife, Sylvia. "The FBI," the report said, "investigated the wrong crime." Not only that, but when it came to Lee, the FBI botched the probe. In the summer of 1998, an FBI officer masquerading as a Chinese official tried to meet Lee. Unfortunately, the agent spoke with Lee in Cantonese, not Mandarin, the official language of the PRC, and Lee, naturally, didn't take the bait.

At the time of the Lee investigation, the prevailing American attitude toward China was one of growing unease. Throughout the 1990s, more than half of those participating in annual Gallup polls said that they had an unfavorable impression of the PRC. In the 1980s, Japan's economy had been America's greatest challenge. When Detroit autoworkers beat Chinese American Vincent Chin to death in June 1982, they thought he was Japanese. But, in the 1990s, China, with its annual double-digit growth and its brusque indifference to American pressure on human rights, elbowed out Japan as a concern. In the minds of many Americans, China combined the nastiest aspects of Soviet Communism with Japan's cutthroat competition. Thousands of Americans lost their jobs as US manufacturers moved production to China, now touted as "the factory of the world."

The biggest China book in a generation appeared in 1991. Jung Chang's *Wild Swans* told the story of three generations of Chinese women and detailed the human toll of the Communist regime. *Wild Swans* arrived as Americans were looking for an approach to help them make sense of China's troubling complexities, and the book reinforced a growing apprehension about the Chinese system. Translated into thirty languages, it sold ten million copies worldwide.

As the decade progressed, Americans saw China doing things that unsettled them, not just in China, but in America as well. Starting in

September 1996, the American press began reporting on a series of dubious campaign donations to the Clinton reelection campaign. On February 13, 1997, the *Washington Post* revealed that the Justice Department was investigating whether the Chinese government was involved. Taking a cue from Taiwan's old China Lobby, the People's Republic of China appeared to be behind efforts to influence domestic American politics.

Paraded before the American public was a cast of characters that included restaurateur Charlie Trie, fund-raiser John Huang, businessman Johnny Chung, immigration consultant Maria Hsia, entrepreneur Ted Sioeng, and more. Congress and the Justice Department undertook investigations and Trie, Huang, Chung, and Hsia were convicted or pleaded guilty to fund-raising–related crimes. The FBI obtained a copy of a check from the Chinese consulate in Los Angeles for $3,000 to a hotel owned by Sioeng. A Senate committee report noted that half of the $400,000 Sioeng gave to the Democratic Party was "funded by transfer from overseas accounts," implying that it could have come from China. Sioeng subsequently left the United States and was not charged.

In testimony before Congress, Johnny Chung spoke of meeting the chief of China's military intelligence department, whom he quoted as saying, "We really like your president." The general gave Chung $300,000, Chung acknowledged. He told Congress, however, that he had spent most of it on himself. The backdrop to all this—a rising China and tensions over Taiwan—combined to make the Democratic Party's fundraising scandal the international counterpart of the Monica Lewinsky affair, which was already roiling Bill Clinton's presidency.

The American press goosed the campaign finance story for all it was worth. In its March 1997 issue, the *National Review* depicted President Clinton, First Lady Hillary Clinton, and Vice President Al Gore on its front cover decked out in Chinese garb, with ear-to-ear grins, buckteeth, and slanted eyes. "The Manchurian Candidates," the headline read. Critics charged the magazine with racism. The *Review* was unrepentant. Cartoons "required exaggerated features," its editor said.

American pundits and China experts grappled with a country that was changing at lightning speed but not in the direction Americans had assumed it would take. China's combination of authoritarian rule and market-oriented reforms could not possibly succeed, many said. "The Communist dynasty is collapsing in China," declared *New York Times* Pulitzer winner Nicholas Kristof in the pages of the *New York Review of*

Books on June 24, 1994. Others predicted not only disarray but a war with the United States. *The Coming Conflict with China*, written by journalists Richard Bernstein and Ross H. Munro in 1997, summed up the fear that trade and cultural relations with China had failed to make it friendlier to America. China looked more like a rival, and America's chief rival at that. Even Richard Nixon, who after Tiananmen had lobbied to keep channels open to Beijing, expressed reservations about how his opening to China was playing out. As he told the *New York Times* not long before his death in 1994, "We may have created a Frankenstein."

In Washington, a group of think tank fellows, political operatives, conservative journalists, lobbyists for Taiwan, former intelligence officers, and academics coalesced around efforts to oppose the Clinton administration's attempts at "constructive engagement." William Triplett, a Republican Senate aide and writer, dubbed the group the Blue Team, taken from the Communist term for the bad guys in Chinese war games. It wasn't simply China's double-digit growth rate that sparked alarm. China's defense budget had grown by double digits as well. China was preparing for war with America, but the United States was asleep at the switch, the story went. Accusations hurled in Congress by politicians looking to capitalize on the shifting mood detached the debate from its factual moorings. In May 1997, House minority leader and presidential hopeful Richard Gephardt, a Democrat from Missouri, alleged that China's export boom to the United States was driven solely by slave labor using Chinese prisoners. The Blue Team successfully blocked the sale of Unocal, an American oil company, to a Chinese oil company, despite the lack of any evidence that the sale would have harmed US security. The team got Congress to pass a law banning NASA from cooperating with the Chinese on space projects. It cried foul when Panama contracted with a Hong Kong–based company to widen the Panama Canal. When a Chinese shipping company announced a plan to lease a decommissioned naval base in Long Beach, California, it wasn't understood as a business decision but as an alleged plot to snoop on the United States. The shipping company chose Boston instead.

In 1997, details emerged about the loss of military technology to China. A year earlier, a Chinese rocket carrying an American satellite had crashed. American firms were suspected of giving the Chinese classified tips on how to improve their launches. Such information would also help the Chinese improve the accuracy of their missiles. Spurred by the Blue Team, Congress created a special committee to look into Chinese espionage.

Chaired by Christopher Cox, a California Republican, the committee released an unclassified version of its report in April 1999.

The report was riddled with exaggeration. It claimed that China's intelligence agencies had established three thousand front companies in the United States when the actual number was around thirty. It charged that China possessed nuclear secrets "on a par with our own" and painted a nightmare scenario of the PRC churning out miniature warheads to counter the United States. Like the 1950s McCarthy-era allegations of "Reds under the bed," these overblown accusations obscured understanding of what China had done in the United States.

By this time, Wen Ho Lee found himself living in the middle of a media hurricane. TV vans were parked outside his home. The *New York Times* and other papers fingered him as a Chinese spy. FBI agents had taken him to a Los Alamos hotel and threatened him with capital punishment, drawing a dark parallel between his case and that of Julius and Ethel Rosenberg, who were executed for espionage in 1953. Many Asian Americans cried foul. The Dr. Wen Ho Lee Defense Fund alleged that all of the charges were "baseless." Lee, the fund claimed, was "unfairly scapegoated because of his Chinese descent." Republicans alleged that the Clinton administration had brought the case because it was desperate to find a fall guy to blame for its criminally lax security. Investigators discovered that Lee had downloaded hundreds of megabytes' worth of secret information on the US nuclear weapons programs. Lee also admitted to misleading federal investigators about the meetings he had held with Chinese nuclear weapons researchers.

On December 10, 1999, the federal government indicted Lee on fifty-nine counts of mishandling defense information, and a federal judge denied him bail. Trial was set for November 2000. Lee would be held in solitary confinement for 278 days.

As soon as Lee was indicted, the government's case began to unravel. One FBI official admitted to giving false testimony. Two government prosecutors quit the case, one over reports of an affair with a woman on his staff, the other to run for office. On September 10, 2000, the prosecution and the defense reached a plea agreement under which Lee pleaded guilty to one felony count of mishandling nuclear secrets and was sentenced to time served. US district judge James Parker blasted Attorney General Janet Reno, Energy Secretary Bill Richardson, and senior officials in the Clinton administration for the questionable indictment and the "demeaning and terribly punitive" conditions under which Lee had been held. Lee sued the

US government and five news organizations for improperly leaking his personal information. In 2006, he won a $1.6 million settlement, of which the federal government paid more than half.

All but forgotten was the central question: How did China obtain information on the W88? An FBI team later determined that the leak could have come from a variety of sources—the Department of Energy, the Pentagon, contractors, even Britain, which deployed the W88 on its nuclear submarines. But, by then, the leads had grown cold.

By the early 1990s, China's intelligence collection in the US had expanded far beyond *Spy vs. Spy* subterfuge to include industrial and trade secrets, inventions and technology, the pilfering of which threatened American competitiveness and prosperity. The Chinese government also established elaborate rules to force foreign corporations interested in investing in strategic sectors of China's economy—such as computer chip manufacturing, automobiles, railways, and aerospace—to share their technological secrets with China in exchange for a chance to sell into the Chinese market. In the United States, Chinese companies, employing Chinese students, scholars, businessmen, immigrants, and spies, along with non-Chinese Americans, searched for a vast array of technologies needed to improve China's economy.

To be sure, the Chinese miracle—the sky-high growth rates, hundreds of millions of people lifted out of poverty, and a revamped military— involved many factors: better policies, the hard work of the Chinese, and a demographic sweet spot that swelled the ranks of the Chinese labor force at the right time. But cheap and unrestricted access to Western, particularly American, technology played a key role, too.

From 1998, China was the principal destination for illegal technology exports from the West Coast. Those technologies ran the gamut from paint formulas, to Ford Motor Company documents, to cellular phone technology, details on oil and gas field bids, and information on organic light-emitting diodes.

Rather than take a final exam at Stanford University in the late 1980s, Brett Kingstone made a light illuminated by fiber optic cables. From there, he went on to found a company, Super Vision International, and to write a guide on student entrepreneurship. In the mid-1990s Kingstone seemed to be coasting to a life of unparalleled wealth. Super Vision's clients included Universal Studios, Disney, and Coca-Cola. But a Chinese engineer stole Super Vision's technology and opened a competing firm, which flooded the market with counterfeits. Kingstone hired private investigators, who purchased Super Vision knockoffs in Shanghai. In 2003, Super Vision won a $41.2 million judgment against its Chinese competitors in a US court. But Kingstone never collected. The Chinese rival had liquidated his assets in America and returned home. Super Vision has limped on ever since.

Kingstone was just one of many American victims of China's way of doing business. In a 2013 book, William C. Hannas, James Mulvenon, and Anna B. Puglisi described China's industrial espionage as a vast operation devoted to identifying foreign technologies, acquiring them by any means possible, and converting them into weapons or competitive goods. There is, they wrote, "nothing like it anywhere else in the world." The writers described China's motives as twofold. On one level, in its desperation to catch up with America, China felt compelled to do anything to get its hands on American technology. But just as important, they wrote, China's government opted to spy because the Communist Party feared the political ramifications of a society where American-style innovation could flourish.

The Clinton administration tried to hold the consensus for engagement together, and despite a long list of problems, the two countries exchanged summits in 1997 and 1998. For the Chinese, President Jiang Zemin's trip to the United States in October 1997 represented the last mile in its diplomatic marathon to expunge the stain of the Tiananmen Square crackdown. Jiang was the first top Chinese leader to visit Washington after the massacre, and from the start the Chinese were intent on fostering a perception of their nation as America's equal. The Chinese obsessed over protocol and symbols, including the size and color of the carpets, Jiang's positioning in photographs of the Liberty Bell in Philadelphia and Harvard's Veritas emblem. They even interrogated the White House about the color of Clinton's tie. The purpose of the trip was to bolster Jiang's image as a statesman and a modern-minded leader.

Some Americans were eager to give the Chinese a hand. An American professor at Harvard University who was angling to gain access to Chinese officials for a book project, censored student questions on human rights. In the rare moments when an uncomfortable query did make it over the Great Wall of big business and geostrategy cosseting the Chinese leader, Jiang answered patiently, the New York Times reported, "as if to slow-witted students who do not understand the complexities of his country."

In his memoirs, Clinton indicated that the two had a freewheeling debate during a private meeting about "how much change and freedom China could accommodate without risking internal chaos." After the discussion, Clinton wrote, "I went to bed thinking that China would be forced by the imperatives of modern society to become more open."

Eight months later, Clinton visited China, starting on June 25, 1998, with an honor guard facing Tiananmen Square. Again the Chinese focused on the atmospherics. China leaned on the White House to ensure that Clinton would not visit Japan en route and that he would stay in China longer than Nixon's historic weeklong trip in 1972. As then premier Zhu Rongji told the party faithful in a speech reported by Hong Kong media after Clinton departed, it was a good thing that Clinton "made no stop-over in Japan on his way to China . . . with the result that Japan has lost face."

In Beijing, the two presidents held a press conference that aired live on Chinese TV. It turned into a polite but spirited debate over human rights and religious liberty. Clinton urged Jiang to negotiate with the exiled Tibetan ruler, the Dalai Lama, and predicted that if they met "they would like each other very much." In his memoirs, Clinton wrote that he wanted to use the press conference to prove to Chinese officials that "greater open-ness wouldn't cause social disintegration." The Americans were pleased with the exchange; the Chinese would never consent to anything like it again.

In the intensifying intelligence competition with China, it often appeared that the United States was dealt a losing hand. But there were coups. From 1990 to 1999, Danny Stillman, director of the technical intelligence division at Los Alamos, took nine trips to nuclear weapons installations in western China that no American had been to before. The Chinese begged him for information on how to secure their weapons and how to maintain their nuclear stocks now that China had agreed to sign the Comprehensive Nuclear Test Ban Treaty.

Throughout his journey to the mountains of Sichuan and to the Lop Nur Nuclear Weapons Test Base in northwestern China, where a midnight barbecue reminded him of a Los Alamos cookout, Stillman ran into elderly scientists who had studied in America during the Second World War. Many of their children were now studying in America as well. Everywhere, Stillman found young Chinese scientists translating American documents and eager for the slightest smidgen of intelligence about America's nuclear arsenal.

Stillman amassed a list of all of China's top nuclear weapons scientists, putting names and faces to the physicists who had brought China into the nuclear age. The Chinese told Stillman the story of how they built the Bomb. The crown jewel, however, was a list of all of China's nuclear weapons tests. This list and other intelligence that Stillman gleaned from his visits confirmed Washington's suspicions. China had proliferated nuclear weapons technology to Pakistan in the 1980s; it had tested a nuclear device for Pakistan and even one for France after Paris had signed the comprehensive Test Ban Treaty. When Stillman and Thomas C. Reed, a former secretary of the Air Force, collaborated on a book, *The Nuclear Express: A Political History of the Bomb and Its Proliferation*, the Chinese pleaded with them not to include one page: the list of the tests. They published it anyway.

At the beginning of the new millennium, the Chinese Communist Party found itself caught in a bind. It understood that it could no longer rely on cheap labor to fuel economic growth; it required innovation. But that meant allowing people to think freely. In 1881, the *New York Times* had predicted that "China cannot borrow our learning, our science, and our material forms of industry without importing with them the virus of political rebellion." The Chinese Communist Party understood that challenge and tried to use espionage to avoid the challenge of a free society.

Americans reacted to the espionage slowly because at heart they were confident that China would evolve into a society like their own. This confidence led the US government and American business, as the nuclear physicist Gordon Prather put it in a report released in July 1999, to pursue a "reckless policy" of unprecedented "openness" with China. Prather was speaking about nuclear weapons and the rapturous enthusiasm that accompanied America's engagement with China in that field. But it held true for business and other areas as well. As the twenty-first century dawned, some Americans began to wonder whether their openness with China had been a mistake.

●

CHAPTER FORTY-FOUR

Welcome to the Club

On May 7, 1999, five American precision-guided bombs slammed into the embassy of the People's Republic of China in Belgrade, Serbia. The attack, at the height of the NATO assault on Serbian president Slobodan Milošević, left three Chinese reporters dead and twenty-three embassy staff members injured.

For the Chinese Communist Party, the bombing of the Belgrade embassy, though tragic, was a godsend. For years, the party had alleged that the United States was intent on keeping China down. Now, it had been handed proof of America's master plan against Beijing. The timing was also impeccable. The tenth anniversary of the Tiananmen Square crackdown was approaching. Although the party had worked hard to expunge any historical memory of the incident, the bombing helped to divert any residual anger onto the United States.

In the early morning hours of May 8, the Standing Committee of the Politburo, China's most powerful decision-making body, gathered in an emergency meeting. The attack would be used, the Politburo ruled, "to enlighten the broad masses" about America's plots. Across the country, the party organized anti-American demonstrations. In Beijing, thousands of Chinese pelted the US embassy with rocks, turning Clinton's ambassador, James Sasser, into a hostage in his own office. In Chengdu, protesters burned down the consul general's residence.

Official American apologies came fast and furious. Secretary of Defense

William Cohen and CIA director George Tenet issued a joint statement, calling the bombing an error. President Clinton admitted to a "tragic mistake" and extended his "regrets and profound condolences" to the Chinese. Clinton tried to call party secretary Jiang Zemin over a hotline, but Jiang would not take his calls. Clinton would apologize five times.

No one in China believed the bombing was an accident. From the top of the party to society's bottom rung, the Chinese had such a deep respect for American technology that they found it impossible to accept that the United States could make such a mistake. During the Politburo meeting on May 8, Li Peng, who ranked number two in the party hierarchy, told his comrades that the attack was "a carefully crafted plot of subversion," according to minutes of the meeting published in a Chinese book, titled *Zhu Rongji zai 1999*. The incident, he warned his comrades, "reminds us that the United States is an enemy." The *People's Daily*, reflecting the Politburo's sentiments, ran a front-page editorial, declaring that "enemy forces in the West" could no longer tolerate China's achievements.

Everything American became a target. America's free press was controlled by cartels and warmongers; its actions in Serbia were triggered by arms merchants; its Hollywood culture glorified violence. Some Chinese made fun of the protesters, pointing out that once American consular officers returned to work, the demonstrators would be first in line for visas. Still, the outpouring of anger and disenchantment was sincere.

Two of the victims of the bombing were reporters for the *Guangming Daily*. The paper created a webpage and posted 281 condolence letters, poems, e-mails, and songs. Taken together, observed the historian Peter Gries, the notes revealed a sense that America had again failed China. "Another dream has been shattered," went one letter, "it was my American dream." America had been "a teacher and a friend," went another, now it was "a scoundrel and a cheat." Some urged a boycott on American goods. (It never happened.) On May 12, the *People's Daily* declared that "the age when people can barge about the world in gunboats" is over. "The wheel of history," the essay claimed, "will not go backward." But in a way, it had.

By stressing the personal nature of the disappointment with the United States, China's state-run media mirrored the campaigns of the early 1950s, when such anti-American testimonials were used to solidify party control. It remained state policy to highlight disenchantment with the United States. Jiang Zemin called the party-sanctioned demonstrations a sign of "great patriotism and cohesiveness."

At the same time, the party remained faithful to the opposing idea that the United States was still necessary to make China strong. So, while one side of the party fanned anti-American fervor, the other reassured American businesses. During the height of the demonstrations, Shanghai mayor Xu Kuangdi stopped by General Motors' $1.5 billion plant in Shanghai and told the American managers to "relax." A vice mayor met with executives from leading US banks and stressed that they were welcome in China. "The bombing is one thing," a Shanghai foreign trade official told the *New York Times*. "Foreign investment is another." A week after the attack, the party was ready to call off the protests, and by May 13, the crowds in front of the US diplomatic installations had dwindled to gawkers and passersby. On May 14, Jiang finally took President Clinton's call, and Clinton apologized again.

While China's Communist Party was encouraging widespread paranoia about the United States in the early 1990s, the US government and Wall Street wizards were laying the groundwork for the Middle Kingdom's remarkable economic takeoff. By the end of the decade, Washington would usher China into the World Trade Organization, triggering a jump in China's trade. Simultaneously, an army of American investment bankers, lawyers, and accountants would open the vaults of global capital to China's state-owned enterprises, creating a string of near monopolies and pouring tens of billions of dollars into the accounts of the Communist Party and its ruling families. These two endeavors fortified the party's rule and made its leading families rich beyond dreams of avarice.

China's government has never publicly acknowledged the US role in either of these enterprises. But internally, China's leaders, at least those at the time, understood that American ideas and capital rescued the state-run sector of their economy. In a 1993 speech, Premier Zhu Rongji told Communist cadres that now that American investment banks were going to invest in China, China's economy would be forever changed.

In 1993, President Clinton appointed Charlene Barshefsky, a straight-shooting international lawyer from Chicago, as his deputy trade representative. Barshefsky took on the office's biggest challenge, the China portfolio. Trade between the US and China was booming. But the Chinese seemed to be cheating American companies at every turn. Chinese firms were churning out fake foreign brands. A whole street of shops called Silk Alley opened up in Beijing selling little else but knockoff North Face jackets and Nike shoes. Within weeks of a Hollywood movie's release, pirated versions, sometimes shot with handheld recorders in an American theater, would surface on Beijing street corners. US software was ubiquitous on Chinese computers, and it was all ripped off.

Reams of internal regulations, protected by state-security provisions, blocked foreign firms from access to China's market. And when foreign firms did set up shop in China, the Chinese exacted a heavy price: the companies had to share their technology with a Chinese subsidiary, which more often than not established its own company to compete directly with the Western firm.

Still, America's leverage over China was considerable. China's economic growth was critically dependent on the American consumers, who snapped up one-third of China's exports each year. In addition, the United States had tools to force China to pay attention. If the United States believed that China was not serious about implementing trade agreements, it could slap punitive sanctions on Chinese goods.

In 1995, Barshefsky threatened to close America's markets to many Chinese products unless China cracked down on its pirating industry. By February, the Chinese government had agreed to provide a measure of protection for intellectual property. But, when Chinese officials in Beijing told Barshefsky that they could not control what happened elsewhere in China, she hit the road. Her first stop was Guangdong province in the south, one of the centers of the DVD trade. There she threatened sanctions against Guangdong's vast textile industry if the DVD pirating didn't stop. In the midst of her crusade, the Chinese offered Barshefsky a meeting with President Jiang Zemin with the tacit understanding that she would back off. Barshefsky shocked the China Hands in the Clinton administration by declining the meeting. Subsequently, some of the DVD factories were closed.

Barshefsky understood that a stick was only useful when it came with carrots. She embarked on a campaign to convince her Chinese interlocutors that if China pirated less and reformed its economy more, it could enter the World Trade Organization. She found allies: Long Yongtu, the head of the International Relations Department at the Ministry of Foreign Economic Relations and Trade and a graduate of the London School of Economics, and his sometime boss, Wu Yi, known as "the iron lady of China." Premier Li Peng and his successor, Zhu Rongji, also backed China's entry into the WTO, seeing it as a way to use foreign-imposed standards to save China's state-owned firms and further boost exports.

Barshefsky's argument was a compelling one. China had done well modeling itself on nineteenth-century America, Great Britain, and mid-twentieth-century Taiwan and Japan, all of which had become economic powers by protecting infant industries against imports, blocking the export of raw materials, and lavishing subsidies on key sectors of the economy. But now, she contended, to become a world power, China needed to move beyond mercantilism, as the United States had done after the Second World War.

Barshefsky's reasoning made sense to Zhu Rongji, who had been engaged since the early 1990s in reforming the state-run sector of the economy. Westerners looked at Zhu Rongji as a Gorbachev-type figure, someone who sought to yank China into the Western world. In reality, Zhu shared more with the legendary banker K. P. Chen and his belief in the bracing tonic of Western competition for Chinese firms. In the way that hatred of the United States was a key pillar of the party's ideology, competition with America had become a mainstay of its economy.

In April 1999, Zhu Rongji traveled to the United States for what he thought would be the final negotiations to seal China's entry into the WTO. China had been trying to get into the international trade body since 1986, when it was called the General Agreement on Tariffs and Trade. Now accession appeared close. As Zhu told reporters in March 1999, "Black hair has turned white, it is time to conclude the negotiations." He came to America with China's latest, best offer. For Clinton, the timing of Zhu's trip could not have been worse. Congress had just released the Cox Report accusing China of stealing US nuclear secrets. The Senate had recently rejected impeachment charges drawn up by the House over Clinton's affair with White House intern Monica Lewinsky. Indictments were being prepared against the hustlers who had funneled money into the Clinton campaign—a portion came from the Chinese government. In his first meeting with Zhu, Clinton asked if the deal could wait. Zhu said it could.

What came next, however, enraged the Chinese premier. On April 8, the US Trade Representative's office released details of China's new offer in an attempt to ensure that China would not backslide later on. In America, business leaders were aghast that the president had passed on such a good deal. Anger roiled Chinese ministries and state-owned industries for just the opposite reason. How could China have given so much to the Beautiful Country? In online chat rooms back home, Zhu was labeled a traitor.

On April 14, Clinton called Zhu at New York's Waldorf Astoria Hotel suggesting that the deal be signed. Zhu demurred. "This is the most arrogant and high-handed imposition," Zhu told his colleagues, according to the book *Zhu Rongji zai 1999*. "The Americans look down on us. This is politics, not child's play." Clinton's feckless handling of the incident was another case in America's long tradition of bungling its relations with China. A month later, the US bombed the Chinese embassy in Belgrade and talks were put on hold.

In November 1999, negotiations resumed, and Barshefsky returned to Beijing. Now she was the US Trade Representative herself. The deal China presented was substantially worse than Zhu Rongji's April offer, and Barshefsky, who had urged Clinton to sign then, was left with the difficult job of salvaging a pact. In Beijing, a handful of American and Chinese men and women made history. Meeting in the middle of the night, in locations such as the women's bathroom of the Ministry of Foreign Economic Relations and Trade, yelling at their own countrymen within earshot of the other side, the two parties reached an agreement. At one point, the Chinese locked the Americans inside the ministry to prevent them from leaving. At another, Barshefsky had already sent her luggage to the airport when Zhu Rongji emerged with a stack of papers and a pen, ready to sign.

On November 15, 1999, the two countries took a huge step toward completing China's reintegration into the global economy. The dream of open access to trade with China that had begun with John Ledyard and Robert Morris soon after the American Revolution, was nurtured by the Delanos and the Howquas in the foreign ghetto of Guangzhou, persisted in the early twentieth century with the vision of the Open Door, and reemerged with Richard Nixon in the 1970s, finally bore fruit in Beijing weeks before the new century. For more than a hundred years, America had sought to pull China into the world, and China had dreamed of becoming rich and strong. WTO membership held out the promise of achieving both goals at once.

To sell the deal to the American people, the Clinton administration again intertwined America's two main threads in dealing with China: the desire to keep it whole and the dream of transforming it into an Asian America. The president predicted that accession to the WTO would exert "a profound impact on human rights and liberty" in China. Barshefsky was not wrong when she told Congress on May 3, 2000, that the deal was "one of the most important trade and foreign policy decisions the United States has made in many years." But she then claimed that it would "promote the rule of law in many fields now dominated by state power and control." Robert Rubin, Clinton's former secretary of the treasury, assured Congress that China's WTO accession would "sow the seeds of freedom for

China's 1.2 billion citizens." In late May, Congress approved the deal. Back in China, Zhu Rongji was aware of the American belief that freer trade meant a freer China. "Western hostile forces are continuing to promote their strategy of Westernizing and breaking up our country," he warned provincial officials in a speech.

Entry into the WTO was a boon to China's exports, but Premier Zhu Rongji also needed help reforming China's lumbering state-controlled sector. After all, the state-owned economy was the main source of income for the Communist Party. Without it, the party risked withering away.

Zhu accepted the suggestion of the chief executive of the Hong Kong Stock Exchange that China grant a select group of state-owned enterprises the right to list on overseas stock markets. As with the WTO, Zhu hoped that Western rules, shareholder participation, foreign competition, and capital would transform Chinese state-owned firms into competitive enterprises.

On October 7, 1992, a company that manufactured minibuses—so small that the Chinese called them "bread boxes"—became the first Chinese firm to list on a foreign stock exchange. Brilliance China Automotive chose the New York Stock Exchange for its $80 million listing. It was wildly oversubscribed. But Brilliance's IPO, one of a handful in the early 1990s, flopped. The firm was technically bankrupt at the time, and its owner, dogged by allegations of financial mismanagement, would flee China for the United States. But at root, Brilliance China's problem was that it was too small.

For four decades, Chairman Mao had kept China on a wartime footing; every province, even every county, had all the businesses it needed, from breweries to brickworks, so that, if one part of China were to fall under foreign occupation, other parts would survive. But when Deng Xiaoping's reforms began in the 1980s, China's state-owned sector consisted of too many companies doing the same thing.

That's where the Americans came in. In 1991, Henry Paulson, then the cochief of the investment banking wing of Goldman Sachs, visited China for the first time. Like Jack Perkowski, Paulson was a star Ivy League lineman who had evolved into a Wall Street honcho. Paulson had a simple idea, one that would end up changing China forever, saving its moribund state-run sector and arguably the Communist Party to boot. Why not use the listings of China's state-owned companies to create international powerhouses? The process would force some companies to merge and create Chinese firms that for the first time would have the reach and revenue to compete on a global scale.

Over the next several years, Paulson and his rivals at Morgan Stanley and other investment banks would marry American financial expertise with the dream of the China market to create a multibillion-dollar windfall for the party. Between 1993 and 2010, Chinese state-owned firms raised $389 billion on domestic exchanges and a further $262 billion on the international market. This was big money no matter how you cut it.

During China's war with Japan in the 1930s, the American government had provided the Kuomintang with what Ambassador Hu Shih had called "life-saving injections." In the 1990s, Wall Street did the same for the Communist Party. Without Wall Street's cash, China's state-owned behemoths would have collapsed. As Fraser Howie and Carl Walter, two investment bankers, concluded in a 2012 book, "Goldman Sachs and Morgan Stanley made China's state-owned corporate sector what it is today."

Paulson framed the role that he and other Westerners played in mythological terms. "Western bankers," he wrote, "were Promethean figures in this process: we jetted in and competed to show the Chinese how to kindle the fire of capital markets." Americans convinced themselves that they were teaching the Chinese how to become modern. "Much of what we did in China in those early days was educational," Paulson wrote. "We might as well have been running a school—indeed, at times it felt as though we were." Paulson and others interpreted Zhu's moves as a way to privatize China's economy. But actually Zhu's goal was to save the state-owned sector so that it could remain the economic pillar of one-party rule. American investment bankers, reaping large profits (in one deal, Goldman is believed to have made $200 million), were more than happy to help him along, although they were perhaps unaware of the consequences.

Paulson convinced Zhu to start the experiment with China's phone companies. At the time, the Chinese phone system was a patchwork of provincial monopolies run out of government bureaus. Goldman Sachs lobbied Zhu to create a national telephone company. Under Goldman's watch, China consolidated what had been fragmented assets into a single firm, called China Mobile. Then Goldman Sachs sold the idea of investing in China Mobile to Wall Street.

China Mobile was a paper company. It had never done a day's worth of business. And yet America and the rest of the investing world loved it. It was the China Dream of the nineteenth century repurposed as a 1990s Wall Street play. At the height of the Asian financial crisis, in October 1997, China

Mobile went public on the New York and Hong Kong Stock Exchanges. It was a roaring success, raising $4.5 billion, dwarfing the listings of the overseas Chinese companies that had preceded it. Following China Mobile, Zhu engineered dozens of similar operations, cobbling together far-flung government assets to transform them into profit-oriented state companies. China listed five state-owned banks, three major oil companies, its state electrical grid, and insurance firms.

Today, China Mobile is the largest mobile phone operator in the world, with over eight hundred million subscribers. Thanks to Western financial guidance, forty-four Chinese companies landed on *Fortune*'s list of the top five hundred firms. The advice of Paulson and a battalion of investment bankers like him laid the foundation for the new New China, where the families of party leaders—such as Zhu's, a premier named Wen Jiabao, and presidents Jiang Zemin and Xi Jinping—became fabulously wealthy thanks to overseas listings. As Frasier and Walter observed in 2012, "The New China of the twenty-first century is a creation of the Goldman Sachs and Linklaters & Paines of the world, just as surely as the Cultural Revolution flowed from Chairman Mao's Little Red Book." In other words, China Inc. was "Made in the USA."

America's influence on China was never limited solely to business. Even in the 1990s when the vigilance of the Chinese government approached an all-time high, Americans strove to bend the arc of China's history. Americans once again doled out advice on how Chinese should treat their women, how they should travel, how they should pass their time, and how they should raise their children. And as in the past, many Chinese were receptive.

On September 5, 1995, First Lady Hillary Rodham Clinton addressed the Fourth World Conference on Women in Beijing, speaking more forcefully on the issue of human rights than any American dignitary in China ever had before. Clinton had nearly skipped the conference. Ties with the United States were still rocky because of the row over Taiwan and human rights. Chinese authorities had arrested an American, Harry Wu, who had exposed a vast network of labor camps exporting products to the United States. Newspapers across America called for Clinton to cancel her trip. "Bag Beijing!" declared the *Richmond Times*. "Clinton Kowtowing to Communist China" editorialized the *Houston Chronicle*. She went anyway.

As thousands of women delegates from across the world listened, cheered, and pounded tables, Clinton chided societies for condoning forced abortions and sterilizations. Her remarks were clearly leveled at China. A day later, Clinton traveled thirty-five miles north to the suburb of Huairou where she addressed the NGO Forum on Women, which the Chinese authorities had moved out of the capital because they feared demonstrations. There, Clinton hailed the work of independent women's organizations and urged them to persist in their labors. In *Living History*, her first memoir, Clinton noted that China's police were out in force as they faced off against a crowd of women's activists. "Seldom does one see so tangibly, in one setting, the differences between living in a free society and living under government control," she wrote.

The reaction of Chinese women to the First Lady was electric. Guo Jian-mei had been dispatched to Huairou to write up Clinton's speech for the All-China Women's Federation. She looked at it as a task. But when she heard Clinton declare that "women's rights are human rights," she thought, "I have found a soul mate." Clinton, Guo later told a Chinese interviewer, "shines with the light of wisdom, self-reliance and self-confidence." If Mother Teresa symbolizes "love," Guo said, Hillary stood for "wisdom." Inspired by the conference, Guo became a pioneering feminist and opened a legal-aid center for women in Beijing.

Hillary Clinton was following in the footsteps of American women who had stirred their Chinese sisters one hundred years earlier. Like her predecessors who fought for women's education and against foot-binding, Clinton was a missionary—for women's rights. Her journey to Beijing underscored the cyclical nature of the relationship between America and China and the reemergence of the bonds between American and Chinese women.

Clinton was not working alone. In the 1990s, as part of her husband's policy of "comprehensive engagement," Americans resuscitated the women's movement in China. Led by the Ford Foundation, Americans poured millions of dollars into projects for Chinese women. They bankrolled independent women's organizations, a hotline for advice on sexual discrimination, a magazine for rural women, a sex-ed center for youth, and a women's law center. Ford funded the translation into Chinese of the 1970s classic *Our Bodies, Ourselves* along with other feminist tomes. American foundations brought Chinese experts out of China and sent Western experts in. As Joan Kaufman, then of Columbia University, declared, "An independent women's NGO sector was born." The goal, said Mary Ann Burris, a program officer at the Ford Foundation, was "creating an empowered women's movement" in China.

Chinese women portrayed Burris the way their predecessors a century earlier had described their American teachers in missionary schools. Before meeting Burris in 1993, one Chinese woman activist said that she had believed American feminists were "relatively extreme . . . masculine, tigerlike." However, Burris molded the minds of her Chinese contacts. Burris, the woman said, "changed my opinions toward feminism."

American support of a women's movement was just one part of an effort to reintroduce Yankee values to the Chinese. Having struck out in its efforts to engage China's leadership on human rights, the Clinton administration and American foundations shifted their emphasis to a bottom-up attempt to transform Chinese society. American lawyers pushed China to build up a rule of law. Echoing Anson Burlingame's work at the Qing court, this was kicked off by translating hundreds of American law books into Chinese. The Clinton administration picked Paul Gewirtz, a professor at Yale University's law school, to lead the program. By assisting China's legal system, the United States, Gewirtz predicted, would "contribute to political reform." Gewirtz dismissed the notion that the effort would just make "the Chinese legal system more efficient at dispensing unfair or brutal punishments."

Just as Protestant missionaries saw female education as a stepping-stone to a Christian nation, so Hillary Clinton, Gewirtz, and their allies saw feminism and law as handmaidens at the creation of a freer China. Ford bet big on Chinese civil society. Between 1979 and 2015, the foundation dispersed a whopping $356 million in the People's Republic, far more than any other foundation. Much of it went into independent groups. Though the goals differed from those of American charities of a century ago, the impulse to bring American ideas to China remained the same. So did the assumptions. Americans involved in these campaigns believed that they were going to change China.

Hillary Clinton's visit was also an instance when China once again played the role of a place where American women could accomplish things that were more difficult at home. Clinton's speech got a huge response from the delegates in Beijing. Women lined up for her to autograph copies of the address. A *New York Times* editorial declared that it "may have been her finest moment in public life." Being tough on China in China resuscitated a political career that had been damaged by her foray into health care policy during her husband's first term. Even Republicans who had called the conference a gathering of "radicals and atheists" were impressed. "My visibility around the world had dramatically increased,"

Clinton wrote. In the past, traveling abroad, the First Lady had limited herself to activities with the spouses of world leaders. After Beijing, Clinton kept her own schedule during trips with her husband, branching off from the president's delegation to push women's issues and equal economic opportunities. In the nineteenth century, China had been a place where American women, denied opportunity at home, could make their mark. It remained that way a century later, even for presidents' wives.

As they had in the early twentieth century, China's traditionalists reacted harshly to the remonstrations of American women. During the late Qing dynasty, Confucianists had accused American female missionaries of plotting to destroy traditional Chinese culture. In the 1990s, the Chinese Communist Party viewed Clinton and other American feminists as equally unruly. In a throwback to "The Record," the nineteenth century's compendium of Western sexual deviance, party officials spread rumors during the Women's Conference that foreign prostitutes were planning to descend on Beijing and parade naked in Tiananmen Square.

There were other echoes of the past. In 1972, the American historian of China, John K. Fairbank, predicted that the People's Republic would never adopt American car culture and instead would teach the United States a thing or two about "a new balance of man and machine." How wrong he was. In the 1990s, China's businesses, planners, and consumers embraced American technology and the American way of life. From automobiles with roomy interiors to a highway construction boom that rivaled Eisenhower's, China's car culture, first birthed by America in the 1920s, woke up with its American pedigree intact.

Americans had begun exporting cars to China in 1902, a year before Henry Ford founded his own company and more than a decade before he started mass-producing the Model T. In 1910, the New York Times predicted that China's "virgin field" would absorb all of America's excess production. American dealers soon dispatched convoys of cars to places where cars had never been. The Reverend Hewlett Johnson, a widely traveled British missionary, bumped into Yankee car salesmen in Xi'an in northwestern China, and came across an expedition of young American dealers from the Dodge Brothers Motor Company in Tibet. American vendors even drove their cars, he wrote, "up the steep angle leading to the wall surrounding the city of Peking."

In the beginning, Britain had the advantage. Automobiles in China traveled on the left side of the road. But Chinese consumers favored American vehicles. Sun Yat-sen owned a Buick; the last emperor, Pu Yi, had two. Mao Zedong drove into Beijing in 1949 in an American car. By the 1930s, US automobile exports to China were outstripping Britain's by ten to one.

Henry Ford was a big believer in the China market. His company trained Chinese mechanics in Detroit and sent them back to man service stations nationwide. In China, the Model T sold for $705—not cheap, but it came with garage space, a chauffeur, lube oil, a service plan, and metal polish to boot. The addition of a chauffeur was a brilliant move. Even today, Chinese bigwigs don't like to drive.

The Americans were also central to China's effort to build roads. From the 1910s, American advisers had urged the Chinese to raze the ancient walls surrounding most Chinese cities and replace them with motorways. In 1919, Guangzhou took the advice. City workers knocked down six miles of the city's thousand-year-old wall and demolished fifteen city gates to create a ring road around that southern metropolis. By 1931, more than twenty cities had followed suit, etching an indelible mark (or scar) on China's urban landscape. Beijing's city walls would not yield until after the Communist Revolution of 1949, but the inspiration, long thought to be Soviet, was of Yankee provenance. As the urban planning historian Thomas Campanella put it, "The walls which had kept out the barbarians fell to Henry Ford." The US car industry received a further fillip in 1946 when US general Albert Wedemeyer convinced Chiang Kai-shek to make Chinese drive on the right.

In the 1980s, Americans were the first Westerners to begin building cars in China. In 1984, the American Motors Corporation contracted to produce the iconic American Jeep in China. The Beijing Jeep deal faced challenges from the start. The Chinese wanted a new army jeep; the Americans wanted to use an old design. The two sides settled on a Jeep Cherokee, to be assembled from kits made in America. At the time, it was illegal in China to send foreign exchange money overseas to buy the kits. So the Beijing city government colluded with project managers to smuggle the money abroad.

Ultimately, though, the venture did well—for a while at least. From 1984 until 1995, the business is believed to have made more than $50 million in profit. But once the Beijing city government stopped forcing government bureaus to buy the clunky vehicle in 1995, sales collapsed. Germany's Volkswagen and France's Peugeot followed AMC into China and developed more substantial operations. But the greatest success story was reserved for an American icon, General Motors.

GM's China story began on a bad note. In 1992, it sank $135 million into an operation to assemble pickup trucks in Manchuria. After about three hundred trucks, the deal collapsed, and both GM and its Chinese partner had nothing but nasty things to say about each other. GM kept at it and launched negotiations with the Shanghai Automotive Industry Corporation (SAIC), the massive city government–owned automaker that was also in a joint venture with Volkswagen. Shanghai officials liked the American story and liked American cars. In the early 1990s, stodgy Buick might have evoked grandma in the United States, but in China, it retained the élan of the days before China's revolution when glamorous coupes cruised Shanghai's Bund. In 2005, GM vice chairman Bob Lutz declared Buick a "damaged brand," but in China, America's oldest automotive make turned out to be a gold mine. In the fall of 1995, GM promised to pour $1 billion into China to make a luxury sedan.

GM's operations illustrated how little China had changed since the days when the British American Tobacco company was its biggest foreign investor and Neil Starr's insurance salesmen ruled the roost. To win the contract, GM took potential Chinese partners to its Brazil operation, which was run by Brazilians. Like BAT and Starr, GM knew that the key to China was empowering Chinese staff.

GM created a design team to cater to Chinese tastes. To its Buick Regal, it added a big washtub-shaped chrome grille and slanted headlights that resembled the face of a smiling Buddha. But in marketing its products, GM continued to rely on its strong suit: America. Ads for the GM Sail, a starter car for a young couple, featured a beefy American surfer. Even Sail's Chinese name, Sai Ou, contained a dig at GM's VW competitor. "Sai Ou" means "better than Europe" in Chinese.

GM's partner, SAIC, illustrated that business ethics in China had not changed much either since the days when BAT bought up loads of Nanyang Brothers cigarettes, let them mold, and then released them on the market. GM signed the deal to make the Buick Century after winning assurances that it would have a monopoly on the luxury car market. But in the spring of 1998, SAIC gave VW the right to make the Passat, as well. And months later, authorities in Guangzhou approved Honda's application to manufacture the Accord. As Philip Murtagh, GM's chief of China operations, said at the time, "We had our moments of agony."

Relations with the government continued to be critical to GM's success. Like the BAT executives who spent countless hours fending off Republican China's plans to create a tobacco monopoly and haggling over taxes with the Kuomingtang's finance minister T. V. Soong, GM executives found themselves in the same position with Communist officials in Shanghai. For GM, the hassles were worth it. Its China operation was the only bright spot for a company suffering from misfortune. From 2005 to 2009, annual car sales dropped in the US from seventeen million to ten million; at the same time, sales in China took off, almost tripling to more than ten million units. In Detroit, GM was closing production lines and dealerships, while its China factories were operating flat out. And just as Duke's cigarette business in China made more money per cigarette than did his companies in America, so GM's profit per vehicle in China was double that in the United States.

In June 2009, GM declared bankruptcy, and the US government stepped in to bail out the firm. That same year, GM China sold more than eight hundred thousand vehicles in China and made a profit of $1 billion. In 2011, GM broke the million-car mark in the PRC. At the end of 2009, however, GM made what could be a fateful choice, one with an eerie parallel to BAT's battle with the Nanyang Brothers. In need of cash for its flagging operations in Europe and elsewhere, GM sold 1 percent of its China operation to SAIC. From the beginning, the China-GM marriage had been a fifty-fifty affair. By ceding the 1 percent, GM handed control of the operation to the Chinese side. This is exactly what James Thomas, BAT's man in China, had wanted Nanyang to do, only Nanyang refused. A chronicler of GM's rise in China, Michael J. Dunne, has argued that GM's decision to dilute its ownership presaged the beginning of its fall.

That's because for decades, GM and other Western automobile firms have been trapped in a Faustian bargain with their Chinese counterparts. To do business, they have been forced to hand their technology to the Chinese and essentially train the Chinese to become their competitors. GM's move to relinquish the leadership of its China operation to its Chinese partner, Dunne suggested, would only hasten that process.

In the early 1990s, China was the scene of a dozen airplane accidents, resulting in 500 deaths, and dozens more near misses. A pilot in Jiangsu botched a takeoff, ran the jet into a ditch and killed 108 of 126 on board. In Guangzhou, a pilot crashed a Boeing 737-300 into a small rise upon landing, killing all 8 crew members and 133 passengers. A pilot on a China Eastern Airlines flight flying high over the Aleutian Islands accidentally adjusted the wings as if to land, causing the plane to drop precipitously; 2 passengers were jostled to death. A China Northwest Airlines flight went down a few minutes after takeoff from Xi'an, killing all 160 aboard. Mechanics had improperly repaired the autopilot system, making the plane impossible to fly. The joke was that the Chinese Aviation Airline Company stood for China Airlines Always Crashes.

In 1997, two Chinese airlines, Air China and China Eastern, won approval by the US Federal Aviation Administration to fly to the United States. A third airline, China Southern, had taken delivery of new Boeing 777s as it readied to open up what promised to be a lucrative route linking Guangzhou to Los Angeles. But China Southern also needed to pass muster with the US Department of Transportation. American officials asked for briefings on China's flight safety protocol. What they discovered alarmed them.

The air disasters and China's growing access to the US aviation market led to another Chinese-American partnership that advanced China's march to modernity. In the 1990s, seventy years after Americans first taught the Chinese to fly, they helped create a Chinese civilian aviation system. In a program funded by Boeing and United Airlines, and staffed by former US officials and American pilots, administrators, and technicians, Chinese aviators and ground crews were run through seminars, tours, training sessions, and a flight school in Kunming to learn how to make China's skies safe. Dozens of American companies, from engine manufacturers to the makers of cockpit equipment, contributed trainers. In the space of several years, the Chinese rewrote their civilian aviation safety procedures. The program integrated US and Chinese civil aviation establishments, binding the two nations together in yet another way.

Among the Chinese leading the program was Yang Yuanyuan. He had joined the People's Liberation Army at sixteen to dodge the political struggles of the Cultural Revolution. At nineteen, he learned to fly. As economic reforms unfolded in the 1970s, he left the air force to become a civilian pilot. By the early 1990s, he was chief pilot at China Southern. In December 1995, as one of a team of officials who took possession of the new planes in Seattle, he became the first Chinese pilot to fly a Boeing 777.

Yang's short memoir of the occasion, published in a Chinese magazine, recalled China's century-old love of American technology. The experience of piloting the 777 on a clear day over Puget Sound, Yang wrote, was "a dream come true." In 1997, he became chief of flight standards with the Civil Aviation Administration of China. Like Zhu Rongji with the WTO, Yang teamed up with Americans to prod China to change.

Yang and his American counterparts identified why China's skies were so dangerous. Pilots were tested by their friends. Maintenance work was rarely done on time. And there were no standard operating procedures for flying in bad weather. Chet Ekstrand, a senior Boeing safety official, marveled at how the Chinese "could be so candid in revealing shortcomings." In 2004, when a Bombardier CRJ-200 crashed in a lake outside the Inner Mongolian city of Baotou, killing fifty-four, Yang gave American investigators access to the site.

The results of this intervention were extraordinary. Guided by the Beautiful Country, China went from having one of the world's worst air safety records to having one of the best. After the 2004 accident, another Chinese plane did not go down until 2010, when a pilot overran a runway and forty-three people were killed. Since then, no fatal accidents have occurred. All this was accomplished as China's air traffic recorded explosive growth. It is now second only to the United States. As Yang Yuanyuan (known as Triple Y to his American colleagues) told the *Wall Street Journal*, China improved because it decided to "adopt a more open attitude" to learning from its own and others' mistakes. Of course, problems remain: 80 percent of Chinese flights are late.

In the summer of 1979, the Washington Bullets arrived in China to face off against the People's Liberation Army team, known as Bayi. The previous January, during his historic trip to the United States, Deng Xiaoping had been wowed by the Harlem Globetrotters at the Kennedy Center. Some of the Bullets were less than impressed with China's many wonders. At a stop at the Great Wall, center Elvin Hayes refused to get off the bus because, he said, he'd seen big walls before. The Chinese, however, were entranced. The Americans' then derriere-hugging basketball shorts and their flashy Converse high tops contrasted vividly with the untailored knits and military-issue green sneakers of the Bayi squad. It was as if the players came from different planets.

With the NBA's entry into China, the Chinese fell in love again with another American product—in this case, the missionary import, basketball. The game drew China into the modern world of professional sports and entertainment. It changed Chinese fashions and became another example of the pull of American culture on the Chinese. The National Basketball Association now counts China as its second biggest market. In 2014, its revenue in the Middle Kingdom hovered at around $200 million.

That's a long way from 1987, when newly minted NBA commissioner David Stern spent a week in Beijing with a demo tape in hand, pleading with the China Central Television (CCTV) to broadcast NBA games. For the next few years, Stern gave the network NBA finals videotapes for free. In 1990, he signed a revenue-sharing deal with CCTV. In 1992, the United States assembled the Dream Team, the first American Olympic squad to feature active NBA players, for the Barcelona Olympics. The Chinese went wild rooting for the American all-stars.

Two years later, China launched the China Basketball Association after seeing what the Dream Team did for America's image overseas. But the CBA, a state-run operation, could not compete with the NBA. Chinese viewers remained enthralled by the American game, watching teams that featured no Chinese athletes beamed halfway across the globe.

By the mid-1990s, basketball, thanks to Stern's vision and the super-stars Magic Johnson, Larry Bird, and Michael Jordan, had become the biggest sport in China, played or watched by three hundred million Chinese, the same number who smoked. National polls found that among males aged fifteen to twenty-four, more than 80 percent declared themselves to be basketball fans. Forty percent said they played the game. Each week during the season, thirty million Chinese watched at least one NBA game, and they were aired on daytime TV. More than twenty thousand stores in China carried NBA-approved merchandise; thousands more sold knockoffs.

Basketball's hold over China wasn't hard to explain. The Chinese had always loved acrobatics, and basketball was acrobatics with a ball. Politically, basketball had never run afoul of Party Central, as had American boxing and baseball. Mao Zedong had played basketball when he was younger, and praised it as the most "democratic" of America's sports. Many Chinese fans focused on African American stars. Though Chinese culturally have looked down on people with darker skins, the raw athleticism of America's black players enthralled the fans. In 1999, a survey of high school students showed Michael Jordan was the most popular athlete in China. On the streets of Chinese cities, NBA jerseys became commonplace, as did a sneaker culture as gung ho as the one in America. Black slang punctuated the lingo of the hip. Tattoos featuring a favorite team became a must-have among the cognoscenti, just as tattoos with Chinese characters festooned the bodies of NBA stars.

The NBA launched a program to teach the Chinese how to run a league. NBA coaches and referees conducted training programs for their Chinese counterparts. Chinese coaches and referees were invited to the United States to study. Promising Chinese players took part in exhibition games and summer camps. US stars began to see China as a lucrative market for sponsorships. Shaquille O'Neal went to China for a month in the summer of 1997, selling his music and his brand. Kobe Bryant followed. The Chinese named athletic-wear companies after the American stars. Michael Jordan unsuccessfully sued a Chinese firm named Qiao Dan, Jordan's name in Chinese, to force it to pay for the rights to his name. The NBA's operations in China mirrored the "constructive engagement" of the Clinton years. America was on a mission to remake China in the image of the United States and to make a few bucks along the way.

Then came Yao Ming.

On June 27, 2002, Commissioner Stern announced that Yao Ming would be the Houston Rockets' first pick in the NBA draft. Yao was the third Chinese player to play professionally in the United States but the most mediagenic by a mile—or at least by seven feet six inches. The Chinese media called it the "Yao Ming Phenomenon." In America, it was the "Ming Dynasty."

The process of getting Yao Ming to Houston pitted the remnants of a sclerotic Soviet-style sports system against the flash of Yankee capitalism. Neither side ended up looking pretty. Prospective American agents swarmed around Yao like sharks, which just happened to be the name of Yao's team in Shanghai. Yao's Shanghai minders demanded $15 million from Yao to let him go; they settled for $7.5 million. Authorities in Beijing also took their pound of flesh, demanding that Yao make a "loyalty pledge" not to "harm the dignity of China." They also forced him to promise to continue playing for the Chinese national team, which would shorten his career.

When Yao was a rookie in America in 2003, American analysts predicted failure. "Sir" Charles Barkley, the voluble ex–power forward for the Philadelphia 76ers, promised to kiss the "ass" of a fellow commentator if Yao ever scored more than 19 points. Barkley soon found himself nuzzling a donkey's rear. Yao led the Rockets to the playoffs four times over an eight-year career. The Yao Ming Phenomenon only intensified China's obsession with American basketball. When Yao faced off against another Chinese big man, Yi Jianlian, with the Milwaukee Bucks on November 9, 2007, an estimated two hundred million people tuned in, making it the most watched NBA game in history. And it was a blowout. The Rockets won 104–88.

In an era of breakneck social change, millions of Chinese followed Yao's progress. He was not only an ambassador from the new New China; he was a pioneer in the battle for personal success in a system that still denied basic freedoms. A plucky privately owned Chinese sports newspaper, *Titan Weekly*, broke story after story about the negotiations between Yao and his bosses in Shanghai, painting them as Communist apparatchiks of the past and Yao as China's future. "Yao Ming Robbed!" read one headline as Communist authorities schemed to siphon off his pay.

Yao's battles over sponsorships became a case study for Chinese as many like him sought, in smaller ways, to become agents of their own fate. Soon after starting with the Rockets, Yao signed a contract with the Pepsi-Cola Company to film ads. In China, however, Yao was featured in ads for Coke, which had a deal with the Chinese national team. Chinese officials claimed Yao's image belonged to them. "All the commercial rights of the intangible property of Chinese national athletes belongs to the state," the government announced at the time. But Yao sued, and in October 2003, Coke removed his image from their cans.

Yao found success during a period in which many Chinese felt that China, despite its booming economy, had not gained commensurate international respect. China's businessmen knocked off everything from North Face to *South Park*, and the government did little about it. But Yao was the real deal. He became China's most globally recognized brand. Yao showed that Chinese could succeed on the international stage, and specifically that they could make it in America. For a nation, a people, and a party that had yearned for American recognition, Yao's success was proof that China had arrived.

American values influenced Yao. From early in his American career, he donated time and money to charities. He gave $2 million after the devastating 2008 Sichuan earthquake. He headlined a "Say No" project to convince the Chinese to stop buying ivory and rhino horn to protect elephants and rhinoceroses. He pursued his passions with the same intensity that drove his game. In 2012, wine specialist Robert Parker gave 96 points out of 100 to the Family Reserve from Yao Family Wines in Napa, California. As Parker noted, "Wines made by celebrities are disappointing, Chinese basketball star Yao Ming's clearly are not."

Still, Yao's values ran up against those of his motherland. After his NBA career, Yao moved back to China and bought his old team, the Shanghai Sharks. In 2016, Yao led an attempt to privatize the China Basketball Association as part of a plan to inject some of the NBA's pizzazz, professionalism, and quality into what had remained a government-run sports operation.

Under the state-run system, CBA teams had to turn over all their revenues to the league, making it impossible for them to recruit talent from China's urban playgrounds, where some of the country's best hoops were played. Instead, the teams relied on China's state-run athletic academies, which chose players because they were tall, not because they were good. As a result, the quality of the game in China was laughably bad, made worse by notoriously corrupt officiating. Some CBA franchises were so strapped for cash that they didn't pay to heat the arenas and players would sit on the bench wrapped in parkas. In 2015, only one of the CBA's twenty teams made a profit. Yao's plan would have allowed franchises to retain a chunk of their revenues and therefore work on player development. But in the spring of 2016, China's bureaucrats blocked Yao Ming's plan, relegating the Chinese version of the game to semipermanent mediocrity. Meanwhile, the NBA in China went from strength to strength. In 2015, it signed a $700 million deal with Tencent, the Chinese social media giant, for rights to its programming in China, the most lucrative digital partnership in the world.

The 1990s witnessed a transformation in China's social mores. Deng Xiaoping's 1992 "Southern Tour" unleashed not only an economic boom but also an obsession with material wealth unsurpassed in modern Chinese history. Unrestrained materialism led to a breakdown in social trust, typical of many post-totalitarian countries. Chinese firms ripped each other off, wantonly stole intellectual property rights, laced milk, toothpaste, pet food, meat, and fish with poisons, and used armed gangs to steal the land from millions of farmers. China's intellectuals declared that the country faced a moral crisis.

This crisis was twinned with one in education. With their emphasis on rote memorization, discipline, and obedience, Chinese schools were turning out generations of Herculean test takers, but as the popular Chinese writer Huang Quanyu noted in 2000, "Not one single adult at a Chinese university has ever earned a Nobel Prize in science." (In 2015, a Chinese researcher was awarded the Nobel Prize in medicine.) Why, Huang asked his countrymen, do Chinese kids so handily beat Americans out of the gate but go on to lose to them at the finish line?

Concern about China's ethical fiber and the future of its children coalesced in February 2002 when three students from elite universities sprayed acid on the bears at the Beijing Zoo over a period of two weeks. Several bears were blinded and disfigured. One of the perpetrators, Liu Haiyang, a standout in mechanical engineering at the American-founded Tsinghua University, told police that he was "curious" about how the bears would react. "I honestly like animals," he said. The public responded to these attacks with shock, wondering whether the moral hole in society coupled with the country's rigid educational system had spawned a generation of twisted kids. Many looked to America for a solution.

Starting in December 1999, with the publication of Huang Quanyu's *Quality Education in America*, Chinese writers churned out a series of books celebrating the way Americans brought up their children. Titles like *How Americans Raise Their Daughters, How to Raise Your Child to Get into Yale*, and *Cornell Girl* flew off the shelves of bookstores around the country. Chinese parents boned up on how American schools and parents encouraged sports, art, and teamwork. The magazine *Must Reads for Parents* ran articles about Americans teaching their children to line up for buses, share, and have fun. Just as Americans were looking to China for answers to their educational concerns, American-style parenting and pedagogy became benchmarks for the Chinese.

Huang Quanyu had come to the United States in 1988 with fifty-five dollars in his pocket and a contract to teach Chinese at York College in Pennsylvania. As he described it, "This was my age of discovery. I was Vasco da Gama. I was Ponce de Leon. And York, Pennsylvania, was the new world." Several months into his tenure, Huang made his biggest find. In May 1989, he was asked to give a talk on China to some fifth-grade students. He rambled through a lecture on Chinese breakfasts and the weather. His audience of ten-year-olds looked bored.

Things began to get awkward when the teacher opened the floor for questions. Huang believed that no child would be bold enough to speak. In China, Huang noted, even university students were reluctant to address a speaker. So it was a shock when a pudgy boy asked him what he thought of the Tiananmen Square protests. Huang muttered a few words about modernization and complexity. "You said a lot of stuff," the boy responded, "but you haven't answered my question." More questions followed. "What's the biggest difference between Japanese and Chinese?" "What part of American culture do you dislike the most?" "What would you change in China?" "What will China be like in ten years?" Huang was stunned by the children's tenacity and self-confidence. That experience launched him on a search for answers. In 1993, he earned a PhD in education from Miami University in Ohio. In 2000, Huang's *Quality Education in America* was one of the top-selling nonfiction books in China. The publisher sold more than one million copies. Pirated editions accounted for hundreds of thousands more.

Huang wrote like a latter-day Xu Jiyu, the Chinese official who authored the first lengthy treatise on America. Underneath Huang's praise of the

United States lay a systemic criticism of the PRC. Huang focused on the education that his son, Kuangyan, received after he brought his family to the US. When Kuangyan was eight, he came home with a research assignment. His parents, both in the middle of their own PhDs, thought he was joking. But they realized that in America, teachers assumed that even a third grader could delve into a topic if given proper direction.

At school, the teachers valued Kuangyan's feelings and encouraged him to express himself. Kuangyan brought these skills home, challenging traditional Chinese family practices. As Huang wrote, a Chinese father would not tolerate a contrary child. But when Kuangyan once responded to Huang's criticism with "when you say that it hurts my feelings," Huang found himself disarmed.

Huang lambasted Chinese education for its overemphasis on controlling the child and requiring mindless obedience. He thought it significant that American students called their teachers Mr. and Ms., not Teacher. The egalitarian principles underlying this habit were one reason why Americans produced successful capitalists, he wrote. They fostered independence and creative risk-taking and the sense that anyone could succeed.

The same year that Huang's book topped the charts, a couple in Chengdu published a memoir about raising their daughter. Called *Harvard Girl, Liu Yiting: A True Chronicle of Quality Cultivation*, the book was a blockbuster, too. Written mostly by Liu's mother, Liu Weihua, the book catalogued the steps she took to cultivate what she called her daughter's "quality." When Liu was eighteen months old, her mother made Liu memorize Tang dynasty poetry. Chores began when she was five. During elementary school, Liu's mother took her to a noisy train station to study so she could hone her powers of concentration. To increase her daughter's pain threshold, she had her squeeze ice cubes for fifteen minutes at a stretch. The culmination of Liu Yiting's education was, of course, admission into Harvard. Liu's acceptance letter was splashed across the book's cover. Facing an uncertain future for their children in a changing world, Chinese parents looked to recognition from America as a sign of success.

The inclination to trust America with China's children ran through all levels of Chinese society. The last three Communist party leaders—Jiang Zemin, Hu Jintao, and Xi Jinping—sent their children to America to study. Deng Xiaoping boasted that a grandson was born in the USA. It is China's particular peculiarity that at the heart of the Communist Party, where fear of America has remained a pillar of state ideology, respect for and reliance on America have rarely flagged.

CHAPTER FORTY-FIVE

Twin Towers

On April Fools' Day 2001, a US Navy EP-3E Aries II signal intelligence airplane was on a surveillance mission in international airspace off the southern Chinese coast when it was intercepted by two Chinese-built F-8 fighter jets, the very planes that the US had once agreed to upgrade for the PLA.

Just ten minutes before the end of the mission, as the EP-3 prepared to return to its base in Japan, the Chinese F-8s approached from the rear at 22,500 feet. One of the Chinese planes positioned itself just under the naval plane's left wing, less than ten feet away. Attempting to inch ever closer to the US aircraft in a game of airborne chicken, the Chinese pilot lost control. The F-8 pitched up into the EP-3's propellers, which sheared the Chinese fighter in half. The front section of the F-8 cartwheeled forward, smashing the EP's nose. Other parts sliced into the EP-3's body. The F-8 fell away, and the pilot, Squadron Leader Wang Wei, was lost at sea, apparently a victim of a malfunctioning parachute.

The EP-3, meanwhile, went into an inverted dive, plummeting 8,000 feet in thirty seconds. "I thought we were dead, no question!" US Navy lieutenant Shane Osborn told *Naval Aviation News*. After pitching down another 14,000 feet, Osborn righted the plane. Unsure how long the aircraft would hold together, he pointed it toward the nearest piece of land, which turned out to be China's Hainan Island. The crew of twenty-four set about destroying sensitive surveillance equipment as Osborn prepared for a crash landing at a Chinese air base.

The Pentagon had become alarmed at China's growing military power and sought to scoop up intelligence on China's enhanced capabilities and keep an eye on China's move to increase its sway in the Western Pacific and the South China Sea. The number of American surveillance operations along China's coast skyrocketed, focused in particular on a Hainan Island naval base and China's growing armada of submarines. China was unhappy with the increased attention. Now that the Soviet menace was gone from the north, the Chinese military had embraced the ideas of Alfred Thayer Mahan and was determined to push foreign militaries, specifically that of the United States, away from its shores.

As he landed at Lingshui naval air base without any landing flaps, Osborn's first thought was, "I just can't believe we're alive!" The Chinese incarcerated the crew. Osborn was kept in a frigidly air-conditioned room and deprived of sleep, he later wrote, as a series of Chinese officers tried to force him to admit that the Americans had rammed squadron leader Wang Wei's plane, not the other way around. Osborn did not budge.

The EP-3 Incident was the first crisis of the new century between China and the United States now led by a new president, George W. Bush. With a crew of Americans incommunicado on Hainan Island, Bush's first thoughts were of the Iranian hostage crisis. "This was not the way I wanted to start my relationship with China," the president wrote.

In America, lawmakers were outraged that the Chinese had insisted on holding the American crew. Duncan Hunter, a Republican congressman from California, introduced legislation revoking China's most-favored-nation trading status. "While we trade with China, they prepare for war," he thundered. Hunter's bill did not pass.

In China, state-run newspapers declared that the collision was more proof that America was intent on keeping China down. President Jiang Zemin did not take a call from President Bush. Secretary of State Colin Powell could not raise his counterpart, Vice Premier Qian Qichen. Throughout the day on April 1, the Foreign Ministry ignored entreaties from US Ambassador Joseph Prueher; he was not called in until 9:00 p.m. Then, Foreign Minister Tang Jiaxuan accused the United States of killing a Chinese pilot and of "gross violations of China's national sovereignty." The foreign minister demanded an apology, reparations, and an end to US surveillance flights. For the next eleven days, the two sides negotiated, privately and through the media.

Prueher had been a naval aviator for thirty-five years before being appointed US ambassador to China. He had led the US Pacific Command during the crisis in the Taiwan Strait in 1995–96. And he was a student of Sun Tzu's *Art of War*. Even though he had been Clinton's ambassador to China, he had remained in Beijing awaiting the appointment of his replacement by the Republican White House of George W. Bush. "I knew more about this subject than anyone else I was dealing with," Prueher told one writer. "It was a wonderful position to be in." Prueher handily countered China's spin that it was all America's fault. The EP-3 was slow-moving while the F-8 was fast. "It's pretty obvious who bumped who," Prueher said. In Washington, the Pentagon released information showing that pilot Wang Wei had been involved in close calls before and had once been photographed in the cockpit holding up a sign with his e-mail address. The Pentagon noted that it had lodged a protest the previous December with the Chinese Ministry of Defense over the behavior of China's Top Guns, who vied with one another over who could edge closest to the American planes.

Beating China at the PR game, however, was secondary to the crew's fate. The Chinese had demanded an apology before they released anyone. It was Prueher's job, with guidance from Washington, to build, as he put it, "a ladder for the Chinese to climb down." On April 6, party chief Jiang Zemin, traveling in Latin America, laid out China's bottom line. "I have visited a lot of countries and seen that it is normal for people to ask forgiveness or say 'excuse me' when they collide in the street," he said. "But the American planes come to the border of our country and do not ask forgiveness. Is this behavior acceptable?" Prueher and his Chinese counterparts agreed on a letter that declared that the United States would say it was "very sorry" for the loss of Wang Wei and "very sorry" that the EP-3 entered China's airspace without clearance. A day later, China released the crew. It kept the plane for months, as its intelligence agencies pored over the hardware for clues about American technology.

The plane crash did not help the United States in China. Even Chinese dissidents were uncomfortable with what they perceived to be the US government's imperious behavior. Liu Xiaobo, one of China's most trenchant writers, noted that the embassy bombing combined with the EP-3 crash aided the party's efforts "to blacken America's name." What was at stake, Liu wrote in 2001, were not simply America's political relations with the PRC but "the spiritual prestige built up since 1972 . . . and America's hopes for a democratic China."

There was an odd but revealing postscript to the EP-3 tale. It was a dying wish of John Leighton Stuart, America's last ambassador to China before the Cold War, to be buried in the Middle Kingdom, where he had been born in 1876. When Stuart died in 1962, China and the United States were locked in the Cold War, and Mao Zedong had singled out the ex-ambassador as a symbol of American imperialism in his famous essay "Farewell, Leighton Stuart." But in the 2000s, Americans broached the issue again. Stuart's family had wanted him to be interred in Beijing beside his wife, who had died there in 1926. But city authorities would not allow it. Finally, in a gesture of what they portrayed to be enlightened benevolence, in 2008 party leaders agreed to let Stuart's ashes be buried in a cemetary in Hangzhou, the city of his birth.

Two years later, the Hangzhou city government built a memorial to the lost pilot Wang Wei in the same cemetery. The five-foot-tall black obelisk was placed in a spot where it loomed right over Stuart's tombstone. It was not as if many Americans would visit Stuart's grave and, even if they did, most would not know who Wang Wei was. But the decision to put Stuart's last resting place in the shadow of a memorial to a man whom the Chinese hailed as a victim of the Beautiful Country underscored the deep resentment some in the Chinese Communist Party nurse toward the United States.

In September and December 2001, two events changed the trajectory of the Chinese-American relationship. On September 11, 2001, the Middle Eastern terrorist organization al-Qaeda launched four coordinated attacks against the United States, killing almost three thousand people in New York City, Shanksville, Pennsylvania, and at the Pentagon outside Washington, DC. Exactly three months later, China formally entered the World Trade Organization.

Al-Qaeda's attack on the United States forced the Bush administration to set aside its plans to challenge China in Asia. On the campaign trail, Bush had called China a "strategic competitor" and had vowed to bolster Taiwan and the cause of human rights. The EP-3 incident only reinforced this view. But now the White House needed China's cooperation in the UN Security Council as it sought to dismantle al-Qaeda and unseat the Taliban. China's president Jiang Zemin was the first foreign leader to call the White House after the attack, and China backed UN Security Council resolutions authorizing the use of force against Afghanistan. The "China threat," which had taken the Republican Party and some Democrats by storm in the late 1990s, was set aside as conflicts in Afghanistan and Iraq demanded Washington's undivided attention.

Bush downplayed human rights, and his plan to support Taiwan like-wise fell by the wayside. In December 2003, Bush did what no American president had ever done before. He publicly criticized the president of the Republic of China in front of a senior Communist official. Premier Wen Jiabao of the PRC was visiting the United States when Bush was asked, at a White House news conference on December 9, his reaction to a call by Taiwan's new president, Chen Shui-bian, for a vote gauging Taiwan's feel-ings about mainland China. When Bush replied that it was unwise, Wen was visibly pleased. Taiwan's president had been put in his place.

Bush also needed China's help with North Korea. Decades earlier, North Korea had started a nuclear weapons program with China's assistance. It had tested missiles through the 1990s and had withdrawn from the Inter-national Atomic Energy Agency in June 1994. It had also concluded deals with the Clinton administration to halt its nuclear program in exchange for technology, food, and fuel, resulting in a visit by Secretary of State Madeleine Albright in October 2000. But by the time Bush entered office in 2001, North Korea had resumed its nuclear program, and in October 2002, Pyongyang acknowledged that it was building a nuclear bomb.

That month at his ranch in Crawford, Texas, Bush appealed to Chinese president Jiang Zemin for help. China was the North's biggest trading part-ner. Pyongyang relied on Beijing for almost everything. Bush asked Jiang to use his influence, but Jiang demurred, telling the president that North Korea "was [Bush's] problem, not his." In January 2003, Bush tried again. Again Jiang didn't bite. Then in February, Bush warned that he was contemplating bombing the North. That got China's attention. In August 2003, under pres-sure from Beijing, North Korea agreed to join China, the United States, South Korea, Japan, and Russia in the Six-Party Talks. Progress was tough, however, and in October 2006, the North conducted its first nuclear test.

Beijing's interests were just not the same as those of the United States. America wanted the North to abandon the Bomb and would have been happy to see the North Korean government collapse. China needed the North to remain communist and a buffer between it and capitalist South Korea, whether it had a nuclear weapon or not. Still, despite this gap, Washington continued to rely on China to somehow solve its North Korea problem.

Formal accession to the World Trade Organization on December 11, 2001, accelerated China's rise. Since then, China's gross domestic product has shot up more than 400 percent and its exports have increased 500 percent.

Its share of world trade has tripled to more than 10 percent. Bush administration officials greeted China's accession into the trade body as another sign that the Middle Kingdom was now locked into the global economic system—more proof that China would inevitably adopt American values and interests. The WTO, declared National Security Advisor Condoleezza Rice, would strengthen "an entrepreneurial class that does not owe its livelihood to the state." The implication was clear: this class of people was going to set China free.

But the Chinese Communist Party didn't share these views. China's entry into the WTO changed the party's calculus toward the United States. The Chinese government had relied on American support to make it into the trade body. But once in the WTO, the Chinese leadership for the first time since the 1970s felt that it no longer needed the United States like it used to. And the US could no longer pressure China as it had before. With China's entry into the WTO, America ceded much of its autonomy to impose sanctions to the trade body. The loss of leverage was extreme. The relationship seemed imbalanced. Officials in Washington asked: Had America given too much to the Chinese?

Against this backdrop, deputy secretary of state Robert Zoellick delivered the most honest speech in decades on the US government's views of China. On September 21, 2005, speaking to the National Committee on US-China Relations, Zoellick noted that the work of seven presidents to integrate China into the international system had succeeded far better than anyone could have imagined. "The dragon has emerged and joined the world," he announced. "China is a player at the table."

Now, Zoellick declared, China needed to make the transition from a beneficiary of the American system to a partner with the United States. Zoellick called for China to become "a responsible stakeholder" in the American-led trading and security system. This was necessary, Zoellick implied, because the alternative—what he called "the traditional ways for great powers to emerge"—could mean war.

The "Responsible Stakeholder" speech underscored a growing unease about China among Americans, and not only inside the government. As Zoellick noted, China's biggest cheerleaders—the American business community—had begun to sour on the Middle Kingdom. He spoke of "a cauldron of anxiety" about China. Smaller American companies faced rampant piracy and counterfeiting by Chinese rivals. And China's policy of keeping its currency cheap meant that China's products were more competitive than similar American ones. Larger US businesses were the targets of state-sanctioned espionage to swipe their technology. American workers were victims, too. The Economic Policy Institute estimated that between 2001 and 2011, 2.7 million US jobs were lost due to China.

In terms of global security, Zoellick noted, China's support of rogue states such as Sudan and Iran, its massive military buildup, its failure to rein in widespread money laundering in its banking system, and its continued close ties to North Korea raised questions about whether China's rise was indeed going to be, as it claimed, "peaceful." "China needs to recognize," Zoellick said, "how its actions are perceived by others." Was China really interested in stopping the proliferation of nuclear weapons? Did it really want to cooperate in the fight against terrorism? More broadly, Zoellick's question was this: Had the Communist Party shed its view of the United States as an enemy or were its mercantilist economic behavior, its ballooning defense budget, and its industrial snooping war by other means?

From the 1970s to the early 2000s, the United States had ushered the Middle Kingdom into the community of nations and helped it grow rich and strong. Now that America was on the brink of accomplishing this mission, Zoellick declared, it was time for China to become America's partner. The dream of a Great Harmony had returned.

Zoellick listed four truths about China that gave him faith that its leaders would choose cooperation over confrontation. First, he said, China no longer sought to spread a radical anti-American ideology around the world. Second, China did not see itself in a conflict with democracy. Third, it was no longer battling with capitalism. And, finally, China had stopped believing that its future depended on the overthrow of the international system. In reality, Zoellick's truths were more of a wish list than a catalog of facts. As the 2000s wore on, China continued to resist democratic ideas. Nor had it embraced capitalism in the way that Zoellick and many other Americans had hoped it would. Finally, its acceptance of the American-led international system was not as wholehearted as many Americans had assumed.

Zoellick's call arose from a sense in America of the growing interdependence between the Beautiful Country and the Middle Kingdom. In 2005, American economist C. Fred Bergsten had argued for a special Sino-American relationship—he called it G2. Bergsten's point was that only with a Great Harmony between the United States and China could the problems of the world be solved.

In early 2006, the Bush administration put Zoellick's call for greater cooperation into action by instituting the Strategic Economic Dialogue with Beijing. Thomas Christensen, the State Department's point man on

Asia, subsequently wrote that the aim of the dialogue was "to help, rather than hinder, China's economic development," and prove to China that America welcomed its rise. Henry Paulson, now Bush's treasury secretary, led the dialogue. On the surface, Paulson's vision succeeded. The first five biannual sessions resulted in thirty face-to-face meetings between US cabinet secretaries and their Chinese counterparts and agreements on energy cooperation and the posting of US Food and Drug inspectors in China to protect American consumers against poisonous Chinese exports. There was even a mini cross-cultural love scandal, which went unreported at the time, when the FBI caught one senior American official in a tryst with her Chinese counterpart.

From his position as the point man in US-China relations, Paulson negotiated the freedom of at least one Chinese dissident and at one point convinced the US Navy not to dispatch a destroyer into the Taiwan Strait. He also leaned on his Chinese interlocutors to allow China's currency to appreciate moderately against the dollar. Congress had been threatening for years to sanction China for keeping the value of its currency artificially low. Americans believed that China had unfairly boosted its exports, contributing to America's $200 billion trade gap with China.

Zoellick and Paulson were unwittingly carrying out Franklin Delano Roosevelt's dream of elevating China into the ranks of global powers. FDR had wanted China to be one of the Four Policemen. Paulson and Zoellick saw China's future role in very much the same way. But to many influential Chinese at the heart of the Communist system, American attempts to pull China into a web of international agreements were nothing more than a plot to encumber the country with responsibilities and derail it from its primary objectives—becoming rich and strong and surpassing the United States. Liu Ming, a scholar at the Shanghai Academy of Social Sciences, summed up the fears of many Chinese when he called Zoellick's "Responsible Stakeholder" speech "a new way for Western nations to pressure and constrain China."

China's rise was the story of the new millenium. If the twentieth century had been the American Century, *Time* magazine said, then the twenty-first century would be the Chinese Century. "Thank you, God, for the Chinese," the magazine quoted one African in a breathless report detailing a vast web of Chinese investments from Botswana to Brazil, Pakistan to Peoria. The Chinese appetite for energy and resources was powering global growth the way the United States had just decades earlier. And Beijing, *Time* noted, "seems ready to challenge—possibly even undermine" Washington's position on top of the global heap. The *New York Times* published a string of stories from China's backyard in Southeast Asia describing China's increasing popularity and America's fading relevance in the region. Thais didn't want to study English anymore, the *Times* claimed on November 18, 2004, they had chosen Mandarin instead. Americans were anxious. Was the world big enough for the two giants?

China's rise was so fast, so compelling, so historic, that it prompted some to argue that the Middle Kingdom would defy all the known laws of economics as it regained its rightful place at the center of the world. In a 2004 essay titled "The Beijing Consensus," Joshua Cooper Ramo contended that China was reshaping the international order by introducing "a new physics of development and power." China, Ramo wrote breathlessly, was "the greatest asymmetric superpower the world has ever seen." It had little need for "traditional tools" of power, like aircraft carriers and missiles, but relied more on "the electric power of its example and the bluff impact of its size." The Beijing Consensus, he wrote, presented a stark challenge to the tired "Washington Consensus," of open markets and open societies. China meant, he wrote, "innovation-led growth." China oozed "productive dynamism," "experimentation and failure," "fast, forward-leaning change," and "intellectual charisma." Ramo called on Americans to toss out all their ideas about China. "Decades-old rhetoric about China makes no sense in a country where two-week-old maps are out of date," he declared. After the Tiananmen Square crackdown in 1989, Americans had been sure that China would collapse. Now, once again, an American was portraying the Chinese as a race of supermen.

Ramo captured US wonder with the rising China. It was indeed unbelievable what was unfolding on the other side of the Pacific as an ancient kingdom modernized at the speed of light. If there were any doubters, all they needed to do was tune in with thirty million other Americans on the night of August 8, 2008, to watch the opening ceremonies of the Beijing Summer Olympics. Ramo was there, serving as the color man on NBC's broadcast, praising China's "harmony" and declaring that China is "a nation about to put a match to the fuse of a rocket."

That evening, fifteen thousand performers celebrated Chinese culture and the Communist Party's rule in a meticulously choreographed performance that fused science (the Chinese government used weather modification technology to prevent rainfall) with art (the gala was engineered by the celebrated film director Zhang Yimou). Synchronized drummers wielded neon-red drumsticks; hundreds of wood blocks undulated like waves, sprouted flowers, and then popped open to reveal people; 2,008 men practiced tai chi; a runner traversed the circumference of the Bird's Nest stadium in midair to light the Olympic flame. Ramo, who was a partner at Henry Kissinger's lobbying firm, predicted that the Olympics would "irrevocably" change China. "They know that their behavior," he said, "is going to have to be different than in the past."

Other Americans saw a darker cast to China's advance. China was a rising power, America was the resident power, and many saw a battle between the two as inevitable. In 2005, Robert Kaplan authored an article in the *Atlantic Monthly* titled "How We Would Fight China." He argued that the wars in Iraq and Afghanistan and the problems in the Middle East were but "a blip." The contest between the United States and China, he wrote, "will define the twenty-first century. And China will be a more formidable adversary than Russia ever was." Kaplan stopped short of predicting a "big war." What was more likely, he observed, was "a series of cold war–style standoffs that stretched out over years and decades."

Kaplan evoked a new kind of Yellow Peril from China to justify his prediction. "Pulsing with consumer and martial energy, and boasting a peasantry that, unlike others in history, is overwhelmingly literate," Kaplan wrote, "China constitutes the principal conventional threat to America's liberal imperium." He did not explain exactly how a literate class of farmers endangered the United States. One critic accused Kaplan of performing a "strategic lap dance for the US Navy and Pacific Command." But Kaplan's fear-mongering reflected growing disenchantment in the United States.

In the twenty-first century, China exploded into American lives in ways that it hadn't since the days when clipper ships brought Chinese exotica to America and old slavers shipped Chinese laborers to the West Coast. Thanks to China's accession to the WTO, Chinese products flooded into the United States. By 2007, China accounted for over 40 percent of the luggage Americans used, the plastic footwear they wore, and the toys they played with. One-third of America's textiles, furniture, electrical appliances, jewelry, and leather goods came from the PRC. Chinese steel undergirded San Francisco's new Bay Bridge. Chinese-made parts powered every laptop and cell phone. Turn over anything—from microwaves to underwear—and there it was, "Made in China." To Americans, globalization, with its peril and its profit, was ineluctably Chinese.

While Washington economists and Wall Street titans heralded globalization and its main by-product, China's rise, as a chance to get fabulously rich, Main Street wasn't so sure. It was no coincidence that as China's manufacturing sector boomed, America's shrank, or that while China added millions of jobs that paid less than twelve dollars a day, America lost millions that paid twelve dollars an hour or more. Entire sectors of the American economy hollowed out. Jobs picked up and moved overseas or just disappeared. Between 2001 and 2013, 63,300 US factories shut down and 5 million factory jobs disappeared. Meanwhile, China's manufacturing workforce added 14.1 million jobs.

Pundits like Thomas Friedman of the *New York Times*, in his 2005 book *The World Is Flat*, hailed this as a great advance, pointing to lower costs for the stuff of American life. Researchers from Princeton University and the Swiss National Bank reported that each time a Chinese product increased its market share in America by 1 percent, consumer prices in that sector dropped by 2.5 percent. They estimated the savings at an extraordinary $780 billion over ten years.

But China's rise had its casualties. In 1973, there were 2.4 million textile and apparel workers in the United States. In 2015, just 232,000 people made clothes. Waves of cheap Chinese goods and a failure to retrain workers brought whole regions to their knees. Henry County, Virginia, had once launched governors, Fortune 500 CEOs, and bigwig politicians on the back of a thriving furniture industry. In the 1970s, there was so much work that furniture makers trucked in convicts to man the factory lines. In the early 1990s, illegal Mexican immigrants took their place. But, by the late 1990s, America's retail showrooms were awash with cheap Chinese wooden furniture. In 1963, there were 42,560 jobs in Henry County. In 2015, there were half that number. In towns that had boasted an unemployment rate of 1 percent, one-third of the families now lived on food stamps. Divorce was up, as was drug use. "Axed by globalization" is how reporter Beth Macy described what happened to American furniture workers in the face of Chinese competition in her beautifully crafted 2014 best seller *Factory Man*. "What good did it do to have access to cheap consumer goods if you had no money to buy them?" she asked.

Did it matter that America no longer made beds or clothes? A chorus of economists let fly with a resounding, NO! But the disappearance of millions of low-skilled jobs ravaged America's working class. China's rise was not the sole factor, but it definitely played a role in furthering the growing income gap in the United States.

This belief that the Chinese had gotten the better of the United States became a powerful political issue in the 2016 presidential campaign when Republican Donald Trump and Democrat Bernie Sanders attacked America's trade relationship with China. It was as if the US had returned to the nineteenth century, when Chinese labor in the western United States had threatened Americans at the lowest rung of the social ladder. In the twenty-first century, the Chinese reprised that role, except from halfway around the world. "The Chinese are not superpeople," Macy quoted one American factory boss as saying. But many believed they were.

In March 2007, a Canadian pet food manufacturer called Menu Foods recalled sixty million cans of cat and dog food that had been linked to the deaths of ten animals in the United States. Subsequent investigations showed that Chinese subcontractors had cut wheat gluten, a common additive in pet food, with melamine, a cheap industrial chemical used in the making of plastics. By the summer, toothpaste from China that contained diethylene glycol, a poison, started showing up in Central America and on the shelves of a discount store in Miami. Then came waves of toy recalls, kicked off in June by 1.5 million made-in-China Thomas the Tank Engines coated with lead paint. That same month, the National Highway Traffic Safety Administration ordered a recall of half a million Chinese-made tires.

By the fall, American newspapers were full of reports about Chinese products. Its food was "filthy and unfit to be eaten," the *New York Times* declared on June 29. "There was a time when the words 'Made in China' immediately evoked 'shoddy,'" the *Times* said on July 8, 2007. "Lately, many Americans are thinking 'danger.'" Nothing so illustrated America's "cauldron of anxiety" about China as the product safety issues of 2007 and 2008. The reaction combined Americans' long-standing apprehensions about China with their worries about globalization. In the nineteenth century, Americans feared Chinese workers; in the 1950s, it was Chinese brainwashing. By the twenty-first century, it was Chinese goods. And as in the nineteenth century, Americans found themselves ill equipped to handle the challenge. For the millions of Chinese-made toys recalled, for example, America's Consumer Product Safety Commission had one full-time inspector.

There was something unsettling about the increasing interdependence between the US and China. In the economic realm, the Sino-American relationship resembled that between a drug dealer and a junkie. The United

States had become hooked on cheap credit financed through China's purchase of US Treasury bonds, which China bought to keep the value of its currency low. China was addicted to its exports to America as it built an economy that consumed too little and invested too much. In 2006, historian Niall Ferguson and economist Moritz Schularick gave this codependency a name: "Chimerica"—the economic amalgamation of overspending Americans and oversaving Chinese. With more than a trillion dollars in US Treasury bonds, China had become America's banker. And with grain exports to China approaching twenty million tons a year, America had become China's farmer.

As early as 2005, the International Monetary Fund warned that the Sino-American economic dance was going to end badly, not just for China or America but for the rest of the world. The combination of cheap money from China and overspending by America accounted for nearly half of global economic growth. It was, the IMF said, an "unsustainable process." Three years later, it came to a crashing halt.

The financial crisis of 2008 strengthened the impression that the future belonged to China while America's greatest moment had passed. The Beautiful Country, once China's model, stumbled badly. The Middle Kingdom, with a stimulus package approaching $600 billion, emerged even stronger from the economic squall. Pundits around the world pointed to an inflection point in the relationship.

America's troubles brought "doubt and discredit to our system in some quarters and boosted China's self-confidence," wrote Henry Paulson. For Paulson, serving as secretary of the treasury, the inflection point occurred in March 2008 at a break during one of the Strategic Economic Dialogues when Vice Premier Wang Qishan approached him to say, "You were my teacher, but now here I am in my teacher's domain, and look at your system, Hank. We aren't sure we should be learning from you anymore." Some 150 years earlier, Caleb Cushing had remarked that Western nations had once learned from China but had become "the teachers of our teacher." Now it was China's turn.

Paulson had known Wang Qishan for fifteen years. A decade earlier, Paulson's firm, Goldman Sachs, had helped Wang, then the executive deputy governor of Guangdong province, manage the largest bankruptcy restructuring in Communist Chinese history. Paulson had later teamed with Wang to list shares from the China Construction Bank on Wall Street. Now the tables—both on a national and personal level—had turned. As

Paulson wrote, "This crisis was a humbling experience and this was one of its most humbling moments."

China had modeled its stock markets, its financial services industry, its central bank, and its commercial banking practices on those of the United States. Its entrepreneurs had copied all the landmark American firms. Apple, eBay, Twitter, and Google had their Chinese counterparts. Two-thirds of the laws passed in China from the 1990s had American roots. But now America was drowning in layoffs, foreclosures, and collateralized debt obligations. The US government even stepped in to bail out giants like General Motors. So much for America's vaunted market forces, the Chinese said.

The Chinese approached the moment with a mixture of triumphalism and concern. They began lecturing Americans instead of the other way around. In January 2008, Wu Yi, one of China's vice premiers, criticized the US policy of letting the dollar fall. For years, America had blasted China for keeping its currency low, and here was a Chinese leader with the temerity to denounce America for doing the same thing, "The Chinese people," she told a group of American officials, "are being hurt because they have invested in your dollars."

But it wasn't just American currency policy that stuck in China's craw; it was the American way of life. At the fourth meeting of the Strategic Economic Dialogue in June 2008 in Annapolis, Maryland, Wang Qishan condemned America's waste. "It's a hot summer day, but it's cold in your offices because you've got the air conditioning on," Wang said. "In the winter you've got the heat blasting out. For exercise you work out in air-conditioned gyms, then take hot showers, then get in air-conditioned cars. This is America! In China, we don't live that way. We can't afford to." Wang Qishan's boss, Premier Wen Jiabao, picked the World Economic Forum at Davos in January 2009 to reprimand the United States for its "lack of self-discipline" and "blind pursuit of profit." America had been weakened, he said, thanks to "an unsustainable model of development characterized by prolonged low savings and high consumption." Clean up your act was China's message to the United States.

The Great Recession only magnified American concerns about a rising China. While the US economy dipped about 1 percent in 2008 and almost 3 percent in 2009, China's growth clocked in at over 9 percent both years. Now it fell to Americans to begin daydreaming about using the secrets of China's system to get their country out of its jam.

*   *   *

In 2008, *New York Times* columnist Thomas Friedman raised the idea of America becoming "China for a day" so that a green revolution of taxes, regulations, and product bans could be enacted to save the world from global warming. Appearing on comedian Stephen Colbert's show in November, Friedman fantasized about a government "that could actually make decisions . . . with the same persistence, focus, stick-to-it-iveness and direction that China does through authoritarian means."

Why was it that China could build a high-speed rail network, other writers wondered, but America couldn't? Why did China have a manned space program now that America had mothballed its own? China once again became the place where American scientists could chart the future. Technologies, such as coal gasification, long since abandoned in the United States, were given a new lease on life in China as part of a multibillion-dollar effort to generate clean energy. "The action is here," S. Ming Sung, a former Shell Oil executive, told the *Washington Post*. "In the U.S., there are too many paper researchers. Here, they are doing things." Medical researchers flocked to China, in some cases to skirt American ethical standards. On May 14, 2002, Harvard University president Lawrence Summers was forced to admit in a speech at Peking University that a massive project to collect genetic material from Chinese farmers had gone "badly wrong."

But these bumps in the road were only bumps because the Chinese were going at breakneck speed. "I'm a sucker for action, and the Chinese were nothing if not active," Paulson wrote. "And frankly, I have to say it was quite a refreshing contrast to the gloomy nay-saying that we had gotten used to back home in the States."

In 2008, the same year the Great Recession emboldened some in China to fancy that the time had come to challenge America, DreamWorks studio released an animated movie about a fat, lazy panda that sent China's intellectuals into a tailspin of gloom about their country's ability to compete with the United States in the intangible realm of "soft power." *Kung Fu Panda* told the story of a pudgy Ailuropoda who leaves his father's noodle shop and, against all odds, saves the Valley of Peace from an evil snow leopard. That a cartoon starring the king of irreverence, Jack Black, should prompt Chinese soul-searching about innovation reveals a great deal about China's mix of triumphalism and distress as it marched into the twenty-first century.

Communist Party propaganda officials huddled to explore a question posed by Wu Jiang, the president of the National Peking Opera Company.

"The film's protagonist is China's national treasure and all the elements are Chinese, but why didn't we make such a film?" Communist Party–approved academics lined up to blast the movie for engaging in "cultural imperialism." One social scientist detected Yankee plots in *Kung Fu Panda* and the movie *Mulan,* both tales of individuals rising above their status. The Chinese artist Zhao Bandi called for a boycott. Now, America was doing the brainwashing; *Kung Fu Panda,* he claimed, was "a tool to kidnap the minds of the Chinese."

Money was thrown at what was perceived to be an enormous gap in the Communist Party's ability to "sell" China's story overseas. Almost $700 million was earmarked for an animated film studio in Tianjin. Its first production, *Legend of Kung Fu Rabbit,* filched the *Kung Fu Panda* story, except in this case a rotund bunny saved China from an evil . . . panda. While *Kung Fu Panda* broke Chinese box office records, the fat rabbit bombed. Later animated movies showed marked improvement.

The Chinese befuddlement at Hollywood's success was a symptom of a deeper issue. China's party chiefs had become obsessed with innovation and with enhancing the country's "soft power." The Communist Party and its propaganda organs strove fiercely to convince people in other nations that China's rise was good for the world. The Chinese government dotted the globe with Confucius Institutes, offering Chinese language courses and programs designed to promote China's interests. It ringed the world with satellite TV broadcasts from its multilingual China Central Television staff. Radio stations in little towns like Galveston, Texas, were taken over by China Radio International. But the results were meager and the payout—billions of dollars—was huge.

In December 2008, as the story of the Chinese economic miracle spread, a group of Chinese liberals drew up a manifesto demanding freedom. The group called itself Charter 08, after Charter 77, a movement of intellectuals in Czechoslovakia that issued a document in 1977 criticizing the country's Communist government for its human rights record.

Though on the surface Charter 08's inspiration came from Eastern Europe, its demands for "free and fair competition among political parties" and a promise to respect China's constitution were deeply American. Issued on the sixtieth anniversary of the Universal Declaration of Human Rights, a document influenced by the Chinese philosopher-diplomat P. C. Chang, Charter 08 argued that freedom and individual rights were not exclusive to Westerners; Chinese deserved them, too.

Liu Xiaobo, a Chinese writer and longtime dissident, spearheaded Charter 08. Almost twenty years earlier, as crowds had massed in Tiananmen Square in the spring of 1989, Liu had been on a teaching fellowship at Barnard College in Manhattan. He made a life-changing decision to return to China. Arriving at the height of the protests, Liu jumped into the movement. Along with three other intellectuals, he began a hunger strike and issued statements calling for democracy. He wrote in a language ripped from the pages of America's past. One statement—"The essence of democracy consists of checks and balances"—recalled James Madison's Federalist Paper No. 10.

In the predawn hours of June 4, Liu was among a group of protest leaders who negotiated the peaceful withdrawal of the remaining protesters from the square, saving hundreds of lives. The authorities then threw Liu in jail for twenty months. For the next two decades, he commuted between prison and his book-filled apartment in Beijing.

Liu was the latest in a long line of American-influenced intellectuals who believed in human rights and democracy as matters of principle and not simply as tools to be used to make China strong. As he matured as a writer, Liu embraced the idea—first proposed by the liberal Lin Yutang in the 1920s—that hate should not be wielded as a driving force for political change. "I have no enemies and no hatred," Liu declared. And in the same way as Hu Shih had opposed Frank Goodnow, Liu Xiaobo battled the presumption that the Chinese were not ready for democracy.

On the night of December 8, 2008, two days before Charter 08 was published online, police arrested Liu Xiaobo at his home. A year later, he was sentenced to eleven years in prison on charges of "slander to incite subversion of state power and overthrow of the socialist system." In 2010, Liu Xiaobo was awarded the Nobel Peace Prize and China reacted hysterically. It detained Liu's wife, menaced his friends, and punished Norway by, of all things, cutting China's purchases of Norwegian salmon. In Oslo, an empty chair substituted for the absent laureate.

From exile in America, Chinese astrophysicist Fang Lizhi wrote that the Nobel committee had "challenged the West to re-examine a dangerous notion that has become prevalent since the 1989 massacre: that economic development will inevitably lead to democracy in China." Not only that. For years, many Americans had viewed men like Liu Xiaobo as not really belonging to Chinese culture. While Americans took Soviet dissidents like Andrei Sakharov and Aleksandr Solzhenitsyn seriously, their Chinese counterparts often got short shrift. Nevertheless, like Luo Longji and other liberals who had fallen afoul of Mao, Liu Xiaobo was very

Chinese, and his award highlighted the century-old struggle between China's dream to become rich like America and its dream to become free like America, too.

Even some former high-ranking Communists shared Liu's vision of democracy. During his sixteen years under house arrest in Beijing following the June 4 massacre in 1989, former Communist Party chief Zhao Ziyang spent a good deal of time pondering his nation's fate. Zhao secretly recorded audiotapes of his memoirs, which were smuggled to Hong Kong and published in 2010. Living a life as a nonperson, confronting a slew of unwritten rules and jailers who masqueraded as functionaries, led Zhao to arrive at positions far more radical than any he had taken when he was in power. On February 26, 1989, shortly before the Tiananmen Square crackdown, for example, Zhao had remonstrated with visiting president George H. W. Bush to stop Americans from supporting "those in China who advocate a Western political system," and predicted that if democracy were to come to China, "chaos will result, and reform will be disrupted." Now, after having been purged and officially forgotten, Zhao concluded that to fully modernize, China needed democracy. He advocated a parliamentary system, as had many nineteenth-century Chinese intellectuals who looked toward Western freedoms as a way for the Middle Kingdom to recapture its greatness. "Why is there not even one developed nation practicing any other system?" Zhao asked.

Echoing the views of Sun Yat-sen, Zhao called for a period of tutelage, during which the Communist Party would prepare China for democracy, freeing the press and tolerating a political opposition. He suggested that China should use Taiwan as its model. Zhao's praise of Taiwan served as a lesson to the many senior officials in the US government who viewed the island as, in the words of one senior American official, "the turd in the punchbowl," complicating America's ties with the PRC. In 2016, Taiwan conducted its sixth direct election for president since 1996. The victory of Tsai Ing-wen was a stunning confirmation of Taiwan's democracy, marking the second time an opposition party candidate won Taiwan's highest office and the first time for a woman.

Zhao Ziyang died on January 17, 2005. At his funeral, plainclothes security officers outnumbered the guests. But his words reached beyond the grave. Writing of democracy, he said, "This is ultimately a worldwide trend that we cannot defy."

●

CHAPTER FORTY-SIX

G2?

In April 2009, a few months after he took office, President Barack Obama scheduled a summit in Beijing with Chinese president Hu Jintao. Obama had entered the White House claiming to be "the first Pacific president," in light of his upbringing in Indonesia and Hawaii where he had attended one of the same schools as Sun Yat-sen.

The Obama administration was faced with a decision. The Dalai Lama was planning to visit Washington on a US tour in October and wanted to meet the president. From George H. W. Bush on, no president had denied His Holiness an audience. Hoping to make a good impression on his soon-to-be Chinese hosts, however, Obama decided to postpone the meeting until after he had seen President Hu.

Barack Obama was the first president in decades to enter the White House without having criticized the China policy of its previous occupant. Focused on the global war on terror, President George W. Bush had shelved the idea that China was a "strategic competitor" and maintained quiescent ties with Beijing. Bush's first secretary of state, Colin Powell, had even announced that US relations with China were the best they had ever been. Obama's team was eager to build on Bush's successes. What better way to show America's sincerity, the White House figured, than starting off the relationship with a concession?

Obama administration officials had given China other indications that their administration wanted to be China's partner, even its friend. Secretary of State Hillary Clinton made Asia the destination of her first foreign trip and China the high point. Clinton expanded Henry Paulson's Strategic Economic Dialogue to include not just trade and investment but all aspects of America's relationship with the Middle Kingdom.

Traveling to Beijing in February 2009, Hillary Clinton signaled that the Obama administration would not let its support of human rights "interfere with the global economic crisis, the global climate-change crisis and the security crisis." Criticism of China for artificially deflating the value of its currency to boost exports was absent from Treasury Secretary Tim Geithner's public remarks. And in the first China-related speech from the administration, Deputy Secretary of State James Steinberg made an unprecedented public call for "a core, if tacit, bargain" between the two powers. Washington needed to show China that it welcomed China's arrival "as a prosperous and successful power," he told an audience at a Washington think tank on October 5, 2009. In exchange, China should convince America that its rise "will not come at the expense of the security and well-being of others." Steinberg called for "strategic reassurance" on both sides of the Pacific.

Critics of the Steinberg speech and other Obama administration moves claimed, as one opinion piece in the *Wall Street Journal* put it, that they marked "a major change in U.S. policy." But the reality was that reassuring China and making China strong had been a mainstay of US policy toward China since the 1800s. Obama's team was simply being more earnest and more public than its predecessors. This impression was bolstered by the joint statement issued by the two sides during the November summit between Obama and Hu Jintao. There for the first time, the United States vowed to respect China's "core interests," which Beijing defined as preservation of the current authoritarian regime, respect for the territorial integrity of China, and the preservation of a positive environment for China's continued rise.

The Chinese reaction to the Obama administration's olive branches was tellingly reminiscent of the Qing dynasty officials who interpreted Anson Burlingame's "cooperative policy" as a sign of Western weakness. "Strategic Reassurance? Yes, Please!" went the headline in the *People's Daily* on October 29. Steinberg, the piece said, "took the words out of our mouth." To start, it said, the United States should reassure China by ending arms sales to Taiwan and military surveillance activities off China's coast.

Just weeks after Steinberg's speech, the Chinese treated Obama to the roughest handling that any visiting American president had ever received.

At the summit, they censored the president's remarks during a question and answer session with students in Shanghai. Whereas the previous Chinese president, Jiang Zemin, had engaged in a wide-ranging joint press conference with President Clinton in 1998, President Hu Jintao did not deign to answer a single question with Obama, nor did the Chinese deign to explain why. Both presidents read short statements and then walked away. The public encounter between the two leaders was so frosty that it ended up being parodied on *Saturday Night Live*. In America, the media portrayed Obama as a deadbeat debtor kowtowing to America's banker, the Chinese Communist Party.

Jeffrey Bader, who was responsible for Asia on the National Security Council, wrote that he and the president felt that the coverage was unfair. Nonetheless, the president could not escape the impression that China was calling the shots. Obama's bumpy China trip reinforced the sense of many Americans that, with the nation's mounting debt, the fallout from the Great Recession, and imperial overreach in Afghanistan and Iraq, the United States was on the wane.

From figurative fisticuffs, the relationship degenerated into a real-life shoving match. In 2009, China surpassed the United States as the largest emitter of greenhouse gases. It was also the year when the United Nations held its Climate Change Conference in Copenhagen. Obama arrived in Copenhagen on December 18 with the conference in disarray. The United States wanted China to agree to cut its carbon dioxide emissions and accept a verification mechanism, but the Chinese, along with other developing nations, were balking.

Late in the afternoon of December 18, White House officials learned that the Chinese delegation, led by Premier Wen Jiabao, was meeting secretly with the leaders of Brazil, South Africa, and India to try to forge a united response to the developed world. The president decided to crash the gathering and set out with Secretary of State Clinton in tow. When they arrived at the door to the makeshift conference room, Bader wrote, Obama strode forward "with startled Chinese security, protocol and others parting like the Red Sea for Moses." Clinton and Bader, however, were left to fend for themselves. Chinese security guards tried to block the secretary from entering the room, but with Bader behind her, the two finally "burst, shoulder down, through the phalanx as in a goal-line plunge."

In the room, the president proposed a nonbinding agreement to lower emissions along with a voluntary verification system. China's climate change negotiator stood up and lambasted the United States. Premier Wen silenced him and after short but intense negotiations with Obama agreed to sign off on the statement.

The agreement was small beer, but the meeting underscored how much the world was changing. Very little could move forward without an understanding between China and the United States, and getting the pair to agree on something was hard. "Coming into this conference, it was about 193 countries," Jake Schmidt, international climate policy director for the Natural Resources Defense Council, observed to the *Washington Post*, "and coming out of it, it clearly came down to a conversation between the leaders of those two superpowers." China had become, albeit reluctantly, a major player, while the United States, with similar unease, had been forced to make room for China at the top.

In 2009, China began to throw its weight around. Since the Tiananmen Square crackdown, Beijing had pursued a charm offensive in Asia, following a foreign policy laid out by the late Deng Xiaoping, who instructed his comrades to "hide your capacities, bide your time." Now, China suddenly started showing off its capacities. It sent scores of fishing vessels into territorial waters surrounding the Senkaku Islands, which Japan had taken in 1895 during the Sino-Japanese War. The Senkaku, or Diaoyu, Islands, Beijing claimed, belonged to China. China continued to demand that Southeast Asian nations recognize its claims to the South China Sea, even though it never actually specified what those claims involved. It faced off against the Philippines, and menaced Vietnam over the ownership of atolls. And it continued its policy of trying to push the United States farther from its shores.

In March 2009, Chinese naval vessels confronted a lightly armed US Navy surveillance ship called the *Impeccable* in international waters seventy-five miles from the Chinese coast. Chinese sailors threw boards into the water to block the *Impeccable*'s path and attempted to detach sonar tracking equipment used to monitor Chinese submarine activity. In late January 2010, the Obama administration announced a $6 billion arms package for Taiwan that included Patriot antimissile batteries designed to counter China's massive rocket buildup across the strait. The Chinese reaction was predictably harsh. China suspended relations with the US military, threatened to sanction the American companies involved in the arms sales, and warned that President Hu might cancel an upcoming trip to Washington in April. The trip went ahead.

In Singapore in June 2010, during a dialogue between officials from both countries, Defense Secretary Robert Gates noted that ever since the two countries had normalized relations, China had known that the United States would be selling weapons to Taiwan. Why the fuss now? A People's Liberation Army general responded simply: then, he said, "we were weak. But now we are strong." Chinese pundits urged their nation on. Liu Mingfu, a retired colonel in the People's Liberation Army, wrote a best seller in 2010 called *The China Dream* in which he called on his fellow countrymen to displace the United States as the next world power.

China's new bellicosity, combined with its expanding territorial claims, gave the Obama administration an opening. Washington tightened US security relations with Japan and South Korea, opened the way to sell weapons to its old enemy Vietnam, resumed military relations with Indonesia, and convinced Singapore to build docking space for an American aircraft carrier battle group. Australia welcomed the basing of US Marines on its territory, and New Zealand allowed US Navy ships back into its ports after a hiatus of more than thirty years. The Philippines, which had unceremoniously tossed the United States from a navy base and an air force base in 1991 and 1992, asked American forces to return.

In July 2010, the foreign ministers of all of the members of the Association of Southeast Asian Nations were gathering in Hanoi for the ASEAN Regional Forum, which also included China and the United States. In March, China's assistant minister of foreign affairs Cui Tiankai had intimated that China now viewed its vague claims to the South China Sea on par with its other "core interests" in Tibet and Taiwan. The Southeast Asian nations were alarmed. Representatives from these countries shared Washington's irritation with China's pressure on countries and companies with interests in the region. China had warned ExxonMobil and BP to stop looking for oil in offshore areas near Vietnam. China's coast guard had arrested fishermen and seized fishing vessels from several countries operating in what it claimed to be its waters.

The US response was unveiled on July 23 in Hanoi when twelve nations—Vietnam going first and the United States last—raised the issue of the South China Sea. Calling freedom of navigation on the sea a "national interest," Secretary of State Hillary Clinton volunteered to facilitate moves to create a code of conduct in the region. Clinton also challenged China's designs on the sea. Many of the land features claimed by China were partially submerged, meaning that they fell outside the international definition of sovereign territory. China's foreign minister, Yang Jiechi, stormed out of the meeting. When he returned an hour later, he gave a rambling thirty-minute lecture full of accusations of an American plot. He poked fun at Vietnam's socialist credentials and threatened ASEAN's smaller states. "China is a big country. Bigger than any other countries here," he said, looking at George Yeo, the foreign minister of Singapore.

In her memoirs, Clinton called the ASEAN meeting a "tipping point," in terms of American leadership and pushback against China's assertiveness. In October 2011, she published an essay titled "America's Pacific Century" in *Foreign Policy* magazine. The secretary of state was announcing what she framed as a significant change in America's foreign policy. The parallel with Henry Luce's 1941 essay in *Life* was made all the more obvious as Clinton argued that just as the United States had stabilized Europe following World War II, it now needed to act with a similar urgency to steady the Asia Pacific. Clinton called for a "strategic turn to the Asia-Pacific" and used the word "pivot" three times. It stuck. America had decided, pundits said, to "pivot" toward Asia.

China, of course, was the reason. Clinton, like other US officials, was eager to assure Beijing that the pivot was not a mechanism to contain China. In her essay, she welcomed better ties with Beijing. "The fact is," she wrote, "that a thriving America is good for China and a thriving China is good for America." However, Clinton's goal of creating a "web of partnerships and institutions" in the Pacific threatened China's interests. China wanted to divide and conquer its neighbors so that it could wield its economic heft to best effect. With the pivot, later renamed a "rebalancing," the United States announced its intention of uniting China's neighbors as never before.

While much of the attention on the pivot focused on America's enhanced security commitments to Asia, trade played an important role as well. Americans first came to the Pacific in the eighteenth century as merchants and in the twenty-first century the Asia Pacific was poised to lead global growth. In 2014, the nations along the Pacific Rim accounted for more than half of the world's gross domestic product. So, while the State and Defense departments worked to tighten US alliances near China's shores, Obama administration officials began pulling together the largest free-trade deal in US history, the Trans-Pacific Partnership linking twelve countries on the Pacific that represented roughly 40 percent of global GDP and one quarter of world exports. The trade deal was concluded in November 2015 and included the United States, Japan, Australia, Malaysia, Vietnam, Singapore, New Zealand, Brunei, Mexico, Canada, Peru, and Chile. China was not on the list. But the US Congress, responding to an American backlash against trade deals, balked at ratifying it.

The pivot marked a break with decades of American policy in Asia. Ever since Nixon went to China, the United States had centered its interactions in Asia on its evolving relationship with the Middle Kingdom. The assumption was that China would evolve toward a system similar to that of the United States. Robert Zoellick's "Responsible Stakeholder" speech in September 2005 had constituted a final plea for China to move in that direction. By 2011, hope for such a change was fading.

Secretary Clinton put China and the rest of Asia on notice that Washington planned to "embed our relationship with China in a broader regional framework of security alliances, economic networks, and social connections." Translated, she meant that the United States was returning to a time when it relied on its alliances more than its hopes for a new New China. The US would continue to engage China, but it was moving to contain it, too. China was welcome to join the TPP trade deal, White House officials insisted, but only if it agreed to follow the rules. In this way, Obama had come to embrace the ideas of John MacMurray, who in 1933 had questioned why China had to be the "sun" around which all of America's relations in the region were merely "planetary."

Like no other president since relations with Beijing had been normalized, Obama was public in his exasperation with China. Several years into his administration, he dubbed China a "free rider" in a global system built by the United States. In an August 2014 interview with the *New York Times*, the president noted that China's unwillingness to shoulder responsibility had "worked really well for them," allowing it to secure the benefits of the global trading system with none of the responsibilities. Of the Chinese, Obama quipped: "Nobody really expects them to do anything."

Yet, at the same time, the Obama administration continued to hope against hope that the United States could further pull China into an ever-tightening embrace. Deep into the president's second term, Obama's trade team intensified negotations with China on a Bilateral Investment Treaty that would move the two countires even closer to a Great Harmony envisaged for decades by both Americans and Chinese. Such a pact would provide Chinese and American companies with unparalleled access to each other's markets; it would reduce restrictions on foreign ownership in China and eliminate policies that had forced American firms to share their most valuable technology with a Chinese competitor. Not only would this tie China's fate more securely to that of the United States, but by further opening China's economy to American companies, it would also allow the United States to reprise its role, envisioned decades earlier by Nationalist banker K. P. Chen and later by Communist premier Zhu Rongji, as the catalyst for China's market-oriented reforms.

But to many of China's Communists the Great Harmony with America always seemed like a plot to weaken China. On November 29, 2012, two weeks after his appointment as the new general secretary of the Chinese Communist Party, party boss Xi Jinping, along with the rest of the all-powerful seven-member Standing Committee of the Politburo, visited the vast National Museum of China in Tiananmen Square. Cloaked in the dour dark suits of the party elite, the seven men toured an exhibition titled The Road to Rejuvenation, about China's history from the Opium War to the present day. It was there that China's new leader revealed his—and by extension, the Communist Party's—profoundly tortured views on the United States.

As he stood at the threshold of an exhibition that offered not a single word of praise for any of the countless Western businessmen, scientists, soldiers, philosophers, diplomats, and educators who had helped his country modernize, Xi declared that the "Chinese dream" constituted a "great revival of the Chinese nation." That the president of China and the head of its Communist Party would frame his goals for his country in quintessentially Yankee terms—a dream—illustrates the messy complexity of China's response to the United States in the early years of the twenty-first century.

If anything, the party acted as though the threat posed by the United States was intensifying. In April 2013, the General Office of the Chinese Communist Party issued a communiqué ordering heightened vigilance against American ideas. The communiqué, called Document Number 9, listed seven political "perils." Among them were the growth of civil society, criticism of the party's mistakes, the promotion of "universal values," a free press, and a privatized economy. The document described China's ideological situation as "a complicated, intense struggle" and framed the purveyors of these "false ideological trends" as enemies. Again, the party had declared war on American ideas.

Unlike Xi's predecessor, Hu Jintao, who in public was so devoid of personality that Obama used the expression "to do a Hu Jintao" to describe a monotone recitation of talking points, Xi swaggered self-confidently and publicly supported China's most virulently anti-American thinkers. In October 2014, he praised ultranationalist blogger Zhou Xiaoping for spreading what he called "positive energy." In a particularly notorious essay titled "Nine Knockout Blows in America's Cold War Against China," Zhou had savaged the tendency of young Chinese to worship the West and declared that America was treating China and the Chinese in the same way that Hitler had treated the Jews. From the late 1800s into the early years of the twentieth century, American presidents had flirted with Americans who despised the Chinese. Now, a century later, Chinese leaders were hobnobbing with those who professed to hate the United States.

In the fall of 2014, Document Number 9 was followed by Document Number 30, which ordered universities cleansed of Western-inspired liberal ideas. Party secretaries of universities were summoned to Beijing to study the document and directed, the state-run press reported, to "enhance their sense of danger and resolutely safeguard political security and ideological security." In November, the *Liaoning Daily*, a party newspaper in northeast China, drew nationwide attention when it declared that ideological laxity was rampant in Chinese universities. Chinese academics, the newspaper complained, were comparing Chairman Mao to an emperor, praising Western notions such as the separation of powers, and advocating "that China should take the path of the West."

In early 2015, Minister of Education Yuan Guiren published a lengthy essay demanding that China's textbooks be cleansed of "wrong Western values" and warning teachers and college students that they could become victims of brainwashing by "hostile forces." Western-leaning Chinese academics came under especially intense scrutiny. Some, like Peking University professor Xia Yeliang, were fired for supporting the growth of civil society and hounded into exile. Others, like Qiao Mu, a professor of journalism and director of the Center for International Communication Studies at Beijing Foreign Studies University, were banned from teaching and relegated to clerical chores as punishment for their advocacy of Western-style freedom of the press.

The party also ended its decades-long tolerance of the boom in Christianity. Ground zero for this assault was Zhejiang province, one of China's richest provinces, which had been at the center of China's evangelical Protestantism as well as its entrepreneurial growth. Starting in 2014, the party authorities in Zhejiang removed fifteen hundred crosses from atop the province's churches. Scores of "unregistered" chapels were demolished. In January 2016, party authorities arrested Pastor Gu Yuese, the head of the largest church in China, the Chong-Yi Church, which was founded in 1902 by missionaries from Britain and the United States. Gu had successfully navigated the perilous shoals between loyalty to Communist Party rule and love of Jesus. But Gu had criticized the crackdown, so he was taken away.

The party identified American-backed rule of law programs as a channel of infiltration for Yankee ideas. It attacked Chinese lawyers who had benefited from the training. In July 2015, it launched the most withering assault on the profession in decades. Within a few days, authorities rounded up more than 250 lawyers and their associates who belonged to a nascent "rights defense" movement that had represented those with grievances against the state. The most prominent human rights lawyer, Pu Zhiqiang, was indicted in May 2015 for inciting ethnic hatred and "picking quarrels." In response to questions about Pu's fate, a spokeswoman for China's foreign ministry declared that "some people in the United States have hearts that are too big and hands that are too long" and advised Americans to worry about their own human rights problems. Pu was convicted in December. But instead of jailing him, Pu's minders ordered him to wear a bulky GPS bracelet to show his friends and colleagues that his every move was being tracked by the state.

In March 2015, security officials expanded their assault on China's nascent civil society to the women's movement, detaining five women in three cities, also on suspicion of "picking quarrels." The women had planned to distribute leaflets and stickers on March 8, International Women's Day, to protest groping on public transport, a widespread problem in China's packed subways and buses. The women, known as the Feminist Five, represented a young, creative approach to women's issues. In New York, New Delhi, and Hong Kong, thousands signed petitions calling for their release. In January 2016, the authorities shut a women's legal aid center run by Guo Jianmei, the lawyer whom Hillary Clinton inspired in 1995. As the party had done so many times before, it felt obligated to justify its crackdown by pointing to the United States. The state-run Xinhua News Agency declared that the detentions and closures were no different from cases in America involving lawyers who broke the law.

In 1998, Paul Gewirtz, who was leading the State Department's program to reform China's legal system, rejected the idea that America's help was actually facilitating the creation of a legal system "more efficient at dispensing unfair or brutal punishments." By 2015, however, it had become hard to make that argument anymore.

Despite the persistent fear of American infiltration, the United States continued to spark change in China. In the autumn of 2006, the air in

Beijing was even more noxious than usual. A cloud of impenetrable smog settled on the city. At the US Embassy in Beijing, the chief of the science and technology section, Deborah Seligsohn, with two children in Beijing schools, was unhappy. Each day the Beijing city government released an average reading for the air quality over the past twenty-four hours. When the reading was high, the schools kept their students inside. When it was low, the schools allowed them outside. The problem was that the reading was only an average so some days the schools forced the students to stay inside even though the air quality had improved, and on others, they let them outside when the air quality had turned horrendous. Seligsohn told the schools they were far better just looking at the sky and judging for themselves but no one would listen. They wanted a number that they could go by.

This launched Seligsohn on a crusade that would help transform China. Within a year, the US Embassy installed a $20,000 pollution monitor on its roof that sent out hourly air quality measurements for PM 2.5, fine particles less than 2.5 microns in diameter that can cause serious cardiovascular and respiratory ailments.

Embassy technicians posted the hourly air quality readings on the embassy's website. Then, as the social media site Twitter, which was founded in 2006, rose to prominence, technicians decided to tweet the results as well. For the first time, Chinese and foreigners alike had access to real-time information about one of the most dangerous pollutants.

The embassy's Twitter feed prompted Chinese to confront on an hourly basis the downside of their nation's breakneck growth: the wanton polluting of their air, water, and soil. The embassy expanded its program to all six of its consulates in China. "PM 2.5" entered everyday vocabulary. Chinese families planned their day around the tweets. Celebrities such as real estate tycoon Pan Shiyi, the children's author Zheng Yuanjie, and a prominent investor named Xue Manzi, who counted tens of millions of followers on their microblog accounts, backed the idea of letting Chinese know more about pollution. On January 29, 2013, Pan Shiyi undertook an ad hoc poll asking whether the government should establish a "clean air act"—like the United States had first passed in 1963. More than fifty-five thousand people took part; 99 percent answered "yes."

The embassy's feed was a huge embarrassment to China's government, especially in November 2010 when the air quality reading surged past 500 and a US embassy technician jokingly called it "crazy bad" on Twitter. Predictably, the Chinese Foreign Ministry accused the United States of "interfering in the internal affairs of China" and demanded that the embassy remove the device. One spokesman said that the air quality reading was not relevant to China because, after all, the monitored air—being on the grounds of the US Embassy—was technically in the United States.

The decision to install the monitoring equipment on the US embassy grounds was never discussed at high levels in the US government. But creating awareness of China's environmental degradation amounted to one of the most significant improvements in human rights in China since the resumption of relations in the 1970s. It also was another example of America's stubbornly high expectations for China. Why had the US government installed such a monitor in Beijing first and not, say, in New Delhi, where the air was similarly toxic?

Once the device was in place, it did prompt a debate among US officials. Some in the State Department and National Security Council argued that America should never do anything to embarrass China. But, at the same time, the Twitter feed marked a return to the days of the missionary campaigns against foot-binding, when shaming China's literati forced them to acknowledge the barbarity of the practice. Now, the US government was shaming China over the quality of its air.

The American move forced China to respond. On December 22, 2011, the Ministry of the Environment announced that it would establish a national PM 2.5 monitoring network in 70 cities. The government pledged hundreds of billions of dollars to clean up the air. In 2014, Hebei province, which surrounds Beijing, committed to shutting many of its aging steel mills, cement plants, and coal-fired power plants. Once again, the Beautiful Country had helped spur change in China.

At 2:30 in the afternoon on February 7, 2012, a drama unfolded at Number 4 Consulate Road in Chengdu, the address of the US consulate in Sichuan province. Standing at the doorstep to the US mission was Wang Lijun, the police chief of Chongqing, China's World War II capital. After exchanging pleasantries with American diplomatic personnel, Wang requested political asylum.

Wang was one of China's most famous police officers. *Newsweek* had dubbed him "China's Eliot Ness" for his bare-knuckled assault on organized crime. He had gained notoriety for torturing his victims, jailing political dissidents, and railing against the United States. In October 2011, he referred to America as a country without a history and called the Chinese who had settled there traitors. But like many Communist officials, Wang also harbored a fascination with America. On the wall of his office, he displayed an MBA certificate courtesy of an American correspondence course. Facing a lawsuit accusing him of torture, he complained to a colleague: "This country is hopeless. I want to seek asylum at the US Consulate."

Wang told his American interlocutors at the consulate a fantastic tale about the murder of a British businessman by the wife of the up-and-coming party chief in Chongqing. Wang said that he had been involved in the cover-up but had decided to come clean. He feared for his life, so he sought protection in the only place he felt had the power to shield him—a US diplomatic mission.

In Beijing, Ambassador Gary Locke, who had arrived in China in August 2011, was called from a meeting to the embassy's secure communications area to hear a report. Wang's information, Locke said, contained "fascinating, eye-popping revelations. My first reaction was 'Oh, my god,' I mean, 'OH, MY GOD!'"

Wang detailed a power struggle at the heart of the party, with Chongqing party secretary, Bo Xilai, conspiring with Zhou Yongkang, a longstanding security and oil industry official, to remove Xi Jinping as China's party chief. The Americans informed China's foreign ministry that Wang was at the consulate and allowed Wang to call officials in Beijing. Given Wang's reputation for mistreating prisoners, political asylum was not an option.

On the street outside the consulate, a standoff ensued. Bo Xilai had dispatched hundreds of police officers from Chongqing to retrieve Wang. Authorities in Beijing had ordered Sichuan province security forces to ensure that Wang stayed in Chengdu. By nightfall, more than seven hundred officers with varying loyalties surrounded the consulate. US Marines protecting the installation donned full battle gear. That night, Beijing dispatched a senior official from the Ministry of State Security to Chengdu to take Wang to Beijing. Based on Wang's revelations, Bo Xilai's wife, Gu Kailai, was convicted of murder and given a suspended death sentence. And Bo Xilai and Zhou Yongkang were put in jail for life. As for Wang, he got fifteen years, but in running to the Americans, he had saved his life.

Cartoonist Wei Ke found it ironic that men like Wang Lijun, who had spent their careers fighting American influence, should seek shelter in an American mission. "Didn't you all hate Americans?" Wei asked in an online posting. "Haven't you deceived a large number of young pigheaded lackeys to rally around your anti-American causes? Why didn't you run to your North Korean friends instead?"

In the early years of the twenty-first century, American reporters reprised their old role as China's conscience. The *Wall Street Journal* broke the story implicating Gu Kailai in the murder of a British businessman, and American reporters filed blockbuster stories charting how politically connected families had used their positions to make hundreds of millions of dollars from China's rise. As they had in the era of Thomas Millard, John W. Powell, and Edgar Snow, American reporters took on a significant role in Chinese society, a role that frightened the Party State.

In October 2012, a delegation of Chinese officials appeared at the Manhattan headquarters of the *New York Times*. Led by Zhang Yesui, the smooth-talking, approachable Chinese ambassador to the United States, the delegation requested that the *Times* kill a story about the financial holdings of the family of premier Wen Jiabao. The story, by reporter David Barboza, detailed how Wen's wife, son, daughter, younger brother, and brother-in-law had enriched themselves during Wen's ascent to the top of China's political pyramid. Based on financial records, Barboza estimated that Wen's family controlled assets worth $2.7 billion.

Ambassador Zhang argued that the story would affect China's ongoing leadership transition. President Hu Jintao was set to be replaced by Xi Jinping. Zhang added that such an article would damage America's relations with China. To the *Times* editors, his argument indicated that despite forty years of engagement with the United States, China's officials still had no conception of how America actually worked. Citing an article's potential explosiveness as a reason for killing it was exactly the wrong approach to take with American editors. It was like a drop of blood to a shark. One *Times* editor mused that Zhang could probably have delayed publication by begging for more time to allow Chinese authorities to comment, but threats and entreaties got him nowhere.

On October 25, the *Times* ran the story on its English and Chinese websites. Within three hours, Beijing had blocked both sites in China. Subsequently, the Ministry of Foreign Affairs declined to approve any new journalist visas for *Times* reporters for three years, accusing the paper of "harboring ulterior motives and blackening China." In June 2012, Bloomberg reporters broke a story revealing that relatives of president-in-waiting Xi Jinping had amassed an estimated $376 million. That, too, resulted in

China's blocking the Bloomberg site in China and denying the firm any new journalist visas.

Whereas the *Times* stood behind its reporters and continued to publish exposés about the nexus between public power and private wealth in China, Bloomberg took another course. Faced with declining sales of its financial information terminals in China, a pillar of its business, Bloomberg was reported to have curtailed its investigative reporting. It spiked a major piece that detailed the financial ties between one of the wealthiest men in China and the families of top Chinese leaders, as well as a story about the children of senior Chinese officials employed by foreign banks. In explaining the decision to his reporters, Bloomberg's editor in chief Matthew Winkler compared the move to the self-censorship practiced by foreign news bureaus trying to preserve their ability to report inside Nazi-era Germany.

The varying reactions of the two media giants underscored the difficult decisions American companies faced as they confronted China's rise. Both the *Times* and Bloomberg had expected their Chinese-language websites to turn into financial bonanzas. But making money in China had to be done according to China's rules. It seems that Bloomberg played along. The *Times* declined to.

American Internet giants took varied approaches to China as well. In January 2010, Google disclosed that it had detected a "highly sophisticated and targeted" espionage attack on its servers originating from China. Further investigation revealed, Google said, that attackers were trying to hack into the Gmail accounts of Chinese human rights activists. Google therefore declared that the company was no longer willing to censor results on its Chinese search engine, as the Chinese government had required. With that, Google rolled up most of its operations in China. By contrast, Google competitor Yahoo! cooperated with Chinese investigations of political dissidents, providing Chinese authorities with access to e-mails and other electronic records. Between 2003 and 2004, at least four Chinese dissidents were sentenced to lengthy prison terms partly as a result. Family members of two of those incarcerated sued Yahoo! and the Internet giant settled with them out of court, ultimately establishing a $17 million fund for human rights victims from China.

Other Silicon Valley executives also pursued deals with China. Facebook cofounder Mark Zuckerberg was particularly eager to gain access to the Chinese market. Since China had banned Facebook in July 2009,

Zuckerberg had worked tirelessly to make it possible for his company to return to the Middle Kingdom. He learned passable Chinese, jogged through Tiananmen Square in the middle of a bad-air day, and when he and his wife, Priscilla Chen, attended a state dinner for President Xi Jinping on September 25, 2015, they asked Xi for a Chinese name for their unborn child. Xi politely demurred.

American investment banks vied to hire the sons and daughters of senior Chinese officials in an attempt to ensure access to their fathers. The practice became so egregious that it prompted a 2012 investigation by the US Securities and Exchange Commission. In one case, the investment giant J. P. Morgan was probed for reversing a decision to fire the son of China's minister of commerce after the minister promised to "go the extra mile" for J. P. Morgan's business opportunities in China. The young man ultimately left J. P. Morgan for Goldman Sachs.

With an eye to China's twelve thousand movie screens, Hollywood also strove to curry favor with Beijing. After 1997, it stopped making films that were critical of the PRC. From then on, as China grew into the world's second-largest movie market, Hollywood labored to shed its image as the polluter of Chinese minds. Chinese censors were feted in Los Angeles, invited onto movie sets, and involved in creative decisions. In 2012, MGM released *Red Dawn*, a cheesy drama about a band of American high school students fighting an invading army. At the last minute, MGM switched the nationality of the invaders from Chinese to North Korean to avoid angering the Chinese.

The Obama administration entered office committed to forging closer ties with Beijing but it found itself confronting a regime that was both increasingly aggressive in pursuing its interests and increasingly paranoid about shielding itself from American ideas. The result was that once again, the United States found itself caught in a cycle of enchantment—the idea that China and America could together solve the problems of the world— followed by disappointment—the realization that the Chinese were not that interested in sharing the world's burdens with the United States.

This disenchantment resulted in a significant change in America's approach to Asia. The US military increased its troop strength in the region, and US diplomats began to work more closely with America's friends and allies to push China to change.

China, for its part, went into a defensive crouch. China's new president, Xi Jinping, seemed as exasperated with the United States as President Obama had become with China. Traveling to Mexico in 2009 before he took over as the new party chief, Xi put America on notice that China was no longer interested in American lectures or guidance. "There are some foreigners who have eaten their fill and have nothing better to do than point their fingers at our affairs," he told a group of overseas Chinese. "China does not, first, export revolution; second, export poverty and hunger; or third, cause unnecessary trouble for you. What else is there to say?"

•

CHAPTER FORTY-SEVEN

End of an Era

Buried in the middle of one of a string of government reports on the loss of nuclear secrets to China in 1999 was a line by former senator Warren Rudman blasting the Department of Energy for a specific problem. "Particularly egregious have been the failures to enforce cybersecurity measures," the report read. Rudman was not kidding.

The Internet was the greatest force multiplier in the history of China's espionage against the United States. By July 2012, Keith Alexander, chief of the National Security Administration, America's signals intelligence agency, was declaring that cyberespionage represented the "greatest transfer of wealth in history." Alexander did not mention China, but others in government did. Less than a year earlier, the Office of the National Counterintelligence Executive had proclaimed that "Chinese actors are the world's most active and persistent perpetrators of economic espionage."

To the Chinese, running intelligence operations from the security of their offices in China made perfect sense. It was far less risky than sending their agents into the field. The murky world of Internet ISPs complicated the task of assigning blame. As Joel Brenner, then the director of the National Counterintelligence Executive, remarked to the *National Journal* in 2008, "Why go to the trouble of running a spy if it can be done remotely?" Brenner noted that China's penetration of America's computer networks was unprecedented. "It's kind of a cyber-militia," he said. "It's coming in volumes that are just staggering." They had been the Yellow

Peril in the nineteenth century and the Blue Ants of the 1950s. Now, Chinese agents were swarming America's virtual universe.

Reports from Internet security firms such as McAfee identified victims among defense contractors, information technology companies, and manufacturing firms. In January 2010, Google's announcement that it had been hacked also noted that Chinese cyberspies had targeted twenty other big businesses. The US government fell victim, too. In June 2006, the State Department's East Asian and Pacific Affairs Bureau was hacked, and, as government engineers struggled to respond, streams of data slipped out the back door. A year later, someone believed to be from China burrowed into e-mails from the office of Defense Secretary Robert Gates. Internet accounts of the presidential campaigns of senators Barack Obama and John McCain were compromised, also in intrusions believed to have originated from China. Chinese hackers downloaded half of the digital archives of the Library of Congress.

Whenever it was accused of hacking, the Chinese government responded like a teenager: it denied everything. In February 2013, when the Mandiant cybersecurity firm linked a series of intrusions to a unit of the People's Liberation Army and included photographs of its headquarters and the unit's designation—91638—the Chinese refused to admit that the unit existed. Foreign ministry spokesmen accused foreigners of "a Cold War mentality" and hinted darkly that "anti-China forces" were stirring up trouble.

In June 2013, Edward Snowden, a contractor working for the National Security Administration, charged that his employer had conducted wide-ranging espionage activities against its Western allies. Snowden also revealed that the NSA had targeted hundreds of organizations and individuals in China as well. Snowden's revelations that the United States was spying on China were nothing new. All nations spy. Nonetheless, his claims were a godsend for the Chinese Communist Party. Since 2000, the United States had accused China of launching cyberattacks on US businesses, institutions, individuals, and government agencies. Now here was proof that the Beautiful Country was no better than the Middle Kingdom.

US officials tried to distinguish between state-to-state espionage to steal information about policies and snooping for commercial ends. China argued that this was a distinction without a difference. "If the U.S. is the true defender of democracy, human rights, and freedom like it always described itself," opined the pro-Communist newspaper *Ta Kung Pao* in Hong Kong, "President Obama should sincerely apologize to the people from other countries whose privacy was violated." Snowden's revelations were published in June 2013 shortly after he had left Hawaii for Hong Kong. US authorities asked Hong Kong to extradite him to the United States, but on June 23, Chinese authorities allowed Snowden to leave the territory for Russia.

The cyberbattles between America and China highlighted the fractious nature of the relationship and the growing disenchantment felt on both sides of the Pacific. The arrival of the Internet in the 1990s had led many Americans to predict that China's march to freedom would accelerate. American computer companies had helped China build its modern information network under this assumption. But the Communist Party learned how to wield the network not to open the country to democracy, but to strengthen its own hold on power.

American officials were left to repurpose the old missionary argument that the Chinese should convert to Christianity because it would help China become rich and strong. Now, they argued that China should embrace a free Internet, not because it was the right thing to do but because it would boost the Chinese economy. As Secretary of State Hillary Clinton said on January 21, 2010, Communist Party officials who interfered with Internet freedom risked "walling themselves off from the progress of the next century." It wasn't that allowing freedom of information was the morally correct choice, it was that such freedom, Clinton declared, underlay "global progress." In a party that had helped engineer a decade of double-digit growth while repressing freedom of speech, Clinton's exhortations fell on deaf ears.

American policy to "free" China's Internet also played into the party's hands. Two months after Clinton's address, the United States awarded $1 million to an organization run by members of the Falun Gong religious sect that offered free software to access websites blocked by China's censors. China had been waging a brutal crackdown on the sect since 2009. Its leader, a former trumpet player named Li Hongzhi, had fled to America. And now the Chinese government could not only accuse the US government of sheltering the chief of what it called "an evil cult," but of bankrolling that cult's attempts to get its message into China.

China's cyberattacks on US targets only intensified. In 2007, Chinese hackers stole production plans for the F-35 Lightning II, the most advanced fighter currently in production, and then apparently modeled their latest stealth fighter, the J-31, on it. In the spring of 2015, Chinese spies burrowed into the database of the federal Office of Personnel Management, filching sensitive personal information on as many as twenty-one million federal employees. The attack on the OPM was the worst intelligence penetration of the US government in the lifetime of most of the readers of this book. The Chinese stole the 126-page security application for every American who had obtained high-level clearances since 1986. At about the same time, Chinese cyberspies penetrated the computer systems of United Airlines, which ferries US officials, including many with security clearance, around the globe.

The American reaction to China's cyberattacks and espionage underscored a powerful sense that China had let America down. Now that it was clear that the Communist Party was not particularly interested in becoming America's friend, many Americans felt obligated to view it as an enemy. One prominent political risk consultant, Ian Bremmer, declared that "China is at virtual war with the United States, and the threat is far higher than that of terrorism." Some congressmen called China's cyberespionage "an act of war."

However, Michael Hayden, the former director of the CIA and the NSA, cautioned that the data from the OPM office was a legitimate focus of intelligence. If he had been in the same position as China's spy chief, he told a conference at the offices of the *Wall Street Journal*, "I'd have launched the Star Fleet and we would have brought those suckers home at the speed of light." Hayden concluded: "This is not shame on China. This is shame on us for not protecting that kind of information."

What was most telling about the intrusions, however, was that so few in the US government were willing to openly blame China. On June 26, 2015, following the attack on the Office of Personnel Management, James Clapper, America's top intelligence official, called China the "leading suspect." But after that, American officials fell silent.

The White House's reluctance to publicly name China continued a decades-old pattern. For years, American officials had avoided openly criticizing China for fear that it would make cooperation on "bigger issues" more difficult. That unwillingness to speak honestly continued to give the Communist Party leverage over the United States. China could rail about alleged American plots at home, but the US government kept mum as it hoped for better days. Keeping China strong and stable had always been an essential aim of US policy toward China. For many US officials, despite the "pivot," China continued to remain the "sun" around which America's interests in Asia revolved. As President Obama told interviewer Jeffrey Goldberg in late 2015, "We have more to fear from a weakened, threatened China than a successful, rising China."

That said, the Obama administration was not without successes vis-à-vis the Chinese. China cooperated with the United States and the rest of the UN Security Council to press Iran to mothball its nuclear weapons program in exchange for an end to economic sanctions. In November 2014, Obama and President Xi Jinping pledged to reduce pollution and greenhouse gas emissions. That agreement laid the foundation for a deal to slow global warming hammered out at the UN Conference on Climate Change at the end of 2015.

But characteristically, American policy toward China was inconsistent, underscoring the difficulty Washington was having as it tried to grapple with the challenge China presented. Even as the White House was soft-pedaling criticism of China for its cyberattacks, US officials undertook a concerted effort to convince other nations not to join an infrastructure bank that China had established in 2015 to fund projects throughout Asia. Ignoring entreaties from the White House, Britain broke ranks with the United States, followed by Australia and other Western countries. The Obama administration's clumsy efforts to block China's Asia Infrastructure Investment Bank gave the impression that Washington was indeed committed to constraining China's rise. As US negotiators closed in on the Trans-Pacific Partnership trade deal, President Obama framed the arrangement as a necessary move to blunt Chinese influence. "If we don't write the rules," the president told the *Wall Street Journal* in April 2015, "China will write the rules out in that region." Just a few months earlier, American officials had said they hoped that China would join the pact.

In some areas, Washington moved to fashion coalitions of like-minded nations to put China on notice that its behavior was out of line. In February 2016, the US joined with the European Union, Canada, and Japan to issue a joint statement expressing deep concern about the deterioration of human rights under China's president Xi Jinping. Washington also worked with eleven other Western nations at the UN Human Rights Council to condemn China's human rights record and voiced alarm again with the European Union, Canada, and Japan at new laws on counterterrorism and nongovernmental organizations that seemingly violated China's commitment to the UN Declaration of Human Rights and its responsibilities under the World Trade Organization.

The Obama administration's efforts to modify Chinese behavior in the South China Sea underscored the challenges of coping with a country that—neither friend nor enemy—remained important to the United States. In April 2012, Chinese fishing boats occupied a lagoon near the Scarborough Shoal, a chain of reefs and rocks between the Philippines and China. The

Philippines, which have long claimed the reef and used it for fishing, sent a naval frigate to investigate. The Chinese responded by dispatching two large maritime surveillance ships. Over the ensuing weeks, Manila withdrew the frigate and replaced it with a coast guard cutter, while the Chinese increased their presence, at one point deploying approximately 80 surveillance ships, fishing boats, and utility craft in the lagoon. Beijing then blocked fruit imports from the Philippines. At that point, the US stepped in and brokered an agreement in June according to which both sides promised to withdraw their ships. But, when only Manila complied, the Obama administration fell silent.

On September 25, 2015, President Obama and Chinese president Xi Jinping announced an agreement to end cybertheft of intellectual property for commercial use. Just a week earlier, Xi had told the *Wall Street Journal* that China did not engage in the "theft of commercial secrets in any form." Was China agreeing to stop a practice that it had denied in the first place? Regardless, days after the agreement was announced, the cybersecurity firm CrowdStrike announced that it had blocked seven Chinese attacks against US technology and pharmaceutical companies. CrowdStrike founder Dimitri Alperovich noted, "We've seen no change in behavior."

China reacted angrily to the Obama administration's inconsistencies, reflecting its own disenchantment with the United States. At times, Beijing appeared to be aggressively xenophobic and basically paranoid. At others, it made perfectly sensible decisions that many in Washington willfully misinterpreted. Obama administration officials described China's June 2014 announcement of the Asian Infrastructure Investment Bank as a gambit to create an international institution beyond Washington's sway. But, in fact, the bank was born more of China's frustration at Washington's failure to live up to its promises than a desire to fashion a Sinocentric universe. Following the 2008 Great Recession, both the Bush and the Obama administrations had committed to reforming the International Monetary Fund to give China more say. But in 2010, Congress blocked the reforms, leaving China with a voting share at the IMF equal to that of France, even though its economy was five times larger. China decided to take its business elsewhere, and when Washington pressured its allies not to join the new institution, the Chinese were doubly miffed. (In late 2015, Congress finally approved the IMF reforms, increasing China's voting share.)

China was furious when the Obama administration encouraged the nations of Southeast Asia to challenge it in the South China Sea. Why should the United States rule the seas so close to China's shores, many in China asked. Wasn't America's much vaunted support for "freedom of navigation" just a smokescreen to allow the US Navy to spy off China's coast? Why did China need to listen to American entreaties to abide by international law when the US itself had yet to ratify the UN Convention on the Law of the Sea? In the spring of 2014, Beijing moved an offshore oil exploration rig into an area claimed by Vietnam. The next year, it launched a massive land reclamation scheme to turn seven rocks into islands in seas far closer to Vietnam and the Philippines than to China. Beijing placed fighter jets, antiaircraft missiles, and other hardware on them as it tried to push US forces farther from its shores.

China seemed to think that its actions would somehow cow its neighbors into submission, but the result was just the opposite. The more China pressed, the more the Southeast Asian nations urged the US Navy to stay in the region. But, at the same time, Washington seemed to be at a loss as to how to roll back China's land grabs. US Navy officers advocated an aggressive response. In the National Security Council, however, officials fretted about pushing China too far. This disagreement was reflected in US action. In October 2015, the USS Lassen, a guided-missile destroyer, sailed within twelve miles of Subi Reef in the Spratly Islands. But when it did so, Obama administration officals called the Lassen's mission one of "innocent passage," which implied that the US government recognized that Subi was Chinese territory. Then, in late January 2016, an American warship sailed within twelve miles of another recently manufactured island, called Triton, in the Paracels. This time, the navy said nothing about "innocent passage," implying that it did not recognize China's claims. In Beijing, the People's Daily took a page out of the 1950s, warning the United States "that China has never been afraid of 'paper tigers.'"

More broadly, President Xi Jinping seemed intent on overturning decades of tacit Chinese acceptance of America's role as the regional policeman in Asia. As Xi said on May 21, 2014, it is time "for the people of Asia to run the affairs of Asia, solve the problems of Asia, and uphold the security of Asia." What he meant, of course, was that it was time for China to replace the United States.

In other areas, the Chinese Communist Party appeared to be reconsidering the very basis of its interactions with the outside world, and specifically those with America. In 2015, the Chinese legislature passed a National Security Law that appeared aimed at creating a digital world walled off from the rest of humanity. Foreign business groups expressed concerns that the law, along with other proposed measures, would be used to restrict foreign investment from the telecommunications, banking, and other sectors. Another law, passed in 2016, placed all of China's non-governmental and nonprofit organizations under the administration of the police, threatening the flow of people-to-people exchanges in the arts, education, science, and philanthropy that Americans and Chinese had fashioned over the previous half century. The Communist Party rang in "National Security Education Day" in April 2016 by plastering Beijing with posters warning female government workers about the dangers of dating foreigners, who could turn out to be spies. The poster, called "Dangerous Love," chronicled the hapless romance of Little Li, a Chinese civil servant, who falls for David, a red-headed foreign scholar, only to end up giving him secret documents. Once again, the party was digging deep into its anti-Western toolkit as its predecessors had done centuries before. Negotiations on the Bilateral Investment Treaty with America sputtered as well, a sign that the officials at China's helm had grown wary of the United States as a catalyst for change. During a meeting in September 2015 between President Xi Jinping and the heads of leading American and Chinese tech firms in Seattle, China's president was clear. American businesses were welcome to come to China to partner with Chinese firms (and hand over their technology). Xi said nothing about US tech firms setting up operations in China by themselves.

On the issue of North Korea's nuclear program, China seemed to be significantly less interested in cooperating with the US to press Pyongyang to abandon the Bomb. Following North Korea's fourth nuclear test on January 6, 2016, John Kerry, who had succeeded Hillary Clinton as secretary of state, hurried to Beijing seeking more Chinese help. Throughout the visit, the Chinese appeared to just barely tolerate his presence. Kerry warned that Beijing had "a fundamental responsibility" to meet the challenge from North Korea. The Chinese did approve tough sanctions on the regime in Pyongyang, but there was no requirement to cut off fuel shipments, which come almost entirely from China. Many in Washington feared that Beijing's goal continued to be the preservation of the North Korean regime and China's influence on the peninsula.

The early twenty-first century found the Chinese alternating between bluster and insecurity in dealing with the United States. Official Chinese delegations returning from the Beautiful Country no longer felt that America was in high gear or that China was stuck in reverse. Now it was, if anything, the other way around. Many of China's elite expressed the belief that China had finally accomplished Mao Zedong's great goal for his nation—*ganmei*—catching up with America. But simultaneously, there was a sense of a yawning gap on other fronts, particularly regarding values. And when the United States dispatched its first Chinese American ambassador to China, this nagging self-doubt burst forth in a public display.

Gary Locke was an Eagle Scout, a Yale graduate, and had been the first Chinese American governor of any state and the secretary of commerce before he was posted to Beijing in 2011. On the way to China, a Chinese businessman in the Seattle-Tacoma International Airport photographed him wearing a backpack and buying his own coffee at a Starbucks. The businessman posted the picture on a microblog site in China. It went viral, touching off a firestorm in a country accustomed to stories of corrupt Chinese officials indulging in privileged lives funded by graft. "To most Chinese people," wrote one Chinese reporter, "the scene was so unusual it almost defied belief."

The Chinese media storm did not subside once Locke and his family arrived in Beijing. His strolls through the capital's diplomatic quarter, his photogenic family, even his workouts—he could hold a plank for fifty-two minutes—became fodder for the adoring Chinese press, which used the ambassador's everyday life to mock Communist officialdom. In that sense, Locke's basic decency and positive attitude fed into a long-standing Chinese belief that the American spirit of self-improvement had something to teach China. That it was a spirit refracted through a Chinese American only made the story more irritating to China's powers-that-be.

The Communist Party tried to limit Locke's appeal. The *Global Times*, an influential tabloid run by the party mouthpiece, the *People's Daily*, took a few swipes at Locke early in his tenure, suggesting that his common touch was contrived and declaring that it was "bizarre and twisted" to regard his public behavior "as evidence of cleanness in US politics." But the party saved its powder for Locke's departure in 2014. Then, the state-run *China News Service* ran a rancorous screed about his tenure, calling Locke "a rotten banana" and accusing him of selling out his race. The rant ended, "Let's bid goodbye to the plague. Farewell, Gary Locke," a cheap reference to Mao Zedong's 1949 essay, "Farewell, Leighton Stuart."

In the face of this new reality, Americans again fell into a cycle of despair about China. One leading China scholar after another emerged to declare a crisis in US-China relations. David M. Lampton, a professor at Johns Hopkins University's School of Advanced International Studies, contended that the relationship had reached an inflection point. "Our respective fears are nearer to outweighing our hopes than at any time since normalization," he wrote in the spring of 2015. "Has U.S. China Policy Failed?" asked Harry Harding, America's preeminent scholar of the relationship, in the fall 2015 issue of the *Washington Quarterly*.

A host of American reports and books tried to grapple with the uncomfortable reality that US bets on China had turned out—at least for now—to be wrong. Some old friends of China's, like Michael Pillsbury, the former Rand analyst who first advocated selling weapons to the PRC, alleged in his 2015 book *The Hundred-Year Marathon* that China had harbored a secret plan to surpass America since the first days of its revolution in 1949. With the zeal of the converted, Pillsbury declared that it was time for the United States to get tough with China. The People's Republic, he declared, "has failed to meet nearly all of our rosy expectations."

Other China Hands urged America to be more, not less, accommodating. In separate books, China scholars Michael Swaine and Lyle Goldstein argued that the United States should cede the Western Pacific to the Middle Kingdom as part of a grand bargain to improve ties. America should withdraw its troops from South Korea, and as long as China offered assurances that it wouldn't attack Taiwan, it should stop selling weapons to the island. Goldstein went so far as to argue that the United States should press Taiwan's leaders to commence negotiations on some sort of unification with China. However, neither Goldstein nor Swaine could explain why China, after decades of American entreaties, would suddenly agree to set aside its threat to use force.

Henry Kissinger argued that the main issue dividing the United States and China was cultural. It was America's inability to understand "their history," Kissinger told *National Interest* magazine in July 2015, that had brought the two nations to their current crisis. "Can two civilizations that do not, at least as yet, think alike come to a coexistence formula that produces world order?" Kissinger asked.

These reactions duplicated the sentimentalism that had been a feature of the relationship for centuries. Thinkers like Pillsbury argued that China needed to be punished for not adhering to American norms. Alternatively, Swaine and Goldstein, in an attempt to turn China into the friend many had always wanted it to be, sought the chimerical Great Harmony that the two nations had chased since the nineteenth century. Kissinger, meanwhile, opted for the mystical Oriental approach. The relationship was difficult, he said, because the inscrutable Chinese do not think like Americans.

The Chinese encouraged Kissinger's view. "It's not that Americans have misconceptions about China," argued Vice Premier Wang Qishan in a May 2011 interview with Charlie Rose. "At root, they don't understand it. . . . China is an ancient civilization. We are an Oriental culture." Compared to the Chinese, Wang declared, "Americans are very simple people."

Was it really that hard to "get" China? With surging economic growth and a stronger military, China's interests now circled the globe. The problem was that the interests of the Chinese Communist Party were diverging from the interests of the United States—and somehow, many Americans had expected that they never would.

In June 2015, China stumbled. A stock market bubble in Shanghai popped, and when the government tried to stop the slide by ordering some companies to buy shares and banning others from selling, the air of invincibility that had shrouded the Chinese Communist Party for decades began to dissipate.

No sooner had Shanghai's shares plummeted than the People's Bank of China engaged in a ham-handed attempt to devalue the Chinese currency, the yuan. Although the bank had decided to make the yuan more, not less, convertible on world markets, the matter was so badly handled that *New York Times* columnist Paul Krugman advised his readers on July 31, 2015, to forget everything they had heard about the competence of China's leaders. Wrote Krugman: "They have no clue what they're doing."

In January 2016, China's contagion spread to the United States. China's stock markets continued their tumble, following the announcement that China's economy had grown by 6.9 percent in 2015, the lowest growth rate in twenty-five years. The New York Stock Exchange posted its worst ten-day start to a year ever. At the World Economic Forum in Davos, Switzerland, hedge fund billionaire George Soros declared that China's economy was in for a "hard landing." China experts such as Arthur Kroeber worried that, in a departure from the past, when China's leaders had reassured domestic and foreign investors that the market would play a larger role, "Today China is a country without a clear economic direction."

While some Americans took a perverse pleasure in China's troubles, with essays heralding "The End of China's Rise," most people registered the tremors from the other side of the globe as an indication of how closely integrated the two great nations that share the Pacific Ocean had become. As China expert Orville Schell observed, "What happens in China matters elsewhere. For better or worse, we are all in a common enterprise from which there is no escape."

Afterword

Over the past five years, I've worked to tell the story of this "common enterprise from which there is no escape." Living in both China and the United States, researching in the Library of Congress as well as in archives around China, I've been struck by the depth of the relationship between these two nations and by the extent to which the patterns of the past permeate the present.

My days have been filled with stories of American and Chinese merchants, adventurers, missionaries, diplomats, thieves, and revolutionaries who forged one of the most complex relationships between any two peoples on earth. From these tales of the past, I've tried to discern a way forward for the future. If there are lessons in the interactions between the Beautiful Country and the Middle Kingdom, what are they?

In the beginning, trade brought China and America together. Other factors—religion, education, art, literature, food, and profound mutual regard—entered the equation. Over time, these have only multiplied, and as China and America proceed into the future, many more powerful bonds will be forged. There are irresistible forces bringing the two countries (as well as individual Chinese and Americans) closer to one another: among them Chinese immigration, Chinese attendance in American schools, investment, economic interdependence, and cultural intermingling. Each week, close to four thousand passenger planes cross the Pacific

Ocean uniting the two peoples; a decade ago fewer than one thousand made the trip.

At the same time, there are those on both sides of the Pacific who continue to resist the creation of a Great Harmony between the two nations. America has no shortage of populists who seek to blame China for the world's ills. In China, anti-American bigots are even more influential. These days their paranoia about American influence and values has infected the highest rung of the Chinese Communist Party.

Still, the United States has no choice but to redouble its efforts to complete its historic mission to pull China into the world and to seek this Great Harmony, even if it is ultimately unattainable. As Richard Nixon presciently noted in 1968, China is just too big to be allowed "to nurture its fantasies, cherish its hates and threaten its neighbors." This task may seem all the more daunting now that China has amassed an arsenal of advanced military equipment and is training a large army to use it. But, it is even more crucial. The United States is the only nation capable of convincing China to become one of the first powers ever to put all that money down, buy all that gear, and never give in to the temptation to pull the trigger.

Indeed, between China and America, the maintenance of peace is the Holy Grail. I would argue that the issue is not whether there will be reunification between the mainland and Taiwan in the future, nor whether there will be peaceful navigation of the South China Sea, but how the transition will go. Botched, a global humanitarian disaster is inevitable as well as disruptions of trade that would roil China and the world.

So far, I'd also argue that the Chinese deserve measured praise. Taiwan and the PRC are far closer now than seemed possible even thirty years ago, and it is not hard to imagine evolution continuing to proceed, in a fashion that keeps the peace and protects the vast web of economic and social interests involved in the reconnection of the two places. The Chinese on both sides of the Taiwan Strait are entitled to credit for this; ditto the US for its role. There is a potential model to offer other nations and it is globally important to show that major disagreements can be resolved without military force and the horrific civilian and other collateral damage we see too often.

To ensure continued tranquility, China needs to change. It is hard for me to imagine both a peaceful reunification with Taiwan and a peaceful accord over the multilateral issues at play in the South China Seas, without a more trusting relationship having first developed in China between the Red Emperor in Beijing who seems these days to be increasingly high and far away and the Chinese people—on the mainland, in Hong Kong, and on Taiwan—who are increasingly sophisticated and politically aware. The notion of a balance existing between the leaders and the governed is a mainstay of traditional Chinese political philosophy. If one sees the relationship between China and America as a historically time-tested friendship, then the United States has an important role to play in righting this balance and continuing the painstakingly slow process of convincing China's government of the need for political reform.

To accomplish this, on one hand, the United States would do well to take a page from the Chinese playbook and work to maintain, if not increase, what the Chinese call "comprehensive national strength." Shouldn't America, faced with the challenge from China, consider some planning in its economic development, more investment in its aging infrastructure, more resources for education, an immigration policy that welcomes job creators, scientists, and artists, and a recommitment to ensuring that its soldiers and CIA officers forever close the dark chapter on "enhanced interrogation techniques?" You're not a useful teacher or a friend, especially to China, which watches America so closely, if you're a hypocrite or weak.

Maintaining peace should also not mean ceding the Western Pacific to China, leaving the South China Sea, or giving in to Chinese demands to stop supporting Taiwan. As we've seen with the case of Anson Burlingame, America's first minister to the Qing court in Beijing, some Chinese would view such solicitude as a sign of vulnerability and would be all the more tempted to pick a fight. Instead, American officials and American businessmen and businesswomen might want to contemplate borrowing another time-worn Chinese tactic and adopting a far more transactional posture in dealing with the Middle Kingdom. Why pay today for a promise of better behavior tomorrow? Why make deals that do not directly and immediately benefit the national interests of the United States or one's company or one's workers? In the pursuit of the Great Harmony, rapturous enchantment is not America's ally; realism is.

If America follows a mixture of containment and engagement with China, my guess is that the two nations will successfully fox-trot, albeit clumsily, into the future, just as they have more or less lurched through the past. I believe this because I believe two other things. China's relationship with America is not as dysfunctional as it often seems. And China deserves more praise than it often gets.

In early 2002, I returned to China after months reporting in Pakistan and Afghanistan following the 9/11 attacks on the United States. Touching down in Beijing, I found myself happy to be in a place where there was promise of a better future and where many people were working to improve their lives. As a colleague from National Public Radio who had also witnessed the destructive madness of radical Islam put it, somewhat tongue-in-cheek, "Go Jiang Zemin!"

I say this even though I've never been a friend of the Chinese Communist regime. As a reporter for the Associated Press, I was tossed out of China in 1989 following the June Fourth massacre. The government accused me of being one of the "black hands" behind the protests. Later, as the China bureau chief for the *Washington Post*, I had my share of run-ins with China's security services and the occasional bigoted Chinese military officer. But I also know, having spent more than a decade of my life covering wars and revolutions in other parts of the world, that things in China could be a lot worse. Like the US, China supports continued trade and investment. It fears radical Islam. Though it perpetrated the world's most egregious act of nuclear proliferation—the passing of a blueprint of a nuclear bomb to Pakistan—it has become far more protective of its status as a nuclear power. It no longer follows the old Soviet model of supporting state terrorism. Both the United States and China understand the importance of addressing climate change. I also am aware that Americans have a hard time acknowledging China's successes. Many of us hold the Chinese in such high regard that we set an impossibly high bar for the People's Republic of China.

In addition, the United States is not doing that bad a job at "managing China" nor the Chinese at "managing America." Both sides are often guarded, sometimes hostile, but overall they are accommodating. China has friends sprinkled throughout Washington think tanks and the US government bureaucracy who can act as a brake on deteriorating ties. In Beijing, a similar, less public core of policy makers and business leaders (many of whom have worked or studied in the United States) do what they can even in today's noxious climate to dial down the anti-Americanism there.

For two hundred years America has held that the stability of China is in the direct interest of the United States. That is not going to change. Indeed, if given a chance, there is a concordance emerging between the two nations. America is getting more of the China it dreamed of for so long: one able to feed itself and stand on its feet with a sense of national purpose and pride. Chinese, as well, are living their halcyon days. Chinese life expectancy has gone from forty-five in 1950 to almost eighty-five today.

It's never been better to be a Chinese. Amid all the discord, there's hope in these ties.

I, too, am a beneficiary of this relationship. I went to China in 1980 as a student, a year after Washington formally recognized Beijing, and I've lived in China, on and off, for the past four decades. I have had a ringside seat at history's most rapid, complete, and positive economic transformation. I met my wife there, and we have raised our children between China and the United States. In that sense, this book also encapsulates my family's story and is born of the blending of the Beautiful Country and the Middle Kingdom.

Notes

●

Part I

ONE • A New Frontier

The best single book on the environment in Guangzhou (Canton) in the early years of America's engagement with China is a novel by Amitav Ghosh, *River of Smoke*, published in 2011. There is a recent history of the early days of US relations with China called *When America Met China* by Eric Jay Dolin. My sources for this chapter are mostly primary, involving letters from US merchants; the diaries of merchants, such as Amasa Delano, William Dane Phelps, and Samuel Shaw; and Chinese archives. Earl Swisher's book of Qing dynasty documents on the empire's relations with the United States—*China's Management of the American Barbarians*—was irreplaceable. The *Chinese Repository*, an American-run newspaper in Guangzhou at the time, remains an excellent source for events that occurred then.

TWO • Founding Fortunes

For this chapter, the Peabody Essex Museum in Salem, Massachusetts, holds significant materials on America's trade with China during the nineteenth century, including a stack of letters between Chinese merchant Howqua and his American clients. This chapter also benefited from John D. Wong's 2012 dissertation on Howqua, "Global Positioning: Houqua and His China Trade Partners in the Nineteenth Century," which includes details of Howqua's investments in the United States. Again, a significant portion of this chapter relied on primary sources, such as letters and writings of US traders, including John Murray Forbes; written records left by Qing dynasty officials, such as Lin Zexu; and reports in the *Chinese Repository*. China had already become a story in the US media, so business magazines, such as *Hunt's Merchants' Magazine and Commercial Review*, accessed at the Library of Congress, were useful in fleshing out the story. Xu Jiyu's *A Short Account of the Oceans Around Us* is central to understanding how the United States was seen by influential Chinese. Frederic D. Grant's thesis on the US-China trade, "The Chinese Cornerstone of Modern Banking," provided an important perspective.

THREE • Blitzconversion

The story of Issachar Jacox Roberts was pieced together through secondary sources, such as Jonathan Spence's *God's Chinese Son* and Stephen R. Platt's *Autumn in the Heavenly Kingdom*, along with primary research at the American Baptist Historical Society in Atlanta, Georgia. Peter Parker's medical work in Guangzhou and his cooperation with Lamqua was spelled out in Jonathan Spence's *To Change China*. This chapter also benefited from the assistance of P. Richard Bohr, professor at the College of Saint Benedict and Saint John's University. Michael Green, of the Center for Strategic and International Studies, was very helpful in teasing out the importance of US consul Humphrey Marshall. Caleb Cushing left behind voluminous reports about his trip to China, which was also covered in the American press at the time.

FOUR • The Calm Minister

Samuel Kim's unpublished PhD dissertation on Anson Burlingame, "Anson Burlingame: A Study in Personal Diplomacy," was very useful in the writing of this chapter, as were the letters of Burlingame's wife, Jane, and Burlingame's writing, much of which is housed at the Library of Congress. Again, contemporary American reporting was used to recount many of the events in this chapter. Earl Swisher's translations of Qing dynasty official reports were used throughout. This chapter also benefited from David Scott's *China and the International System, 1840–1949*.

FIVE • Men of Iron

The story of the Chinese in America in the nineteenth century is told in American newspapers of the day, in letters, and also in a huge quantity of secondary material. Of particular use was Jean Pfaelzer's *Driven Out: The Forgotten War against Chinese Americans* and Charles McClain's *In Search of Equality: The Chinese Struggle against Discrimination in Nineteenth-Century America*. In addition, newer research by Chinese who have recently moved to the United States has provided a refreshing take on the old story, an example being Liping Zhu's *A Chinaman's Chance*. The story of the pulchritudinous Ah Toy is told in the newspapers of the day. Franklin Bee's story is also available in California's newspapers as is that of the Workingmen's Party. Simon Schama has a chapter on Bee in his book, *The American Future*. Yung Wing's story is told best by Yung Wing, in his autobiography, *My Life in China and America*, and by Liel Leibovitz and Matthew Miller in *Fortunate Sons*.

SIX • A Good Thrashing

Jeffrey Dorwart's *The Pigtail War: American Involvement in the Sino-Japanese War of 1894–1895* is an excellent introduction to this conflict. The war was also covered in detail in the American press, particularly in the *New York Times*, which reported extensively about the activities of John W. Foster, a former secretary of state, who aided China's negotiations. William Woodville Rockhill's views on the war and on China are present throughout the archives of the US State Department. The story of Young John Allen, Gilbert Reid, and other missionaries who engaged with China's intellectual elite to try to push reforms is told in the pages of their newspaper, the *Globe*. Kang Youwei's views on foot-binding and Western influence on his reform program can be found in *Kang Youwei Quanji*, his collected writings.

SEVEN • Bible Women

Adele Fielde's story is available in letters and other documents at the American Baptist Historical Society in Atlanta. There is also a biography of Fielde—*Adele Marion Fielde: Feminist, Social Activist, Scientist* by Leonard Warren. The story of Ida Kahn and Mary Stone is told both in Connie Shemo's *The Chinese Medical Ministries of Kang Cheng and Shi Meiyu, 1872 to 1937* and in Jane Hunter's *The Gospel of Gentility: American Women Missionaries in Turn-of-the-Century China*. Fielde, Kahn, and Stone all left behind voluminous writings, both in books and in lectures.

EIGHT • The Door Opens and Shuts

John Hay's Open Door policy is detailed extensively by the newspapers of the day. It is also put into context in *Tournament of Shadows: The Great Game and the Race for Empire in Central Asia* by Karl E. Meyer and Shareen Blair Brysac. The Boxer Rebellion was also of enormous interest to the American press of the day. Records of the State Department have substantial information about the rebellion. The story is told excellently in Diana Preston's *The Boxer Rebellion*. The story of Eva Jane Price is available in a compendium of her letters and journals, *China Journal, 1889–1900: An American Missionary Family during the Boxer Rebellion*.

NINE • Hot Air and Hope

Two scholarly articles were helpful in setting Frank Goodnow's involvement in the constitution of China—Jedidiah Kroncke's "An Early Tragedy of Comparative Constitutionalism: Frank Goodnow and the Chinese Republic" and Noel Pugach's "Embarrassed Monarchist: Frank J. Goodnow and Constitutional Development in China, 1913–1915." Chinese constitutional researchers have spoken informally of their views about Goodnow but have been wary about publishing on this topic due to current restrictions on academic freedom in China. Liang Cheng's role in the decision to return the Boxer Indemnity is told by Chinese historian Liang Biying in *Liang Cheng yu Jindai Zhongguo*. Marie Claire Bergère's biography of Sun Yat-sen was very helpful to the telling of his story. So were Sun's own writings and interviews. Homer Lea's story is told in a biography by Lawrence Kaplan.

Part II

TEN • American Dreams

The story of Hu Shi and Edith Clifford Williams is told by Susan Egan Chan and Chih-p'ing Chou in *A Pragmatist and His Free Spirit: The Half-Century Romance of Hu Shi and Edith Clifford Williams*. Noel Pugach's book on US diplomat Paul Reinsch, *Paul S. Reinsch: Open Door Diplomat in Action*, provided insight into the frustrations he faced in Beijing.

China's story at the Paris Peace Conference is told well in *The Wilsonian Moment: Self-Determination and the International Origins of Anticolonial Nationalism* by Erez Manela.

ELEVEN • Mr. Science

The story of the Rockefeller Foundation's philanthropic enterprise in China is in Mary Brown Bullock's *The Oil Prince's Legacy: Rockefeller Philanthropy in China*. John Dewey's influence on China is detailed in numerous books and articles, among them PhD dissertations by Kuang Qizhang and Wang Ching-sze and again by Susan Chan Egan and Chih-p'ing Chou. Jimmy Yen is the subject of a biography by Charles Hayford, *To the People: James Yen and Village China*.

Sun Yat-sen's disenchantment with America is apparent in the many interviews he gave to Western correspondents. Lydia Liu's research pinpointed the connection between *Chinese Characteristics* and Lu Xun's "The True Story of Ah Q."

TWELVE • Fortune Cookies

The story of America's growing fascination with things Chinese is told in the newspapers, magazines, and movies of the day. Sui Sin Far's short story collection, *Mrs. Spring Fragrance*, Gouverneur Morris's *Incandescent Lily*, and Pearl Buck's oeuvre all evidence a growing American interest in China. Yun-te Huang's *Charlie Chan* is another excellent example of how Chinese immigrant scholars, with little fealty to the dictates of political correctness, are remaking Chinese American studies. Graham Hodges's *Anna May Wong: From Laundryman's Daughter to Hollywood Legend* is a more predictable take on the first nonwhite movie star in the United States. Much of Joseph Rock's work was published in the *National Geographic*. The story of America's fascination with Chinese antiquities is revealed in Meyer and Brysac's book *The China Collectors: America's Century-Long Hunt for Asian Art Treasures*.

THIRTEEN • Up in Smoke

The story of BAT in China is well told in Sherman Cochran's *Big Business in China*. The story of Nanyang Brothers Tobacco company is told in Cochran's book and also in the documents of the company, *Nanyang Xiongdi Yancao Gongsi Shiliao*. The life of a BAT trader is told in the memoirs of James Lafayette Hutchison. The story of Chen Guangfu is told in a history published in Taiwan by Yao Songling and also in the archives of the Hoover Institution on War, Revolution and Peace.

FOURTEEN • The Soong Dynasty

Details of the life of Soong Mayling are available in countless articles and books, among them *Madame Chiang Kai-shek: China's Eternal First Lady* by Laura Tyson Li. T. V. Soong's personal history is well told by Chinese historians Wu Jingping and Tai-chun Kuo. The newspapers of the day reported about the Nanjing Incident, as did Alice Tisdale Hobart in *Harper's*. Her novel, *Oil for the Lamps of China*, was influenced by her experiences in China at this time. American reporter Milly Bennett's writings were edited by Tom Grunfeld and paint a portrait of the increasingly starry-eyed American view of China's left wing. The story of the involvement of Americans in Chiang Kai-shek's crackdown on Communists in Shanghai is in John B. Powell's memoirs, *My Twenty-Five Years in China*.

FIFTEEN • Opportunity or Threat

The story of American jazz and Chinese folk music is told in Buck Clayton's autobiography. Mao Zedong's views of the United States are available in *The Selected Works of Mao Tse-Tung* and also in Liu Yawei's PhD dissertation, "The United States According to Mao Zedong: Chinese-American Relations, 1893–1976." China's evolving views of American women are detailed by Louise Edwards in her scholarly article in *Linglong* magazine, "The Shanghai Modern Woman's American Dreams: Imagining America's Depravity to Produce China's 'Moderate Modernity.'" Chinese scholar Qian Suoqiao has written powerfully about Lin Yutang's role as a Chinese moderate and his troubled relationship with American supporters of Chinese Communism. William Leary tells the story of the US mission to help China's air force in the 1920s in the *Pacific Historical Review*. The US mission to teach China to fly is told in Gregory Crouch's *China's Wings: War, Intrigue, Romance, and Adventure in the Middle Kingdom during the Golden Age of Flight*. The bizarre American silver policy story is told in a PhD dissertation, "American Silver Policy and China," by Michael Blaine.

SIXTEEN • A Red Star

The many lives of Agnes Smedley are told in a courageous biography by Ruth Price, who identified Smedley as a Soviet spy. Edgar Snow tells the romanticized story of Mao Zedong in *Red Star Over China*.

SEVENTEEN • New Life

George Shepherd's story is told in China-born James Thomson's book *While China Faced West*. The kidnapping of Chiang Kai-shek was given prominent play in the newspapers of the day.

Part III

EIGHTEEN • Bloody Saturday

The story of the Flying Tigers is told in T. V. Soong's documents in the Hoover Institution on War, Revolution and Peace; in the autobiography of Claire Chennault, *Way of a Fighter*; in newspapers of the day; and in Daniel Ford's story of the unit, *Claire Chennault and His American Volunteers, 1941–1942*. Minnie Vautrin's story is told by Hu Hua-ling in *American Goddess at the Rape of Nanking: The Courage of Minnie Vautrin* and in the diaries of Vautrin and her colleague Cheng Ruifang. Herbert Yardley tells his China story in *The Black Chinese Chamber: An Adventure in Espionage*, which I highly recommend.

NINETEEN • Little America

Hilda Yan and Li Xiaqing's story is told by Patti Gully in *Sisters of Heaven: China's Barnstorming Aviatrixes: Modernity, Feminism, and Popular Imagination in Asia and the West*. Theodore White tells his own story in *In Search of History*. Chen Hansheng tells his story in his Chinese-language autobiography, *Sige Shidai de Wo*. The Flying Tigers story is from Chennault's autobiography, T. V. Soong's files at Hoover, and Daniel Ford's biography.

TWENTY • Burmese Days

For decades, American views of the US wartime history in China were shaped by Barbara Tuchman's *Stilwell and the American Experience in China, 1911–1945*. But over the past years, other scholars have adopted a broader, more detailed perspective on the war and have relied not only on American sources but also on those from the former USSR, Japan, and, of course, China. For the account of the war years, I relied heavily on research by Hans Van de Ven, Chen Jian, Jay Taylor, Yang Kuisong, and others. Files on Chiang Kai-shek, T. V. Soong, Joseph Stilwell, and H. H. Kung at the Hoover Institution on War, Revolution and Peace were also critical to my research.

TWENTY-ONE • Dangerous Liaisons

Mao's views on the United States are available in his public writings and also in Alexander Pantsov and Steven Levine's biography, *Mao: The Real Story*. For insights into Fei Xiaotong, David Arkush's monograph, *Fei Xiaotong and Sociology in Revolutionary China*, is useful, as are Fei's own writings. Jay Taylor's biography, *The Generalissimo*, tells the story of Chiang Kai-shek's increasing disenchantment with America.

TWENTY-TWO • The Rice Paddy Navy

Milton Miles tells his story in *A Different Kind of War*. Linda Kush also tells it in *The Rice Paddy Navy*. An autobiography by John Paton Davies, a contemporary, provides a different perspective on Miles. Details of Stilwell's troubled Burma campaign are in Charles Romanus and Riley Sunderland's *Stilwell's Command Problems*. Stilwell's fight with Lord Mountbatten is explained in part in the autobiography of John Paton Davies. Maochun Yu's *OSS in China* was essential to an understanding of the competition between the various American intelligence agencies, including details about the outburst of Marine Corps Brigadier General Lyle Miller.

TWENTY-THREE • The East Is Red

H. H. Kung's ill-fated attempts to tame inflation are detailed in Arthur Young's *China and the Helping Hand*. Chiang Kai-shek's philosophy is spelled out in *China's Destiny and Chinese Economic Theory*. Peter Vladimirov's views on the Chinese Communist Party can be found in his Yenan diaries. The story of the Dixie Mission is told by David Barrett in his recollections and in State Department documents and reports by others such as Jack Service and John Paton Davies. American reporters' and scholars' impressions of the Chinese Communists and particularly of Zhou Enlai and Gong Peng are available in memoirs, such as those written by Theodore White, Harrison Forman, and John K. Fairbank. Lin Yutang's spat with Edgar Snow can be found in the pages of the *Nation*.

TWENTY-FOUR • Keys to the Kingdom

Albert Wedemeyer tells his story in *Wedemeyer Reports!* although parts of it are questionable as Wedemeyer had many axes to grind. Patrick Hurley's story is told in the diplomatic cables of the time and in John Davies's autobiography. Chiang Kai-shek's views of the Yalta decision can be found in his diaries at the Hoover Institution on War, Revolution and Peace and also in Jay Taylor's biography.

TWENTY-FIVE • The Beginning of the End

The Amerasia spy case story is told well by Harvey Klehr and Ronald Radosh. The story of the rise of the Chinese Communists in Manchuria is told by Chinese historian Yang Kuisong. The story of Solomon Adler and Frank Coe is told in R. Bruce Craig's *Treasonable Doubt*. Harvey Klehr and John Earl Haynes do a better job in *Venona: Decoding Soviet Espionage in America*. Maochun Yu's *OSS in China* describes Chinese penetration of US intelligence operations in China. FDR and T. V. Soong's interactions over the future course of China's economy can be found in T. V. Soong's papers at the Hoover Institution. Maochun Yu tells the story of John Birch's murder by the Communists.

TWENTY-SIX • Mission Impossible

The mission of George Marshall in China is told in the newspapers of the day and in State Department and White House documents released over the years. John Melby's insights into the mission can be found in his memoirs *The Mandate of Heaven*. The Shen Chong case has never received the attention it deserves among Western scholars, who generally ignore how important it was to the Chinese Communist Party and its campaign to push the United States out of China. Reports such as those by Wang Peilian, a party historian, underscore the importance of the case in turning China's people against the United States.

TWENTY-SEVEN • A Third Force

Chiang Kai-shek's crackdown on China's liberals is detailed in US diplomatic cables of the era. P. C. Chang's role in the UN Universal Declaration of Human Rights is told in part in Mary Ann Glendon's *A World Made New: Eleanor Roosevelt and the Universal Declaration of Human Rights*. Few Chinese sources pay attention to Chang. Mao Zedong's conversation with Soviet representative Anastas Mikoyan is detailed in Pantsov and Levine's Mao biography. The story of the State Department's White Paper and Mao's reaction is told in the newspapers of the time and in Mao's five essays reacting to the report. Private US military support for Chiang Kai-shek in Taiwan is detailed by Ting-ling Hsiao in *Accidental State: Chiang Kai-shek, the United States and the Making of Taiwan*.

Part IV

TWENTY-EIGHT • Hate America

Details on the Korean War are taken from David Halberstam's *The Coldest Winter: America and the Korean War* and from Jian Chen's *China's Road to the Korean War*. Details of the various anti-American campaigns can be found in Robert Loh's *Escape from Red China* and Wu Ningkun's *A Single Tear*. Information about the problems the Communist Party had in carrying out its anti-American campaigns was taken from research by Hui He in the Chinese periodical *Cold War International History Studies*. Details of how Shanghai was given special dispensation to show American films is from Wang Chao-guang's research in the Chinese academic periodical *Shiji*.

TWENTY-NINE • Hate China

Details on Joseph McCarthy's campaign against Communists in the US government were taken from John Earl Haynes and Harvey Klehr's *Venona: Decoding Soviet Espionage in America* and from Arthur Herman's biography of Joseph McCarthy. Perspective on the case against Owen Lattimore was provided by Diana Trilling's essays in the *Partisan Review*. Details on America's China policy in the 1950s were taken from Nancy Bernkopf Tucker's *The China Threat: Memories, Myth, and Realities in the 1950s*. Wang's story comes from his autobiography. Jade Snow Wong's story comes from her autobiographies.

THIRTY • A Cold War

Dwight Eisenhower and John Foster Dulles's nuclear threats against China are detailed in Tucker's *The China Threat*. Zhou Enlai's appearance at Geneva and the Bandung Conference were reported in the newspapers of the day. Details of the US-China ambassadorial talks are in U. Alexis Johnson's *The Right Hand of Power*, as is the controversial non-handshake by John Foster Dulles, which is also discussed in Wang Bingnan's memoirs. The story of Taiwan's economic rise is detailed in Ting-ling Hsiao's *Accidental State*. Qian Xuesen's story is told by Iris Chang in *Thread of the Silkworm*. Details of China's nuclear weapons program were taken from John Wilson Lewis and Xue Litai's *China Builds the Bomb*. Acknowledgment that China faked evidence in its allegations about US germ warfare is in Wu Zhili's article in the November 2013 issue of the Chinese magazine, *Yanhuang Chunqiu*.

THIRTY-ONE • Dead Flowers

Luo Longji's story is told in Jing Li's *China's America: The Chinese View of the United States, 1900–2000*. Wu Ningkun tells his story of his experience of the One Hundred Flowers Campaign in his autobiography. Details about the uprising in Tibet were taken from Kenneth Knaus's *Orphans of the Cold War: America and the Tibetan Struggle for Survival* and Gyalo Thondup's *The Noodle Maker of Kalimpong: The Untold Story of My Struggle for Tibet*. Details about Mao Zedong's worries about peaceful evolution were taken from Qiang Zhai's "Mao Zedong and Dulles's 'Peaceful Evolution' Strategy: Revelations from Bo Yibo's Memoirs," in the *Cold War International History Project Bulletin*.

THIRTY-TWO • Bloody Marys

The story about John F. Kennedy, Bloody Marys, and China is taken from Arthur M. Schlesinger Jr.'s *A Thousand Days*. The account of talks between the United States and China in Warsaw is from Wang Bingnan's memoirs. The account of State Department officials trying to fashion a new China policy is from James Thomson's recollections in the *China Quarterly* in 1972.

THIRTY-THREE • Pictures of Chairman Mao

Details of Mao's support for Vietnam and his increasingly anti-American policy can be found in Jian Chen's *Mao's China and the Cold War*. China's role in the imagination of American antiwar protesters and the 1960s appeared in many newspapers and public documents of the time. Mao's attraction to African American radicals is detailed in Robin Kelley and Betsy Esche's "Black Like Mao" article, which appeared in *Souls*.

THIRTY-FOUR • Out of Bad Things

Details about the persecution, murder, and suicide of American-educated Chinese were taken from a variety of sources, including memorials to their lives on Chinese websites and newspaper reports in China in the 1980s when talk of the depredations of the Cultural Revolution was still allowed. Details about the evolution of Mao's views on America were taken from Jian Chen's *Mao's China and the Cold War* and also from Li Zhisui's *The Private Life of Chairman Mao*. Details of the Ping-Pong diplomacy between the United States and China were taken from Nicholas Griffin's account, *Ping-Pong Diplomacy: The Secret History of the Game That Changed the World*.

THIRTY-FIVE • Not Because We Love Them

Much of this chapter relies on declassified archives from the Office of the Historian of the US Department of State and its records of conversations among American officials and between US officials and the Chinese. U. Alexis Johnson's view of America's "rapturous enchantment" with China comes from his memoirs. Jian Chen's *Mao's China and the Cold War* was also helpful in this chapter. The party document from Pei County is one of dozens I collected during years of research in China. For details on Chiang Ching-kuo's role in a changing Taiwan, I relied on Jay Taylor's *The Generalissimo's Son: Chiang Ch'ing-kuo and the Revolutions in China and Taiwan*.

THIRTY-SIX • Tacit Allies

The story of Richard Nixon's visit to China is told in Margaret MacMillan's *Nixon in China* but also in memoirs and remembrances and in newspaper and TV reports of the time. The story of the resumption of the US-China scientific relationship is told by Sigrid Schmalzer in the academic periodical *Journal of American-East Asian Relations*. Details about China's need for US technology were taken from Vaclav Smil's *China's Past, China's Future: Energy, Food, Environment*. William Gleysteen's criticism of US policy toward China can be found in an interview he gave to the Oral History Project of the Association for Diplomatic Studies and Training. George H. W. Bush's worries about the direction of US policy toward China are detailed in his diary from Beijing, *China Diary of George H. W. Bush: The Making of a Global President*.

THIRTY-SEVEN • We Are Very Sexy People

Details on Jimmy Carter's and Leonard Woodcock's views of Nixon's handling of US-China relations were taken from James Mann's *About Face*. Details of Zbigniew Brzezinski's calculus in pushing for normalized relations with China were taken from his memoirs, *Power and Principle: Memoirs of the National Security Adviser, 1977–1981*. Details of Deng Xiaoping's talks with US officials in Washington were taken from declassified transcripts from the State Department's Office of the Historian.

THIRTY-EIGHT • China Rediscovers America

Details of China's rediscovery of America are in Chinese memoirs, news accounts, and also in Qian Ning's *Liuxue Meiguo*, which tells the story of a new generation of Chinese students in the United States. Details of the poetry and essays written by Chinese were taken from Yang Yusheng's *Zhongguoren de Meiguoguan*.

THIRTY-NINE • Nobody Is Afraid of Anybody

Details of Fang Lizhi's story in China were taken from James H. Williams's "Fang Lizhi's Expanding Universe." The Reagan administration's engagement with China over Afghanistan is chronicled in Steve Coll's *Ghost Wars*. Details about China's proliferation of missiles and weapons of mass destruction were taken from press reports of the day. The story about US support for the Khmer Rouge was taken from Kenneth Conboy's *The Cambodian Wars* and the 2016 reminiscences of Singaporean diplomat Bilahari Kausikan.

FORTY • Deathsong

I own a copy of *Deathsong*, both the book and DVD. I was in China and reported on Fang Lizhi's disappearance from the dinner with President George H. W. Bush, and on the events leading up to the Tiananmen Square crackdown. Details about internal battles in China during and after the Tiananmen crackdown came from senior Chinese diplomat Chen Youwei's memoirs of the period and from *The Tiananmen Papers* and the memoirs of Qian Qichen, James Baker, and Robert Suettinger, and James Mann's *About Face*.

Part V

FORTY-ONE • Kung Fu Fighting

Details from Bruce Lee's interviews are in *Bruce Lee: The Celebrated Life of the Golden Dragon*. Details about the Protect Diaoyus movement are in the academic article by Chinese historian Minghui Lu. For many details on Chinese Americans' engagement in China's science programs, I relied on the work of Wang Zuoyue in such studies as "Transnational Science during the Cold War: The Case of Chinese/American Scientists." Details of Henry Liu's murder and congressional pressure on Taiwan were taken from contemporary news reports and congressional testimony.

FORTY-TWO • Patriotic Education

Details of the Patriotic Education campaign in China are from contemporary Chinese news reports and from Zheng Wang's PhD dissertation, "The Power of History and Memory." President Bill Clinton's zigzags on human rights are detailed in James Mann's *About Face*. Jack Perkowski's story is told in Tim Clissold's *Mr. China*, by Joe Studwell's *The China Dream*, and by Perkowski himself in *Managing the Dragon: How I'm Building a Billion-Dollar Business in China*. Liu Huaqing's views on sea power are in his memoirs, *Liu Huaqing Huiyilu*. Details of US-China tension over Taiwan are taken from reporting from the *Washington Post*. Details of the rising anti-American tone of China's media are in Susan Shirk's *China: Fragile Superpower*.

FORTY-THREE • From China with Love

Details of Chinese intelligence operations in the United States were taken from David Vise's *Tiger Trap: America's Secret Spy War with China* and I. C. Smith's memoirs, *Inside: A Top G-Man Exposes Spies, Lies, and Bureaucratic Bungling in the FBI*, along with my own reporting. The Wen Ho Lee case was covered extensively by the media at the time. Brett Kingstone tells his own story in *The Real War against America*. Danny Stillman's story is spelled out in *The Nuclear Express: A Political History of the Bomb and Its Proliferation* by Stillman and Thomas Reed.

FORTY-FOUR • Welcome to the Club

Details of the Communist Party's reaction to the US bombing of the Chinese embassy in Belgrade are in Zong Hairen's *Zhu Rongji Zai 1999*. Details of the WTO negotiations with China are in James McGregor's *One Billion Customers* and in *Zhu Rongji zai 1999*. Wall Street's efforts to remake China's state-owned sector are detailed in Carl Walter and Fraser Howie's *Red Capitalism: The Fragile Financial Foundation of China's Extraordinary Rise*. Hillary Clinton details her experience in China during the UN Fourth World Conference on Women in *Living History*.

General Motors' story in China is told by Michael Dunne in *American Wheels, Chinese Roads: The Story of General Motors in China*. US efforts to improve China's flight safety were detailed in media reports at the time both in Chinese and English. The NBA's rise in China is told in Brook Larmer's *Operation Yao Ming: The Chinese Sports Empire, American Big Business, and the Making of an NBA Superstar* but also in Chinese press reports, especially from *Titan Weekly*. Huang Quanyu tells his story in *Suzhi Jiaoyu zai Meiguo* and in *The Hybrid Tiger: Secrets of the Extraordinary Success of Asian-American Kids*.

FORTY-FIVE • Twin Towers

I reported on the EP-3 crash in Beijing in 2001, so much of the information is from my reporting and files, including the detail about the Hangzhou cemetery, which I visited. I was in Afghanistan soon after 9/11 and covered China's reaction to the attacks on the United States. The quote from Beth Macy is from her *Factory Man: How One Furniture Maker Battled Offshoring, Stayed Local, and Helped Save an American Town*. Henry Paulson's interactions with the Chinese are detailed in his *Dealing with China: An Insider Unmasks the New Economic Superpower*. Zhao Ziyang's story is from his memoirs, *Prisoner of the State: The Secret Journal of Premier Zhao Ziyang*.

FORTY-SIX • G2?

I reported on the Obama administration's China policy for the *Washington Post*. Much of the sourcing for this chapter comes from my articles and notes. Details of Document Number 9 and Number 30 come from the *New York Times*. The crackdown on China's legal profession was reported in the *Times* and other newspapers. Details about the US air monitor machine came from Deborah Seligsohn, environment, science, technology, and health counselor in Beijing for the Department of State at the time.

FORTY-SEVEN • End of an Era

Details on China's cyberspying on the United States were reported in newspapers at the time and also spelled out in William Hannas, James Mulvenon, and Anna Puglisi's *Chinese Industrial Espionage: Technology Acquisition and Military Modernization*.

Bibliography

Periodicals

Albright, David, and Corey Gay. "Taiwan: Nuclear Nightmare Averted." *Bulletin of the Atomic Scientists* 54, no. 1 (Jan./Feb. 1998): 54–60.

Alford, William P. "Law, Law, What Law? Why Western Scholars of Chinese History and Society Have Not Had More to Say about Its Law." *Modern China* 23, no. 4 (Oct. 1997): 398–419.

Autor, David H., David Dorn, and Gordon H. Hanson. "The China Syndrome: Local Labor Market Effects of Import Competition in the United States." Working paper 18054, National Bureau of Economic Research, Cambridge, MA, 2012.

Barmé, Geremie R. "To Screw Foreigners Is Patriotic: China's Avant-Garde Nationalism." *China Journal* 34 (July 1995): 209–34.

Campanella, Thomas. "'The Civilising Road': American Influence on the Development of Highways and Motoring in China, 1900–1949." *Journal of Transport History* 26, no. 1 (Mar. 2005): 78–98.

Carruthers, Susan L. "'The Manchurian Candidate' (1962) and the Cold War Brainwashing Scare." *Historical Journal of Film, Radio, and Television* 18, no. 1 (Mar. 1998): 75–94.

Carter, Susan B. "Celestial Suppers: The Political Economy of America's Chop Suey Craze, 1900–1930." Online paper, Department of Economics, University of California, Riverside, draft dated September 15, 2008. http://www-siepr.stanford.edu/conferences/GWright2008/Carter.pdf.

Chen, Jian. "The Beginning of the End: 1956 as a Turning Point in Chinese and Cold War History." *Modern China Studies* 22, no. 1 (2015): 99–126.

Cohen, Roberta. "People's Republic of China: The Human Rights Exception." *Human Rights Quarterly* 9, no. 4 (Nov. 1987): 447–549.

Edwards, Louise. "The Shanghai Modern Woman's American Dreams: Imagining America's Depravity to Produce China's 'Moderate Modernity.'" Unpublished manuscript.

Feigenbaum, Evan A. "Soldiers, Weapons, and Chinese Development Strategy: The Mao Era Military in China's Economic and Institutional Debate." *China Quarterly*, no. 158 (June 1999): 285–313.

Finnane, Antonia. "What Should Chinese Women Wear?" *Modern China* 22, no. 2 (1996): 99–131.

Garrett, Charles Hiroshi. "Chinatown, Whose Chinatown? Defining America's Borders with Musical Orientalism." *Journal of the American Musicological Society* 57, no. 1 (Spring 2004): 119–74.

Guo, Xiancai. "Gaigekaifanghou Shoupi Liumeisheng de Xuanpai Jiqi Yingxiang." *Contemporary History Studies* 12, no. 6 (Nov. 2005).

Guy, Nancy. "Brokering Glory for the Chinese Nation: Peking Opera's 1930 American Tour." *Comparative Drama* (Fall 2001/Winter 2002): 377–92.

Hamilton, John Maxwell. "The Missouri News Monopoly and American Altruism in China: Thomas F. F. Millard, J. B. Powell, and Edgar Snow." *Pacific Historical Review* 55, no. 1 (Feb. 1986): 27–48.

Harding, Harry. "From China, with Disdain: New Trends in the Study of China." *Asian Survey* 22, no. 10 (Oct. 1982): 934–58.

He, Di. "The Most Respected Enemy: Mao Zedong's Perception of the United States." *China Quarterly* 137 (Mar. 1994): 144–58.

He, Hui. "Xinzhongguo Minzhong Dui Meiguo de Renshi ji Qita Bianhua." *Cold War International History*, no. 14 (2012).

Huang, Fuhua. "The Globalization of Sport: The NBA's Diffusion in China." *International Journal of the History of Sport* 30, no. 3 (2013): 267–84.

Israel, Jerry. "'Mao's Mr. America': Edgar Snow's Images of China." *Pacific Historical Review* 47, no. 1 (Feb. 1978): 107–22.

Kang, Jean S. "Firmness and Flexibility: Initiations for Change in US Policy toward Communist China, 1961–1963." *American Asian Review* 21, no. 1 (Spring 2003): 109–42.

Keliher, Macabe. "Anglo-American Rivalry and the Origins of U.S. China Policy." *Diplomatic History* 31, no. 2 (April 2007): 227–57.

Kelley, Robin D. G., and Betsy Esche. "Black Like Mao: Red China and Black Revolution." *Souls* 1, no. 4 (Fall 1999): 6–41.

Kirby, William. "The Internationalization of China: Foreign Relations at Home and Abroad in the Republican Era." *China Quarterly*, no. 150 (June 1997): 433–58.

Klinefelter, Katherine. "The China Hearings: America's Shifting Paradigm on China." *Congress and the Presidency* 38 (Jan.–Apr. 2011): 60–76.

Kroncke, Jedidiah. "An Early Tragedy of Comparative Constitutionalism: Frank Goodnow and the Chinese Republic." *Pacific Rim Law and Policy Journal* 21, no. 3: 533–90.

Kuo, Tai-Chun. "A Strong Diplomat in a Weak Polity: T. V. Soong and Wartime US-China Relations, 1940–1943." *Journal of Contemporary China* 18, no. 59 (Mar. 2009): 219–31.

Leary, William M. "Wings for China: The Jouett Mission, 1932–1935." *Pacific Historical Review* 38, no. 4 (Nov. 1969): 447–62.

Ling, Huping. "A History of Chinese Female Students in the United States, 1880s–1990s." *Journal of American Ethnic History* 16, no. 3 (Spring 1997): 81–109.

Liu, Lydia H. "Shadows of Universalism: The Untold Story of Human Rights around 1948." *Critical Inquiry* 40 (Summer 2014): 385–417.

Lu, Minghui. "Liuxuesheng de Diaoyu Yundong He Zuguo Heping Tongyi." *Huaqiaohua-renlishi Yanjiu* 4 (2009).

Madsen, Deborah L. "The Oriental/Occidental Dynamic in Chinese American Life Writing: Pardee Lowe and Jade Snow Wang." *Amerikastudien/American Studies* 51, no. 3 (2006): 343–53.

McMichael, Scott R. "Common Man, Uncommon Leadership: Colonel Charles N. Hunter with Galahad in Burma." *Parameters, Journal of the US Army War College* 16, no. 2 (Summer 1986): 45–57.

Metallo, Michael V. "American Missionaries, Sun Yat-sen, and the Chinese Revolution." *Pacific Historical Review* 47, no. 2 (May 1978): 261–82.

Naftali, Orna. "Empowering the Child: Children's Rights, Citizenship, and the State in Contemporary China." *China Journal* 61 (Jan. 2009): 79–103.

Ngai, Mae M. "Legacies of Exclusion: Illegal Chinese Immigration during the Cold War Years." *Journal of American Ethnic History* 18, no. 1 (Fall 1998): 3–35.

Oksenberg, Michel. "A Decade of Sino-American Relations." *Foreign Affairs* (Fall 1982): 175–95.

———. "On Learning from China." In "China's Developmental Experience," ed. Michel Oksenberg. *Proceedings of the Academy of Political Science* 31, no. 1. (Mar. 1973): 1–16.

Porter, Garnett. "The History of the Trade Dollar." *American Economic Review* 7, no. 1 (1917): 91–97.

Pugach, Noel. "Embarrassed Monarchist: Frank J. Goodnow and Constitutional Development in China, 1913–1915." *Pacific Historical Review* 42, no. 4 (Nov. 1973): 499–517.

Qiao, Xian. "Wo de Fuye Shi Goutong Tuyang." Wenxue Huiyi Lü Zhi Wu, *Historical Materials on New Literature*, no. 2 (1982).

Quigley, Kevin. "A Lost Opportunity: A Reappraisal of the Kennedy Administration's China Policy of 1963." *Diplomacy and Statecraft* 13, no. 3 (Sept. 2002): 175–98.

Radosh, Ronald. "The Legacy of the Anti-Communist Liberal Intellectuals." *Partisan Review* 67, no. 4 (Fall 2000): 550–67.

Sa, Zhishan. "Xin Aiguozhuyi Yu Guojia Yishi zhi Jianli, Yi Kangmeiyuanchao Aiguoyun-dong Weilie, Zhongguo Shehuikexueyuan Wenxue Yanjiusuo." Paper presented at Peking University Chinese Department Conference, Jan. 11, 2014.

Schmalzer, Sigrid. "Speaking about China, Learning from China: Amateur China Experts in 1970s." *Journal of American-East Asian Relations* 16 (2009): 313–52.

Schrecker, John. "'For the Equality of Men—For the Equality of Nations': Anson Burlingame and China's First Embassy to the United States, 1868." *Journal of American-East Asian Relations* 17 (2010): 9–34.

Sewall, Arthur F. "Key Pittman and the Quest for the China Market, 1933–1940." *Pacific Historical Review* 44, no. 3 (Aug. 1975): 351–71.

Shaffer, Robert. "A Rape in Beijing, December 1946: GIs, Nationalist Protests, and U.S. Foreign Policy." *Pacific Historical Review* 69, no. 1 (Feb. 2000): 31–64.

Shen, Zhihua. "Mao and the 1956 Soviet Military Intervention in Hungary." Cold War History Research Center, Budapest, Hungary, online publication, July 2011. http://www.coldwar.hu/html/en/publications/zhihua%20-%20mao%20in%20hungary.pdf.

Sheng, Michael. "Chinese Communist Policy toward the United States and the Myth of the 'Lost Chance,' 1948–1950." *Modern Asian Studies* 28, no. 3 (July 1994): 475–502.

——. "The Triumph of Internationalism: CCP-Moscow Relations Before 1949." *Diplomatic History* 21, no. 1 (Winter 1997): 95–105.

Skidmore, David, and William Gates. "After Tiananmen: The Struggle over U.S. Policy toward China in the Bush Administration." *Presidential Studies Quarterly* 27, no. 3 (Summer 1997): 514–39.

Sohigian, Diran John. "Contagion of Laughter: The Rise of the Humor Phenomenon in Shanghai in the 1930s." *Positions* 15, no. 1 (Spring 2007): 137–63.

Thomson, James C., Jr. "On the Making of U.S. China Policy, 1961–69: A Study in Bureaucratic Politics." *China Quarterly,* no. 50 (Apr.–June 1972): 220–43.

Tsang, Steve. "Target Zhou Enlai: The 'Kashmir Princess' Incident of 1955." *China Quarterly,* no. 139 (Sept. 1994): 766–82.

Tsuchida, Akio. "China's 'Public Diplomacy' toward the United States before Pearl Harbor." *Journal of American–East Asian Relations* 17 (2010): 35–55.

Turner, Sean M. "A Rather Climactic Period": The Sino-Soviet Dispute and Perceptions of the China Threat in the Kennedy Administration." *Diplomacy and Statecraft* 22 (2011): 261–80.

Van de Ven, Hans. "Stilwell in the Stocks: The Chinese Nationalists and the Allied Powers in the Second World War." *Asian Affairs* 34, no. 3 (Nov. 2003): 243–59.

Wang, Chaoguang. "Jianguochu Tingying Meiguo Yingpian Jishi." *Shiji* 4 (2007).

Wang, Peilian. "Zhongguo Gongchandang Lingdao Xuesheng Kangbao Yundong de Douzhen Celue." *Fujian Party History Monthly* (Sept. 1990).

Wang, Shu-Shin. "The Rise and Fall of the Campaign against Spiritual Pollution in the People's Republic of China." *Asian Affairs* 13, no. 1 (Spring 1986): 47–62.

Wang, Zuoyue. "Transnational Science during the Cold War: The Case of Chinese/American Scientists." *ISIS* 101, no. 2 (2010): 367–77.

Wilkinson, Mark F. "American Military Misconduct in Shanghai and the Chinese Civil War: The Case of Zang Dayaozi." *Journal of American–East Asian Relations* 17 (2010): 146–73.

Williams, James H. "Fang Lizhi's Expanding Universe." *China Quarterly,* no. 123 (Sept. 1990): 459–84.

Wood, Eden Y. "Chinese Arms Sales and U.S.-China Military Relations." *Asian Survey* 29, no. 6 (June 1989): 601–18.

Wu, Zhili. "1952 Nian de Xijunzhan shi yichang Xujing." *Yanhuangchunqiu,* Nov. 2013.

Xia, Yafeng. "Negotiating at Cross-Purposes: Sino-American Ambassadorial Talks, 1961–68." *Diplomacy and Statecraft* 16, no. 2 (Aug. 2005): 297–329.

Yang, Kuisong. "Zhongguo Gongchandang Duoquan Dongbei Zhanlüe Yanbian yu Sulian." *Zhonggong Dangshi Yanjiu* (1990): 60–71.

Yang, Kuisong, and Yafeng Xia. "Vacillating between Revolution and Détente: Mao's Changing Psyche and Policy toward the United States, 1969–1976." *Diplomatic History* 34, no. 2 (2010): 395–423.

Yetiv, Steve A., and Chunlong Lu. "China, Global Energy, and the Middle East." *Middle East Journal* 61, no. 2 (Spring 2007): 199–218.

Yi, Guolin. "The 'Propaganda State' and Sino-American Rapprochement: Preparing the Chinese Public for Nixon's Visit." *Journal of American–East Asian Relations* 20 (2013): 5–28.

Zhai, Qiang. "Mao Zedong and Dulles's 'Peaceful Evolution' Strategy: Revelations from Bo Yibo's Memoirs." *Cold War International History Project Bulletin*, nos. 6–7 (Winter 1995/1996): 228–31.

Zi, Zhongyun. "The Impact and Clash of Ideologies: Sino-US Relations from a Historical Perspective." *Journal of Contemporary China* (1997): 531–50.

Books

Arkush, R. David. *Fei Xiaotong and Sociology in Revolutionary China*. Cambridge, MA: Harvard East Asian Monographs, 1981.

Arkush, R. David, and Leo O. Lee, eds. *Land without Ghosts: Chinese Impressions of America from the Mid-Nineteenth Century to the Present*. Berkeley: University of California Press, 1989.

Baker, James A. *The Politics of Diplomacy*. New York: G. P. Putnam's Sons, 1995.

Bao, Ruowang (Jean Pasqualini), and Rudolph Chelminski. *Prisoner of Mao*. New York: Penguin, 1973.

Barrett, David B. *Dixie Mission: The United States Army Observer Group in Yenan, 1944*. Berkeley: Center for Chinese Studies, China Research Monographs, University of California, 1970.

Bays, Daniel H. *A New History of Christianity in China*. West Sussex, UK: Wiley-Blackwell, 2012.

Beal, John Robinson. *Marshall in China*. Garden City, NY: Doubleday, 1970.

Beisner, Robert L. *Dean Acheson: A Life in the Cold War*. Oxford: Oxford University Press, 2006.

Bennett, Milly. *On Her Own: Journalistic Adventures from San Francisco to the Chinese Revolution, 1917–1927*. Edited and annotated by A. Tom Grunfeld. Armonk, NY: M. E. Sharpe, 1993.

Bergère, Marie Claire. *Sun Yat-sen*. Stanford, CA: Stanford University Press, 1998.

Bieler, Stacey. *"Patriots" or "Traitors": A History of American-Educated Chinese Students*. Armonk, NY: M. E. Sharpe, 2004.

Bowie, Robert R., and John K. Fairbank. *Communist China, 1955–1959: Policy Documents with Analysis*. Cambridge, MA: Harvard University Press, 1962.

Brown, Jeremy, and Paul G. Pickowicz, eds. *Dilemmas of Victory: The Early Years of the People's Republic of China*. Cambridge, MA: Harvard University Press, 2010.

Brzezinski, Zbigniew. *Power and Principle: Memoirs of the National Security Adviser, 1977–1981*. New York: Farrar, Straus & Giroux, 1983.

Buck, Pearl. *East Wind, West Wind*. New York: John Day Company, 1929.

———. *The Good Earth*. New York: John Day Company, 1931.

Bullock, Mary Brown. *The Oil Prince's Legacy: Rockefeller Philanthropy in China*. Stanford, CA: Stanford University Press, 2011.

Bush, George H. W. *China Diary of George H. W. Bush: The Making of a Global President.* Edited and introduced by Jeffrey A. Engel. Princeton, NJ: Princeton University Press, 2008.

Chang, Iris. *The Chinese in America: A Narrative History.* New York: Viking, 2003.

——. *Thread of the Silkworm.* New York: Basic Books, 1995.

Chen, Hansheng. *Sige Shidai de Wo.* Beijing: Chinese Culture and History Press, 1988.

Chen, Jerome. *China and the West: Society and Culture.* London: Hutchison of London, 1979.

Chen, Jian. *China's Road to the Korean War: The Making of Sino-American Confrontation.* New York: Columbia University Press, 1994.

——. *Mao's China and the Cold War.* Chapel Hill: University of North Carolina Press, 2001.

Chen, Youwei. *Tiananmen Shijian hou, Zhongong yu Meiguo Waijiao Neimu: Yi Wei Zhongguo Dalu Waijiaoguan de Lishi Jianzheng.* Taipei: Zhengzhong Shuju, 1999.

Chennault, Claire. *Way of a Fighter.* New York: Putnam, 1949.

Chiang, Kai-shek. *China's Destiny and Chinese Economic Theory.* New York: Roy Publishers, 1947.

Clayton, Buck, and Nancy M. Elliot. *Buck Clayton's Jazz World.* Oxford, UK: Bayou Press, 1986.

Clifford, Nicholas R. *Spoilt Children of Empire: Westerners in Shanghai and the Chinese.* Hanover, NH: Middlebury College Press/University Press of New England, 1991.

Clinton, Bill. *My Life.* New York: Knopf, 2004.

Clinton, Hillary. *Living History.* New York: Scribner, 2004.

Clissold, Tim. *Mr. China.* New York: HarperBusiness, 2006.

Cochran, Sherman. *Big Business in China: Sino-Foreign Rivalry in the Cigarette Industry, 1890–1930.* Cambridge, MA: Harvard University Press, 1980.

Cohen, Paul A. *China and Christianity: The Missionary Movement and the Growth of Chinese Antiforeignism, 1860–1870.* Cambridge, MA: Harvard University Press, 1963.

Cohen, Warren I., and Akira Iriye, eds. *The Great Powers in East Asia, 1953–1960.* New York: Columbia University Press, 1990.

Coll, Steve. *Ghost Wars.* New York: Penguin Press, 2004.

Conboy, Kenneth. *The Cambodian Wars: Clashing Armies and CIA Covert Operations.* Lawrence: University Press of Kansas, 2013.

Craft, Stephen G. *Wellington Koo and the Emergence of Modern China.* Lexington: University Press of Kentucky, 2003.

Craig, R. Bruce. *Treasonable Doubt: The Harry Dexter White Spy Case.* Lawrence: University Press of Kansas, 2004.

Crane, Daniel M., and Thomas A. Breslin. *An Ordinary Relationship: American Opposition to Republican Revolution in China.* Miami: University Presses of Florida, 1986.

Crouch, Gregory. *China's Wings: War, Intrigue, Romance, and Adventure in the Middle Kingdom during the Golden Age of Flight.* New York: Bantam, 2012.

Crow, Carl. *Foreign Devils in the Flowery Kingdom.* New York: Harper & Brothers, 1940.

——. *400 Million Customers.* New York: Harper & Brothers, 1937.

Davies, John Paton. *China Hand: An Autobiography.* Philadelphia: University of Pennsylvania Press, 2012.

Delano, Amasa. *Narrative of Voyages and Travels in the Northern and Southern Hemisphere Comprising Three Voyages Round the World in the Pacific Ocean and Oriental Islands*. Boston: E. G. House, 1817.

Deng, Xian, ed. *Under the Same Army Flag: Recollections of the Veterans of World War II*. Beijing: Wuzhou Chuanbo Chubanshe, 2005.

Dennett, Tyler. *Americans in Eastern Asia*. New York: Macmillan Company, 1922.

Dikotter, Frank. *The Tragedy of Liberation: A History of the Chinese Revolution, 1945–1957*. New York: Bloomsbury Press, 2013.

Dorwart, Jeffrey M. *The Pigtail War: American Involvement in the Sino-Japanese War of 1894–1895*. Amherst: University of Massachusetts Press, 1975.

Dunch, Ryan. *Fuzhou Protestants and the Making of Modern China, 1857–1927*. New Haven, CT: Yale University Press, 2001.

Dunne, Michael J. *American Wheels, Chinese Roads: The Story of General Motors in China*. New York: John Wiley & Sons, 2011.

Egan, Susan Chan, and Chih-p'ing Chou. *A Pragmatist and His Free Spirit: The Half-Century Romance of Hu Shi and Edith Clifford Williams*. Hong Kong: Chinese University Press, 2009.

Fairbank, John K. *The United States and China*. Cambridge, MA: Harvard University Press, 1948.

Forbes, John Murray. *Letters and Recollections of John Murray Forbes*. New York: Houghton, Mifflin and Company, 1899.

Ford, Daniel. *Claire Chennault and His American Volunteers, 1941–1942*. Washington, DC: HarperCollins/Smithsonian Books, 2007.

French, Paul. *Through the Looking Glass: China's Foreign Journalists from the Opium Wars to Mao*. Hong Kong: Hong Kong University Press, 2009.

Geng, Biao. *Geng Biao Zhuan*. Beijing: Jiefangjun Chubanshe, 2009.

Ghosh, Amitav. *River of Smoke*. London: John Murray Publishers, 2011.

Gibson, James R. *Otter Skins, Boston Ships, and China Goods: The Maritime Fur Trade of the Northwest Coast, 1785–1841*. Seattle: University of Washington Press, 1992.

Gittings, John. *The World and China: The Men and Ideas That Shaped Chinese Foreign Policy, 1922–1972*. New York: Harper & Row, 1974.

Glendon, Mary Ann. *A World Made New: Eleanor Roosevelt and the Universal Declaration of Human Rights*. New York: Random House, 2001.

Goldstein, Lyle J. *Preventive Attack and Weapons of Mass Destruction: A Comparative Historical Analysis*. Stanford, CA: Stanford University Press, 2005.

Griffin, Nicholas. *Ping-Pong Diplomacy: The Secret History of the Game That Changed the World*. New York: Scribner, 2014.

Gully, Patti. *Sisters of Heaven: China's Barnstorming Aviatrixes: Modernity, Feminism, and Popular Imagination in Asia and the West*. San Francisco: Long River Press, 2008.

Ha, Jin. *A Free Life*. New York: Pantheon Books, 2007.

Halberstam, David. *The Coldest Winter: America and the Korean War*. New York: Hachette Books, 2008.

Hamilton, John Maxwell. *Edgar Snow: A Biography*. Baton Rouge: Louisiana State University Press, 2003.

Hamrin, Carol Lee, and Stacey Bieler, eds. *Salt and Light: Lives of Faith That Shaped Modern China*. 3 vols. Eugene, OR: Pickwick Publications, 2009.

Hannas, William C., James Mulvenon, and Anna B. Puglisi. *Chinese Industrial Espionage: Technology Acquisition and Military Modernization*. New York: Routledge, 2013.

Hayford, Charles W. *To the People: James Yen and Village China*. New York: Columbia University Press, 1990.

Haynes, John Earl, and Harvey Klehr. *Venona: Decoding Soviet Espionage in America*. New Haven, CT: Yale University Press, 1999.

Herman, Arthur. *Joseph McCarthy: Reexamining the Life and Legacy of America's Most Hated Senator*. New York: Free Press, 2000.

Hobart, Alice Tisdale. *Oil for the Lamps of China*. Indianapolis: Bobbs Merrill Company, 1933.

Hodges, Graham Russell Gao. *Anna May Wong: From Laundryman's Daughter to Hollywood Legend*. New York: Palgrave Macmillan, 2004.

Hollander, Paul. *Political Pilgrims: Western Intellectuals in Search of the Good Society*. New Brunswick, NJ: Transactions Publishers, 1998.

Hsiao, Ting-ling. *Accidental State: Chiang Kai-shek, the United States, and the Making of Taiwan*. Cambridge, MA: Harvard University Press, 2016.

Hsiung, James C., and Steven I. Levine, eds. *China's Bitter Victory: The War with Japan, 1937–1945*. Armonk, NY: M. E. Sharpe, 1992.

Hu, Hua-ling. *American Goddess at the Rape of Nanking: The Courage of Minnie Vautrin*. Carbondale: Southern Illinois University Press, 2000.

———. *The Undaunted Women of Nanking: The Wartime Diaries of Minnie Vautrin and Tsen Shui-fang*. Carbondale: Southern Illinois University Press, 2010.

Hu, Shizhang. *Stanley K. Hornbeck and the Open Door Policy, 1919–1937*. Westport, CT: Greenwood Press, 1995.

Huang, Jing, and Xiaoting Li. *Inseparable Separation: The Making of China's Taiwan Policy*. Singapore: World Scientific Publishing Company, 2010.

Huang, Quanyu. *The Hybrid Tiger: Secrets of the Extraordinary Success of Asian-American Kids*. Amherst, NY: Prometheus Books, 2014.

———. *Suzhi Jiaoyu zai Meiguo*. Guangzhou: Guangdong Jiaoyu Chubanshe, 1999.

Huang, Yun-te. *Charlie Chan*. New York: W. W. Norton, 2010.

Hunt, Michael H. *Frontier Defense and the Open Door: Manchuria in Chinese-American Relations, 1895–1911*. New Haven, CT: Yale University Press, 1973.

———. *The Making of a Special Relationship: The United States and China to 1914*. New York: Columbia University Press, 1983.

Hunter, Jane. *The Gospel of Gentility: American Women Missionaries in Turn-of-the-Century China*. New Haven, CT: Yale University Press, 1989.

Hunter, William C. *The "Fan Kwae" at Canton: Before Treaty Days, 1825–1844*. London: Kegan Paul Trench and Company, 1882.

Hutchison, James Lafayette. *China Hand*. New York: Grosset and Dunlap, 1936.

Johnson, U. Alexis. *The Right Hand of Power*. Englewood Cliffs, NJ: Prentice-Hall, 1984.

Kang, Youwei. *Kang Youwei Quanji*. Beijing: Zhonghua Dushu, 2012.

Kaplan, Lawrence M. *Homer Lea: American Soldier of Fortune*. Lexington: University Press of Kentucky, 2010.

Karl, Rebecca E. *Staging the World: Chinese Nationalism at the Turn of the Century.* Durham, NC: Duke University Press, 2002.

Ke, Lin, Xu Tao, and Wu Xujun. *Lishi de Zhenshi: Mao Zedong Shenbian Gongzuo Renyuan de Zhengyan.* Hong Kong: Liwen Publishing House, 1995.

Kingstone, Brett. *The Real War against America.* Specialty Publishing/Max King, 2005.

Kissinger, Henry. *On China.* New York: Penguin Press, 2011.

Klehr, Harvey, and Ronald Radosh. *The Amerasia Spy Case.* Chapel Hill: University of North Carolina Press, 1996.

Knaus, Kenneth. *Orphans of the Cold War: America and the Tibetan Struggle for Survival.* New York: PublicAffairs, 2000.

Kochavi, Noam. *A Conflict Perpetuated: China Policy during the Kennedy Years.* Westport, CT: Praeger, 2002.

Kush, Linda. *The Rice Paddy Navy: U.S. Sailors Undercover in China.* Oxford: Osprey Publishing, 2012.

Kwong, Peter, and Dušanka Miščević. *Chinese America: The Untold Story of America's Oldest New Community.* New York: The New Press, 2005.

Larmer, Brook. *Operation Yao Ming: The Chinese Sports Empire, American Big Business, and the Making of an NBA Superstar.* New York: Gotham, 2005.

Leibovitz, Liel, and Matthew Miller. *Fortunate Sons: The 120 Chinese Boys Who Came to America, Went to School, and Revolutionized an Ancient Civilization.* New York: W. W. Norton, 2011.

Levine, Steven I. *Anvil of Victory: The Communist Revolution in Manchuria, 1945–1948.* New York: Columbia University Press, 1987.

Lewis, John Wilson, and Xue Litai. *China Builds the Bomb.* Stanford, CA: Stanford University Press, 1991.

Li, Cheng. *Bridging Minds across the Pacific.* New York: Lexington Books, 2005.

Li, Jing. *China's America: The Chinese View of the United States, 1900–2000.* Albany: State University of New York Press, 2011.

Li, Laura Tyson. *Madame Chiang Kai-shek: China's Eternal First Lady.* New York: Atlantic Monthly Press, 2006.

Li, Zhisui. *The Private Life of Chairman Mao.* New York: Random House, 1996.

Liang, Biying. *Liang Cheng yu Jindai Zhongguo.* Guangzhou: Zhongshan Daxue Chubanshe, 2011.

Lin, Yutang. *The Vigil of a Nation.* New York: John Day Company, 1944.

Lindsay, Hsiao Li. *Bold Plum: With the Guerrillas in China's War against Japan.* Morrisville, NC: Lulu Press, 2007.

Little, John, ed. *Bruce Lee: The Celebrated Life of the Golden Dragon.* North Clarendon, VT: Tuttle, 2000.

Liu, Huaqing. *Liu Huaqing Huiyilu.* Beijing: Jiefangjun Chubanshe, 2004.

Loh, Robert, and Humphrey Evans. *Escape from Red China.* New York: Coward-McCann, 1962.

Lowe, Pardee. *Father and Glorious Descendant.* Boston: Little, Brown and Company, 1943.

MacFarquhar, Roderick, and Michael Schoenhals. *Mao's Last Revolution.* Cambridge, MA: Belknap Press of Harvard University Press, 2006.

MacMillan, Margaret. *Nixon in China: The Week That Changed the World*. Toronto: Viking, 2006.

MacMurray, John Antwerp, and Arthur Waldron, eds. *How the Peace Was Lost: The 1935 Memorandum: Developments Affecting American Policy in the Far East*. Stanford, CA: Hoover Institution Press, 1992.

Macy, Beth. *Factory Man: How One Furniture Maker Battled Offshoring, Stayed Local, and Helped Save an American Town*. New York: Back Bay Books, 2015.

Madsen, Richard. *China and the American Dream: A Moral Inquiry*. Berkeley: University of California Press, 1995.

Manela, Erez. *The Wilsonian Moment: Self-Determination and the International Origins of Anticolonial Nationalism*. New York: Oxford University Press, 2007.

Mann, James. *About Face: A History of America's Curious Relationship with China, from Nixon to Clinton*. New York: Knopf, 1999.

———. *The China Fantasy: How Our Leaders Explain Away Chinese Repression*. New York: Viking, 2007.

McClain, Charles J. *In Search of Equality: The Chinese Struggle against Discrimination in Nineteenth-Century America*. Berkeley: University of California Press, 1994.

McClellan, Robert. *The Heathen Chinee: A Study of American Attitudes toward China, 1890–1905*. Columbus: Ohio State University Press, 1971.

McGregor, James. *One Billion Customers: Lessons from the Frontlines of Doing Business in China*. New York: Free Press, 2007.

Melby, John F. *The Mandate of Heaven: Record of a Civil War China, 1945–48*. Toronto: University of Toronto Press, 1968.

Meyer, Karl E., and Shareen Blair Brysac. *The China Collectors: America's Century-Long Hunt for Asian Art Treasures*. London: Palgrave Macmillan, 2015.

———. *Tournament of Shadows: The Great Game and the Race for Empire in Central Asia*. New York: Basic Books, 2006.

Miles, Milton E. *A Different Kind of War*. Garden City, NY: Doubleday and Company, 1967.

Millard, Thomas F. *Democracy and the Eastern Question*. New York: Century Company, 1919.

Mitter, Rana. *Forgotten Ally: China's World War II, 1937–1945*. Boston: Houghton Mifflin Harcourt, 2013.

Morris, Gouverneur. *The Incandescent Lily: And Other Stories*. New York: C. Scribner's Sons, 1914.

Nanyang Xiongdi Yancao Gongsi Shiliao. Shanghai: Renmin Chubanshe, 1958.

Pantsov, Alexander, and Steven Levine. *Mao: The Real Story*. New York: Simon & Schuster, 2013.

Paulson, Henry. *Dealing with China: An Insider Unmasks the New Economic Superpower*. New York: Twelve, 2015.

Peattie, Mark, Edward Drea, and Hans Van de Ven, eds. *The Battle for China: Essays on the Military History of the Sino-Japanese War of 1937–1945*. Stanford, CA: Stanford University Press, 2011.

Pei, Jianzhang, ed. *Dangdai zhongguo shijie waijiao shengya*. 2 vols. Beijing: Shijie Zhishi Chubanshe, 1995.

Perkowski, Jack. *Managing the Dragon: How I'm Building a Billion-Dollar Business in China.* New York: Bantam, 2009.

Pfaelzer, Jean. *Driven Out: The Forgotten War against Chinese Americans.* New York: Random House, 2007.

Phelps, William Dane. *Fore and Aft, or Leaves from the Life of an Old Sailor.* Boston: Nichols & Hall, 1871.

Pillsbury, Michael. *The Hundred-Year Marathon: China's Secret Strategy to Replace America as the Global Superpower.* New York: Henry Holt, 2015.

Platt, Nicholas. *China Boys: How US Relations with the PRC Began and Grew.* Washington, DC: Vellum, 2010.

Platt, Stephen R. *Autumn in the Heavenly Kingdom.* New York: Knopf, 2012.

Powell, John B. *My Twenty-Five Years in China.* New York: Macmillan Company, 1945.

Preston, Diana. *The Boxer Rebellion.* New York: Berkley Books, 2000.

Price, Eva Jane. *China Journal, 1889–1900: An American Missionary Family during the Boxer Rebellion.* New York: Scribner, 1989.

Price, Ruth. *The Lives of Agnes Smedley.* New York: Oxford University Press, 2005.

Pugach, Noel H. *Paul S. Reinsch: Open Door Diplomat in Action.* Millwood, NY: KTO Press, 1979.

Qian, Ning. *Liuxue Meiguo: Yi ge Shidai de Gushi.* Nanjing: Jiangsu Wenyi Chubanshe, 1997.

Qian, Qichen. *Ten Episodes in China's Diplomacy.* New York: HarperCollins, 2006.

Qian, Suoqiao. *Liberal Cosmopolitanism: Lin Yutang and Middling Chinese Modernity.* Danvers, MA: Brill, 2011.

Qing, Simei. *From Allies to Enemies: Visions of Modernity, Identity, and U.S.-China Diplomacy, 1945–1960.* Cambridge, MA: Harvard University Press, 2007.

Rand, Peter. *China Hands.* New York: Simon & Schuster, 1995.

Reed, Thomas C., and Danny B. Stillman. *The Nuclear Express: A Political History of the Bomb and Its Proliferation.* Minneapolis: Zenith Press, 2010.

Rhoads, Edward J. M. *Stepping Forth into the World: The Chinese Educational Mission to the United States, 1872–81.* Hong Kong: Hong Kong University Press, 2011.

Ridgway, Matthew B. *The Korean War.* New York: Doubleday, 1967.

Romanus, Charles, and Riley Sunderland. *Stilwell's Command Problems.* Washington, DC: US Army Center of Military History, 1987.

Ross, Robert S., and Jiang Changbin, eds. *Re-examining the Cold War: U.S.-China Diplomacy, 1954–1973.* Cambridge, MA: Harvard University Press, 2001.

Schama, Simon. *The American Future: A History.* New York: Ecco Press, 2009.

Schlesinger, Arthur M., Jr. *A Thousand Days: John F. Kennedy in the White House.* New York: First Mariner Books, 2002.

Scott, David. *China and the International System, 1840–1949.* Albany: State University of New York Press, 2009.

———. *China Stands Up: The PRC and the International System.* New York: Routledge, 2007.

Shaw, Yu-ming. *An American Missionary in China: John Leighton Stuart and Chinese-American Relations.* Cambridge, MA: Harvard University Press, 1992.

Shemo, Connie A. *The Chinese Medical Ministries of Kang Cheng and Shi Meiyu, 1872 to 1937: On a Cross-Cultural Frontier of Gender, Race, and Nation.* Bethlehem, PA: Lehigh University Press, 2011.

Shirk, Susan. *China: Fragile Superpower.* New York: Oxford University Press, 2007.

Smil, Vaclav. *China's Past, China's Future: Energy, Food, Environment.* New York: Routledge-Curzon, 2004.

Smith, Arthur H. *Chinese Characteristics.* New York: Fleming H. Revell Company, 1894.

Smith, I. C. *Inside: A Top G-Man Exposes Spies, Lies, and Bureaucratic Bungling in the FBI.* Nashville: Thomas Nelson, 2004.

Snow, Edgar. *Red China Today: The Other Side of the River.* New York: Random House, 1971.

———. *Red Star Over China.* New York: Random House, 1937.

Spence, Jonathan D. *God's Chinese Son: The Taiping Heavenly Kingdom of Hong Xiuquan.* New York: W. W. Norton, 1996.

———. *The Search for Modern China.* New York: W. W. Norton, 1990.

———. *To Change China.* New York: Penguin Books, 2002.

Stross, Randell E. *Bulls in the China Shop and Other Sino-American Business Encounters.* New York: Pantheon Books, 1990.

Studwell, Joe. *The China Dream: The Quest for the Last Great Untapped Market on Earth.* New York: Grove Press, 2003.

Suettinger, Robert. *Beyond Tiananmen: The Politics of U.S.-China Relations.* Washington, DC: Brookings Institution, 2003.

Sui Sin, Far. *Mrs. Spring Fragrance.* Chicago: A. C. McClurg, 1912.

Sullivan, Regina D. *Lottie Moon: A Southern Baptist Missionary to China in History and Legend.* Baton Rouge: Louisiana State University Press, 2011.

Sun, Yat-sen. *Sun Zhongshan Ji.* Beijing: Zhonghua Shuju, 1981.

Swisher, Earl. *China's Management of the American Barbarians.* New York: Octagon Books, 1972.

Taylor, Jay. *The Generalissimo: Chiang Kai-shek and the Struggle for Modern China.* Cambridge, MA: Belknap Press of Harvard University, 2009.

———. *The Generalissimo's Son: Chiang Ch'ing-kuo and the Revolutions in China and Taiwan.* Cambridge, MA: Harvard University Press, 2000.

Thomson, James C., Jr. *While China Faced West: American Reformers in Nationalist China, 1928–1937.* Cambridge, MA: Harvard University Press, 1969.

Thondup, Gyalo, and Anne F. Thurston. *The Noodle Maker of Kalimpong: The Untold Story of My Struggle for Tibet.* New York: PublicAffairs, 2015.

Thorne, Christopher. *Allies of a Kind: The United States, Britain, and the War against Japan, 1941–1945.* New York: Oxford University Press, 1978.

Tsang, Steve. "War, Co-operation with the United States, and the Future of Post-war China: Re-evaluating Chiang Kai-shek and the Stilwell Affair." Chap. 6 in *Chiang Kai-shek: The Critical Years, 1935–1950.* Edited by Emily M. Hill. Forthcoming.

Tse-Tung, Mao. *Selected Works of Mao Tse-Tung.* Honolulu: University Press of the Pacific, 2001.

Tsou, Tang. *America's Failure in China, 1941–1950.* Chicago: University of Chicago Press, 1963.

Tuchman, Barbara. *Stilwell and the American Experience in China, 1911–1945.* Cutchogue, NY: Buccaneer Books, 1995.

Tucker, Nancy Bernkopf. *The China Threat: Memories, Myth, and Realities in the 1950s.* New York: Columbia University Press, 2012.

Wang, Zheng. "The Power of History and Memory: National 'Patriotic Education' and China's Conflict Behavior in Crises with the U.S., 1991–2001." George Mason University, 2005.

Wilkinson, Mark Francis. "At the Crossroads: Shanghai and Sino-American Relations 1945–1950." University of Michigan, 1982.

Wong, John D. "Global Positioning: Houqua and His China Trade Partners in the Nineteenth Century." Harvard University, 2012.

Yu, Yuegen. "The Bond of an Enduring Relationship: United States–China Scientific Relations, 1949–1989." University of West Virginia, 1999.

Zhu, Pingchao. "The Road to Armistice: An Examination of the Chinese and American Diplomacy during the Korean War Cease-Fire Negotiations, 1950–1953." Miami University, 1998.

Newspapers/Magazines

Hill, Gladwin. "Brain-Washing: Time for a Policy." *Atlantic Monthly*, April 1955, 58–62.

Johnson, E. R. "Operation Matterhorn." *Aviation History*, July 2003, 38–47.

Mosher, Steven W. "The West and Comrade Chou." *National Review*, November 1990, 39.

Sullivan, Roger W. "Discarding the China Card." *Foreign Policy*, Spring 1992, 3–23.

Tong, Tong. "Gaige Kaifang Zhong De Meiguo Yinsu: Xie Zai ZhongMei Jianjiao Ji Deng Xiaoping Fangmei 30 Zhounian Zhiji." *Shijie Yu Zhishi*, no. 2 (2009): 14–25.

Wakeman, Frederic, Jr. "All the Rage in China." *New York Review of Books*, March 2, 1989.

Zolotow, Maurice. "The Dentist Who Changed World History." *Harper's Magazine*, December 1943, 40–53.

Archives and Databases

Association for Diplomatic Studies and Training, Oral History Interviews

Atlantic Monthly

Harper's Magazine

Hoover Institution on War, Revolution and Peace: Papers of Arthur J. Duff, Chiang Kaishek, Sutton Christian, Henry Evans, John Hart's research of Joseph W. Stilwell, H. H. Kung, Paul M. W. Linebarger, T. V. Soong

's Merchants' Magazine and Commercial Review

orker

k Herald Tribune

k Times

eekly

Department of State Office of the Historian

Post

———. *Patterns in the Dust: Chinese-American Relations and the Recognition Controversy, 1949–1950*. New York: Columbia University Press, 1983.

———. *Strait Talk: United States–Taiwan Relations and the Crisis with China*. Cambridge, MA: Harvard University Press, 2009.

Van de Ven, Hans. *War and Nationalism in China*. New York: Routledge, 2012.

Vise, David. *Tiger Trap: America's Secret Spy War with China*. New York: Houghton Mifflin Harcourt, 2011.

Vladimirov, Peter. *The Vladimirov Diaries: Yenan, China, 1942–1945*. New York: Doubleday, 1975.

Vogel, Ezra. *Deng Xiaoping and the Transformation of China*. Cambridge, MA: Belknap Press of Harvard University, 2011.

Wakeman, Frederic, Jr. *Policing Shanghai, 1927–1937*. Berkeley: University of California Press, 1995.

Waln, Nora. *The House of Exile*. New York: Soho Press, 1972.

Walter, Carl, and Fraser J. Howie. *Red Capitalism: The Fragile Financial Foundation of China's Extraordinary Rise*. New York: Wiley, 2011.

Wang, An. *Lessons: Autobiography*. Reading, MA: Addison-Wesley Publishing, 1986.

Wang, Bingnan. *Zhongmei huitan jiunian huigu*. Beijing: Shijie Zhishi Chubanshe, 1985.

Wang, Lixin. *Meiguo Chuanjiaoshi yu Wanqingzhonguo Xiandaihua*. Tianjin: Tianjin Renmin Chubanshe, 2008.

Wang, Shuhuai. *Wairen yu Wushu Bianfa*. Institute of Modern History. Taipei: Academia Sinica, 1965.

Wang, Y. C. *Chinese Intellectuals and the West, 1872–1949*. Chapel Hill: University of North Carolina Press, 1966.

Warren, Leonard. *Adele Marion Fielde: Feminist, Social Activist, Scientist*. New York: Routledge, 2002.

Wedemeyer, Albert C. *Wedemeyer Reports!*. New York: Devin-Adair Company, 1958.

Westad, Odd Arne. *Decisive Encounter: The Chinese Civil War, 1946–1950*. Stanford, CA: Stanford University Press, 2003.

———. *Restless Empire: China and the World since 1750*. New York: Basic Books, 2012.

White, Theodore. *In Search of History: A Personal Adventure*. New York: Harper & Row, 1978.

White, Theodore H., and Annalee Jacoby. *Thunder out of China*. New York: Da Capo, 1980.

Wing, Yung. *My Life in China and America*. Shanghai: Earnshaw Books, 2007.

Wong, Jade Snow. *Fifth Chinese Daughter*. New York: Scholastic Books, 1950.

Wu, Jingping, and Kuo Tai-chun, eds. *Song Ziwen yu Ta de Shidai*. Hoover Institution and Fudan Modern China Research Series. Shanghai: Fudan University Press, 2008.

Wu, Ningkun, and Yikai Li. *A Single Tear: A Family's Persecution, Love, and Endurance in Communist China*. New York: Little, Brown and Company, 1993.

Xu, Guoqi. *China and the Great War: China's Pursuit of a New National Identity and Internationalization*. Cambridge: Cambridge University Press, 2005.

———. *Olympic Dreams: China and Sports, 1895–2008*. Cambridge, MA: Harvard University Press, 2008.

Xu, Jiyu. *A Short Account of the Oceans Around Us*. Beijing: Yinghuanzhilue, 1849.

Yang, Yusheng. *Zhongguoren de Meiguoguan*. Shanghai: Fudan University Press, 1996.

Yao, Songling. *Chen Guangfu de Yisheng*. Taipei: Zhuanji Wenxue Chubanshe, 1984.

Yardley, Herbert O. *The Black Chinese Chamber: An Adventure in Espionage*. Boston: Houghton Mifflin Company, 1983.

Ye, Weili. *Seeking Modernity in China's Name: Chinese Students in the United States, 1900–1927*. Stanford, CA: Stanford University Press, 2001.

Yin, Xiao-huang. *Chinese American Literature since the 1850s*. Chicago: University of Illinois Press, 2000.

Young, Arthur N. *China and the Helping Hand, 1937–1945*. Cambridge, MA: Harvard University Press, 1963.

———. *China's Nation Building Effort, 1927–1937: The Financial and Economic Record*. Stanford, CA: Hoover Institution Press, 1971.

Yu, Maochun. *The Dragon's War: Allied Operations and the Fate of China, 1937–1947*. Annapolis, MD: Naval Institute Press, 2006.

———. *OSS in China: Prelude to Cold War*. New Haven, CT: Yale University Press, 1997.

Zhang, Deyi. *Diary of a Chinese Diplomat*. London: Penguin, 1992.

Zhang, Jishun. *Zhongguo Zhishifenzi de Meiguoguan*. Shanghai: Fudan University Press, 1999.

Zhang, Liang, and Andrew J. Nathan. *The Tiananmen Papers*. New York: PublicAffairs, 2002.

Zhao, Zhihua. *Cong Dajianyu Hui Lai*. Beijing: Xinaiguozhuyi Beixing Ju Publishing, April 1951.

Zhao, Ziyang. *Prisoner of the State: The Secret Journal of Premier Zhao Ziyang*. Translated and edited by Bao Pu, Renee Chiang, and Adi Ignatius. New York: Simon & Schuster, 2010.

Zhonggong Zhongyang Wenxuan Xuanji. Beijing: Zhonggong Zhongyang Dangxiao Chubanshe, 1982.

Zhu, Kezhen. *Zhu Kezhen Riji*. Shanghai: Shanghai Keji Jiaoyu Chubanshe, 2010.

Zhu, Liping. *A Chinaman's Chance*. Boulder: University Press of Colorado, 2000.

Zong, Hairen. *Zhu Rongji zai 1999*. Hong Kong: Ming Jing, 2001.

Unpublished Dissertations

Blaine, Michael Russell. "American Silver Policy and China, 1933–1936." University of Illinois, 1972.

Brockbank, Nancy Ellena. "The Context of Heroism: The African American Experience on the Ledo Road." Eastern Michigan University, 1998.

Cambon, Marie. "The Dream Palaces of Shanghai." Simon Fraser University, 1986.

Carlson, Joana Renée. "Blurring the Boundaries of Cold War Foreign Relations: Popular Diplomacy, Transnationalism, and U.S. Policy toward Post-Revolutionary China and Cuba." Florida State University, 2010.

Chang, Chung-tung. "China's Response to the Open Door, 1898–1906." Michigan State University, 1973.

Chu, Xiao. "Confucianism, Catholicism, and Human Rights: 1948 and 1993." Boston College, 2005.

Cosgrove, Julia Fukada. "United States Economic Policy toward China, 1943–1946." Washington University, 1980.

Finkelstein, David Michael. "From Abandonment to Salvation: The Evolution of United States Policy toward Taiwan, 1949–1950." Princeton University, 1990.

Grant, Frederic Delano, Jr. "The Chinese Cornerstone of Modern Banking: The Canton Guaranty System and the Origins of Bank Deposit Insurance, 1780–1933." Leiden University, 2012.

Grieve, William George. "Belated Endeavor: The American Military Mission to China, 1941–1942." University of Illinois, 1979.

Harold, Scott. "Negotiating Domestic and International Obstacles on China's Long Road to the GATT/WTO, 1971–2001." Columbia University, 2008.

Ho, Zhigong. "Across the Pacific: American Pragmatism in China, 1917–1937." University of Houston, 1991.

James, Stephen Andrew. "The Origins of Universal Human Rights: An Evaluation." Princeton University, 2005.

Kim, Samuel Soonki. "Anson Burlingame: A Study in Personal Diplomacy." Columbia University, 1966.

Koo, Wellington. "The Status of Aliens in China." Columbia University, 1912.

Kuang, Qizhang. "Pragmatism in China: The Deweyan Influence." Michigan State University, 1994.

Li, Jing. "Rhetoric and Reality: The Making of Chinese Perceptions of the United States." Rice University, 1995.

Lien, Chan. "The Criticism of Hu-Shih's Thought in Communist China." University of Chicago, 1965.

Liu, Yawei. "The United States According to Mao Zedong: Chinese-American R[ ] 1893–1976." Emory University, 1996.

Millar, Thomas J. "Americans and the Issue of China: The Passion and D[ ] American Opinions about China, 1930 to 1944." UCLA, 1998.

Park, Jong-chul. "The China Factor in United States Decision-Making t[ ] 1945–1965." University of Connecticut, 1990.

Park, Tae Jin. "In Support of 'New China': Origins of the China Lobb[ ] Virginia University, 2003.

Shaheen, Anthony Joseph. "The China Democratic League and [ ] 1947." University of Michigan, 1977.

Shen, Yu. "SACO: An Ambivalent Experience of Sino-Am[ ] World War II." University of Illinois at Urbana-Cham[ ]

So, Richard Jean. "Coolie Democracy: U.S.-China Politic[ ] 1955." Columbia University, 2010.

Spar, Frederic J. "Liberal Political Opposition in Kuc[ ] Lung-chi in Chinese Politics, 1928–1958." Bro[ ]

Speer, Glenn Michael. "Richard Nixon's Position[ ] Evolution of a Pacific Strategy." City Univ[ ]

Tsang, Kuo-jen. "China's Propaganda in the[ ] Texas State University, 1980.

Tsui, Brian Kai Hin. "China's Forgotte[ ] 1927–1949." Columbia University[ ]

Wang, Ching-sze. "John Dewey to C[ ]

Wang, Jingbin. "Hegemony and R[ ] prochement, 1943–1972." Un[ ]

Acknowledgments

●

Many people and institutions assisted me in writing this book, providing inspiration, places to stay, funds, and guidance. The Smith Richardson Foundation and the Fulbright Scholar Program awarded me research grants. The Council on Foreign Relations gave me a perch in Washington, DC, in 2011, and Peking University welcomed me as a visiting scholar in 2013–2014.

At Henry Holt, my editor, Serena Jones, inherited this orphaned project and treated it like her own. I owe her and Holt's editor in chief, Gillian Blake, enormous thanks for their patience and guidance. My agent, Gail Ross, as always, provided me with invaluable support.

Thanks go to Peter Fuhrman, who helped me hatch the idea in the first place and provided advice throughout the process. Margaret Johnson and Ray Ottenberg gave me unstinting friendship and a home away from home in Washington, DC; Margaret also expertly pulled together the images for the book. Ray arranged for his book club to read an early version and thanks go to John Claringbould, Fred Hart, John Despres, Bert Rein, Tom Reston, and John Wyss.

At the *Washington Post*, I benefited from the help of great colleagues past and present: Phil Bennett, Steve Coll, Len Downie, David Hoffman, and Bob Kaiser, along with former CEO Don Graham, were all very supportive of my interest in China. Without them, I would never have made it back there as a correspondent, and thus this book could not have been completed. Marcus Brauchli, Karen Deyoung, Ed Cody, Jon Randal, Rajiv

Chandrasekaran, Cameron Barr, Scott Wilson, Keith Richburg, Kevin Sullivan, Jackson Diehl, and Fred Hiatt were all helpful in pushing me to think more deeply about US-China relations. At the *New York Times*, Joe Kahn and Phil Pan were particularly supportive of this endeavor. Gady Epstein and Evan Osnos, at respectively the *Economist* and the *New Yorker*, were so as well. Michael Green, Victor Cha, and Bonnie Glaser, at the Center for Strategic and International Studies, provided invaluable perspective on America's role in Asia. Michael was also extremely forthcoming in sharing a draft of his wonderful book on the US in Asia. At the Brookings Institution, Li Cheng, Jeffrey Bader, Kenneth Lieberthal, and Dennis Wilder were helpful. At the Council on Foreign Relations, Elizabeth Economy has always been supportive. William Kirby at Harvard and Lydia Liu at Columbia and Charles Hayford provided assistance, as did Chen Jian of Cornell. Michael, Cosimo, and Debbie Thawley's advice and encouragement were invaluable as were those of Orville Schell and Michael Oren. As always, Jim Mann was an excellent sounding board for my numerous odd theories. And thanks go to Paul French for providing key data and great stories on the Yanks in old Shanghai.

Thanks go to the staff at the Asia reading room of the Library of Congress, the American Baptist Historical Society, the George C. Marshall Foundation, and the Hoover Institution on War, Revolution and Peace, particularly Hsiao-ting Lin. In Taiwan, thanks go to Ch'i Hsi-sheng and also the archives of the Foreign Ministry of the Republic of China.

In China, I benefited from the assistance of many historians and journalists, some of whom cannot be named due to ongoing repression of free speech there. Those who can be named include Shen Zhihua, Yang Kuisong, and Feng Youcai at East China Normal University; Yu Tiejun, Fan Shimin, and Wang Jisi at Peking University; and He Hui at Huanan Normal University. My researcher, Yang Lin, was extremely adept at finding obscure periodicals and documents. Russell Leigh Moses at the Beijing Center opened up its library to me. Special thanks go to Holli Semetko and Emory University's Robert W. Woodruff Library for facilitating my research.

I was aided greatly by the assistance of colleagues and friends who read portions of the manuscript. Ed Gargan and Zofia Smardz suffered through numerous drafts. Historians Maochun Yu and Frederic D. Grant Jr. caught key errors. Dick Butterfield hectored me to give it more voice. Steve and Claire Mufson and M. T. Connolly saved me from embarrassing myself. My father, John D. Pomfret, covered an early version in red pencil. My sister, Dana Pomfret, added her keen eye. In the end, of course, I am responsible for all mistakes and infelicities.

At home, my children, Dali, Liya, and Sophie, generally tolerated their increasingly grizzled dad pounding away at the keyboard night and day. In the spring of 2016 as the project entered the home stretch, my mother, Margaret H. Pomfret, passed away. I deeply regret that she never saw it finished. My wife, Zhang Mei, to whom this book is dedicated, supported me throughout this venture, even through its darkest hours. Neither of us can believe that it actually got done.

Index

Page numbers in *italics* refer to maps.

About the Author

JOHN POMFRET served as a correspondent for *The Washington Post* for many years in China and around the world. He is the author of the acclaimed book *Chinese Lessons* and has won several awards for his coverage of Asia, including the Osborn Elliott Prize. He holds a BA and an MA from Stanford University and was one of the first American students to study in China after relations were normalized. He has been a recipient of two Fulbright scholarships and lives in Beijing and the United States with his wife, the entrepreneur Zhang Mei, and their three children.